NORTHERN RHODESIA
SOUTHERN RHODESIA
SOUTH WEST AFRICA
OLA
BATAWANA RESERVE
NGAMILAND
KHANZI
BAMANGWATO
TATI CONCESSION
MAKARIKARI
ZAMBEZI RIVER
KWANDO
R. Luina
Umgwezi
Chadum
Kaua
Letiahau
Deka
GWAAI R.
Tegwani R.
Marsupe R.
SHASHI RIVER
PROPOSED ROUTE OF WALVIS BAY-LIVINGSTONE RAILWAY
Under construction
Kalomo
Livingstone
Sesheke
Kazungula
Mbala
Mudyua
Lesuma
Siambiza
Kavimba
Lesoane
Simati
Kasinka
Lisho's (Libebe)
Gavegama
Muhembo
Gacha
Ramokwena's
Samusipa's
Lefatsi's
Duma
Mampi
Kashiambara's
Skegau
Tlogoeankws's
Shaleshanto
Joverega
Mutinyane
Masarwa
Massubia
Mokwati's
Rakuku
Levisfontein
Ranwanalenau's
Puluhelo (Samahala's?)
Ramotsaodi
Kharekai
Mochosen's
Mirapene
Maun
Kai Kai
Kogu
Malatshi
Rantsadi
Diroro's
Omdrai
Tsau (Pol. Sta.)
Lempadi
Nengwa
Komane
Makkhalo
Makuba
Makalamabedi (Pol. Sta. & Store)
Mokhopudis
Demarara
Toteng
Motlhatlokho
Kudia Kam
Joani
Makumbe
Muekekle
Molusi
Kwaraga
Kitsuhele
Khasebake
Dauga
Jakops
Khomo Store
Khama Khama?
Segara
Xhane
Tshapatain
Chuma
Gwaraha
Odanakumadona
Madista
Mabole
Tsigara
Thabatskudu
Mekomxana
Nekati
Dodo
Maseme
Sebe
Sebutu
Thamafipa
Gerufa
Gobokonkwane
Matlamanyane
WANKIE
DETT
INTUNDHLA
GWAAI
BULAWAYO
Habangan Stad Store
Kalakamati Store
Masungas
Sebina
Matangwan Stad (Store)
Francistown
Manduyan
SHASHI SIDING
MACLOUTSIE SIDING
FOLEY SIDING
SISI SIDING
Tonoto (Store)
Old Tati
Mphoengs
Karamechen
PLUMTREE SIDING
RAMAQUABANE SIDING
Madabis
TSAMAEA SIDING
Ngwenyana
BOSOLI SIDING
Tlala Mabeli
Ditsinane
Detoie
Sesaloa
Tsipi
Makwa
Kkhobi
Kkhoutsiri
Khanzi
Dekar
Kkhoutsa
Monyalatsela
Khemsbok
17°
18°
19°
20°
21°
22°
23°
24°
25°
26°
27°
28°
29°

Monarch
of all I Survey

Frontispiece Sir Charles Fernand Rey 1877–1968

Monarch
of all I Survey

Bechuanaland Diaries
1929–37
by
Sir Charles Rey, Kt., C.M.G., F.R.G.S.
Commander of the Star of Ethiopia, Member of the
Portuguese Academy of History & late Resident
Commissioner of the Bechuanaland Protectorate

Author of *Unconquered Abyssinia, In the Country of the Blue Nile, The Lady, or the Leopard, The Romance of the Portuguese in Africa, The Real Abyssinia,* &c.

Edited by
Neil Parsons & Michael Crowder
With Illustrations & Map

GABORONE
The Botswana Society

NEW YORK
Lilian Barber Press Inc.

LONDON
James Currey

The Botswana Society
P.O. Box 71, Gaborone, Botswana

Lilian Barber Press Inc
P.O. Box 232, New York NY 10163

James Currey Ltd
54b Thornhill Square, Islington, London N1 1BE

© The Botswana Society 1988
First published in this edition 1988

ISBN 99912-60-00-5 (Botswana)
ISBN 0-936508-22-1 (USA)
ISBN 0-85255-016-2 (UK)

All rights reserved. No parts of this publication may be reproduced in any form by any means without the prior permission of the copyright holders.

Main text and illustrations © The Botswana Society 1988
Editorial matter © Neil Parsons and Michael Crowder 1988

First published 1988
Reprinted 1990 – 1993 – 1994

British Library Cataloguing in Publication Data

Rey, *Sir* Charles
Monarch of all I survey: Bechuanaland diaries, 1929-1937.
1. Botswana — History — To 1966 2. Botswana — Biography I. Title
II. Parsons, Neil, *1944-* III. Crowder, Michael, *1934-* 968.1'102   DT791
ISBN 0-85255-016-2

Library of Congress Cataloging-in-Publication Data

Rey, Charles Fernand, Sir, 1877-1968.
Monarch of all I survey.

Bibliography: p.
Includes index.
1. Rey, Charles, Fernand, Sir, 1877-1968 — Diaries.
2. Colonial administrators — Botswana — Diaries.
3. Colonial administrators — Great Britain — Diaries.
4. Botswana — Politics and government — To 1966.
I. Parsons, Neil. II. Crowder, Michael, 1934 —
III. Title.
DT795.R49AS 1988 968.1'202'0924 87-12570
ISBN 0-936508 22-1 (Barber)

Typeset by Colset Private Limited, Singapore
& printed by Morija Press, Lesotho

Contents

Preface
by Neil Parsons & Michael Crowder
vii

Prologue
by Neil Parsons
xi

illustrations
between pages xxiv & 1

1929
1

1930
11

1931
54

1932
94

1933
114

1934
145

1935
180

1936
194

1937
223

Editorial Notes
237

Appendix:
Notes on the Serowe Incident (1933)
by C.F. Rey
264

Epilogue
by Neil Parsons
269

Index
277

PREFACE

So now I am
His Honour Lt. Colonel C.F. Rey
Monarch of all I survey
What a joke!

With this self-mocking verse, on All Fools' Day 1930, Charles Rey recorded in his diary his assumption of the title of Resident Commissioner of the Bechuanaland Protectorate. Rey had been brought to Bechuanaland from London, as a new broom to sweep out the cobwebs of decades of administrative neglect. He was to stay for eight years, using his talents to tackle, and sometimes to provoke, crisis after crisis.

Trusting few others with his confidences, besides his wife, Charles Rey poured out the impressions of his Bechuanaland years into fourteen hand-written diaries. The diaries were not intended for publication: he considered them too candid and unpolished. They let off steam with biting observations on people and unguarded comments on events, and are written in a relaxed colloquial style. Rey wrote as he is said to have spoken, 'in the warm tones of the born raconteur'.

The diaries of Charles Rey are therefore an invaluable record of the actions and thoughts of a colonial administrator in Africa during and immediately after the years of the Great Depression. Within Bechuanaland (Botswana), the diaries illuminate the continuous personality clash between Rey and his equally headstrong nemesis, the young Regent of the Bangwato, Tshekedi Khama — culminating in the events when the Royal Navy was brought to the Kalahari to crush a fictitious 'native rising' that Rey supposed was led by Tshekedi. Beyond the boundaries of Bechuanaland, the diaries highlight relations with the Dominions Office in London and between Great Britain and the Union of South Africa — the subtle and sometimes not so subtle relations between British imperialism and Afrikaner nationalism in the shadow of the coming World War.

Charles Rey, knighted in 1938, died in Cape Town in 1968 at the age of ninety. He had lived a long and varied life. As a bureaucrat with flair, he had risen rapidly through the ranks of the Civil Service in Britain, which he had joined at the age of twenty-two. By 1918, at the age of forty-one, he was Director-General of National Labour Supply, working closely with Beveridge and Lloyd George. He had also travelled, as a commercial diplomat, to Russia and North America and probably

Preface

China. Then, in 1919, Rey accepted secondment to head the Abyssinian Corporation, a British body vying with the French and Italians for commercial and political influence in Ethiopia. There was then a hiatus within his career in the Ministry of Labour, which Rey made good by extensive travelling with his wife in Abyssinia and by establishing himself as an author of travel books on that country. Finally, Rey was snapped up by Leopold Amery, who combined the new office of Dominions Secretary with that of Colonial Secretary in the British government, to be sent out to Bechuanaland as the next Resident Commissioner — the position from which Rey retired at the age of sixty in 1937.

These cold facts do scant justice to the vigour and spirit of Charles Rey. Rey was, more than most people, a bundle of contradictions. He had been a Tory intimately associated with developing the liberal ideals of social security in Britain. In Bechuanaland he was a social recluse, especially at weekends, and yet he was noted for his gregariousness. He was both an 'office-wallah' with an obsession for filing systems, and a 'bush-whacker' pushing his Armstrong Siddeley automobile across the uncharted wastes of Bechuanaland. He appears to have been intolerant of all women and all children, and yet he was obsessively devoted to his wife and bore the death of his two sons in stoic silence. His relations with Africans veered between racialistic paternalism and a person-to-person directness that was refreshingly unusual for its time. He was frankly atheistic and anti-clerical, and yet he reserved great admiration for the Catholic Church. He is remembered both as a 'hustler' with a bristling moustache and as a man who insisted on all the niceties of being a gentleman — including the well-known and often mocked habit of dressing for dinner each evening 'in the bush'. But perhaps the greatest contradiction, in his Bechuanaland years, was Rey's initial super-patriotic attitude towards Britain becoming transmuted into admiration for Afrikanerdom and its anti-British stance in South Africa.

Rey in retirement looked back on his Bechuanaland experience as the summit and yet the ultimate frustration of his life's achievement. While he continued to hope for recognition of that achievement some day, he saw the tide of history turning ever stronger against all he had stood for in the imperial past. He wrote an autobiography but it was, with his permission, drastically pruned of all his characteristic outbursts. The anodyne result was unpublishable. Apart from a small number of former High Commission Territories officials retired around Cape Town, who do not appear to have been close to him, there was no one left to even begin to understand his Bechuanaland days.

A few years after Sir Charles Rey's death, his Bechuanaland Diaries were bought by the Botswana Society, a learned society based in Gaborone, devoted to the study of all aspects of Botswana past and present. The Botswana Society recognised the value of the Bechuanaland Diaries, and now publishes them shortened but unbowdlerised to retain their original directness and energy. Rey can speak loud and clear to generations who will not dismiss the whole man just because of strong, and sometimes repulsive, prejudices that reflect times past. In particular we can now appreciate, stripped of its colonial rhetoric, Rey's overriding concern with matters of economic and social development. Unlike most of his peers, Rey was schooled in the idea of bureaucracy as the facilitation rather than as the obstruction of change and development. He always had an eye on economic realities. Where he came a cropper was his naïveté about the political realities of development. Tshekedi Khama and the Witwatersrand mining companies ran rings around Rey. But Rey's Bechuanaland Diaries, by revealing the human

Preface

realities, crack the granite face of history to uncover a warm personality inside. The price we pay is sometimes seeing history in excessively personalised terms: 'I hanged my two murderers . . . today', for example.

The Prologue of this book, which follows the Preface, sets Rey's eight years in Bechuanaland against the background of his previous fifty-two years and conditions already existing in the Bechuanaland Protectorate. The Epilogue carries the story of his life up to its end in 1968. A Note on Editorial Principles is appended below this Preface.

The editing and publishing of this book would not have been possible without the active assistance of a number of people. Alec Campbell, Chairman of the Botswana Society, 'discovered' and bought the Bechuanaland Diaries on behalf of the Society, initiated editing, and pushed forward publication. Mrs Fay Longhurst Murphy of Cape Town, Sir Charles Rey's executrix, kindly assisted us with reminiscences and photographs. Our fellow historians in Botswana, particularly Fred Morton and Jeff Ramsay, have assisted us with footnotes. We have also used the insights of Jim McCann of Boston and Tom Killion of Stanford on Rey in Ethiopia; and acknowledge the assistance of the late Anthony Sillery of Oxford and Joslin Landell-Mills of Washington, D.C. Many other people have caught Rey fever on the way, and we respectfully dedicate this publication to the ever expanding circle of their number.

Neil Parsons & Michael Crowder
Gaborone & London

Preface

Note on Editorial Principles

The Bechuanaland Diaries of Sir Charles Rey (1929–37) consist originally of fourteen foolscap 270 × 214 mm carbon letter books, bound with red marbled board covers, with 'Bechuanaland Protectorate' and volume number with dates handwritten on the spine. The carbon copy of each page remains in the volume; the top copies, in blue ink, have been torn out and placed in a loose pile parcelled in brown paper by an antiquarian bookseller after sale by Rey's executrix. It is obviously more convenient to refer to the bound volumes of carbon copies, which also contain extra material such as press clippings. Each volume has one hundred pages, covered in neat handwriting with a minimum of crossings out, to a grand total of about 375,000 words. The volumes were bought from the stationery department of the Army and Navy Stores in London, for the price of two shillings and ten pence each.

The present edition of the Bechuanaland Diaries was prepared by clipping and photocopying a typed copy of the originally handwritten diaries. The diaries have been cut to a third of their original length after much judicious juggling. The main editorial principle has been to keep original observations of people and events that relate to Botswana, while discarding repetitious and simply lyrical descriptions of scenery or matters not based on direct observation by the writer. However, having said this, we are confident that there is sufficient material for at least one more book based on the Bechuanaland Diaries, which could give more vent to Rey's observations on South Africa and Britain as well as to his travels in Europe.

We have standardised rather than gratuitously modernised orthography, as Rey himself tended to be inconsistent in spelling African names. Thus we have standardised the spelling of Tshekedi, and have made corrections such as Barolong in place of incorrect Baralong, but have not attempted to modernise the colonial spellings of Lobatsi to Lobatse or Gaberones to Gaborone. We have also made the decision to spell out expletives such as 'damn' which is inconsistently either abbreviated (as d —) or spelt out in full in the manuscript. To avoid ambiguity we have also spelt out, and sometimes expanded, Rey's abbreviated references to individuals — such as S. for Stanley, simply Clarke for Arden-Clarke who might be confused by the reader with other Clarks. Punctuation has also been modified on occasion. But all substantive modifications by the editors are included in square brackets. Each chapter has editorial notes at its end, indicated by numerals in the text. These notes include biographical and bibliographical details, and relevant explanations and some refutations of the text, aimed at readers who seek a more critical historical understanding of Rey's time in the Protectorate.

Readers may note idiosyncracies that have not been tampered with by the editors. On many occasions Rey refers to the Colonial Office when he meant the Dominions Office, which by that time was a separate institution in London under a separate minister but was housed in the same building. It is Rey rather than the editors who spells develop as 'develope' and who uses 'cucumbers' to refer to concubines, and slang or apparently anachronistic words such as 'hairy', 'brunch', 'O.K.', 'clicked' (as in, 'we clicked together') or 'sky pilot' (for clergyman). It is also Rey whose favourite punctuation mark — giving a sense of urgency to the text — is the dash.

PROLOGUE

Neil Parsons

Charles Fernand Rey was born in London at 6 Montagu Street, Marylebone, on August 31st, 1877 — the year in which Disraeli proclaimed Queen Victoria the Empress of India. Charles Fernand was the son of Edmond Fernand Rey, a French-born merchant in the City of London, and Adina Elidia Rey née Graham.[1] Throughout his life Charles Rey was to retain fluency in French and affection for France, though in every other way he was brought up with the expectations and manners of an English gentleman albeit of mercantile origins.

After a private education at home by tutors, Charles Rey entered the Royal Military Academy at Woolwich as a Gentleman Cadet in September 1895. He thereby followed in the footsteps of eminent Victorian imperialists like 'Chinese' Gordon, 'Bechuana' Warren and 'Sudan' Kitchener, by opting for a career in military engineering. He was later to recall that his interest in African adventures had been aroused by the exploits of an uncle in the Egyptian campaign of 1882.[2]

No sooner had the eighteen year old Charles entered Woolwich, however, than his family had financial troubles, which resulted in his being withdrawn in November 1895. Strangely enough, he just missed by a few days the visit to Woolwich of three Kings or Chiefs (Khama III, Sebele I and Bathoen I) from the country with which he was to be so closely associated thirty-five years later — the Bechuanaland Protectorate.

Charles Rey was sent instead to the Royal School of Mines in the tin-mining county of Cornwall in the West of England, to study mining engineering. This led to his first period of employment in Africa at the age of twenty-one. Rey joined a mineral prospecting expedition up the River Gambia in West Africa. The expedition appears to have been spectacularly unsuccessful. Instead of taking three months and finding minerals, it took more than twelve months and found none. The party proceeded upriver by motor launch and then by canoe to the furthest navigable point, whence it marched overland to Kayes on the River Senegal. It was dispirited by news of a French expedition in the area, whose men, caught in the grip of the dreaded *cafard* or 'desert madness', murdered their officers.

Rey returned home to England reduced to nine stone in weight (under 60 kilograms, or 126 pounds). He was not tempted to continue his African career, but

Prologue

applied to join the commercial branch of the British civil service. In 1900 he was appointed to the Board of Trade, and began to rise rapidly in its ranks. By 1902 he was Secretary to the China Tariff Commission. Apparently this involved travel to North America as well as to China, initiating what Rey later claimed was an intimate acquaintance with the United States and Canada.[3]

In 1903-4 Rey had his first taste of British imperial bureaucracy, as Secretary to the trustees and advisory committee of the Imperial Institute in London. The Institute was a gallery and library, sporting its own Gothic tower in South Kensington, in what has since become Imperial College of the University of London. (Renamed the Commonwealth Institute, it moved to Holland Park after the Second World War, where it is now housed in an enormous blue glass tent.) The Imperial Institute, opened to celebrate Queen Victoria's Golden Jubilee in 1893, had the function of exhibiting to the British their Empire.[4]

From the Imperial Institute, Rey returned to the Board of Trade as Secretary to the 'All Red Route Committee', ensuring commercial communications through Suez (and possibly also the Cape) to India and Australasia. In 1905 he accompanied a British delegation that conducted commercial negotiations in Romania in Eastern Europe, and then continued on as part of a special mission to Constantinople (Istanbul) in Turkey and Sofia in Bulgaria. In 1906 he was assigned to Anglo-Swiss commercial treaty negotiations. On all these assignments Rey was no doubt aided by his fluency in French, then the universal language of diplomacy.

In 1906 Rey had the break that removed him from the ranks of faceless bureaucrats to an administrative field where individual talent and initiative were rewarded. He was sent for by David Lloyd George, President of the Board of Trade in the new Liberal government. Lloyd George directed Rey to Germany to make a special study of the novel labour exchanges there, which helped employers to find workers and workers to find employers. This was the first step towards setting up a similar system of social security for the British working class. However, Rey reported unfavourably on the German experiment, and the British system of labour exchanges was not set up until 1909 — in four frantic months, in response to the agitation of the radical journalist William Beveridge, whose *Unemployment: A Problem of Industry* was published in that year.

Rey was made the first General Manager of Labour Exchanges, within the Board of Trade, second-in-command to Beveridge himself. Rey's task was to set up a national system of local labour exchanges, which registered local job vacancies and locally unemployed workers in a not always successful attempt to match the two.

The climax of Liberal social reform under the leadership of Lloyd George, now Chancellor of the Exchequer (1908-15), was the National Insurance Act of 1911. This provided rudimentary health insurance, on payment by the worker, and an unemployment benefit for workers in the construction, shipbuilding and engineering industries. Rey was given the unenviable task of operating the latter part of the Act as General Manager of Unemployment Insurance (1912).

Charles Rey blossomed as an unconventional bureaucrat in this period. A colleague later recalled how exhilirating Rey was to work with: 'gay, excitable, and most practically energetic . . . always spoiling for an official fight'.[5] Above all, Rey learnt how to fight with the Treasury, the parsimonious stepmother of all British government departments, which controlled them by controlling their budgets. In this, Rey openly acknowledged the prior success of his master, the 'Welsh Wizard' Lloyd George himself. In Rey's autobiography, penned after his

Prologue

Bechuanaland frustrations, he referred enviously to the 'practical freeing of himself and his department from Treasury control' as the key to Lloyd George's success.[6]

Lloyd George found Rey's energies indispensable in setting up new departments in wartime. Lloyd George began to reorganise British society towards 'total warfare', where the whole economy contributed towards victory. When Lloyd George set up a Ministry of Munitions, to manufacture guns and ammunition, in 1915, he took on Rey as one of his 'chief lieutenants' (according to the *Birmingham Daily Mail*) with the position of Director of Labour Supply.[7] When Lloyd George became Prime Minister and a new Ministry of Labour was set up in 1916, Rey became the Director of Employment Exchanges (the new name for the former labour exchanges) in the new Ministry.

During 1917 Rey seems to have been involved in a cloak-and-dagger interlude which cannot be accounted for within his career in the Ministry of Labour. Later memoirs suggest that Rey helped to organise the escape of refugees from German-occupied Belgium into neutral Holland.[8]

Rey reached the peak of his civil service career in 1918. First he was transferred to the Ministry of National Service, a Ministry founded a year previously and folded up after the War, as Director-General of National Labour Supply. As another official, angling to poach Rey for the new Ministry of Shipping in that year, remarked of him: 'He has organised the Ministry of National Service in a wonderful way'. But, later in 1918, Rey was instead transferred back to the Ministry of Labour as the Assistant (Permanent) Secretary, its second topmost civil servant.

Rey's personal file kept at the Treasury notes his 'extraordinary capacity for work'. But, as the War ended and the peacetime ethos of cooperation superseded the wartime needs of coercion and direction of labour, Rey found himself out of sympathy with his colleagues in the Ministry of Labour. An Edwardian Tory, autocratic by nature, he was not in step with the liberal ideals of 'social security' in post-War Britain. As a British labour historian has remarked of Rey after 1919: 'He utterly lost control of the situation in the new Ministry [of Labour] and those entrenched in power were keen to stop him from returning.'[9]

Left in the cold at the Ministry of Labour, but apparently unwilling to resign and lose pension rights, Charles Rey sought secondments elsewhere. In 1919 he moved back to Holland, temporarily, as chief British representative at Rotterdam on the Inter-Allied Commission that was to supply foodstuffs into Allied-occupied Germany. Then, in June 1919, he was given leave to take up the position of General Manager of the Abyssinian Corporation in Africa.

Meanwhile Charles Rey had become a family man. During his years in the Home Civil Service he had met and married Nina (Georgina) Webster, whom he always called by the affectionate French nickname of 'Ninon'. To her, he gives his highest possible tribute in the Bechuanaland Diaries: that marrying her was 'the best day's work I ever did in my life'.[10]

Nina Webster, born May 30th, 1872, was five years older than Charles Rey — and of better 'breeding'. She had family connexions with the Earls of Home in Scotland and with Italian counts, Irish gentry and English admirals. Brought up in London and the environs of Paris, she was — according to Rey — an accomplished pianist, linguist, water-colourist, horsewoman and 'whip', hostess and house mistress.[11] But she was no beauty, and had been passed by in the upper class marriage stakes.

Prologue

Charles Rey fell in love with Nina Webster during his early days with the Board of Trade or the Imperial Institute. Her relatives objected to the match as socially demeaning. They tried to lock her away from him by confining her to a hospital ward, under observation for 'hysteria'. Charles was only able to catch the slightest glimpse of his beloved Ninon, framed in the window panels of a hospital ward door. (He recorded this moment, in poetry or letters since destroyed by his executrix as too personal and painful to be read by outsiders.)

Eventually, after her relatives had relented, Charles and Ninon were married at a Roman Catholic Church in London's West End on March 16th, 1907. He was thirty years old, and she was thirty-five. One of her first acts after the marriage was to join the Royal Aeronautical Club, as a founder-member — attending their flying meetings at Bournemouth, Blackpool, and elsewhere. In 1912 she gave birth at the age of forty to her first child, Roderick; followed by the birth of a second son, Arthur Anthony, in 1917. Notwithstanding the children, Ninon joined Rey in wartime administrative work such as the organisation within the Ministry of National Service of part-time employment for married women. In 1919 she became Honorary Secretary of the Inter-Allied Commission in Rotterdam, of which Rey was Chairman; and together they were almost killed on a 'wild motor trip' from Holland through 'almost roadless and bridgeless' Belgium and France.[12]

During the second half of 1919, with Ninon and the boys at his side, Charles Rey established himself at Addis Ababa in Abyssinia (Ethiopia), as General Manager of the so-called Abyssinian Corporation. The Corporation had been founded in the previous year, probably on the initiative and certainly with the blessing of the British government. Its purpose was to promote British commercial interests in the mountainous Christian empire of Abyssinia — the only independent state left on the African continent besides Liberia. The Abyssinian Corporation had capital of more than a million pounds, including 'disguised subventions' from the British government. The timing of its foundation was critical. The French, with a colony on the coast (French Somaliland) at Djibouti, had almost completed a railway from Djibouti to Addis Ababa, which threatened to monopolise Abyssinia's external trade in the interests of France.[13] France had thereby leap-frogged Italy which held the large coastal colonies of Eritrea and Italian Somaliland, and which had long coveted the Abyssinian interior. Britain also had a coastal colony in the form of British Somaliland, and had more remote placements on the strategic map in its colonies of Sudan and Kenya, which neighboured Abyssinia in the interior. Even the U.S.A. was beginning to take an interest in the 'Horn of Africa'. British and American interests overlapped in political concern for Abyssinia's 'stability' coupled with commercial concern for the country's economic progress.

The key to stability and progress, as Rey soon realised, was to gain the confidence of the 'Young Ethiopians', younger members of the Amharic ruling class led by Ras Tafari Makonnen. Ras Tafari was the young regent, and heir to the throne, who ruled jointly with the Empress Zauditu — who was backed by the powerful conservative forces of the landlords and the clergy. (Ras Tafari was to become Emperor Haile Selassie on the death of Zauditu in 1930.)

The Abyssinian Corporation bought up existing Greek and Armenian merchant firms, and obtained a mineral concession over the frontier area next to British Somaliland. But it lost £150,000 in its first nineteen months, and its one-pound nominal shares shrank to less than two shillings on the stock market. By 1922 the Abyssinian Corporation was bankrupt, and in 1926 it was wound up from its London base. Rey apparently failed to grease the palms of the ruling class, and was

Prologue

out-manoeuvred by established Greek, Armenian and Indian merchants — more adapted to 'local business practices'. Besides, imported British goods were often of shoddy quality, and French interests interfered wherever possible — notably with inflated railway tariffs. It was also reported that Rey got on well neither with his British staff nor with the Abyssinian 'natives'.[14]

Personal tragedy struck early in 1920. Both the Rey sons died of dysentery at Addis Ababa. Roddy, aged seven, died in February 1920. Tony, aged three, died a month later. It was a tragedy from which Ninon never recovered.[15] For the rest of her life her nerves were on edge, despite the brash confidence she sometimes showed in public. Her neck was permanently stiff from the tension, and she often took to her bed. The Reys became a very private couple. Charles was absolutely devoted to Ninon. Yet she remains largely a frail cipher in his Bechuanaland Diaries, and there is no mention of the fact that they had ever had children of their own. When she emerged from her shell, Ninon appears to have sometimes been curiously insensitive to the feelings of others. (A cruel mocking streak emerges in her corrupting the name of a trusted servant into 'Orang Utang', though this merely echoes Rey's muttering 'zoological specimen number one' to the face of an African educationalist at a Bechuanaland board meeting.) Such insensitivity on Ninon's part may have been the price of covering up the deep psychic wound of losing her sons — though people at the time preferred to see it as arrogance born of class snobbery.[16]

Charles Rey resigned as General Manager of the Abyssinian Corporation in June 1920. To be fair to Rey, his successor had as little success. Charles and Ninon retreated to Britain. His colleagues in the Ministry of Labour shunted him sideways into the Unemployment Grants Committee, of which he acted as Secretary. This committee was responsible for grants given to local authorities to provide relief works for the unemployed. It can hardly have been a full-time job, though Rey remained Secretary from 1921 until 1927, as Charles and Ninon continued to take annual trips to Abyssinia — possibly on a retainer from the Abyssinian Corporation, representing the London board to oversee the assets that remained after its 1922 bankruptcy. The Reys returned to Abyssinia three times, on extended tours over rivers and mountains by mule, in 1922–23, 1925–26 and 1926–27. The last visit may have coincided with the sale of the Abyssinian Corporation's remaining assets to a local Greek entrepreneur. But Rey was obviously more concerned with intrepid travels and with cultivating the friendship of Ras Tafari.

In a world where commerce was diplomacy, and diplomacy commerce, Ras Tafari appears to have placed some value on the advice of Charles Rey. Rey was later fond of telling how Ras Tafari had offered him the post of Treasurer of the Empire. Rey said that he could only accept the offer if (as a poacher turned game-keeper) he could apply 'the rigorous auditing system of the British Treasury' to stop 'leakages' in the state revenue. Ras Tafari replied that that would make the Treasurer too unpopular to be effective.[17]

In later years, Rey referred back to Abyssinia as 'a magnificent country with the best climate in the world, and my wife and I are very fond of it'. But, in spite of Haile Selassie doing his best, 'It was sad to watch the passing of the last independent empire in Africa, with its rich tradition and fascinating customs . . . the fact could not be ignored that Abyssinia had suffered cruelly from bad government.'[18]

At the time, however, Rey was aghast when British newspaper reports portrayed Abyssinia as a chaotic empire ripe for revolution. Such reports might

Prologue

alienate the pro-British sympathies of Ras Tafari and his progressive young followers. A particularly ill-informed article on Abyssinia in a London conservative daily newspaper, the *Morning Post*,[19] drove Rey to write his first book. It was titled *Unconquered Abyssinia, As It Is Today*, and was published in London in 1923 and in Philadelphia in 1924.[20] Charles Rey was duly rewarded with the honour of Commander of the Order of the Star of Ethiopia in 1924, a decoration he was sometimes to wear in his Bechuanaland days because of its magnificence.

Charles Rey gave talks on Abyssinia in London during 1922 to the Royal Geographical Society and the (later Royal) African Society, and was elected a Fellow of the former Society in 1923.[21] A string of articles on exploration of remote areas, written in light prose and illustrated by sometimes indifferent photographs, followed,[22] until the publication of a travelogue in 1927 — a book called *In the Country of the Blue Nile*.[23]

Rey finally retired at fifty from the Ministry of Labour, in 1927, after his final trip to Abyssinia. He and his wife celebrated with a visit to Morocco in 1927–28. Ninon was much taken with the *souks* (market-places) of the city of Fez, which had only recently been opened to European tourists, wandering on an ass down dark narrow alleys full of humanity. Back in London Rey tried his hand at full-time authorship, producing two books which were published almost simultaneously in 1929 — and which were reviewed while he was on his way to Bechuanaland. One book, called *The Romance of the Portuguese in Abyssinia*,[24] was a popular historical study of attempts by the Portuguese to contact the mythical Christian emperor Prester John, and then to impose Portuguese Catholicism on the Abyssinians, between the years 1490 and 1633. The other book, *The Lady, or the Leopard*,[25] was Rey's only published attempt at fiction — a 'pulp' mystery novel of travels and intrigues in London and Abyssinia. Rey was delighted when an option on the film rights was snapped up, but no film was ever produced.[26]

Also at this time Rey wrote the entry on 'Abyssinia' that first appeared in the 1929 edition of *Encyclopaedia Britannica* (and which was revised by him for the 1953 edition).[27] He may also have begun revising his first book, which was republished under the new title of *The Real Abyssinia* in 1935[28] — after the Italian invasion had turned world attention to the country.

Rey probably spent much of his time reading and writing in London libraries and gentlemen's clubs. As his manuscripts were handwritten and not typed by him, he was not obliged to stay at home pounding a typewriter. It was possibly in a West End club that Rey met and got to know the man who was to change his life — Leopold Amery.

Amery held the dual portfolio of being both Colonial Secretary and Dominions Secretary in the Conservative government that held power until 1929. A man of undoubted vision, Amery saw himself as the successor of the great 'Pushful Joe' Chamberlain, Colonial Secretary from 1895 to 1903, whose mission was to 'develop' the colonial 'estates' of the British Empire, to make them paying propositions for the Mother Country. Amery had a nightmare of the world becoming increasingly polarised between two giant groupings — the already dynamic and immensely productive 'Pan-America', and the emergent union of the European economies which Amery called 'Pan-Europa'. The British Empire was to be split between the two, with Britain joining Europe and its White Dominions joining America, unless an alternative 'Pan-Britannia' could be created and sustained. (The non-white colonies, on the other hand, were considered as mere appendages without autonomous potential.)[29]

Prologue

With such ideas in mind, Leopold Amery had made a grand tour of the White Dominions in 1927-28, which had included the Union of South Africa and its appendages called the High Commission Territories — Basutoland, the Bechuanaland Protectorate, and Swaziland. Amery was appalled by the economic stagnation and 'very unprogressive form of indirect rule' of the territories, and determined to make them instead into 'centres of progress and development' — which would become strong provinces of a 'British' character when they eventually joined the Union, to counter-balance Afrikaner influence in South Africa. Amery committed himself 'up to the hilt' to reinforce British farm settlement in Swaziland, and to find a dynamic new head for the Bechuanaland administration to lay the foundations for mineral development. ('With mineral development comes farming development and the building up of a nation.')[30] He thought he had found such a man in Charles Rey.

Bechuanaland before Rey

'I have passed, too, in the last two days through that Bechuanaland Protectorate to which Rhodes attached such immense importance as the "corridor", "the Suez Canal" to the North, but which he always regarded as a territory, though perhaps less fertile than some of the countries to the north, with great capacity and well worth developing for the benefit of both its native inhabitants and of European settlers.'[31]

Addressing the white miners and farmers of Kimberley, in the northern Cape Province of South Africa, in August 1927, Leopold Amery tried to recapture the vision of Bechuanaland's potential which had been lost since the 1890s. But the truth was that he had been greatly depressed by what he had seen of British colonial administration in Bechuanaland. As he was to tell Rey, the object of administration had been 'to keep out of the Union, and to keep the natives quiet and happy . . . like a game reserve of wild animals'. 'But it would be impossible to resist the demand of White South Africa for the exploitation of the mineral resources of the Prot[ectorate]. Natives could not do it, and therefore whites must be allowed to.' Incorporation of the territory in the Union, or its division between the Union and the Rhodesias, was inevitable within a decade.[32]

As Amery put it, the administration of the Bechuanaland Protectorate 'was born and had grown up in the country.' Other commentators had been, and were to be, harsher. The great and ancient Tswana ruler, Khama III of the Bangwato, had complained in 1922: 'I receive nothing of the good laws of England but oppression from the Officials.' The missionary Haydon Lewis had written in 1913 that, with the exception of Jules Ellenberger, the administration 'should be washing clothes, instead of Governing nations'. In 1918 Haydon Lewis referred to its 'chief business' as being 'to collect taxes, and receive salaries, a business which seems to exhaust the whole of its administrative energies, if such can be called administration'.[33] The Tswana 'agitator' Simon Ratshosa was even more damning in his manuscript called *My Book on Bechuanaland Protectorate*, completed in 1930: 'The Government is being fast asleep for the last forty-five years to give a thought to our upliftment; thousands of pounds derived from us have been blindly spent to unnecessary purposes.' He added that the officials were 'in many cases replaced by their sons, or friends, that is, their succession is a hereditary one'. The journalist Leonard Barnes, writing in the early 1930s, complained that local administrative officers, mostly drawn from the Bechuanaland Protectorate Police, 'rejoice, as a

Prologue

group, in the mental habits and range of outlook customary in that walk of life'. Barnes referred to the Administration as 'infected' by 'the spirit of sloth'. Even Anthony Sillery, the historian who was Resident Commissioner in the 1940s, remarks in his autobiography that 'Until quite recently the Administration had been a rather inbred closed affair, mildly dynastic'.[34]

The administration of the Bechuanaland Protectorate was under the direct control of the (British) High Commissioner in South Africa, a post held simultaneously by the Governor of Cape Colony and then, after Union, by the Governor-General of the Union of South Africa. The chief administrator of Bechuanaland was therefore always responsible, in his other capacity as Governor-General, to the white settler parliament of South Africa. Even after 1931, when the Governor-Generalship of South Africa was separated from the High Commissionership with two different individuals holding the posts, the High Commissioner continued to be Britain's ambassador to South Africa and was resident in Pretoria.

The High Commissioner appointed Resident Commissioners for each of the three 'High Commission Territories' — Basutoland (Lesotho), the Bechuanaland Protectorate (Botswana) and Swaziland. Each Resident Commissioner was supported by white administrative staff appointed by the High Commissioner, recruited and promoted by a mixture of what could be referred to as the 'old boy' and the 'office boy' networks. The 'old boy' network was predominantly a military one at first: former members of the frontier police forces in Southern Africa. But, in time, a network developed of men trained in and swapped between the three High Commission Territories — whose upper ranks were often drawn from, or cemented by kinship ties with, the families of Basutoland French Protestant missionaries. As for promotion, this was by the 'office boy' system of apprenticeship, beginning as a Magistrate's Clerk or as a junior police officer. This archaic system of appointment and promotion, based on the personal patronage of the High Commissioner, was maintained while all other British African colonies came under the care of the Colonial Office with strict professional standards of entry and advancement. After 1925 the High Commissioner in South Africa was anyway no longer appointed or controlled by the Colonial Office, but by Amery's new-fangled Dominions Office (later Commonwealth Relations Office) that dealt only with Australia, Canada, New Zealand, South Africa, Southern Rhodesia, and the High Commission Territories.[35]

As Rey was to realise, there had been one previous Resident Commissioner who had tried to set the Bechuanaland Protectorate administration on its feet as an efficient and loyal body. Ralph Williams, between 1901 and 1906, had converted a frontier police regime into a civil administration. Williams had failed to get the administrative headquarters moved from Mafeking, sixteen miles outside the Protectorate, to a more convenient 'camp' inside the Protectorate such as Lobatsi (Lobatse) or Gaberones (Gaborone). But he had established a small secretariat, with a rudimentary records system, in the 'Imperial Reserve' at Mafeking, and had removed the Bechuanaland Protectorate Police from the control of the (Southern Rhodesian) British South Africa Police. In future all Resident Commissioners were to head the Police with the rank of Lieutenant-Colonel. Williams reached an understanding with the Chiefs of the seven or eight major Tswana states that had been enclosed within the Bechuanaland Protectorate, that they would be left in charge of the everyday running of their districts or 'native reserves'. He also presided over the demarcation and sub-division of farms for white settlers in Blocks along the borders.[36]

Prologue

Ralph Williams had been appointed as Resident Commissioner by Alfred Milner as High Commissioner, who had himself been appointed by Joseph Chamberlain as Colonial Secretary. But with the passing of Chamberlain, Milner and Williams, and the coming of Union, Bechuanaland had sunk back into inertia — festering rather than ripening in constant expectation of inevitable transfer to the Union. 'Native' development was discouraged as incompatible with the ethos of white settlerdom to which the future of Bechuanaland was committed. Chiefly commercial initiative was stamped on, and indigenous initiatives in education were brought to heel. The whole political economy shifted from relative autonomy towards ever greater dependency on white South Africa. Tswana trading nations were transformed into native labour reserves. 'Development' was equated with the interests of British mining capital and white settler farmers.[37]

In such circumstances, resistance to 'development' became a form of patriotic resistance on the part of some of the more progressive Chiefs — notably Khama III (died 1923) and his son Tshekedi Khama (Regent for Seretse, Khama's grandson, 1926–50). These Chiefs used the argument that the Protectorate of 1885, and its subsequent reaffirmation in London in 1895, was a binding treaty that obliged the British to respect Tswana self-government and land rights. In voicing these assumptions, they were joined by a significant element of the Bechuanaland administration. Jules Ellenberger as Resident Commissioner (1923–28) pressed the viewpoint of the Chiefs. He twice called for the abolition of all concessions to Europeans, and persuaded the High Commissioner and the Colonial Office that the only way to keep Bechuanaland from joining the Union was by stopping European-style development.[38] It was this local 'trusteeship' element, of administrators who saw Bechuanaland as a primarily 'Native' territory, which so aroused the ire of Amery and then of Rey. Amery and Rey turned the previous policy upside down. It was their *volte face* which made the Bangwato, under the leadership of Tshekedi Khama, so aggrieved and obdurate about the revived mining concession in their Reserve.[39]

However, when Rey arrived in Bechuanaland, he was faced by one of the old school of military men as Resident Commissioner, R.M. Daniel (1928–30), rather than Ellenberger. Daniel, following the new Amery line, had already alienated Tshekedi Khama over the mineral concession. Daniel appeared to preside over a moribund regime of bureaucrats who were just holding on to their jobs. Nowhere was this better illustrated than in financial administration, or rather in the lack of it. While the revenue base was shrinking, the administration prided itself on 'good house-keeping' by never allowing expenditure to exceed revenue. Forty per cent of revenue came from direct taxation of Africans ('Hut Tax'), and Africans bore the brunt of indirect taxation too.[40] Yet their capacity to pay was being constantly eroded. Not only was a £25 cow in 1900 worth only £1 by 1922, but from 1924 onwards the Union placed heavy restrictions on the export of cattle from the three High Commission Territories — in order, as Prime Minister Hertzog put it, to 'materially further restrict the development of these territories'.[41] Yet at the same time the European-controlled commercial sector in Bechuanaland was hardly taxed at all. By failing to operate a tax law of 1897 the Bechuanaland Protectorate (B.P.) failed to tax joint stock companies until 1934, to the tune of up to £98,000 a year — the figure lost in 1933–34, and which exceeds total revenue from all sources in twenty-two of the previous thirty-four years.[42] Whereas Rey was to reduce direct African taxation at a time of drought and famine, the B.P. administration in 1922 had actually raised the Hut Tax, as our missionary

Prologue

observer Haydon Lewis put it, 'in proportion to the deepening distress of the public'.[43] To cap it all, Bechuanaland and Basutoland were obliged to loan their 'surpluses' (of revenue over expenditure) to finance white settler development in Swaziland, rather than to spend it on themselves! To be fair, the ideas of development capital and deficit budgeting — essential to capitalist development — were alien to British colonial administrators in general until enshrined in the 1929 Colonial Development Act and its 1940 successor.

The condition of Bechuanaland on Rey's arrival, if desperate for its colonial administration, was however not hopeless for its indigenous population. The major Chiefs had been by no means reduced to mere puppets of colonialism, as they had been in neighbouring Southern Rhodesia and South Africa. Nor had Bechuanaland been uniformly reduced to a social and economic appendage of South Africa. Even in the south-east the Bangwaketse Reserve (under Chief Bathoen II) was less integrated into the South African political economy, as gauged by the rate of labour migration, than the Bakwena and Bakgatla Reserves. The Bangwato (Bamangwato) and Batawana Reserves in the east and north-west were as yet to contribute substantial labour migration to South Africa, and were anyway more contiguous to Southern Rhodesia and South West Africa.[44]

Rey's Appointment to Bechuanaland

The appointment of Charles Rey as Resident Commissioner of the Bechuanaland Protectorate was by no means a foregone conclusion. The Colonial Office attempted to have one of its own men, rather than an outsider, appointed. The names of eminent administrators like Philip Mitchell and Orde-Browne were canvassed. But Amery won through with the argument that Rey fitted Amery's own prescription for the job: 'someone who is enterprising, keen on development . . . a fresh and vigorous personality who will look at the situation with new eyes.'[45] Rey was to sail out in September 1929 to understudy the retiring Resident Commissioner, R.M. Daniel, assuming full responsibility in April 1930.

Rey received an earful about Bechuanaland before he even left England. First he was filled in by the Colonial Office on relations with the Treasury, and by Amery himself on the development possibilities of Bechuanaland. Then Rey was put in contact with a former High Commissioner, Lord Buxton, and two former Resident Commissioners, Sir Edward Garraway and Sir Francis Newton — both with close Rhodesian, rather than South African, connections.

Newton fired Rey with enthusiasm for a railway across the Kalahari, from Southern Rhodesia across Bechuanaland to Walvis Bay in South West Africa — a project strongly opposed by South African interests. Garraway gave Rey valuable personal insights which, as the reader of the diaries will see, helped to prejudice Rey against certain of his future colleagues. Shirley Eales, the Assistant Imperial Secretary in Cape Town, was described as able but 'not sahib'. Dutton, the Government Secretary at Mafeking, was a 'bad man' who had to be watched. Chase, the Chief Veterinary Officer, and Dyke, the Chief Medical Officer, were very good men. Among other pearls of wisdom, Garraway impressed on Rey the need to get his whiskey and champagne free of duty as hospital stores, and the need to be gazetted Lieutenant-Colonel of the Police and to wear its uniform.[46]

Buxton provided Rey with a news-clipping from the *Cape Argus*, entitled 'Bechuanaland: Plea for Reform. By a Native'. (The anonymous writer was Simon Ratshosa, imprisoned and exiled after attempting to assassinate Tshekedi Khama

Prologue

in 1926). Among points that Rey may have absorbed was the plea for a book of native law and custom to guide colonial administrators, and for some form of codification and unification of law from different tribal sources. Rey may have had somewhat more mixed feelings about the author's final statement: 'Native socialists do not wish to overthrow the chief's power, but to have a substantive right in the country and to enjoy its fruits.'[47] But any fears in Rey's mind about 'Young Bechuana', equivalent to the 'Young Ethiopians' of his Abyssinian days, seem to have been set at rest on meeting Kgaleman T. Motsete at a venue in Curzon Street. Motsete was a quiet young man, evidently anxious to please, who was just finishing his third degree at London University (Bachelor of Arts, Bachelor of Divinity, Bachelor of Music), and who was about to return home to the Bangwato Reserve as teacher and preacher. Motsete attempted to teach Rey some Setswana, at least one word of which Rey put to good effect on reaching Bechuanaland. Rey learnt that his own name, with its consonant rolled and spelt 'Rre', was the vocative form of Sir or 'my father' in Setswana.[48]

Rey's last three interviews were with the Assistant Secretary at the Dominions Office, with an expert on the Kalahari, and with Lord Lugard the doyen of colonial administrators. The Dominions Office warned Rey about missionaries and the Bangwato. Tshekedi Khama 'would be helpful if with one, troublesome if not'. His nephew Seretse Khama, the real Chief, was just a small boy but 'very forward. Might be trouble when he grows up.' The Kalahari expert, a Dr Nobbs, acquainted Rey with recent surveys of the area, including journeys by motor lorry by Captain the Hon. Bede Clifford the Imperial Secretary (i.e. chief assistant to the High Commissioner), which probably inspired Rey to follow suit with his own expeditions. Nobbs also underlined the potential of the Kalahari for cattle production and export via Walvis Bay, given the precondition of water development by boring wells.[49]

Rey's visit to Lord Lugard, only a fortnight before leaving England, seems to have been more of a gesture towards the great man than a genuine consultation. Neither Amery nor his new acolyte Rey were really in sympathy with the ideas which Lugard had put forward in his book *The Dual Mandate* (1922). Lugard advised Rey to, in effect, shun the White Dominion model for Bechuanaland's development. Instead he should consult with the Governor of Northern Rhodesia and read up on Nigeria and Tanganyika.[50]

Rey's reading in preparation seems to have ranged from Colonial Office files and Blue Books to popular literature. From Colonial Office files, Rey extracted an item that struck him as being of key importance. It was a letter from Resident Commissioner Williams in 1903, which remarked: 'Khama must be got to understand that he is not King of an independent country but is a Chief under Protection who is granted an area to live in, subject to administration by Government'.[51] Williams's deposition of Sekgoma Letsholathebe, the Batawana Chief, in 1906, was the precedent in Rey's mind for his depositions of Chiefs in the 1930s. For Rey, 'native administration' seems to have boiled down largely to a matter of making and unmaking Chiefs — the handmaids of colonial government who actually did the day-to-day administration of 'natives'. What Rey failed to appreciate was Williams's more fundamental policy of supporting his Chiefs against what he called their 'Earls of Warwick' — the rivals and kingmakers who destabilised the institution of Chieftainship.[52] Instead of recruiting their loyalties, Rey was to make the Chiefs into the main stumbling block in the way of his grandiose plans for developing the impoverished Protectorate.

Prologue

Rey admitted to being influenced by the romance of colonial administration as portrayed by Edgar Wallace's novels on Commissioner Bones and 'Sanders of the River'.[53] It helps to explain why, when he was completely new to the actual situation, Rey could come out with hoary statements like 'they have to be made to realise the moral superiority of the white, or there would be no holding them',[54] so soon after his arrival in Bechuanaland. Rey held onto the central myth of this literature, of the single white man pitted against his human and physical environment. The myth enabled Rey to talk of a single white police officer being in charge of the whole Southern Kalahari — with the ludicrous implication that somehow the whole region would collapse into anarchy were the man withdrawn.[55] It was a myth that had its origins in the literature of the European Age of Exploration. Charles Rey well remembered lines, probably learnt at school, from William Cowper (1731-1800) but supposedly written by Alexander Selkirk — the marooned sailor prototype for Robinson Crusoe:

I am monarch of all I survey
My right there is none to dispute

On Friday, September 20th, 1929, with Ninon at his side and a ferocious new dog called Pongo curled up on a corner seat, Charles Rey left London by train for Southampton, where they all boarded a Union Castle liner. After 'a couple of hairy rows' about Pongo's quarters on board, the ship sailed at 4 pm. Rey compared the sailing with a scene from his own novel: 'we watched and waved until we could see nothing but a blur of moving dots'.[56] He could now turn to making a success of the last phase in a long career of promising starts but few tangible achievements. He looked forward to the fray with unbounded confidence.

Notes

1. Certified copy of birth certificate, in Rhodes House Library, University of Oxford, Anthony Sillery Papers — Box XI/File 54 (hereafter RHL Mss Afr s1611-XI/54).
2. Rhodes House Library, University of Oxford, Charles Rey Papers — Box 2/File 8 (hereafter RHL Mss Brit Emp s1384-2/8).
3. 'Colonel Rey's life of adventure. Retires today after service in 20 countries. Stories of Bechuanaland and Abyssinia', *The Star* (Johannesburg), 23 September 1937; *Cape Argus* (Cape Town), 23 September 1937, pp. 19-20; *Natal Mercury* (Durban), n.d. May 1939; *Evening Standard* (London), 17 July 1939; 'American lunch club', *The Star*, 6 July 1939 — clippings in Botswana Society Rey Papers and RHL Mss Brit Emp s1384-6/2.
4. cf. Kenneth Bradley, *Once a District Officer* (London: Macmillan & New York: St Martin's Press, 1966), pp. 1 & 169; and John M. Mackenzie, *Propaganda and Empire: the manipulation of British public opinion 1880-1960* (Manchester: Manchester University Press, 1984).
5. Stephen Tallents, *Man and Boy* (London: Faber & Faber, 1943), pp. 184-185. Cf. A.J.P. Taylor, *English History 1914-1945* (Hardmondsworth: Penguin Books, 1970), pp. 64-68.
6. Rey Autobiography, fragment of chap. VIII in RHL, Mss Brit Emp s1384-1/3.
7. *Birmingham Daily Mail* (Birmingham), 1 July 1915: *The Times* (London), 23 November 1915 (RHL, Mss Brit Emp s1384-1/1).
8. RHL, Mss Brit Emp s1384-1/1.
9. Rodney Lowe (Heriot-Watt University, Edinburgh) to Sillery, 25 September 1974 & 19 June 1975, citing information from himself and Roger Davidson of Edinburgh University — RHL Mss Brit Emp s1611-XI/54. Cf. 'Sir Charles Rey on labour problems', *Rand Daily Mail* (Johannesburg), 16 August 1939 — RHL Mss Brit Emp s1384-6/2.

Prologue

10 see p. 99 below.
11 C.F. Rey, 'Lady Ninon Rey, an appreciation' (mimeo) 3pp — Botswana Society Rey Papers.
12 ibid; *Morning Post* (London), 18 March 1907 — clipping in Botswana Society Rey Papers.
13 Tom Killion (Stanford University) to Parsons, n.d. (December 1985); information from Jim McCann (Boston University), August 1984.
14 Killion ibid; see also RHL Mss Brit Emp s1384-2/1, 2/2 & 2/3.
15 Interview with Mrs Fay Longhurst Murphy, Cape Town, 27 June 1979.
16 Botswana Society Rey Diaries (Original Mss); A.J. Haile to Sillery, 23 June 1975 — RHL Mss Afr s1611-XI/54; Interview with Peggy and Bruce Little, Mafeking, 27 March 1986.
17 'Talk of the town', *Cape Times* (Cape Town), 27 March 1947; J.L. Park (US Vice-Consul, Aden) to Rey, 10 August 1927 — RHL Mss Brit Emp s1384-2/1.
18 *The Star*, 23 September 1937.
19 'Abyssinia today. Progress arrested. Threat of revolution', *Morning Post* (London), 2 May, 1923.
20 *Unconquered Abyssinia, As It Is Today. An account of a little known country, its people and their customs, from the social, economic and geographical points of view, its resources and possibilities, and its extraordinary history as a hitherto unconquered nation* (London: Seeley, Service & Co, 1923, and Philadelphia: J.B. Lippinscott Company, 1924) 312 pp.
21 'Abyssinia and Abyssinians of to-day', *Geographical Journal* (London), vol. 60 (1922), pp. 177-194; 'Abyssinia of to-day', *Journal of the African Society* (London), vol. 21 (1922), pp. 279-290.
22 *Geographical Journal*, vol. 67 (1927), pp. 481-506; *Edinburgh Review* (Edinburgh), vol. 244 (1926), pp. 276-290; *World Today* (London), vol. 49 (1927), pp. 123-133.
23 (London: Duckworth, 1927) 296 pp.
24 (London: H.F. & G. Witherby, 1929) 319 pp.
25 (London: Martin Hopkinson, 1929) 319 pp. See *Illustrated London News* (London), 12 October 1929 and *East Africa and Rhodesia* (London) of similar date.
26 Interview with Mrs Fay Longhurst Murphy, Cape Town, 27 June 1979.
27 cf. RHL, Mss Brit Emp s1384-2/7.
28 (London: Seeley, Service & Co, 1935 and Philadelphia: J.B. Lippinscott Company, 1935) 291 pp.
29 Leopold S. Amery, *The Empire in the New Era: Speeches Delivered During an Empire Tour 1927-1928* (London: Edward Arnold, 1928), pp. 1-12.
30 ibid, pp. 15 and 19-20. Cf. Ronald Hyam, *The Failure of South African Expansion 1908-1948* (London: Macmillan, 1972), pp. 117-123; Anthony Sillery, 'Protectorate in Action', chap. XI (RHL Mss Afr s1611-3/15), citing Public Record Office (London) D.O.9/7 despatch of 24 September 1927.
31 Amery, *The Empire in the New Era*, pp. 19-20.
32 Rey interview with Amery, 19 July 1929 — RHL Mss Brit Emp s1384-5/1.
33 Q.N. Parsons, *The Word of Khama* (Lusaka: Neczam, 1972), p. 25. Q.N. Parsons, 'Education and development in pre-colonial and colonial Botswana to 1965' (pp. 21-45) in Michael Crowder (ed.), *Education for Development in Botswana* (Gaborone: Macmillan/Botswana Society, 1984), p. 33.
34 S. Ratshosa, 'My Book' (typed mss), p. 101 — Botswana National Archives (Gaborone). Cf. Q.N. Parsons, 'Shots for a black republic? Simon Ratshosa and Botswana nationalism', *African Affairs* (London), vol. 73, no. 293 (1974), pp. 449-458. For Barnes, see his Labour Party document in RHL Mss Brit Emp s1427-1/4; also his *The New Boer War* (London: Hogarth Press/Leonard & Virginia Wolfe, 1932). For Sillery see his draft autobiography 'Working Backwards', p. 211 (RHL Mss Afr s207).
35 Sillery, 'Protectorate in Action', *passim* — RHL Mss Afr s1611-3/15; Ralph Furse, *Aucuparius: Memoirs of a Recruiting Officer* (London: Oxford University Press, 1962), p. 249; Bede Edmund Hugh Clifford, *Proconsul: Being Incidents in the Life and Career of the Honourable Sir Bede Clifford, G.C.M.G., C.B., M.V.O.* (London: Evans Brothers, 1964), p. 148; Louis Alexander Picard, 'Role Changes Among Field Administrators in Botswana: Administrative Attitudes and Social Change' (Madison: University of Wisconsin, PhD, 1977), chap. 3. The best source for the 'Mafora' (French) administrators of the High Commission Territories is Gordon M. Haliburton, *Historical Dictionary of Lesotho* (Metuchen, N.J.: Scarecrow Press, 1976).
36 Cf. Ralph Champneys Williams, *How I Became a Governor* (London: John Murray, 1913).
37 Cf. Q.N. Parsons, 'Khama & Co and the Jousse Trouble, 1910-1916', *Journal of African History* (London), vol. xvi, no. 3 (1975), pp. 383-408; Neil Parsons, 'The economic history of Khama's Country in Botswana, 1844-1930', pp. 113-143 in Robin Palmer & Neil Parsons (eds.), *The Roots of Rural Poverty in Central and Southern Africa* (London: Heinemann and Berkeley: University of California Press, 1977).
38 Sillery, 'Protectorate in Action', p. 187 — RHL Mss Afr s1611-3/15.
39 ibid, p. 200.

Prologue

40 Cf. Quill Hermans, 'A review of Botswana's financial history, 1900-1973', *Botswana Notes and Records* (Gaborone), vol. 6 (1974), pp. 89-116.
41 Stephen Ettinger, 'South Africa's weight restrictions on cattle exports from Bechuanaland, 1924-41', *Botswana Notes and Records*, vol. 4 (1972), p. 21-29.
42 Alan W. Pim (with S. Milligan), *Financial and Economic Position of the Bechuanaland Protectorate* (London: His Majesty's Stationary Office, 1933 — Cmd. 4368), p. 49; see also National Archives of Botswana, S.262/3.
43 Parsons, 'Education and Development', p. 33.
44 John Taylor, 'Mine labour recruitment in the Bechuanaland Protectorate', *Botswana Notes and Records*, vol. 10 (1978), pp. 99-113; Isaac Schapera, *Migrant Labour and Tribal Life: A Study of Conditions in the Bechuanaland Protectorate* (London: Oxford University Press/International African Institute, 1947).
45 Sillery, 'Protectorate in Action', p. 172 — RHL Mss Afr s1611-3/15.
46 Rey interviews with Sir Francis Newton and Sir Edward Garraway, n.d. and 8 August 1929 (RHL Mss Brit Emp s1384-5/1.
47 'Bechuanaland: plea for reform. By a native', *Cape Argus* (Cape Town), Saturday 23(?)February 1929 enclosed in Lord Buxton to Rey, 30 July 1929 (RHL Mss Brit Emp s1384-5/1). Cf. Ratshosa, 'My Book' and Parsons, 'Shots for a Black Republic?'
48 K.T. Motsete correspondence with Rey, 1936-1938 (RHL Mss Brit Emp s1384-5/2). Cf. Dingane Mulale, 'The Life and Career of Dr Kgaleman Tumedisho Motsete' (Gaborone: University College of Botswana, B.A. History thesis, 1977).
49 Rey interview with Dr Nobbs, 16 August 1929 (RHL Mss Brit Emp s1384—5/1); B.E.H Clifford, 'A report on a journey by motor transport from Mahalapye through the Kalahari Desert, Ghanzi and Ngamiland, to the Victoria Falls', *Geographical Journal* (London), vol. 73, no. 4 (1929), pp. 342-358 — followed by further articles on the Kalahari and the Makgadikgadi salt pans in the same journal: vol. 75(1930), pp. 16-26; vol. 77 (1931), pp. 355-357; and vol. 91 (1938), pp. 233-241.
50 Rey interview with Lord Lugard, 5 September 1929 (RHL Mss Brit Emp s1384-5/1).
51 Ralph Williams (Resident Commissioner, Mafeking) to Panzera (Assistant Commissioner, North), 18 April 1903 — typed copy from presumably Colonial Office files in RHL Mss Brit Emp s1384-5/1.
52 R.C. Williams to Rev. W.C. Willoughby, 26 September 1902 — Public Record Office, C.O.417/345; Botswana National Archives, S.178/1. Cf. Williams, *How I Became a Governor*, p. 277 and 306, etc.
53 See Botswana Society, Rey Diaries, (Original Mss), entry for 20 October — 17 November 1929.
54 See p. 5 below.
55 See p. 6 and 195 below. Cf. Anthony H.M. Kirk-Greene, 'On governorship and governors in British Africa', in L.H. Gann & Peter Duignan (eds.). *African Proconsuls: European Governors in Africa* (New York: Free Press, London: Collier-Macmillan, and Stanford, California: Hoover Institution, 1977), p. 230; David Dabydeen (ed.) *The Black Presence in English Literature* (Manchester: Manchester University Press, 1985).
56 Botswana Society Rey Diaries, Mss, vol. 1, p. 2.

1. C.F. Rey in the Resident Commissioner's Office, Mafeking, May 1937. Behind him are photographs of previous Resident Commissioners and of the first government newspaper, *Lebone loa Betsoana (Bechuanaland Torch)*.

2. 'I have had the Camp (Imperial Reserve) straightened up, all the buildings (offices, stores, stables, etc.) whitewashed, the roofs painted red, paths cleaned up etc. etc.' (10 to 13 March 1930)
The Imperial Reserve, Mafeking, towards the end of Rey's reign. Resident Commissioner's Office behind the flagstaff.

3. *'On Thursday I had a meeting with all my Police officers to set new re-organisation proposals going. We were all photographed in uniform, and in honour of the occasion dined together in the evening at the Grand Hotel – the first Police 'mess dinner'.* (30 July 1936)
Standing (left to right): B.P.P. Trooper, Denis Reilly, Hurndall, Poole, Masterman, Bob Langley, B.P.P. Corporal. *Sitting*: Godley, C.F. Rey, Croneen. *Squatting*: B.P.P. Orderly/Messenger. Rey, with no previous military experience, was gazetted Lieutenant-Colonel and Commandant of Police by virtue of his appointment as Resident Commissioner.

4. *'At once, and permanently, we have lost our hearts to the Athlones. Never have I met more charming, kindly, unaffected people, and every hour that we stayed at Government House increased that feeling.'* (8 to 10 October)
The Athlones at Mafeking. Rey's car 'Topsy' and faithful driver, Matsepane ('Marzipan'), in the background. The Earl of Athlone was High Commissioner and Governor-General of South Africa from 1923 to 1930.

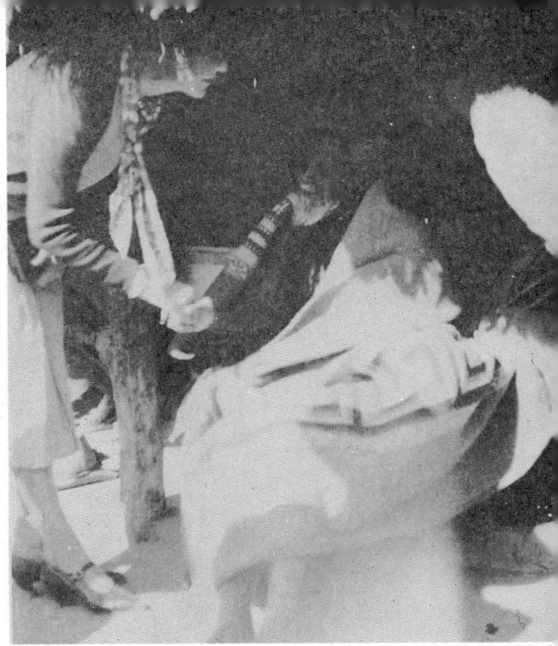

5. (Above left) 'He is a brilliant man, an exceptional brain, very quick, very thorough, quite fearless, an indefatigable worker, a pukka gentleman, and perfectly delightful to work with. We clicked at once'. (20 to 25 April 1931)
'He has as much backbone as a filleted jelly-fish; he is past his job, brain gone to fat and spine disappeared. He is regarded as a joke in Cape Town by the general public; his activities consist mainly in addressing religious gatherings. When a man 'gets religion', it's time he was shut up.' 4 May 1934
Sir Herbert Stanley and Lady Stanley. Sir Herbert Stanley was High Commissioner in South Africa between 1931 and 1934.

6 (Above right) 'I'm sorry to say that old Chief Gaborone has died – he was a wonderfully picturesque figure. 110 years old, and a splendid type of the dignified courteous chief of old times before they were spoilt by European customs and clothes and education and all that rot.' (9 to 15 November 1931)
Lady Stanley greets ancient Chief Gaborone (c1820–1931), August 1931.

7. 'After breakfast Stanley and I arrayed ourselves in top hats and tail coats, and Holbech in uniform, for the ceremony of laying the foundation stone of the church which is being built by the Railway Mission. It was blazing hot, and stiff collars and town clothes don't really go out here.' (29 July 1934)
Sir Herbert Stanley orating after laying the foundation stone of the Anglican church building at Lobatsi. Holbech and Rey on the left; Rev. Lawrence Hands, construction workers and Bishop of Kimberley on the right. Unlike in South Africa, blacks were permitted to do skilled construction work in Bechuanaland.

8 (Top left) *'That little devil Molefi has caused more trouble at Mochudi'* (17 April 1937)
Chief Molefi (1909–1958), with *mopatho* (age-regiment) members in traditional dress.

9. (Top right) *'When in London I found a Mochuana who came to give me lessons in Sechuana in Curzon St.'* (18 to 26 November 1929)
K.T. Motsete (1899–1971) stands in front of his independent Tati Training Institution, built with Rey's aid, June 1936.

10. (Bottom left) *'Sailors and marines with four small field-guns, fit and hard and jolly, doing their drill and field practice, working their camp kitchens, testing their field telephones, and generally bringing a wonderful atmosphere of Britain into the veld.'* (13 September 1933)
Pith-helmeted sailors ready to depart from Palapye Road in Rhodesia Railways lorries, 14 September 1933.

11. (Bottom right) *'Reilly and Neale arrived about 4, and entirely agreed with my view that the only course was to destroy the village by a bombing aeroplane, and to arrest Gobbleman with an armoured car.'* (8 April 1933)
Chief Gobuamang ('Gobbleman') (1845–1940)

12. *'The guard sprang to attention and gave the Royal salute. We solemnly saluted each other.'*
(14 September 1933)
Rey greets Evans on arrival at the Serowe race course.

13. *'A large covered platform had been erected in the middle of the race course... Tshekedi came and stood in front, two B.P. N.C.O.s behind him, and the guns crashed out the salute of nineteen guns, the roar echoing in the hills magnificently... The Admiral then read his speech suspending Tshekedi.'* (14 September 1933)
Rey stands behind Evans and a marine guard at attention. Tshekedi (second from left) stands between four advisers, briefcase bulging with documents at their feet. Local whites have seats on the right of the platform.
'I also had a bad interview with that poisonous little rat Tshekedi, Chief of the Bamangwato. He is a nasty piece of work... The day is rapidly approaching when he will find himself in the consommé.' (4 to 7 February 1931)

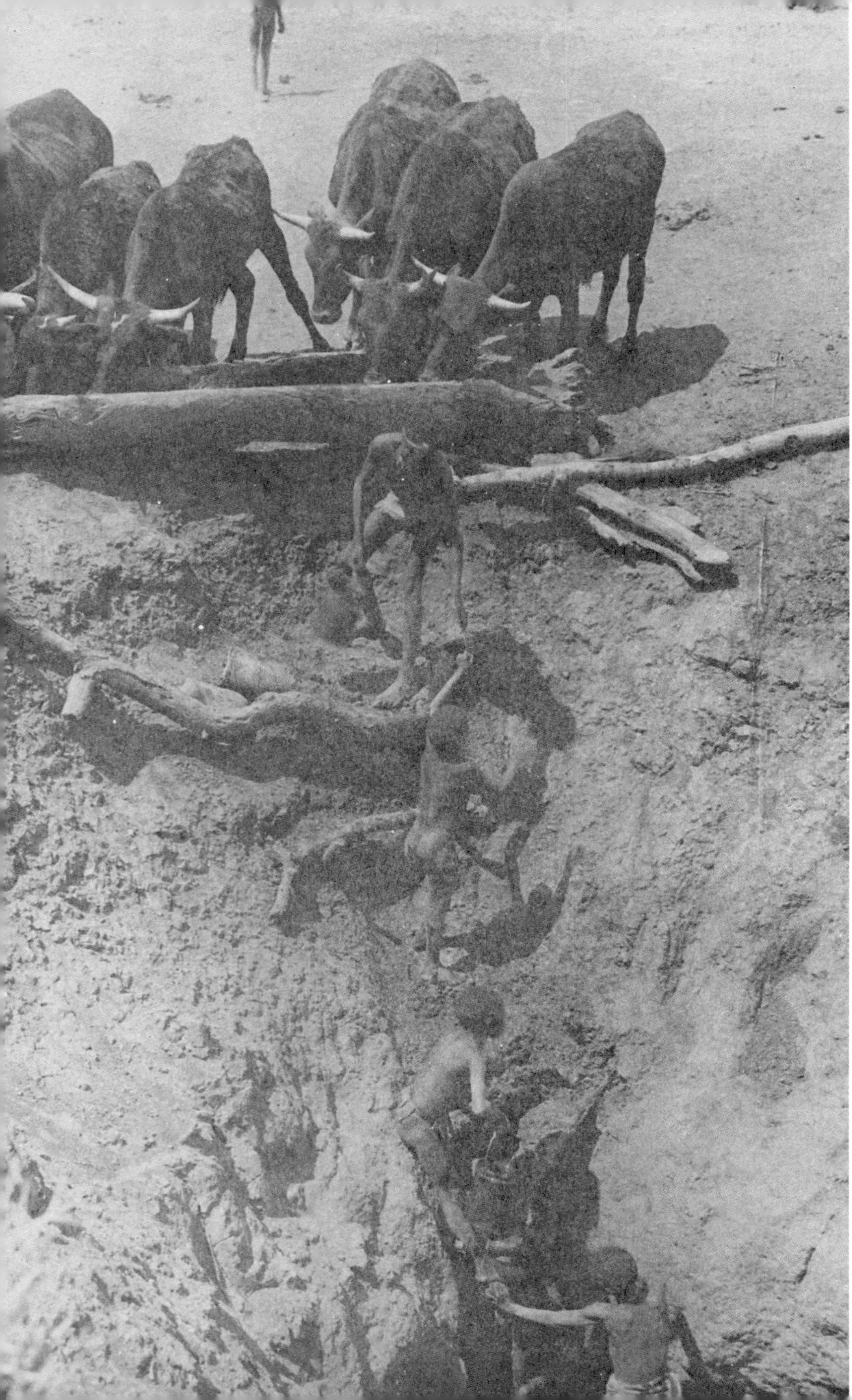

15. (Top left) *'We got news that Foot and Mouth disease had broken out in Southern Rhodesia and was spreading like wildfire... I determined to draw a cordon right along five hundred miles of frontier, and to clear all cattle five miles back.'* (13 April 1931)
Veterinary cordon notice on frontier of Tati District with Southern Rhodesia, with B.P. Policemen, 29 June 1931.

16. (Above right) *'And then after a couple of hard days on Saturday and Sunday, the worst blow of all fell on Monday 9 – a black letter day – those goddamned swine at the Colonial Office cabled refusing my water boring scheme.'* (9 March, 1931)
Serowe dam under construction, 1931.

17. (Below right) *'They were terribly shy. But Ninon and I worked like blacks to make them feel at home... Poor things, it was pathetic to see their garments and to realise that they live marooned in this damned awful place all their lives, seeing no-one and going nowhere.'* (5 September 1934)
Ghanzi white settlers, September 1934.

14. (Opposite) *'Here is another of these huge pans, dry of course, but with a number of wells sunk at one corner... The first well we tried nearly made us sick... We were luckier at the second one however, and got a splendid supply of good clean water at about fifty feet.'* (Khakea 18 February 1931) *'... the grass and veld is eaten out and trampled down for miles around the pan. The usual story showing again and again the necessity for putting down a chain of wells and boreholes right across the country according to my big scheme.'* (Tsabong, 24 February 1931)
Children passing up buckets to a wooden trough from a Kalahari pan well. One of Rey's favourite photographs.

18. (Above) *'The interest taken in our show may be judged by the fact that the day after the official opening people passed through at the rate of two thousand an hour, and we had to enforce one way traffic!'* (2 April 1931)
After the success of 'Bountiful Bechuanaland Protectorate' at the Rand Easter Show (Johannesburg) in April 1931, the theme of the next year's exhibit was 'Progressive Bechuanaland Protectorate'.

20 (Opposite above) *'I was able to tell them that we had got First Prize again, £100 and the special Silver Challenge Cup! Indeed all Johannesburg is talking about our Exhibit, and say it **is** the Show.'* (22 March 1932)
An unusually nervous Rey awaits the award of the Cup.

21. (Opposite below) Colonel Rey sculpted in best Bechuanaland butter, with Basuto pony and his dog Pongo. Rey stands in front of a Bechuanaland exhibit at the Rand Easter Show.

19 (Below) *'At 10.30 we dashed off by car to the flying ground to meet Stuart. He had flown over from the Protectorate with a consignment of 'perishables', the first time that exhibits had ever been brought to the show by air.'* (21 March 1932)
Rey behind tin-bath. Ninon second from left, at a Johannesburg airfield.

C. F. REY. C.M.G.

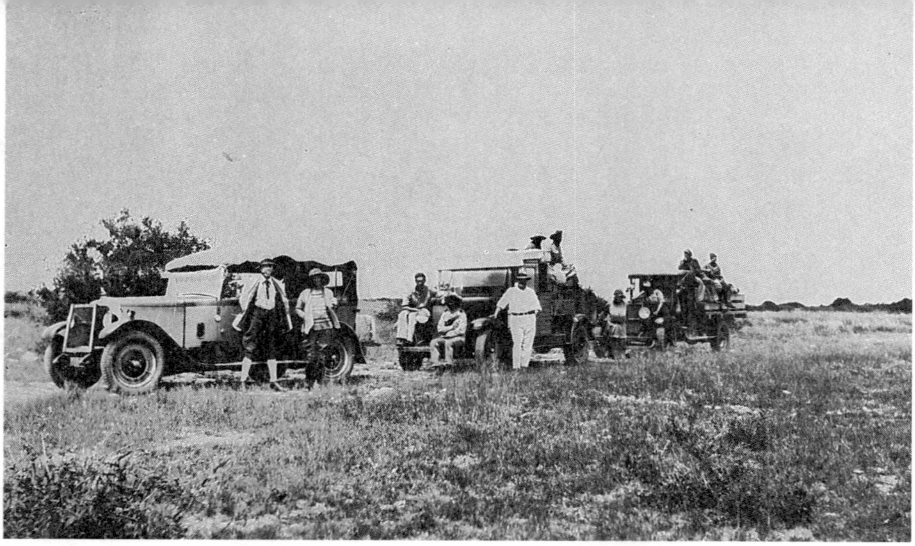

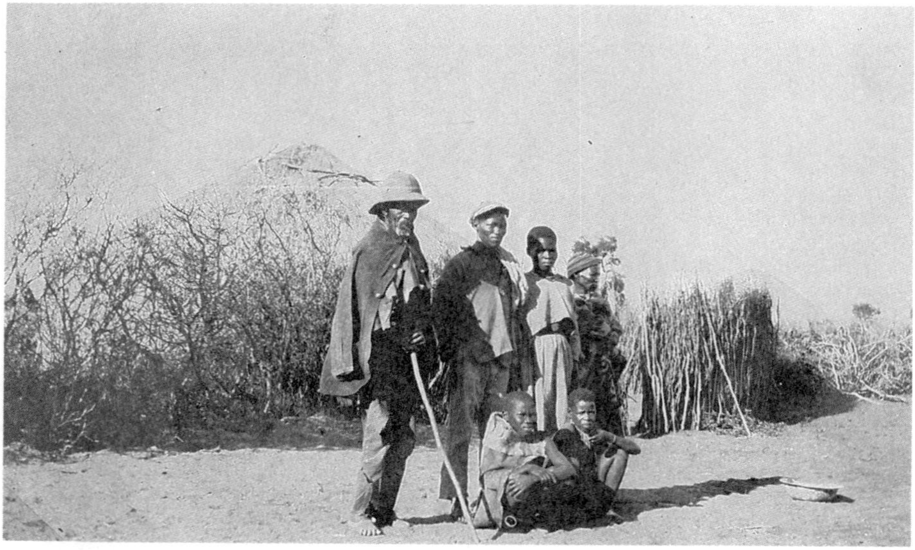

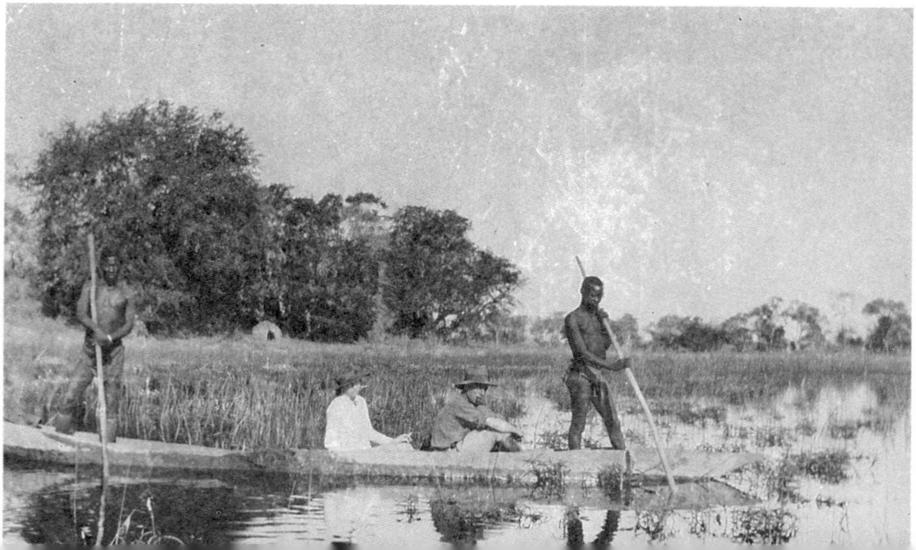

25. (Above) *'It is sad to have to leave Maun today on our return journey – this country is so fascinating and the idea of returning to that hole Mafeking is most unwelcome.'* (28 June 1933)
Ninon, Rey and Ninon's niece Sally in camp at Maun.

22. (Opposite above) *'The day of our great trek has dawned: it is not great in length though it will cover nearly one thousand miles, but it is an adventure as it is across the Great Kalahari Desert'.* (15 February 1931)
Somewhere in the Great Kalahari Desert. Car 'Topsy' at the front, with Rey and Ninon. Lorry 'Jemima' second, with Sharp, Matsepane and Chase. Lorry 'Matilda' third, with Mrs Douthirt ('that wonderful old American lady') and driver. Two policemen and two other people sitting on the backs of the lorries.

23. (Opposite centre) *'They had never seen a Resident Commissioner before (none has ever been here), and they were so overawed that one of them referred to me as his "Second God". I could not help ejaculating "Why second?"'* (*Tsabong* 24 February 1931)
Kgalagadi headman and family at Kalahari cattle post, February 1931.

24. (Opposite below) *'And at 12.45 we arrived at the dreadful village of Maun, chief village of Ngamiland, and most desolate and forbidding of villages in the country.'* (16 June 1933)
Rey and Ninon, punted by two men in a *mokoro* canoe on the Okavango Swamps, Ngamiland, September 1934.

26. (Below) Farewell to Protectorate Government House, Mafeking, June 1937.

27. 'Ninon and I had to bolt off to the Native Sports to be ready to receive H.R.H. there at 3.15. These were held on the aerodrome, yet another site commanding a lovely view. They were admirably organised by Lt. Hope, and included an ox race, chicken race, native dances, displays by Pathfinders and Wayfarers.' (20 March 1934)
Pot-balancing drill by Wayfarers on Gaberones airfield, in honour of Prince George the Duke of Kent, March 1934.

28. 'I see no reason why our B.P. Pathfinders and Wayfarers should not be Scouts and Guides – just like all other natives all over the world, except in the Union of South Africa where the colour bar prejudice is so strong'. (7 February 1936)
'The Crack Troops of the Territory on the March' (B.P. Pathfinders drilling at Molepolole.)

1929

Sunday 6 October (on board ship)
Ninon and I expect to get in about 9 am tomorrow (Monday) morning. After nearly a week's cold weather we shall be glad to get off, for this is a rotten boat in bad weather. If we had not had all the special facilities they have given us, we should have been very unhappy. As it is we have been most comfortable.

Monday 7 & Tuesday 8 October (at Cape Town)
We docked before 9 on the 7th, but unfortunately Table Mountain was wreathed in clouds; there were showers of rain, and it was quite cold.

We need not have worried about our plans or Customs or anything, for everything was managed for us in regal style.

First of all, reporters interviewed and photographed me. Then the Assistant Imperial Secretary[1] came on board to meet us, armed with every kind of Government warrant and pass; and after making himself very pleasant saw us through all obstacles and to our hotel, the Mount Nelson.

The Assistant Imperial Secretary is named Shirley Eales,[2] and the name fits. I don't like him, though he was so very civil. He is too 'eely'. He is I believe a self-made man, which is doubtless to his credit, but I can't help feeling that the Almighty would have made a better job of it. However the creature is one who ought to be appeased, so we did so.

Cape Town to Pretoria

4 pm Tuesday 8 October to 9.30 am Thursday 10 October
The South Africans are very proud of their train service, but I'm damned if I know why. The train was slow, very bumpy, dirty, and lacked most of the facilities you expect on a modern sleeping car train. The food was not too bad, but I can't say we really enjoyed the trip. Fortunately we slept most of the way, day and night, as of course we had a large compartment reserved for us. They have a good bit to learn from the old country.

Our compartment was really one for four. A black gentleman came along while we were at dinner in the restaurant and made up our beds for the night.

An A.D.C. in the undress uniform of the Life Guards met us on the Pretoria platform; relays of servants seized our luggage and belongings; motor cars galore awaited us outside; and before we realised we had arrived we were in Government House and babbling away to the Athlones[3] — and to the Archbishop of Cape Town and his wife who were staying there.

At once, and permanently, we have lost our hearts to the Athlones. Never have I met more charming, kindly, unaffected people, and every hour that we stayed at Government House increased that feeling.

Thursday 10 to Saturday 12 October (at Pretoria)
Government House is a fine building in lovely grounds of about two hundred acres, and Athlone is wildly proud of the gardens which have been laid out according to his designs. He and I had a long talk in the afternoon, and then I went down to see Captain Clifford,[4] the Imperial Government Secretary, and had a long talk with him.

He was my first disappointment. I wanted very much indeed to like him and to get on with him, as I shall have lots to do with him. But I'm afraid I shan't be able to. He is bumptious, conceited, and a cad (tho' he is a nephew of Lord Clifford of Chudleigh); and I could see that he regarded me with suspicion and dislike as a rival. He's clever, confound him, and cuts a lot of ice — but as sure as 'eggs is eggs' he and I will fight like hell one day.

Of course we were as sweet as butter to each other. But he could not hide his feelings as well as I could and — well, *nous verrons*.

Colonel Ellenberger,[5] his son[6] and their wives came to lunch today. He was Resident Commissioner of B.P. [Bechuanaland Protectorate] before Colonel Daniel.[7] My God, what a quartette! They gave me a hump the size of a prize camel's — no wonder Sir Henry Birchenough[8] told me that my predecessors were dead from the neck upwards. I don't believe Ellenberger ever was alive — mentally.

We took a mutual dislike to each other at sight. His wife is a *bonne bourgeoise*. His son is one of my police-officers, and I should think he ought to arrest himself — and the son's wife should have been drowned at birth. (Ellenberger is the son of a missionary, and was born in a cave in Basutoland: need one say more to explain his mentality — or the lack of it).

Sunday 13 to Saturday 19 October (at Mafeking)
Punctually at 6.40 the train rolled into the mighty city (?) of Mafeking. And there on the platform was Colonel Daniel with an escort of six of our Bechuanaland Protectorate Police — khaki shorts with a red stripe down the sides, khaki shirts with red facings; and big khaki hats turned up at one side with a red band round — very smart and businesslike.

An ox waggon took our luggage, and a car brought us to Protectorate House — where Mrs Daniel received us in the lounge (in a dressing gown) and gave us hot tea and rather a cool welcome. Protectorate House made a very unfavourable impression on us. The lounge was dark and shabby, and all the furniture pretty motheaten and out of date.

Mrs Daniel began to thaw, and Daniel continued to be very nice. I wonder they don't try to poison us, as we are turning them out of their job and house. It must be very trying for them and I sympathise with them. We unpacked in the morning, had an infernally bad lunch, and slept till tea time. Then strings of visitors arrived to greet and inspect us.

Heavens, what a gang! I don't know which were the worst, the men or the women — not one with a particle of intelligence or culture or personality. Thank goodness we don't care for a social life, for we certainly shan't get it here. There wasn't a soul one would care to talk to, and if they are a fair specimen of the whole, we shall certainly be able to live a quiet and blameless life here. Perhaps they will grow on one, like castor-oil or ipecacuanha. I hope not.

On Monday (14th) the Government Secretary[9] came round to see me, and I went round to the Office with him in Daniel's car. Daniel had gone off up country for a couple of days.

The offices of the B.P. are situated on a large tract of land known as the 'Imperial Reserve' — which belongs to the Imperial Government, and *not* to the Union or South African Government. On that bit of land (800 acres) we are at home: we fly the Union Jack, have our own Police, and don't care a damn for any beastly South African mongrel Dutchman. It is always referred to as 'the Camp', and the Officer Commanding Police is in uniform — he is one of my eight white officers — a Captain, quite a decent fellow tho' an ass, Gash by name.

I wandered round poking my nose into all the offices, and shaking hands with everybody. And then returned to Protectorate House to lunch, sleep, and discuss plans with Ninon — prior to having a filthy dinner with Mrs Daniel, who is continuing to thaw under Ninon's amazingly tactful handling.

As for the Office — words fail me. I am simply horrified at the utter lack of organisation, the confusion, lack of discipline, and general sense of muddle. Everybody does any and every job: no one is responsible for any one thing; no papers can ever be found when wanted; the Government Secretary (the principal man) loafs in at 10.30 (hours being 9 to 5); the staff is scattered about in five different buildings; and most of their time is spent running about from one office to another and looking for papers.

There *is* going to be a cleaning of the Augean stables.

From the brain point of view the staff are a poor lot — but they are willing enough and only anxious for leadership. They are suffering from an 'inferiority complex' too, because Daniel has always been squashed and so they have come to regard themselves as no good — a fatal frame of mind.

With a good fighting lead I think they'll shape — they'll certainly get it.

Saturday 19 October
Thank goodness our stay with the Daniels has come to an end. We hate staying with people and like to be independent.

We moved into our own bungalow today — all our luggage was transported, and we sorted things out. We have got a cook and two houseboys, and with our two orderlies we made things hum.

Of course none of these people know how things ought to be done, and they'll take a lot of teaching. But Ninon is splendid at handling them, and tho' she is still a bit weary I've no doubt we'll shape soon.

We draw all household utensils we need from the Government stores — also such furniture and rugs etc as they have. That is a help. And with free medical attendance for ourselves, and free veterinary attention for our dog Pongo, a chauffeur and another Police orderly free, and a few other perquisites, I hope we shall do pretty well.

We have put a box on the front door for cards and a notice to say that on medical advice Ninon doesn't receive callers. So we ought to be peaceful and quiet. The bungalow is on the edge of the town, and we walk out of our front door on to the veld. It's really rather nice from that point of view.

Sunday 20 October to Sunday 17 November
It is terrible to think that I have not written up my diary for a month. But I do not think that even in my strenuous life I have often been as busy as during these last four weeks.

In the first place I did not want Ninon to get overtired again. And in the second place the Office! I have had to start from the beginning and organise the whole thing from top to bottom — and at the same time get to understand the work and keep it going somehow — and further to draft several very important reports that Athlone wanted on subjects entirely new to me — besides interview dozens of people who came to pay their respects and see what the new 'boss' was like.

In the four weeks I have been at work I have established a single registry in place of the six different ones they had; set out a complete scheme of office work allotting every man to a particular job; drafted a complete set of instructions for the conduct of business; built on two new rooms and reconstructed two others; brought the staff into line so that now they jump to the word of command and shew signs of life and spirit and even of dawning intelligence; introduced a new system of registering papers and correspondence, handling them and dealing with them; substituted one card index registration for eighteen different registration books; made them use the telephone and orderlies to take messages instead of running about like rabbits to talk to each other; given Daniel and myself a Private Secretary — and all out of *existing* staff and material without adding a man or spending any money to speak of.

Poor old Daniel looks on and gasps — he is quite out of his depth — doesn't mind what I do, and takes a week to understand what an ordinary man sees in five minutes.

I am sorry for him, and sorry to think I am pushing him out. But I am bound to say the interests of our administrative service demand it — things are in an awful state.

I have formed the most serious opinion as to the state of affairs in the Protectorate. The white settlers are seething with discontent at the ineptitude and apathy of the administration. The natives are utterly out of hand: the old chiefs like Khama (who was a great King[10]) have died, their successors are incompetent or drunkards and have no control over their peoples; respect for white men is diminishing, seditious propaganda is starting; progress is nil; and the Dutch in Cape Colony [Province] look on and grin.

Unless things are dealt with drastically and promptly, I foresee an upheaval in the next few years. And so I am going all out with both hands to reform, develope, discipline and organise. It will be a tough job, and a long one. For example there has never been any legal definition of the Chiefs' powers — they practically do as they like — punish, fine, tax and generally play hell. Of course their subjects hate them but daren't complain to us; if they did their lives would be made impossible. And that is only one aspect. Mercifully Daniel disappears into the Protectorate occasionally for a few days at a time, and then I am able to get on with things. But of course until I am really in charge I can't do as much as I want — or indeed anything really drastic and sweeping.

The Regent of the biggest Tribe, the Bamangwato, came to pay me an offical visit in Daniel's absence last week — his name is Tshekedi,[11] and he is regent for his nephew,[12] a boy of nine.

He is a cunning slippery devil I fancy, and made me a clever little speech. I had not expected him, so had to be careful about my answer — but luckily an inspiration came to me. After the usual greetings I said: 'Chief, my name is Rey — in your tongue *rre* means "my father" — so it is clear that I am intended to be father to you and your people.'

This went down like hot cakes, grins spread all round their faces till I thought the tops of their heads would drop off. So I thought that having had the jam they should now have the powder. I added casually that of course I should always be *rre* as long as you are good boys and do what I tell you — in suitable language naturally. That sobered them up a bit — but from what I have been able to gather since, the interview appears to have made a great impression and a good effect. Let us hope so.

In Mafeking I gather that the main topic of conversation is my reforming and devastating energy and zeal, our exclusiveness (we have not received or called on a soul) and speculation as to what we really are and look like!

It's a good thing to keep people guessing — and the notice on our front door is priceless: 'Please leave cards in the box. By medical advice Mrs Rey is unable to receive for some time'!

Mafeking is of course a foul hole — or would be if one expected a 'social' life here. The people are mad, and run about to each other's silly second-rate parties, and can talk of nothing but each other's shortcomings. So we shall know no one, and just give periodical official receptions to the whole damned lot in a bunch. That suits us admirably, and with our horses, car, garden, and our painting and writing and reading, *and work!*, we shall be very happy.

The town is a small place dumped down in the middle of the veld — about one mile long and less than half that width from end to end. There are no houses, all bungalows, and all in their own gardens — wide roads planted with trees — well laid out on the whole. It grows on one. Its primitiveness and wildness (being in the middle of the bush) is what attracts us most. It has a certain fascination but as I said before, if one wanted a *social* life, well — one would be disappointed. But then we don't, and I think we'll be quite happy here.

By the way the proper method of address from servants is *Morena* — which means Lord — very suitable and right and proper.

Our cook is rather a character — she informed Ninon that she had lived among the Dutch and liked them. That they knew how to treat natives and that the natives were terrified of them, which she thought a very good thing. Coming from a native, that was rather illuminating, and an interesting side-light on the infernal nonsense people talk about treating natives as brothers.

They are just big stupid children and need unbending firmness and absolute fairness; they have to be made to realise the moral superiority of the white, or there would be no holding them.

The P.M.O. (Principal Medical Officer) here is a very nice fellow — a new appointment, I met him in London. He told us his wife was coming out to join him, and we shuddered. She arrived last week — Scotch, very Scotch, and very nice indeed — we are delighted as now there is one nice couple here!

By the way, in addition to the P.M.O. I have quite a large staff. Government Secretary, Financial Secretary, Chief Clerk, Inspector of Police (I am Commandant of Police![13]), Chief Veterinary Officer, Inspector of Education, Controller of Stores; those are the principal ones — and about a dozen other white clerks.

All those are at Headquarters here — outside there are eleven Resident Magistrates,[14] one at the head of each district, and in each district are other whites — doctors, vets, police officers and sergeants — *and* my faithful native army 250 strong!

Monday 18 to Tuesday 26 November
The rains have broken at last and very wonderful is the effect. The bare red veld is coated with green and dotted with little field flowers: the mimosa trees are bursting into yellow bloom; birds are singing, and butterflies of gorgeous colours fluttering about; and every variety of insect and beast that crawls and wriggles seems to have come into being.

The sunsets are the most gorgeous I have ever seen — every possible combination of colour blends in one gorgeous blur across the western sky and almost takes one's breath away by its beauty. Bars and streaks and splashes of brilliant crimsons, pale pinks, mauves, yellows, greys, and browns lie across the intensely blue sky — sometimes softened by white clouds, sometimes thrown up by dark storm clouds — it's really lovely.

And then down drops the sun, and soon the whole sky is a blaze of stars, from the great Southern Cross to the myriad tiny pin points that cover it — and the brilliant African moon turns the whole place into a blaze of silver light so bright that you can read easily by it.

Of course — to turn from the sublime to the ridiculous — some of the insects are a little trying. The other night for instance my innocent child-like sleep was disturbed by a feeling of unease. I turned on the light, and my pillow, sheets, and self were *black* with a crawling army of tiny ants — millions and millions of them had swarmed up the leg of the bed, and all over me, head and all. They didn't bite, but they tickled, and it took me about half an hour to clear decks and then coat the floor and bed post with paraffin — so jolly to go to sleep thinking you are a freshly filled lamp.

The work is intensely interesting and I enjoy it very much. One of the most interesting parts of the country is of course the Kalahari (misnamed Desert).[15] We are sending out an expedition to bore for water there, and I had to arrange for it and interview the people. One is the toughest man I have ever seen, 55, hard as nails, a driller all his life, broader than he is long, burnt nearly black, and a long drooping moustache. Rather like 'Ole Bill'.[16]

We have what is known as the 'Desert Patrol' to wander about the Kalahari, collect hut-tax[17] from the natives, and report any signs of trouble. It consists of one white officer and a few native police, mounted on camels. It's a terribly lonely job, and a bit risky too on account of lack of water. So we always choose young unmarried men, and don't leave them there too long. Some of our up-country posts are lonely enough too, and the loneliness has so worked on people that two of our officers have shot themselves in the last few years. It's curious, because if anything would make me shoot myself it would be my fellow-creatures, not their absence. The world wouldn't be such a bad place if it were not for the people in it.

And that reminds me — our card-box hung on the front-door is always full of cards of people we've never heard of, and never want to. We haven't returned one, but there'll be a terrible batch to do one day!

Things are blowing up for trouble with Chief Tshekedi Khama of the Bamangwato tribe, the man I have already mentioned as having come down to see me. He was summoned down here to answer for his alleged misdeeds on six points and arrived on Sunday.

The first thing he did was to call on me and have a very friendly talk. Then all

Monday and Tuesday he was in conference (he and his chiefs) with Colonel Daniel.

I refused to have anything to do with the 'palaver' as I knew it would end in failure. I did not agree with what Daniel was going to say, and I did not want to be tarred with the brush of non-success.

My decision was a fortunate one. The conference was entirely abortive, and nothing was achieved — Tshekedi practically told the Government to go to the devil.[18]

He paid me a second private visit, and I asked him casually how things were going, and he said 'Not very well'. So I looked him straight in the face and said: 'When I rule here, I shall expect things to go differently', and he answered without a moment's hesitation 'When you rule, things *will* be different'. They jolly well will have to be.

When in London I had found a Mochuana[19] who came to give me lessons in Sechuana at Curzon St. To my surprise I received a most interesting letter from him a few days ago. It is an extra-ordinary coincidence that he should be a protégé of Chief Tshekedi, and this should *prove* of immense value and help to me in dealing with him. It is an example of the value of taking advantage of every possible chance of getting knowledge or information about one's job — *and of making friends even with the most unlikely people.*

The R.M. [Resident Magistrate] at Serowe (Tshekedi's place) came down with the Chief. Captain Nettelton[20] is his name, a good man I fancy — he has given me most valuable information about the position there, which he regards as serious — the natives talk of 'the guns speaking' if we do certain things. That I think is rot.

Thursday 28 November (to Lobatsi)
A gorgeous hot cloudless day. Punctually to the minute we pushed off at 8 am, and Ninon drove the first twenty-five miles (half way) in great style. We covered the first five miles in ten minutes, good going as the road was fair — but after that! We bumped into ruts and holes, crossed gullies, ploughed through sand, and scraped between bushes — it was great fun. About sixteen miles out of Mafeking we crossed the border into the Protectorate, *our* own country, and the scenery improved immensely — the ground got more undulating, the bush got thicker; trees bigger and more frequent until we got into really pretty country. There were lovely coloured birds on the way a number of ostriches, and generally the drive was most attractive.

Lobatsi is really a very jolly spot — hilly, wooded and green — an immense improvement on Mafeking. It is to be our new capital one day.[21]

We pulled up at the Residency, and were met by the Resident Magistrate Merrivale Drury, his wife and son. They made themselves quite charming and seemed ever so glad to see us. He is of course brainless, like most of the men here; she has all the brains and all the drive — the son is a nice boy with very good manners, such a refreshing change.

They put us up in a little hut (they call them 'rondavels' here).

Directly we arrived I dashed off with Drury to pick up Brind, the Government Engineer, and we spent the morning inspecting the site for the new town and planning it out.

It's a disgraceful business. They have spent £8000 on the site which wouldn't fetch more than £3000 to £4000 in the market today; three-quarters of it is utterly useless as it consists of steep stony 'koppies' (hills) good only for growing stones or raising baboons — of both of which there are plenty.

The remaining quarter is a strip four miles long and varying from 1000 feet to 1000 yards in width — most unsuitable for a town.

I am putting in a terrible report about it, and someone will be hanged over it I hope and trust.

Back to an excellent lunch, and then off again to inspect offices, camp and official dwellings. All in a disgraceful state of repair and quite inadequate. Water supply lacking — our whole staff is dependent on the charity of a trading company for water because we wouldn't spend £400 to dig a well and pipe up a supply. Monstrous — another drastic report! The staff are fairly good — the white sergeant commanding the troopers and Police especially so — but he had no uniform, tho' he had applied for it in April! Third scorching report! Won't they love me soon!

Off again after tea to inspect the new hospital we are building. Ninon and Mrs Drury came too, so with Drury, Brind and the contractor for the building we were quite a party.

This time no faults to find. The work is being excellently done. The contractor seems efficient and Brind is a first-rate fellow, the best man on my staff. It was quite interesting. It's going to have every modern improvement, electric light, X-Ray room, good water supply, water-borne sewage, etc. But of course it's quite small, only twenty-five in-patients, with a large (detached) out-patient branch.

So off again to the Residency, where I found another big farmer-settler and his wife, Scholz, a Dutchman. They were rough people, but of course intensely interesting to me, as one learned a tremendous lot from them. Funny slow-thinking, slow-moving, great big powerful devils, all muscle and bone, both men and woman. But solid people and hard as nails. I liked the men: they were *men*, not rabbits.

Friday 29 November
Another gorgeous day — we took a fond farewell of our most kind hosts and were off at 9.30. Fortunately Chase,[22] the Chief Veterinary Officer for the Protectorate, a really good fellow, had heard we were there and looked in — so we drove back to Mafeking together, at least our two cars ran along one behind the other.

We stopped at 10.30 at a big farmer's called Adams,[23] and he and his daughter gave us a cup of tea. He is another fine specimen, rough but sterling, an Englishman. They love my looking in on them, say they never see the present R.C., and we got on very well.

But they haven't a good word to say for the Government (*my* Government to be) and by Jove they're quite right. I've learned a lot about the ghastly shortcomings of the administration and I quite realize that it's going to be a tremendous job to put it all right.

I get on with both white settlers (English and Dutch) and with the natives. I think the former like my way of dealing, downright outspoken 'you-be-damned' methods, and the natives appreciate my knowledge of their mentality.

It's a job after my own heart.

The Government Secretary, Dutton, my principal man, is, as I have already said mad. His wife is also mad. She told him to climb up a tree last week to pick some fruit, and the poor fish fell off on his head, shook himself badly and broke his 'artificial snappers' — i.e. false teeth!

The result is that he is madder than ever, in every sense of the word, and so I am going to get him sent away on several months sick leave, and I hope to get rid of him altogether.

Saturday 30 November and Sunday 1 December
A real bad day at the Office on Saturday — that old man Daniel will drive me to murder if he doesn't get out soon, amiable old ass. I have only three good men: the P.M.O. (Principal Medical Officer) Dyke;[24] the C.V.O. (Chief Veterinary Officer) Chase; and the Government Engineer (Brind). The Financial Secretary will pass in a crowd. The rest — also ran.

I disagree with Daniel on every conceivable subject — he is the damnedest old fool I have ever struck, the most incompetent bungler, and the most pig-headed ass. His mind, or what he refers to in moments of enthusiasm as his mind, works at the slowest rate thay any mind could work without stopping altogether; and it invariably works wrong. I shall be so thankful when he goes, and I only hope that one of us will not have murdered the other before then! When the Almighty sets to work to create a fool, he certainly turns out a finished article.

The stupidity of the majority of the human race is always a source of wonderment to me. Why are the vast proportion of people such utter fools? It wouldn't matter if one had not got to deal with them, if one could just live one's life reading, writing, travelling and picking one's associates. But unfortunately one is compelled to deal with fellow creatures who inspire one solely with feelings of contempt and dislike, and who interfere with the progress of one's ideas by their innate imbecility.

Tuesday 10 to Monday 22 December
I have given birth to the first of my big schemes for reorganising this country and putting it on the path to progress and development. I only pray that it may not be killed at birth by the people in London whose lack of vision and of imagination has stifled all advancement here.

It is a big scheme, costing £180,000, and destined to provide the country with the one thing it lacks — water.

Under the Colonial Development Act,[25] passed this year, Colonies may get grants to 'develop trade and agriculture' by means of surveys or water development schemes, especially if these lead to purchases of machinery at Home.

The fools here did not realize the immense opportunity offered. However, it is not too late, and I have evolved four big schemes, involving a water survey of 75,000 square miles of the Kalahari, the formation of a dozen cattle-routes by sinking eighty wells, the survey of many thousand miles of Crown Lands for water, and the sinking of wells and bore-holes on European settlers' farms and in the Native Reserves. Worthless land will become valuable; good land will be doubled in value; more cattle can be raised, grazed and exported; trade will increase; and the place can be opened up and developed. And out of the £180,000 which the schemes will cost, no less than £50,000 will be spent on buying machinery in England to the benefit of British trade; and British settlers can be put on farms out here, once we have proved water and thus proved the value of the land.

Meanwhile other minor things are shaping. My cotton-seed has arrived from Swaziland; it has been distributed to farmers and others for experimental cultivation; reports will be coming in soon; then we must get a ginnery put up for 'ginning' the raw cotton and tackle the Railway company for reduced rates. And then — perhaps — we'll get a big cotton crop going in a couple of years.

Tuesday 23 December to Wednesday 31 December
We spent a very pleasant and quiet Christmas alone together. We enjoyed turkey and plum pudding, and drank the health of all our 'absent friends' at 8 o'clock precisely. In point of fact we had had several invitations to dinner, but of course we declined them.

I got a fool-letter from Cape Town to say that they thought my water schemes were too big, and wanted me to cut them down.

And the weather gets extra hot.

1930

Thursday 2 January (at Mafeking)
The day for my office reorganisation scheme dawned, and everyone of course was expecting it to fail.
So it's been a really hectic time — *but* everything has in fact panned out O.K.

Thursday 9 to Friday 10 January (Mafeking to Cape Town)
At 6 am our B.P.P. [Bechuanaland Protectorate Police] orderly turned up immaculately got up, and drove us to the station, our car 'Topsy' looking like a new pin — the whole turnout very smart. Daniel arrived later in his filthy old car driven by his chauffeur in his shirt sleeves — no orderly — nothing! I regard it as scandalous that he should turn out like that; it lowers the whole prestige of the Administration.
He was sniffling with hay-fever, wore black glasses, and looked like nothing on earth, poor fish.
The scenery for the first day was absolutely ghastly — nothing but miles and miles of veld (bush country) broken only by low stony koppies — a farm here and there — a station now and then — deadly monotony and roasting heat. In some of the sandy country one passed nothing but miles and miles of ant-hills of every shape and size, hundreds of thousands of them — I wonder how many millions of millions of ants there must be there! What on earth was the object of creating the infernal beasts I am at a loss to imagine.
We were very glad when night fell, and after an excellent night's rest and a good breakfast we were able to feast our eyes on some of the grandest scenery the world can show, the Hex River Mountain Pass. It is really grand — and forces one's mind back to the genius of the colossus who conceived the idea of this immense Cape to Cairo Railway — Rhodes whom no difficulty could stop, and to whom England and Africa and the world owe such a vast debt.

Friday 10 to Monday 20 January (at Cape Town)
I lost no time on arrival, and at 3 o'clock Daniel and I started our first conference with Captain Clifford, the Imperial Secretary, and Eales, his deputy.
The general position vis-à-vis the 'High Commissioner and Governor-General of South Africa' (Lord Athlone) has become very unsatisfactory. Owing to the crass incompetence, and lack of energy and initiative of my three predecessors in

the office of Resident Commissioner (Colonel Daniel, Colonel Ellenberger, and Sir James Macgregor) the Governor-General has been compelled to interfere a good deal. This of course I propose to change and I thought it well to make it clear at the start. So there was a certain amount of peevishness, some heat was generated, and not much progress made between 3 and 6.30 pm when we adjourned until Monday.

On Saturday morning I trotted round to Government House to write our names, and ran across Captain Abel-Smith of the Horse Guards, one of the A.D.C.'s, a very nice fellow. He greeted me with much effusion, insisted on my coming in for a drink, and informed me that I had already been given a nick-name, and that it had preceded me to Cape Town. Apparently I am to be known henceforward as 'the Live Wire'.

I went in to see Athlone, and he kept me for one and a half hours, to the rage and fury of numberless other people who were waiting to see him. He was awfully nice, and we did some stout work, notably in connection with my big water schemes, to which I quite converted him — it was an immense relief to me, as if he will back them, they'll probably go through the Colonial Office[1] whereas otherwise they would not stand so good a chance.

On Thursday morning I got my water schemes at last finally agreed to — £180,000 worth of wonderful work, and now they are going on to London. If only the Colonial Office and the Committee[2] that gives the money will agree, it will be the biggest thing ever done for Bechuanaland. Ninon and I are fearfully pleased about it.

On Friday (17th) we had another hectic day. I had a long interview with Sir Drummond Chaplin,[3] the head of the Chartered Company[4] out here — it was very satisfactory. Then another one with Lord Knollys, the head of Barclay's Bank in South Africa.

After lunch the McKinerys took us to the opening of Parliament (Athlone had sent tickets) and we had an excellent view of a most interesting ceremony. Athlone who is a very big man looked magnificent in all his war paint, and Princess Alice (his wife) looked perfectly charming and very royal. The opening speech was read by Athlone sitting, then by some fool in Dutch (what rot this double language business is) and there is all the ceremonial of bowing and backing and the rest of it by Black Rod just as there is at home. The procession was quite fine, and the A.D.C.s looked very grand, especially Abel-Smith in the full kit of the Life Guards, and some of our sailors, the Admiral and Captains[5] and gold lace and medals.

They played 'God Save the King' in great style as they went off and I was glad to see every man leap to his feet — I was afraid some of these filthy Dutchmen might not.

We were very sorry when Sunday (19th) dawned, our last day here. The McKinerys fetched us after lunch and took us for another long and lovely drive through the mountains and out to Simonstown where our fleet's naval base lies. It was nice to see the Union Jack flying everywhere there, instead of that filthy hybrid abomination, the South African flag.

Cape Town and its surrounding mountains are among the most beautiful places I have ever seen — the combination and variety of scenery, rugged hills, big forests, and sea, and the gorgeous climate, make up a whole that is hard to beat. The idea of England in January after that makes me feel quite ill. Why on earth anyone who is not obliged to ever stays in Europe I can't imagine — when these lovely climates are available, amid wonderful scenery and pleasant hospitable people.

Africa is good enough for me!

Wednesday 22 January to Tuesday 4 February
From 22nd until 27th I had a pleasant few days in charge until Daniel returned. He stayed on in Cape Town in connection with a particular matter, which I gather he has bungled hopelessly — as was to be expected.

Poor old thing, I'm afraid I have perhaps been a little hard on him in my judgements. He is of course far from well, and both he and Mrs Daniel have been very poorly since their return here — Mrs Daniel has been in bed the whole time — I'm very sorry for them.

He is rapidly handing everything of importance over to me — I have to preside at the meetings of the European Advisory Council[6] on 3 March, and Native Advisory Council[7] early in April — they are our sort of local Parliaments, and need a lot of handling — also a good deal of preparatory and subsequent work.

The great question I shall have to tackle is the natives: there is a lot of unrest among them in Natal, the Cape, Rhodesia and even in Nigeria — it has not spread here yet, but unless we tackle our difficulties here boldly it may. The chiefs are ill-treating their people, and we shall have to interfere and reduce the chiefs' powers — and then the band will play.

An educated native, Simon Ratshosa[8] by name, has written a book which will be published shortly — it will create a stir as he alleges all sorts of crimes on the part of the Chiefs from whom he has suffered himself — incidentally he tried to shoot Tshekedi, Chief of the Bamangwato the other day just before we arrived. He only wounded him in the arm.[9]

The Chiefs here are a poor lot. The best of them, Isang,[10] of the Bakgatla, was only Acting Chief until the proper Chief[11] of eighteen came of age. He is an idiot boy of eighteen, and was solemnly installed as Chief the other day; the elders of the tribe then promptly sent him back to school! So now there is no Chief.

Imagine the administration allowing this. The incompetence of old Daniel is colossal.

Another amusing thing is cattle-running. The South African Govt. prohibit the importation of our cattle except at certain places and under certain conditions. So there is a lot of cattle-running across the hundreds of miles of frontier by night, and some amusing brushes between the cattle-runners, our troopers and the South African police.

The farmers in the Protectorate find this cattle-running very profitable, and they are coming to protest to me at Lobatsi on Wednesday against our interfering with them!

The ideas of law and order out here are curious.

Wednesday 5 February
A great day altogether, and a most interesting one. I had been invited to attend a big meeting of all the white settlers in the Lobatsi district — partly because they wanted to meet their new Governor, partly because they had a lot of grievances they wanted to air.

We picked up Drury, the Resident Magistrate, at his office in the Camp at Lobatsi, and trotted off to the meeting. And it *was* a meeting! All the settlers from miles around had come in, the place was strewn with cars and carts and traps and vehicles and animals of all kinds, horses, oxen, and donkeys. The meeting was held in the open under some immense shady trees which formed a sort of natural hall, sheltered from the blazing sun, and cool and airy. They had rigged up a platform for myself and the others and the proceedings were opened by the Chairman (a Dutch minister!) making a speech of welcome in excellent English, and then saying that they were waiting to hear what I had to say.

I had not expected this, as I thought it was simply to be a case of listening and answering questions. So I had to let off an extempore harangue on the spur of the moment which went down very well, tho' it had to be translated into Dutch as many of the farmers in this southern district don't speak English.

Friday 7 February to Sunday 16 February
The police force is in a shocking state, and I'm going to reorganise it root and branch: I intend to recruit all officers and N.C.O.s from England, and all natives from Basutoland — Oh Lord, what a lot there is to do to get this place cleaned up.

We are having great excitement here about Tshekedi, the Chief of the Bamangwato. Of course the old fool Daniel can't hold him, and so Tshekedi went off down to Cape Town to interview Athlone. He had a row with him and Clifford and Daniel — and was pretty insolent — he is trying to stop our opening up his country for mining, and is egged on by two poisonous members of the London Missionary Society.[12] These damned missionaries need hanging — they butt into politics and are an intolerable nuisance — I am looking forward to giving them hell when I take over. Meanwhile I am standing aside and watching Daniel get deeper and deeper into the mire — and he *is* plunging!

The Chief is back at his town, Serowe, and Daniel has just had a wire from London instructing him to go up and see him and to prevent his going to England to see the Colonial Office[13] which he wants to do. Of course Daniel will fail. Meanwhile Ninon and I are off on a tour of inspection of the Kanye, Molepolole, and Gaberones districts by car — a week's trip.

Monday 17 to Friday 21 February
A gorgeous morning, as usual, for our trek — we were late in starting as our fool man had tied the luggage on so badly that I had to have it taken off and done all over again.

We were met about 4 miles this side of Lobatsi by one of my police from Lobatse who got on the car as a guide (forty-six miles) and we turned off towards Kanye. At the bordergate[14] (five miles on) we were met by the Resident Magistrate of the Kanye district, Mr Cuzen,[15] in another car with another policemen (we now had three police in all) and drove on towards his headquarters. It was jolly country, hilly and well wooded, but terribly rough going.

With Cuzen I went through a lot of papers I had brought with me, and we discussed matters concerning his district until 4.30 when tea came, and with it *all* the white settlers in the neighbourhood to pay their respects to the new Resident Commissioner and his lady. They were a weird and mixed crowd. I can get along quite happily with the men because they are *men*, not rabbits: but the females leave me guessing. One of the party is the man who is going to be my great enemy here — Lewis[16] of the London Missionary Society who was kicked out of one of the other districts for working against the government and stirring up trouble among the natives. We were very civil to each other, but the fight has got to come — I shall pick my opportunity.

1930

The next day (Tuesday 18th) Ninon was not too fit, and I persuaded her to stay in bed. With Cuzen I went down to Camp and inspected offices and quarters and police, then Chief Bathoen[17] of the Bangwaketse Tribe came in with his followers to pay me his respects.

I made him a speech in which I pointed out that I would always be his friend as long as he did what I told him — and he listened in a rather sulky silence. He is a bit out of hand, and will need rather pulling up — he'll get it.

He's a nasty looking little rat, quite young, recently made Chief. I foresee some fun with him.

I went out with Cuzen and inspected some sites for a big water-dam we want to build to hold up a river for the dry season. It's a wonderful spot — a gorge in the mountains where a small dam about one hundred yards long and ten to fifteen feet high would hold up an immense volume of water.

On Wednesday 19th off I went at 7 am. Finally we ran through a really lovely forest and then up the last hill to the Residency at Molepolole — 51 miles in three and three-quarter hours — pretty good going in this country, especially considering that I had driven myself the whole way.

Captain Stigand[18] the Resident Magistrate was waiting for me and I had a very interesting day with him indeed. He is a brother of the other Captain Stigand the explorer who has written books about the countries round Abyssinia and other parts of Africa — a gentleman and a clever man.

His camp, officers etc. were speckless, his men as smart as paint, and all obeyed 'at the double' — it was a joy to inspect them.

He had arranged for Sebele,[19] Chief of the Bakwena Tribe to come in and pay his respects, and at about 11.30 the Chief and his followers were ushered in. Sebele is an elderly man, a drunken dissolute ruffian, whom we have had to put under a sort of Regency Council lately — he now shows signs of trying to reform, but is hopelessly corrupt — I expect I shall have to depose him before long. However he and his headmen were immensely civil, and received my speech with great (apparent) enthusiasm.

Afterwards I inspected our big new boring machine — a MacNamara Shot Drill that cost nearly £2,000 and is being tested in water boring before being sent out further afield — it's a wonderful toy, but had just started and got down three feet only. We expect to strike water at two hundred feet in about three weeks.

While I was there the other drill foreman in charge of our Jumper Drill out in the Kalahari came in unexpectedly — he had abandoned his drill and his men and was raving mad! The terrible heat and loneliness of the Kalahari had finished him off — and he assured me he was surrounded by men wanting to shoot him, and would I please not send him back to the Kalahari to count oxen.

Poor devil, it was a pretty grim business — this is no country for a man with a weak heart!

Stigand lives quite alone — his wife is half Italian and won't come out to this savage place — she lives in Florence. Stigand is to come on as my Assistant Resident Commissioner after taking four months leave in Europe — I like him immensely.

He gave me an excellent lunch, his servants are drilled to perfection, his place is like a new pin but furnished like a barrack room — camp bed, a few chairs and tables and masses of books and periodicals in all languages — he speaks 10 tongues.

1930

On Friday we went off back to Mafeking — Ninon was better but still a little weary so I drove most of the way, and our policeman chauffeur the rest.

Friday 20 February
We got back to lunch, and afterwards I went down to Camp; and put the fear of God into the office people who had got a little sleepy in our absence.

I found much excitement going on about that poisonous little devil Tshekedi, the Chief of the Bamangwato, and his proposed visit to London.

Of course Daniel had failed completely in his mission — Tshekedi had practically told Daniel to go to the devil, and supported by those poisonous people, the London Missionary Society, had insisted on going to England. Telegrams were flying to and fro, and I thanked Providence that I had kept out of the ghastly muddle.

The reports appearing in the English papers which have been telegraphed out here are grotesque and utterly misleading. They make Tshekedi out to be a fine patriotic fellow standing out for his rights and the liberties of his people against a brutal capitalist company and an unsympathetic Government.

Nothing could be further from the truth. He is a swollen headed young devil, standing out for his personal privileges, ignoring the interests of his Tribe, ill-using them, mal-administering justice, using forced labour to an extent that practically amounts to slavery, and impeding the administration in every way.

Daniel has kow-towed and vacillated to such an extent that Tshekedi thinks he can do anything he likes, and I shall have the devil of a job to bring the little brute into line when he returns. Imagine Daniel's idiocy — some of the Bamangwato reported that in one place their cattle were dying in hundreds for want of water — we were going to spend £600 on sinking a well — Tshekedi objected because he wanted to do it somewhere else, so Daniel gave in and no well was sunk at all! And so it goes on.[20]

Wednesday 26 February
After two days at Mafeking working like a galley-slave I set off today to Gaberones, to do the various jobs I should have done there last week.

I must break off, on my way to Gaberones, to note down some humorous cases of prison laxity in the Protectorate. (That is one of the many things I am reorganising — prisons).

A white man was arrested and brought to the gaol; he asked if he might go and fetch some clothes from his camp. He was refused permission and locked up. So he cut his way out through some loose bricks, fetched his luggage, came back to the gaol, and rang the bell to awaken the sleeping gaoler to let him in. On another occasion the gaoler, who was rather bored having little to do, used to take his one white prisoner out in the evening to play cards with some pals. If the prisoner wanted to stay too late the gaoler used to threaten him that if he didn't come at once, he (the gaoler) would go back and lock the prisoner out!

And in another place the gaoler used to go out periodically and get drunk in the evenings. One of the prisoners would on these occasions climb out of the gaol, hunt round the bars till he found the drunken gaoler, hoist him on his back and bring him back to the gaol in time for the morning inspection.

But enough of this — we must get on to Gaberones.

Firstly I had to meet four native chiefs of the principal tribes round here. Each had to have his formal speech from me, and to make a formal speech in return — and to all I told them that as they said they were my children I would be their father — but the first thing that a father expected was obedience — as long as they behaved well, all would be well — but — .

They all promised everything — we shall see. But it's very interesting dealing with these people, a fascinating study of the native mind. Then followed inspection of camp, officers, quarters, barracks (this is our police training camp), stables, horses etc., interviews with people who had grievances, and settling various minor troubles.

Thursday 27 February
This morning I had a meeting with the principal white settlers in the Gaberones district, a good lot of sound people — a much better type than the crowd at Lobatsi or Kanye. We had an interesting discussion on a number of points, I am getting quite an expert on cattle as well as water boring and crops!

More work at Camp in the afternoon, and then I took my first parade of the corps of which in a month I shall be Colonel and Commandant!

About thirty men were on parade, of whom a dozen will form my mounted escort when I open the Native Advisory Council on 14 April. I took the salute, and then watched some drill, after which I inspected the lines, and retired to the Residency, hot and weary, but well pleased with things. Certainly this is the most interesting job I have ever had.

Saturday & Sunday (1 & 2 March)
I had a tremendously strenuous time preparing for the meeting of the European Advisory Council which starts on Monday 3 March, on which day I take over as Acting Resident Commissioner — Monarch of all I survey.

Monday 3 March
Members of Council (who come from all over the Protectorate — there are six of them) started coming in at 10.30 and first of all we had all to be photographed together. Then business started — I read a message from Lord Athlone, and then made an impassioned harangue of my own — after which we settled down to business.

Monday 3rd to Sunday 9 March
It has been a strenuous week, but I am glad to say an immensely successful one.

Council, who have been damnably treated in the past, told nothing, kept at arm's length, treated me with suspicion and responded rapidly to my new and unorthodox methods — and after the first day they were 'eating out of my hand'.

We got through an immense amount of business, kept everyone in a good temper — and — best of all — they were wildly enthusiastic about my water scheme, blessed it, and enabled me to send off a strong dispatch to London saying that they backed it for all they were worth.

Monday 10 to Saturday 15 March
The Advisory Council sat for three more days and then finished off in a blaze of mutual congratulation.

Incidentally I have had the Camp (Imperial Reserve) straightened up, all the buildings (offices, stores, stables, etc.) whitewashed, the roofs painted red, paths cleaned up etc. etc.

There is a terrible lot of 'cleaning up' to be done in every sense of the word — the police force for example is awful — out of twenty four white sergeants six have had to be sacked in the last year!

Monday 17 March
Mr Vernay and Dr Laing, the heads of the Vernay-Laing scientific expedition[21] passed through today and called on me. The main body of the expedition is awaiting them at Gaberones — they are a wonderfully well-equipped party, fourteen strong, four or five motors, etc. etc. They are going to do scientific work in the Kalahari, collect fauna and flora for various museums and generally enjoy themselves.

Incidentally they are a damned nuisance to me — I have to detach a Police Officer to go with them, arrange for guides and interpreters, and instruct native chiefs to help them. All this because the Colonial Office have fallen in love with them.

Thursday 20 March
Quite an interesting day. N. and I and Chase (the C.V.O.) motored out to Tlapen in the Protectorate to inspect the sheep-dipping that is going on all along the frontier. We have cattle inspectors stationed at various centres where there are sheep dips, and to these places the natives bring in their sheep, thousands and thousands, for dipping against 'scab' infection. Each batch of animals is driven into a pen, then four at a time are pushed thro' a swing gate into the bath and poked under the evil smelling liquid with long sticks (head and all) for two minutes.

We went on to our frontier station, Ramatlabama, where the store keeper, a sturdy Englishman, Smith by name, gave us evening tea, and retailed all the details of a cunning scheme some of these infernal Dutchman are trying to hatch to get hold of land in the Protectorate (under fictitious names) and found a beastly Dutch colony. Smith understands Dutch, and had picked up the threads of the business from overhearing Dutch farmers talking in his store and elsewhere.

Monday 24 March
A real Monday, black Monday — a rotten day. To start with an infernal tooth is beginning to worry me and gave me hell all day long — I have never had toothache or lost a tooth and I don't see why I should — so I must confess that I have not been at my brightest and best!

Then — and much more serious — the natives are starting to give trouble. I imagine that they realise there is a new man as Resident Commissioner and they are going to 'try it on' to see what they can get. I'm afraid they'll get more than they bargain for.

But the really serious matter is with the Bamangwato, the Tribe of which that rabbit Tshekedi (now in England)[22] is Chief.

In Tshekedi's absence Edirilwe[23] is acting-Chief. They rule over a sub-tribe the Bakalaka[24] who in fact are much better people than the Bamangwato who are lazy and diseased and use slaves. The Bakalaka are hard workers, wealthy, and much better men in every way. Their chief is Mswazi, and he laid a string of complaints against his overlord Tshekedi — ill-treatment, robbery, injustice, etc.

So Mswazi was told to bring his complaints in person before Tshekedi at Serowe (three hundred miles away). He refused to come unless guaranteed protection by *us* — which we did.

1930

By the time Mswazi got to Serowe, Tshekedi had gone to England — so the complaints were heard by Edirilwe. The 'trial' lasted fifteen days, at the end of which Mswazi's complaints were all dismissed he was found guilty of disobedience and insubordination, and was told that he and his four chief headmen would be banished from their own territories, and would have to come and live at Serowe under Tshekedi's eye — that is — would be beggared and made perpetual prisoners.

And — here comes the climax — unless they came into Serowe within fourteen days voluntarily, the Makobamotse Regiment[25] would be sent out to bring them in — which of course would mean fighting, burning of villages, carrying off of women and cattle etc. etc.

I heard this on the 24th (today); my damfool of an Acting R.M., Mangan, had never told me — the trial ended on 15th — so it was obvious the regiment was to move on the 29th and I had five days in which to stop what might be a serious native upheaval.

I took charge of the telegraph line (monopolised it) and sent hectic instructions to my R.M. to tell the chief that in no circumstances would I allow any regiment to be moved, that Mswazi had lodged an appeal with me, and that no action was to be taken of any sort in the meanwhile.

And then at 5 o'clock, just before the post offices up the line closed, I got a message that my man at Serowe had gone away, and was four hours journey off — at a place called Mahalapye!

So I had to get a message sent to him via Johannesburg and Bulawayo to return to Serowe instantly.

Wednesday 26 to Friday 28 March
Thank goodness I got a wire this morning (Wednesday) that all was quiet at Serowe — my orders had been given to the chief — he took them without a murmur — And now it only remains for me to arrange about hearing the appeal. But it had been touch and go — .

Saturday 29 March
Tonight's farewell dinner to the Daniels was a perfectly ghastly affair. We were about forty, and N. and I had been particularly anxious to keep in the background, as the position was a little delicate.

So it had been arranged that Dutton, the Government Secretary, as the senior person and Chase, the C.V.O., as the 'oldest inhabitant' would make the speeches — presenting the Daniels with the cheque for £55 which had been collected to buy themselves a present in England.

Dutton's speech was the world's worst — tactless, pointless, long drawn out — really we began to wonder whether it was a farewell speech presenting a gift — or a critical attack! It was awful — and everyone listened in pained silence.

I learned from Stigand and Cuzen that my mortal foes, the London Missionary Society, were owing to lack of funds amalgamating with the Church of Scotland mission, and the latter were going to take over the missions in the Kalahari, at Maun and at Molepolole. Now the Church of Scotland mission run an institution in South Africa called Lovedale where a thousand natives regularly are being educated — and apparently all the unrest among natives is due largely to those who come out of Lovedale[26]. So that is a jolly prospect. I wish I could induce my savages to start a pogrom of missionaries and eat the lot. I always detested missionaries — there was only one good one in all African history, David Livingstone, and he said, *The cause of Christ is better advanced by emigration than by missionaries.*[27]

Monday 31 March
A hectic day taking over finally from Daniel, complicated by the arrival of Ledeboer to act as Assistant Resident Commissioner and of Mangan, the acting R.M. at Serowe, whom I had sent for in connection with the trouble up there.

Thank goodness that is settled — in view of the strong action we took all is quiet, the chiefs have come to heel, and they have got their orders for the future — I understand that the effect has been remarkable and instantaneous — the subject tribes are already singing a song to the effect that the white man has now come to rule and that they will be oppressed by their chiefs no longer! News travels like wildfire among natives in Africa, far more quickly than by telegraph.

Tuesday 1 April
Ninon and I went round at 9 this morning and met engineers and contractors and workmen at 'Protectorate Government House' and started them on their work of tearing down walls, and tearing up floors, and building up fresh walls etc. Everything was in a disgusting state of chaos, but we stayed there all the morning and got everything swinging.

And then at 3 o'clock all the staff mustered at 'Camp' and I formally took over, making them an eloquent and stirring oration.
So now I am
His Honour Lt. Colonel C.F. Rey
Monarch of all I survey
What a joke!

Wednesday 2 April to Sunday 6 April
A hectic few days — taking over at the Office, hustling the workmen at Government House, and dealing with a mass of important stuff including the preparations for the Native Advisory Council at Gaberones on 15th.

Also there's a regular crop of troubles in the Protectorate. I fear this native unrest in South Africa[28] is spreading to my dominion.

I got my fool of an acting R.M. down from Serowe on Sunday (the real R.M. is Captain Nettelton who has gone to England about the Tshekedi business, it is all in Tshekedi's country, the Bamangwato territory). Mangan, the acting R.M., is a more complete ass than I had thought — he has no brain, is slow and heavy, and utterly unable to grasp the essentials of a situation. He has failed entirely in the present case, and so far as I am concerned, he is done.

However I got a certain amount of information out of him, dictated a complete set of instructions to cope with the situation, and sent him back by Monday night's train. On Thursday I got a telegram from him to say he had carried them out, the Acting Chief had collapsed, and all was well — for the time being.

But no sooner is that settled than fresh trouble breaks out farther north, right up at the end of the Protectorate (Kasane) — this time thanks to the efforts of those children of hell, the London Missionary Society. The local L.M.S. man[29] has been encouraging the natives to disobey Government orders, and the R.M. (Captain Neale) has got a most insolent demand from the chief (backed by the L.M.S.) to remove our Police Inspector! who happens to be a very excellent officer.

So I had to get busy with the telegraph again (all telegrams to there have to be taken over a wide river and on by runner for fifty miles), and then sent a dispatch to the L.M.S. headquarters at Cape Town to tell them to remove their man — failing which within a fortnight I would have him expelled from the country as a 'danger to peace, order and good Government.'

One of my pet farmers was caught cattle-running over the frontier into the Union the other day — he ran one hundred and forty head over, was collared by the South African Police and duly brought up for trial. There was no doubt about it, he was caught red-handed, the cattle bore his brand, and it looked as if he were in for a heavy sentence in addition to losing his whole herd. However he engaged a very clever Jew lawyer, the friend of every villain in South Africa, and this fellow got the police so fogged and muddled that they contradicted themselves and each other, and my farmer left the court 'without a stain on his character', got his cattle back (they had been fed at the expense of the Union Government while waiting for the trial!) and is now thinking of bringing a case against the Union Government for wrongful detention of his beasts!

Yesterday and today we have been moving things into Government House amid the crash of falling bricks, clouds of dust, smells of paint, armies of workmen, and general chaos. We have to thread our way on narrow planks over gaping holes in the floors, while walls are being pulled down and built up, and floors relaid, and policemen, carpenters, bricklayers, plumbers, painters and labourers toil about us. We have the Government Engineer, a contractor, the Controller of Stores, and half the police force at our disposal — and the result is awful.

Monday 7 to Sunday 13 April
A hectic week. We moved into our new abode on Monday — it appears to combine in about equal proportions the pretentiousness of a suburban villa, the taste of a Margate boarding house, and the dirt of an East End tenement.

Tuesday 15 April (Gaberones)
The great day for the meeting of the Native Advisory Council dawned, and strange to say it was cloudy and overcast — an almost unheard of thing for this time of year.

I came out with Captain Reilly, the escort came to the salute, and I inspected them. They were faultlessly turned out, men and horses: the brass and steelwork glittered like gold and silver, the horses' coats were like satin, Lieutenant Croneen the O.C. might have been a guardsman. The saddlery and bridles would have done credit to an English hunting stable. The men were speckless, and their carbines like new.

I got into Topsy, half the escort wheeled into a column of twos and went off at a smart trot along to Camp. Topsy came to a halt by the flagstaff, the escort wheeled into line facing the car, and as I got out the bugler sounded the General Salute, the escort came to the present, and then I marched up to my seat, which was covered with a very handsome fur kaross. Facing me were the Chiefs and their followers, sitting and squatting in long lines in the open, and on either side of me under the verandah were the Resident Magistrates, Police officers, Headquarters officials and others. Ninon and Mrs Reilly sat at one end to get a good view.

The senior Resident Magistrate, Captain Stigand, made a short speech introducing me, each Chief was brought up in turn and presented, and then each said a few words of welcome.

Then I let off my oration — it went down very well, and afterwards we got to business.

At previous meetings there had been no sort of show, no escort no uniforms, and the Chiefs had been often truculent, sometimes even rude.

But today they behaved like lambs, and were even at times enthusiastic and cordial. Possibly the escort impressed them, possibly the ceremonial, possibly even the white and gold uniform with the Star of Ethiopia prominently displayed!

Also I made it clear that I was standing no nonsense, tho' I had done everything to make them comfortable, built them a new house and supplied them with rations on a generous scale. We went on till one o'clock, then adjourned until 2.30 and finished off at 5.30 — a record, for in other years they had always taken at least two days.

Wednesday 16 April
At 10 am I walked down to Camp and met the Chiefs to bid them farewell. I said a few words to them and then their spokesman replied in very cordial terms. Amid shouts of 'Pula, pula' — 'rain, rain' (their salute) I retired into Captain Reilly's office and had two or three rather painful interviews with people who had to be 'ticked off.'

Everyone is terribly bucked with yesterday's meeting, the effect on the Chiefs is most marked, and the R.M.s and other officers having had a lead given to them for the first time for fifteen years, have got their tails well up. The more I get about the territory the more disgusted I am with the work of my three predecessors, Colonel Daniel, Colonel Ellenberger, and Sir James Macgregor[30] — a trinity of the damndest fools Providence ever produced.

Thursday 17 April
We had a picnic lunch en route, and got into Lobatsi at about 2.45, putting up at a quaint little hotel there — I found a batch of troublesome dispatches awaiting me that kept me pretty busy, and then the owner of the hotel showed me a 'pan' of gold ore he had been washing, the first gold to be found in the Southern Protectorate. If its genuine and not a 'fake' it will mean a tremendous thing — I'm going to turn the Chartered Company (British South Africa Company) on to it.

Monday 21 April
A holiday: we decided to take a day off, and motored out to Ottoshoop, about thirty miles off, to spend the day with some people of the name of Gubbins.

They have a jolly farm, with some lovely old things in it — but above all, he has the most wonderful library in the world on South African natives, their customs, manners, history, and all about them. It was an intense joy to pore through it, especially as he is a really cultured and well-read man, and we got on famously.

Tuesday 22 April
Alarums and excursions again. A hectic telegram from Francistown (away in the North among Mswazi's people, the Makalaka) to say that reports were rife to the effect that Edirilwe had, in spite of my orders which he had sworn to obey, sent a regiment from Serowe to 'eat up' the Makalaka and that the said Makalaka were very restless and excited.

If this were true it meant big trouble — so I sent off a hairy telegram to Serowe to find out the truth, and, if true, to order the Chief to recall the regiment. Another telegram to my man at Francistown to collect as many men as he could, go out and meet the regiment and order them back. A third telegram to the depot at

Gaberones to order the police officer there to stand by ready to move north by train whenever I wired, with every mounted man he could collect.

I possessed my soul in patience until just on 5 pm when a wire came through to the effect that the Chief Edirilwe had solemnly sworn that no regiment had moved or would move, and that all was peace. I fear it would *not* have been peace if I had not acted promptly — it merely shows for the millionth time that firmness and quick action means peace, and weakness means trouble.

I sat back, wiped my fevered brow, and smoothed my tangled locks. Life is certainly not monotonous here, whatever else it may be.

Thursday 24 April
For once in a while nothing very exciting happened yesterday. Today Motsete, the Mochuana (or rather Mongwato) who taught me Sechuana in London, came to see me, and we had a most interesting talk. He has entirely come over to the Government side, and is absolutely disgusted with Tshekedi and his treatment of the Mangwato people and their subject races. This is very satisfactory, and I propose to use him for a certain amount of 'secret service' work.

Friday 25 April
More native trouble. That wretched Acting Chief of the Bamangwato, Edirilwe, has had the cheek to send two of his men into another part of the Territory (not his Reserve) to hunt for and bring back some Masarwa[31] who had run away. The Masarwa are poor creatures who live in a state of hereditary servitude to the Bamangwato. But we have said again and again that we refuse to allow them to be regarded as slaves, and that they have a perfect right to go where they like.

So I had to send violent instructions to the Chief to recall his men, and ask him what the devil he means by it. In due course I got humble apologies and the men have been sent orders to return — meanwhile the R.M. at Francistown has issued warrants for their arrest for interfering with other natives! So things are keeping lively.

Saturday 26 & Sunday 27 April
All arrangements were completed on Saturday for Captain Gash to leave on Sunday for Kasane to put the fear of God into the people there and turn out the L.M.S. man, and arrest him if he would not go. He left on Sunday morning at 8 am and will pick up his men — all mounted etc. at Gaberones. The railway have fixed up for trucks for the horses, and I have had to wire to the Governor of Rhodesia warning him that an armed party is proceeding by rail thro' Rhodesia to Victoria Falls! From there Gash will have a sixty mile ride across country to Kasane, and another sixty miles ride on to Kachikau, where some of the trouble is[32]. What a game!

And now today (Sunday) yet more trouble. That devil Edirilwe has sent out men to seize the Makalaka cattle (Mswazi's people) and as cattle are the natives' most precious possession there will be fireworks unless I can stop it in time — which I am of course trying to do.

Obviously I shall have to go up myself very soon.

Monday 28 April to Thursday 1 May
Captain Nettelton arrived back from England where he has been to see the Colonial Office in connection with Tshekedi's visit. He was of course present at all the

1930

interviews with Lord Passfield,[33] and gave us a most amusing account of the whole thing. Tshekedi did not get much satisfaction out of it — which is a good thing.

Unfortunately he is entirely under the influence of those devils the London Missionary Society.

I have decided to go to Cape Town to see Lord Athlone as I've had several silly telegrams from his office people, and they make me sick. I won't stand them. They don't come from Athlone, and I mean to have it out with him about his minions, they've got to keep their hands off. So I've written to him.

Friday 2 May
Sub-Inspector Moseley, who is in charge of the Southern Kalahari district, lunched with us today. He is full of interesting information about the quaint people who live there, the Bushmen, the Hottentots, and the Bakgalagadi people.[34] The most interesting of course are the Bushmen, and I am looking forward immensely to meeting them at the end of July.

One of them came to Moseley and asked to be allowed to pay his Hut-Tax (£1.5s. levied on every adult male native). Bushmen, who have no huts, are not liable for hut tax, and Moseley told him so. 'I know', was the answer. 'But if I pay my hut-tax that shows I am a man, not a dog. The Bakgalagadi look on me as a dog, they rob me, take away the skins of the animals I have killed, say I am only their dog. If I pay my hut-tax the Government will give me a paper that will prove that they regard me as a man, and if the Bakgalagadi try to take my things, I will show them the paper, tell them the Government regard me as a man, and will protect me and punish them.'

That's pretty good testimony to British rule.

Trip to Cape Town and Back

Thursday 8 to Wednesday 14 May
At 6 pm I pushed off on my trip to Cape Town and found an escort at the station, carriage reserved and everything in order. It is certainly much more comfortable to travel as His Honour the Resident Commissioner, than as plain Mr Rey, tho' even as Mr Rey we always managed to do things pretty comfortably. The difference is that then I had to do things for myself — now others do them for me.

On Monday I had a fearful rush: a couple of hours with Athlone, then an hour at his office with the Acting Imperial Secretary, Gates, followed by lunch and a talk with the Expert who is coming out to report on our water-boring scheme, thank goodness. I believe I shall get that money — I fairly drove it into Athlone and we sent a hairy cable home to the Colonial Office. But how one does have to fight for things in this world, it is hard on me as a man of peace and patience.

All my kit was packed, and an A.D.C. hurled me into a car and we drove off to the station where I found my reserved carriage O.K. — and at 4 pm we steamed off on our journey back to the beautiful city of Mafeking which was reached at 7 am on Wednesday morning — two nights, a day and a bit — it's a jolly long pull.

All has gone well with my 'Expeditionary Force' to the North. Captain Gash has returned with his merry men (known as the R.M.M. or Rey's Mounted Murderers!) having arrested the missionary and expelled him from the country. Gash had meetings with the chiefs concerned and their tribes, all of whom have expressed unqualified regret for their actions and promised to be 'good boys' in future. The attitude of the population has been most satisfactory — they are delighted to think that there is now a 'Great Chief' who really rules and who will protect them from their own chiefs — they greeted Gash's little party with respect and even pleasure — and peace now reigns.

I await the violent protest which will come from that body of pestilent dogs, the London Missionary Society. I can't think they really love me!

And the trouble which occurred elsewhere has also vanished — the result of a little firmness and immediate action. It's so easy really — the only fatal vices are weakness and indecision.

Friday 23 May
Tshekedi, Chief of the Bamangwato, returned here from England today — and I received a sheaf of dispatches from the Colonial Office concerning matters I have to settle with him.[35] The morning's meeting was ghastly — the worst I have ever had. He has been almost ruined in England by the damned fools who have never lived among Africans but who persist in treating them as brothers, people who regard all of us who have to govern these people (a handful of whites amongst hundreds of thousands of blacks) as bloated tyrannical monsters of cruelty and oppression.

I'd like to plant some of these snivelling holy-boly busybodies down among a native tribe, *with their women folk*, but without anyone to protect them — and then see the gentle African deal with them.

In addition Tshekedi's mind had been poisoned against me (obviously) by his friend Jennings of the London Missionary Society. So the proceedings opened with sullen suspicion and almost hostility on their side, and I struggled in vain to break it down. Finally, towards the close of the meeting, I made an oration, reciting all the facts, pointing out the reasons for and the objects of what I was proposing — and then I dismissed them to lunch, and went home myself feeling like death. These Bamangwato number 60,000, they are the most important tribe here — and if I can't get them going properly I shall have failed as all my predecessors have failed, as Athlone has failed, and as the Colonial Office have failed.

At 2.30 we resumed — and a complete change had come over the atmosphere. I opened the proceedings with some silly joke — they all laughed, they thawed rapidly and visibly, they gave me all the information I wanted, they fell in with my plans, they promised me a warm and hearty welcome when I come up to their country next month, and at 5 we parted the best of friends — and the first stage of the first battle is won.

But it had taken me five and a half hours of the toughest battle of wits I have ever had with natives, and I was as tired as a dog. I walked round to see them in their camp, had a chat with each one, and then rode home, pale but triumphant!

Sunday 25 May
I forgot to mention that on Thursday last 'His Lordship the Right Reverend Bishop Meysing O.M.I.', the Roman Catholic Bishop of Kimberley, called on me and asked if I would be present at the opening of some schools they have built here. Also he wanted me to help him to start work in the Protectorate. I of course said 'yes' to both requests, so we received a formal invitation to the ceremony which was to be performed today by 'His Excellency the Archbishop Gigglefit (or some such name) O.P. and Papal Delegate for South Africa'.

So Ninon and I drove off in style, policeman in front, and to our astonishment found that it was a tremendous ceremony. All the whites in Mafeking were there, and hundreds and hundreds of natives.

Monday 26 May
We had asked the Archbishop and Bishop to lunch here today and greatly to our surprise they accepted. They looked very magnificent, one in black and white, the other in black and purple robes, with their gold chains and big jewelled crosses, both being rather big fine men.

They made themselves quite charming, both able and cultured men, and we enjoyed ourselves very much. They also seemed to. They were very broad-minded and were very much tickled by some of Ninon's characteristic remarks — of course intellectually they are *miles* ahead of anyone else here, and it was refreshing to talk with them.

And it is of course true that the Roman Catholic Missions in Africa do infinitely better work than the others — they send out the right stamp of man, they work like galley slaves, they encourage the people to respect the government, obey the laws, and become good citizens, and they fight Bolshevism and Communism. I am going to help them, and I expect they will help me to down those London Missionary Society vipers.

But I am a little afraid of them, the power and discipline of the R.C. Church are so immense, their resources are so vast, their patience so great. As the Archbishop said to me, 'We are in no hurry, we have all eternity to work for'. Very fine.

Tuesday 27 May to Sunday 1 June
A really terrific week — There were a thousand and one things to clear up before our departure on our 'great trek' of a month, all the preparations for the trek, and a few extras thrown in. I have never worked harder in my life, and never felt better — it's all so interesting.

I had a meeting of all my Heads of Departments and explained my plans and programme for the year — they are all rather delighted, rather frightened, but quite enthusiastic — they've never had anything quite like it before.

Then I found that the damned Union Government (the Union of South Africa) Hertzog's[36] infernal crowd of rebel Dutchmen, have started a new attack on the export of our cattle, and I had to start a fight against them.

Then I had my first murder trial at which I am Chief Justice,[37] with two magistrates to help me — a horrid business. It was held at Lobatsi, and N. and I motored in, a fifty mile run through the bush each way, on a glorious sunny day — like all the days are here. It seemed hard to be going to try a poor devil for his life on a day like that.

The proceedings were most dignified and impressive. The little court house at Lobatsi was spotlessly clean and tidy and quite empty. The prisoner, a Bushman, was brought in and led to the dock by an escort of my Police, the European sergeant in full uniform stood at the back of the Court at attention. On the front bench sat the Crown Prosecutor, and the Clerk of the Court (Price, whose son is now in England).

The official interpreter stood by the box.

With the two magistrates I sat on a raised platform, the interpreter was sworn to interpret 'faithfully and truly to the best of my ability so help me God'. The Crown Prosecutor read over the indictment and moved that the trial be referred to the Special Court (which is presided over by a real judge). I had asked him to do this as I hate trying murder cases.

1930

The prisoner, a wretched Bushman wrapped in a coloured blanket, had killed a man by hitting him over the head with a huge bludgeon (produced in Court) — he was told he could call any witnesses he liked and we would pay their fares down — he was also told he would have a lawyer to defend him whom we would pay. Of course all this conveyed nothing to him really, though it was interpreted well and carefully. I explained everything to him in words of one syllable, and then ordered the case to be removed to the Special Court amid a mass of formalities. I was desperately sorry for him, but justice has to be done, and tho' he will have every conceivable chance, I fear the facts are too strong.

I'm sorry.

Monday 2 June (to Mahalapye)
Off on our trek at last — for a whole month. The police lorry took our luggage, we drove off to the station in 'Topsy' — lots of people at the station to see us off, and at 8 am we steamed off to Lobatsi. We ran past the furthest point North we had hitherto reached (Gaberones) through very jolly hilly country, all in our own Territory, until at 5.30 we reached Mahalapye, our first stopping place.

This is the centre where the annual sports meeting takes place — people come in from all over the Protectorate — by train, by car, by waggon, on horseback and in every way, for the gala week. It is known as our Bisley — there is shooting at the ranges, pigeon shooting, golf, tennis, dancing, concerts and general merriment. I have had twelve tents put up, a big dining tent, a reception tent, two bath tents, etc. and people will also sleep in waggons, in railway coaches lent for the week by the Railway Company, at the hotel (so called) and in their own tents. It's a great show, and people come in from hundreds of miles away, even from Rhodesia and Johannesburg.

It's due to start on Friday 6th but some people are here already.

Several people met us but we were busy getting ready for pushing off tomorrow for Selika (seventy five miles away through the bush) where we are going to stay the night and inspect our post there.

Tuesday 3 June (to Selika)
At 9 am off we went, accompanied by Chase, the Chief Veterinary Officer. We were to break our journey for lunch about forty miles out where I was to address a farmers' meeting, at about 11.

The farmers had brought wives and children, and it was a large crowd, about thirty I should say. Ninon moved off to have a rest, and I tackled my meeting — out in the open, lying on the veld under the trees, really most picturesque and pioneer like. Good fellows too — gentlemen many of them, living the real pioneer life, softened by the car, in which they had come fifty, sixty and even seventy miles over the veld to the meeting. We talked learnedly about cattle, dairying, and farm problems generally — and then at 1.30 we all sat down to a most excellent picnic lunch to which everyone had contributed something. It was really very friendly and jolly — and the farmers (the Tuli Block Farmers Association) were very bucked at our being there — they said it was the first time for ten years that a Resident Commissioner had been out to meet them! They are not merely ordinary farmers — they are the pioneer settlers of this part of the Protectorate and run huge places of ten to thirty thousand acres, with immense herds of cattle — a stout hearted lot of men — real *men*.

At about 4 we parted, Chase returned to Mahalapye, and Ninon and I pushed of

1930

alone without policemen to Selika — another thirty six miles thro' the bush — trusting to luck to find our way. It was lovely country, the track running through bush and trees all the way until at last at about 5.45 we reached Selika Camp — where the R.M., Ellenberger by name, and his wife received us. He is a son of a former Resident Commissioner who was one of the damnedest fools ever born — not as bad as the arch-ass Daniel but pretty nearly.

Ellenberger and his wife were very nice — but the place is too ghastly for words — it's a disgrace to the Protectorate. Ramshackle, tumble-down, patched up buildings — so thick with white ants that if you put a leather suit case on the floor it would be half eaten by the morning. We had to put our shoes on the chairs and our boxes on the tables!

There is no water — it's all brack — so drinking water has to be fetched from twelve miles away in a water cart drawn by oxen twice a week. A grim spot, seventy five miles from anywhere, cut off from the world — no telegraph — no nothing — the one redeeming feature being the lovely country round and masses of game.

But the Camp is situated on a marsh which is a real breeding ground for mosquitoes, so it's very unhealthy — terribly hot in summer.

What a genius the man was who chose the place.

I am going to remove it twenty miles away, lock stock and barrel — *if I find water there*. One of my drills is boring there — they have found *some* water and if there's enough — off goes the Camp.

Friday 6 to Tuesday 10 June (at Mahalapye)
A strenuous five days. We have been out to meals every day — different people at each meal.

On Tuesday morning I struck — and N. and I went off by car with Chase to inspect some of the native creameries which we are encouraging all over the country. It is a very interesting experiment, and it is succeeding very well so far. Three years ago the natives got £600 for their cream — last year they got £6,000 — we have dairy inspectors who go round the country showing the natives how to build their creamery hut and how to work it. The hut is a round thatched contrivance built of mud and whitewashed inside — the floor is cement, the doors and windows netted to be fly proof and the thatched ceiling covered with cotton for the same reason. This costs the native £2! Then he has to buy a mechanical separator which costs anything from £5 to £13, he pays by instalments. This has to be fixed on a concrete block (cost 5s) so as to be perfectly level. The whole thing is then fool proof — he milks his cows into enamel tin pails, pours it into the separator, turns a handle, and the cream comes out one side whilst the skim milk comes out the other — he drinks that of course. The cream goes in sealed tins (supplied by the big dairy at Lobatsi) on donkeys to the railway, is graded 1, 2, or 3 at the dairy, and the man is paid a shilling per pound for it at the end of each month. The cream travels hundreds of miles like this. The big tins are scalded at the dairy and returned to the natives. It's a great scheme, one of the many things I want to expand and develope — there's lots to do here!

At 9.30 we started off in 'Topsy' on our sixty mile run across country to Serowe, Tshekedi's stronghold in the Bamangwato country where we are to stay for two or three days.

Just outside Serowe we found Tshekedi himself awaiting us with a mounted guard of honour of his own troops for us. After a few words we went on into the town and received a magnificent welcome. The way was lined with thousands of troops and people, the women shrilling out the 'el-el-el-el' of the East, the men a deep-throated chorus of 'Pula, pula'. The troops were in weird and wonderful uniforms,[38] and in the setting of the weird native village and the surrounding rocks and koppies it was really very impressive.

N. bowed right and left as to the royal manner born as we passed along, it was really reminiscent of Abyssinia and Gojam. Outside the Residency we halted, where several hundreds of school children were drawn up in long lines, and these then sang us songs of welcome concluding with 'Rule Britannia' in English — it was really very jolly. Some of Tshekedi's principal chiefs were presented, and then after inspecting the guard of honour we went into the Residency and had a well-earned lunch.

After lunch Nettelton and I worked like beavers in preparation for the great Kgotla[39] meeting of the tribe tomorrow, and then Tshekedi brought round his mother (Khama's fourth widow),[40] his two half-sisters,[41] and the mother of Seretse,[42] the nine year old boy who will be Chief and for whom Tshekedi is Regent — to call on Ninon. Seretse came also, an ugly little devil.

Then Tshekedi brought round his stud of horses to show me, his seven prize beasts. Three were very good indeed; one a racer bought in Jo'burg, a pretty little bay mare, and a show hack — the other four were nothing much to write home about.

As he and I were both keen on horses we began to get along very well; drifted on to sport generally; and then very gently I drew him on to business. It was ticklish work because he is quite clever and terribly suspicious, but we began to get along quite well. I rather like him. He has a very pleasant smile when pleased and looks like a devil when he isn't.

He is obviously very nervous about what I am going to say in Kgotla, and to tell the truth so am I! It's a heavy responsibility, for every word I say will be carried through the length and breadth of the Bamangwato country (which is nearly as big as England), repeated to the missionaries, and possibly telegraphed to England if I make a mistake when it will be raised in Parliament. So off to bed early to be fresh for the fray.

Thursday 12 June
In a few minutes we hove in sight of the Kgotla meeting place. It was a most picturesque scene, in the open of course, under some high rocky hills, in the midst of big trees. There were grouped the headmen and councillors from the whole Bamangwato country, between 2,000 and 3,000 in a huge circle, and the size of the gathering nearly took my breath away.

They opened up a passage as we drove up, and Tshekedi came out to greet us, then amid shouts of 'Pula, Pula', Ninon and I walked through the mass and took our seats at a little table, Nettelton, Hope, and the official interpreter (who was shaking with nervousness) beside us and Tshekedi and his secretaries at another table on our right.

Nettelton introduced me in a short and excellent speech, and I had to follow with a formal speech of greeting, very short, but very carefully worded (I learned afterwards that they were immensely pleased at the words I used).

Then Tshekedi rose and welcomed me, and then proceeded to outline six points about which they had a grievance against the Government, the first of which was that until I came they never saw an R.C. as he never came to discuss matters with them, and the main point being of course that terrible mining question which has wrecked all good feeling between Government and Tribe for years.

Then the fun started. Speaker after speaker got up, and in flowery Sechuana (interpreted into English and two other native tongues) held the floor. It was extraordinarily interesting. They raised a number of tricky points — they all complained that they never saw the R.C. — they all said they did not want mining — and they varied this with other troubles and difficulties.

At last I saw we could not finish that morning, and as I had had four hours of it (9 to 1) I said I would give them my answer on all the points tomorrow, and left the Kgotla amid much enthusiasm. The guard of honour escorted me back to the Residency where I shed my butterfly wings and after a hasty lunch met a deputation of traders, farmers and other Europeans at 2.30.

They raised a number of matters which we had to discuss; then at 4 o'clock Ninon and I had to meet the whole of the European inhabitants of Serowe and district, male and female, who had all been invited to tea and tennis at the Residency to meet us. A pretty tiring effort.

And then at 6 o'clock Tshekedi came round for a private interview which lasted till 8.

Nettelton and I had been rather disturbed at the proceedings at the Kgotla because it was obvious that Tshekedi had *not* told his people what Lord Passfield had told him in London. Now T. had told me he *had* done so; he had been told to do so; and my instructions from the Colonial Office were to see that he did so.

How to do this without shewing Tshekedi that we did not believe or trust him, and thus undoing all that I was laboriously building up to win the Chief back to our side, avoid future friction, and smash the L.M.S.?

Some problem. But we solved it in the two hours talk by a policy of perfect frankness and firmness combined.

Friday 13 June
The escort arrived at 8.30 this morning and at 9 we went off to the Kgotla again — it was even more crowded.

More speakers raised more points, and then Tshekedi wound up the debate leaving me the floor.

I must confess that it was a bit of an ordeal to face these 2,000 or more devils, squatting round in perfect silence, their eyes all glued on me, waiting to hear what their New Father had to say. There had been twenty five speakers, beside the chief, and I had to deal with all their points *and* the mining question. And it was the more difficult as I couldn't let myself go on a tide of oratory, but had to use words of one syllable and wait while each sentence was interpreted into three languages.[43]

When once I got going, however, all was well, and I forgot everything but my subject. I took them through the history of the mining concession to the Chartered Company, told them what Lord Passfield had done, gave them my views, and put the position fairly before them.

And when I had done that and answered all their questions I had been on my feet for one and half hours and it was 1 o'clock. Incidentally, I had had enough.

They gave me a tremendous reception, and the guard of honour closed up behind as I drove off, once more pale but triumphant!

I had just time to change out of my war paint, swallow some lunch, and then Tshekedi came up to the Residency to say goodbye, to thank me for the patience I had shown in listening to his people, and for my reply, and to present me with two magnificent fur karosses — one of them was inscribed on the back in Sechuana 'To Colonel Rey on his first visit to the Bamangwato', the lettering being cut out of white leather and sewn on to the kaross most beautifully. All the sewing is wonderful — tiny stitches in gut thread — it is a wonderful example of native work.

Saturday 14 June (to Francistown)
We woke up at Francistown, having arrived there during the night, and our coach having been dropped off.
At 3.30 the Moseleys gave a large party of all whites of Francistown and District at the tennis club to meet us — a fairly exhausting proposition, as everyone has to be introduced, and talked to, and every man has some point to discuss with me.

Sunday 15 June
I thought to have a peaceful morning writing, but not a hope. Moseley dragged me round to meet the 'big noises' in this part of the world, the Haskins trio and a man named Gordon. The Haskins trio consist of three enormous men, father and two sons,[44] very wealthy traders, who own most of the stores in this part of the world. The fool Daniel had practically made an agreement with them for erecting weighbridges for cattle, by which after *we* had paid for them the bridges belonged to Haskins!
I had refused to sign it — hence the meeting. It went off very well — they laughed when I said that the proposed agreement was admirable from their point of view, but the world's worst proposition from ours. It was just a 'try on' on their part and that poor fish Daniel had fallen for it.
We agreed on the basis of an entirely new deal, and left the best of friends.
Gordon is the Managing Director of the Tati Concessions Company,[45] an iniquitous proposition. The Company have an enormous strip of land which they sell or let to settlers; they also do a bit of mining, cattle-ranching, store-running, and dairying etc. But I am against them because they are badly managed, have only once paid a dividend, hold up the settlement of the land by charging huge prices for it (10 shillings and 11 shillings per acre) and cause ill feeling among whites and natives.
Gordon himself is a nice fellow, tho' no businessman. He is really a mining engineer, and has done some prospecting work in Abyssinia where he injured his heart. We had a long yap and he gave me some interesting maps. He has a nice place, and his wife is a very nice woman.
At 2.30 Captain and Mrs Moseley, Miss Perfect, and Dr Drew came to fetch us in two cars to go out about twelve miles to the farm of one Hertz, a wonderful person. His grandfather or great grandfather was a German who had enlisted in the British Foreign Legion to fight first of all in the Crimea and then in the Indian Mutiny. They had then settled in South Africa. The present Hertz had lost his mother when he was six weeks old, had had no education at all, had worked at odd jobs including a black-smith's striker at £1 *per month* and food. At 19 he had joined that magnificent corps the Cape Mounted Rifles, which he left as a Sergeant after twenty one years service. Seventeen years ago he had trekked into the Protectorate with £320 capital and forty oxen (all his savings) and had settled here. Now he owns 20,000 acres, 1,000 head of cattle, besides sheep, pigs, poultry etc. He milks two hundred and fifty cows daily (twenty-three boys do this getting about two hundred and thirty gallons), has built substantial farm buildings, works from 5 am to dark, and is worth £10,000 to £12,000. He sends lots of cream and butter and pigs to

Bulawayo, Lobatsi and Mafeking, has built an enormous dam to hold back twenty six acres of water, and is the most progressive and successful farmer in the district.

But what a life! Never an hour to read, never a moment's leisure, no interest in anything but the most material aspects of life, never a journey outside his district in seventeen years, no culture, no refinement, no comforts. Of course it's very fine as an achievement, but is it worth it? I doubt it.

Monday 16 June
At Ramaquabane I had another Kgotla meeting with Chief Bakwedi of the Bakalanga (or Makalaka), and Chiefs Mosojane and Masunga of different branches of the same tribe. It was a very picturesque gathering under trees in the open, and there were quite a lot of speeches, mainly complaining that they had not enough land, and were badly treated by the Tati Concessions Company. I had no difficulty in answering, tho' the problem is not an easy one, and they certainly have some ground for complaint which I promised to go into.

Sergeant Fox, a very efficient young N.C.O., is in charge of the camp here (Ramaquabane) and gave me some very useful information about his recent expedition when I sent him out to deal with the trouble between Mswazi (of the Makalaka) and Edirilwe (of the Bamangwato) tribes.

He doesn't think much of Mswazi and I am inclined to think he's probably right. Another problem to settle later.

Tuesday 17 June
This is a quiet peaceful place (Tsessebe) and lovely country as I have already said.

This morning we had the most interesting tour, visiting four of the principal farmers in the district. All four farms were beautifully situated on high ground commanding grand views and we drove through jolly country (over awful tracks through the bush) to reach them.

The first was Hoare, the most successful of them. He makes cheese which goes all over South Africa, about eighteen *tons* a year. He gets on the average about a shilling a pound for it, and is going to enlarge and extend the place.

Everything was spotlessly clean, and obviously most efficiently run. He goes on the principle of establishing a chain of native creameries all over the district, run by natives under the supervision of his own trained native foremen. Then the natives bring in their milk, it is bought and separated, the cream sent to the big dairies at Lobatsi or Bulawayo where it is made into butter. He buys every gallon of milk in the district from as far as five to nine miles off and makes it into cheese there. His wife helps enormously.

Forester the next man was a different type, a cultured man living alone. He does a little of everything, and adds tobacco growing — for native consumption — for which he gets about a shilling a pound. It's sweated in sacks, pressed into moulds, and the natives use it for smoking and for snuff. We saw several acres of tobacco plant in flower.

We got back to lunch at 1.15 after a splendidly interesting morning, and at 2 o'clock had to meet a gathering of *all* the [white settler] inhabitants from miles around, as our train was due to leave at 3.30.

They were a jolly good crowd, men and women, and frightfully interested to meet us and hear our plans for the development of the Protectorate. They were as keen as mustard on my scheme for an exhibit of Bechuanaland produce at next year's Johannesburg show[46] — and Ninon roused them to enthusiasm on the subject — she was simply splendid and they all just loved her — their one complaint was 'why didn't you both come out here years ago'.

Friday 20 June (Victoria Falls)
'Topsy' had arrived two days ago (by rail), and our man Matsepane had got her looking spick and span, Union Jack flying and all complete.

Saturday 21 June (Victoria Falls to Kasane)
Off at 9 am, only half an hour late, which for a first day's start is not too bad. We are three cars — a big seven-seater Nash, hired, driven by a youngster named Spencer, who with his brothers runs the garage here; then 'Topsy', with Chase and Dyke in her, driven by our man Matsepane; and finally Lt. Hope's Rugby car driven by himself with his man Ali perched on the top of the luggage. All the cars look like Christmas trees, piled high and strung round with luggage, bedding, food boxes, spare petrol, tins of water, guns and rifles etc. We need fifty to sixty gallons of petrol each, and for one hundred and twenty miles there is no water!
   We (N. and I) are in the Nash as we want to be first so as to see the game, and Spencer is the only man who knows the way so his car must be first.
   Kazungula is on the Chobe River, where the Chobe runs into the Zambesi, an enormously wide confluence. The banks are thickly wooded, and there are some very big trees at Webb's quarters, notably one (German sausage) tree known to history as the place where Livingstone made his camp. It gets its name from its enormous bean pods, eighteen inches long and about three of four inches thick, just like immense German sausages in shape. Kazungula is also interesting as being the spot 'where four Empires meet', or rather four territories of the British Empire, namely the Bechuanaland Protectorate, Northern Rhodesia, Southern Rhodesia, and the Caprivi Strip which is now mandated to the Union of South Africa as part of what used to be German South West Africa.
   Here all our exports of cattle cross the Zambesi; here too the mails are ferried over in canoes. The river is stiff with hippo, crocodiles, and tiger-fish, but as it was very full we did not see any — they get all the food they need brought down by the flood, and so don't need to come to the banks so much.
   Kasane is another lovely spot on the banks of the Chobe River — really lovely, well wooded — the broad river fringed with high feathery reeds in front, and behind it, rolling wooded hills.

Sunday 22 June
We rolled off and early, and had a lovely drive; the 'path' wound up and down and in and out amongst the trees along the banks of the Chobe. Baboons ran across in troops in front of us, and monkeys cursed us from the trees for disturbing them — it was really very jolly and the scenery was perfectly lovely. We were making for Kachikau police post about sixty miles from Kasane.
   Sergeant Davies, an excellent fellow in charge of the post, told me that he had arranged for me to meet the Batawana Chieftainess and her people in Kgotla at their village about three miles off, that he had summoned the two chiefs of the two sections of the Basubia tribe to meet me here, but that only one (and his people) had come.[47]
   Davies seemed to think the other was defiant — this is the place where the trouble was and I had to send the police force to kick the missionary out, and read the Riot Act. So I instructed Davies to send a couple of policemen out to Chief

Chika Leshwane with peremptory orders to him to come in; and if he wouldn't come he was to be arrested and brought in. Meanwhile I settled down to my indaba with the other chief (Sinvala Konguena) and his crowd, and we got very busy.

Just as I was finishing with them, in came Master Chika — voluntarily I am glad to say — so I told him to sit down with his councillors and wait while I went off to the Batawana village in 'Topsy' to meet that little lot.

This was very picturesque — in the open-air of course, all these meetings are — under some big trees in the midst of rather a well built village. The tribe were squatting round in a big half-circle — the headmen, about a dozen, in a row in front, and alone in front of them all, on a stool was the weirdest figure I have seen for a long while. She looked very like the pictures of Gagool, the old witch in *King Solomon's Mines*. She must have been very old, was huddled up, and muffled in leopard skins; on her head was a native made plaited straw basket thing, under which two piercing eyes glared at me. As a chieftainess, she certainly looked the part.

We had quite a good 'indaba' — the usual long speeches, and I picked up some quite useful information.

Then I got up. Hope saluted, the cars came up, and I stalked solemnly into the first, Chase and Dyke into the second, and we drove back to camp when I had my third 'indaba' with Chika and his Basubia.

Monday 23 June
We did not roll into Satsarogo Pan until after 2 o'clock. The remains of the Vernay-Laing scientific exploring expedition were camped here and Dr Laing came over to greet us, just as we were walking round to see him. He insisted on sending us some tables and chairs, and a large dish of stewed fruit as a contribution to our lunch.

Their camp is on a large scale. Three closed motor lorries in which they sleep and keep their gear. Some of them used tents, as they were fourteen. Other tents are used for preparing and sorting the skins and skeletons of their specimens; they have everything from a bull giraffe eighteen feet high to tiny fish.

Tuesday 24 June
We did forty miles through Mopane tree forest,[48] exquisite scenery, saw the spoor of elephant and leopard, little steinbok, reedbuck and duiker; pretty little antelope, dashed away or stood blinking at us — and of course birds galore including the lovely blue jay.

Then our troubles began. We had left the other cars behind so waited a bit — then went back — and found them broken down — Hope's car had struck work — an hour's delay — then on again — then again we were alone — back again — poor old Hope had struck another puncture and couldn't get his wheel off. Of course the track was enough to wreck any car — stiff bushes scraped our sides, deep sand held us up — holes, ruts, mounds, tree and bush stumps added to the liveliness of things — and it was a hungry and weary party that sat down to lunch, or rather brunch for we had had no breakfast. We were now in the Tsetse fly belt — they infest a narrow strip about twenty-five miles wide, and they worried us a bit — but we were too hungry to bother, and watched with famished eyes eggs, sausages and bacon frizzling on the fire which we had lighted instantly. How we did enjoy them!

At long last at about 2 o'clock we bumped into Maun and drew up at the Residency, where the R.M. Captain Potts was awaiting us — he was a great contrast to our party, clean and neat and dapper — whereas we!

Even Ninon's face was streaked with black dust, and as for the rest of us! Unwashed and unshaven and coated with dust from head to foot we were enough to frighten a criminal!

Thursday 26 June
Maun is the administrative centre and principal village in the Ngamiland district. The main tribe are the Batawana, and there is perpetual trouble between them and a subject race, the Makoba, and also with the Damara, a tribe that was allowed to migrate here from German South West Africa some years ago owing to ill-treatment by the Germans after the Herero rebellion.[49]

The Chief of the Batawana is Mathiba,[50] a poor fish. He is quite loyal, and very pleasant, but as weak as dishwater — also tho' he is only forty-five he is so riddled by disease and drink that he can hardly walk.

Maun is on the Okavango River, a very lovely broad stream, and the country round is jolly, well-wooded and grand ranching country — the cattle are in splendid condition, fine big beasts and lots of them. But the native village is too ghastly for words — nothing but sand — not a blade of grass — dirty, straggling, and untidy. There are four European stores, representing wealthy trading interests as this is a great cattle buying centre. But the Europeans mostly a bit mixed in blood, are a ghastly crew. Of course this is a tropical place and very malarial, hot, and unhealthy in the rains and hardly anybody from the outside ever comes here. I am the first Resident Commissioner to come for twenty years, and no female R.C. has ever been here — Ninon the first.

We went down to Camp — a dilapidated collection of huts — and first of all I had a short talk with the Chief alone and tried to stir him up a bit. Then we met the whole tribe in Kgotla — Ninon was there, and sat through it all. They gave a sort of dance first — then a speech of welcome, and then got up and voiced their troubles, not many, and not serious.

After this I gave them a lecture — told them they were lazy, ignorant, unprogressive and helpless — explained what I proposed to do for them, and what they had got to do to help — arranged to build a school — told them I was sending the Chief's son away to be educated and to get some military discipline at our police training camp at Gaberones, and generally raised Hail Columbia. I am bound to say they took it very well.

Various matters were discussed and a few complaints raised: but in all these places they are so pleased to see a R.C. in the flesh for the first time that they are most amenable. The fact of being in uniform too makes a *tremendous* difference to the native mind — it is difficult for a European to understand this.

The meeting lasted till past 1: then after lunching at the Residency I went back to Camp and met all the European men — traders, cattle-buyers, and storekeepers, mixed blood mostly, some Greeks and a couple of Jews — no self-respecting person could live here through the rains.

Saturday 28 June
It was sad to have to leave Maun today on our return journey — this country is so fascinating and the idea of returning to that hole Mafeking is most unwelcome.

1930

Monday 30 June
We got in to Kasane at about 12.45 where they gave us a hearty welcome and an excellent lunch — after which N. went out in the barge paddled by native police to try for tiger fish, and look for hippo — whilst I inspected the camp buildings etc. and worked with Midgeley, the acting R.M., rather a young ass I fear.

Tuesday 1 July
After a lovely run through forest where we saw a fine herd of kudu, we arrived back at Victoria Falls — very sorry indeed to be back in civilisation. We've had a grand time, been through lovely country finer than anything I've seen in the world except Abyssinia, met lots of interesting people and things, and seen more game than I've ever dreamed of — zebra, giraffe, warthog, wild pig, kudu, tsessebe, wildebeest, duiker, sable, steinbuck, reed-buck, impala, ostrich, pauw (greater bustard), turkey buzzard, tick-birds, heron, duck, wild goose, pheasant, guinea fowl, monkeys, baboons, meer-cat, koran, Lehututu bird — and lots of smaller things.

Dyke and Chase very kindly insisted on giving us lunch and dinner at the Victoria Falls Hotel — a large and sumptuous place beautifully furnished and arranged with a gorgeous view of the Falls. But the food was pretentious and filthy and Ninon agreed that we *infinitely* preferred our bacon and eggs out of a dirty frying pan on dirty plates in the bush, eaten round the camp fire, and washed down with tea, to the finest meal any hotel could give us.

I'm afraid we're both hopeless savages!

Friday 4 July (Back at Mafeking)
Our train was very late and we did not arrive at Mafeking until after 5 o'clock. Dyke had been met at Lobatsi (fifty miles up the line) by his wife in their car and motored home from there. There was a great crowd at the station to meet us, and they gave us a royal welcome. Of course Pongo was there, and after nearly knocking us down by jumping all over us he hurled himself in sheer light-heartedness at an Airedale and had him down in a moment! Fortunately we got him off before he had time to get a grip. He is really a grand dog.

Sunday 13 to Tuesday 15 July
We were dog tired and after 'brunch' we retired in 'Topsy' to a secluded spot in the veld far from the madding crowd and wrote and read and dozed in peace. 'Topsy' is a Godsend: I don't know what we should do without her. As a means of conveyance, a bedroom, a refuge in times of stress, and a few other things, she is 'It'. Monday and Tuesday were devoted to hectic days at the office, and much cursing of all my heads of departments who seemed to have developed signs of incipient sleeping sickness during my absence.

And at 7.30 pm Colonel Ellenberger, former Resident Commissioner before Daniel, arrived here to stay for a couple of days on his way through. He has been doing a bit of frontier delimitation work for us away in the North-West where we touch Portuguese South West Africa [Angola] and what was German South West Africa — now belongs to the Union of South Africa.

He is unintelligent, small-minded, cunning, and generally about as fit to be a Resident Commissioner as I am to be a Bishop.

1930

Wednesday 16 July
Another dash off into the Territory — for a day only, this time. We have to attend a farmer's meeting at Lobatsi so I took Chase with us.

I had a great piece of luck. Colonel Robbins was at Lobatsi, he is the General Manager in South Africa of all the Chartered Company's business, a most important man, and with him was Major Cholmondeley who manages all their farms and cattle, a huge job. I had a long private talk with Robbins after the meeting, and established the most friendly relations. I believe it will be the beginning of a new era in the relations between the Government and the Company and may lead to big results. Robbins and Cholmondeley both attended the meeting and apparently were much impressed.

Thursday 17 to Sunday 20 July
A damnable few days. Ellenberger left at 7 am and had to get up at 6 am in the dark as all the damned lights went out. Then we had a complete domestic upheaval which means that most of our servants are going just when we've got the brutes trained. Our cook's husband is a jealous old fool and objects to her playing the fool with the other men. As if it mattered. He wants to take her away and the others turned out, and generally we've had a rotten time. However we may compromise by giving the cook a month's holiday, and sacking one or two of the others. I've wired to the Native Commissioner at Livingstone to send down another (Northern) Rhodesian boy.

Monday 21 to Thursday 24 July
A very interesting spell, dealing with native problems in the Bamangwato Reserve. Chief Tshekedi came down to see me, and also Simon and Oratile Ratshosa (husband and wife) who are the Chief's cousins and his mortal enemies. Simon shot at Tshekedi in Serowe and got him in the shoulder: we collared him and stuck him in gaol for a bit, and turned all the Ratshosa family out of Serowe. Tshekedi grabbed Oratile's patrimony (her father was Sekgoma, son of the Great Chief Khama and brother of Tshekedi) and burned all the Ratshosas' houses. They brought a case against Tshekedi, won it, and Tshekedi has appealed to the Privy Council. Now there are continual rows, intrigues and quarrels, and sooner or later there will be bloodshed if we can't fix things up.[51]

So I spent three days listening to all the parties and weighing the arguments. They are a set of mules, tho' of course Oratile, being a woman, is much the worst. She went off the deep end (just as I was getting things straight) because Tshekedi rather tactlessly suggested that she was not the daughter of her father (!) and this aspersion on her mother's virtue caused a dreadful scene.

However I suggested certain terms of settlement, told them all to go away and think over it; and warned them that if they did not come to agreement voluntarily I should settle it in my own way, and carry out my decision by force. I think it will pan out all right.

Thursday 31 July
Great news. *We've won the first round of the fight for my water-boring schemes.* The Treasury have agreed in principle, and a preliminary grant has been voted for the detailed scheme to be prepared by Dr Du Toit,[52] the biggest water expert in South Africa, whom I had recommended.

It's taken me seven months hard fighting, and we're not through yet — but it's a great step forward, and now I'm certain we'll get it through. A great triumph. So I dispatched telegrams, fixed up meetings with Du Toit, and generally made everything hum. We *are* going to be busy — tho' we haven't been exactly idle hitherto!

And then, so that we should not get too uppish, our new servants struck and walked out of the house! That was the limit, and was more than my sweet and patient nature could stand. So I reported them to the Magistrate here, and they'll get it in the neck.

Friday to Monday August Bank Holiday
On Saturday the servants were arrested, and a Sergeant of Police came round for me to sign the necessary papers. They will be brought up in Court on Tuesday and of course I shall have to appear. Ninon is delighted, and the other servants chuckled and grinned with joy, and seemed to think it a huge joke. I expect the men will get fourteen days imprisonment, and as I've reported them to the Magistrate at Livingstone they'll probably get another fourteen days when they get back there. I hope so.

Sunday was a gorgeous day, and we went off in Topsy and basked in the sun on the veld, taking our lunch and tea with us, our work and some books. It was most peaceful and lovely.

And now I have an extra strenuous week ahead, as Dr Du Toit the water expert is coming over to stay with us, and we have to launch the first stage of THE WATER SCHEME!

Tuesday 5 August
A week of real triumph — my eight and a half months of fighting is beginning to bear fruit in abundance. Directly I got the telegram about the water boring grant I dispatched Dutton (the Government Secretary) to Kimberley to see Dr Du Toit, the great expert who is to start the work for us, rope him in, make him an ally, and bring him over here.

I spent today preparing for them, varied by intervals in the police court where after giving evidence I had the pleasure of seeing my servants sentenced to periods of hard labour varying from one to four weeks as a punishment for deserting me. That's the way to handle them.

Wednesday 6 August
A great day. Du Toit arrived at 7 am and I brought him here, bathed and breakfasted him, and settled down to work at 9 am.

Captain Neale, the R.M. from Molepolole, is also staying here: he has come down to discuss my scheme of deposing Sebele, the Chief of the Bakwena, who is a ruffian. We have got to manage it without any fighting or bother, and it's no easy job. But it's got to be done.

We had a very jolly dinner, and felt that life is really pretty good.

Thursday 7 August
Du Toit left by the 6.30 am train. He started talking water to me at 5.45 am.

On arrival at the office I was met by another ripping telegram. Athlone asking me to represent him at Bulawayo on 14th at the ceremony of the re-interment of Sir Charles Coghlan (Southern Rhodesia's first Prime Minister) at Rhodes's Grave in the Matopos. It's to be a wonderful ceremony — all South Africa is to be represented and as I represent the 'High Commissioner and Governor-General of South

Africa' I shall be Lord of the Universe there for the day! Its really awfully nice of Athlone, and a great feather in the cap of the Bechuanaland Protectorate, and of C.F. Rey.

Then at 11.30 we launched another of my schemes, the first meeting of the Committee for the B.P. exhibit at the Jo'burg show next March. Ninon is a member of it, and the idea has been taken up with enthusiasm throughout the Protectorate — it will be a tremendous advertisement for us as it's never been done before. We're going to show all our products, cattle, cheese, cream, fruit, jams, jellies, native arts and crafts, woods, pottery, skins and lots of other things. It went off splendidly, and we formed three sub committees to work out all details and stimulate the local committees which we have formed in every district of the Protectorate.

And then to cap it all, I got another telegram to say the Colonial Development Committee had agreed to our sharing in the Walvis Bay Railway survey, a scheme for a railway right across the Protectorate from East to West, for which I had started fighting before I left England — and ever since! And they've given us £2000 to start with; Southern Rhodesia puts up £2000, and South West Africa another £2000.[53]

It's great.

The afternoon was devoted to discussions with Captain Neale in regard to our friend Sebele. It's going to be a ticklish business, but they've accepted my plan for doing it (Neale, and the others I've consulted here) and as soon as we've got a little more evidence, which will take about a couple of months, out goes Sebele. He ought to have been kicked out eight years ago, but two High Commissioners and three Resident Commissioners funked it. He is a drunken, diseased, dishonest scoundrel, who oppresses his people, flouts the Government, and lives by robbery and worse.

Saturday 9 August
Another telegram from the Colonial Office to say they had agreed to another grant of £3,000 for an investigation into Tsetse fly here — the jolly little fellow that brings sleeping sickness to men and cattle. We have got a belt of them, we went thro' it on our recent tour, and it's spreading. So they must be exterminated, and an expert is coming out from England to help us.

Monday 11 August
A really devilish rush all day. I had to launch the preparations for the meeting of the European Advisory Council and the opening of the Lobatsi Hospital next month — and it is surprising what a lot of questions are involved. I fear I lost my temper over one of them — namely how many of the seventeen different religious bodies who infest this unhappy country are to be invited to blither at the opening ceremony of the hospital!

First of all I said *none*. Then in response to unanimous and pathetic entreaties I agreed to *one* viz the Church of England, which after all is the official religion I suppose. But when it came to Dutch Reformed Church, Lutherans, Wesleyans, Baptists, Seventh Day Adventists, London Mission Society, *and* a lot more fancy religion, I struck. As a matter of fact the only missionaries that are worth a damn are the Roman Catholics — they get on with their job, teach the natives useful trades and discipline and respect for authority; and don't interfere with the Government.

Tuesday 12 August
At 8.30 pm after an excellent dinner we ran into Bulawayo. Sir Cecil Rodwell's[54] A.D.C. met me, and rolled me up to Government House, or rather to Sunrising the

house near Government House belonging to the Chartered Company.

There was a dinner party on — a lot of Ministers, Rhodesian and South African as well. General Kemp[55] was amongst them, the Union Minister of Agriculture, a poisonous brute, ex-rebel and anglophobe, but mightily civil these days — a dangerous clever rogue.

They cleared out to catch a train, and then Rodwell took me over to Government House leaving his A.D.C.s to entertain a couple of Dutch sweeps.

We had a long and very interesting talk, and ranged over a number of subjects — high politics, Walvis Bay Railway, water-boring, relations between Rhodesia and the B.P., the Union's native policy etc. etc. He is a *very* able man, and a most pleasant one — and I was most grieved when it was time to go to bed. He has arranged for me to have a private interview with Moffat[56], the Prime Minister of Southern Rhodesia, tomorrow.

Wednesday 13 August
We went down to the Roman Catholic church for a Requiem Mass for Sir Charles Coghlan[57] (he was an R.C.). A very impressive ceremony. Pirow, the Minister of Justice in the Union Government, was due to arrive by aeroplane — but as he had not materialised we presumed he had broken his neck *en route*. He will be no loss.

Then back to Government House where I had another interesting talk with Rodwell — he is a top hole person — and then after an excellent lunch I met Moffat at 2.30. We talked 'solid' till nearly 5!

And by Jove it *was* worth while. Of course I can't put it all down here, but I think we've started to make history. They've never considered the B.P. before — simply ignored it. Now they've begun to realise that we count. Moffat was simply delighted to learn the line of policy I wanted to follow — the push north to Rhodesia instead of south to the Union, cooperation with them in trade and development and railway construction and politics, joint work over the Walvis Bay Railway that will link us together in the future. And finally the ultimate goal, the great dream of the future — a solid *British* block under the *British* flag — Northern and Southern Rhodesia, Bechuanaland, and Nyasaland — a British counterstroke to those damned Dutch sedition mongers that have turned the Union of South Africa into an anti-British camp.

It's a great dream — but I don't see why it shouldn't come off.

Thursday 14 August (Trip to Rhodes's Grave)
Pirow[58] had arrived at 7 am and came with us, clever but poisonous person. Fortunately I was with Rodwell, so we beguiled the thirty mile drive with much useful talk.

On foot and very slowly we wound up between the great grim rocks, the grey sky lowering above us, the cold wind whistling round us, and so to the grave side. The grave was blasted out of the solid rock, the coffin covered with a huge Union Jack beside it. Around it a detachment of that magnificent corps the British South Africa Police, picked men, nearly all public school, smart as paint in the speckless cavalry uniforms and spiked helmets. The Governor, Sir Cecil Rodwell, and A.D.C.s were waiting there and we all took up our positions, and the service became a little blaze of colour amid the surrounding masses of people in dark clothes that stretched back and round us. The singing was very fine, the service most impressive, and the Bishop's address admirable. Then the B.S.A. Police lowered the coffin into the grave, the buglers sounded the Last Post — and slowly

1930

and seemingly reluctantly the masses began to move away.

I drove back with Rodwell and had another interesting talk — but I was frozen to the marrow.

We had an amusing lunch. Pirow is a very able man, and tho' he is anti-English and talks a lot of unmitigated rubbish he can be — and was — very amusing.

Friday 15 August
What a different atmosphere there is in Rhodesia. It is really English there, virile, breezy, blunt and open — such a refreshing contrast to the sly tricky underhand Dutch mentality which is so utterly repulsive.

Saturday 16 to Monday 25 August
There's a terrible lot to do preparing for the meeting of my 'Parliament' (the European Advisory Council) and the opening of the Lobatsi Hospital, both of which take place early next month.

A poisonous man called Ballinger[59], a Communist, has descended on us and wants to tour the Territory. I stopped him here and said I'd put him in gaol if he moved without my permission. Meanwhile I've wired to the police at Cape Town, Jo'burg and Pretoria to find out all about him. It's amusing to be able to handle people like this.

Tuesday 26 to Thursday 28 August
Another trip into the Territory and a very interesting one. We left early, N. and I, motored to Lobatsi, and lunched at the Residency with the Drurys. Before lunch I inspected the Cold Storage works, where they make ice and butter and where I hope they will be killing cattle for export before long. It all depends on whether a new type of refrigerating car, now being tried on the railway, is good enough for the long pull to the Coast. It will be a great thing if it comes off.

We got to Kanye about tea time — we are of course staying at the Residency there with the Cuzens who seemed delighted to see us. After tea I inspected the new water supply arrangements — a splendid scheme. We sank a borehole, got water at fifty feet, installed a pump which sends the water up to a tank holding 25,000 gallons. From here it gravitates down a pipe underground from which rise fifteen stand pipes with taps. Here as many as four thousand natives a day can come and draw water — it is a perfect Godsend to them.

On Wednesday morning was the great Kgotla meeting, Chief Bathoen and all the Bangwaketse Tribe. I got into full uniform and with Ninon drove off to the meeting where we were received in great state. It was a wonderful gathering — N. and I and the Cuzens sitting in the midst of nearly 2,000 natives, who had come in from miles. It was a tremendously animated meeting as there was bad trouble between Bathoen the young Chief, Kgampu an ex-councillor of the old Chief, and Gobuamang the subordinate chief of a branch of the Bakgatla tribe who had fled for protection to the Bangwaketse one hundred and twenty years ago when chased out of the Transvaal by Moselekatse (Mzilikazi) the great Matabele Chief.[60]

Kgampu had been exiled and wanted to come back: he wouldn't stay in his place of exile, and the tribe asked me to force him to stay there, which I agreed to do.

Gobuamang pronounced 'Hobuaman', or as my predecessor called him, Gobbleman, was a much more difficult problem. He is a stubborn old man of 70 who has defied the Chiefs of the Bangwaketse and three Resident Commissioners (my predecessors) for twenty years. He was in the Kgotla, and after he had been

1930

vigorously denounced he got up and said that he didn't recognise Bathoen as Chief of the people — but only chief of the rocks and earth — that he, Gobuamang, was Chief of the people, that what he had said he had said, and then talked about guns going off!

The stolid natives almost gasped, and as I got up to answer there was a sort of rustle of expectancy, and 2,000 pairs of eyes glared at me. I could see Cuzen fidgeting and wondering what on earth I was going to say — only Ninon was quite unperturbed.

I had just about five minutes to make up my mind what to do — while I was answering the other points that had been raised. Then I said I was sorry to hear Gobbleman's remarks, reminded him of what had happened a hundred and twenty years ago, told him he had been a nuisance for twenty years and that he was going to be a nuisance no longer. I said he had been warned again and again — and that now it was finished — I therefore directed that he should cease to be Chief of the [Mmanaana] Bakgatla, that his son should take over the direction of affairs, and that within one month he was to leave his place and tribe and come into Kanye to live there under the protection of the Chief Bathoen and the eye of the Government. And then I sat back, mopped my brow, and hoped for the best — I had three police with me!

However it all went down like butter — they accepted my dictum, and later on, after all the speeches were finished and we left the Kgotla, they gave us a tremendous reception. Natives don't understand anything except an *order*: they like to be *governed*, and as long as one is fair and just, the more despotically one governs the better. But I wonder what our Socialist friends at Home would say!

Friday 29 August to Friday 5 September
September 1st was a Red Letter Day. My first survey party under my big water scheme *started!*

Dr Du Toit the biggest geologist in South Africa, Mr Leeson the Chief Boring Superintendent of the Union Government (lent to us), and Brind the Government Engineer of the B.P. arrived at 6.45 am, bathed and break-fasted with us, and then we wandered down to Camp. Here the two big lorries were awaiting them, packed with camp kit, food, petrol, water, survey instruments etc. and at 10.30 amid scenes of tremendous enthusiasm from the entire staff the *EXPEDITION STARTED!*

And by today's post I received another dispatch to say that my proposals for the Walvis Bay Railway Survey (for a Railway right across the B.P. from Rhodesia to South West Africa) are approved, that there is to be a conference between the Governments of B.P., Rhodesia, and South West Africa to settle the route of the survey, and that I have been appointed to represent the B.P. and the High Commissioner at this Conference! Another triumph!

Saturday 6 to Saturday 13 September
On 8th my Parliament opened — that always means a fearful lot of work for both of us; problems and debates for me, and entertaining for Ninon.

There are thirty subjects down for discussion this session, some of them very tricky, and its always difficult to keep the balance between the interests of the white settlers and those of the natives — *vide* Kenya!

Saturday 20 September
I had a nasty smash on Saturday.

I was riding a young untrained Police horse on the veld before breakfast: he was as wild as a coot, and I had just had a battle with him and had reduced him to peace — we were going at a walk and I was wrapped in thought. Suddenly a piece of paper blew out from behind a bush into the horse's face — he threw up his head and gave me an awful crash in the face, and then before I could recover my senses reared and came down with me — my hand underneath him, and as we afterwards discovered, smashing my finger in three places.

It hurt like the devil, and it wasn't easy to mount again as the pony was dancing about like a dervish. But we got home all right, and then Dyke came round, trotted me off to be X-rayed, and then put it in a wire splint, a very neat dodge.

But of course it's an awful bore, as I have to pack and get everything ready to go off to Pretoria.

Ninon was very angry with me, and said I wasn't fit to be trusted out alone! A bit hard.

Thursday 25 September
The Walvis Railway Survey Conference was a huge success from the B.P. point of view. All the other delegates had their own ideas as to the route the survey was to follow. So when they had expounded their views I got going and explained mine *which eventually were carried unanimously.* We sat all the morning and all the afternoon, and fixed up everything; practically all the arrangements are left in my hands, as the Railway covers three hundred and fifty miles in B.P., about fifty in Rhodesia, and about a hundred in South West Africa. The Rhodesian delegate, Mr Downie,[61] Minister of Mines and Railways, dined with us at the Hotel. He is going to be Rhodesian High Commissioner in England, so he should be very helpful to us there.

Friday 26 September
The Conference met again this morning to settle a few final details and sign the Report. Then I had to go to Union Government Buildings to see Mr Grobler, Minister of Native Affairs,[62] whose speeches have been creating a lot of fuss in the newspapers here and at home lately. We got on very well and made an excellent arrangement.

We left Pretoria at 1 taking our lunch with us — the road to Johannesburg is grand, and we ought to have done sixty miles an hour the whole way. But 'Topsy' wouldn't pull, so we didn't get in till 3.30 and then had to leave 'Topsy' at the garage of the Armstrong agents. We went to the Carlton Hotel, a really very fine place indeed, where one meets everyone in South Africa.

N. and I went to our first 'talkie' — it was supposed to be a very good one as 'talkies' go — but we didn't like it at all.

Saturday 27 September
Jo'burg is a foul place. Too much money, too much traffic, too much noise, too many Jews, too many Corona cigars. But it is wonderful to think that forty years ago it was bare veld!

We much prefer Pretoria, which is smaller, quieter, more countrified, and more African.

Sunday 28 September to Monday 6 October.
We got back to Mafeking for tea on Sunday pretty weary, but having had a *very* successful time.

And then on Tuesday the blow fell. I got a report from Cuzen, the R.M. Kanye, that Gobbleman had refused to come in as ordered by me. Cuzen had sent out a white sergeant with a regiment (unarmed) of Bangwaketse to bring him in. The [Mmanaana] Bakgatla had shewn a threatening front, brandished weapons, and said their chief was not going. The sergeant, having walked into a trap and being surrounded, feared bloodshed if he persisted, so very wisely withdrew.

The next day Cuzen himself dashed off to Moshupa only to find that Gobbleman had completely disappeared and that the tribe professed complete ignorance of his whereabouts.

Then he sent in a runner to me with a report, and to ask for instructions.

I received the report at 4.30 pm. By 4.45 I had telephoned orders to R.M. Lobatsi to send for Cuzen, by 5 pm a runner was on his way out to Kanye and by 9 am. the next morning Cuzen was in the office.

After consultations we made the following arrangements. All my available police at the Gaberones depot were to come down to Lobatsi by train on Friday morning, with arms, rations and saddlery but no horses; they were to be met by motor lorries on arrival at Lobatsi, and moved directly to Moshupa via Kanye. The officer commanding was to come on ahead to Mafeking, get his orders direct from me, go back to Lobatsi, meet his police and go with them to Moshupa. Meanwhile Cuzen was to go back to Kanye, arrange with Chief Bathoen to supply horses for the police, and move all available police from Lobatsi to Kanye to await the reinforcements.

On arrival of the combined force Cuzen was to draw a cordon of police round the village, to enter the village with ten men, and send for the Chief. If found he was to be arrested at once and conveyed to Kanye. If not the village was to be 'combed' by the police and ten headmen arrested as hostages.

The police were then to watch the village until further orders. Meanwhile all R.M.'s were warned and a general search was ordered for Gobbleman.

This is only an outline of the order — there was of course a mass of detail.

On Thursday evening I received a report to the effect that Gobbleman had been trying to refuge with various chiefs who had refused to take him in, and that it was believed he was with one Seboko near Gaberones. At 9 pm Cuzen's second-in-command, Langton, with three police went off by motor lorry to fetch him, and at 5 am Friday morning ran him to earth in Seboko's kraal (Ramoutsa).

Langton went straight into the hut, woke up Gobbleman and told him to come along. Seboko objected to his going, said he could only be handed over after a general meeting of the tribe. Meanwhile the tribe were gathering (it was now just before daybreak) and as Langton had only three men the position was awkward. So he told Gobbleman 'I have police outside, hundreds are coming later, will you come voluntarily, or must I arrest and handcuff you'. There was a moment's pause, while Langton sweated almost audibly — then Gobbleman said he would come. Langton bundled him into the lorry, jumped in with the police and drove like smoke through the village back to Lobatsi, which he reached at 9 am Friday morning.

They telephoned me at once, and I was just in time to stop the police reinforcement from Gaberones.

They conveyed Gobbleman to Kanye, and Langton slept for twelve hours! Meanwhile Cuzen and Croneen, the officer commanding police, rode into Moshupa with one white N.C.O. and six native troopers — they found five hundred and fifty natives drawn up in the kraal. They ordered them to cross the river without arms, and examined them as they came across four at a time through a gap to see that they were unarmed.

Then Cuzen harangued them, told them what had been done, ran up a Union Jack

1930

on a post there, and made the whole lot file past and salute it, while the majesty of England's power (represented by one white officer, one white N.C.O. and six native troopers) presented arms!!

Then Cuzen went home and went to bed. I heard all this on Sunday morning when he came into Mafeking and reported — a fairly breathless week-end.

But I fear our troubles are not yet over, tho' Gobbleman is fixed. Reports have come in that a man is promenading the Southern Kalahari, saying he is a sort of Messiah, that the land is his, that people must not pay taxes to Government but to him, and generally stirring up trouble. We shall have to tackle him next.

Other troubles have occurred during the week.

On Thursday 2 October
Tshekedi Chief of the Bamangwato came down to discuss various matters with me. He had written me a letter saying very rude things about Lord Athlone and the Government so I told him he must withdraw and apologise before I would talk to him. He said he wanted time to think about it![63]

So I sent him back to Serowe with a flea in his ear, and said that when he had learned manners he could come back and see me — not before. And that meanwhile I would not even consider any of his requests.

Tuesday 7 October (to Lobatsi)
Off again — this time to Mochudi in the Bakgatla native reserve, a place about thirty miles north of Gaberones. We motored to Lobatsi, starting after lunch, and rolled in there for dinner — sleeping at the hotel which is really quite clean and comfortable for this Godforsaken country.

Wednesday 8 October (to Mochudi)
I did some business at the Gaberones Camp, interviewed Croneen the O.C. Police there, and saw young Moremi, the son of the Chief Mathiba that I saw up in Ngamiland at Maun. I had arranged for him to come down here to be educated and to have six months preliminary military training with our police — it has worked wonderfully successfully: the boy is quite changed, cheery and bright, and filling out well. He loves the life and we shall make a man of him. It's a great success, and now I hope to have a Chief in the making who will be a lot better than some of the rotters we have now.

Got into Mochudi soon after six, being met just outside by Mr Reyneke of the Dutch Reformed Church Mission who is our host for two days.

They seemed delighted to have us and did everything humanly possible to make us comfortable — a worthy couple, and about the only decent missionary I have met, tho' he is a Dutchman. We had a foul room, and a horrible dinner — and afterwards — prayers! I expect it did us good, and anyhow it was quite short — he let out a special prayer for his 'honoured guests' which was rather nice of him, and no doubt needed.

Thursday 9 October
A strenuous day. We started off by inspecting the village — most interesting. It is the best-built village in the Territory, the huts are beautifully thatched, the walls cleanly plastered and decorated with most artistic designs, and quite clean. Each hut is surrounded by a courtyard and a wall, built of rock and mud and plastered with a mixture of earth and cowdung which keeps out ants and is smooth and

polished and very clean looking. The village is built among rocks on a number of koppies, and very picturesque. The ex-chief Isang is very progressive, insists on all huts being properly built and kept, has started quite a good scheme of education, built a splendid school and a church, and established a first-rate water-supply. He was only Regent for his nephew Molefi to whom he handed over about a year and a half ago. Molefi was going wrong, but I've managed to pull him up and now he looks as if he might shape well.

After this we drove to the show-ground to have a preliminary inspection of the cattle exhibits. This is the first native agricultural show to be held in the B.P. Imagine such backwardness. I've been egging them on to this for months, and they have organised it themselves — a wonderful effort.

There are three hundred cattle exhibits alone, besides a lot of others, sheep, poultry, pigs, pottery, basket and wood work, sewing, thread and cloth made of aloe fibre, and best of all one hundred and seventy exhibits of different grains.

The official opening and judging was in the afternoon, and N. and I drove up in great style and were formally received and conducted to a really very well built stand, decorated in red blue and white cloth and hung with Union Jacks.

The principal Europeans were on the stand behind us, and on another stand were the chiefs and their followers.

There were tugs-of-war between teams representing the different native 'regiments' — of course the Chief's regiment won. I imagine there might have been trouble if it hadn't!

'Tiger-men' did weird dances for us — a portrayal of a leopard hunt. One was wrapped in a leopard skin, most realistic, the leopard's head covering his own; the others in long streaming tiger-cat skins and armed with axes and spears stalked the leopard and chased him.

Then there were ox-races, the sight of oxen galloping is very odd, but the riders sat their unwieldy mounts very well. The donkey race was chiefly remarkable for the fact that the boy who eventually won fell off early in the race, remounted, and won chiefly by beating off the other competitors with his whip — Jockey Club Rules!

Then they brought up a witch-doctor, covered with dried skins, blown-out animal bladders, and bones — he was going to do some witchcraft 'stunts' for us, but much to my regret I felt that we could not really encourage him as we have recently issued a Proclamation against witch-craft! So we decided to move on to the school buildings and have a look at the 'Arts Crafts and Agricultural Section'.

They had built the school (an excellent and very large building) at the top of a steep koppie, so we arranged for a chair in which Ninon was carried up to the top, and after we had examined hundreds of exhibits and were nearly dropping with weariness they gave us an excellent tea which was a very welcome interlude.[64] Then Ninon presented prizes. I let off another (short) speech and as 'the shades of night were falling' we trooped back to the village. We had to stop on the way at one of the Europeans' houses to meet all the 'White People' — an exhausting performance, but relieved by the fact that they provided us with whiskey and soda 'en masse' — very grateful and comforting as our hosts the Reynekes are teetotal.

Friday 10 to Sunday 12 October
We motored back to Lobatsi on Friday — quite a fleet of cars came to see us off. We lunched at the most filthy hotel at Gaberones as I didn't want to go to the Residency being annoyed with Ledeboer, the R.M., for his behaviour yesterday.

Instead of being with us, playing a star part, and taking an interest in things, he spent nearly all his time talking to females. He will get it in the neck from me later.

Monday 13 to Sunday 19 October (back at Mafeking)
Another hectic week. On Monday Dr and Mrs Du Toit arrived at 7 am to discuss *the* water-boring report with me. They stayed on till Tuesday afternoon.

On Wednesday Dr Hale-Carpenter arrived. He is the expert from England who is to enquire into the Tsetse fly business for us during the next six months.

On Saturday Ninon and I and Hale-Carpenter motored out to Ottoshoop to lunch with the Gubbins, to have another look at his wonderful library and also to discuss further the question of the establishment of an experimental grass-station. Our idea is to do it on Gubbins' farm of 16,000 acres, Gubbins to supply the land, housing and cattle; I to get a grant from the Colonial Development Committee at home and organise it; and to bring in on a cooperative basis the scientists from Pretoria and Johannesburg Universities, and from the various South African Government bodies interested.

If we can improve the feeding-value of the grasses on the veld by cultivating some and eliminating others, we can treble the value of the land for grazing purposes, carry more cattle to the acre, and grow a better beast. No one is doing this in South Africa and it will be a great achievement if we can bring it off.

Monday 27 October to Sunday 2 November
That little devil Chief Tshekedi of the Bamangwato put in a rude letter some time ago and I told him that I would not see him or do any business for him or his tribe until he withdrew it. He withdrew it on the 16th and so I arranged to see him about business on the 28th. On Monday 27 Captain Nettelton, the R.M. of that district, arrived for a preliminary discussion with me. He, Mrs Nettelton, and Miss Chase lunched with us — Miss Chase is the younger daughter of our Chief Veterinary Officer. She works in the Johannesburg hospital and is about as dull as its humanly possible to be, grins like a Barbary ape and says 'Yes Colonel Rey' and 'No Colonel Rey' when I speak to her until I could scream with rage.

On Tuesday I got down to business with Tshekedi. He had brought six headmen with him and being evidently very sore at my having made him withdraw his letter was offensively obstructive, until at about 4 I could stand it no more. So I kicked them all out, swore myself into a state of calm and said I would have nothing more to say to them, and that they could all go back to Serowe.

My remarks were carried to the young man: and his own headmen got very much annoyed with him — so much so that on Wednesday morning he sent me a full and ample apology, and after a good day's discussion we settled a number of outstanding difficulties that had been going on for several years.[65]

On Sunday 2nd Dr and Mrs Du Toit arrived at 7 am and stayed for the day, leaving at 4. He brought me a copy of his report which he had handed in on the 30th. It is MAGNIFICENT. He and Leeson support all my proposals entirely — say they are perfectly feasible and urgently necessary — that from the geological, practical, and financial points of view there is nothing to prevent their being successful — and they recommend £200,000 instead of £180,000!!! After which I went to bed, and dreamed that one of my new drills was boring a hole in my chest.

1930

Monday 3 to Sunday 9 November
I had one rather interesting interlude: an interview with a native — Sol Plaatje by name — who has translated three of Shakespeare's plays into Sechuana! A useful fellow, and I want to get some of his books for our native schools.[66] One's work is varied!

On Sunday morning Gubbins and I went round to see another educated native — a Dr Molema,[67] who took his doctor's degree at Edinburgh. He is a very enlightened man and we discussed Sechuana literature with much interest.

Monday 10 November
I had the first meeting of my newly-formed 'Board of Advice' on native education today — a great event. It consists of about a dozen people including five missionaries of different breeds and four native chiefs, with some officials and myself as Chairman — a weird body. My Inspector of Education (Dumbrell)[68] worried me again about starting the proceedings with a prayer, and I really had to get angry and tell him to go to the devil. Why, the five missionaries would have cut each others' throats if one had been asked to pray and not the others — and fancy five lots of prayers — or my letting one off myself!

I made them an eloquent oration, and then left them to quarrel among themselves, which they did successfully for two whole days — Incidentally that little beast Tshekedi made some offensive remarks on the first day for which he had to make a public apology on the next day. That young man will I fear find himself in sore trouble soon; my patience is almost exhausted.

One good omen today was that it rained, our much needed and long-overdue rain for want of which the cattle are dying in hundreds, and half Mafeking has to go without baths.

Tuesday 11 November
In the evening after the meeting I had a long and very straight talk with Haile,[69] the London Missionary Society man who runs the big native training college at Tiger Kloof, and told him I would *not* have missionaries interfering with politics or administration. He was very nice about it and thanked me for my frankness. He is an Oxford man and much better than the ordinary L.M.S. ruffian.

Wednesday 12 to Sunday 16 November
On Thursday the big Enquiry opens at Serowe. A number of the Bamangwato have presented a petition[70] against Chief Tshekedi, alleging all sorts of brutalities, and so I have ordered this public Enquiry. There is great excitement about it and I expect I shall have to go up there, as the feeling against the Chief is rising and Captain Nettelton the R.M. talks of 'shooting' and 'rebellion'. Personally I don't believe this; I think he is losing his nerve. And one can't afford to lose one's nerve in this country with three hundred native police to control two hundred thousand natives!

Tuesday 18 November (at Palapye Road)
Lieutenant Lawrenson met me with a car and we covered the thirty five miles to Serowe in one and a half hours, an almost record run for bush tracks.

After a bath and a second breakfast, and short talk with Captain Nettelton, he and I, with interpreter and shorthand writer, escorted by Lawrenson went down to the Kgotla where we met the Chief, his Councillors and about fifteen hundred evil-smelling ruffians at 10.30 am.

I spoke to them for nearly an hour, mostly about mining, explaining what it all meant, telling them the story of the Mining Concession for their country granted by King Khama to the Chartered Company in 1893 and generally trying to make the thick-skulled perishers understand what they were throwing away by opposing mining and starting litigation with the Company.[71]

But it was like talking to a brick-wall and as various speakers got up to answer, I could see that they had grasped nothing, and their only idea was that if mining started they would be handed over by the Government to the Company, and that the Government was their father and mother and would I please protect them against the Company and everyone else.

We adjourned at 1 for lunch, and after an interval for rest, Tshekedi came up at 4 and I had him alone till 6. I talked to him like a father and abused him like a pick-pocket, telling him he was heading straight for rebellion and the disruption of his tribe, and pointing out to him all the silly things he had done and was doing. He took it very well I am bound to say, thanked me, and promised to mend his ways — I wonder!

Then a little air and exercise being indicated, I went for a walk alone, and poked my nose into various parts of the village: the people seemed surprised, — but exceedingly courteous and glad to see me. They couldn't understand where my escort and motor-car had got to! A bath, dinner, and bed.

Sunday 23 to Sunday 30 November (to Johannesburg)
A wonderful week at Jo'burg. The Transvaal Chamber of Mines asked Ninon and I to be their guests for a week to see everything connected with the working of the Mines and the recruiting of labour for them.

On Monday morning I got busy early, as Sir Drummond Chaplin, the Managing Director of the Chartered Company in South Africa, had come up from Cape Town on his way to Rhodesia and had stayed over to see me. We met at 9 am and had a most interesting talk concerning mining operations he wants to do in the Protectorate, the law-suit with Tshekedi of the Bamangwato country, the removal of the Batlokwa Tribe from land belonging to the Company, the development of the Territory generally and the vexed and difficult question of the Company's Preferential Rights in the Crown Lands which has been outstanding for twenty years and which I have now got to settle![72] It will take me months of work.

At 10 o'clock Wellbeloved called for me in a car and we went off to inspect the Witwatersrand Native Recruiting Corporation Compound, a wonderful bit of organisation. They recruit natives from all over South Africa — from Portuguese Territory; from what was German South West; and from the three Protectorates, Bechuanaland, Basutoland and Swaziland.

The Compound is an immense place, with accomodation for thousands; a hospital with three hundred beds; big kitchens for preparing their food; shower baths; swings and roundabouts to amuse them; a staff of six fully qualified doctors for examination purposes, etc. Each doctor does nearly two hundred a day! It's all specklessly clean, and the food good and plentiful: as I have already said the system of records is unique.

I spent the whole morning visiting every corner of it and then we dashed back to the Rand Club where the Gold Producers Committee were giving a lunch to meet me. It was a most interesting party and I enjoyed it thoroughly. They were a wonderful collection of men including all the principal Heads of the various big mining groups. Wolfe Davis[73] came to see me in the evening: he is the Managing

Director of the Imperial Cold Storage Company, an extremely shrewd and able Jew. He came for five minutes and stayed over an hour — we 'clicked' at once and laid the foundation of quite a good business deal for the Protectorate in regard to cattle matters.

Tuesday 25 November (to Pretoria for the day)
After lunch I went off to a meeting with eight professors of Pretoria University and other agricultural experts to discuss the joint establishment of an Experimental Grass Cultivation Station to carry out practical experimental work to improve the grazing value of the grasses on the veld in the Protectorate — a most important matter for us. They were all very nice and keen and interested, and I think we'll get that going early next year.

Friday 28 November
Another most interesting day — we spent the whole of it visiting the 'Modder B' Mine, one of the best and most up to date on the Rand, tho' by no means the largest. The main vein is about 3,500 feet below ground, they employ 2,900 natives below ground, six hundred natives above ground, and about two hundred and fifty whites. Over 250,000 persons are employed in the Rand mines altogether.

It was about an hour's run by car along the Reef, a lovely morning and a grand road. When we got there we were received by the Mine Manager, the Assistant Manager, the Underground Manager, and one or two others — all of them Englishmen (no damned Dutch) and all perfectly charming.

I could write for hours about the interest of this wonderful work — but I'm afraid no one would read it. It is sufficient to say that all these thousands of men, all these millions of pounds worth of machinery and plant, all this work and ingenuity and organisation — *all* gets its reward out of the *half ounce* of gold that one ton of rock contains — it's simply marvellous to contemplate.

After a wash and change we went off to inspect the surface working — which was in its way just as interesting. The arrangements for the reception of the natives when they come in — fingerprints again — another medical examination — shower baths — sleeping cubicles — play ground — and most remarkable — the feeding arrangements. The men are astonishingly well fed — as much as they want to eat — meat in great cauldrons stewing with masses of different kinds of fresh vegetables and beans of various sorts — porridge — bread — mealie-meal — cocoa — kaffir beer — etc.

I tasted the food and found it excellent, so it is hardly surprising that the natives put on fifteen to twenty pounds weight on an average in their first six weeks!

They are weighed every pay-day (once a month) and if one loses over five pounds in weight in the month he is sent to the hospital attached to the mine (three hundred beds!) for examination.

So when people talk damned nonsense about the 'poor wage slaves' in the mines, and their dreadful conditions, and the awful lives they lead you can point to some of these figures and facts, and compare it with the *really* awful life they lead in their native villages — filthy huts full of vermin, no medical attendance, irregular food and not enough of it, ill-treatment by their own chiefs, not even enough water to drink sometimes.

At the mines if a man gets *even a scratch* on him, hand or foot, up he goes to the top (he's bound to) and its painted with iodine and bound up in a little special dressing station run by two natives — we went in there and they treated Mrs. Stubbs' hand as she had got a scratch against some rocks.

Just think of it — regular work, good wages, promotion for the smarter man to be 'boss boy', as much excellent food as he can eat, medical and hospital attendance, clean sleeping cubicles, bathing and lavatory arrangements of the most up to date character — arrangements for his wages to be banked and sent home if he likes — etc. etc. what more could be wished for?[74]

And yet these damned missionaries are doing their best to stop my introducing mining into the B.P. where the people are verminous, half-starved and where most of them, probably ninety per cent, suffer from venereal disease.

I'd like to stick my missionary crowd down a mine on to a stick of dynamite and blow the whole damned lot to the heaven they're always bleating about.

(From which it may perhaps be gathered by the careful reader that I really don't like missionaries very much!)

Monday 1 & Tuesday 2 December (back at Mafeking)
There have been quite a lot of happenings during my absence. The native chiefs have held a secret meeting all together at Serowe greatly to the alarm of the R.M. who sent in all sorts of rumours — as a matter of fact they are alarmed at what they think I may propose to do about limiting their powers — forced labour, flogging especially of women, burning of huts etc. etc. — and they have sent in a petition to be allowed to come and see me — great fun.[75]

Then Athlone is so bucked by Du Toit's report on my water boring proposals that he suggests asking for £250,000 instead of £180,000!

Also they have agreed to my proposal to appoint ex-chief Isang as my Native Adviser[76] — the railway survey arrangements are nearly complete — and my draft scheme for grants for £30,000 for hospital extension and £150,000 for roads and bridges are almost complete.

Wednesday 3 to Monday 8 December
Rather a hectic spell. Old Gobbleman, the troublesome chief whom I kicked out of Moshupa, arrived to see me to beg to be allowed to go back. But he wouldn't do as I told him so the answer was 'nothing doing', and back he was sent to Kanye. He has got a beast of a grandson who has imbibed Communist ideas from some school he has been to at Cape Town, and he is at the bottom of the trouble, I fear. That young man will get into trouble soon: I like him not.[77]

Then Dr Duke of the Witwatersrand University and Mr Franz, Inspector of Schools in the Union of South Africa, arrived to stay with us for a couple of nights to attend an Orthography Conference I have arranged to try and settle on a unified form of spelling Sechuana for all South Africa. We are taking the lead in this.[78]

On Friday that poisonous person Jennings (known as Fat Albert)[79] of the London Missionary Society turned up and wasted half my day trying to justify himself in regard to some matters about which I had read the Riot Act to him — he is a fluent liar.

Wednesday 10 December
The celebrated White Train came in at 6. It is so called because all the saloons are white — it is the Governor-General's private train — bedroom, dining-room, drawing-room, bath rooms etc. etc. Probably the most luxurious train in the world.

At 8.55 the party got into cars to go to the Camp — in the fullest of full uniform. First of all six troopers; then the first car with Athlone, the Princess and myself; then two more troopers; then the second car with Lady May Cambridge, Ninon and the Imperial Secretary; two more troopers; then the third car with the A.D.C. and four more troopers at the end; the O.C. escort and the N.C.O. rode each on one side of our car. Everyone dropped into his place perfectly; all kept their distances like an escort of Life Guards. We turned under the triumphal arch (put up the day before) and drew up at the red carpet in front of the marquee which was of course open all round on account of the heat and double roofed, the passage in between being covered with Union Jacks.

The R.M., Drury, and Mrs Drury received the party, Mrs Drury giving the Princess a native basket of really gorgeous flowers. We all sat at one end of the marquee; opposite us were the bulk of the Europeans, on the right members of Advisory Council; on the left the Native Chiefs of the Southern Protectorate. It was really quite a good show.

Then one of the Europeans read a farewell address and handed it in, one of the Chiefs then read the native address and handed that in. (I had approved both the night before lest anything 'controversial' should creep in).

Athlone then read two addresses in reply, one to Europeans, one to natives. After this everyone was marshalled up and shook hands with Athlone and the Princess and finally there was a certain amount of informal conversation.

At 9.55 the cars and escort formed up again and at 10 off we went 'amid the cheers of the populace' as the papers say, back to the train.

One anecdote of the Princess I must tell — it is so characteristic. Athlone and she were receiving a lot of natives for the first time and in the course of his speech Athlone introduced her as the granddaughter of Queen Victoria, the great white Queen overseas. The Princess turned round and in an aside said 'He always says that, it goes down awfully well you know'!

Friday 12 to Sunday 14 December
Friday and Saturday were terrific days. I had a wild mad rush clearing up everything at the Office prior to our departure for Cape Town on Sunday, and worked like the devil himself 'from early morn to dewy eve'.

But we're going to have a grand holiday at Sea Point — NO WORK — no entertaining, no parties — just sleep and eat and bathe and bask in the sun.

From Tuesday 16 December (at Cape Town)
Some quite exciting things have been happening in the B.P. during our absence — mostly of a tragic nature.

One of the white settlers at Lobatsi was murdered by natives on Christmas Eve. He was a very much liked and respected man, a bachelor seventy years old, Kingdon by name. He was reading his Christmas mail when it happened.

Then the old Chieftainess of the Batawana at Kachikau died, and there'll be Hail Columbia about her successor — another little job for me on return.

And finally, Tebogo, the mother of the nine year old Chief of the Bamangwato (where the devil Tshekedi is Regent) has also died — which means that the boy's education becomes a more pressing problem, and I've got to keep him out of the clutches of the missionaries.

During the last few days of our stay I had to do a little work and browsed through our Estimates for the budget for the coming year. Very gloomy — we are faced with a possible drop of £30,000 in income tax as the Railway has been relaying the line and wants to charge it to income — so that there will be no income and so no income tax from them. Of course I shall fight it, but it's a beastly nuisance.

Then I saw Jennings of the London Missionary Society and Buchanan, the lawyer who acts for Tshekedi, about the mining concession in the Bamangwato Reserve. They showed me the letter they proposed to send into the Chartered Company terminating the concession. But this means long and expensive legal proceedings which they are desperately anxious to avoid, and so they want me to come in and try and arrange a compromise.

It's a ticklish business, but I want mining, so I'll try.

Buchanan is a pleasant fellow, able up to a point, but obsessed by a missionary complex — if only he would drink or smoke or swear *a little* he would be so much more interesting. A worthy soul. I tried hard to convince him of the error of his ways as regards the Mining Concession, and what a disservice he was really doing the natives, and I think I made some headway.

1931

On *Monday* night *5th January* we dined with Lady Cromer and her son Evelyn Baring.[1] He is a splendid specimen of a young man, about 6ft 3 and broad. He's in the Indian Civil Service and is over here on behalf of the Indian Government trying to soften down the anti-Indian legislation which the South African Government are proposing to pass. He was extremely interesting about the position in India, very moderate in his views and obviously liking the Indian peasant. He is going back to a Frontier Station where his work will be mostly political, and he is very keen on it. I should think he ought to do well.

Friday 9 to Tuesday 13 January (back at Mafeking)
Pongo is an intense joy, and sticks to me like a shadow — trots along by my pony to the office and back, curls up in my office all the morning and occupies the best chair in my study when I work at home. We are known as the 'fighting dog and man' and I'm bound to say he'll go for anything that walks or crawls, other dogs, bulls, goats, spiders, scorpions, rats, snakes or anything else. He's a great comfort and is as quick as lightning after mice.

Altogether things aren't too bad, though official troubles never cease. The latest are a threatened invasion of locusts and rumoured spread of Tsetse fly.

So we are busy preparing plans for a locust campaign, enrolling volunteers, instructing natives, laying in a store of drums of poison stuff and pumps to spray fire and poison on the locusts if and when they arrive — a warm welcome.

Tsetse is more difficult — but we are experimenting with a new fly trap invented by one Harris which is supposed to be wonderful — it catches them by the millions apparently. However I believe the Tsetse scare to be unfounded — but as I have to send six hundred miles to verify the reports, I can't decide in five minutes!

Africa is a hard country to live in. In spite of its beauty and its wonderful climate one has to fight ceaselessly to live — drought, floods, hail, locusts, Tsetse, cattle disease, fever, etc. But after all, it's all this battling that makes life worth living — it would indeed be dull to have to sit down in Whitehall and deal with papers after this!

Monday 26 January
A telegram just in reporting a fracas near Francistown (three hundred miles up north) between Bamangwato and Masarwa — apparently a few dead and

wounded. So I'm off by the night mail, leaving here 8.30 pm and arriving at Francistown midday tomorrow — I hope to be in time for the fun.[2]

The Drurys left this morning by car for Rhodesia — they stopped at the Camp on their way and everyone turned out and gave them a rousing send-off. I'm sorry they're leaving as he is a good fellow, and Mrs Drury is the ablest woman in the Protectorate. The pity is that she always ran him, and people didn't like it — really they were jealous of her.

Tuesday 27 January
The fracas is not as serious as was thought at first. Apparently a party of five Bamangwato raided another cattlepost belonging to other Bamangwato and seized and took away three Masarwa (two men and one woman). The Masarwa are a subject race whom the Bamangwato regard as slaves — which of course we won't tolerate.

They beat one Mosarwa to death, and almost killed the other two — they were all left lying in the bush until the woman crawled to the nearest native huts and gave the alarm. Then our police got busy, motor-cars were rushed out, and the Medical Officer brought in the Masarwa. Police scoured the country, got on the spoor of the raiding party and captured several. The Medical Officer told me he had *counted* over three hundred wounds on the body of the man who died! I inspected the other two: the man had over two hundred wounds and the woman over seventy! I have never seen such a foul sight in my life — and by heavens if it can be brought home to these devils they shall hang.

I caught the 10.30 night mail home. Just as the train was starting a trooper rode up and reported that they had captured all the Bamangwato concerned in the murder and that they had confessed. So now I'll have two murder cases to try — a nasty business.

Wednesday 28 January
After a good night I spent the morning on the train talking to Jennings the London Missionary Society man. A poisonous toad who has been responsible for most of the trouble we have had with Tshekedi and the Bamangwato tribe about mining and other matters.

I spoke to him for the good of his soul and I think we've fixed the basis of an agreement — but whether he'll stick to it or not is another matter.

Thursday 29 to Saturday 31 January
Thursday and Friday were a really terrific drive completing the budget proposals for 1931-32 — a ghastly business as the Railway Company are trying to rob us of £30,000 in income tax and I can't see easily how on earth I'm going to make it up. But it's got to be done.

On Saturday morning we made up our minds to dash off to inspect Lehututu, an outpost in the desert, four hundred miles away and very little known. No Resident Commissioner has ever been there! and I have always meant to go as soon as possible.

Wednesday 4 to Saturday 7 February
A very strenuous week in the Office preparatory to our departure for Lehututu. I have made up my mind that we cannot stand this enslavement of the Masarwa by the Bamangwato any more, and I have proposed a cocked hat official enquiry into

the whole question.³ This will raise Hail Columbia and make the Colonial Office wild — as the policy hitherto has been hush-hush. But there is bound to be a row about the Masarwa sooner or later, and then I shall be damned for having allowed it to go on. So I've decided to make the row myself and a drastic dispatch has gone Home — great fun, another hairy battle.⁴

I also had a bad interview with that poisonous little rat Tshekedi, Chief of the Bamangwato. He is a nasty piece of work. He has now deliberately disobeyed an order issued by the Secretary of State for the Colonies⁵, the High Commissioner, and myself! The day is rapidly approaching when he will find himself 'in the consommé' — and that will mean another good old row with the tribe, who are about 60,000 strong.

On Saturday I signed *at last* the budget estimates for the coming year — I'm afraid they are not too good.

Sunday 8 February
Mrs Douthirt arrived today. She is that wonderful old American lady, who goes wandering about Africa, Asia, Australia and America, all alone with a couple of handbags and a cheque book. We met her some five or six years ago in one of those poisonous little boats that potter about the Red Sea when we were trying to get to Aden and had got to Berbera instead. Her latest effort was to drop down in South West Africa, reach Windhoek, and get the taxi driver there to take her on to the Portuguese Congo! The papers were full of it last year. Directly she heard of our trip to Lehututu was on she had to come too.

So now the party will be as follows:
Lorry No. 1. Driven by Sharp our guide, with Chase perched on the seat beside him. Behind, one hundred gallons petrol, fifty gallons water, food, kit and tents and bedding, on to which two native police will cling.
'Topsy'. Ninon and I with Dr Dyke, driven by our faithful Marzipan (Matsepane), who is convinced we shall all die of thirst in the desert.
Lorry No. 2. Driven by an unknown white man with Mrs Douthirt perched on the seat next to him. More water, petrol, spare tyres and food etc. One more native servant will cling on to the top.

Wednesday 11 February
I had a hugely successful meeting with a crowd of L.M.S. missionaries who had had the cheek to write me an offensive letter and go back on arrangements formally agreed with us. So I had the pleasure of telling them just where they got off — and generally wiping the floor with them — it was real joy. Of course they climbed down and said they meant nothing of the sort etc. and they took back their letter and we parted as brothers!

A bad crowd — they ought to be doing 'time'.

Across the Kalahari

Sunday 15 February
The day of our great trek has dawned: it is not great in length though it will cover nearly one thousand miles but it is an adventure as it is across the Great Kalahari desert, and we have to face lack of water, deep sand to plough through, and thick bush to get over, round or through.

1931

We got off finally at about 8.40 and had a very pleasant and easy run out to Kanye (eighty two miles), the last outpost of civilisation we shall see for some time.

The Resident Magistrate, Cuzen, and his wife met us and gave us an excellent lunch — then while they were putting in some more petrol and water, I interviewed the Chief of the Bangwaketse, Bathoen, and we got off at 3.30.

Our difficulties started almost at once. The heat was intense, the sand soft deep and dry, and the lorries boiled furiously.

We were only able to cover thirty eight miles by 7 o'clock (one hundred and twenty miles in all) and then we outspanned and pitched camp. We were dog-tired and turned in immediately after dinner, N. and I sleeping in 'Topsy', Mrs Douthirt in a tent, Chase and Dyke in the open.

Monday 16 February

A bad night. It was suffocatingly hot in 'Topsy' and we couldn't sleep so we shall sleep *à la belle étoile* in future — hoping that it won't rain.

We got off at 7.10, fighting hard all the way in heavy sand through thick bush. We pushed along slowly, the bushes crashing against car and lorries, hitting us in the face as they were swept back — sometimes we crashed into and *over* small trees and bushes higher than the top of the hood of the car. The bumps were awful, and 'Topsy' must be a wonderful car to stand up to it as she did.

Forty three miles for the day. The country had been lovely all day, alternate bush and plain, excellent grazing, lots of 'woolly-finger' grass — woolly-finger contains seven times the amount of nourishment for cattle that ordinary grass does.

So it can be seen what rot it is to call the Kalahari a desert — certainly it is waterless on the surface, but the vegetation is grand, and there is heaps of water underground, and when my scheme of boring is at work, it will be the finest cattle ranching country in Africa.

That is *one* of the reasons why we are doing this trek — to prove the value and feasibility of my water proposals.

Wednesday 18 February

Reveille at 4.30 am, off at 6.15 and then we ran into a little rain-storm which was very pleasant, as it cooled the air, and set the sand a little.

We reached Khakea (9 miles) in an hour after digging ourselves out of sand holes twice. Here there is another of these huge pans, dry of course, but with a number of wells sunk at one corner where as usual the limestone formation holds the water. The first well we tried nearly made us sick, the smell of the water was so awful. We were luckier at the second one however, and got a splendid supply of clean good water at about fifty feet. So all hands were set to work to fill up our drums, refill radiators, and boil some for a cup of tea. We found a friendly donkey and three or four horses standing by looking rather thirsty so we filled up a trough hewn out of a log and gave them all the drink of their lives. They had never had so much in their lives before and swelled visibly!

We inspected the trader's store here — a ghastly filthy hovel with a few dust-covered things in it — some traps, old helmets, bottles of oil, skins, pieces of cotton goods, and a few cheap showy toys for natives. He had a 'creamery' (save the mark!) where he made ghee. It stank of rancid cream and was a solid mass of flies. But I think we could help the natives by sending out trained native demonstrators to show them how to make ghee properly — there is a great demand for it in South Africa, and they import it from India. So why shouldn't we make it here? It all depends on my water scheme going through so as to make the roads possible for transport.

We reached Kokong (forty seven miles) at 4.30 — another big dry pan with wells in the limestone where we filled up. I interviewed the headman of the district meanwhile: curiously enough he is a Morolong[6] and is of course more intelligent than the Bakgalagadi. There is actually a sort of school here run by a L.M.S. native — and the old headman who seemed to have an enormous number of wives and scores of brats encourages it, and also tries to make his people sink wells and grow crops. But he says the land is drying up and the grazing getting worse, and altogether seemed in a pessimistic frame of mind. However he seemed better after a chat and a few presents.

Friday 20 February
We covered about twenty seven miles to Tsane (the police post and headquarters for the Lehututu district) reaching it soon after 11 after crossing a flat dry pan about three miles across, and were greeted by Lieutenant Moseley who was immensely relieved to see us — he had been very worried as he had not expected we should be able to get through! He has three nice little round brick huts and N. and I stowed ourselves in one and unpacked our gear and had a much-needed wash preparatory to a large and excellent 'brunch'.

Afterwards N. had a rest and I interviewed the headmen of the Hottentot tribe who live at Kartlwe about sixteen miles off. Their language is extraordinary — it's a series of clucks and clicks and hisses, and their feature are distinctly Malayan in character — they are also much lighter in colour than the other tribes.

They laid various grievances before me, their main one being lack of food, and I'm bound to say they looked it — they wanted permission to shoot game for food, which I granted them. They also wanted permission to move up into another part of the Kalahari where there is supposed to be more water. I undertook to send an officer up to explore and report when I would consider the matter further.

Note: The place they want to go to is between Nojane and Ukwi about a hundred miles northwest from here, near the Beacon fixing the border between South West Africa and the Protectorate. They say natives have dug pits there lately and found good water in plenty, and grazing.

Also by going there they will get further away from the Bakgalagadi who have been giving them trouble lately — there are very few Bakgalagadi at Ukwi whereas here at the Hottentot village there are fifty hut-tax payers, probably three to four hundred souls.

They say they *must* get more food: formerly they could shoot all the game they wanted — now they can't shoot any.

So I told them they could shoot wildebeest, gemsbok, and springbuck — *for food only* — for six months on trial but that if I found any meat being exported as 'biltong' I would stop the shooting.

Incidentally Moseley told me I should have difficulty in getting in hut-tax if I didn't, as they would be too poor to pay.

I had to read the Riot Act to them about a fracas which had occurred last week between them and Bakgalagadi in which the latter used knobkerries and the Hottentots had fired — wounding one of the others. Dyke doctored him; he will recover.

These Hottentots are extraordinary people: they came here in 1909 under the leadership of one Simon Kooper, fleeing from the Germans over the border in South West Africa with whom they were having a lot of fighting. We made a treaty with them, granting them a piece of land about 5,000 square miles on certain conditions which they have observed faithfully. Their present leader is also called Simon Kooper, a younger brother of the original, who is dead. I saw the old Treaty, a remarkable document, and told them that that was the signature of the King's Government and would always be observed as long as they followed its provisions.[7]

After which being weary I had an hour's sleep, then — a BATH! — and after tea motored off to Hukuntsi about eight miles away to inspect the place.

There is one white storekeeper there, and how he remains sane all alone in this God-forsaken place cut off by hundreds of miles of sand and bush from everything, beats me. As a matter of fact he did seem a little cranky, tho' very polite and of course delighted to see us.

The natives grow and cure tobacco (of a kind!) here and I bought some from him of two kinds — so called 'Boer' tobacco and 'native' tobacco. Both smelt dreadful but are very curiously made up. Here they were also able to grow beans and mealies which help them out for part of the year.

There is wonderful water at Hukuntsi which enables this tobacco, and also crops, to be grown. In one corner of a pan there are quite a lot of wells, in the usual limestone formation — excellent water and lots of it at only twenty feet deep. Just imagine what could be done with this magnificent grazing country by carrying out my scheme for sinking these wells all along the cattle routes at twenty mile intervals!

A few words about this Kalahari. The district administered by Moseley is 50,000 square miles, more than half the size of England! The population is roughly estimated at 7,000 — the amount of hut-tax collected from them last year was £1,200 — and the total force at Moseley's disposal in one European sergeant and ten native troopers! So when these rotten Socialist dogs at Home get up and talk of 'Extravagance of Colonial Administration', and 'brutal military force overawing the natives' etc. my blood boils, and I should like to dump some of them down in the middle of Kalahari to live there — if they could.

It's wonderful grazing country — as good as any in South Africa: and if only I can get my water scheme going it will be the world's best ranching proposition.

Saturday 21 February
We had arrived at Tsane yesterday morning, and in the afternoon had pushed off to Hukuntsi. Today we went to Lehututu, our 'journey's end'. But first of all I had a meeting with the headmen and their followers from all these places (except the Hottentots from Kartlwe whom I had seen yesterday). They were a miserable looking crowd and practically repeated everything that Simon Kooper and his crowd had said yesterday. They were as follows:-

Retoro (sound but weak), Headman of Barolong — Lehututu
Montsine (ditto), Headman of Bakgalagadi — Lehututu
Tekone (good), Headman (minor) of Bakgalagadi — Lehututu
Mochage (foxy), Headman of Bakgalagadi — Tsane
Moapare (-?-) son of Mosiwa, Headman of Hukuntsi.

Mosiwa by the way is under arrest awaiting trial at Kanye for brutal torture of a man arising out of a charge of witchcraft — which I will explain later.

The first four spoke, also a Mokwena who had recently come into these parts — and I gave the same answers as yesterday, with a few embellishments added. They all want to move away, some as far north as Ghanzi — they were however delighted with the permission to shoot game for food.

As regards our friend Moapare. The original chief of the Bakgalagadi in these parts was called Moapare — he is dead. His son Mosiwa was away for over twenty years, and returned in June last bringing *his* son Moapare with him. Mosiwa has been an infernal nuisance ever since he returned, and was mixed up in this torture business which arose as follows. Three wretched men were accused of witchcraft because some old man had died mysteriously, so the council of headmen condemned them to be tied up in nets until they confessed. This is a ghastly business: the man's head is shoved down between his knees, he is rolled up in a ball and tied up in a net — the net is squeezed tighter and tighter — sometimes on the ground, sometimes hung from a tree — the victim generally gets ruptured, loses consciousness, and in half an hour to an hour dies if not released. Moseley caught them red-handed, arrested the whole council of headmen (with two policemen!) and sent them off to Kanye for trial. I'll see they get a jolly good sentence. There is a terrible lot of this sort of thing existing here, and the only way to stamp it out is by a rigorous sentence when it can be proved.

After seeing my deputation we got into cars ('Topsy' and Moseley's) and drove over to Lehututu — across a wonderful pan of level hard dry mud two miles wide on which we travelled at nearly sixty miles an hour!

Sunday 22 February
I had hoped to have a day's rest here but it could not be managed as Moseley has to be at Kanye this week to prosecute in the witchcraft trial, and he sails for England on leave next week. We have decided to go back by another route, via Tsabong, to the south instead of the east in order to see more of the Kalahari and of the people. But it's a bit of a risk owing to shortage of water on the route. So we must have Moseley with us.

We did not get off until 7.50 waiting about for Moseley, and while doing so had a parade of the police camels which were in splendid condition.[8] There were two baby ones a few months old and they were most attractive.

The road was heavy sand and not at all the easy going that Moseley had told us. It got worse and worse as we went on, the lorries stuck and had to be dug out, the cars all boiled furiously and by the time we had done thirty miles they had drunk twelve gallons of water between them in the radiators! A bad look-out if we do not find water soon.

It took us nearly four hours to struggle over thirty miles. Then the going was not quite so bad and in a little over two hours we covered the twenty miles to the pan where we were dismayed to find no water! This began to look serious and Dyke and Chase and I took private counsel. Moseley had misled us rather badly as to the road, etc. (his information was evidently out of date) and if his further statement as to the certainly of finding water at mile 76 (twenty six miles further on) was wrong we should indeed be in sore straits. Was it therefore better to risk it, push on twenty six miles and trust of finding water — or push back the fifty miles we had already come from Tsane (if we could) and return home by the route we had come in by.

We decided to take the risk of pushing on (I *loathe* turning back) and so on we went. But the road was so ghastly that we could not cover more than another twelve miles in just under two hours, and by 6 o'clock we halted, very weary, by a beautiful grass pan, a couple of miles in diameter, but of course no water. We had come sixty two miles in ten hours (eight hours trekking) and were fourteen miles from the alleged water.

Monday 23 February
At 8.30 pm we saw the pan in the distance — was there water or not? The sun shone on it and glistened. Was it hard white mud and sand — or was it water? IT WAS WATER and never was I more pleased to see that fluid.

Near the pan was a wretched village (Kgothi) with one or two more decent huts in it, and while the lorries went down to the pan to fill every drum and tin with water we explored the village. The people were Bakgalagadi — very poor and ill fed. They live near the pan during the four months in which it generally has water (February-May), afterwards roaming about in search of odd waterholes or the melons from which they get a little water.

This pan is known as Mabuasehube — is nearly a mile across (quite circular like they all are), and it holds just a little water in the middle. At one corner is quite a steep, straight rise, almost a small cliff, and below this the natives have made a poor sort of dam to try and hold up the rainwater draining from the higher ground. It is badly made, and in the wrong place, but it was in fact holding up a fair supply of muddy water. It was here that the lorries filled up every available receptacle that we carried, for we have another eighty miles stretch of waterless country to cross now.

Tuesday 24 February
Sergeant Fox and his camel patrol met us on arrival at Tsabong. They have got a delightfully situated camp under a big tree. He is a *very* efficient sergeant and had made every kind of preparation for us. The one and only local trader, an ex-German, Brown by name, also met us. He had got masses of water already boiled for us, had killed a sheep and sent this in with fresh milk, new bread and eggs. Really a friend in need, and a friend indeed.

I inspected the police camp, and Brown's store. There are a quantity of wells here (at one corner of the pan as usual) containing excellent water and lots of it. At least twenty good wells with water at thirty-five to forty feet, wall-timbered and *clean*. But as there is no water for sixty miles around (the nearest is at Madaline), the grass and veld is eaten out and trampled down for miles round the pan. The usual story shewing again and again the necessity for putting down a chain of wells and boreholes right across the country according to my big scheme.

There was one curious point I noticed here however: the wells are situated not in the usual limestone formation but in red granite, and there are low red granite hills around the pan.

As soon as we had outspanned and pitched camp I held a meeting of the headmen and representatives of the various tribes — about fifty or sixty of them. They were:-

Matlara Tribe	Headman *Lorekan*	a scoundrel
Hottentot Tribe	Headman *Petrus Koartse*	good
Damara Tribe	Headman *Jan Januarie*	weak
Bakgalagadi Tribe	Spokesman *Tepa*	neutral
Barolong Tribe	Not represented	

They were generally of a very low type, especially the Bakgalagadi, who were almost indistinguishable from Bushmen. Amongst them were not a few refugees from across the border, who would probably be better in gaol. Of them all the Hottentots were undeniably the best.

I made them a speech, and then invited them to hold forth. They spoke very timidly. Poor creatures, they are little above the animals, and I am bound to say I have immense sympathy with them. They had never seen a Resident Commissioner before (none has ever been here) and they were so over-awed that one of them referred to me as his 'Second God'.[9] I could not help ejaculating 'Why second'?

They told the usual story of hunger, but I was in a difficulty here, as there being no police post here I could not authorise the killing of game as there would be no control, and they are so near the border that they would smuggle over 'biltong' and would massacre all the game for that purpose.

So I said that I would send them up an Agricultural Demonstrator (native) to help them to grow crops (beans and mealies) and when I had established a police post I would consider the question of allowing big game hunting. I warned them that I had heard of the smuggling of arms and ammunition, and of poaching all along the border, and said I would take stern measures if it did not cease.

I learned one thing which annoyed me. The L.M.S. have no church or school here, yet they send natives over to collect subscriptions from these people once a year, ten shillings from men and five shillings from women, though they do nothing for them. It's an outrage and it must be stopped.

Wednesday 25 February
Sergeant Fox came up with his patrol mounted on their camels, and we got some good photographs for them. Then after giving a few instructions, and making a few arrangements, we left this very fascinating spot at 7.30, everything being rather wet owing to heavy dew after yesterday's rain. We travelled through very fine veld, lots of woolly finger and other good grass, and then we crossed the frontier, sixteen miles south of Tsabong, into what used to be Cape Colony. It was a curious thing that a few miles over the border the grazing got less good and there was no game at all to be seen other than a few of the lesser bustard or Koran.

The country further on had been divided up into farms and we passed a number of wretched looking 'poor Dutch' places. Hard, treeless veld not like our Protectorate.

Saturday 28 February to Monday 9 March (back at Mafeking)
The world's foulest ten days. Monday lived up to its reputation. Dutton and Gash returned from Cape Town full of bad news about finance and we had another rotten morning. Worse followed in the afternoon. I saw all the Chiefs who had come down en bloc to see me, headed by that nasty piece of work Tshekedi. They were none too civil and so I kicked them all out of my room. They had had the cheek to bring thirty five followers with them and insisted that I see them *all* in my room! So out they went.

The next day (Tuesday) they fired in a joint letter repeating their request and as it wasn't couched in too civil terms I told them to go to the devil again.[10]

Mrs Douthirt went off on her journey north to Elizabethville, the Congo, Rhodesia, Tanganyika and elsewhere, and no sooner had she gone than one of the servants burst in in tears to say that someone had pinched the tip — a golden sovereign — that Mrs Douthirt had given her! She and the cook accused one of the other servants, our very best boy of course, and demanded his instant dismissal.

So they also were all told to go to the devil, but I had to get the police in, and a mutton-head idiot (the typical detective of the detective novel) blundered about, annoyed everyone, and made the most complete ass of himself.

On Wednesday, the Chiefs departed en bloc without seeing me, and missionaries descended on me and bored me to tears for hours; and on Thursday I had to spend the whole day dictating a three-volume novel about our Budget to try and mitigate the damage.

And then, after a couple of hard days on Saturday and Sunday, the worst blow of all fell on Monday 9 — a black letter day — those goddamned swine at the Colonial Office cabled refusing my water boring scheme.

The cursed brainless visionless dunderheads. They throw money about like water on rotten schemes to bribe the damned electors at Home. They fire three million pounds to the Zambesi bridge, a poisonous scheme that can only result in diverting trade from British to Portuguese ports.[11] They waste hundreds of thousands on those damned Jews in Palestine. They fire more hundreds of thousands to rich Colonies like Rhodesia and Kenya and the West Indies; and they haven't the sense to see that the one way of keeping the British Flag flying in South Africa and holding up the Dutch, who are openly hostile, is to build up a rich, prosperous territory here; a territory bigger than France, potentially enormously wealthy but utterly undeveloped; a territory that linked up with Rhodesia on one side and South West Africa on the other would make a grand British 'bloc' right across Southern Africa. And they can't see that if they *don't* do this everyone in it will get discontented and disloyal and demand incorporation in the Union of South Africa, that poisonous Colony that makes anti-British treaties with Huns and Japanese, and doesn't even fly the Union Jack.

I suppose they *want* to smash up the Empire; they are certainly doing their best to, and they want to chuck away our natural allies like the French and make friends with all those who want to smash us. Huns and Bolshies, etc.

Having cursed myself almost into a state of coma I shut my office and went home.

Tuesday 10 March
A lovely day. Ninon has made the garden really beautiful. It was delightful to sit in it all day and recuperate.

Wednesday 11 to Sunday 15 March
Are we beaten? Are we downhearted? Not a bit. We have evolved a fresh plan or scheme. If the Government are such accursed idiots that they won't do my scheme, then we must get it done by private enterprise.

A man called Dr. Nobbs[12] wanted to do it before — he told me all about it in England. So I've telegraphed him at Cape Town to come up here at once, and will give him a fat concession to do it — if he will.

Monday 16 to Wednesday 18 March
Nobbs arrived 7 am and we set to work. It was a tremendous business putting him wise as to the whole story of all the negotiations, going through reports, memoranda, schemes and plans, etc.. Though he is a very able man, being a South African he has a mind that does not work as quickly as I should like.

1931

And in addition I had all the preparations to make for my Parliament, the European Advisory Council, which meets on the 19th; preparations for work; and what is worse, entertainment.

However we got through all right, and worked out an entirely new plan of operations. Nobbs met all my Parliament at their hotel one night and got them to support the new scheme unanimously and whole heartedly, and I promised to get a resolution passed by Council. So now we're off on another tack, though it's not as good as my original scheme and will take a lot of working out yet. It means a big, private company, at least £250,000 capital, and in these days money is not too plentiful or too easy to find.

Thursday 26 March to Thursday 2 April
From 26 to 28th I was busy clearing up the work left by the European Advisory Council and dealing with arrears of ordinary work that had accumulated, and then on Sunday 29 we motored off to Jo'burg for the great Show. On Monday morning Ninon and I with Chase and England went down to the Showgrounds for a preliminary inspection of our Exhibit.

Right across the entrance to the Exhibit was a large wooden arch inscribed 'Bountiful Bechuanaland Protectorate'; the woodwork was entirely hidden in bundles of the different pasture grasses with which the Protectorate abounds and which make it such grand ranching country. The rest was closed in with a selection of different karosses made of the very fine furs of the country.

The Exhibit itself was divided into two sections: European and Native. On one side ran the timber and mineral part; home industries; cheese, butter, eggs; the meat exhibit; agricultural produce of all kinds; pasture grasses; grains; fruit; etc.

On the other was the native part: scores of karosses; piles of skins; basket work; bead work; pottery; curios; school children's work; wood work; and native produce of all kinds. At one end were two native women making pots; at the other end a man making a kaross.

Scattered about everywhere were large mounted photographs illustrating the resources of the Territory, scenery, animals, and other features of interest. The benches were covered; the walls were covered to the ceiling; the gallery was nearly a hundred feet long.

Heads and horns were displayed, and several huge Union Jacks, flanked by a record lion skin. IT WAS GOOD!

The interest taken by the public in our show may be judged by the fact that the day after the official opening people passed through at the rate of two thousand an hour, and we had to enforce one way traffic! All the karosses and many other things were sold, and we booked hundreds of pounds of 'repeat' orders.

And my cup of joy was complete when it was announced that we had been given the First Prize. A cheque for £100 and a special prize of an immense Silver Challenge Cup.

Monday 13 April (back at Mafeking)
Being Monday and being 13th something foul had to happen. And it did.

We got the news that Foot and Mouth disease had broken out in Southern Rhodesia and was spreading like wildfire. 20,000 cases and four hundred fresh ones daily! All cattle export stopped — trade in hides, milk, cream, butter at a standstill. It had reached Beit Bridge on the Crocodile River, less than one hundred miles from our border.

I realised instantly that at all costs it must be stopped coming into the B.P. So I determined to draw a cordon right along five hundred miles of frontier, and to clear all our cattle five miles back from the frontier along the five hundred miles! Some job. I held a Council of War in bed, drew up complete plans with my principal officers, ordered all police to the frontier, concentrated all our veterinary officers there, commandeered motor transport, ordered four native Chiefs to mobilize six native regiments under European supervision, enrolled some well-known European cattle owners and cattle thieves as special constables, despatched over twenty telegrams, arranged for co-operation with Transvaal and Rhodesian Governments, and then went to sleep for two hours. Some morning for a convalescent. But it did me a lot of good.

Matters are complicated by the facts that it is raining heavily and the rivers are impassable, being in flood. I have neither bridges nor railways and the tracks through the bush are under water or washed away. These things don't help much. Also some damned fool has burnt my best motor lorry complete with driver! What fun.

Sunday 19 April
I packed for my journey to Cape Town to interview Sir Herbert Stanley;[13] then Chase returned from Pretoria where he has made excellent arrangements with the Transvaal Government who are delighted with all we have done.

Monday 20 to Saturday 25 April (to Cape Town)
A long hard day's work in the train — three dispatch boxes full of papers. In bed by 8 o'clock and sleep till 5.30 am Tuesday morning.

We got in at 6.30 sharp. The High Commissioner's car was waiting for me and we were whirled off to Rondebosch about eight miles out where they have temporarily taken a furnished house for him.

A bath and a shave, and then I met the Stanleys.

I will summarize now the impression I formed during my four days stay and work with them. At last I see daylight, the dawn of great things.

He is a brilliant man, an exceptional brain, very quick, very thorough, quite fearless, an indefatigable worker, a pukka gentleman, and perfectly delightful to work with. We clicked at once, see eye to eye generally, and got through an enormous mass of business working together from 10 to 7 daily with a break for lunch. Curiously enough we have very much the same tastes — both love books, both hate golf, both hate bridge, both smoke a lot, and both frightfully keen on our job.

He is nothing to look at — rather fat, and red faced, wears glasses, and doesn't bother much about clothes. He was at Eton and Oxford, was a friend of Ninon's uncle, Sir James Harrison, and we have a number of acquaintances in common.

Lady Stanley is years younger than he is: very pretty, very modern, and quite charming. They have three jolly kids, and their oldest boy is on his way out from England.

So that's that, and now I feel I'm going to be helped and not hindered, and with our two brains together we'll move mountains!

Sunday 26 to Thursday 28 April (back to Mafeking)
Quite a good day on the train working hard, and on Monday arrived at Mafeking at 7 am, starting a hard day's work at 9.30.

On Tuesday I was snowed under with trouble about our Foot and Mouth disease arrangements. The farmers and natives are furious, but we can't help it; we *must* keep the disease out of the Territory, and the infernal Union Government won't let our cattle in until we have got water-tight arrangements for keeping Rhodesian cattle and products out.

They have 30,000 cases in Rhodesia, but fortunately it's a very mild form and only one per cent are dying. But it spreads like wildfire. The symptoms are a hanging head, saliva dropping out of the mouth, a temperature, and little pustules that form on tongue and in hoofs, no appetite. It lasts about a week or so, and the period of incubation is a week. No cure or preventive has ever been found.

I have to use all my motor lorries to feed my long lines of police and native auxiliary patrols; and to make matters worse one of my few lorries is burnt! They were filling up with petrol in the dark, had no torch or lantern, and so put a candle on the running board. It fell over and the petrol caught fire, and was in a blaze in a moment. It was loaded with ammunition and petrol! Lt. Hope, the white driver, the native corporal and four troopers worked like Trojans. The driver crawled under the blazing lorry and cut off the petrol; Hope and the corporal climbed *on* to the lorry and hurled the boxes of ammunition and the petrol tins off (it might have blown up at any moment). The corporal was overcome by fumes and fell into the flames and was pulled out by Hope just in time. They got all the stuff off and saved the chassis and engine by heaping sand on it, but it will cost us £120 to repair. A plucky effort.

Wednesday 29 April
The people who murdered Mr Kingdon at Lobatsi, and the others who murdered the Masarwa at Francistown are being tried today at Lobatsi. There is great excitement locally.

Captain Neale, the R.M. from Molepolole, is down to work out the plans for removing and deposing Sebele, the Chief of the Bakwena (the people of the Crocodile).

It's not going to be an easy matter, as we've got to avoid any fighting, though how we're to do this and at the same time depose, arrest, and remove him, I don't quite see. He has a largeish following of ruffians, and I shall have about a dozen police! The Tribe numbers several thousands, and probably from one to two thousand will be present. I shall have Captain Stigand (Assistant R.C.), Captain Neale, the R.M., a white police officer and a white sergeant, and twelve native troopers. What fun!

If all goes well, nobody will say anything: if anything goes wrong and we have to shoot, the Colonial Office will of course curse *me*. But it's all in the day's work.

Thursday 30 April
My worthy Court has condemned the murderers of Kingdon to death, but has found the Bamangwato who killed the Masarwa guilty only of 'culpable homicide' — so I can't give them more than fifteen years and a flogging. I am much annoyed as they ought *all* to be hanged. People will say that we hanged the first lot because they killed a white man and let off the others because they killed a native.

And of course the papers are full of lurid articles — Slavery in the Bechuanaland Protectorate, Man Skinned Alive, etc. The poor devil had three hundred counted wounds. The Bamangwato are devils.

However there was a technical flaw in the evidence and so the Court couldn't convict of murder, though I'm afraid I should have done so, evidence or no evidence!

The man was asked had he any dogs? He said 'Yes'. So they said 'Would you beat your dogs like that?' 'Oh, no', was the answer: 'I would always beat Masarwa harder than any animal'.

I am having a man out from England to conduct an independent enquiry into the conditions under which the Masarwa live and work, and I hope the result will enable me to give the Bamangwato hell.[14]

Friday 1 May
Russell England, our Dairy Expert and Agricultural Officer, came to stay for a couple of days. We planned out a series of Native Agricultural Shows, to culminate in a 'Royal' Show at Mochudi. England was rather amusing about the Johannesburg people: they were rather impressed by my work, speeches, etc. at Jo'burg, and as they can't understand anybody working for anything except money they asked England what mining interests I really represented! They felt sure that I really represented one of the big groups and had merely come here to spy out the land preparatory to starting mining!

I quite forgot to mention that on Thursday last (30 April) I had a long interview with Jennings, the London Missionary Society man, about settling the law suit between the Chartered Company and Tshekedi over their mining concession. Jennings has great influence with Tshekedi and so we evolved a scheme whereby Tshekedi will withdraw his opposition if we give him a certain piece of land. I believe it will work and it will be a great thing if it does because it will help mining to start everywhere.[15]

We have got trouble on in several places now owing to this infernal revival of certain native ceremonies of a secret kind known as Bogwera[16] and Bojale.[17] They are connected with male and female circumcision and cause much excitement. They last for several months. 'Schools' are formed out in the bush away from everyone and all sorts of secret initiation rites (which no white men have ever seen) go on. The trouble now is that some of the natives don't like this, so others are taking them by force, not only boys and girls, but grown men and even married men. Some of them are resisting, and there has been some shooting — if we *don't* stop it there may be fighting among themselves; and if we *do* stop it they may fight us, as it is an ancient custom, centuries old, and the natives hate interference with them. We don't interfere if they don't harm other people, but if they do, then we stop it.

Monday 4 May
We've had a plague of locusts in the North and had to mobilise hundreds of natives to deal with it under European supervision, and arm them with pumps to spray poison on the brutes. In this way we've destroyed over five hundred swarms of locusts, and what a swarm means may be gauged by the fact that *one* of them flying over Ghanzi covered a space three miles long by two miles broad. It threw a deep shadow over the country as it passed overhead. Fortunately, it flew on over Ghanzi into South West Africa as there was a high wind blowing.

Another swarm dropped near Ghanzi and our people rushed out in cars and lorries and ox waggons and on horses to deal with it. But when they got there they saw an amazing sight. The locusts were being attacked by a swarm of locust-birds (pretty white, long-beaked birds like small storks). As the locusts tried to get up

1931

the birds beat them back to the ground, and never desisted until they had destroyed the whole swarm. It took several days!

Of course 'locust birds' are 'royal game'; no-one is allowed to shoot them under heavy penalty.

Tuesday 5 to Friday 8 May
A really terrific four days, starting with having a tooth pulled out. Then a dozen difficulties cropped up about our Foot and Mouth disease arrangements, and I have had to fight the Union Government like a cat to get their restrictions taken off which are killing our trade. I have worked out a lot of new plans for this, and it means pages of telegrams and arguments.

Then the Colonial Office got 'cold feet' about my removal of the recalcitrant Chief Sebele. They agree to his going but are afraid of my plan of whisking him off by aeroplane. Newspaper articles: 'Abduction of a Bechuanaland Chief by air across the desert', etc. What if there is an accident? People will say we murdered him, and all that sort of rubbish.

Really the funk that the Home Government gets into on the least excuse is pathetic. It makes me sick.

So I've got to get out a new scheme which will cost twice as much, and not be nearly so quick or so safe, and probably cause a row.

Saturday 9 May
A long cable from the Union Government who appear to be inclined to accept my proposals to remove the embargo on our cattle. Another from Stanley who is apparently panting to see me, and wants me to bring down that little devil Tshekedi to pull off the deal about mining which I mentioned a day or two ago.

So I drafted two huge telegrams, had conferences lasting till 7 pm and arranged to go off to Cape Town tomorrow.

Wednesday 13 May (at Cape Town)
Another hectic day. Thank goodness the Union Government agreed with my proposals and I am taking back the agreement in my pocket, signed, sealed and delivered. And now our cattle can be exported again and we'll get trade going once more. It's a huge triumph, especially as everyone said we shouldn't be able to get it through. The mining proposition looks hopeful too.

Stanley and I worked all through the day: they brought in some sandwiches at 1 o'clock and we wolfed them as we worked. We finished on the stroke of 3.45. They hurled me into a car, and I caught the 4 o'clock train back with five minutes to spare. The Imperial Cold Storage man (they buy 20,000 head of cattle a year from us) was at the station nearly delirious with joy. He has got six train loads of our cattle ready and waiting.

Chase came back with me, as we have a lot to do together. We have to work out plans for a new cordon of police and natives right across the Protectorate, so as to make a hundred mile buffer between us and Rhodesia — and cattle in that hundred miles can't go out yet. That will be the next step. We sank back in our seats as the train went out, and grinned at each other. We were both deadly weary but exceedingly triumphant.

1931

Thursday 14 to Friday 15 May
Chase and I worked all day on the train on Thursday, and we rolled into Mafeking at 7 am on Friday. Several people met us including a cattle man. 'Have you got the embargo lifted?' he asked, and when we said 'Yes' I thought he was going to burst into tears! He threw up his arms and cheered, and said he had never thought it could be done yet.

Monday 18 May
At 9 am I had a meeting with all the Resident Magistrates of the districts that are not too remote and we did an hour's useful work. Then at 10 am I met the Chiefs and their councillors to discuss their grievances about the proposed new Hut Tax Law I am issuing and to listen to what they had to say about the other new Law (which is not yet drafted but on which I have a lot of work) to define the Powers of the Chiefs and the Jurisdiction of the Native Courts.[18]

After that I had a long talk with Tshekedi on various matters affecting the Bamangwato Tribe. Butter would not melt in his mouth. He was extraordinarily polite and civil, and agreed with everything I said. I only hope that this does not mean trouble later!

Tuesday 19 May
Meeting of the Native Advisory Council, my native Parliament. We had representatives from all over the Territory, including (for the first time) some Batawana from Ngamiland where Ninon and I went last year.

We had a most interesting meeting. Dr Dyke gave them a most interesting lecture on health, hygiene and food, and told them they were the poorest physical specimens in South Africa! They took it very well, and the more intelligent agreed. It is of course due to the fact of bad and inadequate feeding. As they can't get enough water, they can't get enough vegetables or milk. That is one of the main reasons for my water scheme, for which, by the way, I am still fighting hard.

We discussed a variety of other subjects — schools, dams, wells, cattle, the constitution and functions of the Council, etc., and eventually I managed to close the discussion at 5.30. They had had a good innings since 10 am.

Wednesday 20 to Thursday 21 May
Both days, all day long, I had interviews with individual Chiefs about matters concerning their own territories, one thing after another.

But there is not a single Reserve in this Territory in which there is not trouble of some kind, more or less serious. I suppose it is typical of all Africa just now. Let us hope it won't get serious.

The *Batawana* have got trouble with the Damaras with whom they are always fighting. They have trouble with the Tsetse fly, and have just got over trouble with locusts.

The *Bakwena* have a villainous Chief, Sebele — a drunken, diseased brute, with whom they are always fighting, and whom I have got to remove. He has started the Bogwera ceremonies, people are being forcibly abducted, and they have had some shooting cases.

The *Bamangwato* are always a source of trouble; I have got to have this enquiry into the condition of the Masarwa whom they treat as slaves and ill-treat brutally, and that will mean a jolly old row.

The *Bangwaketse* are starting the Bogwera in defiance of their Chief's orders. He

(Bathoen) burned down their Bogwera 'school' so they started it again outside the Reserve on a farm hired from a Dutchman, abducted some people forcibly and two men got shot. I am issuing an edict about it — more trouble.

The *Bakgatla* are dividing up against each other, some in favour of the present young Chief (Molefi), some in favour of the ex-Chief (Isang) who was Regent during the minority of his nephew, the present Chief.

The *Batlokwa* are grousing because their Reserve is not big enough and want me to get them a few thousand more square miles, and none of their neighbours will give them an inch.

And so on. These of course are only *some* of their troubles. They have lots more!

Saturday 23 to Monday 25 May
I hanged my two murderers at Gaberones today. I had to sign all sorts of black-edged, black-sealed documents. Our gallows was got out of cold storage here and sent up to Gaberones. A hangman was imported from the Union (we had three applications for the job — funny tastes people have). Captain Neale and a doctor were in charge, but I did *not* go up there. That sort of thing does not amuse me, though I was very glad the brutes were hanged.

Tuesday 26 to Thursday 28 May
Mr and Mrs England and Mr MacFarlane lunched. England is a most capable man, my Chief Dairy Expert, who did so much to organise the Jo'burg Show. MacFarlane is a big rancher and cheese producer, member of the European Advisory Council, a rather pompous ass, but a useful man. I've recommended him for the O.B.E. in the King's Birthday Honours List, and they are going to give it to him.

I tried two cases today, which bores me to tears. Listening to lawyers splitting hairs makes me tired. I've no use for lawyers; I like people who *do* things, not people who let off hot air.

On Thursday I breakfasted in bed and shook off my threatened cold by working at home all day. To my great joy I got a telegram from the Colonial Office agreeing to my kicking out Chief Sebele of the Bakwena. The Colonial Office were in an awful funk and were afraid of starting a 'tribal war'. They hope I shall be able to avoid fighting, etc. etc. Poor fish. They do suffer from cold feet.

So now I've completed all my plans, issued my orders, arranged for my 'army' to be ready, and shall strike on Tuesday next.

Friday 29 May
I am arranging to give General Kemp, the South African Government Minister of Agriculture, a week's shooting (lion) here in order to 'bribe' him to relax some of his iniquitous restrictions on the importation of our cattle on account of the Foot and Mouth disease in Rhodesia. I loathe Kemp, who fought against us as a rebel, but one must do these things to push on our interests.

In connection with this tour I ran up against a good example of the hatred between English and Dutch. I told Captain Gash, the head of my police, that I wanted him to go with the party. He got rather pink in the face and said nothing. Later on he came back, and asked me if I really meant it, and when I asked why he said, 'If I go out shooting with General Kemp the only thing I shall shoot will be General Kemp'. Gash is a very mild man usually, so I asked him why, and he then told me that Kemp had fought against his (Gash's) cousin in the rebellion, captured him, and had him flogged. So Gash's Irish blood is up, and his one desire in life is to shoot Kemp.

What a dreadful state Home affairs appear to be in. Reading the papers makes me quite ill. The criminals who are in power[19] now seem to be absolutely bent on destroying the Empire and the country, and they seem to be succeeding pretty well, too. I can't imagine why that 'goof' Prime Minister Baldwin doesn't put up a better fight. He's got the backbone of a filleted caterpillar and the pluck of an emasculated rabbit.

Saturday 30 May
I was full up with plans and arrangements for the deposition of my friend, Sebele, and for our tour. I had to discuss with Roos, the South African Government magistrate of Mafeking, various arrangements for dealing with Sebele if he tried to bolt from here. So he's to be 'shadowed' by police and detectives, and generally shepherded. I've warned the three local garages that they must not let him have a car, and the police all along the line have also to be warned. But the warnings and instructions can't go out until after I've seen him on Tuesday. If he got an inkling beforehand of what was coming to him he might bolt into one of the Reserves, and try to raise one of the other Chiefs — and then 'battle, murder and sudden death'.

Sunday 31 May to Wednesday 3 June
On Sunday afternoon Captain Neale, the Resident Magistrate of the Bakwena country, arrived from Molepolole, Sebele's abode, and came to stay with us. Jolly old Sebele, his two senior uncles, and the four councillors we had appointed to rule for him last year also arrived, and were accommodated in tents on the Imperial Reserve. They are frightfully keen to know why they have been sent for, and haven't an inkling. So our secret has been well kept. Rather a triumph.

On Monday we perfected our arrangements and completed our plans, and on Tuesday the balloon went up.

At 10.30 Sebele, complete with uncles and councillors, was marshalled into my room, at one end of which I sat in state, with the Assistant Resident Commissioner, Government Secretary, Staff Officer, A.D.C. (L. Hope), and the Clerk of the R.C.'s Court, grouped gracefully around.

And then off we went. I recited his crimes and misconduct, the lamentable conditions of his Tribe, the warnings he had been given, the revolts in his Tribe, etc., during the fourteen years since he had been Chief. When I had drawn a picture that almost caused me myself to melt into tears, I wound up.

'The patience of the Government is very great, but it is now exhausted. Your rule has come to an end. You are no longer Chief. You are relieved of your functions, and the decision of the Government is that you be banished to Ghanzi, and if you leave that place you will be arrested and put in prison'.

Then the Clerk of the Court read the full sentence and decision, handed a copy to Sebele, and I sat back and waited for the band to start.

But they were all so stunned and amazed that they could find nothing to say. For eight years the Government has been dithering and blethering and warning and weakening, and that the new R.C. should really have decided on this momentous step fairly dumb-founded them.

At last Sebele got up and having cheerfully remarked that he was dead, and that I had 'killed' him, and that he would never reach Ghanzi alive, asked when he had to go and how.

I told him he would go as soon as his personal effects and family arrived here from Molepolole; that his things would be packed and sent down, and any members of his family (he has unlimited wives and cucumbers[20]!) and servants *who wished to go* might accompany him. He would be sent by rail to Gobabis (in South West Africa) via De Aar and Windhoek, and by motor lorry from Gobabis to Ghanzi.

I then sent him back to camp and addressed the others, told them that the two uncles were appointed Regents by me until a new Chief was elected, and that the four councillors would carry on and help them.

They all spoke, said that they knew this would happen one day, and had continually warned the Chief not to play the fool (liars!), and that they would faithfully carry out my orders. I told them they must go back to Molepolole tomorrow at 7 am, have Sebele's things packed, count his cattle, and maintain order until I came up and met the Tribe.

They were in a fearful funk and said that 'the streets would be full of dead bodies'. I told them not to be fools, said the Resident Magistrate was going back that night and would be there before them and would help them. They were to summon the Tribe to a big Kgotla to be held in a week's time at which I should be present, and would deal with any trouble myself, but that if difficulties arose before then I would come at once. I should anyhow be on my way via Lobatsi and Kanye where I had engagements.

Thursday 5 June (at Lobatsi)
We went to inspect the Creamery run by the Lobatsi Cold Storage Co. They turned out 88,000 pounds of butter last month, and sent 15,000 pounds to the Congo — pretty good. There was a remarkable young woman there who was wrapping the butter in paper — she did 1,200 lbs in an hour — good going, and didn't know she was being timed.

Everything else is done by machinery, and we have the most modern machinery in the world — it is most fascinating to watch the different process. We are working up at last. And the farmers who sent their cream to creameries outside the Territory before the embargo, and *had* to send it to Lobatsi when the embargo came on, are so bucked with their treatment at Lobatsi that they are going to stay on there.

Friday 6 June (Lobatsi to Mafeking)
A 'school' morning — school inspection is a new role for me and I'm getting quite good at spotting the weak points, making drivelling speeches to the children, and asking for a holiday for them in honour of our visit! First of all we visited the Lobatsi school for Europeans — very poor, a wretched two-room building, dilapidated, a poor type of child (largely Dutch), but the two teachers seemed keen and good. We ordered a large box of sweets from the local store to be sent and distributed amongst them. Then on to the European school at Hildavale about ten miles out. This was better and larger, and the two teachers quite good. The children were all drawn up in two long lines and sang 'God Save the King' very nicely as we arrived. They were a better type, but the building was awful. I should imagine it would fall down on them one day. We repeated the dose as to sweets.

From Pitsani we went on about another ten miles to the Barolong Farms Native School — which was the best of the lot. It is called 'Good Hope' and is run by Chief Lotlhamoreng[21] of the Barolong Tribe — his wife is one of the teachers there.

There were fifty two children on the roll, and forty seven were present. It was an excellent large airy building, tho' it needs a ceiling under the roof. Their craft work was excellent — basketwork, woodwork, pottery, needlework, etc. I encourage all that sort of thing and agricultural teaching among the natives, as I do not believe in the rot we have taught in India and elsewhere. Bookwork only — what on earth is the use of that to natives?

From here we went on to inspect the Barolong Bull Camp — another effort of mine to improve the breed of their cattle.

After this, being somewhat weary, we lunched on the veld. Captain and Mrs Reilly, Ninon and I. Mrs Reilly had brought an excellent meal, and just as we were finishing Dumbrell, our Inspector of Education, rolled up.

I told him that I thought a lot of his work was rotten, and he had better work more and talk less, do more inspection and less writing of circulars.

Sunday 7 June (Mafeking to Kanye)
About 11.30 we got off in 'Topsy' on our way to Kanye — a lovely drive through wooded veld, and at about 12.30 stopped in a jolly place to have our picnic lunch (just Ninon and I), after which we composed ourselves to rest. Ninon had just dropped asleep when we heard a car coming along furiously — it was Reilly (and Madame) who had received an urgent dispatch from Captain Neale, Resident Magistrate of Molepolole, for me, and thought I ought to have it at once as of course he knew all about our efforts at kicking out Chief Sebele. The dispatch was very alarming. Neale reported that the Regents I had appointed to carry on the Chieftainship (until I got there and put in a new Chief) had got cold feet and lost all control, that the people were fed up with them and wouldn't obey them; that they refused to allow the Regents to collect and send off Sebele's things; that the police sent up to help them had withdrawn in face of a threatening crowd; and that generally there was Hail Columbia.

I will *not* alter my plans and hurry to Molepolole; it would look as if I were 'rattled' and make the natives imagine all sorts of things. So unless things really get too bad we are going through with our programme at Kanye 'according to plan' and shall arrive at Molepolole on Wednesday.

Before dinner I went round to see Lewis, a viper, the local representative of the London Missionary Society, and squared him about the 'Pathfinders' so as to make it easier for Ninon to organise these among the natives. The L.M.S. have a poisonous movement called the 'Life Brigade' which might have been a nuisance — so I squashed that as far as Kanye is concerned and also knocked out of Lewis' head any idea of his Mission running the Pathfinders and Wayfarers — it must be undenominational, no Bible-thumping and psalm-singing.[22]

Tuesday 9 June
I sent off messenger by motor bicycle and car to Stigand (via Lobatsi) and to Neale at Molepolole and then went on with my business. I had an interesting interview with ten Bakgalagadi prisoners who were doing six months for torture (I have already mentioned the witchcraft torture case at Lehututu). They were not a bad lot, and they wanted me to appoint one of them as Headman over all the other headmen of the scattered branches of the Bakgalagadi in the Kalahari — when he had finished his sentence and went back home. An amusing request, but rather a good one; it is easier to deal with one Headman than with a dozen. The one they wanted to appoint traced his descent back for generations to the original chief who

came into those parts ages ago. So as they all agreed and all seemed to want him, I said I would go into it — I think I shall do it. The gentleman's name was Mosiwa.

Then I had another interview with Kabosetse and two others of the Bakgatla people at Moshupa — they wanted me to let Gobuamang go back. I told them they must make their peace with their overlord Chief Bathoen of the Bangwaketse first of all, and then I would think about it, as it was Bathoen's Reserve. When I asked them if they had anything else to ask me, they started the same story over again, so I got angry and told them to get out. Of course I only *appeared* to lose my temper, one must never do that in reality with these people — but I gave them hell.

We all motored out to Rowlands' asbestos mine. Rowlands is a half caste, but a most cultured and well-educated man, very sensitive on account of his colour, for people won't meet him because of that, and so he wouldn't accept Cuzen's invitation to meet us at tea yesterday. As a matter of fact he is streets ahead of most if not all the other white traders here — he was educated in England and married an English girl whom he leaves at Home.

Wednesday 10 June (to Molepolole)
And now the day has dawned for our visit to Molepolole and for dealing with Sebele's refractory people. We pushed off at 10.30. About five miles out Captain Neale and Captain Gash met us in a car, and reported all peaceful but anxiously expecting our arrival. Then just outside Molepolole a party of Bakwena horsemen met us and escorted us in, galloping furiously behind us in a cloud of dust.

Thursday 11 June
The great day. Neale and I had laid all our plans previously and perfected them yesterday evening.

One great difficulty had been the *place* of meeting, as the kgotlas are usually held on the Hill, but the people in the Plain (the opposing section) feared to go up there, as Sebele's supporters all live on the hill.[23] So we had arranged to have the meeting about half way between the two, on the parade ground in the Government Camp, and people began pouring in there from an early hour. I had one European Officer (Captain Gash), three European N.C.O.s and twenty two native police. The people at the meeting (all men of course) numbered about 2,000 — so really the odds were about even.

I may mention that I had a new Chief 'up my sleeve', one Kgari Sechele,[24] a young brother of Sebele, aged twenty four, who was being educated at King Williams Town. I had telegraphed for him and kept him at Gaberones in 'cold storage' until this morning when I brought him over by lorry at 9 am.

I had a few words with him and told him what I expected of him — a nice lad, but in rather a funk — however I told him we would see him through and he gradually brisked up a bit, especially after some breakfast.

As we sat down and faced the assembled multitudes I cannot say that we were greeted with uproarious enthusiasm! They were all extraordinarily still and silent, all rose as we came in, then sat down again and waited in such tense quiet that one could have heard the proverbial pin drop.

So I heaved myself up and began. I told them of Sebele's continuous bad behaviour, of his ill government of the Tribe and of its lamentable results, and of his defiance of the Government's orders. And then I finished up by saying that the patience of the Government was long but that it was now finished. That its decision was that Sebele be removed from the Chieftainship and banished to Ghanzi, that the Tribe be invited to elect an Acting Chief, and that if they elected a suitable one the Government would approve him and install him as Chief.

After which I sat down (no cheers!) and waited for the band to play.

After a chilly pause speaker after speaker (headed by the Regents I had appointed to carry on *pro tem*) got up and said that Sebele had brought this on himself, that he had only got what was coming to him, that it was no use challenging the Government decision and that they had better elect Kgari, who was next in the Royal Line to be Chief, and ask the Government to confirm this.

My spirits began to rise and after a long succession of speakers had supported Kgari's election, and none had opposed it, I thought I might put it to the torch and risk a vote. So I did so, and after a few words invited all those in favour of Kgari as Chief to hold up their hands.[25]

About three quarters of them did so, and I was looking round to make a rough estimate when an old villain, seated among the Hillmen (Sebele's supporters) on my left, jumped up and yelled 'We want Sebele!' Tableau! Murmurs began to rise and people to move, so I saw it was necessary to act quickly. I moved towards them, told them they could not have Sebele anyhow, but said that if anyone wished to oppose Kgari they could say so freely. I asked them twice, but now nobody moved. So then I came back and asked those who wanted Kgari to hold up their hands again. This time I should say over eighty per cent did — so I snapped the chance, declared him duly elected, and walked across and shook hands with him — and this time there *were* some murmurs of approval. Tableau No 2.

After which I dismissed the meeting, marched solemnly back to 'Topsy' with Ninon, the guard saluted! and off we drove. And as we got into the house Ninon opened her handbag and showed me her revolver, nicely loaded and all ready to wear! I hadn't the faintest idea she had got it, and she wouldn't tell me!

After which whiskey and soda was clearly indicated.

Friday 12 June
We inspected three schools where great preparations had been made to receive us, one European and two Native. The European school was very poor, the teacher a Dutchman, De Villiers, the nineteen pupils very poor type, some half-caste I think — anyhow a miserable lot.

The native schools were much better. One, which we have taken over from the L.M.S., was quite good, about two hundred children all arranged in classes, neatly dressed in a simple school uniform. The other native school, taken over from the Church of England, was also good, though not quite up to the first one. There were about fifty pupils — their craft work and singing were very good.

We got back to camp about noon where we found the old Chief and his advisers and the hut-tax collector Martinus Seboni[26] all in a great state of alarm. Apparently the Hill people (where Sebele's adherents lived) were all buzzing with excitement; as some blighter had told them that I was going to burn all the huts on the Hill and make them all go and live down on the Plain, as a punishment for having backed Sebele. So they were up in arms and there were all the makings of a pretty little row.

I sent messengers up the Hill to tell them to keep quiet and that I would come up to the Hill in the afternoon myself and meet them. I told the Chief and his councillors that they had got to come with me, so they turned green and gave at the knees, and asked how many police I was going to take with me. I told them 'None'.

Confidence begets confidence, and then they got greener still! These people have got the backbone of a filleted sole.

After lunch we met all the Europeans for an early tea at the Residency and Ninon discussed Pathfinders and Wayfarers with some of them. And then at 4.30 off we went up the Hill, N. and I with Captain Neale, and the Chief and his people looking as sick as owls. We found the assembled multitudes rather glum and anxious, so I let off another speech, told them not to be asses and believe rubbish spread about my mischief-makers, and if they heard any more silly stories they were to come and ask the Magistrate for the truth — and so on. They began to perk up a bit, some of them made speeches professing loyalty to the Government and the new Chief and some asked questions, and soon I had got them grinning all over their faces — and finally when I announced that oxen would be distributed for a feast, all was beautiful in the garden! Then we strolled about amongst them through the village, visited the graves of the former Chiefs — and left amid quite an ovation!

Sebele's home was a disgraceful ramshackle affair, but the 'national office' where the tribal business is done was quite a respectable building.[27]

I was weary enough by the time we got back to Camp but there was a good deal to do. We must rig up a telephone from here to Gaberones. It costs £3.10s now to get a message out and back by car! And we must get some more money somehow for school supplies. There is a terrible lot to be done in this country.

Saturday 13 June (at Gaberones)
We visited the old Chief Gaborone in his hut; he is supposed to be 110 years old — quite blind, and can't stand. But he can speak slowly and understands though very deaf. He is a native of the old school, very courteous and dignified and looked most picturesque lying wrapped in new blankets propped up against the wall of his hut. He was very touched that N. and I should have been to see him, and so were the rest of the villagers.

The land the Tribe are on (40,000 acres) belongs to the Chartered Company and the Tribe are supposed to have to clear out when the old man dies. But we shall have to prevent this somehow.[28]

Then we motored on to Khale, the R.C. mission, where we were met by Bishop Meysing, three priests and three nuns. They are doing good work here, teaching the natives agriculture, carpentry and other things — they have just imported some splendid Swiss bulls to improve the native breed.

The Bishop has a great scheme to buy up the whole 40,000 acres where the Batlokwa tribe are in order to develope it for them — it would be a great idea, and he is going to write to me about it. But I fear there would be great opposition.

Monday 15 June (at Mochudi)
The Chief Molefi sent us round a present of a white ox — a very special mark of friendship according to old Bechuana custom.

Then an escort came to fetch us to take us to the Kgotla and they gave us a great reception — leopard dancers ran along beside us, guards of honour tried to present arms, and a special party who had served in the Labour Corps in France turned out with their medals displayed. The Chief read us a most cordial address of welcome, and ex-Chief Isang his uncle spoke well also.

Then back to the Reynekes' (Dutch Reformed missionaries) where I found that verminous Ballinger-Barnes party waiting to see me.[29] They are from the

1931

Witwatersrand University, wretched people who are carrying out an 'Investigation into the Economic Effect of the Impact of Industrialism on Natives in Africa'. My heavens, how can fools give people like this money to waste. They go about disturbing the natives by talking to all the scallywags — and all the decent natives hate them.

I told them I wouldn't have them, but they have pursued me here to beg for permission to go on, as they have made all their arrangements and they'll lose a lot of money and fail in their beastly job if I turn them back now. So I gave them a limited permit for certain districts and sent them away — they comprise Ballinger, an ex-trade unionist from the Clyde; Miss Hodgson, a flat-footed, flat-chested history lecturer from the University with a face like a horse; Barnes, one of the sub-editors of *The Star* — and his wife, a rabbit.

Tuesday 16 June
We lunched on the veld in a top-hole spot under some big trees and had a rest, and finally reached Wetherilt's place, Palla Ranch, on the Tuli Block[30] about 5.30 having enjoyed our drive immensely.

Wednesday 17 June
Wetherilt is a very interesting personality — over 70, but active and keen as a youngster. He is the doyen of the European Advisory Council and the most knowledgeable and helpful and interesting man in the Territory. Palla Ranch covers about 36,000 acres; he has another ranch in the Tuli Block, 'Ellington' about seventy miles away, of about 20,000 acres; a third near Lobatsi of 8,000 acres; and a fourth in the Ghanzi district of about 30,000 acres. So owning as he does nearly 100,000 acres he is a person of some consequence. His wife is a South African, a very nice woman and his boy is going to Cambridge this year. His daughter is at Roedean School in Jo'burg.

Friday 19 June
Thank goodness N. was ever so much better today, and we were able to push on — we left at about 10.30. It was a very pretty drive of about a couple of hours to Stuart's Ranch through jolly wooded country over quite a fair track; we put up a herd of impala on the way.

The Hon. John Stuart[31] is a splendid type of young settler and pioneer — a brother of Lord Moray — he was in the Navy during the war, after which he left and bought a Ranch of about 30,000 acres in the Tuli Block, and another of about 20,000 acres further north. He married an extremely pretty girl, the daughter of the well-known pioneer 'Matabele' Wilson,[32] and they have the two most delightful and fascinating children I have ever seen.

Then at about 2.30 on we went again to Jousse's Ranch, a household of a very different kind. Jousse has built himself quite a good sort of rambling farmhouse, but everything is very primitive and rough. He is an astonishing character of French-Swiss origin, a tremendous worker, very capable, most cantankerous and hated by every soul in the place.

Until I came along he quarrelled with all the R.C.'s and all the administrations, and as he plaintively remarked to me nobody will speak to him! He was for some years in the Ngwato Reserve as a trader, but was ruined and kicked out by Khama, the then Chief.[33]

He bought a farm in the Tuli Block (he owns about 20,000 acres now) and

1931

started dairy ranching. Now he is one of the wealthiest farmers here and the biggest cream producer in the country. On this particular ranch he has twelve hundred head of graded Friesland cattle, milks four hundred and sixty a day and has another eight hundred head on another ranch further north.

I made him a loan of £1000, and with this and £1000 of his own he has installed an electrically driven mechanical milking plant, cold storage room, separator and cooler — it's a wonderful bit of work, the most up to date in South Africa.

Saturday 20 June
We had another lovely drive through jolly country through the Tuli Block to Mahalapye, where we arrived at Russell England's[34] house at about 6 pm.

Sunday 21 June
England is by far the ablest man in the whole service — he has a first rate brain, sound judgment, and indefatigable energy, and he is worth more to me than all the others put together, except perhaps Dyke and Chase. Apart from those three I have no-one I can really fully rely on. Unfortunately England (like myself) does not 'suffer fools gladly', and so he quarrels with people as his tact is not first-rate, but I am trying to break him of this.

Tuesday 23 June
A good morning's work with England, *inter alia* planning our High Commissioner's tour — then an early lunch, a short rest for Ninon, and off at 3 for Serowe. The Englands came with us in their car as far as a big native creamery run by a villain called Mathiba[35] — about sixteen miles off.

Wednesday 24 June (at Serowe)
We went to the Kgotla meeting of all the tribe at 10 am. That little snake Tshekedi is away (with my permission) conducting some investigations in the north as to the value of land concerning which we propose to do a 'deal' in regard to mining so as to buy off his opposition to mining in his Reserve.[36] It will be a great thing if it comes off.

The Acting Chief Edirilwe (Tshekedi's uncle) is a good old thing — he sent the escort again to take us to the Kgotla, and we had an excellent meeting: no complaints, and everything lovely in the garden. Mrs Page-Wood,[37] the sister of Captain Nettelton the late R.M. here, took notes for the newspapers.

Thursday 25 June
The new dam delighted my heart. It is a huge thing in course of construction to be finished by September. Hundreds of tons of earth have been shifted to hold up the Metsemotlhaba River and its tributaries — it is being reinforced with 20,000 pounds of cement, the whole making a wall three feet high; it will hold up to ten or fifteen million gallons of water according to the season. It's costing about £1,200 and the Tribe are supplying all the labour in addition — so it's a pretty big job for this Territory.[38] I shall just love to see it when the rains come down in October.

Friday 26 June
We pushed our way through quite jolly country, out over a bad track to Palapye, inspecting the veterinary cordon posts on the way — I have got a complete line a hundred and twenty miles along from Serowe to Palapye and thence right along

the Lotsani River to the Tuli Block — divided into three sections, each under the control of a European (one N.C.O. and two special constables). Distributed over the cordons are ten native police and thirty native auxiliaries in little camps ten miles apart — they patrol the whole line twice daily. The whole was in charge of one of my officers called Knoll — it was not good, and when I got in to Palapye I cursed him roundly, took the job away from him, and put another man in charge. He is a lazy incompetent ass.

Saturday 27 June (to Francistown)
We ran into Francistown at about 5.15 and were received by Captain and Mrs Nettelton at the Residency. They are very pleasant and kind, but have two of the worst mannered children I have ever seen.

Sunday 28 June
With Nettelton in his car, we motored out to lunch with Gordon and his wife (Manager of the Tati Concession Company) at his prospecting camp, in a most delightful spot at the junction of the Tati and Sekunawe Rivers (both dry of course).

He showed us a wonderful collection of old flints (arrow heads, cutting implements, and hammer heads and all in stone) very old, Paleolithic or Neolithic, and mineral specimens he had found; one of the latter shewed visible free gold to the naked eye.

Then back to the Residency — Dr and Mrs Drew dined; a damned dull dinner party. She has just had her first baby, the only one in the world.

Monday 29 June
Nettelton and I with Holmes and Hay (veterinary officers) motored over the area we have cleared for the veterinary cordon along the Tati-Rhodesian frontier. It's a wonderful bit of work — for a hundred miles we have cleared back all the cattle from five to twenty miles — established cordons of police all along it, 'blazed' a line of trees, put up notice-boards, evacuated whole villages, and moved altogether 10,000 head of cattle and 14,000 head of small stock! That of course is in addition to what we have done along the Ngwato-Rhodesian and Tuli-Rhodesian and Tuli-Transvaal frontiers, and the Serowe-Palapye-Lotsani cordon.

In the whole of our trip today we saw only two animals — one dog and one mongoose.

Tuesday 30 June
At 8.45 I went off with Nettelton to Ramaquabane for a Kgotla meeting with a number of tribes — poor devils they are in a bad way owing to the cattle embargo being still in force in the northern part of the Territory. They can't sell a beast, as no-one will buy; their grain crop is a partial failure; they can't get work outside the Territory owing to the general trade depression, so they can't pay their hut-tax or buy anything they need.

Then at 2.30 we had the big meeting of all the white farmers and settlers of Tati, Tsessebe and Francistown. They were terribly sore, all their business being paralysed by the cattle embargo, and as they are largely Scotch it may be imagined what this drain on their pockets made them feel like! So the speeches were very bitter and things didn't look too well.

1931

Wednesday 1 July
I had an interview with Dr Romyn who is going to do the Economic Survey on the line of the Walvis Bay Railway Survey route.[39] I disliked him at sight — he is an ignorant opinionated mule, and I hope he breaks his neck on the survey.

Thursday 2 July
Then another tribal meeting. Samuel Moroka of the Barolong tribe, an old man of ninety, who fought the Boers in the Orange Free State at Thabanchu forty years ago, killed lots of them, was defeated and exiled and wants to go back — of course they won't have him.[40]

He presented another knotty problem. That branch of the Barolong are 'squatters' on Tati Co. land. They pay the Tati Company thirty shillings a year rent each, also three shillings a head grazing fees for cattle (reduced from six shillings in 1927). There are about a thousand of them (adult men) so the Tati Company get a goodish rental. But they have to pay twenty five shillings a year hut-tax to us also, so they have a pretty heavy annual bill to meet, poor devils.

But if we move them on to Crown Lands we ruin the Tati Company to whom we also pay £1,000 a year for the lease of the Reserve on which yet other natives are housed. So we move in a vicious circle.[41]

Friday 4 to Sunday 12 July (at Mafeking)
On the 11th the Bishop of Kimberley arrived to stay; and we had a tea party, tennis, etc. in the afternoon; and finally on Sunday Mrs Rheinallt Jones came to stay arriving at 7 am. She is the 'moving spirit' in the Pathfinders and Wayfarers movement in which Ninon is so interested. Her husband is Professor Rheinallt Jones[42] of Jo'burg University with whom I have had many dealings on native questions affecting the Protectorate.

The Bishop spent most of Sunday in Church, and thank goodness he and Mrs Rheinallt Jones both left by an early morning train on Monday.

Monday 13 to Sunday 19 July
Tagart arrived from England at 8 am on 13th. It's a lucky thing we have several spare rooms and some good servants!

Tagart is undertaking the Enquiry I asked for into the conditions under which the Masarwa live in the Bamangwato Reserve, which I maintain are akin to slavery, but which have always been glossed over until now.

Meanwhile in addition to being R.C., I am also Assistant R.C. (while Stigand packs his things preparatory to retiring on 1st August), Government Secretary (while Dutton is away) and Chief Veterinary Officer (while Chase is on leave in England). And my Chief Clerk and two Resident Magistrates are on leave.

Dutton got off on Sunday. He very nearly missed the train and was so excited that at one moment he refused to go! Quelle hope.

Monday 20 July
A bad day — Black Monday. Telegrams came in from Rhodesia reporting a spread of Foot and Mouth disease towards our border which will make my Conference with Kemp at Pretoria more difficult — also it increases our danger, tho' it it still nearly a hundred miles away.

1931

Tuesday 21 July
More trouble — this time at Serowe. A telegram from Captain Potts saying that he has received five deputations all pressing for the expulsion of Moanaphuti[43] (the blighter who went round with the Ballinger crowd) and he fears a serious explosion if something is not done. Expelling people seems to be becoming my speciality, and so I have given instructions for the necessary papers to be prepared and for a long telegram of instructions to be drafted for Potts.

Monday 3 August (at Bulawayo)
Arrived Bulawayo 7.30 am (twenty four hours travelling). Then off to the Club where I met Mitchell, the Minister for Agriculture, and three veterinary officers, and planned Foot and Mouth disease measures all the morning. Then an interview with Dr Romyn the agricultural expert who has been surveying the Walvis Bay Railway Route. Then back to Government House — where I lunched with Admiral Tweedie, the Admiral commanding the South African Station.[44]

Wednesday 5 August (to Pretoria)
Off again — to Pretoria this time. After a hectic morning at the Office, I caught the 4 pm train to Pretoria. No peace for the wicked.

Thursday 6 August
Hay and I went off to do battle with General Kemp, Minister of Agriculture, in regard to getting the embargo lifted for our cattle in the northern part of the Protectorate. We had a fearful argument for nearly two hours, at the end of which they agreed that if at the end of two weeks there was no further extension of Foot and Mouth disease in Rhodesia towards our borders they would agree to my proposals.

Friday 7 August
We reached Mafeking at 6.40 am. Potts going on in the train to Serowe. After a hectic morning at my office I'm off again, this time by car.
    I left at 4.30 arriving at Lobatsi at 6.45.

Saturday 8 August (to Kanye)
Off at 10 am with England in 'Topsy' to Kanye, where we arrived at 11.30, the object of my visit being to open the Native Agricultural Show.
    It was a great show and a splendid thing for the natives. To get the whole tribe laughing, the women singing and the children playing, means that there is not much wrong, and the Bangwaketse are now a changed people. They were frightfully keen about the Show too — but to give an idea of how suspicious these people are, I may say that a lot of the older people would not exhibit because they thought we should confiscate the winning exhibits!

Monday 10 to Thursday 13 August (at Mafeking)
A bad four days struggling with all the preparations for the High Commissioner's visit. We are going to have Sir Herbert and Lady Stanley, Captain Clifford, and Captain Holbech on our hands for a fortnight.
    I have had every detail for every day worked out to the last detail — but it's a tremendous bit of organising — trains, cars, guards of honour, lunches, dinners, balls, meetings, speeches, etc, etc. And if I leave anybody out of any of the parties

they will be mortally offended; and if I ask the wrong person, all the others will be offended. And when one has to consider the feelings and precedence of half a dozen native 'Kinglets' in ragged trousers, and all their Tribes, as well as all the European settlers and farmers — life becomes a little complicated, not to say hell.

Visit of High Commissioner for South Africa

Monday 17 August
At 8.30 Hope rolled up in his car, and at 8.45 in 'Topsy' I rolled up at the station, and met Sir Herbert and Lady Stanley, Captain Holbech A.D.C., and Captain Clifford, Imperial Secretary. They all came along to Government House where Ninon met them: they were highly delighted with the house, and Clifford, who had seen it some years ago, was amazed at the changes and improvements we had made.

Wednesday 19 August (at Lobatsi)
Punctually to time we steamed into Lobatsi — Captain Reilly the R.M. and Mrs Reilly and staff met us, the cars (which had gone on by road) were awaiting us, and arrayed in top hats and morning coats off we drove at 10 am to the meeting of European settlers.

We got back to our coaches, changed and lunched at the Residency — then into full uniform and up to the marquee again to a meeting of all the Native Chiefs of the Southern Protectorate and hundreds of their followers. More guards of honour, more speeches, etc, then back to the coaches, change again and off to inspect the Cold Storage works where we make our butter, etc. They had the whole thing running well, and it was quite interesting to see all the processes, the big machinery, the ice making, etc. Last year they made 450,000 lbs of butter for export.

After dinner Bongola Smith[45] rolled up. He is the biggest cattle dealer in South Africa, and one of the biggest villains — he has a monopoly of the Congo market for meat, and I want him to come into the B.P., erect killing works, buy our cattle, and export meat to the Congo and elsewhere. We had a most interesting discussion until after midnight, and I think he'll play. It will be a great triumph if he does, as it will make us independent of those damned Dutchmen in the Union — rogues and villains they all are.

Thursday 27 August (at Serowe)
Off early and back to Serowe again. Lunch at the Residency as yesterday — afterwards a long and painful interview with Tshekedi in regard to mining.

Everything had been 'so lovely in the garden' up till then that Sir Herbert Stanley felt quite sure Tshekedi would come into line at once this afternoon — but I know my man and guessed otherwise.

And so it was — the little devil was as obstinate as a team of mules, stuck his toes in, and wouldn't budge. So after nearly four hours of it we told him to think over our proposals and to come down to see us on the coach at Palapye tomorrow.

Friday 28 August (at Palapye)
At 2.30 Tshekedi arrived, evidently in a foul temper, and for the first time since I have met him Stanley really got annoyed. I confess that secretly I was rather pleased!

Tshekedi would agree to nothing, and finally just at the end he produced two memoranda, which he handed in — one was a protest against the removal of Chief Sebele, and the other a most lying statement about my having ordered the use of 'forced labour' to build their dam for them.

So I saw red, told him he was 'not speaking the truth' and asked him to produce the letter that I had written him about it. After shuffling for nearly twenty minutes he produced it and of course it made the whole thing clear and showed him up badly. Then Stanley got really angry. We told him that if he didn't want the dam we would call off our men and our plant, stop the work at once, and pay for any assistance they had given.

That called his bluff; he said he would consult the Tribe and let the R.M. know tomorrow. And the interview ended in what one might call a minor key. The dirty little rat.

Sunday 30 August (Tati District)
The train took us on to Tsessebe at 8.30 where we arrived at about 10. Off again by car to see Hoare's cheese factory at Vukwe. He is a wonderful old man, uses native milk to make his cheeses, and for this purpose has established a chain of twelve native milk collecting stations. The other Europeans hate him because by buying native milk instead of keeping his own cows, as they do, he can manufacture and sell more cheaply. Went on to tea at MacFarlane's Ranch. He is the member of the Advisory Council for this District for whom I got an O.B.E. in the last honours list — a tiresome old devil, but quite useful. He gave me some shocking bad news, namely that Foot and Mouth disease had spread to within a few miles of our border, so I was itching to get back to the coach to deal with it.

Monday 31 August
My birthday: age 35 [actually 53] — feel 25! We went off at 9 am by car to Ramaquabane to meet five native tribes. Quite a good show — the chiefs and many hundreds of their followers.

We dined with the Stanleys, and had a very jolly evening, made all the pleasanter by the fact that telegrams had come in saying that the Foot & Mouth disease report was not true, and that Tshekedi had come to heel about the dam.

Tuesday 1 September (Gaberones to Molepolole)
We were 'unhooked' at Gaberones Station soon after 10 am this morning — Captain Neale the R.M. met us, and drove us out to Molepolole, about thirty five miles over an excellent track through lovely country. We have to assist at the formal installation by the Tribe of Kgari Sechele as the new Chief of the Bakwena in place of the former Chief Sebele that I kicked out.

Afterwards we all drove off to the new Kgotla where we found a huge assembly — over three thousand I should say, all dressed up for the show — lots of Europeans, traders, missionaries, etc., etc.

First of all one 'sky pilot' said a prayer, then the Chief's uncle made a speech, then I had to address the multitudes. Ninon said my speech was a great effort, and I hope so, as it was rather an important occasion. The Bishop then gave a blessing, and the proceedings concluded by half a dozen speeches from the more important headmen.

1931

Wednesday 9 September (to Pretoria)
Off to Pretoria for a conference with Stanley, the Resident Commissioners of Basutoland and Swaziland, Tagart who has been sent out here by the Home Government at my request to enquire into the Masarwa question, and Patrick Duncan[46] the Legal Adviser who is also the leader in the Parliament here of the South African Party.[47] He is a most able man and very charming.

Friday 11 September
A long day's work at our conference on Native Affairs to consider my great effort, a new Law to 'define the powers of Chiefs and establish and define the duties and jurisdiction of Native Courts'. It is very important, as if successful it may be a model for the British Territories in South Africa. But it's a very difficult and thorny subject.

Monday 14 September
A hectic day at the High Commissioner's Office with a brief interval for lunch — the Round Table Conference consists of Sir H. Stanley; C.F.R.; Sturrock, R.C. of Basutoland; Nicholson, Acting R.C. of Swaziland; Tagart, late Native Affairs Commissioner for Northern Rhodesia; Patrick Duncan K.C., Legal Adviser to H.M. Government on Africa and deputy leader (General Smuts is leader) of the South African Party; Dutton, Government Secretary of B.P.; Clifford, Imperial Secretary; and Eales, Assistant Imperial Secretary — quite an imposing gathering, and all to discuss my new scheme!

We wrangled bitterly of course, but made good progress — anyhow I am getting my way which is the main point!

MacFarlane the member of my 'Parliament' and England are down here for the meeting of the Dairy Control Board, both staying at Polley's. I got England to do some underground negotiation re Foot and Mouth disease — and arranged for MacFarlane to receive his O.B.E. Why people like these rotten decorations I am at a loss to understand.

Wednesday 16 September
Stanley wanted to see me as an idiotic telegram had come in from the Colonial Office about our proposal to put up a new cattle-slaughter and cold storage works at Francistown. The Colonial Office are the damnest fools; they *can't* see a point, and are swathed in red tape. However we composed a devastating answer (three foolscap sheets of telegram); Stanley came out to the car where Ninon was sitting and took a tender farewell of her; we dashed off to the hotel, picked up our luggage and started off for home at 12.30.

Monday 21 to Sunday 27 September
Nothing of very much interest to record during the week, which was largely devoted to putting the fear of God into my Office which seems to have got slack in my absence, and driving work through — there's plenty of it — also plenty of trouble. That little devil Tshekedi has got influenza thank goodness, so the Bamangwato are quiet for a moment. Also the Bakwena are behaving beautifully since I kicked their Chief out. But there is trouble among the Bakgatla owing to the young Chief and the ex-Chief (his uncle who acted as Regent) quarrelling, and my friend Reyneke is very worried. I shall have to send Captain Neale up there, and may have to go myself.

Bathoen — the Chief of the Bangwaketse came in, and I had to talk to him for the good of his soul. My Acting Magistrate has played the fool in Ngamiland, and the Batawana are being silly — also the Europeans are up in arms against the Acting Magistrate. And owing to the cattle embargo in the north the wretched people are in a terribly bad way.

On Wednesday we had a murder trial at Lobatsi, and Duncan the President of our Court found the fellow guilty and sentenced him to be hanged. Afterwards he motored on here (Duncan, not the criminal!), dined with us and stayed the night. He is a very able and interesting man, though exceedingly quiet and reserved till one knows him.

Monday 28 September
Really the people at the Colonial Office are the outside edge, the frozen limit. How they dare try and fight big schemes that Stanley and I present and support — some damned office-boy must be trying to be clever I suppose. However we fight on and pray that a taxi will run over his face.

Wednesday 30 September
An interesting report from Lt. Hope, whom I have sent round inspecting the frontier 'cordons' on our Rhodesian border — he is doing his work very well, loves being out in the wilds and wanders about in the minimum of clothes, generally with a bag of monkey nuts tied round his neck for food!

Thursday 1 October
Captain Neale arrived and we had a conference about affairs at Mochudi. I am afraid they look bad, and I shall have to go up. We arranged that N. and I should go up and camp there for a few days while I wrestle with these devils. The Chief and the ex-Chief will certainly be at each others throats before long, and that must be stopped, or we'll have another 'Great War'. Neale lunched, and we made all arrangements.

Friday 2 October
I forgot to say that Bongola Smith came through on Wednesday and I had 40 minutes with him — he gave me some very valuable confidential information about affairs in Northern and Southern Rhodesia and the Congo. The Imperial Cold Storage and the Southern Rhodesia Government have been trying to stop our scheme for putting up an 'abattoir' at Francistown by intrigues in London, Bulawayo and Brussels, damn them — so I had to do some hectic telegraphing. Stanley is backing me grandly and the telegrams that go to London from the two of us are worth reading. I should like to crucify those clerks at the Colonial Office.

Thursday 8 October (at Johannesburg)
At 9 am I was interviewing Gemmil, the Chairman of the Native Labour Recruiting Association — the body that recruits all the labour for the Gold Mines.[48] I have a new scheme that I want him to adopt that may bring us in some money I hope.

Then I saw Bongola again, and afterwards wrote up notes of my interviews. After lunch more interviews — Trevelyan, the Chief Inspector of Mines, about our new Mining Proclamation which will I hope be published on the 16th; that *is* going to make a splash — then Major Weil[49] about establishing some refrigerating works in the B.P. An interesting man who went through the Raid and all the early pioneering days out here.

Then Dr. MacDonald the Editor of *Sun and Agricultural Life* who has published such nice articles about the B.P. in his paper. Then he brought in two of the directors of the XL Bazaar, the biggest retail place here — who are anxious to do trade with us — a splendid opportunity which I seized at once. They buy £800 worth of bacon monthly, 1000 dozen eggs a week, £1000 worth of butter a month, etc.

Friday 9 October
A telephone message came through from Pretoria to say the Colonial Office had at last cabled *agreeing to my F'town Scheme*. I am afraid I did a war dance in the hotel hall.

By 10 o'clock we got off — not a bad early morning's work, and we had quite a pleasant drive back though it was much colder and terribly dusty.

Saturday 10 October (at Mafeking)
Shocking bad news about Foot and Mouth disease — its spread to within five miles of our border near the Tuli Block. So I sent out long telegraphic instructions, ordered every beast that came near our border to be shot, sent Captain Gash from F'town and another Veterinary Officer up to the border — and strengthened the patrols.

Then I had a poisonous interview with a vile fellow called Moanaphuti who caused a lot of trouble up in Serowe and whom I had to expel from there — I'm afraid I gave him hell, and if looks could have killed I think I should have been a corpse!

In the afternoon I packed and worked and got ready for our jaunt tomorrow — there is trouble up at Mochudi, and we're off to Gaberones to deal with it.

Monday 12 October (at Gaberones)
I had my morning's interview with the young Chief of the Bakgatla, Molefi, the ex-Chief Isang his uncle, and Reyneke the missionary.

It was a long and complicated business; there has been trouble between the ex-Chief Isang (who acted as Regent during Molefi's minority) a very capable and progressive man — and Molefi the young Chief. It's perhaps natural, for as the saying here goes you can't have two bulls in one kraal, and the older man hates to give up the power and to see his work being spoiled by the young one — but if the trouble is not stopped it will spread and sooner or later there will be fighting.

I patched up an arrangement which seemed to please them all, but I don't believe it will last — and I shall have to station an officer at Mochudi.

Tuesday 13 October
Ninon and I went down to the Camp, and by way of a cheery start inspected the new gallows! The former arrangement was an absolute disgrace — the wretched man had to walk fourteen feet up a scaffold which was in full public view and quite wobbly.[50]

The rest of the Camp was much more cheery, and was in spotless order — everything beautifully clean and neat and tidy — and in the brilliant sunshine and warm atmosphere the white-washed buildings looked most attractive. It is our biggest camp, and a very nice one — if I had to be stationed anywhere I should like to be here.

Thursday 15 October (at Mafeking)
The Mining Proclamation is appearing in tomorrow's Gazette — we shall have to get out an Immigration Proclamation to prevent our being flooded out by undesirables under the guise of mining.

Friday 16 to Sunday 18 October (to Pretoria)
A hard morning at Office and then off to Pretoria by the 4.15 pm train.
  It's as I feared: the Imperial Cold Storage are trying to block our scheme, claim monopoly rights and say they will put up the factory themselves — which I know they can't and won't do.

Thursday 22 to Saturday 24 October (at Mafeking)
That infernal European Advisory Council sat for these three days, and by the end of it I was fed up to the teeth with them and never want to see them again. Of all the peevish stupid ungrateful grousing dogs I have ever met, they are about the worst. There had been a silly public meeting at Francistown on 17th, and as I couldn't be there to guide them they went off the rails and passed foolish resolutions. Their representative, MacFarlane, is a member of the European Advisory Council; he tries to run with the hare and hunt with the hounds — so I went for him bald-headed and we had quite a cheery little dust-up. Their tails are all down because of the financial depression, and I had to try to buck them up and put a little backbone into them — but they're a poor lot.

Sunday 1 to Saturday 7 November
The week and the month opened well by good rains, but from every other point of view it has been absolute hell. Clifford and the rest of the High Commissioner's Office mucked up the negotiations with the Imperial Cold Storage at Cape Town completely and finally, and the Imperial Cold Storage have been clever enough to kill my whole scheme for a cold storage works at Francistown.
  First of all the damned fools at the Colonial Office held the whole thing up for a month — then when they agreed there was further delay before dealing with the Imperial Cold Storage and now the psychological moment has passed. Bongola Smith has ratted (he has of course been 'got at' by the Imperial Cold Storage) and the thing is dead. It is a tragedy. But it is also a lesson — unless I handle every single detail myself and especially all negotiations, it is hopeless to expect anything to go through.
  I am struggling to frame Estimates for next year — a perfectly heartbreaking job, all receipts are down and I don't see how we can possibly balance our budget. The one hope I have is the Mining Proclamation. It has been published, the Magistrates are explaining it to the natives, the European Advisory Council have agreed it unanimously, and the last (and most difficult) thing to be done is to get it through the Native Advisory Council. This I propose to do myself early in December.

Sunday 8 November
After a foul week we both felt very weary and spent Sunday in Topsy on the veld, reading and sleeping. The only person who is always cheerful and full of beans is

1931

Pongo — nothing seems to damp his spirits. He is always ready to come out riding with us, or for a game with us, or for a fight with other dogs.

Monday 9 to Sunday 15 November
This week may be described as less foul than last — distinctly so. In the first place we have had magnificent rains here and throughout the Protectorate. In the memory of the oldest inhabitant there have been none better! Pans that have never held water are full — rivers running bank high — and dams everywhere holding up good stores. Grass is sprouting already and the wretched cattle are beginning to look more cheerful.

My new dam at Serowe has stood! The river came down in a great wall ten feet high, crashed against the dam, rose and washed over it, carrying away some of the plant. But the dam stood, and is now holding back ten solid feet of water, a few million gallons — though many dams in South Africa have burst. It's a great triumph.

The rivers are so full that in some places they can't be crossed, and several of my stations — Molepolole for example — are entirely cut off.

In view of the failure of the H.C. Office to bring off the arrangements for the Francistown factory, I have decided to try to open up a new cattle export route from the B.P. through Northern Rhodesia to the Congo. I have sent a man out to explore the route and report on it, and I have decided to go up to Livingstone *myself* next week to fix up preliminaries. The Governor, Sir James Maxwell,[51] a friend of Lord Lugard's, has asked me to stay with him, and I've made all arrangements for a whole series of interviews there.

At Livingstone I shall also deal with two other Schemes I have — the establishment of a Game Reserve in Ngamiland, and the building of a hotel there. The idea is to protect all the wonderful game in Ngamiland from extinction, and to attract visitors there to see them. Thousands of people go to the Victoria Falls every year. If we can put up a good hotel at Kasane and protect the game, the visitors will come on into Ngamiland, spend money, and open up and develope the Territory. It's a great scheme, and I think can be done without our having to spend money. There's wonderful fishing there too and altogether I don't see why it shouldn't be one of Africa's show places.

I'm sorry to say that old Chief Gaborone has died — he was a wonderfully picturesque figure. 110 years old, and a splendid type of the dignified courteous chief of old times before they were spoilt by European customs and clothes and education and all that rot. But it means a row — as their land belongs to the Chartered Company who allowed the Tribe to have it during Gaborone's life only and the Tribe (the Batlokwa) will certainly refuse to move! More fun and games!

We had the annual meeting of my 'Board of Advice on Native Education' — Church of England, Roman Catholics, Lutheran, Dutch Reformed Church, and London Missionary Society are all represented on it — I managed to keep out the Wesleyans and the Seventh Day Adventists. Also some native Chiefs and a few others.

Wednesday 18 November (to Bulawayo by train)
Bulawayo at 2.30 pm where I had a three hours wait before going on to Livingstone — a very full three hours in which I did some very successful work. I had telegraphed to the Rhodesian Cooperative Creameries for their Chairman and Managing Director to meet me there to discuss the question of erecting a creamery

and butter factory and cheese cold storage at Francistown. *They have agreed to do it*, and I telegraphed to some of my F'town people to meet me here (Bulawayo) on my way back on Saturday to settle all details and get it going. It's splendid because it will help the F'town district immensely and create new trade and industry in the North.

Off at 5.30 pm. again *en route* to Livingstone.

Thursday 19 November (at Livingstone)
A terrific day. I arrived at 6.30 am. and was met at the station by Captain Hopkins, A.D.C. to the Governor Sir James Maxwell, who whisked me off to Government House where I am staying.

Government House is not much of a place, as they have been meaning to move the capital up to Lusaka three hundred miles north for twenty years and so would not spend anything on existing quarters. They are starting next year and will take five years and £350,000 to do it!

I went around and had a talk with Sussman, the biggest cattle exporter in the North, about my scheme for bringing cattle up from Tati on the hoof through Northern Rhodesia into the Congo — which I had also discussed (amongst other things) with the various people mentioned above. It is perfectly feasible, but there are a lot of cross-currents. The Ngamiland people don't want it because it would compete with them. The main difficulty however is that the demand in the Congo has fallen because, owing to the slump in the world price of copper, production has fallen off in the Congo and Northern Rhodesia, thousands of people have been dismissed and the consumption of meat has fallen. It all depends on a conference of copper producers sitting in New York now — so does the price of copper in London and New York affect the sale of cattle in Bechuanaland! And there are other factors too; all the meat contracts in the Congo (the Union Minière, the Railways, the Government, and the other big mines) are controlled by my villainous friend Mr Bongola Smith. His directors sit in Brussels — Mr Carton de Wiart, Count Lippens, ex-Governor of the Congo, one of the Rothschilds, etc., and they in their turn control the Belgian Government who control the Congo Government! A dirty game — and a network of intrigue covering Cape Town, Salisbury, Bulawayo, Livingstone, Elizabethville, Brussels and New York.

Friday 20 November
I spent a very interesting morning attending the Session of the Northern Rhodesia Legislative Council. It is a very formal and dignified business modelled (on a very small scale) on the House of Commons at Home. The Governor sits on a raised dais alone; and a chair had been put there for me beside him, so I sat in dignified state and listened to the proceedings. Their finances made my mouth water — a Revenue of nearly £800,000 and, *in addition*, expenditure on public works of nearly £250,000 out of Loan moneys!

All this as a result of mining. A few years ago they were as poor as we. If our fools at Home had allowed mining here we might have been in the same position — now as a result of two years fighting I've just got our Mining Law published. I hope to have it finally passed next month — and then — *Nous verrons*.

Saturday 21 November (at Bulawayo)
After a sticky night in the train I arrived Bulawayo 6.30 am. I went to the Grand Hotel and had a much needed bath — and breakfast. Then followed the usual

crowd of interviews. First that arch scoundrel Haskins — the man who has been pretending outwardly to support the Francistown factory scheme, and then was bought by the I.C.S., and at their dictation wrote them a letter saying that people up there didn't want it! The letter was shown to Sir H. Stanley who sent it to me! So when Haskins saw me he was just the most unhappy man in Bulawayo — I greeted him sweetly, guided him to a chair (he didn't seem to want to stay!) and after talking hot air for about ten minutes I asked him was he still in favour of the Francistown scheme? 'Oh yes'. And was his brother? 'Oh yes, we were only talking of it last Wednesday'. Then, I observed, 'the people who say you wrote a letter damning it are mistaken?' 'Oh yes, I never wrote any such letter'. 'Nor your brother?' 'No. . .' 'Ah', I observed, 'then is this a forgery?' And I shewed him the letter. To say that he turned green is putting it mildly — he gasped like a fish hauled out of water and if he could have killed me I rather think he would. Because now I can break him and get him kicked out of F'town if and when I choose.

The rest of our interview was *not* terribly cordial and when I'd finished telling him what I thought of him he departed.

Then Dewar of the Tati Company and Holmes our Veterinary Officer, whom I telegraphed for from F'town, came in, and off we went to meet the Board of the Rhodesian Creamery Company. *And we completed the deal* — it's all signed, sealed and delivered. They're going to put up the Creamery at F'town at once — butter factory and cheese cold storage complete. And thank goodness I've done it all myself and no devils have been able to interfere and bungle it.

Sunday 22 November (to Mafeking)
Bongola Smith was on board the train and we had a heart to heart talk. Eventually he said that if I would write him a suitable letter he would sign it saying he would buy 10,000 head of cattle a year from us! I don't believe him, but I'm going to try. He's a marvellous man, can't read or write, and yet controls ninety per cent of the cattle trade in the Congo, and a large proportion of it in the Union.

Monday 23 to Wednesday 25 November
The Reillys and Moseleys lunched on Tuesday. On Wednesday I got a nasty knock — locusts in Ngaminaland, the most awful curse of Africa. Fortunately they're flying and have not settled — yet — but there are enormous swarms. It was six miles long by two miles broad! I've telegraphed full instructions, sent up cases of poison and pumps — called for volunteers, recruited natives, etc. etc. What a life! We seem to get all the ten plagues of Egypt. But are we down-hearted? Not a damn bit of it.

Thursday 26 November (to Cape Town)
Off to Cape Town by the 6.15 am train to settle, I hope finally, the row about mining between Tshekedi and the Chartered Company and so clear the last obstacle out of the way.

Friday 27 November (at Cape Town)
After a hasty lunch we started working at once, Sir Herbert Stanley and I. Then I had to see that vile renegade Colonel Williams of the Ministry of Agriculture about cattle. He is an Englishman who has gone over to the Nationalists and is more Dutch than the Dutch. We do not love each other, he and I, but the infernal fellow is clever confound him.

Then came the great interview with Tshekedi *and we won again!*[52] We settled everything except a few details to be finished off tomorrow — it's a huge relief.

Tuesday 1 to Wednesday 2 December (at Mafeking)
Two tough days preparing everything for the meeting of the Native Advisory Council on Thursday. It is *vital* that I get the new Mining Law understood and agreed by them so as to avoid delay. Of course we should overrule them if they did not agree, but that would mean delay as the Colonial Office would certainly be silly.

The Resident Magistrates arrived on Wednesday afternoon and so did all the Chiefs except Tshekedi who has to come from Cape Town, where he is settling finally the Mining Concession with the Chartered Company — it is going through all right. The other Chiefs are palavering in the big marquee I have had put up in the grounds at the Imperial Reserve, getting ready to yap tomorrow.

Thursday 3 December
Then the Native Advisory Council meeting started, and I made a long speech pointing out the necessity for and advantages of Mining — all day long the discussion went on and at least at 5 o'clock I got a *unanimous* vote of support! It was a great triumph and I was simply delighted, but by Jove terribly weary. There were one hundred and ten clauses in the Mining Law, and forty-five clauses in the explanatory memorandum.

Saturday 5 December
A hairy morning at the Office, but a very good one. A long interview with Tshekedi in regard to Mining, and now I think everything is satisfactorily terminated, both as regards to Mining Law and the Mining Concession. I have made final arrangements with him; he seems to have turned over a new leaf, and to be extraordinarily amenable. He was present at the Native Advisory Council on Friday, although previously he had always refused to come.[53]

In the afternoon we had a tennis party of about twenty people, and then in the evening the farewell dinner to Dutton and his family — about forty people. Of course I had to make a speech, a very difficult one as Dutton has been perfectly hopeless as Government Secretary, but it went off all right. Then there were two or three other speeches and finally Dutton's reply — a perfectly awful effort that I thought was never coming to an end.

Monday 7 & Tuesday 8 December
I have now started everyone in the Office on the great drive to get the Estimates for next year finished off. The real hard work is all done: the results have to be put together, added up, and the picture made. I've invented £17,000 worth of new taxes which will make everyone swear, cut down the expenditure by another £5,000 (making £16,000 in all) and pinched £17,000 out of reserve — thus we acquire £39,000 and just balance. But it's a heartbreaking job.

Professor MacMillan[54] descended on us — he is Professor of History and Bantu Studies at Witwatersrand University — a very able and pleasant man. We agreed on many points — notably that the Protectorate should be administered by the Colonial Office and not by the Dominions Office. The Dominions Office has to do with all the self-governing Dominions and is terrified of them. Our interests (B.P.) are directly opposed to those of the Union of South Africa, and the Colonial Office is far more likely to fight for us than the Dominions Office. Also we agreed that as a measure of economy and practical efficiency there is no need for a High Commissioner for South Africa — it is quite an unnecessary complication and expense. Let each one of us run our own show. I wish I could bring these things to pass! I must have a try when I get to London next year.

Saturday 12 December
Some of my people have been having rather adventurous times. Hurndall, the Police Officer in charge of the Kalahari, very nearly died on the same route that we followed coming out of the Kalahari between Lehututu and Tsabong. He was in his car with only one native boy when he found that all oil had leaked out. He filled up with his spare can, but in about two miles it had all gone again and the car stopped. He was then one hundred and twenty miles from Lehututu and fifty miles from Tsabong and had practically no water or provisions left. He started to walk in to Tsabong. The heat was terrific, he had only thin shoes on. The deep sand worked into his shoes and cut his feet to pieces, and he had a dose of fever and other things. He pushed on until he was all out — and then twenty miles from Tsabong collapsed under a tree, and sent the native on to Tsabong to bring help. A day and a night passed and no help. So he struggled on again. Halfway he found the spoor of the native going right away from the track out into the bush! He just managed to struggle into Tsabong, and get a search party to go out for the native and then collapsed for a week. The search party found the native in the bush alive but off his head. They brought him in and he recovered. It's no picnic wandering about in some parts of this Territory, and now I understand why people said N. and I were mad to go off on that Kalahari trip.

I had sent up a cattle dealer Reilly by name to explore a new route I want to open up for exporting cattle via Northern Rhodesia to the Congo, *not* through Southern Rhodesia. He reports the route to be magnificent, plenty of water and grazing — but he had the very devil of a time. He saw many lion and shot two, and also saw thousands of head of game. His car stuck in the mud during rain on the way back, and he had to walk miles to a native village and borrow oxen to pull it out. Then twenty miles from home it broke down altogether and he had to walk on — and so on.

I also sent Ellenberger to explore some choked-up rivers in Ngamiland with a view to seeing if we could clear them, and so let the water down to irrigate land further south. Hippo attacked his boats (steel) and knocked holes in both of them. They just got to shore in time to save the boats from loss, and themselves from crocodiles. It's an interesting country.

Sunday 13 December
I had to wander down to the Office with the last sheaf of notes on the Estimates and found Goodman (Financial Secretary) and a bevy of female typists putting the finishing touches to the great effort. My dispatch consists of eighty-one sections and covers twenty-eight foolscap pages! The Estimates themselves and the explanatory notes cover double as much. So the jolly old Colonial Office will have something to scratch their woolly heads over. The infernal thing went off at 4 pm by train mail — and so that's that.

Monday 14 to Wednesday 16 December
Chase has done very well at Salisbury, has held up our end of the stick, and gave way on nothing — we maintain the embargo on Southern Rhodesia into our Territory of course, and also through Northern Rhodesia. But on the other hand he has almost

completed the arrangements for our cattle to go from Tati on the hoof inside our Territory to Northern Rhodesia and the Congo through Kazungula.

Friday 18 to Sunday 20 December
On Saturday I had another stiff morning at the Office. When I had started packing quietly in the afternoon I got a cipher telegram and had to go down to Camp to open the safe and get the cipher book.

I proved to be a telegram from the Colonial Office to say that the 'Secretary of State proposed to put my name before the King for the Honour of a C.M.G.' and would I like it! So I had to send off an appropriate reply but no sooner had I got back home than Chase arrived with another telegram to say that thirty-six valuable cattle had broken across from Rhodesia into our Territory and that the owner, Haskins, begged they might not be shot, and what about it? I wired back two words: 'Shoot immediately'.

Christmas Day & 26-27 December (at Cape Town)
A pleasant three days loaf and basking in the sun, swimming, eating and sleeping. Also a jolly mail from home, seventy-six letters. We enjoyed it immensely. There was one sad bit of news — poor Gubbins has had a large part of his library destroyed by fire. He has spent the last twenty years out here collecting a wonderful lot of books, and he had given them to the Witwatersrand University at Jo'burg to form the nucleus of a library and literary work on South Africa subjects. About half the library had gone to Jo'burg, and the University caught fire and of course his library was amongst the parts burned.[55] Curiously enough he had shewn me in the library in his home a black streak along the wall where lightning had struck it, and had said that he didn't think it right to keep his books there lest they should be burned!

1932

Saturday 2 January
A heavy morning at the Office. Case and I interviewing the Imperial Cold Storage people until nearly 1 o'clock. They are a slippery lot of devils and tried to wriggle out of their obligation to buy ten thousand head of cattle from us by saying that there weren't enough! When I had proved that there were, and they had been forced to admit it themselves, they fell back on the argument that they couldn't get them at their price — which ridiculous argument of course cuts no ice. We have got to resume the fight again on Monday.

Sunday 3 to Tuesday 5 January
We had another stiff day on Monday at the Office arguing heatedly with the Imperial Cold Storage directors — finally they agreed to send representatives up into the Territory to buy (which I had told them to do from the beginning), if they could not arrange for the whole lot by telegram which I know they can't do.

Wednesday 6 to Sunday 10 January
On Wednesday and Thursday I spent the whole day in Cape Town with Stanley and our legal adviser Patrick Duncan going through the revised drafts of my two big Proclamations dealing respectively with the Powers of the Chiefs and the Jurisdiction of the Native Courts — it's my 'magnum opus' and I've been nearly a year at work on them. They have been put into legal shape by Patrick Duncan who has done it very well, and now I have got my last amendments put in. They are now going Home to the Colonial Office, and if they agree I am going to break them to the Native Chiefs at a special meeting in March, give them the months while I am at Home to argue about them with the Resident Magistrates, and then have a final meeting and get them passed into Law when I come back.

Monday 11 to Tuesday 12 January
Colonel Venning came round at 10 am. He is head of Posts and Railways in South West Africa, an early pioneer in this country and a most interesting man. He came to discuss with me various points relating to the Walvis Bay Railway scheme. (He was the S.W.A. delegate at the Pretoria Conference where we started the ball rolling).

He was anxious that we (the B.P.) should have a representative on the Walvis

Bay Harbour Board in order to have a voice in getting us a fair share of the cattle export from Walvis Bay up the coast to the French and other colonies; and also that we should have a corridor through South West Africa from our frontier at Sandfontein to railhead at Gobabis for export from Walvis Bay. He suggested I should start the ball rolling with Werth, the Administrator of South West Africa.

Wednesday 13 January
Last night or rather this morning at about 4.30 am we received the attentions of a burglar in our hotel room. We always sleep with our doors and windows open, and one of the doors is a French window leading on to the big *stoep* in front — we are on the first floor.

We were both asleep, but Ninon was woken up by a board creaking and thought I had got up. She looked round to see, and caught sight of a strange figure of a man with a soft hat on, walking in a crouching position across the room. She shouted out 'What are you doing?' That woke me, and as I woke I saw a man silhouetted against the skyline in the open doorway. I roared at him like a bull and jumped out of bed to get at him, slipped on a loose mat on the polished floor, came down the devil of a crash. Of course I was up in a moment and after him but when I got out on the *stoep* he was not to be seen.

The police and C.I.D. people came round in strength and took finger prints and statements from Ninon and me. It was all very amusing.

Friday 15 January
I had a splendid report on the water from the medicinal springs I discovered up at Kasane where I propose to start a Game Reserve and have a hotel built for visitors to see the Reserve and enjoy the tiger fishing in the Chobe and Zambesi Rivers.[1]

The analysts say the water is rich in medicinal properties and is similar to the old springs at Harrogate and in certain parts of Germany — another attraction.

Sunday 17 & Monday 18 January (back at Mafeking)
Reilly looked in and said he hoped I should not come down to the Office too early as they were not quite ready for me! He had written me a very amusing letter to Cape Town in which he said they all hoped I should come back very fit and well but not with any *more* energy.

Sunday 24 January
I also heard that that poisonous fellow Eales is not going to be made Imperial Secretary vice Clifford but is going to be sent to some Railway post in Rhodesia. I am very glad because it will make things easier for me, with both Clifford and Eales out of the way.

I further heard that after my row with Clifford, when I had told him a few home truths, he complained to the Colonial Office and it set him down good and hard. That was apparently why Clifford has been so amazingly polite to me — very amusing.

Monday 25 January
There is a most ghastly water shortage in this one-horse dorp owing to the poor rains, and I fear very much that there will not only be much suffering among natives, but possibly illness among Europeans, especially the poorer type.

The rules are that you can only water your garden twice a week for an hour! — a rule to which of course I pay no attention. We the B.P. Administration pay the municipality immense sums in rates, and for water and electricity, and spend thousands a year here — and I insist that they give us what we pay for — or we won't pay.

Tuesday 26 to Thursday 28 January
I went over the house previously occupied by Dutton, the Government Secretary I have just got rid of — as I am having it got ready for some new arrivals. It was in a shocking state, but the most amazing part of it was the garden. The man must have been raving mad as he had dug tunnels under the garden in every direction — one was twelve feet deep and then ran for twenty or thirty feet right out under the road! It was so big one could almost stand upright! Another had run under the wall of a neighbouring house and the wall had to be propped up at Government expense.

It must have taken the man years to dig all this out at night and bring out all the earth and deposit it outside. No wonder he was no use in the Office. I also gather now that in the hot weather he used to perch in the trees at night *in puris naturalibus* and study the stars. It was about time I fired him.

I am having all these excavations filled in and the place cleaned up, but really I think I might have made some money by letting people visit our catacombs at sixpence a time.

On Wednesday Captain Potts arrived from Serowe to stay with us — and on Thursday I had an all day meeting with that tiresome devil Tshekedi, Chief of the Bamangwato, who had no less than eight different problems for me — all of them annoying and some of them very important.[2] I had to read the Riot Act to him about two of them and gave him very definite and distinct orders which he didn't like but had to do. That young man ought to come to a bad end soon.

He started wrangling about the piece of land we are giving him in connection with mining — tried to refuse to hear a petition against himself by his own sister or to allow it to be heard — wanted to impose a compulsory levy of an ox per head on a whole tribe he doesn't like.

Monday 1 February
Frightfully hot again, and everybody rather slack. I had a long interview with Bathoen, Chief of the Bangwaketse who had put forward rather an impudent demand for more land as a bribe to allow mining in his Reserve! Not a hope — was heavily defeated and went away with his tail between his legs.

Tuesday 2 to Sunday 7 February
On Wednesday I sent off a record mail to the Colonial Office. Fifteen dispatches covering sixteen foolscap sheets of typing — they *will* swear! But if only they'd get on with what I tell them to do and not worry me, I'd leave them alone.

Captain Cash came in in the morning to consult me about a matter I am sending him up to enquire into, on the frontier. One of the native Chiefs has reported that one of my white sergeants of police was drunk on duty, arrested a man, and kept him twenty nine days without trial! I don't believe it but must have an enquiry — as our police must be above suspicion.

Monday 8 to Sunday 14 February
I have balanced my budget by the most horrible expedients — cutting down expenditure ruthlessly; increasing European poll-tax by fifty per cent — from £2 to

£3; putting three shillings on to native hut-tax; an export tax of two shillings and six pence per head of cattle; many other details, *and* cutting ten per cent off all salaries! What might be called a really popular budget! But I'm getting £8,000 (I hope) from my new issue of stamps, and £6,000 from a tax on railway tickets. Now I know what it feels like to be a Chancellor of the Exchequer — as I think I've said before.

The European Advisory Council sat all day on Wednesday, and my opening speech lasted nearly an hour. I'm bound to say it was very well received, and then they retired to consider it and pick holes in it.

Thursday was a triumph. They came back and with the exception of a few small points practically agreed with all my proposals, and made most flattering speeches. So I rushed the whole agenda through, and got finished by 6 o'clock — an absolutely record performance.

On Friday I had a series of interviews on various points with individual members, and then told them of my new scheme to cooperate with Southern Rhodesia — to get a cattle export route fixed up from Southern Rhodesia right across the Protectorate to South West Africa and Walvis Bay (for Protectorate and Southern Rhodesia cattle jointly), and a joint attack on the Colonial Development Fund for a grant to sink boreholes right across the route, and so not only establish the route but also create an Empire meat trade by shipping to England from Walvis Bay.

The Southern Rhodesia Government are frightfully keen, and will cooperate wholeheartedly with us. Needless to say my Parliament are truly pessimistic. One member observed that if only I had come out here twenty years ago, we should now be on velvet.

Monday 15 to Sunday 21 February
A stiff day on Monday morning and on Tuesday preparing for Wednesday's meeting at Francistown which threatens to be a very troublesome one. They have invited — almost challenged — me to go up and meet the public at a public meeting where they will air their grievances (very real ones) and abuse the Government, I sympathise with them (I am generally agin' the Government myself!) for they are having an awful time owing to this Foot and Mouth disease embargo, and are suffering real hardship not being able to sell their cattle and produce and export them. But we have done all we can; we cannot go to war with the Union of South Africa, much as I should like to — as I've only got three hundred men in my army!

Then at 10.30 on Wednesday we met the Tati farmers and settlers — they let off steam pretty hard, and being mostly Scotchmen — hit in their most tender place, their pockets — they spoke with feeling. I spoke in answer for over an hour, told them what we had been doing, what we were doing, what we hoped to achieve — reminded them of the Butter Factory I was putting up, the new cattle route to Kazungula I had opened by which over a thousand head of cattle were on their way north — told them the new Mining Law would be out very soon now, and ended up with a purple patch of oratory!

There was one interruption only and I had to tell the man not to talk damned nonsense, to sit down or get out.

The meeting gave me a great reception, much cheering and then the Rhodesia Creamery people told them all about the new factory, and the generous terms they were offering them to come in as cooperative shareholders, etc.

The Union Government have suggested a conference at Cape Town between themselves, ourselves, Basutoland and Swaziland to settle outstanding differences. I am entirely opposed to this as we have no big stick to beat them with. So that means a mighty dispatch and a ten-page memorandum of argument. My shorthand writers earn their pay!

Monday 22 to Sunday 28 February (to Tiger Kloof)
Tiger Kloof is the great native industrial training centre near Vryburg (Cape Province) run by the London Missionary Society, the principal being the Rev A.J. Haile, a very good fellow. It's a marvellous place, where they have five hundred natives in training — carpentering, cabinet-making, bricklaying, masonry, building, spinning and weaving, tanning, and leather work, furniture making, boots and clothes making, rugs, carpets, table and bed linen, etc. We slept in the 'guest rooms', a series of excellent bedrooms in a separate and well-built house — lots of hot and cold water in the bathroom!

I was the first Resident Commissioner who had ever addressed them, and only the second who had even been there.

There are over fifty boys and girls from the Protectorate there, and they *are* fortunate to live in such a place when compared with their own filthy hovels. They even have a most excellent water-borne sewage system, and of course admirable washing arrangements.

Afterwards, I visited cattle kraals, and then the native teachers came in to tea, and I had a few words with each.

Monday 29 February to Sunday 6 March
Bad reports from everywhere about crops; these recent rains seem to have come too late. We had good early rains in October and November — then bad drought in December and January and the sun burnt up all the young grass and crops. Our only hope is if the rains now go on through March we may get a second crop which may save the position.

Then I got a damfool telegram from Stanley about my Butter Factory scheme — that dog Eales has been instilling poison into his ear about it. I believe, and he's afraid now. But it's going through.

On Thursday I got telegrams finally agreeing to my Butter Factory in Francistown, and to another scheme of mine for clearing the grass away in three rivers in Ngamiland so as to let the flood waters of the Zambesi[3] come right down to Tsau and irrigate the dry lands there — a great scheme that I have been fighting for for ever so long.

On Sunday 6 March
Chase went off for the conference at Salisbury with the Southern Rhodesia Govt. for a great joint scheme — a cattle route from Rhodesia right across the Protectorate through South West Africa to Walvis Bay — it means a joint application to the Colonial Development Committee for a grant to sink bore-holes and wells right across. It will be a great scheme.

Chase will also I hope sign the agreement with the Rhodesia Creamery people at Bulawayo, en route, for the Factory.

Thursday 10 to Sunday 13 March
Our exhibit at the British Industries Fair in London has been a huge success. The Queen was immensely interested and was photographed at our Pavilion: we have

sold the whole exhibit, lock stock and barrel; taken large numbers of orders; established agencies for our products; and generally put the Bechuanaland Protectorate on the map. The Queen admired one of our karosses very much made by natives of six hundred tails of the *tsipa* cat, so we telegraphed asking if Her Majesty would accept it as a gift from the administration, and the Queen said she would.[4]

Some triumph. And in 1929 my predecessor wrote an official dispatch to say that the B.P. could not possibly send an exhibit to London and that it would be many years before it could even think of it!

Monday 14 March
Strange to say a good day: in spite of it's being Monday. I heard that the 1,062 cattle sent up by my new route to Kazungula for Northern Rhodesia and the Congo Belge have arrived in better condition than when they started; and that only two were lost en route. This is another great success — it means at least £4,000 coming into the Territory. Then Stanley had had the bad taste to disagree with one of my dispatches to the Colonial Office, and they have agreed with me and overruled him. *Mon Dieu.*

Then Amery,[5] late Colonial Secretary, has written to me that he wants me to address a joint meeting of the Royal Empire Society and the African Society in London about the B.P., and that Lord-Buxton[6] is very keen on it — also he wants me to address the Compatriots Club, a dinner club composed of members of the House of Lords and House of Commons on the subject of the B.P. And the Royal Geographical Society also want a lecture. So it doesn't look like being much of a holiday.

On Tuesday 15 March
I signed the Rhodesian Creamery Factory agreement so that is now all over, bar the shouting, and erection of the buildings will start at once: £4,000 worth of machinery is being ordered from England by telegram.

Wednesday 16 March
Our silver wedding day — 25th anniversary of the best day's work I ever did in my life. We celebrated the occasion by motoring over to Ottoshoep to Gubbins' place: he and family are still at Johannesburg, but his secretary, Bertram, did the honours and gave us an excellent lunch.

Sunday 20 March
Off to Johannesburg for the Rand Easter Show.

Monday 21 March (at Johannesburg)
After dealing with a fresh lot of telegrams, letters, callers, and telephone calls we got off to the Showground soon after 9 and went straight to our Exhibit. It was simply wonderful — far better even than last year. We had got much more space and England had broken it up into bays; in each bay was a different class of exhibit, native on one side, European on the other. Among the skins and karosses were stuffed animals of the type from which the skins came; curios of all kinds, carved wooden toys; purses, bags, belts, tobacco pouches and watch bracelets made of python skin; native head dresses; pottery, stone and basketwork galore; two native women making baskets, and a man carving wooden toys; clothing made at the schools; a huge ostrich (stuffed) sitting on its eggs; cheese, butter and

1932

eggs; poultry and game; whole antelope and buck kept in cold storage, half a huge shorthorn ox hanging up: minerals; stamps, wood and timber, blackmiths' work, and hundreds of enlarged photographs etc., etc., etc. It was a really wonderful show, and everyone was wildly excited about it — they said it was the finest thing that has ever been done here.

At 10.30 we dashed off by car to the flying ground to meet Stuart. He had flown over from the Protectorate with a consignment of 'perishables', the first time that exhibits had ever been brought to the Show by air.

He brought with him some *live* fish caught in the Crocodile River, game shot the night before, vegetables, fruit and flowers. The fish and flowers are going to be frozen into blocks of ice and exhibited on our stalls.

The head of the flying place, Captain Douglas, was a very keen and enthusiastic man and we then and there evolved a scheme for flying services into the Protectorate — I shall have to get flying grounds made, and he will provide the service — I have undertaken to rope in the Chiefs to help in making the grounds. It ought to be a great thing if we can bring it off.

Tuesday 22 March
I gave an interview to a representative of the *Rand Daily Mail*, then off again to the Rand Club where Gemmill had arranged a lunch for me to meet about a dozen of the principal mining people, including Sir Ernest Oppenheimer,[7] Sir George Albu,[8] Sir William Dalrymple,[9] Martin[10] (the Chairman), etc. A most interesting meal, which gave me the opportunity of speaking about the new Mining Law, and the general development of the Protectorate.

Then back to the Show for a little business — and by 4.30 I was at the station to meet Sir Herbert and Lady Stanley and Captain Holbech who arrived by train from Cape Town to open the Show officially tomorrow morning. I was able to tell them that we had got First Prize again, £100 and the special silver Challenge Cup! Indeed all Johannesburg is talking about our Exhibit, and they say it *is* the Show.

Wednesday 23 March
At the hotel I found six people waiting to see me, including the stamps man, and the representatives of the Aircraft Operating Company who want to do an aerial survey of the B.P. They have developed the art of aerial photography to such a point that the photos now reveal the *nature of the soil*, i.e. whether fertile or not, whether suited for cattle or crops etc. etc.

(By the way I quite forgot to mention that Tshekedi had signed the agreement for Mining with the Chartered Company on Tuesday, and I had told Oppenheimer so — he was fearfully excited and I think that things will now move.)

Monday 28 March (back at Mafeking)
Hope returned from the frontier cordon for a month's rest. He had done extraordinarily good work in stopping Foot and Mouth disease and is quite convinced now that the position is safe!

He told me incidentally that the northern Bamangwato are furious with Tshekedi for having delayed the signature of the Mining Concession for so long! That is most amusing and interesting, as I always maintained that the natives really wanted it, and the wise fools at Home thought they know better and were terrified of my pushing it through — as I have done.

Hope also told me that the South African Government sent a native spy through

1932

to our veterinary cordon to see what we were doing — our native police got him and — needless to say without orders — dealt with him so faithfully that he was just able to crawl away.

Tuesday 29 March
A really hectic morning getting my speech ready for the Native Advisory Council tomorrow. I fear it will be a very difficult meeting as I have to announce an increase of three shillings in the native hut-tax, but I believe I can carry it without trouble, at least without real trouble.

Wednesday 30 March
Ninon and I drove down in state to the Native Advisory Council meeting on the Imperial Reserve (Mafeking). The Chiefs had all arrived the night before, and held a preliminary meeting among themselves, and were all gathered in the marquee to greet me. The guard presented arms, I inspected them, and then in we went and I let off my speech. It went down very well, and then one after another the Chiefs got up and — while pointing out how bad the times were and how difficult it was to pay tax, — not one opposed the increase! It was a great personal triumph for me as it demonstrated their confidence in my administration, and everybody was most terribly pleased. In the afternoon we went on with the meeting and disposed of the rest of the Agenda, thus finishing off the meeting in one day, a record.[11]

Then came the *revers de la medaille*. A telegram came in from the Northern Rhodesian Government to say that lung-sickness (the most dreaded of all the diseases except rinderpest) had broken out in the Caprivi Strip — that is the long narrow strip of land that runs between Barotseland (part of Northern Rhodesia) and our northern boundary. They have always had the disease in Barotseland and apparently it had crossed the river into the Strip. I telegraphed to Livingstone asking them to send out a runner to Kasane with my orders — which were to establish a guard along the river (the Chobe River very broad and deep, runs between us and the Strip), to shoot at sight any cattle or other animal that crossed, and to keep up a regular system of patrols.

The next trouble was with my accursed old friend Gobbleman who has been making himself an infernal nuisance to the Bangwaketse Tribe again — and the Chief Bathoen now wants me to turn him out of the country. However I've got another plan and am trying to induce Molefi, Chief of the Bakgatla at Mochudi, to take him in and keep an eye on him — as he belongs to that Tribe really, tho' settled among the Bangwaketse.[12]

The third trouble was about the Pathfinders. Cuzen came along with a yarn that the Pathfinders' rules made it obligatory for them to study and carry the damned South African flag as well as the Union Jack! Of course all my people were up in arms at once, and rightly so. We won't have that filthy 'Union Joke' anywhere in our territory. So that had to be argued out in preparation for our meetings tomorrow about Pathfinders and Wayfarers which Ninon and I are both going to take.

And finally and worst of all, I fear Pongo is very ill indeed.

Thursday 31 March
Mrs Rheinhallt Jones was able to dispel our fears by producing new and revised regulations which did away with all questions of the filthy Union flag and so dispelled all difficulties on that score.

At 2.30 I had a meeting of the Pathfinders' Council — and at 3.30 we all went out to the tent and met all the Chiefs again when Mrs Rheinhallt Jones explained the objects of the two movements in an excellent speech. The Chiefs took it very well, all seemed very enthusiastic and promised to support both movements wholeheartedly in their Reserves.

Friday 1 April
I had the representatives of the Batawana Tribe in and gave them an awful dressing down on account of the misbehaviour of their Chief and council and generally. I told them they were the worst Tribe in the Protectorate, that they were thieves and loafers, that they had stolen hut-tax money, did no work, did not carry out the orders of Chief or Government, and that I was sick of them. I said I would give them six months to reform and that then, if they had not mended their ways, I should have to depose their Chief and establish a new form of rule.

They received my abusive remarks in a very penitent manner, thanked me (!) and swore they would be good boys! Of course they won't and the first thing I shall have to do when I come back from leave will be to put in a new Chief.

Then I spent a good time with Pongo — he seems a little better.

Saturday 2 April
Pongo died.

Sunday 10 to Tuesday 12 April
Our last three days in South Africa for some time. Sunday morning we finished off our packing and at 4 pm rather weary, we steamed out of the station.

The entire staff turned up to say goodbye, male and female, all were there.

On Leave in London

I am afraid I kept no diary and very few notes when in England.

My lecture at the Royal Geographical Society went off very well, and everybody congratulated me and was very nice. I showed about a hundred slides that the Royal Geographical Society had prepared very well from my photos, was invited to dine at the Geographical Club first — met Vernay there of the Vernay-Laing Expedition.

On Tuesday 21 June
I had to go to Buckingham Palace for the C.M.G. investiture — another magnificent show — the uniforms were simply grand — the King was again very well and cheerful and shook hands cordially. The arrangements were beautifully carried out — we were marshalled in groups, received detailed instructions what to do — went in in single file — marched singly to the middle of the room opposite the King — walked up to him — he put the order round my neck, and shook hands — then I went out, a man took off the order, put it in a box and handed it to me — then off I went to face a battery of photographers outside the Palace.

At the dinner of the (Royal) African Society at the Dorchester Hotel Sir P. Cunliffe Lister[13] was the guest of the evening, and made a rotten speech — really bad. He blethered about receiving natives properly in this country and told silly stories about Africa that every child knows — and this to a roomful of people who have spent their lives in Africa!

We had a talk with Cunliffe Lister — he was very nice but displayed dreadful ignorance — he didn't know that the B.P. was not in the Union! And that for the Colonial Minister!

But of course the greater part of my time was taken up at the Dominions Office where I saw *everybody* about every conceivable subject. They were all very pleasant and helpful, and most complimentary about what I had done, which was satisfactory but it took up the devil of a lot of time. However I got through many things and in addition saw various people about the disposal of our furs and other produce and laid the foundations (I hope) for financing the Walvis Bay Railway, as well as the cattle route scheme.

I lunched with Tomlinson of the Colonial Office on 1 September, a very able and pleasant person in charge of the 'Personnel' Branch. He was very helpful; had Sir Alan Pim[14] to lunch with me at the Junior Carlton Club on 5 September — he is coming out to report on the finances of the B.P.

We had a demonstration of a very admirable portable wireless at our rooms this evening after dinner — the 'Eldeco' — and decided to buy one to take out with us (£25).

I met the directors of the Tati Co. at their offices on the afternoon of the 14th and had an interesting talk with the Chairman — the other directors are dull old dogs, dead from the neck upwards. In the evening we went to our last theatre, *The Cat and the Fiddle*, and on Friday 16th we sailed for South Africa again. Quite a party to see us off at the station, where we also saw Moffat the Prime Minister of Southern Rhodesia, and Downie the Southern Rhodesian High Commissioner — they had come to see off the South African delegates back from Ottawa on their way to South Africa. They were very cordial.

Back to Mafeking

Friday 16 September to Sunday 2 October
Like a good many of our trips we started by quarrelling vigorously with the ship's officials, and our dog Orlando was the cause of the first upheaval.

The captain has made himself most amiable, and so (unfortunately) have other people on board — we know too many of them plus their beastly females. However we have a lovely corner on the very top deck where we hide and read and write — and Orlando comes up morning and afternoon and plays about. So we are really very happy and comfortable.

I had a long talk with Stokes, Moffat's secretary, and am trying to induce him to persuade Moffat to put the Walvis Bay Railway scheme in his election programme — the general election in Southern Rhodesia comes off at the end of this year, and it would be a great stunt. Stokes is much tickled with the idea, and it would be great if Moffat would do it. If only I can get this Railway thro' it will be a small edition of Rhodes' Cape to Cairo Railway scheme — and it would be *mine*.

Thank goodness the beastly sports are finished — the prizes were given away last night — and peace reigns today. Tomorrow everybody packs and we arrive on Monday at 8 am.

And then we shall no longer see the aristocrat who sits at the table opposite to us with his three diamond shirt-studs, and his two huge diamond rings, one on each hand.

1932

Monday 3 to Tuesday 4 October
We ran into Table Bay at about 6.30, a beautiful sunny morning, and before 7 we were being bombarded with messages and callers. I had to have my final row with the Union Castle people about Orlando and got away without paying anything — letters and telegrams of welcome came pouring in.

Soon after 8, Captain Reilly and Mr Chase came on board to greet us. The Government Veterinary Surgeon arrived to inspect Orlando! The Immigration people made fools of themselves, and generally life was fairly hectic.

The train journey to Mafeking was quite uneventful and very comfortable. Reilly and Chase gave me all the news, and we talked business most of the way — and pretty bad most of the news was.

We ran into Mafeking punctually five to 5 on Tuesday afternoon, and there *was* a gathering! The whole staff and their wives, and they all seemed really pleased to see us, it was really wonderful — quite affecting. Our trusty police collected our things — the faithful Marzipan [Matsepane] had got 'Topsy' looking as tho' she had just left the makers, and off we went to the house. Here a guard of honour was posted and presented arms very smartly, fixed bayonets etc. complete and after inspecting them we wandered into the house and garden.

And so we are back again, and it's really rather jolly, and there's lots to do, and Ninon is ever so much better — so all promises well.

Wednesday 5 October (at Mafeking)
My office looks very nice — it has been done up, and round the walls are the photographs of all previous Resident Commissioners, from Dr Jameson onwards, our exhibits at Johannesburg and in London, our prize cups, etc.

I found rather a melancholy state of affairs. Firstly there has been a bad — a horrible — scandal at Kanye. At about 5 am one morning the police observed the offices to be on fire — they tried to put it out and the interpreter went to awaken the one white clerk in charge of the station. (Cuzen, the Resident Magistrate, had been transferred to Ngamiland and his successor, Ellenberger, was to arrive on the next day). The clerk Langton was found on his bed tied by his hands and feet to the bedposts. The offices meanwhile were burned to the ground including the safe with £300 in it and all books, accounts, receipts, stamps, etc.

Then investigations began, and things began to look ugly. Langton had been tied up loosely with office string which a child could have bitten through. There were no marks on his wrists or ankles such as must have been caused by the string if he had made the slightest effort to free himself. He said he had been beaten by his assailants as he lay on his face, but the marks of beating were in a convenient place which could have caused him no real hurt. He claimed to have shouted for help, but the police in huts thirty yards away had heard nothing.

Then police dogs were brought in and they went for a native, Langton's servant. He was so terrified that he gave the whole thing away — confessed that he had carried petrol into the offices by Langton's orders, had sprinkled it over the papers hung on the walls and on papers in the safe — also that he had had criminal relations with Langton, etc. etc.

So Langton and the boy were both arrested, and are both now in gaol. They will be charged with falsification of records, theft, arson and other crimes too beastly to mention — a foul and loathsome case — the first thing I had to deal with.[15]

Then there have been several deaths — one a very sad one, a most promising young officer of mine, Gray, stationed in Ngamiland. Gray, Hyde and Dr Gerber went out to shoot lion near Maun (where we were). They saw one and fired, wounding it. They followed it into the bush, and it sprang on Hyde and knocked him down — Gray (whose rifle was empty) attracted the lion, hitting it on the head with the butt-end of his rifle, and then getting hold of its tail tried to pull it off Hyde! Gerberhen came up and killed the lion — they patched up Hyde and somehow got him back to camp. Hyde died of his wounds, Gray went off his head and died, and Gerber has gone all to pieces with nerves — a bad business.

Commander Combe who was out shooting near there and got mauled by a lion some time ago has had a relapse and is in a bad way. He had got five lion, but the sixth got him and he has had to have his leg amputated. He is pretty bad.

Influenza has played Old Harry here too and we've lost a lot of people, mercifully none of our staff. But Dr Henderson at Lobatsi seems to have gone to pieces; his *locum tenens* nearly died of pneumonia. Mrs Ledeboer has to have a dangerous operation next Monday — and appendixes seem to have been pulled out by the half-dozen.

It's really a chapter of tragedies. Generally speaking things are not going too well — people seem to be down-hearted, there seems to have been nothing but trouble everywhere, both with natives and Europeans — I see that I've got all my work cut out to restore the morale and swing these people into line again.

Saturday 8 October (at Lobatsi)
We had a very pleasant drive into Lobatsi. After lunch I had long talks with Ledeboer, the Resident Magistrate here, and with Ellenberger, the R.M. from Kanye. Trouble everywhere. Old Gobbleman the head of the Bakgatla at Moshupa and Bathoen the Chief of that district have been at loggerheads — refusal to pay hut tax led to Bathoen sending a party of forty men to get it. There was trouble, then fighting, the forty thieves were chased away. So I've had to take what they call 'strong action' and read the Riot Act to both. I hope that Ellenberger will carry out my instructions properly, but he's damnably weak.

Then the Lobatsi farmers have been passing idiotic resolutions about what they are going to say to the Economic Commission that is coming out, and that fool Ledeboer was not present at the meeting and does not even know exactly what passed. He is infernally lazy, and if his wife were not going to have a severe and dangerous operation I should have given him a terrible dressing down. However that will come later.

Dr Henderson, in charge of the hospital here, is far from well — he has not recovered from his nervous breakdown, and the rupture of his engagement — so the work of the hospital is suffering.

On the other hand my scheme for building the hospital extensions entirely by skilled and unskilled native labour is succeeding admirably. The work is excellently done, it is going to cost less than the estimate — and not a single man has been dismissed during the job. It's rather a triumph and my natives are delighted — they are not allowed to do skilled work in the Union!

Sunday 16 October
We went off to Pretoria in 'Topsy'.

Monday 17 & Tuesday 18 October (at Pretoria)
Monday was a very strenuous day. I had a dozen matters of first class importance, and many others, to discuss with Stanley as a result of my visit to England — and they are all so damned slow at the uptake out here.

Then I had the most extraordinarily interesting and important interview with

Colonel Williams, the head of the Department of Agriculture. It all arose out of the Ottawa Conference.[16] A huge scheme for exporting meat from there to England (instead of Argentine meat), pooling our resources — the Union, Southern Rhodesia, South West Africa, Bechuanaland Protectorate, Swaziland, and Basutoland. It should be a wonderful effort, and there is to be a big Conference next month between all the States concerned to discuss it, and work out details. More work! Dumbrell (our Inspector of Education) looked in, and I had a talk with him — I am not very pleased about some of the educational developments and I shall have to look into them.

Captain Holbech, the A.D.C., is very bad — arthritis — we're terribly sorry as he is such a nice fellow. I fear he is not getting on too well with Sir Herbert Stanley which is a pity. Herbert Stanley is ageing — he needs a holiday — and his mind is not as alert as it was. He's too fat, and of course that cursed fellow Eales is a ghastly influence to have about.

Mrs Rheinallt Jones came in to see Ninon in the morning about Wayfarers — she's being a bit of a nuisance I fear and I shall have to stamp on her enormous body. Ninon motored her over to Jo'burg to lunch with Mrs Patrick Duncan who is the head of the whole thing in South Africa. Patrick Duncan is an eminent King's Counsel, official legal adviser to the H.C. He was on Lord Milner's[17] staff and has great administrative experience — able but dull — too fat.

Wednesday 26 October
I had an interview with Bathoen, Chief of the Bangwaketse who has been misbehaving, and I twisted his tail good and hard — he's a nasty piece of work. His people had had the infernal cheek to stop a European driving a lorry laden with the Magistrate's goods, and fine the driver ten shillings for coming into their country without a permit! I made him write a letter of apology and generally gave him hell for that and other things!

Friday 28 October (at Mafeking)
An alarming telegram came in from Captain Potts from Serowe — a Pretender to the Bamangwato Chieftainship has arisen — an illegitimate son of the late Chief by his legal wife's sister.[18] And Potts wants police sent up and wants to arrest him and generally everyone up there is very excited.

Tuesday 1 November
The first member of the Economic Commission arrived today — Lee,[19] the representative of the Dominions Office who also will act as Secretary to the Commission. He is exceedingly able and shrewd, but a shocking little bounder. However he is obviously out to make himself pleasant, and I have impressed on everyone the necessity for giving him every assistance and a good reception.

Monday 7 to Thursday 10 November
A terrific four days with the Economic Commission. Sir Alan Pim and Mr Milligan[20] arrived at 7.15 am, and their train being twenty minutes ahead of time they got to the house before I was ready. Alan Pim is rather a dried up stick, the other man quite a cheery soul. Pim represents the Treasury, Lee the Dominions Office, and Milligan is the economic expert.

Of course we spent all four days down at the Camp and I shewed them the whole organisation, introduced everybody, gave them masses of reports, papers, memoranda, statistics etc. and handed over my room for their use. They interviewed lots of people, asked innumerable questions, and eventually paid me the compliment of saying that I knew more about the working of each individual department than the heads of the departments. Which incidentally I knew already.

I have planned a great six weeks tour for them — every detail worked out for every hour of every day, and I should think they would be jolly tired at the end of it.

Our white servants arrived on Tuesday evening but of course we couldn't let them come here while the house was full, so they had to go to a boarding house until Friday.

Friday 11 to Wednesday 16 November
On Friday Pim and party (called Pimbo for short) left at 9 am, thank God, and left me with four days arrears of work to make up.

Being Armistice Day we had a ceremony at the Cenotaph, laid a wreath and mounted a guard of honour of the B.P. Police. They were frightfully smart and immensely admired, a wonderful contrast to the slovenly South African Police who (both European and native) looked like nothing on earth, and almost fell over each other when ordered to right turn — a rotten crowd.

Our new white servants came in, and I should think the sooner they go out again the better — they seem to be useless.

Afterwards we spent the day in 'Topsy' on the veld, writing: the last bit of comparative ease I was to have before the worst and most strenuous six weeks since I have been in South Africa.

Things get more and more hectic, more and more difficult. I really think that we shall have to call a halt for we cannot go on at this pace much longer. Much depends on the result of Pimbo's efforts.

Thursday 17 November
A great invasion. All the Chiefs and their followers, over forty of them, arrived for the Native Advisory Council. Some of the Resident Magistrates arrived too. Captain Neale and Captain Potts are staying with us. It's going to be a terrifically important meeting as I am to launch my two new Proclamations to limit the powers of the Chiefs, and to set up Native Courts of Justice — the greatest step forward in native development in the last forty years here. There will be terrific opposition from the Chiefs[21] and I've got to fight the fight alone as Sir Herbert Stanley and the Dominions Office are both frightened to death of what may happen. It's taken me two and a half years of hard work — and now it's going to be put to the test. If they go through, it's the biggest thing of my career — if they fail, then I go down with a bump. But they *shall* go through.

I issued copies of the Proclamations to the Chiefs, and told them to spend the day reading them, and that I would explain them fully at the official meeting tomorrow.

Meanwhile I went on with a meeting of Resident Magistrates where a very nasty incident occurred. For some reason I cannot fathom Ledeboer was first of all most obstructive and then downright rude — so I had to give him hell at the meeting — and after lunch I saw him alone and simply wiped the floor with him. Result — amazing. He apologized profusely and at the afternoon meeting butter wouldn't melt in his mouth, and he was most helpful and pleasant!

Then the first blow was struck by the Chiefs. They sent in a deputation of two of their members to see me to say that these Proclamations were very drastic, that they wanted a long time to consider them, and would I postpone further action for a year! To which I replied 'certainly not', that I would explain them fully tomorrow and tell them exactly what I proposed to do.

Friday 18 November
A great day. N. and I drove down 'in state' to Camp to the opening of the Native Advisory Council and were received by the guard of honour. N. presented the 'swagger-stick' to the most efficient trooper in the last training course, and then we got to business. My opening speech on general matters lasted nearly an hour, and my explanatory speech on the two Proclamations over two hours — so I was speaking for about three hours — a bit of a strain, especially as it was infernally hot in the big marquee I had had erected.

Ellenberger, the Acting R.M. at Kanye, and his wife lunched with us, and afterwards we resumed. There was little opposition from the Chiefs at this stage — except of course Tshekedi, who made a rambling speech to say that this was not the time for these Proclamations, they ought to have been enacted forty years ago![22] I replied that because they had been wandering in the Wilderness for forty years was no reason for wandering for another forty years — rather should they regard themselves now as within sight of the Promised Land! I also told them that Magistrates would explain the Proclamations to the people in each district, and that when they were better understood I would meet the people in Kgotla in the bigger centres and deal with any difficulties and consider any suggestions; and that I would not rush the matter, but that they should have plenty of time to digest the new Proclamations before they became law. (*In my own mind* I give them until June — then finish).

It went down better than I expected, but of course the real opposition is to come. Later on I had private talks with various people, and got quite favourable reports. All the more enlightened natives are enthusiastic and say it marks a turning point in the history of the Bechuana — the opposition will come from the Chiefs and reactionary old men, and those whom they may influence or intimidate.

Sunday 20 to Tuesday 22 November (to Pretoria)
A lovely run to Pretoria and wonderful to say — cool. We got off at 8 and got in at 6.15 — including a two hours break for lunch and rest on the veld, and half an hour at Rustenburg for tea and petrol. We are staying at High Commission House, as are also Sturrock and Dixon, the Resident Commissioners of Basutoland and Swaziland. I don't like either of them — Sturrock is an ass, though a gentleman and pleasant enough, and Dixon I don't trust. He is not stupid but a bit of a sycophant. Also I should not be surprised if he had a drop of coloured blood somewhere back. The Stanleys were very nice and we had quite a pleasant evening, but Herbert Stanley does nothing but grouse.

On Monday we started our Conference — a rotten waste of time, the subjects don't interest me — foolishness started by the damn body of male and female old women the League of Nations, and passed on by the Dominions Office. My object is to block everything and I'm doing it quite successfully so far.

Hertzog has made a foolish speech about the conditions on which Southern Rhodesia could come into the Union, and as a result has killed the idea for many a long day — a good thing. We don't want to increase the Union but to smash it.

Hertzog would insist on bilingualism for Southern Rhodesia. The idea is too funny for words.

Monday 28 & Tuesday 29 November
A hell of a dog-fight! But quite a victory after all. We all met at 10 at the Union Government Buildings — and we *were* up against it.

The Union Government paraded all their big guns and experts and at the word 'go' went off full pelt with long speeches about the Ottawa Conference, and what a chance it was for South Africa *as a whole* to get chilled (not frozen) beef on the English market, and how we must all cooperate and all do the same thing etc.

The point is that England has agreed to reduce the imports of chilled beef from the Argentine so as to let in South Africa as a whole — not only the Union but all of us — and so the Union Government has *got* to bring us in — but they wouldn't if they could avoid it.

Then after all the 'pretty-pretty' speeches came the cloven hoof. They wanted us all to agree on conditions which would have made it *practically* impossible (tho' *theoretically* feasible) for us and Southern Rhodesia and the other Protectorates to export! That was the moment for C.F.R. to hurl himself into the fray, and he did so — good and hard. And except for Bagshawe of South West Africa the others just sat back and watched the fight — and left me (as I had feared) to carry on. However that didn't trouble me, and by about 5.30 we had reached a fairly satisfactory agreement on the main points.

But when we met at 10 am on Tuesday, the damned Union delegates went back on it and tried to pretend they hadn't agreed! So the fight started again; but we reached agreement by lunch time on lines satisfactory to us, and wound up the Conference in a blaze of beautiful and wholly insincere speeches which pleased everybody and deceived nobody.

Then we all lunched at the Pretoria Club with that arch villain General Kemp, the Minister of Agriculture — a very good lunch incidentally though much too ample and too long. Then we adjourned to Polley's and resumed the negotiations about the Walvis Bay Stock Route, and after several hours came to a comfortable complete agreement — a huge success. So now we can go ahead on that basis at last and apply formally to the Colonial Development Fund for the grant. And I was tired.

Wednesday 30 November to Monday 5 December (at Mafeking)
There is trouble at Mochudi where the Chief Molefi wants to resign the Chieftainship which would mean the devil of a row. I had letters from Reyneke and the Magistrate to say the position was very serious, so I telegraphed I was coming up. Really these people are very trying.

Tuesday 6 December (to Mochudi)
I went off alone this time as it's going to be the very devil of a rush. Started by the 9 am train, arrived Pilane at 2, picking up Neale (the R.M. at Gaberones) at 1, and lunching with him on the train. At Pilane Reyneke and Rutherford met us and motored us to Mochudi (five miles) and then the fun started. Molefi was as sulky as a bear. He says his uncle Isang, who was Regent during Molefi's minority, has robbed him of all his inheritance; that the tribe doesn't make him any allowance; that he has no money; that he is sick of it all, and is going to resign and get a paid job of work somewhere else! Now that would be a catastrophe for the next heir is

Molefi's younger brother aged eighteen now at school at Tiger Kloof, and if he came in there would be chaos as he couldn't manage the Bakgatla — who are the most warlike tribe in B.P. and who wouldn't have Isang back as Regent, as they hate him for his strictness when Regent. He made a splendid Chief, the best we ever had and brought the Bakgatla to their present state of high development.

Well, I went into the whole question in a series of interviews, arranged for the tribe to have a big meeting about it all in a week or ten days, which I said I would come up to address, and told Molefi not to talk any more damn nonsense about throwing in his hand.

Wednesday 7 December (at Francistown)
Arrived Francistown 6 am and proceeded to the Gordons: he is the General Manager of the Tati Company. After bath and breakfast we plunged into the Tati troubles. Against my views the High Commissioner issued a damn fool Proclamation making it a penal Offence to pay natives in anything but the new legal tender. Now the new legal tender is this damned South African currency. Tati have never used it. Being so near Southern Rhodesia they do all their business, trading, and banking in Southern Rhodesia and English money (which is all on a Sterling basis of course). To force them off this on to gold *without any warning* simply means general stoppage of all the industries I have been fostering there — mining, dairying, cheese-making etc. and ruination to the districts. They *sell* all their produce north — i.e. in the Rhodesias on a sterling basis; and if they have to make all their *payments* on a gold basis it means paying £1 for an article and selling it for fifteen shillings! Hardly a business proposition.

So I sat down and wrote out a terrific telegram pointing out that the Proclamation must be cancelled (it was only issued ten days ago!).

At 12 noon the Dairy Factory was fully opened, the Chairman of the Company made a speech, and then I had to hold forth — after which they presented me with a gold key. We went in and inspected the place — it's top hole. The latest and most modern machinery and plant, and up to date in every way — all the stuff is *English*. They turned out 250,000 pounds of butter at their Bulawayo Factory from cream bought in B.P. last year, so all that will be made here now and lots more too, I hope and expect. A great triumph.

Then there was a dreadful lunch — thirty people — at the hotel, and I had to make another speech. After which we had more discussions about the currency troubles and left for Mafeking by the 5.30 train.

Thursday 8 to Saturday 10 December (at Mafeking)
Three really heavy days at Office exchanging infuriated telegrams with High Commissioner about the currency question in the Tati. I got in from F'town at 8.30 and after a hasty bath and breakfast plunged right in. An extraordinarily foolish cable came in from the High Commissioner, with a perfectly futile suggestion made after a discussion with McFarlaine of the Tati Company who is a double-faced idiot. At last at 1 o'clock on Saturday a telegram came in from the High Commissioner giving way and adopting my proposal to repeal the Proclamation. (I had previously telegraphed to Sir Alan Pim who is a financial expert, and he had telegraphed to the High Commissioner supporting me).

1932

Sunday 11 to Friday 16 December
December 16 is Dingaan's Day,[23] a Union public holiday to celebrate a massacre of some natives by Boers. I don't recognize it as a holiday and won't have the Office closed on that day.

Sunday 18 December (to Lobatsi)
Quite fit again. Went off early by train to Lobatsi, inspected the new hospital building put up by Robertson entirely with native skilled and unskilled labour — a wonderfully successful effort; lunched at the hotel (a foul meal), and met Sir Basil Blackett[24] on the train. He is the Chairman of the Colonial Development Fund, and is passing through on his way back home from Rhodesia.

We had a most interesting two and a half hour talk — it passed like five minutes. He is strongly in favour of my Walvis Bay Cattle Route scheme and is going to support it when I send home my application for a Grant. He quite agrees with my views on the currency question, and as he is a financial expert, that is very satisfactory. He is writing direct to Thomas[25] (the Secretary of State) about things in B.P. and when he gets home, he will, I can see, be extremely helpful. He agrees generally with my policy and my schemes.

He told me he feared that Sir Herbert Stanley has become almost a defeatist. He is so overwhelmed by his own financial troubles, by the difficulties of his position, and by the scant support that he gets from Home, that there is no fight left in him. It is a pity.

Blackett gave me some very interesting inside news about the political position here. Blackett says the Union Government cannot keep on gold much longer — a year at the very outside, probably less — or else the country must crash. Blackett also told me that the big people in Jo'burg were all very bucked with me, and that they were much interested in my efforts to develop and open up B.P. That is good news.

Tuesday 20 December
We bumped along and got into Lobatsi at about 1. Here we got our first shock or shocks. There had been the devil of a row at Mochudi yesterday culminating in a bit of a fight, and apparently the one thing that was still keeping the peace was the fact that I as on my way up.

Molefi (the Chief) had been drinking, and worked himself up into a fury over his uncle the ex-Regent's alleged thefts of his patrimony. So, armed with a rifle, he betook himself to Reyneke's house. Isang (the uncle), also armed with a rifle, went off to Rutherford's house, Rutherford being the one and only official at Mochudi (with *no* police), and stalked on to the verandah complete with rifle. He had, the evening before, telegraphed to the Magistrate at Gaberones that his (Isang's) life was not safe, and that he appealed for help, and meanwhile would defend himself by arms.

Molefi, on Reyneke's verandah (Reyneke is the missionary), saw Isang go into Rutherford's; picked up his rifle; jumped on his horse; rode across; and burst onto the verandah with his gun — the two were out to finish matters. Rutherford however with much calmness got in between them — shoved them apart and tried to grab their guns. At this moment Lt. Moseley from Gaberones who had received Isang's wire arrived by car, and between them they calmed the two savages.

Then Molefi said that there was a big tribal meeting on in the veld about the matter and asked Moseley to go with him, which he did, Moseley taking the Chief in his car. Now this meeting was not a Kgotla such as I often attend but a *letsholo*,[26] which is held not in the village but in the veld. It is a dangerous thing because people come to it armed, and an unpopular person is apt not to return. Isang had been invited and had refused to go. But when he saw Molefi go off to it with Moseley he thought he would be safe — a European officer being there. He said he must go or they would slander him in his absence, and in spite of Rutherford's efforts to keep him, jumped in his car and drove off! Rutherford's car was in the garage. So he lost some time in getting it but — then it wouldn't start for a bit — so he was delayed, but as soon as he could dashed off after the others!

Meanwhile there had been striking developments.

Lt. Moseley had arrived at the *letsholo* with Molefi to find about a thousand men — all armed — rifles, knobkerries, etc. — rather excited. Molefi very excited, strutting up and down shouting 'Am I the Chief?' — answering shouts of 'You are'. Up came Isang — Molefi was grossly insulting to him, said he wasn't a man etc; and then Isang struck the Chief! Hail Columbia and hell let loose. Fighting started fortunately only with knobkerries as the rifles weren't loaded. With great coolness, Lt. Moseley who is a big powerful man — the only European there — grabbed Molefi and Isang and shoved them apart — pushed away some of the fighters, and calmed the crowd. He told them I was on my way up and would give them hell if there was any bloodshed — he said I would deal with the whole thing on arrival. Peace was restored and the meeting dissolved until my arrival. He then telegraphed a full report to me which I received on my arrival at Lobatsi on Tuesday midday.

Unfortunately the special Court is sitting at Lobatsi, consisting of Patrick Duncan and two Magistrates (Neale and Ledeboer) to try that awful brute Langton, and of course the beastly case was not finished today. So, I shall have to deal with the Mochudi business alone tomorrow.

Wednesday 21 December (to Mochudi)
Ninon and I off to Mochudi early by car with Moseley, a foul road that shakes one to bits. Fortunately there was no water in the Metsemotlhaba River so we got straight through to Mochudi where everything (on the surface) was peaceable. After a short preliminary interview with Rutherfold, Reyneke and Moseley I got to grips with the Chief who was in a foul mood. He brought four reptiles with him who would have been better under ground. He roundly accused Isang of having filched £22,000 of his inheritance and says Isang has got to be cleared out, and that he will give him no compensation for houses, cattle or anything else left behind. Then I had Isang and four of his ruffians in. He denies the whole thing, says he won't go, and demands large compensation. So then I cursed them both, said I would appoint a native Commission to examine all the charges, with a Magistrate as Chairman and meanwhile I would deal drastically with anyone who broke the peace or played the fool. After lunch (which we had at the Rutherfords — very nice) I summoned a meeting of all the headmen — about a hundred or more, and made them a speech, told them what I had decided to do and abused them roundly. I told them they must get on with the job of selecting two nominees for my Commission; the Chief and Isang to select two each and I would select two. I said I would meet the whole Tribe early next morning, and expected them to get on with the good work meanwhile.

After which we motored our thirty miles back to Gaberones. Neale had arrived, but he brought me bad news that owing to bad bungling on the part of Minchin

(Crown Prosecutor), Langton had got off on the first of the charges brought against him — though everyone knew he was guilty. I sent off some dreadfully rude telegrams in consequence and being dog-tired went to bed early.

Thursday 22 December
When we got to Mochudi we found the people had been so much impressed by my remarks and disliked the idea of my Commission of Enquiry so much (which was what I intended) that they had decided to get on with the enquiry themselves on the definite lines I had indicated (which was what I had hoped). So I left them to it for a bit. It's never possible in dealing with natives to go straight at one's object, if it can be helped. Later I drove down to the Kgotla and met the assembled multitudes and gave them a few words. Later on the Chief came up to Rutherfords and reported progress — Isang had accounted for £25,000 out of £34,000 left by Linchwe, and they were now on the remaining £9,000. Finally he came up and reported that they had practically settled everything satisfactorily.

I decided to push off back to Gaberones, sleep there and if all is quiet tomorrow return to Mafeking. They are not likely to raise trouble during the Christmas and New Year holidays.

Friday 23 to Saturday 31 December (at Mafeking)
And on Saturday 31 we got the great news about South Africa going off gold. It is magnificent, the best bit of news since we've been here. It will make all the difference to B.P. and simplify many of our troubles.

To some extent it is of course due to that clown Thielman Roos,[27] but he has merely precipitated things — it was bound to come soon. The Germiston election started the rot, Roodeport followed it up, and £3,000,000 left the country this week![28]

And, now on New Year's Eve it's raining again heavily, and as we're off gold at last everything promises beautifully.

And so a Happy New Year to all.

1933

Sunday 1 to Wednesday 4 January
A bad start — spent in bed, owing to an attack of gastric flu aggravated by an over-strenuous bout of work while I ought to have been going easy.

On Tuesday morning I (in bed) had a two hours confab with Reilly, How and Goodman. Reilly goes to Cape Town in my place this afternoon for a Conference with the High Commission about currency. He takes with him a deputation from the Tati.

This currency business is maddening, but it's shaping better. Now the Union is off gold, I hope we shall link up with Sterling. Their man Roos is a mountebank and also a knave. No doubt the Mining interests have bought him, and a good thing too — for he has undoubtedly accelerated going off gold which will help the Mines enormously.

Of course all South African politicians are corrupt. Some of the low Dutch (poor white) farmers have been poaching and gun-running, over our borders. We issued summonses against them, and the Union Government won't serve them because they are their political supporters! We caught four others and have now got them in gaol. Another one, caught poaching, deliberately loosed off his rifle at one of our native policemen — who behaved most gallantly and went for him unarmed. But the swine got away. However we've got his name and five witnesses: I've issued a warrant for his arrest for attempted murder, and a Union magistrate has endorsed it, so we ought to get him. As regards the other cases I got Stanley to put in a hell of a stiff letter to the Union Government. So I'm hoping for a first class row.

Sunday 8 January
Reilly is back from Cape Town and came in at about 10.30 to tell me all the news. He has been very successful at Cape Town, and has carried all our points; the High Commission has given way all along the line. The stupid currency proclamation is to be repealed for the whole Territory at once. It's a pity he didn't take my advice at first.

Sir Alan Pim came in at 11.30, and stayed to lunch. He is a dry old stick: he seems to have enjoyed his tour in the Territory very much, and to have appreciated all we did for him. He didn't tell me much: of course we start battling next week in earnest.

1933

Monday 9 January
I rode down to the Office this morning for the first visit there since before Christmas, and did a good morning's work — part of it unpleasant. I had to ask old Minchin, the Crown Prosecutor, who is 67, to resign — he's long past his job.

I tried my new Basuto pony that Sir Herbert Stanley sent me for the first time, and was not very pleased. He's a bit on the small side and rather short in his paces. However I didn't canter or gallop him, so perhaps he'll improve.

Tuesday 10 to Wednesday 18 January
Nothing of great interest occurred during this week. Pimbo (by which I mean Sir Alan Pim and Pals) were here, and of course this meant that I had to spend a lot of time working with them.

I am having a series of twenty-four injections as a tonic, which seems to be doing me a lot of good. I have persuaded N. to have them also — so we are 'pricked' together every morning after breakfast.

We had a dinner party for Pimbo on 18th. Quite good fun.

Thursday 19 January
As I anticipated, the South African Pound is now about on a parity with Sterling — a bit of good news, and the only bit of good news I'm likely to have for a mighty long time.

A terrible catastrophe has fallen on us, the worst thing that could possibly happen — Foot & Mouth disease has broken out near Mafeking and is therefore probably in the B.P.

At about 1, just as I was leaving the Office, Chase came up and said he wanted to speak to me. He said that a farmer (T. Smith by name), who owns three farms and runs our cattle quarantine station at Ramatlabama on the Protectorate-Union border about sixteen miles from here, had just told him that he had noticed signs of sickness among his own cattle and among the cattle coming thro' from the Protectorate which looked suspiciously like Foot and Mouth. (All our cattle exported to Durban have to be detrained at Ramatlabama, fed and watered).

Whereupon we had to sit down and make plans. I arranged for Chase to go up to the Tati (Francistown) by train tomorrow morning (Friday), get to work at daybreak looking at cattle on Saturday morning, and wire me early Saturday. Trainloads of cattle had been coming down from Tati to Ramatlabama route for export via Durban for some time.

I didn't have much of a night on Thursday.

Saturday 21 January
The blow fell. A wire came in from Chase to say that we had Foot and Mouth in the Tati. It was an absolutely crushing blow. But we had to get busy at once, telegraph to all the neighbouring Governments, stop all movements of cattle, inform all our Magistrates, arrange for the telegraph lines and offices to stay open all this afternoon and all Sunday, etc.

Monday 23 January
We have arranged for five columns under officers of our Veterinary Department to go north from Palapye Road towards the Tati, spreading out in a fan-shape as they go to pick up the disease at its furthest point south. Then we shall know exactly where to place our defensive cordon. Meanwhile we are planning the cordon to

run from where the Nata River crosses the Rhodesian border down the Nata to the Makarikari Salt Lakes; south along the east shore of the lakes right down to Shoshong — keeping twenty-five miles west of Serowe — and from Shoshong east along the Mahalapye to where it crosses the Tuli Block to the Transvaal. It's over four hundred miles long, and I'm rushing up three officers, twelve N.C.O.s and twelve special constables (all white), and three hundred native police and auxiliary levies. It's a terrific job, like an operation in the Great War! They've got to be instructed, placed, tented, fed, inspected, and generally directed. And there are no roads or railways in that district. I've got to hire, beg, borrow, or steal motor transport, and push it through thick bush, and when established keep control of the whole cordon.

I've withdrawn our old cordon along the Rhodesian border and the Transvaal (two hundred and fifty miles long). It's no good now, but to evacuate all those men is the very devil.

Wednesday 25 January
Chase's conference today at F'town with the Southern Rhodesian people to determine origin of disease: no good. They stoutly deny that it came over their border to us; and as the Union people deny equally stoutly that it came from them, where did it come from? Did it drop from heaven — or hell? More bad telegrams as to spread of disease — it's awful.

Thursday 26 to Sunday 29 January
On Friday we gave Sir Alan Pim and Milligan a farewell lunch. Thank goodness they are going, now we can get on with our work.
In the afternoon N. and I went to an Intercession Service called at the Mafeking Town Hall by the Mayor on account of Foot and Mouth disease. The Church of England and Nonconformist parsons both officiated, but of course the Dutch Reformed Church kept out — rotten people.

Wednesday 1 February
We have decided to accept Colonel Ellenberger's generous offer to come and help us as a volunteer in our Foot and Mouth disease campaign. They left early this morning by car for Jo'burg where he is going to collect things and then go at once by train to Mahalapye to organise No. 3 section of our big cordon. It is very sporting of him, and I think he should be a real help.

Thursday 2 February
I have definitely decided that we must have a big campaign to stamp out Foot and Mouth. It is no use standing on the defensive, making cordons and hoping for the disease to die out. So I dictated a huge report for the Colonial Office setting out my plans, and asking for £50,000 spread over two years to stamp it out by inoculating all the cattle within my cordon. The cordon is over four hundred miles long — within it are enclosed 40,000 square miles (nearly half England) and 200,000 head of cattle at least. It means six veterinary surgeons, twenty five stock inspectors, and two hundred native assistants, with transport. In each different district the European farmers or natives will build scores of 'crushes' — big wooden pens, tapering to the end, where one beast comes out at a time. All the cattle in each district are collected, driven through the crush, and inoculated by squirting up their noses. They react in four days and are well in a fortnight. Meanwhile they are

kept in big zaribas, and when well are branded. All cattle not brought in within the given time in each district will be shot. It's a colossal task to organise and they say I can't do it. But Chase and I have made up our minds, and we're going to have a jolly good try. Our joint report for the Colonial Office went off today, and now we must wait for a telegram back from Home. But we are not going to wait: we're going right ahead with the organisation. If we don't, then the disease will spread all over the Kalahari and Ngamiland, become endemic, and the B.P. is ruined forever, as we could never export cattle again.

Tuesday 7 to Sunday 12 February (to Serowe)
Saturday was perhaps the biggest success of all, as it was certainly the most difficult. I had to meet Chief Tshekedi and Bamangwato Tribe in Kgotla, and carry them with me, and it's infinitely harder to do that than to deal with Europeans. There were between two and three thousand natives, a big gathering, and I spoke for one and a half hours (including the interpretation). Then they spoke, and then I went away and came back in an hour — when the Chief said that he and the whole Tribe agreed entirely with all I had said and would support and work the scheme wholeheartedly. It was a triumph because to work it in that huge Bamangwato Reserve without their help would have added enormously to the expense and difficulty and caused endless trouble.

And then to crown it all, when we got back to the Residency for lunch, I found a telegram waiting for me from the High Commissioner saying he had discussed my scheme with Sir Alan Pim. They both agreed on it, and they had telegraphed on to London asking for telegraphic answer. So in the words of the prophet: that is that.

Monday 13 to Saturday 18 February (at Mafeking)
My efforts are now concentrated on trying to keep the Lobatsi Creamery open, so that farmers can sell their cream and the Creamery shall go on exporting butter — a very difficult job on account of infection from Foot and Mouth and Union Government restrictions.

Sunday 19 February
A Coalition Government in the Union of South Africa now seems a *fait accompli*.[1] I'm sorry about that as it bodes ill for B.P. The S.A.P. (Smuts' party) is really little better than the Nats (Hertzog's crowd) and I fear they will cause us trouble now they are united. The Nats have made the S.A.P.s swallow the language question and their rotten flag and their vile Native Policy — so where is the difference?

Monday 20 February
The Imperial Cold Storage directors at Cape Town have turned down the agreement I made with their representative the other day about the Lobatsi Creamery — and have put forward the most scandalous proposals — the dirty dogs. I've had to send hectic telegrams to Cape Town and I've now got the Mafeking Creamery — an opposition show — on the run to try and lease or buy the Lobatsi Creamery and run it for us.

Tuesday 21 February
A telegram from the Dominions Office to say that they, the Ministry of Agriculture and the Treasury, all approve my big inoculation scheme, and give me a free

hand, and say carry on as quickly as you can! What a triumph. And so we must get at it like the devil, tho' in fact I have already started.

Wednesday 22 & Thursday 23 February
Captain Douglas of the De Havilland Aircraft Company and John Stuart flew over from Jo'burg and landed on my new aerodrome here at Mafeking. We had a long discussion about aeroplane development in B.P., and then they lunched with us.

They are going to give us a man and a plane *free* for a one thousand mile experimental flight over our Foot and Mouth cordon to inspect it. I do hope this may prove the beginning of air development here. I have got eight aerodromes cleared in the B.P. and it is time we made a real beginning now.[2]

Friday 24 February
A very hectic day. The Union Government are proposing a scandalous Meat Control Bill which would paralyse our trade, or at all events give them power to do so. And my fools here had not realised the inwardness of it. So I had to draft a hell of a dispatch and to propose a number of amendments, and may have to go down to Cape Town to give evidence.

Meanwhile, I've got to dash off to Pretoria tonight to see General Kemp and his crew of devils to try and get the Lobatsi butter factory opened up for export. Telegrams have been raining in today from Cape Town and Pretoria about it.

Saturday 25 February (to Johannesburg and Pretoria)
Arrived Jo'burg at 6 am, and was met at the station by Lavin, the Mafeking Creamery man, who told me he had failed in his underworld efforts regarding Lobatsi owing to the change of Ministers due to the Coalition coming off. There was no one definite person whom he could bribe (it cost him £150 to get the Mafeking Creamery open). The way he put it was really delightful. Owing to impending changes the usual channel is not now available, and a new one has not yet been formed!

I walked up to the Carlton Hotel where I had a bath etc., and then caught the 8.25 to Pretoria. They give you an excellent breakfast on the train. There was a scandalous article in the *Rand Daily Mail*, implying that B.P. were responsible for Foot and Mouth disease in the Union. So I sent for the Pretoria representative, gave him a letter to the Editor for publication which I wrote then and there, and also some home truths.

Afterwards I spent a very hectic morning at the Ministry of Agriculture — *and as a result I believe I've succeeded in getting Lobatsi opened for export*. They'll telegraph me on Monday to confirm it, but I feel confident it's right — though it was the devil of a fight.

Kemp does not arrive until tonight — by aeroplane — and then leaves again at once. So it's no good waiting to see him. But I've got his people to see daylight, tho' they tried to put up some dirty work on extraneous matter such as branding our cattle on our border and fencing the Tuli Block — all to prevent cattle running! Damn it, it's *their* law that prevents cattle movement and it's for *them* to enforce it. I don't see why we should spend time and money trying to enforce an unjust law of the Union against our own people.

Monday 27 & Tuesday 28 February (at Mafeking)
Black Monday. It started well, a telegram from Kemp to say it was all right about Lobatsi, so I was successful at Pretoria on Saturday as I had thought. Then came a letter confirming it. Then Chase came in and said he was unhappy about some beasts

at Ramatlabama, and was going out to look at them again and would be back in the evening. Meanwhile bad reports about the spread of the disease came in by telegram until the evening when Chase came back and said there was no doubt it was Foot and Mouth at Ramatlabama.

That means that all my success at Pretoria is no good and all my efforts wasted. Lobatsi can't open, and the farmers in that district will pretty nearly starve. God damn and blast!

Wednesday 1 to Sunday 5 March
The Dominions Office seem to be more idiotic than the usual Government Office intellectual level — and heaven knows that is low enough. We have had a very important law case on against the Southern Rhodesia Railway Company involving £30,000 this year, and more in subsequent years. As may be imagined it was of vital interest to us that we should win, and I have been working at it like anything. We won in the Special Court here, but the Company appealed to the Privy Council in London. We considered whether we should brief a South African barrister and send him to London, but this would have cost us £1,000 to £1,500. So we arranged with the Dominions Office that we should get a barrister here to prepare the case (which had to be decided according to South African Law) and send it to the Dominions Office — who got the Attorney General to appear for us. We paid a hundred guineas for this, and put in a lot of work. Then two days after our brief had left South Africa we got a cable from London saying the case had been heard *without waiting for our brief!* — tho' they knew the importance of it, knew that we were doing this, and knew that it had to be decided by South African Law.

And now today we get a further telegram saying that the case has been decided against us! The damned fools at the Dominions Office will now have to pay £30,000 for their folly — we simply haven't got it.

Monday 6 March
Bad news from the cordon. Reilly, Gash and Ellenberger all telegraph that Hope has let us down badly. He was shell shocked in the War and it comes out sometimes. He has had a breakdown, and the No. 3 section of the cordon is all to bits and has been pierced.

Tuesday 7 to Saturday 11 March
These politicians are a dirty crowd whatever party or race they belong to. Patrick Duncan, who is General Smuts' second-in-command, and supposed to be the leader of the English out here, made a speech saying that they must not call themselves British but South African! Selling his birthright for a mess of pottage just because he wants to get into Office in the Coalition Government — it's filthy. My friend Gemmill of the Chamber of Mines went for Patrick Duncan in the press about it, and Patrick Duncan's reply was too feeble for words.

On Thursday morning Chase had had a frightful row with Major Keppel, the Union vet, who had had the infernal cheek to put a padlock and chain on *our* gate in *our* territory near Ramatlabama — to prevent our coming in and out of our own territory on account of Foot and Mouth disease. Chase smashed the padlock, but when he came back he found another padlock and a Union policeman on duty in *our* territory. So then there was the father and mother of a row. I sent off an infuriated telegram to Pretoria — and police and padlocks etc. have all disappeared and we've received an apology. Damn all Dutchmen.

Tuesday 21 March
That disgusting Langton case has been cleared up. He has been found guilty on eight counts, and is recommended for dismissal. The papers go forward for confirmation tomorrow.

Wednesday 22 March
I had Chief Bathoen down this morning and told him the Government decision about Gobbleman — the old devil has been giving trouble again. So we've decided to kick him out finally and to take various others steps. I am going off to Kanye on Monday to do the job, and have summoned a full meeting of both tribes. Bathoen is delighted and agrees to everything. He has been helping splendidly in regard to Foot and Mouth matters, and has cleared a strip sixty miles long and five miles wide of cattle all along his border. This has been a great help to us.

Friday 24 March
A most interesting day, spent in inspection of the cordon and inoculating work in the Lobatsi and Barolong districts. As the animals go through the crush, loose bars are dropped across, a short noose at the end of a short stick dropped over the nose, the inoculation is squirted up each nostril, another man brands the animal to shew he has been done — and then the next animal is tackled and so on.

The work is done amazingly quickly — it starts at daybreak and goes on all day. At the first post we visited, eight hundred had been done by 2.30; at the next, eight by 3.30. The rate is estimated to be a thousand a day by one white man with native assistants at each post!

We have done the Tati District, 50,000 head; in the Barolong we have done 7,000. It is all a question of getting and maintaining a constant supply of virus — that is our difficulty. The virus is made of the blood of three infected animals mixed together and added to some glycerine solution and a preservative. It can only be obtained from an ox, at a particular stage of the disease, generally the fourth or fifth day when his temperature is over 104 degrees and the lesions on the mouth (gums and tongue) and on the feet have not or have only just burst.

The whole thing — inoculation and everything — was a wonderful sight. The herds of cattle waiting under the trees, crowds of natives squatting about; the inoculators working like beavers, clouds of dust standing up over the zaribas and the crush; swarms of flies; and the work going on steadily and methodically without break of pause. We have electric prodders to urge the animals into the crush. This does not hurt them, but makes them move quickly — otherwise the natives would hammer them with sticks (they hate going into the crushes) and this is brutal — also it damages the animals by bruising.

The whole thing is a triumph of organisation and hard work. It's never been done on this scale anywhere in the world, and it may revolutionise the whole future treatment of Foot and Mouth disease everywhere. It is obviously far better than shooting. We don't lose one per cent by this method — whereas by shooting you lose them all, millions of pounds are lost, and you don't immunise any of the cattle that don't get the disease — so it may always break out again.

1933

Sunday 26 March
I wrote letters and diary all day — a pleasant spell in the garden which is still quite lovely with lots of roses and other flowers. A very curious thing has happened in the Territory. Some time ago we arrested and tried a man for attempted murder. He was a witch-doctor, and he threatened all sorts of things at his trial — so much so that it was very difficult to get natives to give evidence. He was convicted and sentenced to a term of imprisonment with hard labour. Since then, Lt. Hope who tried and sentenced him, Sergeant Mitchell who prosecuted, and the three native police who gave evidence, have all five fallen ill! The natives shrug their shoulders and say of course — he has 'put medicine on them' and their faith in witch-doctors has gone up ever so much. Of course that's all rubbish, but it's a very curious coincidence to say the least of it.

Monday 27 March (to Kanye)
Called 5.45, breakfast 6.45, off at 7.30 in 'Topsy' for Kanye where I have to deal with that old villain Gobbleman!

There was a huge gathering of Bangwaketse tribesmen, and several hundred Bakgatla had come in with Gobbleman from Moshupa. I made a long speech, told Gobbleman what I thought of him — that he was an obstinate foolish old man, that he caused trouble for thirty years; and that he was no longer headman of the Bakgatla, that he was to leave Moshupa and come and live at Kanye, and that if he was not there in a week I should send police and bring him in by force. I appointed his son Kabosetso as headman, and said if there was any further trouble he would be dealt with drastically like the rebels at Serowe last month who got seven and eight years hard labour.

My remarks evidently made some impression as they were listened to in dead silence, hardly a man moved. Then the Chief said a few words cordially agreeing with what I had said, and I drove over to the Office in the Camp. There I saw, the Chief, then Kabosetso and finally old Gobbleman. The old devil was absolutely unrepentant and truculent, and said he wasn't going to come in, and if we wanted him we could jolly well fetch him, or words to that effect.

So I gave him hell, and the old devil went off in a rage. He pretends to be deaf when he doesn't want to hear, but can really hear as well as I can if he chooses. He had defied three chiefs and four Resident Commissioners in thirty years, and now he has met his Waterloo. But I can't help admiring the stout-hearted way in which the old sinner stood up to us all, and practically told us all to go to the devil!

Wednesday 5 April
I wanted action and I've got it. Mangan the Magistrate at Kanye arrived by car last night full of news, which he poured out this morning. I had given Gobbleman a week to come in. The week was up on Monday and he had not arrived. So yesterday Mangan went out with waggons etc. to bring him in. He found him in council at Moshupa with about four hundred of his tribe, all very excited. They said they were not going to give him up, that if Mangan tried to take him they would resist, and that they didn't care a damn for the Government and generally sent us all to the devil. Mangan reasoned with them for about two hours, but he had no force with him, and could do nothing. So he returned empty handed, and came into Mafeking to report and ask for instructions. There is neither telegraphic nor telephone communication between here and Kanye — so jolly and so helpful in an emergency.

Well we then sat down to think it out. It was a very awkward position. Old Gobbleman can muster about a thousand fighting men, all armed, many with rifles. Moshupa is a natural fortress, a stronghold up in the hills surrounded by rocky koppies which give splendid cover. Three roads lead into it, all up hill, and all commanded by hills. They have water in the village, and probably a store of provisions.

Against this I have no trained men available at all. All my trained men are on these cursed Foot and Mouth cordons or holding isolated posts away up country — and I have exactly twenty untrained native police in camp who don't know one end of a rifle from another — two machine guns with no one to work them, no aeroplane and no armoured car.

But the Government has been defied and I've got to act. So after much deliberation I decided to collect two officers and eight N.C.O.s (all European of course) from the nearest posts, and send them up with my two machine-guns as a guard for Captains Reilly and Neale who are ordered to arrest Gobbleman. The idea is that they are to proceed in six cars from Lobatsi at daybreak, drive straight into the Kgotla (Gobbleman's huts are next door to it) arrest him and get him away in the first car — the others to cover it. We rehearsed it all over and over again in detail, and it seemed all right. I trust to the appearance of so many (twelve!) Europeans to prevent any attack — of course it's not a punitive force, but merely a guard to protect Reilly and Neale. I meant to go myself, but they all fought me hard, said it was not suitable for the R.C. and if he were insulted or attacked; it would lower the prestige of the Government, etc. etc. So at last I gave way, very unwillingly. Sickening.

They are all to assemble at Lobatsi on Friday, and on Saturday at daybreak the balloon goes up. Of course if it goes all right, it's all right and no-one will say anything except 'of course'. But if it goes wrong — then naturally it's my fault and I should have done something else.

Saturday 8 April
A grim failure. The party left Lobatsi at 4 am according to plan, picked up Mangan the Magistrate at Kanye, and proceeded on to Moshupa. All was quiet, and they drove their cars to the entrance to the Kgotla, turned them round, left the engines running, posted two men as a guard, the one machine gun (the other would not work) being mounted on the last car and trained on the entrance under the charge of native Sergeant Ndandala,[3] a splendid old warrior from the King's African Rifles, and the only native member of the party except the interpreter. All the European officers and N.C.O.'s were armed with revolvers, but my orders were that there was to be no firing except in self defence.

There was only a handful of natives in the Kgotla. Gobbleman was not there — only his son Kabosetso. Reilly asked him where Gobbleman was — he said he was ill! Reilly told him to lead the way to his hut — and then Reilly and Neale with a few N.C.O.s went through three enclosures, palisades with narrow entrances, thro' several huts and there found Gobbleman. As they did so, whistles were sounded and hundreds of men all armed appeared from nowhere and poured into and around the huts, surrounding the whole party with a dense mob. Reilly read out my order to Gobbleman and asked him if he understood it — he said yes. Reilly then asked him if he was going to obey it — he said emphatically *no*. Then Reilly ordered two of the N.C.O.s to arrest him — they seized him, and then all hell was let loose. Hundreds of natives pressed round and fought to get

Gobbleman away — the other N.C.O.'s came in — Gobbleman was dragged through the first palisade, but then they were stuck and couldn't move forwards or backwards. The natives did not *use* their weapons but beat on the ground with them, waved them in the air and yelled.[4] Reilly and Neale kept perfectly cool. Reilly got on a stool and addressed the mob — warning them of what was coming to them if they persisted. They wouldn't listen. Then he got hold of Kabosetso, dragged him outside and told him to call the people into the Kgotla so that he could talk to them. No good. Meanwhile one of the N.C.O.s came in and reported more natives outside with piles of rocks ready to smash the cars. Our native sergeant, old Ndandala, was perched on the back of one car where the machine gun was mounted, his finger round the trigger, his face twitching with fury, panting to let drive! The N.C.O.'s were beginning to finger their revolvers, and it was obvious that in a few minutes there would be firing which, completely surrounded as our ten men were by many hundreds of savages, could only have one result. They might have blotted out twenty or thirty but that would have been all. So very reluctantly Reilly gave the order to withdraw, and they fell back slowly, and drove off. It was a wonderful example of coolness and discipline — if one of our men had lost his temper or self-control (and they were being roughly handled) and fired a shot, not a man would have got away alive. The natives were temporarily mad, a howling mob of fanatics.

Reilly got to Lobatsi at about 12 and immediately telephoned this news to me. I saw at once that this meant war! A punitive exedition on a large scale, for Moshupa is a regular fortress, and they can muster nearly a thousand men if they call them all up. I realized that I should have to borrow men from Rhodesia, which meant applying to the High Commissioner. So I telegraphed him I was coming to see him at Pretoria on Sunday's train, and sat down with what patience I could to await Reilly and Neale and lay fresh plans.

Reilly and Neale arrived about 4, and entirely agreed with my view that the only course was to destroy the village by a bombing aeroplane, and to arrest Gobbleman with an armoured car. By this means no lives need be lost, the object would be attained with a minimum of loss and expense, and the moral effect on the natives would be immense.[5] Also it could all be carried out in a few days if we could get the plane and armoured car from Southern Rhodesia.

But can't I see the panic of the High Commissioner and the Colonial Office when they get our jolly Easter egg!

We had one good bit of news — inoculations for Foot and Mouth in the Tati is completed — 63,900 cattle done, and they told us they had 25,000 to 30,000! We've done it in seven weeks — an average of 1,280 a day in that district alone — while we have done many thousands more in other parts.

Monday 10 April (to Pretoria)
We got to Jo'burg at 7, had a bath, and caught the 8 o'clock train to Pretoria — one gets a jolly good breakfast on the train.

Then we went on to break our good news to the High Commissioner.

He — much to my surprise — took it like a lamb, agreed to all my proposals — but said we must report to the Colonial Office before starting a war! So Reilly and Eales went off to draft a really fine telegram to London and the High Commissioner and I discussed many other matters.

Tuesday 11 April (at Mafeking)
We got in at 7.40 am and by 9 I had bathed, shaved, breakfasted and was at Camp, where there was an immense amount to do for the 'war'. I blocked all roads leading to Moshupa, stopped all communications, all transport, ox waggons, cars, horses etc. and cut them off from the world. Then I had to issue orders for finishing off the aerodromes at Mochudi and Gaberones (the two nearest to Moshupa) and arrange for concentration of police from all over the country. These orders I allowed to leak through to Moshupa to worry them a bit.

Wednesday 12 April
Colonel Naus[6] lunched with us — a very interesting man. He was in the French army (sappers) then Belgian, English and Irish, for the latter of whom he rebuilt two hundred bridges destroyed in the Civil War. He has been living in Ngamiland for the past year, running about all over the country in a little Baby Austin. He never eats meat or drinks alcohol, lives mostly on roots, vegetables and fruits, drinks river water without boiling it, never sleeps under a mosquito net, and has never had fever! He has travelled all over Africa and is extraordinarily well-informed. He wants to bore for water in Ngamiland, and has put up a very good proposition — he finds the machinery and puts down the boreholes and we only pay if he finds good water.

Thursday 13 April
A cable from England that our three new veterinary surgeons were sailing today — thank goodness — at last.
 Dr Henderson telephoned from Lobatsi to say he had heard a rumour that old Gobbleman was coming in to surrender. So I sent him out to Kanye to find out — he returned at 8 pm to Lobatsi and telephoned that it was true. Reyneke, the Dutch parson from Mochudi, had been out to Moshupa (he had wired to ask me if he might go) and had found them very shaken by it all.

Good Friday
A telephone from the High Commissioner to say the Colonial Office agree that the tribe must be dealt with, but they won't give me an aeroplane or armoured car, and say I can go out and deal with the village with my own police, or if necessary borrow a few men from Southern Rhodesia. They are raving mad — it would mean heavy fighting and lots of loss of life. However it doesn't matter as I got telegrams to say that Gobbleman had surrendered himself this morning, and that the tribe would surrender publicly and unconditionally to me on Tuesday next. Reilly and Ninon returned at 10 pm and confirmed all this — it is splendid news. Apparently the blocking of all communications, preparation of aerodromes, order for concentration of police, etc. have broken their morale, and they're in an awful funk. They informed Reilly and Ninon they would agree to whatever punishment I chose to order.

Saturday 15 to Sunday 16 April (Easter)
Not much of a rest. We had to plan all arrangements for Tuesday's show — draft in lots of police, arrange for their transport, etc. It *may* go off all right, but it *may* be a trick, and I'm not taking any chances about it. All police are to concentrate at Lobatsi on Sunday and Monday, proceed to Kanye Monday afternoon in lorries, and to Moshupa at 7 am Tuesday. The tribe's to assemble five miles outside the

village by 10 am, and on my arrival hand over all arms and make public submission and hear their penalties.

Monday 17 April
Gordon Store (who flew from England to South Africa with Miss Peggy Salaman) arrived and lunched with us — a very nice quiet boy — I liked him. I have arranged for him to fly over to Mochudi tomorrow, test our new ground and give the natives a display — it will produce a good effect.

Tuesday 18 April (to Moshupa)
We left at 8 am for the 'great surrender', Ninon and I in 'Topsy', Reilly and Neale in Reilly's car. At Kanye we had some tea, and I got into uniform — then off we went to Moshupa. And fortunately we had arranged that the Bangwaketse Chief should follow us in his car for the little devil nearly upset the whole show just at the end. I had told him he was to be present but that none of his Tribe were to be present. I knew they would love to come and gloat over the surrender of the Bakgatla, and I knew equally that if they did there would be trouble. But in spite of my orders, we kept on passing parties of Bangwaketse, armed to the teeth, pushing along to Moshupa. So I stopped the car, sent for Bathoen and told him these people were to stop. He said that a lot more had gone on on horseback, and were probably at the rendezvous by now! So after cursing him freely I said that I should stop my car some few hundred yards short of the rendezvous, and that he must send on a messenger to pull his men out. Then we pushed on praying that trouble had not already started.

When we got within a short distance of the rendezvous we found hundreds of armed Bangwaketse on horse and on foot. Apparently they had gone right into the rendezvous and mercifully Mangan the R.M. had sense enough to stop the first lot and send them back. So we breathed again and I gave positive orders that they were to come no nearer. Then we drove in.

It was a fine sight: under a huge tree was a table covered with a Union Jack, half a dozen chairs behind it. At one side a flagstaff had been planted and a Union Jack hoisted, beside it were the piled rifles of the European N.C.O.s. On the right the European Officers and N.C.O.s were drawn up in line under Lt. Croneen. On the left the native troopers under Lt. Lawrenson.

About one hundred yards away on the right were the whole male population of Moshupa, about a thousand strong, all armed. Opposite my table the cars were parked behind two in which the machine guns were mounted in case of trouble — hidden under tarpaulins — under the charge of Sergeant Ndandala, my faithful old K.A.R. warrior who was (I was told) praying for a scrap!

The thousand Moshupa tribesmen marched forward in single file and at a given spot where the European N.C.O.s stood, they passed between them, dropped their arms in a pile and walked past my table to a position opposite.

It was a wonderful and almost unique sight and it was a tragedy that we had not a cine-camera for it would have made a grand picture. The sullen sulky natives, the pile of weapons getting bigger and bigger, guns, spears, axes, knobkerries, sticks etc. The deathly stillness only broken by the clatter of the arms falling on the pile. The statue-like immobility of the police standing straight as darts — expressionless and motionless as the sphinx — only their eyes bulging with excitement. One by one the whole thousand passed over and took up positions opposite and near my table, until at last it was all done — they were all unarmed and between the two lines of the guard. I gave a sigh of relief I must admit! Men gathered up the arms and piled them onto a lorry which was parked behind the cars. Then Reilly called on Kabosetso, Gobbleman's son, to make submission on behalf of the tribe. He hated doing it I could see, but he got through with it. And then came my oration, and I gave them hell for nearly a quarter of an hour, and announced the Government decision. Gobbleman was to be deposed forever — he was in gaol and would be tried for his crime. The tribe had saved themselves a terrible punishment by their submission — they would be fined a hundred head of cattle — they would have to build a police post for the man I should station there — if they offended in any way again their village would be destroyed and they would be removed to another part of the country — Kabosetso would act temporarily as Headman — any trouble and he would follow his father to gaol. The Government (I said) was very merciful and very lenient because they had surrendered unconditionally — but any more trouble and there would be no leniency and no mercy.

Then Kabosetso formally recognized Bathoen as Chief, and promised to obey him. I told the tribe to return to their village, and much chastened but very much relieved, they filed off.

I inspected the guard, dismissed them, and drove back to Kanye for lunch. And that was that.

Wednesday 19 to Sunday 23 April (at Mafeking)
There's been trouble at Serowe over the Native Proclamations, that devil Tshekedi of course, and the R.M. had a row in the Kgotla.[7] But Potts expects to get over it. Also a very unfortunate murder case — a white man aged twenty lost his temper with an old native woman, hit her with a stick, and she's dead — apparently she used to steal his beans. The case came before me on the question of bail, and as the Crown Prosecutor reduced the charge to one of 'culpable homicide' I granted bail on two approved sureties of £250. A beastly case.

Monday 24 to Wednesday 26 April
Three stiff days sitting in Conference all day long with the R.M.s Reilly and Neale considering the various amendments proposed by the different Tribes to my two Native Administration Proclamations.

On the whole, with one or two exceptions, the amendments proposed were not unreasonable, but it was a big job going thro' them all. We have got them all in with the exception of the Bamangwato, who are always more troublesome than all the rest put together; and Tshekedi is coming down on Friday to be duly cursed by me for his delay. Potts had four days in Kgotla with him and four thousand of his Tribe about this last week.

In the afternoon today Ninon came down to Camp and we had an inspection of tents, beds etc. for our trek. They were all put up for us to see. It's going to be a great trek — right up the cordon from Mahalapye past Serowe, north along the Makarikari Salt Lakes, along the Nata River to the Southern Rhodesian border, then two hundred and fifty miles through forests along the Southern Rhodesian border to Kasane on the Zambesi — and then right on thro' Ngamiland to Maun — and back to Victoria Falls — train from there to Francistown and then trek on back here — about fifteen hundred miles trek in five weeks.

1933

Monday 1 to Wednesday 3 May
To add to our troubles April has come to an end without rain. It's been the worst drought for twenty years, and we are faced with terrible distress, and even starvation amongst the natives, on account of this — the Foot and Mouth disease restrictions which stop all sale and export of all produce. So we've got to get to work and organise relief measures for Europeans and natives alike — small loans to settlers, grain for feeding natives, rations for destitute whites, etc. etc. We have evolved several schemes and I've sent in a big report about it. It's going to be telegraphed to London and they are to be asked to telegraph back authority to spend all this additional money — it's ghastly.

I'm also trying to get Lever Brothers to put up a soap factory here to use up the cream and tallow. Their head man from Durban (Seals-Wood)[8] is going to be in Jo'burg next week and I'm sending England over to see him.

Then we've had trouble with Dutch poachers from the Union again. The Union Government objected to our arresting them, and when we've got over that they're sending the Government Attorney to defend them! The case is at Selika — so I'm sending up the Crown Prosecutor to prosecute. It's disgraceful that the Union Government should defend these scoundrels just because they're Dutch.

Monday 8 May
Not the usual Black Monday — for a change. On the contrary, a telegram announcing that H.M. Government are placing £100,000 to my credit to enable me to carry on! Very nice of them. I wish it were for myself.

A further telegram, in answer to mine of 1 May, agreeing to *all* my proposals for relief of distress. This is really very satisfactory — I fancy Sir Alan Pim must have been working the oracle in London.

Cattle inoculation going strong — we've done nearly 200,000 now — but I fear there's another 300,000 to do. However Chase agrees with me that he *may* finish by the end of this year, which will be a huge triumph — less than half the time we estimated.

Wednesday 10 May (to Johannesburg)
Arrived Jo'burg 7 am. England met me at the station and we jogged off to the Carlton for bath and breakfast. Then we had our most important interview with the Lever Brothers people. Seals-Wood is the head of their whole South African business, an extraordinarily able and very pleasant man. He had with him one Whitehead, their principal chemist, and another member of the firm, Lever by name. They were all three most helpful, very able men, and obviously all out to do what they could to help. We came to quite a useful agreement on main lines, then I arranged for England to meet Whitehead again in the afternoon to thrash out details. We telephoned to the Ministry of Agriculture, Pretoria, for an interview for England and Whitehead tomorrow to settle the terms upon which our butterfat may be exported. We have given up the idea of a soap factory as Lever's people said it wouldn't pay; and anyhow we can get more for our butter fat if used for manufacturing purposes for biscuits, cake, pastry etc. (sixpence to a shilling per lb) than if used for soap for which we could only get threepence.

Monday 15 May
Today we had the great meeting at which Ninon launched her big scheme, the Bechuanaland Protectorate Relief of Distress Fund — a Central Committee at

Mafeking, Local Committees at every centre in the B.P., money to be raised by bazaars, plays, dances, bridge drives, tennis tournaments, etc. Ninon is President of the whole thing — and is organising lots of it herself. The whole staff attended today's meeting, and the wives of all the married people. Ninon made a splendid speech; we appointed a committee, and organisers for all the different branches of work — a depot for receiving gifts of food and clothing, etc. It was a huge success.

The object is to help the poorer Europeans who have been so terribly hit by the Foot and Mouth disease restrictions on trade, and the awful drought — the worst for twenty years.

Tuesday 16 May
Bishop Meysing has come back from his long tour in Europe, and lunched with us today.

He was very interesting about the state of affairs in Germany. The R.C. Church first of all opposed Hitler and refused the benefits of the Church to those who voted for him — then Hitler made certain concessions to them, and, as Hitler is violently opposed to Socialism, the R.C. Church came round. Meysing seems to take quite a mild view of Hitler's excesses — he says they are exaggerated by the press of the world which is run by or influenced by Jews. Meysing says that Jews who were in Germany before the war, or fought in the war, are not molested, but only the Russian, Polish, Lithuanian etc. Jews who have come in since and exploited the country.

The *Bulawayo Chronicle* has got an article and a leading article on my big Game Reserve scheme — full of praise, and urging cooperation between the Governments of Southern Rhodesia and B.P. for their mutual Game Reserves and for attracting tourists to both territories! It's splendid, and I'm terribly pleased, especially as I've now got a definite offer to start building my hotel in Ngamiland at once, from some commercial people. A move on at last.

Friday 19 May
Splendid news. The Union Government have agreed to our proposals for the export of our butter-fat as melted butter for industrial purposes.

That means that all our people in every part of the B.P. can start producing cream; we are going to improvise a plant at Lobatsi for preparing it — melting it down etc., pay them monthly for their cream, and market the produce thro' the big South African firms including Lever who are all out to help us! It's splendid, and will go far towards saving the situation: we hope to get a million pounds out by the end of the year. Work starts today (I've started it all by telegram). We are going to work twenty four hours a day in shifts to be ready to receive cream on Monday next — messages have gone out today all over the B.P.

Are we ever beaten? Never — till we're dead — and not always then.

Also I've every hope we may be able to induce the big dealers to buy our hides and furs at once, because the Union Government have agreed that if they are stored under our Government supervision for three months they may then be exported. I have sent Chase to Pretoria to negotiate the final arrangement.

1933

On Trek

Wednesday 24 May (at Serowe)
The drought here is awful — my beautiful dam has dried up, and the one thing that keeps Serowe alive is the borehole and pump I put up. Hundreds and hundreds of women can be seen all day long carrying their pots to the stand pipes, filling them, and carrying them away on their heads — a wonderful sight. I am also supplying the natives with explosives to deepen their wells as even these are drying up. Incidentally one party touched off the fuses for the dynamite in one well too soon, and five of them will need no more water in this world — tho' they are probably wanting it pretty badly where they are!

Friday 26 May (Serowe-Botletli road)
The water in the washing basin by my bed was frozen when I woke this morning! But I had noticed nothing in the night and had slept like a log in my flea-bag out in the open.

We lunched at Morokoro, and afterwards had a look at and photographed the people and the place. It is a Bamangwato cattle post, herded by Masarwa, and I have rarely in my life seen anything more dreadful than the appearance of those unfortunate Masarwa. They get no pay, and practically nothing to eat except the milk from their master's cattle, and roots and berries they dig up or pick. Their bones were sticking out, and they seemed too cowed and dejected to take any interest in anything. We had shot a springbuck — a large one — and gave it to them. I feared that their Bamangwato overlords might take it, so I stood over them while they skinned and cut it up. A dreadful sight — it was like a pack of starving wolves fastening on to their kill.

There was trouble at Dinokana — sixty head of cattle belonging to one Rasebolai,[9] one of Chief Tshekedi's Headmen, had crossed the cordon line, and been caught and brought in by our cordon guards. This was the second time this man's cattle had been over, but everyone was afraid to shoot them because of Tshekedi.

I considered the whole matter very carefully, and discussed it at length with all my people — Potts, Hurndall, Moseley, Barton, and Tarr (the stock inspector in charge here, a bright and able young man). No one would definitely say 'shoot' — so I decided it myself and ordered the whole herd to be shot the next morning — sixty of them — a beastly job.[10] But one can't risk the success of the whole of this vast inoculation scheme for the sake of sixty oxen.

Saturday 27 May
We got off at 9.10 with Lt. Hurndall, and had a perfectly wonderful drive. At first the track was a bit bumpy, then it improved a lot and was really very good except for a quarter of a mile of heavy sand where the lorries stuck and had to be manhandled out. For an hour we ran through really beautiful scenery, wooded and hilly — then we crossed an arm of the Great Makarikari Salt Lake, a wonderful sight. As far as the eye could reach there was this vast stretch of cracked *white* dry mud, flat and featureless — stretching to the horizon — dust devils were spiralling up into the air to huge heights — a bitter cold wind blew across and cut like a knife. On one side miles away was a very beautiful mirage of waters and trees, the 'trees' reflected in the 'water', one of the finest mirages I have ever seen. After this we ran into *mopane* forest for about an hour, then crossed another arm

of the Makarikari where we met with conditions similar to the other, including a bitter wind again. We came across springbuck and guinea fowl and shot a couple of the buck and some birds for our larder. Then on through more jolly scenery reaching Tsheagaki before noon — a good run of forty-four miles.

The native headman here had built a really excellent concrete tank for watering his cattle, instead of the usual muddy hole in the ground which wastes about half the water and takes the cattle three or four times as long to drink. I photographed this; the idea must be extended elsewhere.

Tuesday 30 May (near Nata)
It was bitterly cold during the night and when we woke up this morning, the camp fire was very welcome. Overnight I had sent for Tshekedi's representative from the other side of the river (the Bamangwato Reserve) and he arrived this morning. I put the fear of God into him about allowing cattle to stray across the cordon — and I also told him that he could not put his cattle into the strip of country between the Nata and Maitengwe Rivers recently ceded to him until the Foot and Mouth restrictions were raised. That piece of country is now occupied by about two thousand head of cattle belonging to an ex-Basuto policeman of the B.P. Police and he cannot move out yet awhile.

Monday 5 June (beyond Pandamatenga)
Off at 8.15 — a foul piece of travelling over dried cracked black cotton soil — fissured and full of bumps and holes, forming the beds of numerous valleys running east to west, which we crossed.

We reached Kazuma at 12.45 — thirty-two miles — and were horrified to find the pan dry — this had not been known to happen before, and stray people who had got in here from time to time across the Southern Rhodesian border had said this pan never dried. Incidentally we came across spoor here that indicated the presence of poachers from Southern Rhodesia. I shall have to get our police on to this.

This country teems with game. We saw a herd of about three hundred tsessebe grazing quite close to us, and picked up the spoor — quite fresh — of a lion stalking them. He must have been in the bush close to us.

We shot an oribi and a couple of tsessebe[11] for the 'pot'. Our natives eat a fearful lot of meat and we don't do badly ourselves.

Tuesday 6 June
A lovely morning, rather warmer. We got off at 8.05 and actually shot a brace of pheasants a hundred yards from camp. We had three miles good going across the flats. Kazuma Pan lies in some flats about five miles by three miles. I collected some dom-nuts and Mukwa pods[12] for my 'museum' which is getting quite well-stocked.

Then we had the most trying bit of going that we've had on the whole journey. We had to cross a valley of which the soil was the unbroken continuation of hard cracked lumps of black turf, studded with tufts of coarse grass growing on small mounds. There was not one yard of level ground. We bumped and crashed over bumps, and into holes and cracks, until I thought the car *must* be smashed. The lorries heaved and rolled like ships at sea. This lasted for eight miles without a break, and it took us two hours to cover it!

When we got to the other side we were all simply battered, and cursed the place freely. We called it 'The Happy Valley' — a dreadful spot.

There was a lot of mopane fly about, sometimes called 'mopane bees'[13] — they are an awful curse in the wet weather, tiny things. They make quite good honey in the hollow trees, sealing up the entrance with wax, and leaving a tube sticking out thro' which they go in and out.

Ninon had thought the man who was telling us about this had said that the flies were good to eat, so she promptly caught one and started chewing it up! Said it was very sweet and nice — until stopped by yells from all of us. Ninon will try *anything* new to eat.

Thursday 8 June (Kasane to Livingstone & Victoria Falls)
Sir Ronald Storrs,[14] Governor of Northern Rhodesia having asked us to lunch at Livingstone, we shed our trek garments, arrayed ourselves in (rather crumpled) 'purple and fine linen' and started off at 9 in 'Topsy'.

Sir Ronald Storrs was quite charming; he is a very cultured man, and incidentally hates his present job and Livingstone. He spoke very bitterly of the Colonial Office and of things generally. We had a long and most interesting talk, including the question of the amalgamation of the two Rhodesias with Bechuanaland and Nyasaland, and also the question of our exports of cattle etc. from B.P. into Northern Rhodesia and the Congo.

We went off to Victoria Falls Hotel for tea where we meet Reilly and Dyke who had come up by train for a conference with the people of Northern and Southern Rhodesia about Native Affairs. They thought we looked awfully fit and well, and Dyke especially was amazed at N. having come thro' it all so well.

Friday 9 June (back at Kasane)
A really lovely day in this very lovely spot. We had a late breakfast at 9, and then took some photographs and I collected some of the mahogany tree bean pods.

Then we all packed into Beeching's car, and went off to the hot water springs, about seven miles off. Wonderful possibilities there.

There are about eight different springs, all very hot and possessing properties like the waters at Harrogate, and some of the German spas. Beeching had dug out a sort of small swimming pool round the biggest one, enclosed it with poles, and made steps down into it. Near it he had put up a shelter of reeds, and an old bath in which people could wash the mud off themselves after coming out of the pool. The mud in the pool is supposed to possess healing qualities, and by using it as a 'mudpack' on his neck, Beeching had cured himself of headaches and neuralgia which he had had constantly.

We must however put up a dam round the springs to prevent their being flooded out by the river when it comes down after the rains.

Saturday 10 June (Kasane to Kachikau)
The scenery was lovely and the track good as we rolled along by the river. We passed our old friend the giant baobab tree that I photographed three years ago, and which figures on our new stamps[15] and saw lots of game — a herd of roan antelope, lots of baboons and monkeys. We shot four guinea fowl 'for the pot' and a few pheasants and partridges, as our larder is low.

Further on we ran through huge herds of cattle. Engelbrecht (Sussman's agent) has alone about 5,000 head. They were of a good type, and seemed in good condition; being along the river they can of course get water and grazing.

Engelbrecht is a good type of Dutchman. His post is about 16 miles out of Kasane and he came with us; he pays all his wages *in cash* unlike most of the sweeps up here.

At Kachikau we had a very strenuous and interesting time. The two Basubia tribes and the Batawana[16] were drawn up in two groups to greet us, and about fifty children from the Basubia (Munga) school (Headman Sinvula's lot) were also on parade in a separate group. There were no children from Headman Chika's Basubia crowd (about twenty miles from here) as they don't go to school, and the Batawana children from Kachikau school had not paraded as their teacher was ill.

The other children gave us a great reception. They marched, drilled, and sang songs including 'Tipperary' and 'John Brown's Body', besides native songs. Quite amusing.

I had a Kgotla meeting with the tribesmen and listened to their grievances, lots of them — partly against the native police who they said treated them like monkeys (they want white police here they say), but mostly against their own (Batawana) Headman whom they accused of interfering with their wives, killing people by witchcraft, drinking, and lying to them and to the Government! He appeared to be a popular fellow! Also he seemed quite keen to resign his job.

As a matter of fact these tribes are a lazy good for nothing lot, and will do nothing to help themselves. They grumble about not being able to pay their hut-tax, but as a matter of fact Beeching got an offer of fifty jobs for them on Sussman's timber camp just over the border and only fifteen turned up for it! Corporal Maketta, the native N.C.O. in charge here, took an awful lot of trouble to show them how to grow cotton for sale.

I gave them a good talking to, and cursed them freely, but I don't suppose it will do any good.

They have a rotten native missionary here — one Samuel — who like all the L.M.S. (London Missionary Society) people is nothing but an intriguer. He is trying to work the teacher out of his job here, because he wants it for his own wife. I gave him a good choking off. I detest nearly all missionaries, and all *native* missionaries.

Wednesday 14 June (on the Mochaba River)
This is the most divine spot amid trees, parkland all around us, and game. As we are staying here today we got up lateish, and enjoyed a bath, there being plenty of water. After which Ninon and Reilly and I went off up the Mochaba to look for game — and we were not disappointed. After covering about ten miles we ran into herd after herd, in such numbers and of such variety as I had never imagined. And when I describe the different species it must be remembered that there were many hundreds of each, thousands in all. There were zebra, wildebeeste, impala, tsessebe, lechwe, all in hundreds. *They galloped along beside us and in front of us.* They were in such numbers and raised such clouds of dust that we actually had to turn 'Topsy' away from them! It was a marvellous sight.

And then there were smaller parties of other animals, reedbuck, waterbuck, warthog, wild pig, baboons, monkeys, ostriches, marabou storks. A small impala was resting in the shade of a bush and when we stopped 'Topsy' close to him he blinked at us, got up and ambled slowly off. We saw about twenty zebra standing and lying near one that seemed to be dead. We were quite concerned about it; it was stretched out flat on the ground with legs extended. So we drove up quite close when it jumped to its feet and raced off as lively as a cricket.

We could have shot dozens with the greatest of ease, but of course we weren't out to kill. When I hear of these so-called 'big game hunters' and their arduous treks and their record 'bags', it makes me sick. I should think we could have had the world's record 'bag' if we'd wanted to, on this trip.

The natives do a certain amount of damage to the game but very little comparatively, as there are few natives here (and those only come in periodically to get meat) and they don't use fireams, but traps.

Friday 16 June (to Maun)
Running along the Thamalakane we came across some family parties of Makuba[17] with all their household goods piled on quaint looking sledges with high sides, mounted on wooden runners, and pulled by oxen. We got some good photos of these interesting folk, who were very friendly and jolly.

Soon after 12 we struck the drift across the Thamalakane, where we had had to be pulled thro' by eight oxen when we were up here at the same time of year in 1930, and where we stuck good and hard. This year it was bone dry — a tragedy, showing that the flood water from the Okavango River had not even yet reached Maun. The river banks were full of birds, the lovely Egyptian ibis, the quaint-voiced Lehututu bird (ground hornbill), herons, storks, duck, etc.

And at 12.45 we arrived at the dreadful village of Maun, chief village of Ngamiland, and most desolate and forbidding of villages in the country.

Saturday 17 June
I did not enjoy sleeping indoors at all, missed the freshness of the open air and found it very stuffy. A trying day too. We spent all the morning in the Kgotla, a great gathering of the Batawana Tribe and some oddments from their subject tribes. The Batawana are hopeless: lazy, immoral, stupid, thieving, lying blighters, and I gave them hell. They would discuss nothing except a rotten boundary question, which they raised because they wanted to be able to go into Crown Lands (my Game Reserve) and trap game for food instead of working to produce food themselves. They have got lots of game in their own Reserve, but it's a bit far and in the Tsetse fly belt so they can't take their horses there and they're too lazy to hunt on foot. There was a poisonous fellow Moanaphuti Segolodi,[18] who has been kicked out of two other Reserves. He dared to argue with me, so got suppressed good and hard.

Sunday 18 June
More work at the Office, then a general inspection of some very interesting irrigation work being carried on along the river bank by a German, Dr Lucan. Unfortunately I couldn't see Lucan as he was down with black-water fever, but his work interested me more than he did, especially as he is supposed to be a bit of a dog and causes havoc among the frail ladies of Maun. The idea is to bring the flood water (when the river rises) thro' deep channels at right angles to the river into lines of irrigation channels along and parallel to the river, in which are planted acres and acres of food crops. There were two acres of very good crops of beans, mealies and kaffir corn, all killed by the frost. This was watered by two big trenches ten or twelve feet deep bringing the water to a well at the end. From here it was raised by long poles acting as levers on the old Egyptian system — indeed the whole thing was very like the system in force on the Nile. It was most interesting and seemed very efficacious.

1933

Tuesday 20 June (to Makalamabedi)
Off at 8 am and into Makalamabedi by 8.30 — good going on a hard track. We put in a tremendous morning's work — four hours of concentrated effort.

Our stock-inspector, Hoyle, in charge of this wild district, met us here, also Gopolang, Chief Tshekedi's representative, and a number of headmen from neighbouring villages. They were a terrible looking crowd of savages, half-starved, wholly stupid, clad in filthy rags, more like animals than human beings. They were overawed by seeing a Resident Commissioner (none had ever been in this district)![19] and a Mrs R.C., and it was a work of great patience to get any facts out of them. However after I had addressed them all together I tackled them in different groups and got a fair idea of the position. To the north of Makalamabedi, up towards Maun where we had come from, it was not so bad, but from Makalamabedi on southwards it is apparently worse and worse — no crops for two years, no water this year, cattle drying up and no milk, cattle dying etc. etc.

While I was doing this work, and discussing the buffer-zone arrangements with Hoyle, Dr Henderson was conducting a medical examination of the people, not only the sick ones, but generally in order to find out their general condition — which he reported as bad, suffering from malnutrition, and verging on scurvy.

Potts meanwhile was going thro' the hut-tax register with the village headmen, tracing up defaulters — some had not paid for ten years! Ordering some to come down to Serowe for trial, cursing others, and letting others off with a warning — altogether a remarkable picture of Native Administration in the bush. How the Colonial Office people would smile if they realised how we do our work — sitting on boxes in the shade of a tree with a couple of planks for a table, and administering justice there and then straight off the reel — no lawyers, no courts — just commonsense fairplay. And then and there we began to lay the plans for our relief scheme — it's going to be a big job.

I examined the historical blazed tree that forms the end of the boundary between the Batawana and Bamangwato Tribes, a source of perpetual dispute, and photographed it.

Then I addressed the multitudes, telling them the Government would feed them, and that they had got to behave properly, herd their cattle as directed, and pay hut-tax. Poor devils they haven't a kick left in them, and we shall have to let most of them off their tax.

Wednesday 21 June (to Rakops)
We reached Rakops at 4.45 — fifty two miles from our last camp, and eighty three from Makalamabedi. A delightful spot under some big trees.

We were greeted by Gopolang, the Chief's representative, Sergeant Corcoran in charge here (all alone with some native police), and a very decent white youth who runs the store for R.A. Bailey & Co. The two Europeans (Corcoran and the trader) dined with us and were very interesting, especially Corcoran. He had been in the U.S.A. police, and had been a detective in Chicago of all places. His stories were lurid of the bribery there. Any policeman who did not take bribes would never hold his job.

Thursday 22 June
I woke at daybreak about 6. Birds were sitting in the branches above me intensely interested in the new specimen below. Two small green and yellow birds hopped onto the ground-sheet on which my bed stood, and came quite close to investigate.

Lots of quaint insects were crawling about, and some big birds of the bustard and heron types flopped over the trees. It was so very peaceful and lovely, a real example of a place where 'only man is vile' — for the people here are very vile.

To begin with, the local Headman, Makala Kopo,[20] was an intolerable nuisance, but has recently quietened down, tho' I'm bound to say when I saw him later in the day he looked to me as if he was cheating the gallows. His people are steeped in witchcraft. They have a sort of school for witchdoctors at Mopipi not far from here, where the people come to learn these damnable practices from a sort of local 'god', and they certainly carry them out pretty thoroughly. Corpses are dug up and made to speak; twins are killed at birth; the witch doctors 'put medicine on people and they die for no apparent reason, and we *can't* get at them for not a single native will dare to give evidence. They all take orders from their local 'god' but not from us. If I could find him he'd hang as high as Haman.

Another meeting of headmen of riverine villages. Then whilst Potts resumed his hut tax and other magisterial dealings I dealt with the Damara[21] people and their rascally headman Nicodemus, old Nick for short. His infernal people are on the Bamangwato border, and while the Damara go over and poach the other blokes' game, they come over and plough the best lands usually used by the Damara! All the makings of a troublesome little row which has got to be dealt with; and I've appointed Corcoran to enquire into it with three representatives of each tribe, and told them they'll be smacked if they fight.

Friday 23 June (to Mopipi)
It was bitterly cold when we woke this morning, 32 degrees, but we got away at 8.10 am and passed several large lots of springbuck. We reached Gomo at 9.20 — twenty miles of very good going, fifteen from Rakops camp.

Here we found a store run by a degenerate white man — but he saved our lives by giving us hot coffee while we waited for the lorries to catch us up. I believe he has about fourteen half-caste children. He has been stuck in this God-forsaken country for thirty years, and says this is the worst year from every point of view that he has ever known. His total *takings* last month were £3. Owing to the drought the natives have no food and are scattered looking for berries. Even the berries have failed owing to frost. The temperature fell to 23 degrees on the night of 26 May. His name is Ingleton. We bought a fine squirrel kaross from him for £5 to cheer him up and left his depressing place at 10.20, by which time the sun was blazing hot. It's amazing how the temperature changes out here.

We got to Mopipi at 11.20 — forty-one miles in all — and here we struck the worst hunger position of all; it was really too terrible for words. They have had little or nothing in the way of crops for four years — this year nothing at all. They go out searching for berries and are found dead from exhaustion and hunger. Owing to the drought the milk from their cows is all drying up. The children's food is one cup of milk a day — nothing else. I made Dr Henderson come with me into the huts and examine the people. They are *all* terribly undernourished, and many show signs of scurvy. It's a tragic picture. I have decided to start the feeding campaign by telegraphic instructions from Serowe when we strike that delectable spot, but we've some way to go yet.

I looked over the school, a dreadful tumbledown place run by a bad type of native. Seventy children last year, twenty five this, only up to 3rd Standard. The teacher claims to be Standard Six, but I should put him and his pupils all lower than he says. His name is Kitso. The headman is Rethatoleng[22] — both scoundrels I should say.

Like Rakops, Mopipi is a collection of small separate villages — all equally squalid and miserable, and we could not face a meal in the village. So we pushed on five miles (forty six in all) and camped for lunch while we interviewed groups of tribesmen. One lot of Makalaka were too dreadful for words, emaciated with dull eyes like animals, under headman Madilsa. I bought oxen from Ingleton's son who runs another store near here and gave them to the people to eat. They were like wolves when they heard the news, poor devils, and hardly believed me.

Here we said goodbye to Gopolang, Tshekedi's Headman in this district, and his hut-tax men, all of whom had been perched like crows on our lorries from Makalamabedi for the last few days — and pushed on to a store kept by Ingleton's half caste son, a wretched place with practically no goods for sale. He gives no cash for the cattle he buys in normal times, so the wretched natives have to trek their cattle all the immense distance from here to Serowe to sell!

Monday 26 June (at Serowe)
I had quite a hard day with Potts at the Office, dispatched a number of telegrams, and had a long interview with Tshekedi — he is a tiresome little devil but I rather like him in some ways.

Things are in a shocking condition at Serowe — no grazing for the cattle, the big dam dried up, very little food, hundreds of starving, diseased dogs howling all night and most of the day. The one thing that has saved the position is the bore-hole I put down three years ago. If it were not for that, the people would be dying for want of water and disease would be rampant. As it is the pump engine runs all day, and thousands of women draw water from the stand-pipes all day long. And to think that I had to *force* the borehole through against the wishes and opposition of Tshekedi.[23] Who is the friend of the Tribe, he or I?

I fixed up all arrangements for sending out the grain supply along the Botletli River — arranged to have the dam cleaned out, argued with Tshekedi about various other matters, and finally had a pow-wow with Bishop Gibson (Bishop of Kimberley) about his people from Tonota whom Tshekedi won't allow to go back to Tonota because he is afraid of their plotting against him — or so he says. Really Tshekedi has a down on them because they are Church of England, which is why the Bishop is interested. Tshekedi loves his damned London Missionary Society people to the exclusion of all other brands of Christians.[24]

Ninon went round to see Semane, Khama's widow and Tshekedi's mother, and had a pleasant interview with the old lady.

Matsepane has cleaned up 'Topsy' wonderfully, really that car is a marvel. Although she was scratched to bits she is already beginning to look quite new again, after only one day's polishing.

Thursday 29 June (to Mochudi)
At 5.40 ran into Reyneke's place at Mochudi. Reyneke was away but Mrs Reyneke was delighted to see us and had some people in to a late tea to meet us. She and the children are very nice people. It is curious that the best missionary in the Territory, and my best friend among them, should be a Dutchman and a member of that poisonous body, the Dutch Reformed Church — a politically-minded anti-English institution which has done terrible harm in South Africa.

1933

Friday 30 June (Mochudi to Mafeking)
And so we completed one of the best trips we have ever done. About two thousand miles through extraordinarily interesting country. Some of it practically unknown, some of it reported impassable, all of it delightful.

Sunday 2 to Sunday 9 July (back at Mafeking)
The Office has got a little somnolent in my absence, and I stirred them up vigorously; I kept three shorthand writers going hard and generally got a move on things.
   I had to tick off that sweep Van Rensburg, the member of the European Advisory Council for Lobatsi. He has been up in a Native Reserve trying to get the Chief to say his people would like to go into the Union. And then he lied about it and said he had never been there!
   Tshekedi called in to see me about what he called 'private business', really to try and prevent my dealing with certain points affecting the Native Proclamations at the forthcoming meeting of the Native Advisory Council.
   I am very busy preparing for this meeting, which will be an important one as I have to deal with all the amendments proposed by the various Tribes — a lengthy and difficult business.
   The Foot and Mouth disease campaign is also going well, but we shall have to make a great effort to speed it up and get the whole work of inoculation completed before the rains. It will mean a huge drive, but we must do it.

Monday 10 July
The Native Advisory Council opened with the usual formalities, and then I got down to it and spoke for over three hours on the various amendments to the Proclamations, dealing with every detail, point by point, an exhausting performance. When 1.15 o'clock came I was very glad of the adjournment for lunch, though that wasn't much rest as Rutherford (Resident Magistrate, Mochudi), Towne (Resident Magistrate, Molepolole) and Mangan (Resident Magistrate, Kanye) came to lunch.
   Then at it again at 3 when the obstruction began, principally inspired by Tshekedi. So I told them they could have a couple of days to yap among themselves and consider my speech which had been taken down in shorthand and typed as we went along — a good effort — and at 5 adjourned the meeting for that purpose, after they had passed a resolution about Pathfinders with which I had a good deal of sympathy. The Union Minister of Native Affairs, Grobler, had refused to issue passports to allow native Pathfinders from the Union to go to the great Scout Jamboree in Hungary — a ridiculous act on his part — and so the meeting passed an infuriated resolution of protest about it which I duly telegraphed on to the High Commissioner for South Africa.

Thursday 13 July
The meeting of the Native Advisory Council was resumed, and the Chiefs put in a lot of damned silly proposals and fresh amendments which if accepted would have had the effect of killing the Proclamations. So I made them a short speech telling them how disappointed I was, and ticked them off well. Then we went on with the rest of the Agenda which was not very thrilling, except that they passed a very good resolution unanimously, objecting strongly to any idea of going into the Union.

Friday 14 & Saturday 15 July
Admiral and Mrs Evans,[25] his Flag Lieutenant, and his two boys arrived for breakfast at 7.30 and left at 9.15 on their way north to Bulawayo. They are all perfectly

delightful and charming people and we lost our hearts to them — it will be a pleasure working with him while Stanley is away on leave in England and Evans will be acting as High Commissioner for South Africa.

The Resident Magistrates and the Chiefs all left for their various destinations in the Protectorate on the 9.15 train, and I then had to get busy preparing for my visit to Cape Town and my interview with Stanley on many subjects prior to his departure for England. This involved a great rush on both days.

Friday 1 to Thursday 7 September
Although it rained after dinner tonight (a good omen) this month ushered in the biggest trouble we have had in the B.P. — the row with Tshekedi. The first rumblings were heard on Friday and Saturday. Tshekedi had sent in a letter about my Proclamations addressed to Sir Herbert Stanley (who is in England) requesting an interview with the Secretary of State, and completely ignoring myself as the R.C. and Admiral Evans as the (Acting) High Commissioner. He practically refused to take it back or to acknowledge his error — of course, a definitely planned piece of insolence and defiance.[26]

Admiral Evans was on the train from the north going to Pretoria, so I joined it and went with him, having telephoned on Friday to Eales to come up to Pretoria from Cape Town for a conference, as the matter seemed serious.

On Monday 4, we conferred all day, settled what to do and I returned to Mafeking by the night train. The Admiral went on for a tour in the Game Reserve (Kruger Park).

And then on Thursday 7, the storm burst, and I got a telegram from Capt Potts, R.M. Serowe, to say that Tshekedi had flogged a European publicly in the Kgotla![27] (I am detailing the matter with some care as this will be probably the only complete and true account ever written. No one else knows or could know *all* of the facts except myself.[28])

Friday 8 to Wednesday 13 September (to Pretoria and Serowe)
Now the offence committed by the European, i.e. striking a native, a common, indeed everyday occurrence in South Africa, took place 'early in August', the flogging on 6 September and the report to me was made by telegram on 7 September.

On 8th, I telegraphed to various likely places in the Kruger Game Reserve to catch Evans, and telephoned to Eales at Cape Town to come up by the afternoon train which would reach Pretoria on Sunday morning 10th.

I myself went to Pretoria by Friday night's train arriving there early Saturday morning when I met Evans and Liesching,[29] the Political Secretary, an exceedingly able and very delightful man. We were in conference all day. The first thing I learned, much to my surprise and rather to my alarm, was that the Admiral had already (on Friday night) telegraphed to Cape Town for a detachment to come up from the Fleet with guns.[30]

I handed in a dispatch which I had written on Friday, reciting all the facts and recommending the action to be taken.

On Sunday 10 morning, Eales and Leslie Blackwell[31] (Legal Adviser) arrived from Cape Town and we conferred all day, despatching orders and telegrams to make all arrangements, a long and tiring day.

Ninon had been going to spend a few days in Jo'burg, and arrived there by car. I motored over there from Pretoria to sleep at the Carlton.

1933

On Monday 11, I went back to Pretoria very early and after further conferences all day, Liesching and I left for Palapye Road by train in the Admiral's coach at 6.20. Ninon had returned to Mafeking by car.

On Tuesday 12 we reached Mafeking at 7.30, where Ninon joined us and all three in the Admiral's coach (he had remained at Pretoria) were hitched onto the special train carrying the sailors and marines who had arrived from Cape Town. We left at 8.20 — I had just had time to rush to the house and collect some clothes and uniform, etc.

All the way we were planning and organising, receiving and sending telegrams — the last one I got being one from Potts warning me to expect an outburst at Palapye Road.

On arrival at Palapye at 8.30, I found all quiet however. Potts and Neale met us, told us that in spite of my orders to the contrary Tshekedi had brought thousands of his men down from Serowe — the very thing I had wished to avoid as the Enquiry which we had ordered to take place on the next day (Wednesday 12) was likely to create trouble, and I didn't want to have to deal with a huge crowd. That was why we had the Enquiry at Palapye instead of at Serowe.

However it was reported that Tshekedi was exhorting his people to keep quiet, so after decoding telegrams up to 11 pm we went to bed and slept on the coach. Incidentally, I had developed a foul cold or flu, and had a temperature of over 100 degrees for the next few days.

On Wednesday 13 the Enquiry was held. The sailors and marines had detrained and camps were run up everywhere; field telephones fixed up in the twinkling of an eye from all the strategic points to the train, e.g. from the Court House where the Enquiry was to take place, etc. A guard of marines was posted at the Court House — another guard of the only twenty police I could raise under Captain Croneen at the Enquiry itself.

At about 8.30 Buchanan (Tshekedi's lawyer from Cape Town whom *we* had brought up, by telephone from Pretoria) came to see me and asked if I wouldn't stop the whole thing! At 9.30 I summoned Tshekedi to the police camp, and formally read to him the order suspending him from exercising the functions of Chief and directing him not to leave the precincts of the camp.

And at 10 am the Enquiry started, Captain Neale in the Chair, aided by Liesching. Captain Nettelton had withdrawn by permission, as it appeared that Tshekedi might bring certain charges against him.

I then had a little leisure to inspect the naval detachment — a wonderful body of men — a hundred and sixty five in all. Sailors and marines with four small field-guns, fit and hard and jolly, doing their drill and field practice, working their camp kitchens, testing their field telephones, and generally bringing a wonderful atmosphere of Britain into the veld. The officers were a jolly crowd, and by Jove weren't they all efficient and keen. One old quartermaster was priceless. I heard him remark: 'My Gawd, fancy me after thirty years in the Navee just goin' on pension and now come up to this Gawd forsaken sand bin to be stuck in the bloomin' stumick by a bleedin' Kaffir'!

The Enquiry (which I did not attend) was a most impressive affair. It was in the open under some trees. Neale and Liesching at the table, officers of the Court beside them. Tshekedi and his lawyers and friends in front. Drawn up at the side were my twenty native police, like statues, and all around were thousands of natives squatting motionless on the ground drinking in the interpreter's words.

Behind the Court House, out of sight but ready for any emergency, was a party of marines complete with tin hats, rifles loaded, etc.

The report of the Enquiry is a long official document which I won't quote here; the result is well known, the facts were not denied, and the report is merely a summary of the facts which we knew already.[32]

By 3.30 the Enquiry was completed, and then I had to hold a further short enquiry into certain allegations made by Tshekedi against the Magistrates, Captains Potts and Nettelton, as to alleged dilatoriness in dealing with the Chief's complaints against the white villain. These proved quite unfounded;[33] the real fault lay with Tshekedi himself who had failed to produce the evidence asked for by the R.M.

In the meanwhile Ninon and I had moved over to the Palapye Hotel (!) leaving the coach for the Admiral. I got into uniform and drove up to the aerodrome. He arrived by air with his Flag Lieutenant and Eales at 5. After a preliminary talk we adjourned for dinner, then afterwards conferred in the coach till 10 pm, when we all came back to the hotel and made all final decisions and arrangements for the formal suspension of Tshekedi at Serowe on the next day. We finished at 12.30, and I was glad to stagger into bed, dead to the world, with a foul headache and a beastly temperature, cold and cough.

Thursday 14 September (at Palapye and Serowe)
We were up at 7 and saw lorry after lorry push off laden with the sailors and marines and their guns, in the midst of a blinding dust storm, the worst ever — a ghastly morning, hot as hell, and a stifling wind. We all left in five cars at 10.45 — all in full uniform — the Admiral and I in the first car, Ninon, the Flag Lieutenant and the Director of Operations in the next, Eales, Leisching, Neale, etc.

The heavy lorries had a devil of a time in the deep sand and stuck again and again, but the sailors pulled them out in great style. We passed several of the lorries on the road, and waited outside Serowe for them to get up and into position. Tshekedi had been sent on ahead.

Then I went on and arrived at the scene of action — a most impressive sight. A large covered platform had been erected in the middle of the race course, a flagstaff in front of it from which a huge Union Jack was flying, chairs on the platform, and in the middle a table covered with another Jack. On either side a guard of marines with fixed bayonets, tin hats (battle-bowlers); away along to the right stretched out in a long line was the naval detachment, the four guns each with its gun's crew kneeling or standing by it; a small group of Europeans on the right of the platform; behind it a naval guard on one side, and my guard of twenty B.P. Police. All as smart as paint and motionless as statues. Stretched in a long line five or six deep in front of the platform behind a whitewashed line were thousands of tribesmen, squatting on the ground.

As my car drove up, the Police saluted and I met Major Webber commanding the troops and the other officers, ran a rapid eye over everything to see things were all right, and then up came the Admiral and staff.

The guard sprang to attention and gave the Royal salute. We solemnly saluted each other. The guard was inspected, and then the Admiral and I and our A.D.C.s and officers got on to the platform. Tshekedi came and stood in front, two B.P., N.C.O.s behind him, and the guns crashed out the salute of nineteen guns, the roar echoing in the hills magnificently. The tribesmen jumped up, prepared to bolt, but we had foreseen the possibility of this and men had been posted near them to reassure them.

The Admiral then read his speech suspending Tshekedi. The guard saluted. We got into our cars and drove off to the Residency in an impressive silence. There Mrs Potts had got together a most excellent light lunch which we all needed very much — it was past 2 o'clock and we were famished.

Meanwhile Tshekedi had been driven off in a car back to Palapye Road; the aeroplane had come up from there to Serowe; we drove down to the flying ground. Admiral Evans, his Flag Lieutenant and A.D.C., Liesching, Eales, and the naval writer all got into the plane and off they went back to Johannesburg to pick up the night mail back to Cape Town. Altogether a sound piece of organisation.

Later on Ninon and I went back to Palapye Road by car. The sailors went back, the marines staying at Serowe. We were utterly tired out and simply flung ourselves into bed.

Friday 15 September
Trouble started early. Tshekedi was reported ill, so I sent an urgent telephoned message to Serowe for Dr Morgan to come down. However it proved to be nothing, so we arranged to send him to Francistown by the 9 pm train — he is ordered to stay there. Meanwhile I heard from Potts that the Tribe had refused to appoint an Acting Chief,[34] so Ninon and I went back to Serowe in the afternoon. I interviewed the Headmen and told them they had jolly well got to do so at once, and then after further consultation with Potts returned to Palapye Road having arranged with Major Webber that if all continued quiet tomorrow he could withdraw his men on Sunday.

Saturday 16 September
A busy day telephoning, telegraphing, and writing despatches. Tshekedi had gone to Francistown last night and had arrived this morning. He had refused to occupy the government quarters provided, or to eat any of the food we had got in, and went off to a private farm in the neighbourhood.

Monday 18 to Sunday 24 September (back at Mafeking)
A very hectic week telegraphing and telephoning Cape Town, and telegraphing London. On Sunday I had two telephone talks with Cape Town lasting fifty-five and sixty-five minutes!

The net result of everything is that Tshekedi has climbed down, expressed regret for his action, promised never to interfere with Europeans again and undertaken to work loyally with the Administration. So now we are going to terminate his suspension and reinstate him.[35]

It has been a huge triumph, and I think our friend is flattened out for all time, or at all events for a long time to come. Everyone is simply delighted, except of course the rotten missionary-inspired Press, and the missionaries themselves. I have received any amount of congratulations.

Sunday 1 to Sunday 8 October (and lasted well on into November)
An awful month owing to Ninon's illness which started on 1st and lasted till well on into November — the worst time I've ever had since her great illness in England. I think she got over-tired and chilled at yesterday's bazaar and that started one of her usual attacks which got steadily worse.

I had to go up to Serowe with the Admiral on Tuesday afternoon — leaving at 4.45 pm and getting back to Mafeking at 6.30 am on Thursday morning.

It was a simple ceremony held in the same place as the suspension but without any naval guard, just a detachment of B.P. Police. The Admiral and I, his Flag Lieutenant and Director of Operations left Palapye by car on Wednesday morning, and drove to the Residency at Serowe where we got into uniform; then to the place of meeting where the Admiral read his speech terminating the suspension on the ground of Tshekedi's apology and undertakings as to future behaviour. Then back to the Residency where we lunched. Afterwards we had an interview with Tshekedi and some of his Headmen, when he asked if he might be allowed to go to England about the Proclamations! Evans said he would telegraph on his request.

On Thursday I got a cable from Home definitely refusing to allow Tshekedi to go to England, and on Friday 13 Buchanan and Jennings sailed to represent his case.[36]

On Sunday we had a few drops of rain — the first of the season here.

Monday 23 to Sunday 29 October (to Pretoria)
Ninon continued to improve so I was able to leave with Chase for two days (Wednesday and Thursday) for a most important Conference at Pretoria regarding exports from the Territory. Wolfe Davies of the Imperial Cold Storage met us at the station at Jo'burg. Chase and I had a very satisfactory talk with Wolfe Davies who agreed to start killing at Lobatsi and exporting to Durban the very day we got leave to export.

We slept at Polley's Hotel and went off early for the Conference. The Conference at Pretoria was most successful, General Kemp met us very well, and we can now start exporting everything except cattle — that will come shortly, he says, probably April. I tried for January, but he sticks to eight months since the last case of Foot and Mouth, which was in August.

I drove back to Jo'burg alone after lunch for a conference with Gemmill regarding our natives for the mines — a very satisfactory interview, he is going to take 2,000 more.

Monday 6 November (at Johannesburg)
I had my big cattle and meat Conference — representatives of farmers and traders — Wolfe Davies of the Imperial Cold Storage and Colonel Robins[37] of the British South Africa Company from Southern Rhodesia. My proposals for organisation of cattle improvement and meat export were discussed exhaustively and adopted and it was agreed to form a cattle owners association to regulate, control and stimulate the whole question of cattle and meat raising and export. A great triumph.

Monday 20 to Sunday 26 November (back at Mafeking)
Very busy all the week with preparing the Estimates for next year; a terribly difficult job in view of our bad financial position.

I am thankful to say that we had good rains on Wednesday, Thursday, Friday and Sunday. A great joy after the awful drought.

On Thursday I had a meeting of all cordon officers to discuss the question of shooting cattle that cross the cordons: it has got to a serious state now, as we have shot nearly 3,000 cattle and small stock. But it's the only way to force people to obey the instructions and save the rest of the Territory from becoming infected, and so prolong the period during which we can't export.

The Estimates were completed and sent off. I got a letter from General Kemp confirming all the arrangements made with him in Pretoria — and so we are making a little progress.

But this is a heart-breaking job.

Monday 27 November
Rains all over the country — splendid for us, but I gather rather overdone in other parts of South Africa. Reports from everywhere of burst dams, roads flooded, railway delays, even deaths of people and cattle from lightning and drowning. Extraordinary country this — it's either as dry as a man's throat in hell, or else torrents fall, and the water rushes away to waste sweeping the good top earth with it, and so causing soil erosion. What with drought, deluge, cattle diseases (Foot and Mouth, Redwater, East Coast Fever, Anthrax, Lung Sickness, etc.), hail, locusts, insect pests, terrific heat, and frost — the lot of a farmer in this much over-rated country is hardly an easy one. However, thank goodness we've good *ordinary* rain in most parts of B.P., which is most important especially as I've got the Francistown Creamery opening for butter manufacture at once, and the Lobatsi Creamery opening on 11 December — a tremendous achievement, and one that will be of immense benefit to farmers and natives.

Friday 1 December
I had a perfectly delightful letter from Admiral Evans today on his relinquishing the High Commissionership. Sir Herbert Stanley arrives back tomorrow by air. Evans is the finest man I have ever worked with — he is a *man* — and in this age of decadent rabbits it is refreshing to find one. He says the nicest things about our work together,[38] and looks forward to our coming to stay at Admiralty House when we come down to Cape Town.

Indeed all this week I am getting a very satisfactory series of dispatches and letters, either congratulating me on the various successful 'coups' I have brought off last month, or agreeing to fresh proposals of mine.

It's infernally hot again, and dictating all day gets a bit wearisome — the concentration of mind, and forcing out all one's ideas and plans in full detail and in terms of money like sausage meat coming out of a machine. Everyone is working at top pressure, and looking rather boiled. I wish it were not quite so hot for Ninon's sake — she feels it just now.

Saturday 2 & Sunday 3 December
My morning ride before breakfast is the saving clause in life just now — it is heavenly getting out for an hour in the early cool and galloping over the veld. I can't understand why some of the others don't do it.

Wednesday 27 & Thursday 28 December (at Cape Town)
I spent all day, both days, with the High Commissioner and had tremendous success all along the line. My Estimates and all my applications to the Colonial Development Fund for grants for my development proposals have all gone home already, all approved here, so now it only rests with London. Sir Herbert Stanley agrees and supports all my schemes and ideas: he solemnly said: 'I think it's time we adopted a forward policy'! That is screamingly funny, considering that I have been urging it and fighting it for four years, and putting forward scheme after scheme for fools to criticize — as Kipling says 'to see the words uttered twisted by knaves to make a sport for fools'.

However, at long last it looks as though we are really going ahead. It will be a huge triumph if, after wallowing through all the troubles we have had, we really start progressing.

Stanley told me a number of things of interest, the most important being that the Colonial Office have definitely decided (and have told the Union Government) that they will *not* hand over Bechuanaland to South Africa. That is confidential, but it's jolly good news.

Also the Colonial Office have decided to get rid of that poisonous ass Leslie Blackwell, the Legal Adviser to the High Commissioner and President of my Special Court, and to send out a real good man from Home. I begged Stanley not to appoint Blackwell who is a politician as well as a lawyer (a rotten combination) and a nasty piece of work. But he would do it, and as it was for his own Legal Adviser I couldn't stop it. I am afraid Stanley is a bit sick with things, and I imagine the people at Home were not too pleased with him. They seem to have supported me in several things where he (Stanley) did not agree, and probably told him to be a bit more energetic. He is so terribly fat, takes no exercise, and smokes like a funnel all day.

However everyone seems to be supporting *me*, *I* am happy!

Friday 29 December
I had a long and very satisfactory talk with the Imperial Cold Storage people about beginning to slaughter our cattle at and export from Lobatsi and Walvis, and also in general support of my Walvis Bay Cattle Route scheme. They are frightfully keen on it, and are writing me an official letter supporting the idea, saying it is a sound proposition commercially, and undertaking to kill and export 20,000 chilled and 20,000 frozen carcases annually. Good enough.

1934

Friday 5 January
An extraordinarily satisfactory interview with General Kemp at the Ministry of Agriculture; he agreed to all my proposals for restarting export trade from the B.P. Hides, skins, karrosses, butter, etc., had already been agreed to, and now he has agreed to meat and also cattle to Durban, he entirely agrees with my Walvis Bay Route proposals, and to my scheme for getting cattle out of Angola through the Caprivi Strip. We also discussed other matters very amiably, and I am to see him again on our return from Walvis Bay. Altogether a very good morning, and in the afternoon I wrote dispatches and did a lot of other useful work.-

Trip to South West Africa

Monday 8 January (from Cape Town)
Off to Walvis Bay. The ship (*Watussi*,[1] a German boat, 10,000 tons) did not sail until 5.15, but we drove down in 'Topsy' at 4.30, a perfectly lovely afternoon, warm calm sea, and generally delightful.

Thursday 11 January (to Walvis Bay and Swakopmund)
We got into Walvis about 10 am and had a lovely day. The ship's band performed again as we came alongside the quay, and there seemed to be quite a lot of people on shore. We were met by Major Drydale, representing the Government, Neale representing the Imperial Cold Storage Company and Gordon Store with his aeroplane retained by the Government to fly us over to Swakopmund. His plane was a small Puss Moth — so Ninon and I went off with him first — Chase and the luggage will follow. We had a perfectly lovely flight — smooth and calm as if we were not moving at all. Swakopmund is a pleasant little spot built on sand dunes right on the mouth of the Swakop river, as its name implies. The Germans started building a huge pier, as they intended that the place should rival Walvis as a port, but the War stopped that, and the pier has never been finished.

Friday 12 January
We started our official negotiations at 9 and had a *most* successful day, obtaining agreement on all the points we had come over about. The principal ones were of

course the Walvis Bay Stock Route, and the passage of B.P. cattle across the Caprivi Strip into Angola (Portuguese South West Africa). As regards the former we got all the concessions we needed: a passage through South West Africa from our frontier to rail head at Gobabis — about eighty miles; and a water-tight set of conditions to ensure that we have these rights in perpetuity and for nothing! Of course it is to their advantage, too, for the cattle will go by rail from Gobabis to Walvis where they will be turned into chilled and frozen meat for export to England and Italy. This will mean a great benefit to the town and port of Walvis Bay and to the railway.

Chase and I drafted the Agreement in the form of a Treaty and after some further discussion it was agreed to — it has to be copied out and signed tomorrow.

We also got our proposal to cross our cattle through the Caprivi Strip to Northern Rhodesia agreed to, and this will be signed tomorrow. They will cross the Chobe at a place called Andara,[2] and this will be a great help to the Ngamiland European and native cattle owners.

Saturday 13 January
We finished off our negotiations in the morning, signed the Treaties, exchanged dispatches ratifying them, congratulated each other all round.

Monday 15 January (at Walvis Bay)
Chase and I went off to inspect the Imperial Cold Storage slaughter works that are going to take our cattle, and the wireless station — both most interesting. The Imperial Cold Storage works are the most modern and up-to-date in South Africa.

We shall trek our animals across the Protectorate (three or four hundred miles) and I am getting a grant from Home of £20,000 to put down wells and boreholes to water the cattle along this route. It will be a *crime* if they don't give it to me, for I have overcome every other obstacle, and every single soul, official and commercial, supports the idea.

Tuesday 16 to Thursday 18 January (Walvis Bay to Cape Town)
A perfect passage back to Cape Town: lovely weather the whole way, though rather colder than on the way up.

It was very interesting talking to the Germans and getting their different viewpoints on Hitler. The officers, crew, and most of the 1st class passengers are Hitlerite to a man; but in the 3rd class are a number of refugee Jews, and naturally they are *not* Hitlerites! The day before we got on board one of them spoke disparagingly of the Swastika flag which all German ships now fly in the bows — so one of the crew 'set about him' properly and wiped the deck with him!

There is no doubt in my mind that the world's Press is run much too much by Jews, that affairs in Germany have been much exaggerated by them, and that Hitler has done good work in stamping out Communism in Germany, even if he has trodden a bit heavily on Jews in doing so. There is a wonderful spirit among Germans today. I told one of the stewards on board, when tipping him, how well satisfied we were and how admirably we thought everyone did their job. He thanked me and said that 'in the new Germany, we are taught that everyone must do his job to the best of his ability, whatever the job is, for the good and for the credit of the country'.

A fine spirit, and a good contrast to the damned trade union spirit in England, and the living-on-the-dole complex.

1934

We got into Cape Town at 5 pm on Thursday. The faithful Matsepane was on the quay with 'Topsy' all ready for us. They were a longish time clearing the ship through Customs and Immigration Officers, owing to the number of German Jews in the 3rd Class. They go through them with a tooth-comb, and I don't blame them.

Wednesday 24 January (back at Mafeking)
All the morning I spent at the Office, and again all the afternoon, planning out the locust campaign with the Union locust officers who have come here from Pretoria and elsewhere to see me. It's going to be an infernal nuisance and a horrible waste of money, and nothing that we can do can really exterminate the beasts; we can only protect the food lands. One of my people who has been in the country for forty years told me he had never in all his experience seen such a visitation — he drove through one swarm sixty miles long!

Chase is back from the interview that he and Liesching had with Kemp in Pretoria re-locusts — a bad show. They told Kemp that the Imperial Government would not agree to his demand to pay half the total costs of the campaign in B.P. (estimated at £100,000), so Kemp lost his temper! and shewed himself in his true colours. He said that in that case it was time the Union took over the B.P., and that he would have to go back on all the export concessions he had agreed to give me! He is a dirty dog, and still of course a Boer rebel at heart.

Monday 29 January
A hectic morning at the Office. Dyke has got to sack two of our doctors — one is no good, the other has got seriously entangled with an undesirable female. A great bore.

Then I had interviews with Shepherd of the Scotch Church and Tongue of the Seventh Day Adventists as to establishing a mission hospital at Maun. The latter people put up by far the better proposition, and I shall propose to accept it. I am still waiting for the Roman Catholic offer.

Thursday 1 February
Much to my surprise I had a very pleasant and satisfactory interview with Tshekedi (my first since his suspension!) regarding the arrangements for fighting locusts in his district, much to his delight.

I also saw Moremi, the prospective Chief of the Batawana who is being educated at Tiger Kloof. He is a hopeless youth I fear. He complained that his tribe would not even give food to his mother, the late Chief's widow, and that his cattle and possessions were not being looked after by the tribe in his absence, and wanted to chuck any more schooling and take up his job as Chief. I refused and told him to go back at once. But that means that we must look after his mother and his Tribe.

Monday 12 February
I had a long talk in the morning with Bishop Meysing about his medical mission work in the B.P. I fear that Dr Dyke with his beastly Scotch low church evangelical prejudices has not been giving him a fair show, so I gave Dyke a talking to in the afternoon and I fancy things will be better now. Extraordinary thing how religion warps even good men's judgement.

Tuesday 13 to Friday 16 February
Tshekedi is an amazing problem. I mentioned that I had had a very pleasant and satisfactory interview with him lasting nearly all day on 1st February.

Today he came through Mafeking on his way to Cape Town and called in at the Office to pay his respects. Most pleasant, friendly and courteous. He had been told to draft an address of welcome from his Tribe for H.R.H. Prince George. He sent it up to the Office late on Wednesday and I only saw it on Thursday morning after he had left. An amazing production, most insolent and even threatening, and utterly impossible! So I posted it back to him at Cape Town with a letter from myself saying it wouldn't do, and he'd got to draft another. Goodness knows whether we shall have another row about that now.

I had to draft (myself) most of the addresses to be presented to H.R.H. and *all* his replies. It's really very funny. I wonder if people realize how much work a Royal visit entails on the authorities responsible for it. If it all goes right, well it's taken a matter of course, but the tiniest thing wrong means hell.

Saturday 17 February
An infernally annoying thing happened this morning — my Police Sergeant (European), who is helping Captain Croneen to train H.R.H.'s escort, has been found out in a joint scheme with an ex-convict to buy cattle illegally for a commission and run them through our cordon and over the border!

I shall have to arrest him, have him tried by a Board of Officers, and dismissed if found guilty — it's simply maddening.

Sunday 18 & Monday 19 February (to Cape Town again)
I worked at papers all day in the train on Monday. *Inter alia* I read some amazing letters from the Dominions Office reporting their interviews with those two limbs of hell, Buchanan and Jennings, in London. The lies, bare-faced, damnable lies, that the lawyer and the man of God told were simply amazing. I suppose they thought they were perfectly safe as there was no-one from here to contradict them. It is of course monstrous that the Dominions Office should see people like that without the presence of a representative of the B.P. The lawyer talked about the 'dishonesty' of the local officials, and the man of God told the deputation that the poor Bechuana natives couldn't even understand my new Proclamations because they were only published in English! In fact they were published in *Sechuana*, and I explained them in two long speeches, one lasting three hours, the other three and a half hours, both of which were translated into Sechuana sentence by sentence as I went along; and all my Magistrates explained both the Proclamations to *all* the different Tribes in their own villages again in Sechuana![3]

How I loathe parsons of every breed, and everything to do with every Church. Damned cowardly liars.

Friday 23 February (at Cape Town)
I did some shopping and lunched at the Club with Liesching. And then at 3 began the great object of my visit — the meeting with Tshekedi and the other Chiefs about my new Native Proclamations.

It was a bad show. Sir Herbert Stanley handled it very badly; he doesn't know how to deal with natives, and he doesn't know the native Proclamations. The natives tumbled to this and talked the most awful rot, and the proceedings dragged on until nearly 7, and then we didn't finish and I am to go on again tomorrow.

Saturday 24 February
All the morning we blethered on with the Chiefs about my Proclamations: a heart-rending performance that made me sick. It's dreadful to see one's work bungled.[4]

Wednesday 28 February (back at Mafeking)
The Sergeant at Gaberones has confessed fully about the illegal cattle buying basis, and I have allowed him to resign instead of dismissing him. I want to avoid the public scandal which would be caused by a court prosecution. He has left the Territory today.

Thursday 1 March
Ninon and I off by car to Gaberones to inspect all arrangements for H.R.H. Prince George's visit.

Friday 2 March (at Gaberones)
After dinner I discussed various other official matters with Ellenberger. Things are not too good up here, and I can see trouble coming. The Chief Molefi is heavily in debt. He wastes his time drinking and fooling about in Johannesburg instead of attending to his Tribe's business, and they are getting very sick of him. His uncle, ex-Chief Isang, is gaining influence, and there may be a sort of revolt to kick out Molefi. One old headman said plainly: 'If you (the Government) were not here we should have killed the Chief long ago'. Moreover Molefi has 'pinched' some hut tax money and handed in a cheque that was dishonoured, and he is also going to be sued for debts by a Jo'burg firm in the Magistrate's Court.

Saturday 3 March (back to Mafeking)
Witch-doctors are playing a large part in the trouble between Isang and Molefi at Mochudi. They say that the four years drought they had on Molefi's accession was because he was never given the Chief's rainmaking 'medicine' held by his father. The old man said it was not to be given to him until he shewed signs of being fit to rule, and it has been hidden in a secret place and so no rain could be made! The obvious fact that the drought extended to other districts as well makes no effect on them — *their belief in this business is so deep-rooted that nothing will eradicate it.*

Sunday 4 to Sunday 11 March
A lovely morning in the garden, writing. The day was however marred by an unfortunate episode. Mrs Mildenhall, coming into Ninon's bedroom, found Lazarus and Lydia, our two prize domestics, grovelling on the floor, and in due course told Mildenhall who reported to me. So I had a hell of a row with them both, carried on by Ninon with Lydia. I offered Lazarus the choice of a devil of a thrashing, or a fine of two months wages, or to be handed over to the Magistrate. He chose the middle course after a fearsome scene. They are dreadful people, all pigs and liars.
    On Tuesday I had a very interesting letter from Sir Alan Pim on his return from British Honduras where he has been on an economic mission similar to his jaunts out here, and to Zanzibar etc. Certainly our Colonial Administration needs looking into, as I discovered when I came out here. But the first thing to do seems to be to hang most of the Colonial Office officials at Home on the lamp-posts in Whitehall.

1934

Sunday 18 March (at Gaberones)
The real start. Various small troubles and difficulties had to be settled in the morning, and then after an early lunch, the train came in at 1.30 bringing Sir Herbert and Lady Stanley and Captain Holbech. The escort turned up, smart as paint again, and H.E. (His Excellency, i.e. Stanley) was delighted. I introduced a few people to him (MacFarlane and Glover[5] of the Advisory Council) and then at 4.15 took them 'over the course' for H.R.H.'s visit. They were obviously delighted with all the arrangements. At the Camp we presented a medal 'For Valour' to a Pathfinder boy. He had saved three lives by pulling people out of a hut struck by lightning, although injured himself, a fine effort.

Tuesday 20 March (at Gaberones)
At 10 H.R.H. Prince George[6] left his coach, and with his suite walked down to the flagstaff where Ninon and I were waiting. We were presented by Sir Herbert Stanley and then H.R.H. inspected the escort, being very pleased, and complemented Croneen. Of course we were all in full war-paint, white uniforms and decorations, and it was rather an effective sight. Then I presented the senior officers of the Administration and their wives to H.R.H., after which we all got into cars and went off to the European meeting. The cars were all numbered, and everyone had a list shewing exactly what he had to do and which car he belonged to.

The European meeting was held in a huge marquee about half a mile from the station under big trees among the bush.[7] The floor was covered with native skin karosses. H.R.H. inspected a small detchment of Girl Guides and a party of about twenty ex-servicemen all wearing their medals. An address of welcome was read by MacFarlane, the senior Member of the Advisory Council present, and presented to H.R.H. Then H.R.H. read his reply (which I had written for him!) and handed it to MacFarlane. After which all the Europeans came up one by one and were presented. H.R.H. shook hands and said a few words to each — that was that.

Then the cars rolled up, the mounted escort closed around the Royal car, and in the same order we moved off slowly over the two and a half miles thru jolly country to the Native Meeting.

As H.R.H. drove up there was tremendous cheering and shouts of 'Pula, Pula', and after saluting the crowd, he walked along the lines of Pathfinders and Wayfarers and inspected them, then returned to the platform. After a few words of introduction from Stanley, each Chief came forward in turn, gave his address of welcome to the interpreter who read it out in English and handed it to H.R.H.. At the same time the Chief presented his gift — karosses, lion skins, which were all piled up in front of the Prince. Each Chief then came forward and was presented by the Prince with a silver mounted walking stick bearing his Crest and an inscription. The Prince handed his present to each Chief and shook hands with him (including our friend Tshekedi of Serowe fame, whose presents of karosses and skins were very fine indeed).

Led by ex-Chief Isang of the Bakgatla, the whole huge multitude sang 'God Save the King' and gave three cheers for the Prince — after which once more the cars came up, the party embarked and off we went back to the station.

Under a big tree by the station a deputation of some twenty Indians hung a garland round his neck in the usual Indian way (which he discarded as soon as possible!) and that was that. The whole morning's proceedings had gone like clockwork.

Eventually at about 3 pm back we all went to the train, and then Ninon and I had to bolt off to the Native Sports to be ready to receive H.R.H. there at 3.15. These were held on the aerodrome, yet another site commanding a lovely view. They were admirably organised by Lt. Hope, and included an ox race, chicken race, native dances, displays by Pathfinders and Wayfarers. H.R.H. seemed to enjoy them thoroughly, as did everyone else, and stayed for an hour. Then he went off for a quiet walk — or so we thought. H.R.H. got into shorts and went for a five and a half mile run along the railway track with one of the pressmen who had been a professional runner!

Friday 23 to Sunday 25 March (at Mafeking)
Masses of arrears of work to be picked up at the Office, where I had a hectic day on Friday dictating and writing at home all day Saturday. I had a perfectly foul letter from the Dominions Office; they are the world's damnedest fools. Actually trying to stop my exporting meat to England, when they are allowing meat to come in from Argentina, Brazil, Australia, New Zealand, South Africa and Southern Rhodesia! And that would mean ruin to us, and the British taxpayer would have to support the Territory for ever. They are mad.

Wednesday 28 to Friday 30 March (Good Friday)
A couple of idiotic letters from Rheinallt Jones about Pathfinders. He wants to cooperate with the L.M.S. movement 'Life Brigade', or some such rot, and I won't have it. I want to work towards amalgamation with Scouts. So I had to write and 'tick him off'. On Friday Ninon went to church and I worked at home all day.

Monday 2 April
Chase arrived early from Pretoria — likewise a telegram with the amazing news that General Kemp, the (South African) Minister of Agriculture, had calmly announced his intention of coming uninvited into the B.P. to see how the locust work was getting on! The amazing cheek of a Minister of another State doing this almost took my breath away. I also realized the political repercussions that might follow, the row at Home, and the effect on the natives here. But we can't afford to quarrel with the brute, as he has the power to stop our cattle exports. So I sent off a very polite telegram saying I had heard he *wished* to come, inviting him to do so and offering to arrange facilities if he would let me know when and where he would arrive, and inviting him to stay here! Then I told Chase to leave on Tuesday morning by car at 6 am, head Kemp off at the point of entry and stick to him — also to warn all my officers all along the line.

Wednesday 4 April (at Francistown)
With a great flourish of trumpets the Monarch Mine was opened at 10 am. Dr Cullen, Mr Glassman, Mrs Cullen, the Mine Manager, Major Pillatt the new manager of the Tati Company, Mrs Pillatt, and lots of others were there, and of course many hundreds of natives. The mine Manager made an excellent speech explaining the policy that they were to follow — very sound i.e. development for a year to see exactly what payable ore they had before starting any extraction. Then I followed and the spirit moved me to one of my more successful efforts. *Inter alia* I told them that I hoped this was the dawn of a new era.

Then the pumps were turned on, the sirens blared, and out poured the first stream of water. They have got about twenty Europeans and two hundred natives employed at the mine, and about four hundred natives are employed at other workings nearby. So things are beginning to move.

1934

Monday 9 to Friday 13 April (at Mafeking)
A tiresome and uninteresting week. That wretched Chief of the Bakgatla (Molefi) disappeared with £350 of our hut tax money and in spite of every effort to bring him in he has given no sign of life. So I had to hand over the matter to our Police to deal with. That probably means arrest, which in the case of a Chief always means trouble. However, by the mercy of Allah he turned up on Wednesday as if nothing had happened, and paid up in full! I think he spent all the money and then went off to borrow some more from his missionary friends.

Locusts don't seem to be doing as much damage as was anticipated, certainly they are not worrying us much. *Per contra* there are millions of 'mealie crickets', great fat black things like beetles about three inches long. They fight the locusts and eat them. It is interesting to see how the different animals eat each other. Ants eat locusts starting from the tail, mealie crickets start at the head, and locusts eating each other don't touch the head at all.

I am glad to say that Sir Herbert Stanley has supported strongly my protest to the Dominions Office against their monstrous attitude in regard to meat exports, and has sent my memorandum home by air mail. I trust sincerely that it may produce some effect.

Saturday 14 to Sunday 22 April (at Mafeking)
Every other country is in a bad way financially. Roosevelt the damn Socialist seems to be raving mad, and I should think he'll land the U.S.A. in bankruptcy.

On Friday Haile arrived for breakfast. He is the head of that very good native training institution at Tiger Kloof, the only decent thing the L.M.S. have done in South Africa. Haile is also head of the L.M.S. in South Africa and is the only decent man they have got; he's not a bad fellow, if only he were not a missionary. He came to discuss with me Government cooperation with his mission in running a joint hospital. We have also got the Seventh Day Adventists on the same tack, and I got them all to agree to run an L.M.S. show at Rakops on the Botletli River and an S.D.A. show at Maun in Ngamiland. So we shall get two more hospitals, if my deal comes off, for the price of half-one! And in remote districts where they are terribly badly needed for natives.

Stupid letters from the Dominions Office, who seem to understand about as much about Africa as I do about the Kingdom of Heaven — and nothing could be less. Then I am not satisfied about the work Colonel Naus is doing for me up in Ngamiland in regard to the clearance of the Okavango River. He seems to have launched out on a scheme of damming rivers instead of clearing them. I shall have a look into this when we go there in June.

They now propose to admit women to every branch of the Civil Service except the Colonial Office. My God, with hundreds of thousands of men unemployed, the growing effeminacy of the race, the decrease in families and the increasingly strenuous nature of competition between nations they propose to make every one of these things worse by letting women into jobs which are crowded out, and so taking them away from the jobs they can and ought to do. It's enough to make one despair of things.

Japan seems one of the few sensible nations left. They realise the ghastly muddle and mess that Europe has made over Chinese affairs, so they tell Europe to go to the devil and keep their hands off China which they (Japan) propose practically to annex. I take my hat off to them.

I had Molefi (Chief of the Bakgatla Tribe), his uncle the ex-Chief Isang, and three of their Headmen down for a conference. They are fighting and quarrelling among themselves and I had to knock their heads together — metaphorically — and read the Riot Act to them. It took all day, and then we didn't finish.

That unspeakable brute Jennings, the L.M.S. Missionary who went Home about the Tshekedi affair, lied pretty heavily when in London and especially at the Colonial Office. When I got the report of what he had said, I wrote infuriated letters pointing out his lies to the Colonial Office. Now he has written to Thomas admitting he lied, and apologising, and has sent me a copy of his apology! But of course it's too late. The lies have got a good start and can't be overtaken.

Wednesday 25 April
An awful shock on Monday, a report from Tshekedi that one of our Magistrates had hit a prisoner in the face in court! Telegraphic enquiry now reveals the fact that the incident actually happened, but not a Magistrate thank goodness, tho' it's bad enough as it is. Apparently one of our police officers, Hope, was performing magisterial functions on the Foot and Mouth cordon a year ago; a prisoner was abusive and so Hope stopped the proceedings, hit the man twice, and then went on again. Thank heavens we have already invalided Hope out of the service on account of nervous breakdown, otherwise there would have been an awful row, and we should have had to have a public enquiry and sack him. On Lord, as if we hadn't enough troubles.

Thursday 26 April
Got information by wireless of Hertzog's statement about taking over the Protectorates, and Du Plessis'[8] monstrous and lying statement in the Union Parliament about the B.P. I am awaiting full confirmation tomorrow before taking action.

Friday 27 April
I have now got the full report of the statements in the Union Parliament about taking over the Protectorate, and a more complete example of false statement and muddled thinking I have rarely seen. Du Plessis lied in every conceivable way and on every conceivable point, and as for the Prime Minister (Hertzog) his remarks would have discredited a schoolboy. They complain about our competition in exports, but were we part of the Union we should of course have *unrestricted access* to all Union markets, which we have not now got — and so the competition would be keener! These people have the brains of rabbits. I have telegraphed to Stanley urging him to make a public statement denying these lies.[9]

Capt. Masterman came to lunch. He is going on leave for a bit and then comes down here to relieve Gash who goes on inspection tour. Masterman is an awfully nice fellow with charming manners. He came from the Sudan Civil Service. I am very proud of the three recruits I have brought in — Masterman and Arrowsmith, and Sinclair from Oxford.[10] Arrowsmith has gone out to take charge of the Kalahari. Sinclair is acting A.D.C. to me. He has passed both 1st and 2nd grade examinations in Sechuana already, and has an Honours Degree from Oxford in Jurisprudence.

Tuesday 1 May
Our latest recruit, a young man, Batho[11] by name, has joined us from the High Commission Office. He is a cheery youth, and I think should do well. He says he feels

1934

thoroughly at home already as everyone has made him very welcome. Lawrenson[12] is in from fifteen months in the Kalahari where he has done very well. He is one of my most promising youngsters, full of good ideas for development. Arrowsmith has gone off to take his place.

Wednesday 2 & Thursday 3 May
A series of tragic bits of news. Poor Engelbrecht has been killed by a lion at Kazungula (where we are going next month). He was such a nice fellow, the very best type of solid Dutch settler. He was with us in Ngamiland last year. I have not got details yet, only a telegram giving the news. George Haskins of F'town has died after an appendicitis operation in Bulawayo Hospital. He was a huge strong man, quite young and full of life. He was the owner of the Monarch Mine that I opened in Tati last month. Then I was drinking champagne with him at his house after the opening and wishing him every kind of good luck. I am so sorry for his very nice little wife.

Friday 4 May
Chase returned from Cape Town after a difficult negotiation with the Union Ministry of Agriculture about complete re-opening of our export trade. He has done as well as could be expected. We shall get cattle out via Durban almost at once, and to Jo'burg soon — also the other irritating restrictions will I hope be removed. The negotiations were to some extent hampered by the attitude of funk, weakness, and vacillation of poor old Stanley who is shaking like a jelly over the row with the Union about taking over the Protectorates. He has as much backbone as a filleted jelly fish; he is past his job, brain gone to fat and spine disappeared. He is regarded as a joke in Cape Town by the general public; his activities consist mainly in addressing religious gatherings. When a man 'gets religion', it's time he was shut up.

We went to the cinema tonight as they are showing the film of H.R.H.'s visit to Gaberones. It was very good and quite interesting. The first time I have seen myself on the films, and Ninon as well. The rest of the show was too awful for words.

Sunday 6 May
I think the world's worst day. Ninon and I went over to Dyke's to meet all the survivors of the Mafeking siege, who had been assembled to greet young Baden-Powell, Lord B.P.'s son, who is staying a day or two on his way north. We had not been there five minutes when the blow fell. A Boy Scout came in to say that Chase was outside and wanted to speak to me. So I left the gathering and went out. I could see by Chase's face that something pretty bad had happened, and then he told me — a suspected case of Foot and Mouth disease had been reported at Rakops towards Ngamiland, two hundred and fifty miles N.W. of Serowe, and two hundred miles away from our nearest cordon. The blow was awful. We have reported all clear since August. The Union Government are going to relax restrictions, and now, if this is true, we are back again in a worse state than before. It's too utterly ghastly to be able to visualize.

I had just time to change for our dinner party for young Baden Powell — an awful ordeal, trying to be merry and bright when one was practically heartbroken. It was a dreadful evening. Young B.P. is rather a cub — manners not too good. He was at Sandhurst but failed to pass out, so he is joining the Southern Rhodesia

Police as a trooper at £150 a year. That is what a distinguished general and peer's son has to do in these days.

Monday 7 May
A heartbreaking morning at the Office. I had to break the news to the whole staff: they took it splendidly, expressed real sympathy with me and promised all support. Then we had to go into all the thousand and one details of restarting all our cordon arrangements — the cordons had been lifted on 22 April.

Wednesday 9 May (at Johannesburg)
I went off with some wireless/telephone experts to see a demonstration of a new w./t. set for my outstations. It was perfectly marvellous and will solve all our difficulties of intercommunication between stations like Ghanzi, (350 miles), Maun (450 miles). It takes us weeks now to send a letter and get answers.

The cost is trifling; £250 for our installation at Mafeking, and £150 for each of the out-stations. We don't need engines, just batteries, and it requires no more technical knowledge than is required to work an ordinary wireless set.

Thursday 10 May
A hectic day. First of all I interviewed Russell at 9.30. He is going to be our new Financial Secretary and I think he will fill the bill quite well. Then I had an interview with Major Wood and others representing the Aircraft Operating Company, with regard to the aerial survey they are going to do for us, and also as regards carrying our mail and our officers by plane. I think we ought to do business.

We lunched with Captain and Mrs Douglas. He is De Havilland Aeroplane representative, also the moving spirit in the Jo'burg Light Plane Club. I want him to hire us a plane for our Foot and Mouth work along the Botletli and Kalahari, and also to tender for our flying postal services. He has agreed to do so. He also gave me some astonishingly interesting information regarding the way the Germans are worming their way into the African Flying Service. They will shortly have a ring right round Africa and will cut out Imperial Airways and the other British concerns.[13] It's a tragedy and our damn Government does nothing, while the Union Government is giving everything away to these Huns.

Hands, the Church Railway Mission[14] parson, was on the train. Quite a good fellow for a parson. He told me he had asked Stanley to come up and lay the foundation stone of his church at Lobatsi. And of course the old fool, who is 'gagga' and has got religious mania, jumped at it. A great waste of time and money and not the sort of thing for the High Commissioner to do at a time of crisis like this.

Saturday 12 May (back at Mafeking)
A really gorgeous gallop over the veld before breakfast puts new life into one, and I needed it for it was a grim morning at the Office. Telegrams poured in and out, and Cape Town was busy too. Stanley is panic-stricken at the news I have telegraphed him — that the Chiefs have had meetings and are beginning to favour the idea of going into the Union, because the British Government have not carried out any of my big development schemes to help them in their life and trade! It's a marvellous turn of the wheel, and justifies everything I have said and done in the last four and a half years. As everyone in England is foaming at the mouth at the

idea of handing the Protectorate over to the Union 'because the natives don't want it', it will produce the most astounding results when it is known.

I have sent in the very devil of a dispatch quoting all my four and a half years' recommendations, and pointing out that the present trouble is entirely due to the Dominions Office. I hope they like it — damn them for a set of incompetent timorous rabbits.

Monday 14 to Wednesday 16 May
Horrible days, driving thru' the organization to cope with our latest tragedy, heart-breaking uphill work. Telegrams pouring in and out all day, one difficulty after another. I don't think anyone who has not done it can realize the difficulty of organizing a campaign of this sort four to five hundred miles away — no communications, improvising everything out of nothing, all the responsibility for every decision on my shoulders. So much at stake, everything to be done at once, but everything to be weighed and considered. Negotiations by telegram with South West Africa, with Northern Rhodesia, with Southern Rhodesia; reports Home by telegram; moving men, horses, rations, fodder, tents, equipment; hiring motor transport or waggons; and trying to keep up everyone's spirits. Meeting attacks from the Union and from the dirty swine at Home in England — inspired by those thrice accursed missionaries. Damn them.

I had to clear up things with Captain Reilly, who is off on Tuesday for ten days to Kasane — to settle the timber concession with Southern Rhodesia and the contractors (it may make all the difference to Ngamiland), and to look into other troubles up there.

On Wednesday, I learned definitely that the aeroplane for service up North is fixed up. It will be at Serowe on Saturday, £60 a month and £2 per flying hour, about four pence a mile.

Mr and Mrs Ellan, the acting Assistant R.M. at Ghanzi, lunched with us. They are too awful for words. He is the most colossally fat man I have ever seen, with a brain like a linnet. She was too shy to eat anything; it was awful.

Thursday 17 May
More bad news. Foot and Mouth has broken out badly in Northern Rhodesia right on our border by Kazungula and Livingstone. South West Africa want us to inspect the Caprivi Strip, their territory, thro' which the disease has probably broken thro' to B.P. from Angola. It needs a map to follow all this.

Friday 18 May
At last a telegram from Chase but a bad one. The disease is widespread in Ngamiland. He and his men are still scouring the country to trace it up. He wants more police and motor transport. Three officers, six N.C.O.s and fifty native police have gone. I'm getting veterinary officers from Southern Rhodesia. I've fixed for the aeroplane to call here at 8.30 tomorrow morning and go right on to Serowe, Rakops. Maun — taking masses of telegrams and mail.

There is terrible malaria, people dying, in the Kalahari at Tsabong and Lehututu, also at Ghanzi, also in Ngamiland. I have sent dispenser Brookes with masses of quinine to the Kalahari.

I've sent Dyke up to Francistown to look into trouble there in connection with the health, feeding, and housing of the natives employed on the Tati gold mines — seven hundred now shortly rising to fifteen hundred.

1934

Saturday 19 May
Our aeroplane arrived at 8.30 and the pilot, Mr Francis, came to breakfast. I wrote out his instructions, provided him with maps, and fixed up insurance of passengers for £1000 each (£10 for the lot for one month), and handed him our first air mail — a tremendously heavy lot for Serowe, Rakops and Maun.

We drove down to our aerodrome, and off he went in great style. A great milestone, our first air service in B.P. It is a very jolly little plane, carries two passengers besides the pilot, sitting side by side, and a large locker for baggage. It is a new model, a 'Leopard Moth' which has superseded the 'Puss Moth'. He left at 10.30.

Then I inspected the new lorry we have bought: a one and a half ton Chevrolet, a fine big powerful fellow. I have had to buy American, as the English firm that we got our last from are such damn fools that they have no spares out here. When they did send them, they sent the wrong ones. One tries to help English firms, but it's no good.

Sunday 20 May
At 3.20 I was at the station to greet Sir Hubert Young,[15] the Governor of Northern Rhodesia, on his way to Cape Town. I brought him up to the house for tea where he and Ninon clicked in great style. He is very pleasant, an able man, old Etonian, quite amusing and very quick at the uptake. Dr Huggins, the Prime Minister of Southern Rhodesia, was also on the train. I don't care for him so much, but then he suffers from the disadvantage of being a politician.

Tuesday 22 & Wednesday 23 May
A series of acid telegrams between Stanley and myself at intervals through both days, ending up with an absolutely rotten cowardly telegram from Stanley which left me no alternative but to cancel our trek. He is a damn swine with 'cold feet' because of possible native trouble about incorporation in the Union — which can't possibly happen until July (the trouble I mean) and can't amount to anything when it does happen. He is also beastly jealous of my knowledge of and power in dealing with the people in the Protectorate. He hates my being able to say that I know about B.P. problems from personal contact, and is of course inspired by that foul hound Eales, the Administrative Secretary. Well, we're enemies now, for good and all.

I telegraphed all over the country cancelling all arrangements and telegraphed to Chase to come down from Maun to consult with me about Foot and Mouth disease up there. I must know all the facts, and I don't know them yet and can't find out.

The Chiefs have been meeting each other all over the place talking about this incorporation in the Union business, and have decided to hold a joint meeting at the end of June — and to ask me to send a representative. They will then pass 'resolutions' etc., all hot air.

John Stuart has presented his petition to Hertzog from the Europeans in the Lobatsi, Gaberones, and Tuli Blocks — asking for their incorporation in the Union, and I must say I sympathize with them. The Imperial Government either can or will do nothing for them. They can't sell their produce in the Union; and they see nothing ahead but pain unless they go into the Union and so get markets.

Thursday 24 to Sunday 27 May
Empire Day on Thursday, but I have been much too dispirited and busy to think of arranging for it. Besides, in this country Empire Day is a farce. A lot of damn disloyal Dutchmen run it, who are out for one thing and one thing only — and that is to down everything English and get out of the Empire as quickly as they can.

We should have started on our trek today (Sunday 27), and it was utterly sickening to be unpacking and putting our things away instead. It froze last night, but only slightly; the roses are still going strong. We went out on the veld in 'Topsy' directly after lunch, and sat out in the sun all the afternoon: it was very pleasant. And then, as most of the house is shut up and the servants gone or going on their holiday, we started taking our meals out and dined at the Grand Hotel — not at all a bad meal. We went to the Grand as most people go to Dixon's Hotel, but the latter is run by Jews and we hate Jews. A touch of Hitler is needed out here.

Monday 28 May
Still beastly cold. I've got a touch of lumbago, due I imagine to the bad blood engendered by the foul temper I've been in for some days now.

I got a telegram from the D.O. saying that the King is being recommended to give Chase the C.B.E. in the Birthday Honours on 4 June and asking me whether he would like it. I've been pushing this for nearly eighteen months and of course I'm delighted, and I know Chase will be. So I telegraphed accordingly. He has jolly well earned it and everyone in the Territory will be enthusiastic. The B.P. doesn't get much in the way of Honours.

Our aeroplane arrived this afternoon from Maun which it had left this morning! Breakfast in Maun, tea in Mafeking, and coming back via Ghanzi too. Direct from Maun here by ordinary means would be over a week! and via Ghanzi nearly three weeks!

As to Foot and Mouth it's quite clear that it came over from Angola (Portuguese South West Africa), across the Caprivi Strip between Andara and Mohembo, down along the west side of the Okavango River to Nokaneng, Tsau, Tokeng, and Maun. From Nokaneng it was taken to Ghanzi by oxen, and from Maun to Makalamabedi down the Botletli River to eighteen miles north of Rakops. This is quite clear in the light of all the veterinary inspections we have made by car and plane. It's nowhere else — not at Lehututu where Hobday went by plane. But it has not crossed our old cordon, which is very satisfactory.

So now we've got to go on with the fresh campaign (inoculation) in Ngamiland and Ghanzi, which we've already planned. It will take five or six months strenuous work, and we shall have to keep the cordons on for another six to eight months after that.

Thursday 31 May
Its 'Union Day', a public holiday in the Union of South Africa but *not* in the B.P. I won't recognize it.

Saturday 2 June
I worked at home but telegrams kept pouring in about my veterinary conference on the 6th. That thrice cursed fool Stanley had a whole week to arrange it, and did nothing except bungle. I telephoned him at Cape Town last night about it. He could hear me very plainly (so he said) but he mumbled so that I could only catch about half of his remarks — probably I lost nothing.

Monday 4 June
The King's Birthday, a holiday in the B.P. and of course in our Office here, but not in the Union.

1934

Tuesday 5 June
Four out of the five delegates got here today. Dr De Kock representing the Union arrived this morning by car from Pretoria; Hooper-Sharpe (Southern Rhodesia) and Macdonald (Northern Rhodesia) by train from Salisbury and Livingstone respectively this afternoon; and McNae (South West Africa) by train from Jo'burg this evening. The first three came up with Chase and Reilly to the house for sundowners at 6, and we broke the ice. They are all pleasant fellows, but it's going to be a difficult job.

Wednesday 6 June
The conference started at 10 this morning, and Wagner (South West Africa) arrived by air — a little late. Things were very sticky at first, but gradually I got them going and brought them together and they all thawed little by little — De Kock, the Union man, being the most difficult. He is a very able man, but too much of a theorist. He was bitterly suspicious that they only *raison d'être* for his presence was that he was going to be attacked by all the four other governments for not letting their cattle into the Union. When he realized that the object of the conference was something much bigger and broader than this, being indeed no less than the first attempt to bring all the States of South Africa together to work for their common benefit in the eradication of the scourge of Foot and Mouth disease, he came round whole-heartedly. By the evening, we were going ahead grandly, but we did not quite finish.

Thursday 7 June
The conference resumed and we concluded by lunch time. A great success, everyone highly pleased. We propose to meet again with representatives from Portuguese East Africa (Mozambique), Belgian Congo, and Angola. So the seed I have sewn is growing rapidly.

I have also heard that Stanley is coming up here to lay the foundation stone for the rotten church at Lobatsi on 29 July, a rotten waste of time and money. He wants to stay in the B.P. for a week, which is an infernal nuisance.

Sunday 10 to Wednesday 13 June
I've adopted a new plan: Office in the morning; and then immediately after lunch N. and I go out on the veld in 'Topsy' and I work on my papers We do this because it's so beastly cold that if N. rests after lunch it's too late to go out in the car afterwards. Also I can't get any peace at the Office to read my papers and work quietly.

Thursday 14 to Saturday 16 June
A rather mysterious thing happened. On Thursday a definite statement came in at midday over the wireless that Stanley had been appointed Governor of Southern Rhodesia in succession to Sir Cecil Rodwell, and that Sir William Clark,[16] now High Commissioner in Canada, was to succeed Stanley here. In the *Rand Daily Mail* of that day it was given as a 'report', not an official announcement, and their photographs were published. But neither in the *Star* of that day or following days, nor in any further issues of the *Mail*, is the matter referred to at all — neither confirmed nor denied. So we don't know where we are and can't telegraph to congratulate Stanley, or condole with him. I know he *wants* Southern Rhodesia, but Clark's appointment here would be a thoroughly bad one. He knows nothing

of natives, nor of Africa, and is very 'official' — the last man for South Africa. I was at the Board of Trade with him years ago and know him well, so from a *personal* point of view it would be very nice.

I got a dispatch from Stanley on Friday to say that the Union Government wanted a conference of *all* the South African States about locusts to be held end of July. It would be perfectly futile as there is profound disagreement on the subject. Northern and Southern Rhodesia and the B.P. hold that poisoning of locusts is utterly useless and costs immense sums of money. The Union on the other hand believes in it. The Portuguese, of course, do nothing, as usual, and the Home Government believes in aeroplanes attacking locusts.

On the other hand I want our Foot and Mouth disease conference, and so I sent a really hectic telegram urging this point and suggesting that the two should be held together.

We have got trouble witch our with-doctors who are doing a good bit of murdering, but it's almost imposible to bring it home to them because all natives are terrified of giving evidence. However we got at one gentleman. He was tried last week and sentenced to be hung, in spite of bungling by that fool of a President of the Court, Leslie Blackwell — who is an ass and a politician, as well as a rotten bad lawyer. The case was an awful one, the murder of a child as the witch-doctor wanted human fat to have in his 'medicine box'. They have lion and other animal fat, but like human fat best. They generally cut a bit out of the backside, and off the thigh, and also cut off a hand. They killed the child by wringing its neck and then battering its head with a club.

We were not so fortunate in the case tried by Hope some time ago. That was a particularly foul case of the murder of a woman. The witch-doctor was a bit of a mesmerist, and terrified and influenced the witnesses so that they all collapsed. He was so offensive that Hope lost his temper and hit him, a dreadful thing to do. Even the Chiefs are terrified of witch-doctors and pay them a sort of tribute, blackmail I imagine, tho' they also make the witch-doctor pay a license fee. But the Chiefs daren't interfere with them.

I read a most delightful remark by the President of the Seychelles Planters' Association in welcoming their new Governor. He said: 'The mistake of imagining the Colonies as dependencies to be administered, rather than estates to be developed, has been made here: much in the present situation is due to it, and everything in the future depends on its correction'. That might be said very truly of the B.P.! I have tried to bring that point home to the Dominions Office often enough. He went on to say '. . . we hold that to organize and develope industry and commerce in these small backward countries is just as truly a function and duty of Government in this fiercely competitive new age as it is to maintain law and order'. Hear! Hear!

We were all very delighted that the King has agreed to my recommendation of giving Sergeant Ndandala of our Police the medal of the British Empire Order. He is a splendid specimen of a native, a fine fighter, full of pluck and a great disciplinarian. He is as tough and wiry today at 60 as the average man of 30, more so.

Sunday 17 June
It's bitterly cold and we've got our electric fires going all over the house, four large and four small. The new imitation log fire with a flickering flame is a great success.

There's a wood famine in Mafeking, partly owing to supplies from the B.P. being cut off on account of Foot and Mouth, and partly owing to gradual deforestation round here. I'm told that there's no wood for forty miles from here.

Dumbrell looked in after tea and we went for a walk together. He is an amusing person, quite cultured and very well read and I think he is jolly good at his job, i.e. Inspector of Education. He has achieved wonders in the short time he has been here, and with the utterly inadequate resources in staff and money at his disposal.

Wednesday 20 June
Not quite so cold, but I have to wear gloves when riding before breakfast as my hands get numb! Stanley's appointment as Governor of Southern Rhodesia, and Clark's appointment to succeed him here, are gazetted at last. So we duly sent off the usual congratulatory telegrams. Clark is not made 'High Commissioner for the Territories' but 'His Majesty's Commissioner for Basutoland, the Bechuanaland Protectorate and Swaziland'. I wonder what on earth that means.

Another interesting note I found about cattle. They are brought down from the north by train to Jo'burg and enroute are off-loaded at Ramatlabama to rest, water, and graze. There is a regular path round the enclosure there where they have walked round and round trying to find a way out. Tho' they have come by train they congregate at the *north* end of the enclosure, which is in the direction they have come from. Poor beasts, the cattle trade is a horrible business, and yet hundreds of thousands of natives depend on it for their living and there doesn't seem to be any substitute.

Tuesday 26 June (at Johannesburg)
I had a very interesting interview with Dougal Malcolm[17] of the Chartered Company, or rather British South Africa Company, at the very palatial offices of the Anglo-American Corproation. We discussed mining in the B.P. The Bamangwato Concession is *no good* and the Victoria Prospecting Company are throwing it up. And diamonds, they want De Beers to look around and see if there are any there.

We also discussed the general position of the B.P. and the question of incorporation in the Union. I think Malcolm will be very helpful to me in London; he is a nice fellow and an able man.

Thursday 5 July
A telegram came in from the Dominions Office today approving my Foot and Mouth disease campaign proposals and the expenditure of £50,000. Just one month after I had started the work! It was lucky that I didn't wait for it.

Tuesday 10 July
Dr Du Toit of De Beers came along to have a discussion about diamond mining in the Bamangwato Reserve. The British South Africa Company have found no minerals, so they are going to have a smack at diamonds. Tho' they don't want to find any more diamonds just now — there are too many in the world! — they don't want anyone else to. If they find any, they will work them on a small scale.

For some obscure reason Tshekedi doesn't want them to. So I fixed up a working arrangement with Du Toit, and wired for Tshekedi to come down and see me on Thursday.

Wednesday 11 July
The aeroplane people arrived from Jo'burg to have a discussion as to a new three month agreement, and we made a very satisfactory deal. For £500 they will arrive in

Mafeking every Sunday morning at 9 am, pick up mails, fly on to Maun via Serowe and Rakops, arriving Maun Sunday afternoon, spend all the week there on Foot and Mouth work — and fly back to Jo'burg via Rakops, Serowe, and Mafeking on Saturday morning.

Thursday 12 July
Tshekedi came down in the best of humours, and we had a most satisfactory talk, and fixed up the diamond mining business very pleasantly. We also settled some other matters.

Dr Fourie of the Union Government came thro'. He is doing a trip in the Protectorate looking for rats and other rodents in which he is interested, especially from the point of view of plague. A pleasant and agreeable man, quite able, I should say.

Thursday 19 July
I had to receive a deputation from the Indian inhabitants of the B.P. who are full of grievances. They are a poor lot, no use to the Territory, living like and with natives and robbing them, spending no money in the B.P. but sending all they make away to India. I don't encourage them, so they complained to the Indian High Commissioner at Cape Town who complained to Stanley who passed it on to me. However, I was able to deal with their point satisfactorily and they accorded me a vote of thanks — rather to my astonishment.

More trouble with that little devil Molefi, the Chief of the Bakgatla at Mochudi. I fear there will never be peace there as long as he and his uncle, the ex-Chief Isang, are both alive.

Sunday 22 July & Monday 23 July
Ninon won't be well enough to come with me and the High Commissioner on his tour this week. It's bad luck and I *hate* going up country without her.

I finished up everything and put the finishing touches to the arrangements for the High Commissioner's tour starting tomorrow, and packed my gear. It's an awful bore and a shocking waste of time.

High Commissioner's Tour
Tuesday 24 to Tuesday 31 July

Tuesday 24 July
Stanley and Holbech arrived at 7.30 and I met them at the station with Reilly and other senior officers.

Wednesday 25 July (at Francistown)
A very busy day and a fairly successful one. We started off by inspecting the Camp, gaol, etc., then three schools (European, native and coloured), and then the Monarch Mine (Tati Goldfields Ltd.) and the engineer's house, Brown by name. There is not much to see at the mine, as they are simply de-watering and opening up. The native compound where several hundred natives are housed is a disgrace, and they will have to improve this, especially the lavatory arrangements.

1934

Thursday 26 July
We visited the Lady Mary, Phoenix, and Leonie Mines; and at the second of these I have never seen richer gold ore in my life. When they stopped the stamp battery, and the water had run off the blankets, they were positively yellow with gold. It must have been several ounces to the ton — eight I was told afterwards. Of course one could not expect a vein to run on at this richness, and it is doubtless just a pocket, but it indicates much gold about the place.

Friday 27 July (at Mahalapye)
A bad day, being Friday probably the reason. It was as poisonously hot as the last two days have been, and altho' Stanley pretends not to mind the heat, I'm afraid that it affects him. For once in a way Russell England failed to come up to his reputation, and the show he staged today was much below the mark. Stanley did not take much interest in the demonstration dairy or seed samples, nor in the demonstration cultivation plots (spineless cactus, etc.) — possibly because it meant walking about in the sun. Then we went to the school, where he gave them a lengthy 'pi-jaw', and after that he had over an hour's interview with Tshekedi in the railway coach, which took us up to lunch time. Then a run out by car to see the effect of de-horning cattle about twelve miles out — but only a small and poor lot had been got together, and they did not make much of a show. Back to tea at England's house to meet the European residents of the Tuli Block, Palapye, Serowe, and Mahalapye. Only about twenty turned up, which showed great lack of interest (to put it mildly) in the High Commissioner and anyhow it didn't go too well.
And to wind up we had the most appalling dinner party.

Saturday 28 July (to Kanye)
We drove up the hill along the splendid new road that Rowland has made with the labour (native and European) to whom we have been giving food rations — a wonderful bit of work. The whole Tribe were gathered at the top of the hill around the big reservoir that Rowland has also made. The Chief and Tribe were cooperating very well, and they gave us a rousing reception. Another long speech by Stanley.
We had a delightful drive back to Lobatsi in the cool of the evening. Met Molefi and Isang and four headmen, and ticked Molefi off properly for his abominable conduct of tribal affairs, drunkenness and general misbehaviour. Stanley gave him four months to put his house in order, failing which he would be pushed out.
The Ledeboers dined on the railway coach, quite a pleasant evening after a very successful day. After the guests had gone Stanley inquired who was for early morning (Communion!) service tomorrow! Silence followed, so he asked me. I explained it was against my principles, so the wretched Holbech has to be dragged out.

Sunday 29 July (at Lobatsi)
While dressing comfortably at a reasonable hour for breakfast I had the pleasure of observing Stanley and Holbech *returning* from their early morning devotions. It does not seem to have done them much good if one can judge from their tempers.
After breakfast Stanley and I arrayed ourselves in top hats and tail coats, and Holbech in uniform, for the ceremony of laying the foundation stone of the church which is being built by the Railway Mission. It was blazing hot, and stiff collars

1934

and town clothes don't really go out here. There was quite a big crowd, about a hundred and twenty, and the ceremony was quite nice. The Bishop of Kimberley looked very fine in his episcopal robes, and Hands who officiated is a jolly good sportsman and a very nice fellow. Of course it was the hottest part of the day and we had to stand out in the open, with the sun beating on our bare heads for part of the time. Most of the people will have headaches, I imagine.

Hands, the Ellenbergers, and the Hendersons came to dinner — a bad show. Stanley had got a headache from the sun, and would hardly talk to Mrs Ellenberger and Mrs Henderson who were next to him. Also he contradicted me flatly on a point of fact, which I can't stand, so we had quite a passage of arms.

Tuesday 31 July (to Mafeking)
'Topsy' arrived early and we all went off to Mafeking, inspecting the Hildavale and Pitsani schools on the way, both dreadful shows — the two worst European schools in the Territory. We arrived at Protectorate Government House in good time for lunch, where Stanley and Holbech had a row over their mails.

Then at 3 the whole Headquarters staff, complete with wives, over sixty in all, turned up to meet Stanley and we had a really good show — delicious ices and etceteras all beautifully served. Stanley enjoyed it thoroughly, I think. Ninon organizes these things wonderfully.

I made a little farewell speech, and Stanley made a very charming reply, after which we all adjourned to the station, and Stanley and Holbech departed for Pretoria at 4.20. And that was that — a very successful conclusion to a very trying episode, except that I twisted my knee which hurt like the devil, made me limp like a cripple and invoke Dr Dyke's assistance. He talks of water on the knee, which I don't believe.

Wednesday 1 to Saturday 4 August
A strenuous four days picking up the arrears that have accumulated during our week's tour. In between I had a long talk with Schapera,[18] who is going to do the work of compiling 'native law and custom' for us during the next year or so. Also with Dumbrell regarding education questions, about which I am not happy.

Wednesday 8 August
A very 'secret and personal' telegram from Stanley offering me a new job if I care to retire. I am very doubtful about staying on here, anyhow, and still more doubtful as to accepting any new job. I think both Ninon and I want a good long rest and change.

Thursday 9 August
Meeting of our 'Board of Advice on Native Education', of which, of course, I am Chairman. It was a very successful meeting lasting all day, and it gave me an opportunity to loose off a homily on what we mean by native education and what we think we are driving at. I am strongly opposed to the lines followed in India and some parts of Africa resulting in creating lots of disgruntled so-called 'educated' natives all wanting jobs as clerks that don't exist. We don't want all this theoretical stuff, and I summed up our objects as character formation, training in agriculture and industry, hygiene, etc. In other words teach them to be decent law-abiding citizens; teach them to become a sound peasant population; to build their houses better, plough and sow their lands better and raise better crops; and teach them to

live more healthily and cleanly than they do, and bring their children into the world properly and feed them properly.

The missionary element didn't like my remarks one little bit, but the sound people were all highly delighted amongst them some very distinguished visitors from outside the B.P. who had been attending the big international education conference at Cape Town and Joburg. Ninon and I gave a biggish luncheon party of sixteen at the Grand Hotel which went off very well, and then Professor Victor Murray[19] (from England) dined with us.

Tuesday 14 August
Sir Cecil and Lady Fforde[20] arrived to stay. He is the newly appointed President of our Court and Legal Adviser to the High Commissioner. They are both charming, and we like them immensely.

He is furious at the idea of my retiring, but I've written to Stanley saying that I propose to do so.

Thursday 16 August
The Ffordes left by car at 10.30 for Lobatsi. They are going to do a few days tour in the Territory to get the hang of things, a very good idea. I think he will be a great acquisition, and we all four clicked at sight, so that he should be a very helpful addition to the High Commission Office. He gets on very well with Liesching. As Liesching was with Sir William Clark in Canada, and likes him immensely, and Clark was with me at the Board of Trade in England, we ought to be a very happy family now.

Friday 17 August
Rutherford arrived by car from Mochudi bringing with him the resignation of Molefi, the Chief of the Bakgatla. This is rather a blow, as the legal successor is a poisonous pup, Mmusi by name, at school at Tiger Kloof; and his accession could make confusion worse confounded. Also it is maddening that this should happen just now when I am starting off on trek in less than a week. So, after consultation with Reilly, I dispatched a message to Ellenberger the R.M. at Gaberones, telling him to see Molefi and tell him not to be a fool, and to await a meeting of the Tribe to be held in a month's time when the whole position would be carefully examined. I had a long talk with Dr Molema about it. He quite agreed with this course. He is a wily devil, one of the cleverest natives I have ever met: he took his degree in Scotland.[21]

I had a wire from Stanley about my proposed retirement.

Saturday 18 August
A wire from Ellenberger to say that Molefi won't play and intends to resign at once. So Reilly and I had a bit of a consultation, finished off some work at the Office, rushed home, had some lunch, hurled a few things into a bag, hired a car, and pushed off for Gaberones at 2.30.

Sunday 19 August (to Mochudi)
We left just before 7 am for Mochudi (thirty miles) and got there in record time, starting work at once and having a series of interviews with Molefi and Isang in turns separately all the morning. We managed to settle the position temporarily, arranged for a big Tribal meeting to be held in September at which I am to preside,

fixed up some of the main troubles, and settled that Molefi would not play the fool meanwhile.

Maun — Ghanzi Trek
Friday 24 August to Friday 21 September

Saturday 25 August (to Serowe)
We got into Serowe after a pleasant run by car about 12. Unpacked an enormous case containing two huge framed portraits of the King and Queen, which Ninon is giving to Tshekedi's mother, Semane.
　In the afternoon, there was a tea party at the tennis club which we attended to meet local (European) inhabitants. I motored out with Nettelton to inspect the new aerodrome — a magnificent effort — the best in Southern Africa I should say, except the military one at Roberts' Heights (Pretoria).[22]

Sunday 26 August
Tshekedi and his mamma, Semane, arrived at 10.30 and Ninon presented the pictures to her in a delightful little speech. Ninon does these things wonderfully well. Then I had a long palaver with Tshekedi when we discussed a number of points, he being very sensible and reasonable.
　Duggan-Cronin[23] came into the Residency to show us his photographic studies of natives. They are simply marvellous — he is a real artist and must have a very wonderful camera to obtain the results he does.
　We inspected the hospital after tea — it falls short of Lobatsi by a long way, and there is something rather depressing in the atmosphere of it. Rather to my annoyance Dr Morgan was not there, nor was the matron, it being her 'afternoon off'.

Tuesday 28 August (to Maun by plane)
At 9 sharp the big six-seater Dragon Moth plane arrive from Jo'burg bringing the pilot, a director of the Aeroplane Company, and a ground engineer. We gave them breakfast and then got off all together soon after 9.30, flying straight through to Maun where we arrived about 12.30. It is a gorgeous plane; one can walk about in it whilst in flight. The pilot in his little compartment in front, six very comfortable seats for passengers, and a little compartment at the end complete with lavatory basin and tap.

Wednesday 29 August
We are seizing the opportunity of having the big Dragon up here to fly over the Okavango Swamps and inspect from the air the work that Naus has been doing on the rivers. So at 9 am sharp Colonel Naus, Captain Potts, Ninon, Sally and self took to the air again and had the most wonderfully interesting flight. First of all we flew up the Thamalakane River to its junction with the Santandibe River, noting on the way the barrages, dams and weirs built by Naus. Then turning north we flew up the Santandibe to the junction with the Gomoti River at Chief's Island. Here Naus had built the biggest dam, a thousand and fifty feet long, twenty four feet wide at the top (wider as it goes down), and fourteen feet high — a colossal undertaking, involving the shifting of thousands of tons of earth by hand labour. Then we went on to the North West and saw the colossal amount of water lying in the swamps that we want to bring down into the territory. Finally we turned south

and came down over the Taoge River, past Tsau and Toteng and over Lake Ngami — now perfectly dry tho' it was a huge sheet of water when Livingstone discovered it eighty years ago.[24] Now one has to dig fifteen feet to get to water in the bed of the lake.

Thursday 30 August
A really strenuous day for me. I worked all the morning in Camp with Potts and Naus at his water schemes — going into every detail, work done, cost, water gained, future plans etc. He has built seven dams — the smaller two hundred and fifty feet long, and five about five hundred feet long. Motors and carts can go across them, boats can go thro' the weirs — the water rushes thro' the weirs at six to eight miles an hour, ever drawing down the supplies from the swamps above. Between the dams the water is kept at weir level, to maintain a constant river during the whole year. It is a great scheme and so far has cost under £900! Now we want another £3,000 spread over two years to complete the work — work which I conceived three years ago and which everyone said: (a) couldn't be done; (b) if done would cost hundreds of thousands of pounds; (c) anyhow we could never get any money for it. It is some triumph.

In the afternoon I worked in Camp with Chase, who also has done a marvellous bit of work in this second Foot and Mouth disease eradication campaign. To tackle this job as we did it in 1933 was big enough; to tackle it here is just marvellous. A vast area. No tracks away from the river; it is either swamps or no water at all; no communications; no local staff or European population to speak of; tremendous heat and fever. Well, we've organised it and nearly finished it. Chase established a depot at Maun for making the virus for inoculation. Tons of virus were dropped by aeroplane in parachutes at his various inoculating centres; tracks were cut, aerodromes cleared; motor and boat transport bought and hired; veterinary staff and extra police recruited and posted. Cordons six hundred miles long established, fed, inspected and paid; crushes and zaribas for inoculating cattle put up at fifteen mile intervals in all the cattle districts; transport of men (as well as virus) effected by aeroplane. In less than five months we shall have inoculated 250,000 head of cattle and stamped out the disease, in an inaccessible district with no communications.

The whole veterinary and Police staff have worked magnificently, and Captain Potts, the Magistrate, has been simply invaluable. Not only that, but he has changed the whole atmosphere of the Tribe here (the Batawana) and has got them into line in a really remarkable way. The difference in the position now as compared to when I was here last year is most cheering.

With three good men like Potts, Chase and Naus, one can achieve anything. I shall describe later on[25] the work Potts has been doing to discipline the Tribe, improve the position, create agricultural demonstration lands, and generally develope the district. This is a wonderful country — but what an enormous amount there is to be done!

Friday 31 August
My birthday — I forget how old I am, either 37 or 97 [57] but as I can still walk, ride, shoot, fly, play tennis and work twelve hours a day, I can't honestly say that I am fully qualified for an old age pension. This morning I inspected every building in the Camp on foot in the midst of a dust storm.

It is of course splendid that I have got the money to establish a hospital here in cooperation with the Seventh Day Adventist Mission — that will make a great difference. We looked at various possible sites for the hospital.

Dyke came in in the evening for a sundowner and to say goodbye. He is off by plane tomorrow morning to Mafeking, stopping on his way to attend the opening of the new hospital at Molepolole. It is being run by the 'Continuing Church of Scotland' Mission, and has been built by our man Robertson and his gang of trained skilled and unskilled natives — no whites — great achievement.

Monday 3 September
A very satisfactory day. Full Tribal Kgotla all the morning which went off very well in remarkable contrast to last year's effort.

The only point they seemed nervous about was the arrival of a new form of religion — i.e. the Seventh Day Adventists! I expect they were put up to this by Sandilands and his beastly L.M.S. crowd, and I can see I shall have a little difficulty here.

The new Acting Chief Dibolayang seems a very good fellow and a vast improvement on his predecessor, Monnaamaburu — a worthless lump whom I had to kick out.[26] Altogether it was a very good show.

I interviewed various people in the afternoon and in the evening we went out shooting — birds for the pot.

Tuesday 4 September (to Ghanzi by plane)
Ellam, the Ghanzi Magistrate, and Chase met us and we drove to the 'Residency', so-called, where they had given us the 'guest room' — a detached building, quite roomy and very nicely arranged. They had evidently taken a lot of trouble to make it nice for us. But my God what an awful place Ghanzi is! The Camp is just a few white-washed buildings stuck in the middle of flat veld, dusty, wind-swept, and baked in the blazing sun. A few stunted trees, a few bushes, and nothing else but flat veld all round. No wonder that no Resident Commissioner has ever been here. I cannot understand how anyone could live here without wanting to commit suicide. And yet Ellam has applied to stay on for another two years! No-one who had any brain at all could stand it — there's nothing to do. I lost no time in getting to work and after seeing our luggage (one bag) stowed in our room, I went round inspecting the Camp. The Residency is tiny — two rooms, kitchen and bathroom and the guest room outside, quite neat and clean. No garden — just sand and dust. The Office — two rooms and a storeroom, small but adequate — not too tidy. Obviously hardly any work doing — tho' the Magistrate here is magistrate, O.C. troops, public prosecutor, postmaster, gaoler, chairman of school committee, director of works, and a few other things.

The gaol was rather depressing. I walked into the first cell and saw a body lying under a blanket — a prisoner, shot whilst trying to escape a few days ago, died last night, to be buried this morning. The next cell, another prisoner lying under his blanket motionless, a Bushman just pining away and fading out. Bushmen can't stand captivity; they just die. This man had a sentence of six months for cattle theft. I ordered him to be released at once and given as much food as he could carry away. After which I thought lunch and a whiskey and soda was indicated.

This place was colonised by Rhodes about forty years ago — a bunch of English and Dutch farmers, mostly Dutch, trekked up here, and were given pretty large farms, and rather larger promises. The scheme never has been and never could be any good, and the farmers have steadily dropped in the social scale until today they are little better than 'poor whites'. Then the embargo on cattle exports hit them hard two years ago, followed by an outbreak of malaria after the drought and the next season's heavy rains. They were not able to stand up against it, having no resources in money or food. So we had to send in doctors and quinine by aeroplane, tens of thousands of pounds of grain by lorry, and Ninon's fund for relief of distress provided them with clothing and other necessaries. And now they have got their own outbreak of Foot and Mouth, poor devils.

How they live I cannot understand. Formerly they sold cattle which were trekked down south and run over the border into the Union — but they cannot do that now.

Wednesday 5 September
I invited over Sebele, the Chief of the Bakwena whom I had kicked out of Molepolole some years ago and exiled to this place. He looked very smart but pretended to be ill, and complained that the place did not agree with him. As a matter of fact he is better off than he has ever been in his life. He has had four good brick-built huts erected for himself and two wives; he has as much land to plough as he wants, water, and £20 a month Government allowance. He had the infernal cheek to give me a letter asking: (a) that he should be sent back to Molepolole; and (b) that his allowance should be increased to £30 a month!

Captain Potts had arrived for breakfast by plane from Maun, and, at 10, I had my meeting with the farmers. They had all come in to see me from the whole district. It was a very good meeting; they were much interested in my plans to establish a creamery and to start a Karakul sheep industry. We would pasteurise the cream and send it in to Gobabis in South West Africa to be made into butter, and there is of course a good demand for Karakul sheep pelts. But the trouble is that they have three years accumulation of cattle that they have not been able to sell, and they feel grave doubts as to being able to take on dairy work whilst looking after all these cattle until they can sell them. They *can't* see that if they don't start these new industries they will starve, as there is no market for their cattle, and the Government can't go on feeding them. As it is we are feeding ninety per cent of the Ghanzi (European) population. Our August bill was 4,700 pounds kaffir corn (sorghum), 3,600 pounds mealies, 160 pounds sugar, 35 pounds tea, 35 pounds coffee — and a few other things too. It's a tragic outlook.

Then we trotted back to the Residency, where not only all the farmers but all their wives and children had assembled. They had come in from miles around in every variety of vehicle, ox waggons, donkey carts, two lorries, a battered old Ford car, etc.

They were terribly shy. But Ninon and I worked like blacks to make them feel at home, and, with the help of tea and a case of whiskey I had sent over, we got them into quite a jovial frame of mind before long — comparatively speaking! Poor things, it was pathetic to see their garments and to realise that they live marooned in this damned awful place all their lives, seeing no one and going nowhere. They were wonderfully grateful to Ninon for the clothes she had sent them. Some of the women told her that they could not otherwise have sent their children to school, as they could not even clothe them in decency.

Tuesday 11 September (back at Maun by plane)
At 10 I went over the river to meet Chief Dibolayang and some of his councillors. We discussed a number of points and had quite a good meeting. He is quite a good

man and is instilling discipline into the Tribe which they needed badly. I heard an amusing story about him today. A few nights ago we heard a lion roaring about the camp, and apparently his lordship moved on to the village and killed an ox and a donkey. So the Chief called on two or three 'regiments' to turn out for a lion hunt. About thirty five heroes appeared, armed with every variety of weapon from an old muzzle loader to a sjambok, and very half heartedly followed the lion's spoor, losing it as often as they could, and finally returning unsuccessful to the village. The next day in the Kgotla (Tribal council) the Chief recited what had happened, and called on all men of the 'regiments' summoned who had come to stand on one side. Then he told all the men of the regiments summoned who had *not* come to stand in another place, and informed them that he was going to flog the lot! Great consternation, but they took off their coats and got down to it. Then he said, 'Let this be a lesson, I'll not flog you this time but you can see what's coming to you if you don't obey my orders'. A jolly good effort, and I told him so.

I then inspected the demonstration agricultural plots and irrigation plots started by Potts with the help of a native whom we have had trained for three years at Domboshawa[27] in Southern Rhodesia. A splendid bit of work: four acres broken up into ten plots: mealies, kaffir corn, melons, pumpkins, cowpeas, all grown from special seed to produce seed. We shall give this to the natives who will then be able to produce vastly better crops in quantity and quality. They will give us in exchange some of their poor grain which we need for horses, native rations, etc. They will also be shewn how to sow these crops properly. The whole of the pupils from the school are to be brought down once a week to be instructed in this work, and so the good work should go on. That is what I understand by 'native education', and not all this damned nonsense of literary stuff. We are also growing in irrigated beds along the river vegetables and fruit, bananas, oranges, lemons, lettuce, spinach, tomatoes, shallots, potatoes, and are going to educate the natives in this as well — to improve their diet (which is very bad and making them unhealthy), and enable them to make a bit by selling the vegetables.

Wednesday 12 September
Terribly hot today, and N. was a bit weary as well, so I proceeded to inspect the schools myself. The native school was the one I started in 1930 — the only one in the whole of Ngamiland. There were some eighty-three pupils, all Batawana except about eight Makuba. No industrial or agricultural training, only this rotten bookwork which is no good for natives. I started changing it at once — arranged for the weekly school visit to the agricultural plots as already mentioned. And I'll make a radical change throughout when I get back. It's all the doing of this thrice accursed London Missionary Society and their vile representative here (Sandilands).

Thursday 13 September
A deputation of five from the Seventh Day Adventist Mission arrived last night and camped near the Residency. They have come up to go into the question of the hospital we are putting up as a cooperative effort with them.

I went round to see them before breakfast this morning and found them to be a cheery crowd — very different to those L.M.S. killjoys. Two of them I knew already; the others were new to me, but all good fellows. They were certainly travelling light — no tents or paraphernalia — just beds and food — all in one lorry from Serowe. They had pitched camp near the Residency under a tree, and seemed full of beans.

1934

I forgot to mention that yesterday after I had seen the schools I went round to see Mma-Moremi, widow of the late Chief, and mother of the Chief-to-be, a nasty little beast at school in Tiger Kloof, where he is doing no good. She was 'all dressed up' and very much on her dignity. A nasty old thing, whom the Government are practically supporting, as the Tribe are too poor to give her food (except grain) or clothes befitting her estate! She looked very well and very smart, and I don't think she is to be pitied.

Friday 14 September
The Seventh Day Adventist people have agreed on a site for the hospital with the Chief. I spent most of the day in the Kgotla discussing theology with the Tribe! The natives are much interested and a little alarmed at the arrival of a new religion. But I reassured them, and explained that any form of religion was as good (I longed to say 'as bad') as any other. What damn nonsense all these dogmatic religions are. I am completely unable to understand how in these days it is possible for any educated and intelligent European to believe in any of them.

Saturday 15 September (to Palapye by plane)
Off at 6.45 in the Leopard Moth — a single engine monoplane seating the pilot and two passengers — rather tightly! A perfect morning — everyone, including the Chief — was at the aerodrome to see us off — the Seventh Day Adventist party cheery as usual — the only absentee being that son of a yellow dog, the L.M.S. Sandilands creature. We had a perfectly gorgeous flight, the finest I have ever had in my life. We were flying at nearly 11,000 feet and for part of the time were *above* the clouds — so that no earth was visible at all — just the steel blue vault above and masses of snow-like billowy clouds below. It was too grandly impressive for words, the most fascinating thing I have ever done or seen.

Tuesday 18 September (to Mochudi by car)
There was quite a mail awaiting me in Mochudi, including letters from Stanley saying that the Dominions Office wouldn't let me go to the Southern Rhodesia railway job, and a telegram from the Dominions Office saying that although they recognised I was entitled to retire if I wished to, they hoped very much I would stay on for two or three years to see all my schemes through! Very complimentary — but I think not. *Nous verrons*.

Wednesday 19 September
A busy day at Mochudi. Tshekedi and Molefi came in from Artesia, to pay their respects and explain their *indaba* together. We had quite a pleasant and interesting discussion, but these people are very tricky to deal with, and one never knows what they really think. Our discussion lasted all morning. After lunch I interviewed the Chief's tax collector (who has not been paid for years), and had a long talk with Ellenberger (who had come over from Gaberones) and Rutherford about Tribal affairs. I inspected the water supply, which is entirely broken down and doesn't function, and the hospital which was in a shocking condition — untidy, neglected, and not too clean. Everything is in a deplorable state here now owing to the incessant quarrelling between Chief Molefi and ex-Chief Isang, and the drunken habits and neglect of duty of the former. It's most unfortunate that we have had to postpone the Tribal meeting owing to Isang's illness. The doctor reports that Isang is getting on all right, and should be fit by the end of the month.

1934

Thursday 20 September (to Khale)
Off at 10.30 and after a pleasant drive arrived at the R.C. mission at Khale for lunch — passing a largeish snake on the way by the roadside that seemed interested in our progress, but wouldn't stop to be photographed.

The Khale people gave us a wonderful reception. Father Rittmuller and Sister Karan are delightful people. We had a most excellent lunch, beautifully cooked and served; everything is always so spotlessly clean in this place.

After lunch Ninon went off to a bedroom to rest, and I went off with Father Rittmuller to look over the farm. They have a marvellous place, splendidly organised and run, thousands of orange trees, and crops and fruit of all kinds. They have a grand water supply from a well from which they pumped 40,000 gallons in seven hours without lowering the water level — and the Notwani River, now dry, runs along their borders. I must get Naus to dam this river as he has done the Okavango tributaries in the north. If so we should get marvellous results here. In fact I don't see why we shouldn't apply the Naus scheme to all the southern rivers. I must go into this directly I get back.

For some idiotic reason the Union Government have stopped the export of oranges from here — I sent off a hectic telegram about it and shall hope to get that put right at once.

Friday 21 September (at Lobatsi)
I saw our Veterinary Officer, Hay, and went with him to the Imperial Cold Storage works where at long last I saw in actual progress the results I have been fighting for for five years — the slaughter and export of our own cattle at our own works in our own Territory! At last! It was an intense joy and satisfaction.

Now we have to make it permanent — and we must fix up the definite arrangements for this — five hundred head of cattle a week for twelve months, or 25,000 head in all. It will make an enormous difference to the Territory as all export of cattle has been stopped for three years. We can't even export now; and we never have exported meat, altho' the works were put up in 1927. Of course the price is terribly low — only £1 per head, but there are three years accumulation that will simply die of old age if we don't get them out.

The man in charge, Fish, seems very capable, and I am glad to say they are slaughtering with the humane killer.

We got off at 10.45, and stopped at Fincham's at Pitsani for a chat. They have bought hundreds of bags of grain from the natives — a pity, because the natives will want it themselves later on and will have to buy it back at increased prices.

Thursday 27 September (at Mafeking)
Chase is back from Ngamiland for good, thank heaven. That devil Wolfe Davies of the Imperial Cold Storage did not turn up as promised, to settle about the meat contract. So I telephoned to Cape Town and he confirmed it over the wire. But I want it in writing — please!

We are have a first class row with the Union over the export of oranges from Khale. They can't say that oranges carry Foot and Mouth disease, so they talk about 'citrus canker' and want me to give a certificate about it signed by a 'mycologist' whatever that may be, and to send out each consignment in a sealed railway truck! We are having a very pretty row, but we shall of course win.

1934

Tuesday 2 to Thursday 4 October
Three days of very strenuous Meat Conference. Gilman, representing the Federated Meat Industries of South Africa, arrived on Tuesday to make a contract with us for 25,000 head of cattle to be slaughtered at the rate of five hundred per week *at Lobatsi*, and exported to England as boned meat. Price in England two pence halfpenny per pound, which means twenty to thirty shillings per ox here. We shall have to give a subsidy of five shillings per head. But it means that we shall get it all back in hut-tax as the natives owe us £27,000 and can't pay because they can't sell their cattle. If this comes off, they will be able to. And above all it means the start of a meat industry here, and a footing in the English market.

On Monday morning Hay, our Veterinary Officer, and Gilman went off to look at the Lobatsi works, and we resumed our discussions here in the afternoon. And again on Thursday morning when we reached agreement. It now all rests with the English Government and I sent them off the devil of a dispatch about it in the afternoon.

Mrs Rheinallt Jones lunched on Wednesday, and Mrs Reilly on Thursday — Ninon had her meeting with Wayfarer leaders who had come in to camp here from the Protectorate and from other places outside. She made two excellent speeches that went down very well indeed.

Friday 5 October
An idiotic telegram came in from London about meat export, so I sat down and wrote them another tremendous dispatch. Wired Stanley that he must see me on Monday at Pretoria, so that both my dispatches and his can go off by air mail to London on Tuesday. It was infernally hot, and a stifling wind blowing, clouds of dust everywhere.

Monday 15 to Sunday 21 October
More trouble at Moshupa with old Gobbleman. There was very nearly a fight between the Bangwaketse and his Bakgatla, but fortunately Ledeboer was there, and calmed them. That young ass Bathoen, Chief of the Bangwaketse, came into Moshupa with five hundred of his men on the way back from a boundary survey. And Gobbleman's Bakgatla, who were having a meeting, about a thousand of them, very nearly started a new 'war'. They were beating on the ground with their sticks, and generally raising Hail Columbia.

Tuesday 23 & Wednesday 24 October
Ellenberger (from Gaberones) and Ledeboer (from Lobatsi) arrived to confer. We have trouble in three Reserves at once now. In the Bakgatla we have the Isang-Molefi row, which is getting worse and worse. The Tribe are furious at the renewed postponement of the big meeting. They believe that Isang is simply doing this in order to hang it up until the rains come on when the people won't be able to come in.

In the Bakwena, Kgari, the Chief, is being attacked by a section led by two of his brothers, and he wants our help to squash them.

In the Bangwaketse, Bathoen the Chief is giving trouble about the removal of the followers of old Gobbleman, whom we have removed bodily from Moshupa to Thamaga in the Bakwena Reserve. Bathoen went to Moshupa with five hundred men, as related above. Bathoen has also established some of his men in a post between Moshupa and the Bakwena frontier, which will certainly lead to trouble.

So I ordered him to move them back. He did not like it, but he's jolly well got to do it.

Friday 26 October
A good rain-soaking during the day. A monstrous and outrageous dispatch from Home, covering a note of an interview at the Dominions Office with a deputation from the 'Save the Children Fund'. Led by some infernal woman called De Bunsen,[28] they informed Thomas that medical services and health conditions here were very bad — missionaries had told them so!! — and that something ought to be done. That swine Thomas never told them that I had been reporting this for years, had begged for funds to put it right, and had submitted plans every year for doing so! These political Government Office people in London are the limit. The dirty yellow dogs shelve the blame onto us out here for their own damnable misdeeds, and take the credit for everything that goes right. I wrote a terrible dispatch home, setting out the facts, and lashing out about the false impression they had given to the deputation. Missionaries indeed! — why, the only English mission here, the L.M.S., have not got a single hospital or doctor or trained nurse or dispensary in the whole Territory, and all they do is try to prevent other missions coming here. The other missions are all doing good and useful medical work, but the L.M.S. make me sick. They are useless, lying idle, hypocritical, canting swine.

Saturday 10 November
A very hectic morning at the Office, getting ready for the great Mochudi trial, which starts on Monday. It's going to be a devilish difficult show, and I hear that thousands of natives are coming in for it from all the country round and even from the Transvaal. Reyneke fears fighting, but I don't believe it, and am only taking two policemen (natives) and my staff officer (Capt. Gash). Of course Reilly comes too.

Monday 12 November (to Mochudi)
Off at 7.30 am by car to Mochudi which we reached soon after 8.30, shooting a guinea fowl on the way. I changed into uniform, and off we went to the meeting of Headmen which is to precede the big Tribal meeting. There were over a hundred Bakgatla Headmen and the six Chiefs from the other districts. They blethered on for hours, and twice I pulled them up and tried to bring them to the point. At last they really began to lash out about iniquities of the Chief and of Isang. We adjourned for a picnic lunch on the stoep of Germond's[29] house, and then as rain began to threaten we continued the meeting in the church — a huge building like a barn. A strange setting for such a meeting. Things warmed up and feelings began to run high, mostly against Isang, and I managed to bring the proceedings to an end at about 6.30. A tremendous storm then burst, and we drove back to Gaberones in sheets of rain, thunder and lightning — water and mud splashing over the top of the car, rivers filling up. Fortunately the Metsemotlhaba River had not had time to come down in flood, and we got over it all right, but it's going to be tricky tomorrow.

Tuesday 13 November
Off at 7.30 again. We left one of our cars on the Gabs side of the Metsemotlhaba as the flood was beginning to come down, and went on in the other. The meeting was

a huge one, at least four thousand Tribesmen had come in, and the sight under the trees was most picturesque. Half a dozen of us, with two native police! in the midst of this tremendous concourse. Its speeches got more and more violent, and I had to intervene once or twice with a joke to relieve the tension. Certainly the feeling is almost unanimous against Isang. I quite believe what Reyneke said, i.e. that if I had not been there they would have shot Isang. I allowed no weapons at the meeting, but of course they all had them handy in the village. One man suggested flogging the Chief and giving him a dose of his own medicine — and then shooting Isang. So to ease matters I told him that I had re-christened him, and his name was no longer Kgari Pilane, but 'Kgari Mussolini'. Of course they didn't understand, but as the Chief laughed the whole meeting roared with laughter! A little thing like this helps. We went on till nearly 7 — then off again back to Gabs. The Metsemotlhaba was a torrent, roaring bank to bank — so we left our car, climbed over the railway bridge, and picked up the other car we had left on the other side. We got back to Gabs about 9, very weary and starving.

Wednesday 14 November
Again off at 7.30, and strange to say found the river had gone down; we were just able to drive thro' it. This morning the Tribe was divided into Kgotlas, and each Kgotla was asked if they agreed with what had already been said — if so, to sit down. Anyone disagreeing and wishing to speak to remain standing. It took some time — then Molefi, the Chief, spoke and made a bitter attack on Isang, repeating the facts about the case of attempted murder on Kgari Pilane. Apparently Kgari Pilane and Isang had a case before the Kgotla in 1931 or 1932. Molefi had given it against Isang, who had then followed Kgari Pilane into the bush, beaten him unconscious — blood running from ears and mouth — pitched him into a cart, taken him to the Kgotla, dragged him out and thrown him at Molefi's feet, saying 'There is your dog'. A pretty grim effort, and the effect of this on the meeting may be imagined.

Isang then spoke. I warned him to be careful what he said about this matter, as 'anything he said might be used against him' if we had to take proceedings. He spoke for three hours, not a very good effort and not very convincing.

I then adjourned for a few minutes to try and get a line from the other Chiefs — but the dirty dogs wouldn't say a word to me. Led by that yellow dog Tshekedi, they said they were going to speak at the Kgotla, and wouldn't say a word beforehand.

By this time it was getting late, and it was obvious we couldn't finish tonight. So I had to arrange for Captain Reilly to carry on tomorrow. However the back of the thing was broken, the danger was over, and it only remained for the Chiefs to speak and for the Tribe to pronounce 'verdict and sentence'. I imagine I know what that will be!

Monday 19 November (at Pretoria)
Quite a good day, tho' a very strenuous one, at the Office with Stanley all day. Good telegrams from Reilly re the Mochudi affair, which he seems to have finished off well. All the Chiefs spoke — all against Isang, tho' recognising Molefi's shortcomings. Isang sentenced to banishment to his farm for six months and fined £350. Reilly announced my decision to appoint a 'tutors council' of six to look after Molefi; also the appointment of a Magistrate at Mochudi; also a committee to

investigate the question of the estate of the late Chief Linchwe (Isang's father and Molefi's grandfather). It all went down very well.

Tuesday 20 November
I had a very satisfactory interview with General Kemp, Minister of Agriculture, at 9.30, and got agreement on various points affecting exports from the B.P. and shooting of cattle on the border. Then some work with Stanley. Then an interview with Colonel Whalehan, late Commissioner of Police for the Union, whom I *may* get to reorganise my police for me. After which Ninon and I went off to lunch at Government House where the Clarendons[30] were as usual perfectly charming. I sat next to Lady Clarendon and she was full of horror at the idea of the next Governor-General being a South African. Of course it would be too ghastly, like that poor fish Isaacs they have made Governor-General in Australia. In point of fact everyone would hate it, nobody really wants it; and yet these rotten politicians will probably put it forward to catch the votes of the back-veld Boer farmers.

Monday 26 to Wednesday 28 November (at Mafeking)
Beastly hot — detestable hole this place. Then very high winds, then good rains. Riding this morning I bumped into clouds of locusts, or rather they bumped into me; they hurt like anything when they hit one on the face galloping through them. It was very curious to see them in the high wind on Tuesday flying backwards! They were trying to fly against the wind to get to the B.P., but the wind pushed them steadily but rapidly backwards. Quite funny to watch, I was of course delighted for they were being driven into the Union.
There is a terrible lot to do to get ready for the European Advisory Council meeting on the 3rd December and, to add to my troubles, Cuzen, the R.M. at Francistown, has played the fool hopelessly, and got the whole of F'town staff in a state of mutiny. He and his wife are a hopeless couple — pin-pricking their staff the whole time. I've had to send for him to come down here.

Saturday 1 December
Arrowsmith came in from the Kalahari, where he has been doing particularly good work. He has some trouble too with the Bakgalagadi out at Kang, who mobilised their womenfolk to impede the police and prevent their searching for smuggled ammunition and poached skins — saying that the British Government would not fire on women! So Arrowsmith *backed* his lorry into the crowd and onto their toes, and they scattered promptly like rabbits — all the others laughing at them, and the situation was saved. Very good of the boy: he will do well.

Sunday 2 December
All the members of the European Advisory Council arrived today and came up to the house for sundowners in the garden about 5.30. They were a mouldy lot, an offence to God and Man most of them. The only redeeming feature of the party was Captain and Mrs Martin from the Tuli Block, who are *sahibs* and know how to behave and talk.

Monday 3 to Thursday 6 December
Meetings of this infernal Council proceeded spasmodically during these four days, and got worse and worse. They started off by bringing a newspaper man with them, and asking that he should be admitted to all the sessions. I refused, but

agreed to telegraph to Stanley for his views. He agreed with me; so that was that.

Then they asked me to telegraph Stanley to ask him to ask the Union Prime Minister to receive a deputation from these European Blocks in the B.P. regarding General Smuts' speech about regarding the B.P. as 'foreign territory'! Of course I had to agree to send the wire. Stanley, who was in Basutoland, wired back that as he was in Basutoland, and Smuts in the Orange Free State, it wasn't possible to arrange a meeting in Pretoria! So then the silly blighters wanted another wire sent to the Prime Minister asking to see them when he came back to Pretoria!

Meanwhile business proceeded. I let off my opening oration, gave them the Estimates and told them to go away and study them. They returned on Tuesday, and let off some futile remarks in reply to my speech, and then began to talk the most awful nonsense about various points. They led off by objecting to my policy of encouraging native creameries, because there was enough butter in South Africa already, and if I allowed the natives to produce more it might harm the Europeans in the B.P. (!) by inducing the people in the Union to object. A perfectly priceless argument, which England trampled on, and I buried. And so it went on, until Wednesday morning when they handed in a fatuous and drivelling document which they said they wanted circulated to every member of the House of Lords and House of Commons and every English newspaper! It was a series of misstatements, exaggerations and general rot, and after a hasty glance at it I went off the deep-end properly and gave them hell. I told them it was a grossly misleading document, that I would have nothing to do with it, and that if they wanted to send it to heaven or the other place they could do it themselves. Then I told them what I thought of them. They had come down with a tame journalist with the sole idea of getting publicity for their own views, regardless of the facts. That for two years the Government had fought every disaster and difficulty without any help from them; that they had done nothing but grouse, nothing to help the Territory or even themselves, etc. etc. etc. After half an hour of unabated and rigorous abuse, I stopped. Their eyes were sticking out like prawns, and all they could say was a request to adjourn for half an hour.

Then their leader came back, saw Reilly, and asked him to tell me that they desired to withdraw their request to see Smuts!

A quiet triumph; and on the next day (Thursday) we completed the rest of the business rapidly and peacefully, and they asked *me* to draw up a statement of their grievances to present to the Imperial Government. That really was too funny, and of course I agreed to do so.

Thank God they all went off home in Friday morning's train — and we're clear of them until February.

Friday 7 to Sunday 9 December
Fforde got back on Saturday about 3 pm and dined and slept, bringing more rain with him. He was very amusing and interesting about Basutoland and also about Union Ministers and the Protectorate and Stanley's departure. Apparently Basutoland is still even more firmly asleep than the B.P. was five years ago. Sturrock the R.C. is a confirmed somnambulist — nothing is even attempted, much less done, and nothing ever happens. In the one hotel at Maseru, the capital, there is no liquor licence, and you can't buy drinks. You can't even get a drink at the Club, and members keep their own bottles of whiskey in their own lockers! Rip Van Winkle seems to be a live wire compared with Sturrock, who has killed every atom of initiative in his staff — which I suppose is why they knighted him when he retired last month.

Fforde also tells me that since Eales has been ill and away from duty, and his deputy Smith is in Basutoland with Pim, they get thro' more work in a day at the High Commission Office than they did formerly in a week. I shall have great pleasure in telling Eales this when he rises from his bed of sickness. Thank God he is leaving for Bulawayo in February. His successor, the new Administrative Secretary, is Priestman[31] or Priestley who comes from West Africa, but doesn't arrive until May.

Monday 10 to Wednesday 12 December
I had good news from Mochudi. Everyone has accepted everything that I settled. Isang has gone to his farm. Molefi is working like a beaver, and peace appears to reign.

Visit to Cape Town

Wednesday 19 December (at Cape Town)
I trotted off to the High Commission Office, and saw Stanley and various people. Stanley was very nice and cordial and we did a good bit of work. Also Fforde and Liesching. Thank goodness Eales is still ill, and Smith away with Pim in Basutoland, so there was no obstruction, and Cohen who was in charge was most helpful. Lunched with Liesching — he is a very able and most pleasant fellow.

Thursday 20 December
We saw what was supposed to be a really good 'talkie' film with Marlene Dietrich — *Song of Songs*. I did not care about her at all, nor did I think her good-looking. It's so damned silly these women having all their eyebrows pulled out and a straight black line painted on their foreheads — that fashion is one of the most striking proofs of the mental inferiority of women that I have met with.
After the show everyone went on to drink beer at some place, but I thought N. had had enough so we drove home.

Friday 21 December
A morning at the High Commission Office, where I got three bits of good news. Firstly the Dominions Office have at long last agreed to my Native Administration Proclamations, and they are to be published on 4 January! For three years I have been fighting to get them through. I drafted them originally, and they have been discussed, argued over, amended and battled over ever since. I have had to fight London, the missionaries, the Chiefs, and the High Commission Office; and I think that most people would have given it up long ago. It is a great triumph, the greatest I have had out here, and now I have definitely got Mr Tshekedi in his place. It is the only large bit of constructive reform in regard to Native Affairs that has been carried out in South Africa for a very long time — indeed the only thing of its kind ever done in the Protectorate. I *am* glad.
Then the Colonial Development Committee have sent me a most flattering dispatch about the work done in Ngamiland in clearing the Okavango rivers, and have moreover given me £3,000 to go on with the work. That's very good. And finally the Dominions Office have agreed to my recommendation to give Captain Reilly a C.B.E. in the New Year Honours.

1934

Monday 24 December
A very busy morning in Cape Town. N. shopped while I dashed around and left cards at the French and Italian Legations (Dr Simonin and Count Labia), and after getting my golden curls trimmed did some work with Stanley. An idiotic letter in from Tshekedi complaining bitterly of the attitude of the other Chiefs, and saying that he won't work with them any more. Now that he can't quarrel with us, he is quarrelling with them — I am very glad. It will make it easier for us. *'Divide et impera'* as the old tag goes.

Tuesday 25 December: Christmas Day
We had a pleasant morning in 'Topsy', reading our Christmas mail. Over a hundred letters and cards came in yesterday and today — quite an undertaking, tho' a very jolly one.

In the afternoon we revelled in the Empire broadcast, a truly marvellous and inspiring effort, sitting on the *stoep* of the hotel listening to Australia, New Zealand, India, Canada, the Rhodesias, South Africa, and above all England talking to all the rest of the Empire. It was really wonderful, and brought home in a way otherwise impossible the immensity of the Empire and all that it stands for. The best of all was of course the King. We heard every word perfectly — a grand effort, a splendid speech, and a fitting climax to the proceedings. And to think that these foul Little England dogs and other stay-at-home sewer rats would break up and give away this unique and marvellous edifice of great nations.

Thursday 27 to Saturday 29 December
On Friday we went to the Admiral's big dinner at Simonstown — farewell to the Stanleys and reception of the officers of the German training cruiser *Emden*. We were twenty-six at dinner, a very jolly dinner and evening which we enjoyed muchly. In addition to the Evans and Stanleys there was the German Minister and his wife. He was very clever and pleasant, but we didn't like her — and a number of German officers. We were all very much in war-paint, decorations, etc. It was quite an imposing sight, the most imposing being of course Evans' perfect blaze of medals and decorations. I should think that he has got everything that could be got in that way.

Monday 31 December
We were in bed before the Old Year ran out, I am glad to say.

1935

Saturday 5 January (at Cape Town)
A great send-off at the station for Stanley. The Union Government provided a very large, smart Guard of Honour, and all Cape Town was there — all in full war-paint came from Government House; Admiral Evans and his staff also in full uniform; Sir Cecil Fforde, Liesching, Dickson (the Swaziland R.C.), Sims (Basutoland Acting R.C.) and self, all in top hats; all our ladies of course; most of the *corps diplomatique* and lots of Government people. The guard saluted, Stanley inspected them; and then we are trooped *en masse* to the platform, where there was a very cordial and impressive send off. Both Stanley and Lady Stanley quite affected by it all.

I forgot to mention that in the New Year Honours List, Evans has got a K.C.B., at which we are all delighted; Reilly has got the C.B.E. for which I recommended him; and to our utter disgust that jelly-fish and poisonous reptile Eales has got a C.M.G. It is a public scandal, and everyone is exceedingly annoyed.

I have received all the addresses to present to Clark on Monday, nine in all! From the European Advisory Council, the Indian Community, and seven Chiefs — Tshekedi's is a wonderful effort, illuminated in colour.

Monday 7 January
A very busy morning helping to receive Clark. At 9.15 we went on board the *Armadale Castle* (the ship we came out in five years ago), everyone in uniform or top hat. Clark was very nice indeed and seemed really glad to see me. Lady Clark and the daughter also seemed nice. After chatting to all and sundry for about half an hour, Ninon and I drove off to the High Commission Office where I changed my uniform. We drove out to Milnerton, where there was another gathering, smaller but more official. Sir Cecil Fforde, in robes, did the 'swearing in' very impressively; then the other two R.C.'s and I presented our addresses from our respective Territories. After which, drinking of champagne, press photographers dashing about, some more chat, and we all broke off for lunch. Evans was magnificent in uniform; he is simply covered with medals, orders and decorations.

Tuesday 8 January
All morning at the Office with Clark and the two other R.C.'s — a very interesting talk. Apparently the Imperial Government would like to hand over the Territories

if they dared, but they are frightened of public opinion at Home and in Africa. Clark does not seem to know very much of our work out here, tho' he realises there is a tremendous lot of it and that it is very difficult.

Wednesday 9 to Friday 11 January
Ninon went to the Guides and Wayfarers Council Central Meeting. Very important business: it was decided to accept the offer of the Guides for the Wayfarers to join up. Very satisfactory. Lady Clarendon presided one day, Mrs Patrick Duncan the other. Ninon says Mrs Duncan is the ablest chairman she has ever met, man or woman. She is a very able woman, wife of the Minister of Mines.

Saturday 12 January
Heard that Sir James Macgregor, a former R.C. of the B.P., died in Cape Town yesterday, and is to be buried tomorrow. So I had to send a telegram and order a wreath. He's no loss, one of the worst R.C.s we ever had, and that's saying a good deal.

Monday 14 January
A very hectic morning. We were all packed and ready early, and I went round to see Colonel Deneys Reitz,[1] the newly appointed Minister of Agriculture, *vice* Kemp — an admirable change. We had a most satisfactory interview, and I think we'll be getting cattle out soon. He assured me that he would never be party to any policy of trying to squeeze the Protectorates into the Union by imposing veterinary restrictions on our cattle exports for other than veterinary reasons. He spoke quite disparagingly of his predecessor, General Kemp, now Minister of Lands. He said that he quite realised that to try and *force* the Protectorates into the Union would only result in antagonising the natives and creating an immense feeling in England — possibly a sort of 'Chinese Labour Election'.[2] Tho' he thought the ultimate destiny of the Protectorates, one day, would be to join the Union.

Back at Mafeking

Monday 21 to Wednesday 23 January
On Wednesday I had a terrible row with Brind, our Government Engineer — the worst I have ever had with any official, ending in my turning him out of the room. He had the damned insolence to say that Colonel Naus's river clearance scheme in Ngamiland is all wrong in theory; that the work should be taken from him, and given to him — Brind! He protested against my action in dealing direct with Naus, and he put in an infernal memorandum asking that it should be sent to the Secretary of State. He's dug his own grave.

Thornton, the newly appointed Agricultural Adviser, also arrived on Wednesday morning, and contrary to my fears and expectations we had a very pleasant and satisfactory interview. I think he should be of much help to us in our agricultural work. But it is very amusing how these 'experts' differ. Milligan, who came out with Pim to advise us, said we ought to have a Stud Farm to improve our cattle, instead of the Bull Camps we had started. So we applied to the Colonial Development Fund for a grant for a Stud Farm and got it. Now Thornton says we ought to have Bull Camps; that they are much better; that he has run them very successfully in the Union; and that he originally got the idea from us!

1935

Thursday 24 January
Huggins, the Prime Minister of Southern Rhodesia, and some of his Ministers and technical advisers were going through on the train today to attend the Customs Conference with the Union Government at Cape Town. It is going to be a tremendous battle between the two Governments, and if they can't agree Southern Rhodesia are going to break off their present Customs Agreement and start a sort of tariff war. I got on the train at 6.30 am and, after completing my toilet, breakfasted with Huggins and Chapman in the latter's private coach. Chapman is the General Manager of Rhodesia Railways. Huggins and I had a most interesting talk after breakfast on many matters affecting Southern Rhodesia and the B.P., and our respective relations with the Union. He said he would oppose strongly any question of the transfer of the northern portion of the Protectorate to the Union as it would mean the encirclement of Southern Rhodesia by the Union. He pressed me to come up to Salisbury to discuss commercial and other questions with him and his Ministers.

Smith, Minister of Finance, and Harris, Minister of Agriculture, lunched and I had a most interesting talk with them afterwards — Walvis Bay Stock Route, and other matters of mutual interest.

With them and with Chapman I also discussed the linking up of our new air service with theirs. 'Rana' (Rhodesia and Nyasaland Airways) is the name of their company. It is a branch of Imperial Airways. By that means we should have a really British air service linking Northern and Southern Rhodesia, Nyasaland and B.P.; and that would be the first step to a closer union between us all round, and a counter-blast to those Dutchmen here with their Union Air Service — which is staffed by Germans with Junkers and Dutch (Fokker) machines. I think we can do it, and I must get busy on it.

Monday 28 January
Today the Customs Conference started between Southern Rhodesia and the Union at Cape Town. I was to be there to represent the B.P., but in view of the very heavy pressure of work here I wired off. I *loathe* that long boring journey to and from Cape Town in the hot weather, especially the nights in the train. One gets choked with heat and dust.

Friday 1 February
After further discussion with Thornton I finished my big memorandum on trade relations between the B.P. and the Union — an undertaking that has meant a lot of work, digging into past history and planning for the future. It ought to make them sit up.

Saturday 2 February
Hope, our retired police officer, has written a book of his adventures entitled 'Swashbuckler'. I fear it will have no success, but as he asked me I wrote a 'foreword' for it. He appears to be immensely delighted and most grateful, but I don't think it will help much.

Monday 4 & Tuesday 5 February
Late on Thursday Captain Thompson arrived from Bulawayo. He is the chief flying man of 'Rana' and was sent down by Chapman, the Chairman of the Company, to discuss with me the question of linking up our proposed flying

service with them so as to form the first link towards something bigger in the way of an Imperial chain. We sketched out a very promising looking plan of operations. Now I must get it approved by London, as it means joining up with Imperial Airways. I fancy they will agree.

By the way, I think I should mention that my native orderly who rides with me every morning, has been presented by his wife with twins whom he had christened 'Colonel Rey' and 'Captain Gash'. He informed me yesterday with much glee that 'Colonel Rey' was quite black, and 'Captain Gash' was white! I think this latest scandal in the B.P. is quite good. Anyhow it lets me out, but I don't know what Gash will say when I write and break the news to him.

Monday 11 February
A great triumph at the Native Advisory Council. Realising that at long last my two Native Proclamations are law, all the Chiefs accepted them fully — and there will be no trouble! I always maintained that directly they became law, the artificial and fictitious obstructions of the Chiefs would cease, and now I am justified. And I have had everyone against me — the Chiefs, the High Commission Office, the Dominions Office, and even some of my own people. Now of course everyone says — how beautiful! It is an immense weight off my mind.

Of course Tshekedi did not attend. But his 'jackal', Bathoen (Chief of the Bangwaketse), howled with all the other Chiefs.[3] We had a long day of it, and the R.M.s and Dr Schapera (who is getting on splendidly with my native law codification) all came to the house for sundowners.

Friday 15 February
I got sick of seeing Chiefs, so turned them all over to Reilly, whose day they entirely filled. I forgot to mention that amongst those I saw yesterday was Molefi, Chief of the Bagkatla at Mochudi. He has quite come to heel, and I was able to settle various difficulties without any trouble, including the difficulty of the duties of the six 'guardians', whom we had appointed to look after him at the recent big *indaba at* Mochudi.[4]

I dictated my memorandum about the position of the European settlers in the B.P. — as I've heard they have again asked to see the Prime Minister (Hertzog) about incorporation into the Union, and Clark must be 'briefed'.

Tuesday 19 February
Spent the whole day arguing with that poisonous little beast Tshekedi — finance, Masarwa questions, Proclamations, Khama School, agricultural plots at Mahalapye, miscegenation, etc. His new attitude is not to oppose, but to say that none of our plans will work — to say he will cooperate, but in reality to try and make them fail. A nasty piece of work.

Wednesday 20 February
Rain this morning, but it did not prevent my having a very jolly ride. A pleasant letter from Count Labia, the Italian Minister in South Africa. As I have reason to believe that he is interested in B.P. cattle for Italian colonial markets, I am writing to try and arrange a meeting with him at Cape Town to discuss the question of starting a meat canning factory in the B.P.

1935

Thursday 21 February
Those wretched European Advisory Council people arrived here today for a preliminary pow-wow before the meeting of the Council on Monday next. They are a bore and a pest. They have asked to see Hertzog about incorporating them in the Union and want to send a deputation down for 1st March. I wish the Union would take them and drown the lot. They are no use to themselves or anyone else — helpless and hopeless — and when one tries to help them they do nothing but grouse.

Colonel Wilkins and Colonel Bezeidenhout arrived from the Union Government to ask me if I would allow them to send men and lorries over our southern border (Tsabong to Kuis and Bokspits), to deal with enormous swarms of locusts that have settled there. Of course I agreed, but stipulated that one of our officers must accompany them and they must not shoot game except small stuff for the pot! They were very decent specimens of Dutchmen, much better than our rotten farmers.

Monday 25 February
That poisonous little beast Tshekedi, after discussing matters with me all day long on the 19th and agreeing everything with me, has now telegraphed saying he wants to see Clark with me at Cape Town before I sail — and go through it all again! He is a poisonous little swine. I have wired Clark asking him to say 'No'.

The European Advisory Council met today and, wonderful to relate, everything passed off peacefully and we finished before 4 pm. They were like lambs, due no doubt to the tremendous dressing down they got the last time. They are to see the Hertzogs on 1st March. Four of them are going — MacFarlane, Glover, Van Rensburg and Going — all blighters.

I got an extraordinarily nice dispatch from Clark, enclosing a copy of one he had sent Home saying all sorts of nice things about the way I had handled the last meeting of the Native Advisory Council — also a private letter from him to the same effect.

Tuesday 26 February
It is alleged that a diamond pan has been discovered in the Kalahari at Kai-Kai, near Lehututu.[5] Dutch and natives are alleged to be illegally digging up diamonds and smuggling them over the border. Arrowsmith is on their trail with some police trying to find the place. No easy job. Masterman goes off on Thursday to consult with him and Major Brinton of the Union Police, and we hope to have a great round-up. It will be good fun, and I wish I were there — they may show fight.

Saturday 2 March
In the afternoon a telegram from the Union Government to say they would allow our cattle in — *at long long last!* But they want to impose some rotten conditions that we must fight. So Chase and I will have one last battle together against the Union on Wednesday next. I got Chase and Reilly round and we concocted a diplomatic telegram, which we got away before 5.30. We certainly do keep things going on till the end! Then Ninon and I had a last drive in 'Topsy' — very sad. I hate parting with her. She is sold and to be handed over tomorrow.

1935

Sunday 3 March (en route to Cape Town & Mafeking)
A final burst of packing one's own things and packing up the house. Then at 4.30 — away. A big crowd at the station, guard of honour, everyone to shake by the hand. Rather an exhausting and almost an affecting ceremony — especially as it was frightfully hot. Everyone was there, even Chief Lotlamoreng from the Barolong village.

Started work almost immediately on the train with Chase on this infernal cattle question. Then at 6.30 (by which time it had started raining and was much cooler) Captain Masterman and Arrowsmith (in charge of the Kalahari) boarded the train. We discussed this new and rather exciting diamond business that is giving us a good deal of food for thought — and action. Apparently a solicitor, Freylinch by name has got hold of a letter from a scoundrel named Rautenbach, offering to hand over a parcel of diamonds he got from Hottentots out of the Kalahari to one Johnson.

Freylinch gave Johnson away to us, and will help us to get the what-nots in return for a prospecting licence! A pretty party of crooks. We accordingly arranged that Freylinch go off at our expense to collect the what-nots at Bokspits, followed (on the skyline) by Arrowsmith and one of the Union Police. Then when we've got them, we'll make the people tell us where the diamond pan is and go out and collar the lot. Freylinch and Major Brinton (Union Police) came on board. We told them what we had decided; they agreed. So the balloon ought to go up next week — great fun if it comes off. Incidentally that's the way the Kimberley Mines started — by working a pan in the bush. But these diamonds may have been stolen from the South African diamond mines and been smuggled over the border. However, *nous verrons*.

Tuesday 5 March (at Cape Town)
All ready at 6.30 am and we got in punctually at 6.40 — very cold. I put on my clothes over my pyjamas and an overcoat over that.

Clark told me all about the interview that the deputation from our European Advisory Council had with the Prime Minister. Apparently old Hertzog was most polite to them, but told them he didn't want the European Blocks only, but the whole Protectorate. He is going to press for it when he goes over to England this year, and moreover to press for it to be done within a certain time! Clark cabled all this Home, and shewed me the answer. They are rather worried about it. The Home Government has taken a nasty knock about Unemployment Insurance, another one about India on account of the volte-face of the Indian Princes, and a third by reason of their White Paper on armaments. A fourth about the Protectorate might bring them down, for there is a large body of opinion at Home that feels very strongly on these native questions. So it looks as tho' I should have quite a lively time on arrival in Downing Street.

Wednesday 6 March
Dog-tired this morning after my third not too good night — my mind working top pressure.

I was at the Office early and did a bit more dictation. Then at 10.30 Tshekedi arrived for his interview with Clark and self. He was most sweetly reasonable, as is his way at a first interview. But in spite of that was rather silly about the Masarwa question, and Clark put him down over that. We finished by 12 and then Clark and I did some more work. Ninon and I lunched alone together again at the hotel.

Then I went off to meet Count Labia to discuss B.P. meat for Italy: not a very useful meeting as he was woolly and ill-informed on the subject. He was very keen to know my views on the Italian-Abyssinian question (!) which incidentally looks bad.

I was so tired last night and tonight that I did not dress for dinner! — an unheard of lapse on my part.

Thursday 7 March
Our historic interview with Colonel Reitz at 10 am about re-opening the Union markets to our cattle. A great fight and a marvellous victory. Chase and I were so excited afterwards that we wanted to cheer! We got them to agree to re-open at once and drop their absurd conditions about branding our cattle on the border. Moreover they are going to give us a quota of 10,000 head a year, which is double the amount they have given Southern Rhodesia! They are going to give us a hundred a week at once, and are calling a meeting of the Meat Quota Board by telegram, to ratify the remainder — a perfectly wonderful result. We have to send them out thro' Quarantine Camps, and we have undertaken to cooperate in stopping smuggling cattle over the border. Chase goes to Pretoria tomorrow to settle details with Du Toit and to see the Secretary of the Meat Quota Board. He will attend the meeting of the Board later. A huge victory. We came back to tell Clark, and he was fearfully pleased and excited and could hardly believe his ears. He congratulated us most cordially and enthusiastically.

On Leave

Wednesday 20 March (on board ship, off Gibraltar)
Our first glimpse of Europe — cold, misty, raining, thoroughly loathsome and depressing. We can hardly see the Rock thro' the mist. The only cheering sight is the British Fleet, and that is a joy, tho' the huge ships are veiled in mist.

Wednesday 27 March (in London)
Walked over to the Dominions Office and saw Sir Edward Harding, Sir Harry Batterbee and Sir Geoffrey Whiskard.[6] They all seemed very pleased to see me and made themselves very nice. A letter from Amery asking Ninon and me to lunch on Friday.

We went to the theatre again — *The Dominant Sex* at the Aldwych. Too hopelessly rotten for words — just married couples ranting at each other. Wives saying who they'd played the fool with before they were married, equality of sexes etc. We were bored to tears.

Wednesday 10 April
At 3, I had meeting at the Dominions Office re Stud Farm versus Bull Camp trouble. We came to a compromise after winged words with Milligan.

Thursday 11 April
Interview with J.H. Thomas at Dominions Office in morning — very pleasant — asked many questions, said they were very pleased with my work in B.P.

Monday 15 April
At 5, meeting at Chatham House [Royal Institute of International Affairs], where held forth about B.P. They asked me lots of questions — a lot of stiffs mostly. The

best was Miss Marjorie Perham,[7] who has written a series of articles about B.P. in *The Times* in opposition to Lionel Curtis.[8]

Wednesday 21 August to Thursday 5 September (Marseilles to Cape Town)
Count Labia is on board with his wife and children, and has made himself exceedingly nice to us indeed. He comes up to our corner of the deck and has long talks with us, mostly about Abyssinia, which is indeed the main topic of conversation on board. Mussolini obviously intends to go right ahead and there seems no doubt about war. Labia put the Italian case very fairly and forcibly, and cannot understand England's attitude in siding with barbarous savages against their old allies. I am bound to say I sympathise a good deal with his views, and with Italy's grievances against Abyssinia — tho' I cannot think that Mussolini's methods could be regarded as justifiable.

Return to Africa

Sunday 8 to Tuesday 10 September (at Mafeking)
Almost the whole staff met us on the station at Mafeking, and all seemed really pleased to see us. It was a great joy to see the new car 'Topsy II' looking really very beautiful, and I must say the house and garden looked very nice indeed. Hector (the dog) was all over us, and the servants grinned until I thought their faces would split in two. Thank goodness the weather is cool. Really hectic days, unpacking, sorting out our things, picking up the threads at the Office and getting ready to go to Pretoria. My goodness, there is a lot of work to be done. They have been doing a good deal in my absence, but they have mucked one or two things badly, and many more have been held up for discussion with Colonel Rey on return. It's funny how people hate taking responsibility, and how often they muck things when they do take it.

Friday 13 to Sunday 15 September (at Pretoria)
A great day's work with Clark. We had forty different items of business to discuss and got thro' them all. I can do as much business with him in one and a half days as I could with Stanley in a week. We had a pleasant dinner party on Friday night with the Swedish Minister and his wife.

On Saturday morning I saw old Grobler (Minister for Native Affairs) at his request. Thank goodness I had ridden him off coming up to Mochudi to interview Molefi and Isang. He was very pleasant and wants to come up to Ngamiland next June. He was quite amusing about Tshekedi, and said that if he (Grobler) was still Minister when the Union took over the Protectorates Mr Tshekedi would be brought into line good and quick. I should love to see it.

Monday 23 to Sunday 29 September (back at Mafeking)
On Friday Ellenberger and Towne (the R.M.s from Gaberones and Molepolole) lunched after a palaver at the Office in the morning. They are both doing very well, and their Chiefs are being good boys — especially Kgari at Molepolole. It's wonderful how we've got the Bakwena Tribe into shape since we kicked out the former Chief Sebele. At Mochudi I hear that Molefi has given up drinking for the time being and is behaving beautifully. He has brought back his uncle ex-Chief

Isang, about whom there was such a row, and they are almost on kissing terms. Wonderful what a little firmness does.

Of course Tshekedi is as ever a damn nuisance. He has disappeared into the bush and can't be found. His cousin, Bathoen of the Bangwaketse, has come into line this week, but I shall have to go up there to smack him.

Those ungrateful beasts, the European farmers on the Council, in spite of all I've done for them — got them an opening for 10,000 head of cattle a year at Johannesburg, freed the country of Foot and Mouth, and got lots of grants from Home. In spite of all that, they do nothing but grouse — dirty, idle, stupid bone heads.

Monday 30 September
I finished off the great Meat Dispatch embodying my new proposals for meat export from Lobatsi — 15,000 head a year; subsidy of £800 a month; minimum price ten shillings per hundred pounds; fixed annual quota for exporting to England. It's been a difficult negotiation and a difficult dispatch to write.

But everything is improving and showing signs of going ahead. The natives are more prosperous and cheery; revenue is going up; and generally the indications are that the tide has definitely turned and we are on the up-grade — rather a mixture of metaphors.

Tuesday 1 to Sunday 6 October
The Native Proclamations are going quite well everywhere, except in Serowe where Tshekedi as usual is making a nuisance of himself. He has disappeared somewhere in the Nata country. I am specially pleased with the progress made at Molepolole where, since we kicked the Chief out, matters have steadily improved. Now they are leading the way as regards the Proclamations. They are appointing paid Councillors to try big cases, and taxing themselves to do so. A very remarkable and satisfactory development.

Monday 7 to Sunday 20 October
The event of the week was the arrival of Sir Malcolm Hailey[9] and his secretary Donald Malcolm. He is on a tour throughout Africa to report generally on British Administration in all the Colonies, a huge job.

Hailey, a brilliantly clever man, very amusing, keen sense of humour and immense and varied experience over half the world. We got on like a house on fire. Malcolm is a very able and pleasant fellow too.

On Thursday morning I took them down to the Office and we had a further talk after which I brought in my prize exhibit, the native Dr S.M. Molema, and left him with Hailey for an hour. Malcolm went off in the cars to Palapye to wait for Hailey who is coming on by train. They have two Ford V 8 cars, fitted with enormous tyres. Marvellous cars for desert work; they get through sand as if it were a macadamised road — tremendous engine power and acceleration, and very cheap.

Monday 21 October
A really terrific week, the labours of which were made much worse by the fact that Ninon again spent it all in bed. She still runs a slight temperature and an infernal cough that worries her a lot. It's damnable.

I spent the whole day preparing for the Resident Commissioners' Conference to be held at Pretoria on the 24th and 25th. The agenda has been in the Office since 10th August and my blasted Office people had never given it to me. Mercifully I know most of the subjects to be discussed by heart, backwards and forwards, but of course one must be word-perfect for these battles. Luckily my memory is as good as ever and my mind still works pretty rapidly. So it was possible to do a week's work in a day. But it was a bad effort on the part of my people, and I cursed them properly. The terrific heat didn't improve matters: it was 95 degrees on our *stoep* and 104 at Mahalapye.

I should like to get some of these Whitehall theorists out here and turn them onto some of our difficulties and make them work under our conditions.

Tuesday 22 October
Conference about our water schemes which have been held up by these damned theorists in my absence, notably by Thornton — the so-called Agricultural Adviser — and his tame engineer Roberts. They are always theorising and proposing vast impracticable schemes, instead of getting on with the jobs which *can* be done with available means. I don't know which I dislike most — theorists or missionaries.

Five of my schemes have been held up in my absence, *altho' we'd got the money for them:* Ngamiland waterways; general water development; Stud Farm; pasture research; and skin tanning factory. It's a business to kick them all into life again, but they'll all be in full swing in a month at most.

Thursday 24 October (at Pretoria)
A very hectic day. The conference began at 10, but I had telephoned twice to Mafeking before then — to Ninon (who was better) and the office. The Conference was held at the High Commissioner's house, as there was no room big enough at the Office. Among those present we noticed Sir William Clark, Sir Cecil Fforde, Major Furse[10] from the Colonial Office, Richards the new R.C. for Basutoland, Marwick[11] the new R.C. for Swaziland, Priestman (Administrative Secretary to the High Commissioner), Smith the Deputy, the Assistant R.C. and the Financial Secretary from Swaziland — quite a gathering. Richards is a hairy-heeled ranker, and he and I fought at sight. We disagreed on every conceivable point, and he being rude of course I was not exactly polite. However the conference went very well and I got thro' what I wanted, and blocked what I didn't want. Clark was very good as chairman, tho' of course he doesn't know very much about things yet.

A telegram from Reilly to say that little pipsqueak Tshekedi had asked for a further delay until February before putting the Proclamations into force. He had been given until November 15. Clark of course agreed with me that the request was preposterous, and I sent him a stiff telegram telling him to get on with the job. We shall have fun and games after the 15th November I am certain.

Marwick the newly appointed R.C. for Swaziland is a pleasant old fish. He has been in Swaziland since the Year One, and has only got another year or so to go. He is slow but not stupid and knows a devil of a lot about his job. We get on very well: he is keen.

Saturday 26 October (to Mafeking)
Off by the 9.54 train. A very successful day, discussing, planning, and dictating. With Naus' help I was able to tear to pieces the damn silly reports written by those two children of shame Roberts and Thornton. And, as I had agreed with Clark for

1935

Naus to go ahead again on my line, I hope all may be well in the future.

Reached Mafeking 7.40 pm, where thank goodness I found Ninon much better.

Sunday 27 October
Major Furse arrived by train from Pretoria for bath and breakfast. He is a most delightful person; everyone loves him. It is a thousand pities that he is so deaf, but he manages to understand wonderfully well. He is of course exceptionally able. He is the head of the Personnel Department of the Colonial Office and chooses the staff for the whole of the Colonies on the new selection method. He does it extraordinarily well too.

After breakfast I took him down to the Office to meet Reilly and all my heads of department; then back to lunch. Captain Masterman took him by car to Kanye after tea. He is going on via Molepolole, Gaberones, Palapye, Serowe and to Ngamiland.[12]

Thursday 31 October
Gale all day, clouds of dust, overcast and dark, cooler. Glover, the Gaberones member of the Advisory Council, came and whined to me about our police stopping the smuggling of cattle over the border into the Union. He had the cheek to suggest that our Gaberones police were too active and ought to be moved. I handed him over to Godley,[13] who gave him hell: Glover used to be a trooper in Godley's regiment of Light Horse.

The L.M.S. people came over today for a conference about their joint effort with us for a hospital at Tswapong, near the Tuli Block. We have got an extra £1,000 out of the Treasury for sinking a well, so they can get on with it now. They are a rotten lot. Haile (the best of them), Gavin Smith and Burns came over and I handed them over to Reilly to deal with.

I sent Brind and Dr Stirling over to Johannesburg — the former to get boring machines for my water-scheme which is at last about to start; the latter to get our two new motor travelling dispensaries for which we have now got authority.

Tuesday 5 November
England got back from Maseru, where he had been completely successful in converting that amiable theorist, Thornton, in regard to the skin tanning factory. So we got the dispatch drafted to the Colonial Development Fund for £3,000. Another scheme on its way; we ought to get something done soon.

Wednesday 6 November
Dispatch from home agreeing to my application for £3,000 to start the Karakul sheep industry here. I am afraid we are getting such a devilish lot of hay on our fork that we shall be smothered if we're not careful. More rain.

Friday 8 November
After a hectic hour at the Office dealing with damn fool telegrams from Home about meat export and water boring, I drove over to Zeerust to see Colonel Reitz (Union Minister of Agriculture) about getting 25,000 head of cattle into the Union for trek and store purposes. The Western Transvaal farmers want them — trek oxen for ploughing, store cattle for fattening on their surplus mealies (which they can't sell), and eventual sale to Johannesburg. Jo'burg too is getting short of meat for their 250,000 natives on the mines.

Reitz was interviewing a succession of deputations, but we lunched together and had a most satisfactory interview. He said he was entirely in favour of the proposal, and would put it up to the Cabinet next week. He also said it was entirely impossible to stop cattle smuggling over our four hundred mile frontier, even if he had regiments of soldiers and lines of blockhouses. Their cordon was costing them £60,000 a year and was useless.

Later on he saw a deputation of B.P. farmers and told them much the same thing. Obviously the only way to stop smuggling is to provide a legitimate market and Reitz sees this. Whether the Cabinet will is another matter.

Reitz is a well known author and his book *Commando* is a classic. So we had much in common. He was very nice about my writings.

We got back — under the hour again — soon after 3, and went to the Office. Tshekedí has now practically told us to go to the devil with our Proclamations. He was given a month, i.e. until 15 November to comply, held a Kgotla yesterday and said 'nothing doing'. So now we must get ahead and apply sanctions — in other words to depose him. This will be final and will also mean another hell of a row. I started drafting a cocked-hat dispatch about it, but shall wait till Monday for the Magistrate's report of the Kgotla before sending it off. He is a devil.

A cold evening at last.

Monday 11 & Tuesday 12 November
Meeting of most of my Resident Magistrates from up country. Ledeboer, Cuzen, Ellenberger, Nettelton, Lawrenson, Mangan. A very interesting and useful meeting on native affairs. It is most unfortunate that while the Southern Protectorate is so splendidly prosperous, the Northern Protectorate, which has been doing very well, is now threatened with the worst drought for twenty years. No rain has fallen in the Northern part of the Bamangwato Reserve, the Tuli Block or the Tati. There is no grazing left. The cattle are dying at the rate of a thousand a day; and the ones left are so weak that even when the rains fall they will be too weak to plough for weeks — so they'll miss the season and have no crops.

Friday 22 November
I went down to the Office in the afternoon, and was busy with the big dispatch that has come in about the political negotiations regarding transfer of the Territories to the Union. Grobler, the Minister of Native Affairs, had had an interview with Fforde, at which he had been talking out of his turn and contemplating wild proposals to enable transfer to be made in two years. He wanted to send men and machinery into the B.P. and take charge of all our water-boring, paying about £65,000. Of course we could not let him do that, unless we definitely agreed to hand over in two years — whether the natives wanted it or not. We couldn't do that, as it would mean violating our pledges to the natives. And to accept Union Government financial help in those circumstances would be taking money under false pretences. So we had to say 'nothing doing' on those lines. But Fforde and Priestman had been rather silly at the interview, and I can see I shall have to go over to Pretoria soon. Anyway, there is no question of any immediate transfer — or for many years.[14]

Sunday 24 & Monday 25 November
Sunday was terribly hot and we melted. I had my secretary up to the house and dictated all the morning. In the afternoon Ninon and I lazed in 'Topsy' on the veld.

As I expected, I've got to go to Pretoria. Frantic telegrams from Clark who, tho' in bed, is alarmed at our opposition to the silly proposals discussed with Grobler by Fforde and Priestman, and wants to see all three Resident Commissioners.

Wednesday 27 November (at Pretoria)
After a preliminary pow-wow with Fforde on the subject of Tshekedi's fat-headed action against us, we three Resident Commissioners, Fforde and Priestman, journeyed over to the High Commissioner's house and interviewed Clark in bed. A most amusing show lasting nearly two hours. Clark was immensely impressed with our arguments and as a result decided to send the devil of a long telegram to London, going back on a good deal of what had been said before. He said that he ought to have consulted us long ago — before the idiotic interview with Grobler — but had been prevented by illness. Quite so, but Fforde ought not to have seen Grobler before talking to us — and I said so with some force, by way of making myself popular.

I lunched at Polleys with Marwick, the new R.C. for Swaziland, a pleasant old bird but timid as a rabbit and divided between alarm and admiration at my drastic and outspoken methods. Very funny.

Friday 6 December (back at Mafeking)
More infuriated telephoning to Pretoria — this time about Bathoen, the Bangwaketse Chief, who is making a fool of himself by trying to copy Tshekedi's example. Also more trouble about that poison-pot Tshekedi.

Tuesday 10 December
A fiendish day finishing off Estimates, but they are nearly through. Our ordinary (non-capital) expenditure for this year is £168,000. The Dominions Office told me to put them *down* to £148,000 for next year; so I have put them *up* to £183,000. That will take some justifying and arguing. More arguments about the Tshekedi case. Why will people argue? The world would be a better and a happier place if only everyone would agree with me.

The first stage of the Tshekedi case took place in the Resident Commissioner's (my) Court today, when I heard Counsel's argument asking to be allowed to bring the case. It was all very correct and formal, and I think Counsel were astonished and a little alarmed at my ruling (accepting the case). They were expecting opposition *at this stage* — and hope to make capital out of it later. But we are watching our step.

Wednesday 11 December (to Pretoria)
The Tshekedi affair develope. He refused to put the Proclamations into force, and all the time I was away on leave the affair was allowed to drag on.[15] Clark summoned him and Bathoen to Pretoria. Bathoen came, but Tshekedi was supposed to be 'ill' and didn't (of course he wouldn't come).

I made it clear to Clark that this sort of tomfoolery could not go on, and a letter was sent to Tshekedi on October 14th giving him one month to comply or take the consequences. November 15th came and of course no action. Indeed Tshekedi held a Kgotla a few days before the 15th, and practically said he wouldn't.

Clark got ill and we couldn't go on. Tshekedi went to Cape Town, saw his infernal lawyer — that wretched negrophilist Buchanan — and came back and asked two Magistrates to attend Kgotla at which he executed a complete *volte face* and nominated twelve Councillors to comply with the Proclamations. It was of course only camouflage. He left out most of the important men and put in mostly duds — the idea being that he could say he was complying with the Proclamations and at the same time wreck them. And meanwhile he had handed in a process against the High Commissioner to ask the Courts to declare that the Proclamations were illegal. Of course he didn't announce this in Kgotla.[16]

I went over to Pretoria and saw Clark and Fforde (the Legal Adviser). We decided to instruct the R.M. to call another Kgotla at Serowe to put to Tshekedi certain leading questions, and to inform him that he was obviously only pretending to work the Proclamations while trying to defeat them — and that we refused to anwser the questions without consulting his legal adviser. So the R.M. said his piece, and that was that.

This Kgotla took place today (11 December).

Wednesday 18 December
Yesterday and today was held the big Native Conference at Bloemfontein to consider the Native Bills that the Union Government propose to bring in.[17] All the natives are dead against them, and there is going to be a big row and lots of repercussions. It's going to strengthen very much the hands of those who are against incorporating the Protectorates in the Union.

Natives have the franchise in the Cape, but nowhere else in the Union. They want it everywhere, but the Bills take it away even from the Cape people. The Bills give Natives four (instead of seven) white representatives in the Senate where they can do nothing — instead of in the House of Assembly where they would be some use.

Christmas Day (at Cape Town)
A really jolly hot day, the hottest yet. After a pleasant morning's loaf in the garden, we drove out through the woods to a very jolly little tea place up in the mountain — the Round House by name, which used to be Lord Charles Somerset's shooting box when he was Governor here umpty years ago.

Just as we got out of 'Topsy' the wireless began giving out the King's Speech. It was a marvellous bit of luck. We heard every word as clearly as though we were at Sandringham.

There was a children's dance at the hotel in the evening, but I managed to survive it by reading the celebrated Chapter XV of Gibbon's *Decline and Fall* — peculiarly inappropriate to the occasion.

Monday 30 December
All the morning at the High Commission Office in an interview with Fforde and Priestman. The former very nice, the latter detestable. I'm afraid I see rows ahead.

Tuesday 31 December
A pleasant interview with the dentist at Cape Town. As there were three hundred people to dinner and two hundred more coming into the dance afterwards at the hotel, we went out and saw a cheery film entitled *Murder at Penguin Pool*. Not too bad. And then saw the New Year in — in bed.

1936

Monday 6 January
'Topsy' went to Armstrong-Siddeleys to be overhauled as a measure of precaution, and I had another cheery go at the dentist's — as a measure of necessity. Captain and Mrs Wanklyn came to tea; he was at the Ministry of Munitions with me during the War; is out here on holiday, and seeing our name in the papers rang us up. Very nice people indeed.

Tuesday 7 & Wednesday 8 January
At the High Commission Office with Russell, getting my Estimates through. A great success: the whole £183,000 approved with some minor amendations and changes. It was a real triumph and I am tremendously pleased. Lunch with Sir Cecil Fforde at the Club. I had a short half hour at the dentist, and Ninon and I lunched with the Clarks at Milnerton on Wednesday. He was up after his operation and looks a bit shaky. They were very nice: Lady Clark gains very much on acquaintance.

Thursday 9 January
We had a terrible shock today. Count Labia died suddenly of heart failure this morning. We were both at the Races with him on Saturday, and he was so nice and jolly and full of life. It is impossible to imagine that he has gone. We were both genuinely fond of him and are really distressed.

Friday 10 January
I had an interview with the head of the Customs in the morning. They are trying to rob us of some of the Customs Revenue they ought to pay us. Then I saw Fforde, and afterwards drove to Muizenberg to leave condolences on Countess Labia. He was lying in state guarded by Fascists in their black shirts, a tragic spectacle amid all the magnificence of their lovely house.

Tuesday 21 January (at Johannesburg)
We heard the news of the King's death on the wireless at 7 am this morning at the Johannesburg station. The announcer could hardly speak. The effect here is profound. I would never have believed that it would have produced so deep an impression in this country.
It would be a tragedy at any time, but now it is doubly so at a time of

international danger — when we have nitwits for Ministers in England. The King's influence was invaluable.

I spent most of the morning telegraphing instructions all over the country re the formalities to be observed, and the ceremonies to be carried out. There is a great deal to be done on an occasion of this sort in a native territory.

Thursday 23 January (back at Mafeking)
Blakeway, our Attorney General, had agreed with me at our conference yesterday as to the necessity for amending our Law to enable the Tshekedi case to come before our Special Court. It was obviously necessary for otherwise either the case could not have been tried at all, or it might have to be tried twice over — if the Privy Council (to whom it must go on appeal) refused to admit the validity of our Court, and so refused to hear an appeal from it. I telephoned to Sir Cecil Fforde (at C.T.) this morning and he agreed with the view come to by Blakeway and self.

I worked on the Tshekedi case. It gives me a lot of trouble as I have to run it all myself — legal procedure, witnesses, my own evidence, etc.

All arrangements are made for celebrating the King's Accession up country in every district. It's rather marvellous to think that, in remote native villages all over the Protectorate, the King's death and the King's accession are mourned and hailed respectively by wild savages and civilised beings, drawn together at the instance of a single white officer in common loyalty to the head of this vast Empire of ours. And to think that there are fools who don't understand it, who've never seen it, and who would cheerfully throw it away for some rotten theory.

Monday 27 January
I heard the Bathoen case today, sitting as Judge in the Resident Commissioner's Court. He wants to join with Tshekedi in the case against us and applied thro' his lawyer for leave to sue in the Special Court. I granted him leave in the terms as before.

Monday 3 February
Opening day of the European Advisory Council. I let off my oration in which I reviewed the great progress made in the last year — really quite a good effort, altho' I say so. And it was received in stony silence. They are a surly lot of dogs, and if they are out for a fight they shall have it. But I really don't know what their trouble is. Everything is so much better in the Protectorate and everyone is so much more prosperous that really they can have little to grouse at.

I went into Conference with Captain Nettelton, Ellenberger the R.M. Gaberones, and Kelly our Legal Adviser, about the Tshekedi case and that took up all the rest of the day.

Tuesday 4 February
MarFarlane, Glover, Going and Van Rensburg — four members of the European Advisory Council — lunched with us. Captain Potts arrived back from England after six months leave, looking very fit, and we discussed affairs in the Batawana Tribe in Ngamiland, where trouble appears to be brewing.

The future chief Moremi, a nasty piece of work at school at Tiger Kloof, has been up there on holiday, and prompted by that devil Tshekedi has stirred up trouble. He so worked on the Acting Chief Dibolayang, that the latter is now afraid to put the Proclamations into force (tho' he started to do so) and wants to resign.

1936

Wednesday 5 February
Resumed session of the European Advisory Council. An ominous speech from MacFarlane in answer to mine; then we disposed of some minor items. Then, as they were protesting about the cattle levy, I let fly. It's simply outrageous their opposition to this. They send 10,000 head of good cattle to Jo'burg a year for which they get a jolly good price. We levy ten shillings a head on them and use that money to subsidise the export of beef from Lobatsi — thus getting another 10,000 head exported. All the money goes back into the Territory — the export of good cattle helps the export of inferior cattle as meat by the levy and subsidy, and we build up an export trade.

Moreover as eighty to ninety per cent of the export of cattle is native produced cattle, the native really pays the levy and so it's only fair he should get the subsidy.

Afternoon meeting of Council — very successful. I was able to swing them round by the exercise of tact and patience and we really parted most amicably — but it does mean a lot of oratory and self-control. We got over the most dangerous part of the agenda, their criticism of the creation of an Agricultural Department under Russell England whom they hate.

Friday 7 February
Colonel and Mrs Walton and their niece Miss Mackay arrived to stay. He is Baden-Powell's chief of staff, and is touring South Africa as B-P's representative about Boy Scouts and Girl Guides.

I discussed the whole future of Pathfinders and Wayfarers and their relation to Scouts and Guides with Walton. I see no reason whatever why our B.P. Pathfinders and Wayfarers should not be Scouts and Guides — just like all other natives are all over the world, except in the Union of South Africa where the colour-bar prejudice is so strong that of course they won't have them. There is a frightful row on here about the proposed joining up of Wayfarers and Guides, even with all the restrictions proposed. The Transvaal (where the colour-bar is strongest) are up in arms against the proposal, tho' it has been discussed for years, and was finally agreed to by a committee of Guides and Wayfarers white leaders.

There is a similar row on about Pathfinders and Scouts, in which needless to say I am taking a hand. I am writing a very stiff memorandum on the point — and the final decision is to be taken at Durban on the 25th February. Unfortunately I can't be there.

Monday 10 to Friday 14 February
A hectic Office week, largely occupied with the Tshekedi case in regard to which a good deal of unnecessary work was caused by the damn folly of the High Commissioner's Office. They (that's Fforde) actually want to send the Tshekedi case straight home for trial by the Privy Council on a direct reference. That would mean no trial here, no cross examination of Tshekedi's lying witnesses, no speeches by Counsel, loss of most of the value of my evidence, and the case decided on legal quibbles by the theorists, the old dry-as-dust dead-heads who sit in the House of Lords. Of course I am fighting this like a cat — our lawyer Kelly here, and our Attorney-General Blakeway at Johannesburg, agree with me absolutely. Imagine our case, which is a mass of detailed fact of which only I am master, being argued in London by a damn lawyer before the Privy Council who knows nothing of conditions out here, and whom I couldn't coach. And of course Tshekedi and his lawyer Buchanan would go Home and stuff their men full of lies

which I couldn't contradict being 6,000 miles away, and which our fool lawyer wouldn't have the knowledge to answer. My God, it makes my blood boil to think of the folly that ruins the lifework of men.

Two flashes of intelligence from Whitehall — they have approved my skin dyeing and tanning factory, and my meat export subsidy proposals, so now I can get on with some more of my development work. But it's hard going.

There is a fearful row on here about the Union Government's Native Bills. They propose to take away the vote that the natives had in the Cape province for years, to give the natives land and then to try to keep them there — in other words to relegate them to a permanently inferior position and to carry out a policy of segregation. How can you go on educating people with one hand and denying them all right to progress with the other?

There are 6,000,000 natives in the Union and only 2,000,000 others. There must be trouble if that sort of policy goes on, and of course they are making any question of handing over the High Commission Territories practically impossible.

The European situation seems to us out here as bad as it could possibly be. Every country piling up armaments, a loan of £200,000,000 for that purpose in England, and every other country following suit. What a triumph for the League of Nations and its peace ideals! I don't suppose there's ever been such a war atmosphere in all the world. And all thanks to that damn lunatic Wilson's idea of a League of Nations — a collection of intriguing dago politicians.

Saturday 15 & Sunday 16 February
The first number of the newspaper I am starting in the Protectorate arrived today. Dumbrell is editing it and sent the first copy of the first number to Ninon as the First Lady in the Protectorate. It is called *Lebone loa Betsoana (The Bechuanaland Torch)*,[1] and has created quite a stir. I have been fighting for it for several years and we've got it at last.

Thank goodness I have finished my stuff for the Tshekedi case: the draft of my evidence, a 'thesis' on native law and custom, the rebuttal of his absurd plea. But it meant a lot of time and work — a dreadful waste of time.

Thursday 20 February
Molefi the Chief of the Bakgatla came in to greet me, and incidentally said that trouble was going to start again between him and the ex-Chief Isang. It's actually awful; I thought that was really settled. But there's an ammunition and gun smuggling case on before Lawrenson our Magistrate at Mochudi, and I fear Isang is in it. And if so, what does he want rifles and cartridges for?

Tuesday 25 February
An interview with Bishop Meysing about his agricultural school at Khale and his new one at Ramoutsa. He had had trouble with his people. One of the Fathers got too fond of one of the Sisters, and they've both had to go. I like to see these human touches.

Then a most interesting long talk with Edirilwe, the uncle of that plague-spot Tshekedi. Edirilwe is a very sound able old bird, and he is going to give evidence for us against Tshekedi in the trial. He told me some astonishing things. It just shows how right I've always been that the people want the Proclamations, and that it is only that rat Tshekedi who engineers opposition for his personal ends.[2]

1936

Wednesday 26 February
I observe from the papers that political people in England are trying to interfere with the Union Government's policy in regard to the new Native Bills. Now in the first place, the Home Government has got no legal or other right whatsoever to interfere with legislation in the Union. In the second place people at Home don't understand anything at all about Native Affairs or the Native Question out here. In the third place it is attempted interference by meddlesome busy-bodies at Home, in matters that don't concern them and of which they are ignorant. It will cause heated feelings out here, increase disloyalty, and make the position of the natives worse instead of better.

I quite understand why Colonies break away from the Mother Country. They do not dislike England or the English really, and they are intensely loyal to the King. But they detest and loathe Whitehall and Government Offices and the old women in Parliament — and they won't be dictated to by them on matters in regard to which they are profoundly ignorant.

I sympathise with them entirely — the little wood pavement-gods of Whitehall make me sick.

Thursday 27 February
A long conference with Gelman the managing director of Federated Meat Industries. We came to a satisfactory arrangement to re-open the Lobatsi works for the export of meat in March for three months, during which we are to pay a subsidy of £800 a month. Meanwhile we shall draft a permanent arrangement for a period of years at half the rate of subsidy to handle 15,000 head of cattle a year. It looks very promising.

They seem to be having big trouble in Japan. I suppose they will have another Mussolini there — but of course they are merely savages with a veneer of Civilization. East can never meet West, and all the rot that is talked today about equality of races and difference being merely superficial owing to education etc., is the most unmitigated drivel. Centuries of education will *never* convert a black, brown or yellow man into a white man.

Friday 28th February
Very hot again. A huge triumph today — the Dominions Office have turned down Fforde's ridiculous proposal to take Tshekedi's case straight to the Privy Council, and have agreed with my proposal to alter the constitution of our Court so that it can try the case. It's a great victory for me and a bad smack in the eye for Fforde and 'I fear' for Clark. I am afraid they won't love me any more. I fought the proposal very hard because I *knew* I was right, and now I have been justified. It's surprising that an experienced judge like Sir Cecil Fforde should make such a bad mistake and be so obstinate about it. He must be pretty sick now.

Saturday 29 February
The following extract from one of my Magistrate's reports is not unamusing — Midgeley of Selika:

> About 9 pm on Sunday I was summoned from my bath to a cattle post about three miles away where three native females and two males had partaken of tea boiled in a locust poison drum. One boy was in a bad state. I took salt, mustard and castor oil, and with the help of Sergeant

Roberts made all the poisoned natives as sick as possible. All their lives were saved.

Midgeley is only a youngster, and is only Acting Magistrate. Our people have some quaint jobs in their day's work.

Monday 2 March
The imbecility of the High Commission Office is past praying for. They have negotiated with the Union Government an arrangement to give us reduced railway rates for the export of *chilled* meat. We export no *chilled* meat, all ours is *frozen!* And they have written to the Union Government to thank them for something that is perfectly valueless.

Our two travelling motor dispensaries arrived from Jo'burg this weekend: they look very imposing. It's been a fight to get them. I was arguing for them in London in 1932 and everyone said I'd never get them. They should be a great boon in our remote districts. They carry water, oil and petrol for three hundred miles, and are fitted up as a complete dispensary with drugs, instruments, and bedding for European doctor and native dispenser.

These two form the first unit — another is under construction. Canvas shelters let down from each side, so that when the cars are halted there can be a little tent-room on each side of each car — for consulting room, sleeping, eating etc. They are the first of their kind in South Africa, and I am very proud of them. They are fitted with a little electric light plant to make their own electricity, driven off the car engine.

Tuesday 3 to Thursday 5 March
Cattle running over our border into the Union is getting worse and worse. They estimate that they are going over at the rate of 5,000 a month. Everyone is in it. The Union Police are bribed, and the young bloods amongst the Union farmers on the border go into it for the sport of the thing. Unfortunately there was a fracas last week and a Union policeman got knocked on the head. Fortunately he recovered, but the cattle runner got two months hard. It is like rum running in America was — a bad law will always be broken.

The Abyssinians seem to have had a really nasty knock. They must be idiots to try fighting pitched battles against Italian guns, tanks and aeroplanes. If only they would stick to guerrilla warfare, cutting the Italian communications, raiding their bases, they might have a better chance. As it is, it looks as if they were being knocked out.

Friday 6 to Sunday 8 March
Reilly came around to tell me that Ledeboer was dead, a most tragic and sudden calamity. He was playing cricket this morning up to about 1 o'clock, then said he wasn't feeling too well. His wife drove him home when he collapsed, and in about half-an-hour all was over, in spite of the efforts of two doctors who were there. It was really too dreadful, and a truly bad shock and sorrow.

Friday 13 March
Two interesting interviews today. Dr Schapera and young Ashton.[3] Schapera has been and still is doing our Report on Native Law and Custom and has just come back from a trip to England. I telegraphed him to come up here as I wanted him to give evidence in our Tshekedi case. I was just in time, as the other side tried to get

hold of him. He saw those awful people in England, the Anti-Slavery Society, John Harris[4] and the L.M.S. crowd. They asked him what he thought of Tshekedi — he said that Tshekedi seemed to be the last surviving exponent of the doctrine of the divine right of kings, and was out entirely for his own rights and privileges. All these blighters agreed with Schapera — and yet they support Tshekedi against us. They are a dirty lot.

Young Ashton is a Rhodes Scholar and did three years at New College, Oxford, and a year at London University. He is exceptionally intelligent, and a good athlete too. I am going to appoint him here — he has a wonderful academic record and is a very pleasant fellow. So now I shall have for my four last recruits, two Rhodes Scholars and two Oxford men chosen by the Colonial Office — a strong element of brains and culture.

Tuesday 17 & Wednesday 18 March
Dr Schapera's Report on Native Law and custom is extraordinarily interesting. Four hundred tyepwritten foolscap sheets.[5] He certainly has gone into it pretty thoroughly, and it will be a great help to us for the Tshekedi trial. Those wretched mugwumps at Cape Town are still havering about the date. I suppose they have got minds, but they don't seem able to make them up. I love Lady Phillips' definition of mugwumps. A creature that sits with his mug on one side of a fence, and his wump on the other.

My veterinary people nearly let me down over the import of cattle from the Caprivi Strip into the Chobe. Sussman & Co., who are running the timber concession there, wanted to bring in four hundred trek oxen to help in hauling the timber they cut. Imagine *importing* cattle into this country when we are screaming to be allowed to *export* more. And then the Caprivi Strip borders on Angola, where the Portuguese have lung-sickness and Foot and Mouth and everything else and no proper control. And South West Africa wired us advising against it, saying it might encourage smuggling from Angola and thereby increase the chance of disease. And yet my people were going to do it. I put my foot down good and hard.

We have no more news about the Foot and Mouth outbreak in Southern Rhodesia, but I've stopped all imports of everything from there and established a police and veterinary cordon all along the frontier — it's a damn nuisance and will cost me about £2,000 or £3,000. Rain again last night.

Thursday 19 March
Ninon and I went off in 'Topsy' to visit and inspect the agricultural experimental work and stock improvement work being carried out on the Government farm at Ramatlhabama. It is under the charge of one of our Stock Inspectors, Wright by name. He has got a number of different plots of from five to twenty acres under different crops suitable for human or cattle food — all grown by dry farming without irrigation just as the natives could grow them — but properly ploughed and planted, good seed. For example, sun-flowers for making oil, seed cake for cattle, the stalks for ensilage or paper manufacture. Mealies grown side by side, one batch manured with cattle kraal manure (which all natives have), the others without — showing the enormous difference. Amber cane and cow peas — for hay and for ensilage. Soudan grass for cattle either as grass or hay. Stacks of hay made from our ordinary veld grass (which is very rich in the valuable woolly finger grass) and from amber cane and cowpeas mixed.

Also our stud bulls, cross between Shorthorns and Afrikanders, our black-head

Persian rams, our Swiss goats (Tockenberg fawn, Alpina black and Saanen white) which, crossed with other breeds, give goats with a milk supply running to four pints a day — a most valuable thing for human consumption, thus leaving the cows' milk for the calves and for the butter making.

We are going to have eight farms of forty morgen (eighty acres each) — one at each of our Bull Camps — this will act as a series of agricultural educational centres for the natives, and should result in general agricultural improvements all round. The natives come from miles to see what is being done, and are immensely interested.

Friday 20 & Saturday 21 March
I had a great day at the Office on Friday clearing up all my arrears of work, and so was able to devote Saturday to finishing off my reply to that amazing Dominions Office Memorandum about the future of the B.P. which has been written obviously by the office boy.[6] My reply covers sixty-nine foolscap sheets! I have had to smash a series of the most damfool arguments ever advanced by the brain of a nit-wit. I have rarely come across such a perfect example of ignorance and folly.

The Dominions Office has excelled itself. They have sent around a printed circular to all Colonies explaining that all Church of England priests in future will receive a number! What a brain — what a triumph of organisation — to think they have discovered this marvellous method of recording. I wonder who told them of it.

Wednesday 25 March
A telegram from the High Commission Office to say that Tshekedi's lawyers are trying to put off the case until July. It nearly drove me wild — I only got it late in the evening so I can do nothing about it tonight and so shall miss the Cape Town mail.

Thursday 26 March
Very cold again, but a pleasant ride. I drafted the very devil of a dispatch about the Tshekedi case. I think Fforde is cracked: he seems to be playing the fool properly. I am recommending that we take action to enforce the proclamations in Tshekedi's country at once, and damn the trial.

The Baden-Powells arrived at 5 instead of 6 — fortunately we were all ready. They are perfectly delightful and I simply love them. He is so interesting. He and I went for a stroll round Mafeking after tea, and he recognized every place and building, and had a yarn or an anecdote about them all. Here a shell burst and blew in a wall. There a shell fell and didn't burst. Here a shell went clear thro' a house under a man's bed, wrecked the place and the man was unhurt. There was Lady Sarah Wilson's dug-out that she lived in during the siege. Lady B-P is a very intelligent woman too, full of energy — about thirty years younger than he is. She was typing letters in answer to all their correspondence before and after dinner! The two daughters are about twenty — very nice, too, clever and energetic. One acts as his secretary — does shorthand and has got her own typewriter with her.

We had a very pleasant evening, and thank goodness went to bed early.

Friday 27 to Sunday 29 March
The B-P's visit has been a huge success. I think they really enjoyed it. Of course he loved being back in Mafeking and they loved seeing the place that he defended. He

1936

is a marvellously versatile man — sketches beautifully with either right or left hand, writes delightfully, has a vast fund of knowledge on a number of subjects, and is a very clever actor. His imitation of an old man beating his daughter was too lovely for words. I laughed till the tears came. His account of his interview with Mussolini was most amusing. He says Mussolini is quite an amusing person, with a keen sense of humour — an aspect of him which the ordinary man never sees. They cracked jokes together, and then when Mussolini walked to the door with him to say goodbye, and saw the sentries outside, his whole expression changed and he became the man we all know in photographs — chin sticking out, complete with scowl.

On Friday morning the whole B-P family went off in their car to go round the siege positions. Then at 6, the eight or nine survivors of the siege still in Mafeking — and Col. Godley who was with the Relief Force — came up to the house to meet him and have sundowners. It was really quite a pathetic gathering.

On Sunday they all went off by the 9.15 am train. There was a gathering of our own people at the station, and we gave them a great send off. It was really sad to see them leaving, for they are so lovable. He is a really great man, and there is no doubt about it that he is the only man in the world who has founded a great work and seen it come to success in his own life-time in every country of the world. A work that more than any other single effort must make for international peace, as the Scouts and Guides meet their brothers and sisters from every country, of every race, colour and religion, at Jamborees, and otherwise get to know one another. And to think of him at 79 wandering over the world carrying on this wonderful work, when he might be sitting down comfortably in his own very delightful home in England.

Wednesday 1 & Thursday 2 April
My natives do not seem to appreciate the Union Government's offer of financial cooperation. I have got reports from all my Magistrates and they say the natives' attitude was one of deep suspicion. They saw the 'catch' at once; does this mean a bribe or a price for incorporation? They all want to come and discuss it with me — very awkward.[7]

Friday 3 April (to Lobatsi)
To Lobatsi for the day — mainly for a farmers' meeting.

The meeting promised to be lively and hostile — these farmers are impossible to please. They've had a wonderful year. Everything's booming. Markets are open for cattle: they've sold 10,000 to Jo'burg, 5,000 for the Italian contract, 10,000 to my meat works. 30,000 ran over the border. The Lobatsi meat works are open again. The rains have been splendid. They'll have excellent grazing, and so be able to get lots of cream to be sold for butter-making. I've opened markets for pigs and poultry. I am starting a skin factory at Lobatsi to tan and dye wild animal skins. Lobatsi is on the railway; they have the meat factory and the butter factory at their doors as well . . . , and yet the damn wasters grouse. What they like to do is to pay piccanins five shillings a month to watch their cattle, while they smoke and drink on their stoeps and curse the Government. One infernal Dutchman actually had the cheek to move a vote of no confidence in the Government. So I jumped up and asked for a seconder — of course there wasn't one. And then I let go and gave them hell. Most of them liked it, and things went much better afterwards.

I lunched with the Bruortons — he is the manager of the Chartered Company's ranch here. They are very decent people, English of course. He told me a funny story about cattle running, showing the corruptness of the Union Police. Some of the local farmers came to him (Bruorton) and asked if they might put some of their cattle through the farm over the border. Bruorton said that he didn't mind smuggling, but he couldn't let them use his farm as it wouldn't do for his company's name to be brought into it if there was a row. 'Besides', he said, 'it would be no good if I did agree, for there's a Union Police post just over the border opposite my farm'. The farmers laughed. 'Yes', they said, 'and it is the policeman in charge of the post who advised us when and where to put the cattle over'.

Wednesday 15 April (to Mahalapye)
A very hectic day. Bitterly cold, fortunately, so it was not too tiring. We were out at 7.30 and spent an hour and a half going round Russell England's agricultural work here — forty acres of intensive cultivation of various kinds. Wonderful bit of work. Mealies, kaffir corn (sorghum), *inyati* (millet), cactus, Soudan grass, Johnson grass, beans of various kinds, cowpeas etc. All tractor ploughed and sown in proper rows, wonderful results and a great object lesson to the natives. The stuff when reaped is being turned into ensilage for winter feed. Russell England has dug a huge silo pit, holding fifty tons, and it's nearly full.

One very interesting experiment had been carried out on a piece of land given by Tshekedi — two acres of derelict land on which everyone said nothing could grow. It was tractor ploughed, and on it I saw an excellent crop of beans of which the cash value was £8, fully equivalent to any native crop on good land. The natives only get about three bags of grain to the acre, and at ten shillings per bag that would work out at £3. Robb was enthusiastic, and he is supposed to be the biggest expert in South Africa.

We got back at 6 and some people came in for sundowners, and after dinner we played *vingt-et-un* until it was time for me to catch my train (9.30). The fools had not reserved my compartment, so I had the Immigration Officer kicked out of his, and took that. And didn't I sleep!

Tuesday 21 to Thursday 23 April (at Mafeking)
I had a very interesting talk with my native orderly who rides with me every morning. He told me that some of the Chiefs write to him, and that they have told him that they are all against Tshekedi and in favour of the Proclamations — that they think they are splendid things for the *people*, who are all for them. Formerly if a Chief didn't like a man he could (and did) take all his property on any trumpery excuse. Now he can't do that, because the case has to come before a regularly constituted Tribunal — of natives of course. He told me that Bathoen's people had had a real row with him after the last Native Advisory Council meeting because he had spoken against the Proclamations.

This cattle running over the border is getting serious. The smugglers are now *stealing* cattle to run over, and bringing back guns, ammunition and liquor in payment. It is getting a real scandal, and if the damn fools at the Dominions Office won't agree to my Police reorganisation scheme, and the Union Government won't let the cattle in legitimately, there'll be the devil of a row soon. The other day a Union policeman got knocked on the head. I suppose they will wait until one is killed before doing anything.

1936

Tuesday 28 & Wednesday 29 April
There is no doubt but that there will be a nasty row if we try to press on the natives those silly proposals of financial help from the Union, and I trust they will be dropped. They ought never to have been started, and they wouldn't have been if I had not been in England when they set the ball rolling. The natives in Swaziland and Basutoland feel just as suspicious as mine do. They think (and rightly) it is merely a bribe to make them agree to incorporation.

The Star publishes a nice tribute to the state of the B.P.[8] It is wonderful to see the results of six years' work materialising at last, everything booming — people happy, trade expanding, and of course, all helped by this year's rains, which though late were very heavy.

Thursday 30 April
Off by the 6.30 am train to Cape Town.

Friday 1 May (at Cape Town)
Clark, Fforde and Priestman were all very nice, and I got everything through that we tackled. Of course there's more tomorrow!

Saturday 2 May
Back to the hotel, where I found that poisonous bounder Richards, the Resident Commissioner of Basutoland, and his wife were staying. He introduced me to his wife; we did *not* click. Then I threw some things into a bag and went off for a short weekend to Vergelegen at Somerset West, the Phillips' place. Lady Phillips had been ordered away by her doctor. I am afraid she is very far from well, but she had sent me a message by Mrs Struben asking me to go out and stay anyhow to see Sir Lionel.[9]

Mrs Struben is the widow of the M.P. for Grahamstown who dropped dead in Parliament here the other day — a very nice and clever woman. Her son by her first husband Ashton (whom she divorced) is my latest recruit to the B.P. service — a Rhodes Scholar and a very able pleasant boy.

Sunday 3 May
After another talk with Sir Lionel, a Mr and Mrs Watermeyer and their daughter came to lunch. He is the General Manager of all the South African Railways, and a brother of Judge Watermeyer[10] who is coming up into the territory to take the Tshekedi case for us.

Back to Cape Town as I had to dine at Milnerton with the Clarks. Smuts, who was a guest, had quite a long talk with me about Abyssinia and also the Protectorates. He is terribly worried about the world position arising out of the Abyssinian affair, and asked me a lot about affairs out there. As regards the Protectorate, he is inclined to let the question of financial assistance from the Union drop in view of the native opposition. He said that it was unfortunate that there was this attitude of suspicion — 'tho' God knows we have given them cause for it' — which was very funny.

Tuesday 5 to Saturday 9 May (back at Mafeking)
On Wednesday a meeting of Heads of Departments to discuss Cape Town results. All very pleased, especially Dumbrell, who at last has got the Education estimates

through after three years of fighting. Now we can get ahead with our Native Education proposals.

Sunday 10 May
The Bishop of Kimberley arrived to stay — at 6 instead of 4, having been delayed by a broken spring in his car near Molepolole. Our Protectorate roads!

Monday 11 May
We discussed with 'Bish' that dreadful woman Deaconess Townsend, who is causing such trouble at Molepolole. She is a sort of unattached missionary, a pillar of the Church of England, and is supposed to be running the Wayfarers at Molepolole; but of course she quarrels with everyone. Archdeacon Mogg came in this morning, and we all agreed she had better go, and we left to Mogg the pleasant job of telling her so. These sex-starved women who develop emotional religious tendencies are very trying.

A long conference all the afternoon with Reilly and others re the Tshekedi case, and also about a row at Mochudi where my young friend Molefi has been burning down huts belonging to a man who annoyed him. We decided that Kelly must go into Jo'burg tomorrow for a conference with Blakeway. A most foolish telegram from London about this 'Cooperation with Union' business. The fools won't realise that when natives ask questions one must say yes or no — to hedge merely arouses suspicion and then causes trouble.

Monday 18 to Thursday 21 May
The Native Advisory Council was in session for these four days, greatly to their own satisfaction, tho' not so much to mine, as I have a lot of work on hand. However it went off very well, and was altogether about the best meeting we have had. A snag was the bitter cold; and as we have to meet in a big marquee which I always have erected in the Camp, one feels the cold.

After my opening speech on Monday morning, and a certain amount of palaver, I let them discuss the agenda among themselves on Monday afternoon and Tuesday morning. During that time I was able to have conferences with my Resident Magistrates (who are now called District Commissioners[11]) and with Russell England about various matters.

On Tour

Sunday 31 May to Friday 19 June
We took our private railway saloon from Mafeking to Francistown. From Francistown we did the rest of the tour in 'Topsy' — about fourteen hundred miles over some appalling and even dangerous roads. We went to Tsessebe and the Gungwe Reserve, back to Francistown, then to Palapye and Serowe, and thence down the Tuli Block — through the new government camp at Machaneng to Mochudi, Molepolole and home.

It was a bitterly cold morning when we started at 9.15. There were icicles hanging on the train when we got on board.

The country throughout the tour was lovely, and the late rains had kept every thing wonderfully green. And everybody is so prosperous: development work of all kinds starting; cattle export booming; lots of cars and lorries about; and generally

1936

a really cheerful outlook. It is a sheer joy to get about, and what a contrast to our last tour in 1934. Of course we were in England at this time in 1935.

We motored out to Tsessebe where I held a Kgotla of the five tribes there. They seemed wonderfully contented, although they have lost a lot of cattle owing to last year's drought.

We went on to the Gungwe Reserve where we inspected Motsete's cooperative native school, entirely built and run — both school, and living houses — by natives with the help of a grant from us.[12] They grow their own food too. They turned out a good show of Pathfinders and Wayfarers, and gave us a wonderful reception.

After the usual inspection in Palapye on the morning of the 7th, we motored over to Serowe for tea and to stay with the Netteltons for a couple of nights. On Monday I had a Kgotla in the morning, very crowded but peaceful. They are all dead against accepting the Union Government offer of financial assistance.

We drove over to the proposed site for the new hospital at Sofala, [Sefhare], about eighteen miles from Selika. A lovely place and jolly drive. They are still boring for water before we start building, but the prospects of water are not too good. The water is reported brack, and not too plentiful — only three and a half thousand gallons a day.

Friday 12th — a very busy day. We went off to inspect the new Camp at Machaneng. Very nearly finished, very nice indeed — a vast improvement on the old one. How we have changed things in the last few years. While there, I had a meeting of all the (white) residents of the Tuli Block and the Railway people to discuss the Railway's lorry service — which carries all the locally produced cream to the railway, and also their mails, parcels and goods. A very successful meeting, and we came to a very good and mutually satisfactory arrangement for an altered and extended service. A very amusing picnic lunch in the veld afterwards.

On Monday 15, I went over to Mochudi and back, seventy miles from Gaberones. We, Ellenberger and I, had a very successful day, lunching in the new Residency. We have built an entirely new Camp here about a mile and a half out of the village, on the slopes of some hills. I had a pow-wow with the Chief Molefi and some of his followers. Settled a few troubles, made a short speech, and then had quite a good drive back. We crossed one of the new bridges I am building, over the beastly (Metsemotlhaba) river that held me up once when I was going to Mochudi. These low-level bridges will make a wonderful difference.

On Tuesday Ninon and I and the Ellenbergers went over to Molepolole and had a very good Kgotla meeting. We settled finally the trouble about moving the hill people down to the Chief's house and Kgotla. There is a wonderfully good water supply we have put in here. The borehole gives eighteen thousand gallons in twenty four hours, and it's all pumped up to a big reservoir from where it gravitates to the various centres. The natives we have trained run the pump etc. very well.

On Wednesday we had a busy morning at Gaberones, and ran over to look at the Chief's cattle — splendid beasts, all 'improved' cattle, and quite a jolly lot of sheep. Chief Gaberone is an awful grouser, poor chap, tho' he is doing very well.

An amusing incident here was provided by the cattle smugglers who ran a hundred head over the border. The Union Police caught them and handed them back to our Police. During the night the smugglers stole twenty of them and ran them over the border again! We were going to sell the rest by auction, but the local farmers agreed to buy them in at lowered prices by not bidding. So I got the slaughter works at Lobatsi to send up a man; he outbid them all and we got a nice little sum! After lunch we drove the fifty miles to Lobatsi, crossing two more of our low-level bridges, and got into the Cuzens for sundowners.

Friday morning the Cuzens gave a really very nice morning tea party at the Residency, about twenty people. Then I went down to the Skin Factory and raised hell. They were not getting on at all well, so I telephoned Brind (the Government Engineer) to come over at once from Mafeking. After lunch we turned the whole place inside out, and I sacked two of the people. I understand the place has since been rechristened the 'Skin and Fur-Flying Factory'.

Saturday 20 to Tuesday 30 June (at Mafeking)
These ten days have been devoted almost entirely to work on the Tshekedi case, which comes off on 6 July. I am rather worried about it, as Blakeway, the Attorney-General, who lives and works in Johannesburg, is so busy with other things that I am afraid he hasn't time to read the enormous mass of stuff we have sent him.[13] He ought to have been here at least by now, and I had to go over to see him in Jo'burg, and had to send Kelly over to him also. The amount of work involved has been tremendous. Quite apart from preparing notes and memoranda on every conceivable point, there have been Blue Books to read, and all sorts of arrangements to organise. The High Commission Office have been damn silly in my absence, trying to interfere with my arrangements at Lobatsi for housing and feeding all the people coming up for the trial — Judge, counsel and solicitors on both sides, officials, witnesses and general public. The hotel is hopelessly inadequate and very bad, so I arranged with the Railway Company to send up three carriages and a restaurant car, and to leave them there. Also I took a small house for Blakeway the Attorney-General, Isaacs[14] our other counsel, Kelly our solicitor, and myself. And lots of other details. And then I find on my return that those fools have been interfering, knowing nothing of past conditions or requirements or anything else. However I have sent off telegrams telling them to go to hell and have re-confirmed everything I did originally. But it all means unnecessary work and bother — which is maddening when one is driven to death with very difficult and tricky work, and lots of it. The High Commission Office has always been useless. Now it is becoming a nuisance. When I am away that fat ass Priestman, the Administrative Secretary, is apt to spread himself.

Thursday 2 to Saturday 4 July
Our witnesses all arrived this morning and last night — officials, natives etc. And conferences have gone on all day and part of the night for three days. The witnesses all have to be schooled and the evidence prepared: it's a big job. My own evidence, which of course is the most important, is being left until we get to Lobatsi. . . . of course I prepared it long ago.

Sunday 5 July (to Lobatsi)
Blakeway, Isaacs and I left for Lobatsi by car soon after breakfast. We installed ourselves in the home of the Manager of the Native Recruiting Corporation, which had been very nicely arranged for us. Then we went down into the Court House and re-arranged it all, and gave the Police their orders for controlling the crowds. Two thousand natives have turned up, and the Court House will hold fifty.

After lunch we called on Judge Watermeyer, who had arrived by train in the morning, and then got down to work good and hard until 11 pm — with a short break for dinner.

Monday 6 to Friday 10 July
What a week! The first thing was a row about the few people who could hear the case because of the smallness of the Court. Buchanan, the counsel for Tshekedi and Bathoen, wanted to have the case tried in the open air so that the natives could hear. This was too silly for words, and the Judge pointedly remarked that it was not a theatrical performance. Then they suggested fixing up some sort of a big tent arrangement by means of buck-sails tied to and around the Court House. This I flatly refused to allow.

Finally I suggested that I would try to get loud-speakers from Jo'burg — which idea was hailed with enthusiasm. It took our people two days hard work to find the infernal things and get them sent down here complete with engine on a motor car. The result was wonderful. All remarks in the Court House could be heard half a mile away, and even further amongst the hills. It cost £120, and I made the other side pay.

All arrangements are working smoothly. Everyone is delighted with my train accommodation and the excellence of the food there. The two thousand natives sit outside in long lines and listen delightedly to the loudspeakers, which they do not understand. The weather remains perfect; and the case drags on.

Buchanan's opening speech was rotten, but Tshekedi's evidence was good. Blakeway, who is a very bad cross-examiner and who did not know his brief, could not shake him. However most of the other witnesses were badly rattled — tho' the Judge, I am sorry to say, seems to lean to the other side.

We are in Court all day until 4.30, then back to our quarters and work on the case until 10 or 11, with an interval for dinner. It's exhausting and most of it falls on me.

Monday 13 to Saturday 18 July
On Monday and Tuesday I gave my evidence and was cross-examined, and enjoyed it thoroughly. The other side were all out to stop me in every way possible, objected to as many of Blakeway's questions to me as they possibly could, and cut short their cross-examination to the lowest possible limits. I managed to turn some of their questions to ridicule and made the Court laugh at them — which made them mad.

Unfortunately my Magistrates got nervous — heaven knows why — and were not effective. Nettelton was weak; Cuzen tried to bluff and failed; Ellenberger was the best of them. Our native witnesses were good. Molefi, the Chief of the Bakgatla, who was called for the other side, gave valuable evidence for us! Bathoen, Chief of the Bangwketse, one of the plaintiffs, broke down badly in cross-examination.

Buchanan's closing speech was poor but Blakeway's speech was admirable, especially on the legal points — and obviously impressed the Judge.

The other side's argument that our Proclamations were *ultra vires*, because Sir Charles Warren had in 1885 made a treaty with the natives saying they could make their own laws, broke down completely when we produced a telegram from Sir Charles Warren saying he had made no treaties!

Nevertheless I am anxious about the results in view of the Judge's attitude. He seems to favour their view that our Proclamations do not respect Native Law and

Custom and that they ought to. Our contention is that they do, except where Native Law and Custom is against Order and Good Government.

Sunday 19 to Monday 20 July
On Monday morning Blakeway finished his speech, and Buchanan replied in the afternoon. The case closed at 4 pm, when the Judge reserved judgements. I think it will be a long time before we get his decision, as he is probably going to address certain formal questions to the Secretary of State. He is empowered to do so under the Foreign Jurisdiction Act, when any question arises as to the 'Extent of His Majesty's Jurisdiction' in any country such as a Protectorate, which is technically a foreign country. He asked counsel on both sides to draft the question for him. As of course we could not agree with the others, he took both sets of questions to draft the final version himself.

I came back home in 'Topsy' to dinner thoroughly tired out and sick to death of the whole business. A most shocking waste of time and money, which ought never to have been allowed — the result of weakness, vacillation, and indecision.

Tuesday 21 to Sunday 26 July (back at Mafeking)
I burst no blood vessels by overwork this week, as I really was tired as a result of the previous three weeks, which were a great strain.

On Wednesday Judge and Mrs Watermeyer came over from Lobatsi to lunch with us, and played golf afterwards with Major Reilly and Capt. Masterman whom they defeated. They (the Watermeyers) are very good at golf and their two sons are in the championship class. Watermeyer is staying on for a day or two to finish off some cases for us, which Fforde should try as Judge of the Special Court, but which he cannot as he is Acting High Commissioner in Sir William Clark's absence.

At long last we received (on Wednesday) approval from London of my Police re-organisation scheme, which I sent in in October or November last. They have now approved it word for word *exactly* as I sent it in. So they might have saved all this delay and argument. They are dreadful at Home.

Friday was inclined to be hectic again, as I had a longish interview with Du Toit representing the De Beers Company to negotiate an agreement for diamond prospecting. The Dominions Office in London are prepared to agree to rotten terms; Fforde and Clark in Pretoria failed to move Oppenheimer; and so it was thrown back on me. I was successful in improving the terms offered by nearly fifty per cent, which was very satisfactory.

Also another long conference with Russell England and others regarding our Fur Factory at Lobatsi, in connection with which various hitches have occurred. It should go all right now, and should prove a wonderful asset — enabling us to turn out skins and furs beautifully tanned, dyed, and made up.

The wireless generally is pretty good now, especially Germany. But London has gone off a lot, and cannot compare with Berlin. It is a pity we let ourselves be out-classed by these aliens. I suppose we shall try to improve and beat them again. But the first thing to do is to rebuild our Navy, Army and Air Force!

Monday 27 to Friday 31 July
I sent off a fairly full report of the Trial and I hope I've heard the last of it for some time.

Tuesday was a bad day. In the first place Hobday smashed up his aeroplane. He was off to Maun complete with wife and luggage, and was, I suppose, overloaded. The beastly thing wouldn't take off properly and crashed into the fence, damaging the machine badly, Fortunately neither Hobday nor his wife were hurt. He wasn't insured. Next we had a daylight thief in the house . . .

The third trouble was that one of our temporary officials shot himself. He had committed a loathsome crime up in the Territory and come down to Mafeking, where I had him arrested by the Union Police on Saturday. He was handed over to our Police on Monday, and one of them was escorting him back to Gaberones by train for trial. He asked for a drink of water and as our man was getting it, the prisoner (who had concealed a cartridge in his sock) grabbed the rifle and blotted himself out. It was a ghastly business — tho' a good thing in a way.[15]

On Thursday I had a meeting of all my Police officers to set new re-organisation proposals going. We were all photographed in uniform, and in honour of the occasion dined together in the evening at the Grand Hotel — the first Police 'mess dinner'.

Heard that our water-boring at Sofala for the new hospital there is no good, owing to the water being unfit for human consumption. It's a bore because it means trouble with Tshekedi and the L.M.S.

Saturday 1 to Saturday 15 August
Having lost my notes for the fortnight I cannot make any records, but I don't think anything of much moment happened.

Tuesday 18 to Sunday 30 August (back from Pretoria)
Got into Mafeking from Pretoria on the 7.30 am train and had a hard day at the Office before Captain Arden-Clarke,[16] my new Government Secretary, arrived at about 4. He comes from Nigeria and I picked him out of a list of half a dozen people recommended by the Colonial Office. He seems a very nice fellow and appears to have a brain, for which I am devoutly grateful. I hope he will come up to first impressions. We had a sundowner party at the house.

Reilly is very far from well. He looks a complete wreck and retired to bed on Wednesday. He has never really got over his motor accident some months ago when his car was knocked right over, his arm-bone cracked (and I think a rib), and his son thrown clean thro' the sunshine roof — unhurt.

On Monday 24 Reilly had to be sent in to Lobatsi hospital and Ashton had to go in for an operation for appendicitis. Black Monday!

Monday 31 August
My birthday! I meant to have a day off, but instead had to spend a cheery day at the Office interviewing Tshekedi about the trouble that has occurred at Sofala (Sefhare) over the water for the proposed hospital. We struck a 'dud' hole, and so want to use the surface spring water. But Tshekedi objected because he wanted it for his own farm, altho' the hopsital is for his own people and is a joint affair with the L.M.S. However we arrived at a satisfactory settlement.

1936

Transport Conference & Opening of Empire Exhibition at Johannesburg

Sunday 6 September
Ninon and I left in Topsy for a hectic fortnight in Jo'burg. The first week we stayed at the Carlton Hotel as the guests of the Union Government for the Transport Conference. The second week we stayed with Sir William and Lady Dalrymple for the opening of the Empire Exhibition.

Monday 7 September
The Conference was opened in great style this morning.

The objects of the Conference were to promote cooperation between all the Southern African States in the matter of Transport, whether by road, rail or air.

The proceedings were formal only: two committees were formed to do the real work, one for land and the other for air. I was on both, with Brind to help me. We started at 2.30 and it was obvious quite soon that we should be more concerned with air than land, and so I decided to concentrate on that one.

We had a State Banquet tonight, a tremendous affair, everyone being present. It was given at the Carlton, so we hadn't far to go. The dinner was quite good, and the evening a pleasant one until the catastrophe came, the toast to the King. This was a most amazing 'gaffe' and an outrageous insult to all of us representing different Colonial Governments. They had the infernal insolence to propose the toasts in the following order:-

1. King of the Belgians
2. President of the French Republic
3. King of United Kingdom of Great Britain and Northern Ireland
4. President of the Republic of Portugal
5. King Edward VIII Sovereign of the Union of South Africa.

A more damnable thing I have never read. If I had not been an official guest I should have walked out. As it was, Colonel Stallard[17] did walk out.

Of course there should have been just 'The King' as the first toast — that is the universal rule. To stick the King of the Belgians first, and then sandwich the King in between the Presidents of two stinking Republics, and then separate the King into two parts by bringing him in last again as 'Sovereign of South Africa', was an outrageous and abominable insult. These beastly disloyal anti-English Dutch dagoes make me sick.

Tuesday 8 September
Quite a busy day at my Transport Committees. The Portuguese, French and Belgiques don't speak much English, so I interpret. It's amusing, and they are all very appreciative and grateful.

Friday 11 September
An amazing phenomenon — a really heavy snowstorm and so cold that the snow was lying on the housetops, in the streets, on the tops of the cars and everywhere. Snowballing was general, the favourite targets being natives on bicycles. Shop girls from the upper storeys of buildings threw down large snowballs — some

being so hard and heavy that they went thro' the hoods of cars and smashed the car windows. That was not too funny.

Monday 14 September
Final sitting of the full Transport Conference. A purely formal meeting when everyone made back-scratching speeches, and it was decided to meet again in 1940 at Lourenzo Marques.

Tuesday 15 September
The opening of the Empire Exhibition was really a remarkably good effort. The organisation was admirable and the ceremonial simple, dignified and impressive.

Thursday 17 September
We (the B.P. exhibitors) gave our big lunch at Bien Donné Restaurant today, a huge success. We had taken a lot of trouble to order something really good, and by Jove, it was! We were thirty, including some very jolly people. They clicked well and it went with a swing. General Smuts was in great form, chaffing Sir Herbert Stanley like anything. After lunch most of us whirled down to the B.P. exhibit. They thought that was huge fun. Smuts and Stanley were fooling about like schoolboys. Our exhibit was much admired, and our party spent nearly £200 there — so Russell England told me afterwards.

Saturday 19 September
I had a most interesting talk with John Mackenzie, a very big business man here, and a very pleasant one too, about prospects of business for me when I retire. He was very encouraging and hopeful, and I was quite bucked.

Monday 21 to Sunday 27 September (back at Mafeking)
A filthy attack on me in that disgusting rag at Home, the *Manchester Guardian*, reproduced in the *Star* here. I consulted the Attorney-General as to whether I could go for them, but it is too subtly worded for that. Some damn 'Little England' Exeter Hall lawyer.[18]

A conference with Cuzen and Cairns regarding Bathoen's levy. He proposes to impose a levy on his people of an ox a head to pay for the cost in the case against us, including a possible appeal to the Privy Council. As may be imagined, this is causing trouble, especially as some of them — Gobbleman's Bakgatla at Moshupa — are refusing to pay.

Monday 5 October
Ellenberger (D.C. at Gaberones) and Parker (D.C. at Mochudi) motored down through the night arriving at 4 am to report trouble at Mochudi. They came round with Arden-Clarke immediately after breakfast. Apparently Molefi has been having a few more drunken orgies and has gone beyond the limit. He collected thirty or forty of the young men of his own regiment; picketed houses of people he didn't like; beat some of them; terrified the people in the church and at a concert so that they jumped out of the windows; stripped and flogged some girls and boys publicly in front of the whole school; and generally raised hell.

After consultation I got a wire sent through to Lawrenson, who has just returned from leave in England and who is now taking charge in Mochudi, instructing him to have all the hooligans arrested and to tell the Chief to call a Kgotla to meet me at

Mochudi on Tuesday morning. I arranged to have all the police at Gaberones ready to move in motor transport at a moment's notice. And after lunch I went off by car to Gaberones with Ellenberger and Parker, leaving Arden-Clarke in charge here. On arrival at Gaberones in the evening I found Arrowsmith who had just come in from Mochudi. He reported thirty arrested, all quiet, and the Kgotla called for tomorrow. But he says the position looks ugly. I slept at Gaberones.

Tuesday 6 October (to Mochudi)
A very strenuous day at Mochudi. I motored off good and early and had a consultation at the Residency at Mochudi on arrival. Ellenberger, Parker, Lawrenson, and Capt. Croneen O.C. Police. (I left all police at Gabs, ready to move). All was quiet, but much excitement under the surface. The situation needed very careful handling. I met the Tribe in Kgotla and dressed them down, including the Chief, telling them they had brought disgrace on the Tribe and village and blackened their good name. I told them the Government would not allow this, and all those responsible must be punished — but before announcing the Government decision, I asked them what they had got to say about it.

They were very crestfallen and sulky and I had a great job to make them speak. The twenty [sic] men who had been arrested were marched into the Kgotla and squatted in a corner — a murderous looking lot of thugs.

Gradually the old men of the Kgotla began to speak. They deplored the recent happenings, blamed the Chief's drunken habits, but put forward no ideas for action. So I said I would leave them for a bit, and went off to see Krige, the Dutch Reformed Church missionary. He seemed very unhappy about it all, and said that all his work and all the education work was being brought to a standstill by the impossible behaviour of the Chief. He said there was a sort of reign of terror and people went about in fear of their lives.

I went back to the Kgotla after lunch, when Isang addressed me on behalf of the Tribe. He admitted the truth of all I had said, deplored the troubles, and said they were all ashamed. He concluded by asking the Government to have the twenty arrested hooligans tried by the D.C. in the Magistrate's Court, and to allow the Tribe to try the Chief in Kgotla.

I pointed out the difficulty of trying people in different courts for the same offence, and after some further discussions, said I would give them my decision in the morning.

Wednesday 7 October
Over to Mochudi again in the morning and to the Kgotla. I decided, and the Tribe agreed, that the Government should try all concerned, including the Chief. I said I would make arrangements for this, and gave them a stern warning as to what was coming to them if there was any more trouble.

Friday 9 October to Sunday 11 October (at Mafeking)
Poor Reilly seems definitely sinking. Mrs Reilly has been staying with us for some days, and today I telegraphed for the two sons to come and stay with us also — and for Reilly's brother and sister to come from Johannesburg. One son is in our Police and has to come from Palapye Road, the other is in the Swaziland service.

1936

Monday 12 to Wednesday 14 October
Rain on Monday. Reilly died at 5 am on Tuesday after dreadful suffering. The funeral took place on Wednesday, and everyone combined to try to show their sympathy to the greatest possible extent. We got a firing party of the B.P. Police down from Gaberones, and as it was a military funeral we were all in full uniform.

It does seem a damn meaningless shame that he should die like this. After thirty four years service he and his wife were so looking forward to the evening of their lives together after a long day's work, on a reasonable pension.

And now she is left alone without enough to live on. Her two boys, having only just started in their careers, can't help much.

Friday 16 October
I got a damn fool telegram from the High Commission Office about the Mochudi affair. They seem to have got cold feet about the steps I am taking. So I sent Arden-Clarke off by car to Pretoria with my answer, to try and make them stand up.

Saturday 17 October
Frightfully hot. Arden-Clarke returned in the evening, having done very well at Pretoria. They agree with my views now and have telegraphed to London for authority to suspend Molefi. I should have done it without authority and reported afterwards.

Sunday 25 & Monday 26 October
We got the cable from London on Sunday morning early, authorizing me to act at Mochudi as I had proposed. So we got a telegram off to Lawrenson good and early, instructing him to collect the Chief and Headman for a meeting Monday at 5 pm. The news was to be broken to Molefi that 'unless he could show good and sufficient cause to the contrary within three days' I would come up and deal with him.

It is all very trying because there is a conference of Resident Commissioners from all three Territories with the High Commissioner at Pretoria on the 28th, which means going there on the 27th, and I was going to take Arden-Clarke with me.

So now we have to divide. Arden-Clarke goes up to Mochudi on Monday, like John the Baptist, to prepare the way for me to come up later. I go into Pretoria for the Resident Commissioners' conference. Arden-Clarke has to do a lot in Mochudi, arranging for the enquiry to be held and for the trial. Meanwhile Ninon and I have to cancel our visit to Johannesburg which we were going to do after the R.C.s' conference — as of course I must come back here to go on to Mochudi. Damn.

But the science of organisation is to be able to change one's plans at any moment to meet changed circumstances.

Wednesday 28 October
The R.C.s Conference started at 9, lasted all day and went very successfully. From what Sir William Clark told us, the people at Home seem cracked about the question of incorporating the Territories with the Union. They *won't* realise that it must come about some day, and that there will be the devil of a row with the Union Government and with the natives if something is not done to prepare the way.

1936

Thursday 29 October
Very busy with various appointments all day, including a long discussion with Heddon on our Customs Agreement with Southern Rhodesia.[19] We agree on all points, and the beastly thing is now ripe for signature. It has given us a lot of trouble.

Friday 30 October
Sir William Clark's meeting with the Chiefs of B.P. and Swaziland — not too good. Our people had bungled the arrangements badly. The Chiefs, after spending the night on Johannesburg platform, arrived late and in a very bad temper. Sobhuza, the Paramount Chief of the Swazis, was also late, and brought with him a lot of naked savages in their national Swazi dress — very fine, much better than our scarecrows in their shabby European kit.

Sir William Clark's speech was vague and general, very anodyne. There was no answer, and no discussion. And the Chiefs all seemed rather puzzled as to why they should have been brought up to Pretoria, to hear something that they had already heard repeatedly from me.

Tea and cake were served on the lawn afterwards, and after a certain amount of desultory conversation the meeting broke up. I fear it did not do much good. I spent all the rest of the morning and all the afternoon with Sir William Clark discussing various matters. Quite satisfactorily, but we couldn't finish as he was very tired, and we had to break off soon after 5. I fear he is far from well.

Monday 2 November (at Mochudi)
My mounted escort of ten native troopers under Sergeant-Major Lord had ridden in yesterday, and looked very smart this morning. We inspected them at 9, and they then moved off towards the village to await me about half a mile outside. I was of course in full war-paint.

After ticking them off good and hard, I read the formal notice suspending Molefi from the Chieftainship in dead silence in a Kgotla of two thousand people. Then I announced the result of the formal trial of the hooligans, whose number had grown to about forty people arrested. Then I announced the Enquiry to be held by Captain Nettelton.

Finally I told the Tribe that there being now no Chief, they must nominate an Acting Chief.

After which — consternation and silence!

Unfortunately the weather was terribly hot. The heat and stink in the Kgotla, amid these two thousand unwashed, was dreadful. And as they were suffering too, they kept on going out to refresh themselves with kaffir beer.

No progress was made; the young men of Molefi's regiment began to get truculent, and so I adjourned the meeting to let things simmer down a bit.

When I returned after lunch, things were worse. Some of them were very drunk. A drunken tribal policeman tried to arrest a still more drunken tribal man; and there was a comic scuffle, ending in help being forthcoming and the offender being hurled into the guardroom.

So, as things were really looking rather bad, I told them that I would give them until tomorrow morning to make up their minds. If they could not settle by then, I would settle for them. I arranged for the heads of the five wards, into which the village is divided, to speak in the morning, and said I would not listen to anyone else, or to any discussion except on who was to be the Acting Chief.

1936

Tuesday 3 November
A complete change this morning. Evidently my remarks had penetrated, and they were thoroughly ashamed of themselves. Each head of a ward got up in turn and nominated Mmusi, Molefi's brother, as Acting Chief, to rule with the advice of his uncles and headmen. Then I put it to the Kgotla, and they were unanimous. So I confirmed their choice, gave them a solemn warning as to their future behaviour, and left the Kgotla.

I then had a meeting elsewhere with Mmusi, his uncles including Isang, and the headmen and elders. I gave them a good 'talking to' — saying they were partly responsible for the troubles that had occurred, and they had got to stop it. We discussed various points, and then I left them to get on with the good work.

Wednesday 4 to Saturday 7 November (at Mafeking)
A busy few days at the Office, clearing up arrears, dictating reports, seeing people. There is a devil of a lot to do always, and I am glad to say that my new Government Secretary, Captain Arden-Clarke, is a great help. He is really first class, able, energetic, tactful, lots of drive and initiative, and very pleasant. We finished the week packing once again, as Ninon is going in to stay with the Dalrymples at Jo'burg for the week's Conference of the National Council of Women. I shall stay at the Rand Club, and do a lot of business I have at Jo'burg and Pretoria.

Tuesday 10 November (at Johannesburg)
I had a very interesting interview at the Rand Club with some people who want to come into the B.P. to prospect. They are, they say, prepared to spend quite a lot of money. They say they represent the African-German Investment Company at the head of which is Dr Merensky, the well-known millionaire.[20] I told them of course I wanted guarantees, and that if these were satisfactory I was prepared to negotiate for a concession.

At 11.30 I had another interview, also at the Club, with Rheinallt Jones about Pathfinders — very satisfactory. We discussed the new Pathfinder-Scout Constitution, and I insisted on certain changes, notably as regards the flag. I won't have two flags in the B.P. — nothing but the Union Jack. They can keep their beastly Union Joke for the Union.

We went on to a cocktail party at the Country Club given by Mr and Mrs Hans Pirow.[21] He is *the* Government Mining Engineer for the Rand — a great noise out here, and incidentally a very able and pleasant person, with a nice wife. His brother, Oswald Pirow, the Minister of Railways and Airways (and the ablest man in the Government), was there too. I had a longish talk with him. He offered to do our flying service for nothing (!) from Mafeking to Maun, on to Ghanzi and Windhoek, and back via Lehututu. It would be a splendid thing, and I am all over it. I propose to take it up at once, and I do hope that the Home Government will agree.[22]

Thursday 12 November (to Pretoria)
Off to Pretoria by the 8 am breakfast train. A series of interviews at Union Buildings with Ministers, starting at 9.30: Senator Clarkson (Public Works) about a new bridge over the Crocodile River; Grobler (Native Affairs) about the Mochudi business; Hofmeyer (Interior) cooperation and general; Reitz and Viljoen (Agriculture) about cattle etc. questions. All very satisfactory. Clarkson agreed to build the bridge at Union Government expense. Grobler was delighted to

hear I had kicked out Molefi, and offered to help in any way. He explained that tho' Molefi has got part of his Bakgatla on the Union side of the border, the Union Government don't recognize Molefi as Chief there. But he is a great nuisance all the same, and they will help to get him out altogether. Hofmeyer, a most able and cultured man, was perfectly charming, and wants to meet Ninon and I when we go to Cape Town. Viljoen was fearfully interested in my reports of Lung Sickness in the Caprivi Strip — and undertook to stir up South West Africa to do something. He was also alarmed about the invasion of rabies in Ngamiland, from Angola. He further undertook to go into the questions again of my Walfish [Walvis] Bay cattle route, and also my scheme for an Inter-State Bureau for dealing with cattle diseases — which was agreed to by all the States represented at the Mafeking Conference in 1934, over which I presided.

Friday 13 November
I forgot to say that on Monday I had had a very interesting interview at the Club with Ludorf, the Chairman of the Union Government National Park on the Nossop River — a reserve for game, especially gemsbok. He wants us to cooperate with them by removing from our borders a settlement of coloured people, known as Bastards.[23] Being well mounted and well armed they poach into the game reserve and do a lot of harm. I promised to go into the matter and do what I could.

Sunday 15 to Sunday 22 November (back to Mafeking)
Heavy rains all the week and much thunder and lightning. The Protectorate is being washed away, and everyone is delighted. The road to Lobatsi was completely impassable on the 19th from here.

Our broadcasting station here was completed on Saturday 14, and on Sunday 15 we started testing. And have been testing all the week with splendid results. We have got excellent reports from Maun, Beira, Natal, Cape Town, Luderitz Bay and Windhoek in South-West Africa. Salisbury and Bulawayo in Rhodesia. It's a wonderful triumph.[24]

I broadcast a message to the High Commissioner on the 19th, and he telegraphed that the reception was 'perfect'. And those fools in London said my proposals were impracticable, and the Marconi Company would do it for us for £11,000. My scheme is costing £1,500. Now we are sending the transmitter out to Ghanzi, Lehututu, Tsabong, and Maun, to test sending messages back here. We shall install the machines there. I am ever so pleased, and so is everyone else.

Ciring who owns the Lobatsi Hotel, Seamon who runs the one at Mahalapye, and a representative of the Railway Company on whose land the hotels are built, all came to a conference on the 19th. I have warned them that if they don't improve their hotels I shall refuse to renew the licences on 1st January, and they are all in a blue funk. As a result I think we shall now see better hotel accommodation in the Territory. The Gaberones Hotel people have spent £4,000 on extension and improvement, and the Francistown (Tati Hotel) people £3,000. We do develop!

The appointment of Patrick Duncan to succeed Lord Clarendon as Governor-General of the Union is a tragedy and a scandal. It is a monstrous thing that such an appointment — the one link left between the Crown and South Africa — should not be made from amongst distinguished Englishmen of high rank and noted service. It is a scandal that it should be given to a politician out here, and an active politician at that. Duncan is a fool: he drinks, his wife is of half foreign and quite indifferent origin, and they possess no qualifications for the job.

All Johannesburg is furious I have not met a single soul, English or Dutch, who is pleased. It is a real tragedy.

Monday 23 to Sunday 29 November
My greatest triumph! The Judge has delivered his judgement in the Tshekedi case, and *we win on all points, with costs!* I am immensely bucked and everyone is fearfully pleased and excited. The papers have great headlines.

What a fight — nearly six years of argument, and now I am justified. My Proclamations stand, and Tshekedi is defeated.[25]

Of course he may appeal to the Privy Council, but I don't think we need worry about that.

We got the sealed copies of the judgement on Wednesday morning, and arranged to have it read in Court at Lobatsi on Saturday morning at 9.30. The reading was finished by 12.10, and I got the telephone message saying so at 12.12. At 12.30 I broadcasted a summary of the results from our wireless station here: we had previously warned all officers in the B.P. to stand by to receive the message from me.

Everyone is sending in congratulations; even our native staff are overjoyed — police, messengers, etc.

Sir William Clark is of course immensely pleased, and our solicitor here is delighted. I have sent telegrams of congratulations and thanks to our two lawyers, Blakeway the Attorney-General and Isaacs.

I interviewed Chief Bathoen of the Bangwaketse and Chief Seboko of the Bamalete with regard to the proposed mining in their Reserves. Both are delighted at the idea, and I shall now arrange for representatives of the Company to negotiate with them.

Cattle smuggling is also beginning to be a nuisance again. The Union Government are alarmed at the large numbers of cattle (about five thousand a month) being moved from the north of the Protectorate to the south near the Union border. They have wired and written me about it. This smuggling is really Gilbertian. Not only do these trainloads move south regularly within the Protectorate, but the station master at Mafeking tells me he has been asked to arrange for the trains south to be punctual, so that the cattle can be detrained and run over the border to be entrained on the Union side! No less than forty thousand head have been moved south from Ngamiland and Ghanzi in the last twelve months!

This leads of course to cattle stealing, and Bathoen complained to me bitterly of his brother Chief Seboko, allowing stolen Bangwaketse cattle to trek openly thro' the Bamalete Reserve.

Monday 30 November
Moremi, the Chief-to-be of the Batawana, came in this morning. They have let him out of Tiger Kloof, where he was at school, nearly a fortnight before his time, which is a beastly nuisance. He is a hopeless youth, slow and stupid. It is sad to think we have got to install him as Chief and add another to our list of incompetent Chiefs. What a waste of energy it is trying to bolster up these incompetents. We ought to abandon this make-believe Indirect Rule,[26] and run the tribes thru' our District Commissioners. This fetish, of pretending that to-day the Tribes can be run as they were a hundred or even fifty years ago, is responsible for more waste of

money and energy than any other of the shibboleths that guide our sloppy sentimental administration.

Tuesday 1 December
Inspired no doubt by the recent Conference of the National Council of Women, Ninon gave a luncheon party here for women only, and turned me out to lunch at the hotel!

Wednesday 2 December
Another 'feminist' effort on Ninon's part! She gave a tea party consisting only of women! This is getting serious.

Thursday 3 December
One unit (two cars) of our travelling dispensaries came in from the Kalahari. It has been out since July in the charge of Dr Thompson. He has had a wonderful time, covering about fifteen hundred miles a month, and doctoring hundreds of natives. At one time the natives came in to get medicine, asking for it to be put into ostrich eggs that they brought with them! Dr Thompson brought back two baby ostriches, about six weeks old, funny fluffy little things, quite tame and cheeky.

Friday 4 December
This morning we got yesterday's papers with the ghastly news about the King. As a matter of fact we had heard rumours before, and Fforde told us about it last night. It's too utterly awful for words, and everyone is simply dumbfounded. It's incredible that he should insist on doing this horrible thing, and at this moment. The whole world is looking to England and the Empire, and the whole Empire is looking to the King, as a great steadying influence in the troubled state of world affairs today. And now the King proposes to throw it all away, and risk the future of the Empire — and more — for this rotten American street woman.

There is a lovely story going round about Buchanan, Tshekedi's lawyer and adviser. Buchanan has had thousands of pounds out of Tshekedi in costs. When Tshekedi married, Buchanan sent him a rotten Bible as a wedding present! On the flyleaf it is alleged that he wrote 'Count not the costs'!

Saturday 5 December
Tshekedi arrives from Cape Town tomorrow morning. I wonder what he has decided about appealing against the judgement. He will be a fool if he does.

Arden-Clarke came round at about 9 pm with a cypher telegram, which seemed to make it pretty clear that the King is going to abdicate — and asking me what I propose to do about letting the natives know. It will be a damn shame if the King has to go, through the damn folly of Baldwin and the interference of those blasted Bishops. But how on earth I am ever to explain it to the natives, I can't imagine.

Monday 7 December
COMPLETE VICTORY: Tshekedi and Bathoen came to see me this morning, and handed in a letter saying they were not going to appeal to the Privy Council! The Judge's decision was so crushing that it was obvious that an appeal would stand no chance.

It's a tremendous score for me, and I am delighted.

They want an interview with Sir William Clark and myself to settle finally how to set about working the Proclamations. So I telephoned to Clark, who was simply delighted, and fixed up an interview for Wednesday morning — which means I must go into Pretoria tomorrow.

Ninon had to preside over her Wayfarers Council, and took my room at the Office for the purpose. So I took Arden-Clarke's room for my interview with Tshekedi and Bathoen, which was most satisfactory. They are greatly chastened, Tshekedi told me he had had enough of fighting the Government, and was going to devote his energies to development work — schools, cattle improvement, water etc. So I have won indeed!

I also fixed up with Tshekedi about the Bull Camp for our cattle improvement scheme, which has been hanging fire a bit, and made a satisfactory arrangement with him. He wanted, and I agreed, to buy a farm in the Tuli Block for the purpose. He is using for this purpose the money he raised by levy on his Tribe to pay the costs of the Appeal Case. Very amusing.

Wednesday 9 December (at Pretoria)
A preliminary talk with Sir William Clark, Fforde and Priestman at the Office, and then our interview with Tshekedi. Not too good. Sir Wiliam Clark is not very good at handling him, and Tshekedi was rather troublesome, raising quibbling points of law which annoyed both Clark and Fforde. However Clark was quite firm, and told Tshekedi he must discuss all these matters with me. The interview finished soon after 12, Clark remarking that Tshekedi was an irritating little devil!

Tshekedi's points boiled down to three regarding the Proclamations — i.e. the Council; the appointment of Tribunals; and appeals from the Chief's Court to the District Commissioner's. Then he raised his fourth, which was: 'What was the status of the B.P. Tribes in the light of the Judge's judgement?' The answer seems obvious, and none of us could understand what he was driving at. So it was left that he should write out his point and send it in.

But everything else is overshadowed by the ghastly news of the King's decision to abdicate. It's too utterly awful for words — and the effect will be grim. Of course Ireland will become a Republic, at least in all but name. And the Malanites here will get tremendous encouragement in their republican efforts. And how are we to explain it to the natives? — I wish some patriot would murder that infernal woman.

Saturday 12 December (back at Mafeking)
Hobday returned from the Meat Control Board Conference at Pretoria, where he seems to have done very well. He has maintained our position against the Union Government efforts to reduce our cattle export quota by the number of additional cattle sent a few months ago. And then he fought them over cattle smuggling. That is a difficult question, but the fault lies entirely with the Union Government. It started because the Union Government broke their Customs Agreement with us, which provides for mutual free importation. It is Union subjects (not B.P. people) who come over, buy the cattle, and run them over.

The Union Police connive at the whole thing, and are bribed. The fee for running the cattle is ten shillings a head of which the police get a quarter. Union people are coming over to lease farms on the border in the B.P. to facilitate running over. There are big financial interests in the Union behind the smuggling. Everyone who can raise £5 comes over, buys a beast, and sells it for £7. People are even stealing cattle to run them over. There is no doubt but that there will be the very devil of a row one day, and I am thankful that my conscience is clear in having warned all concerned.

We heard the ceremony of the new King's accession through the wireless — and then the latest news about the late King's departure. I am glad he went as Prince Edward and not as 'Mr Windsor', and that he had the Admiralty yacht and an escort of destroyers.

Sunday 13 December
Pretty hot again. A loathsome morning packing. Ninon had arranged for a party of Pathfinders and Wayfarers to go from the Protectorate to the Johannesburg Exhibition, and to break their journey at Mafeking so as to come up to Protectorate Government House to have refreshments. We arranged for the lorry and cars to bring them up in the afternoon. They rolled up in great style, formed up in the garage as it was raining, and as we came in sang 'God Save the King'. Then Ninon spoke to them; I said a few words; two of them replied (very well); and they sang the native national song.[27]

Then the rain stopped; they formed up on the tennis court; had lemonade and a currant loaf each; and Ninon presented every one with a shilling. Off they went to the station, and we followed them down and saw them into the train — a great afternoon.

Monday 14 December
A hairy morning at the Office. England came over from Johannesburg to report very unsatisfactory interviews at Pretoria with the Ministry of Agriculture about our proposed Customs Agreement with Southern Rhodesia regarding butter and cheese exports. Captain Potts arrived from Ngamiland, and we interviewed Moremi the prospective Chief of the Batawana, who has just left school (Tiger Kloof) and appears to be a pip-squeak. We had to hammer the Proclamations into him, then arranged for him to go to the Jo'burg Exhibition. Then to return to Nagamiland, when I suppose we shall have to make him Chief.

Wednesday 16 December
Kelly came round to tell me about the costs in the Tshekedi case. Those devils were trying to wriggle out of paying, and I am all for making them pay to the uttermost farthing.

Cape Town

Saturday 26 December
Much colder. A heavy mail from Home and Mafeking — nearly seventy letters including forty-five more Xmas cards — nearly a hundred and fifty cards in all now. An idiotic letter from Arden-Clarke. He has mucked the interview I told him to have with Tshekedi about the Proclamations. My God, must I do *everything* myself? Arden-Clarke has actually agreed to let the Tribunals for the administration of justice consist solely of the Chief for the principal one, and of the Headman of each village for each of the others.[28] So that the Tribunal would consist of one man only, and the Chief and headmen would be confirmed by law as complete autocrats for judicial administration. This would thus defeat the whole

object of my Proclamations which I have fought for for five years, and won in the Courts! Of course I shall have to turn it all down, but it's maddening.

Sunday 27 December
I received a ghastly piece of news by telephone from the Railway Company, just as we were going in to dinner. Young Alistair Martin was struck by lightning and killed at Tsabong last night at 6 pm. Apparently he and his young wife were in the same room when the lightning struck — she was not injured but merely given a severe shock.

The tragedy of it is that they had just come back from their honeymoon in England. He was one of my most promising young officers — a nice straight clean-living boy — fearfully keen on his job. I had just recommended him for promotion.

Killing him like that was an act of senseless and fiendish cruelty, such as even the worst man could not do or even imagine. And we are told that not even a sparrow falls without God knowing about it. I cannot understand there being a single person left in the world who believes in religion.[29]

Wednesday 30 December
We've got the London papers about the King's abdication. What a tragedy it all seems. And what a damn interfering set of blighters those Archbishops and Bishops are. Certainly the Church has out-lived its utility, and ought to go — Bishops first.

And the American comments make me sick. They have the morals of the jungle, and the manners of the gutter. Their ignorance of English conditions and English mentality is simply marvellous. Very like back-veld Boers.

Thursday 31 December
John Gunther's book *Inside Europe* is very interesting. It has gone through fifteen editions this year; so it is evidently appreciated.

I don't agree with some of his views. Some are very sound, especially those on Hitler and the German position. But he is much too 'Left' — much too socialistic.

1937

Saturday 2 January
Telegrams and letters from Arden-Clarke regarding the ghastly blunder he has made about the Proclamations. He can't see it. The High Commissioner is entirely against him I am glad to say; and of course I'll never agree.

We left cards on Generals Hertzog and Smuts at Groote Schuur and Smuts' private house. Groote Schuur, Rhodes' house which he gave to the nation as a sort of Chequers for the Prime Minister of the day, is a lovely place. Smuts appears to live like a pig — a smallish villa, kept anyhow. I saw his married daughter — not an exhilarating sight.

Monday 4 January
Telegraphed Captain Arden-Clarke to come down for discussion by tomorrow's train.

We went to the Alhambra in the evening to see Shirley Temple's latest film, *The Littlest Rebel*. That child is a marvellous little actress, if she is really only six, and the film was excellent. The films in the first part of the programme — both American — were beneath contempt.

Wednesday 6 January
A hectic day, and a very hot one again. I went in by bus for the interview with Sir William Clark and Arden-Clarke, Fforde, Priestman and Smith, regarding this unfortunate Tshekedi business. We had a terrific wrangle all the morning and afternoon — and eventually I carried my point. Tshekedi is to be told that we won't accept his proposals, and that he must nominate more members for the Tribunals.[1] But it *was* a fight!

Friday 15 January
After lunch I went into Cape Town and had a longish and very pleasant interview with Wilson, the editor of the *Cape Times*. I arranged with him to write a series of articles on the B.P. for his syndicated papers — the *Cape Times*, *Rand Daily Mail*, and *Natal Mercury*, to be published as soon as I retire. That should bring a bit of much-needed grist to the mill, and will fill in my spare time.

The world's greatest tragedy — for us — broke tonight. A telegram to say that Foot and Mouth disease had developed at Palapye Road in a herd of six hundred cattle belonging to R.A. Bailey & Co. It's too utterly ghastly for words — heartbreaking — disheartening — after all we have done to stamp it out and develop the Territory. I am utterly miserable about it. Just as I was hoping and expecting to leave the Territory in such a happy and prosperous condition. It is the most damnable piece of cursed luck.

Back at Mafeking

Wednesday 13 January
The whole country is being systematically inspected, and already fifty thousand head of cattle have been inspected. No further trace of infection has been found outside the herd of six hundred at Palapye — and if this is borne out by further investigation I think I shall shoot the lot. We shall see.

Thursday 14 January
I find from my notes that I forgot to mention an amusing remark made by Sir William Clark in a speech at Cape Town. He was referring to Cohen's predilection for wireless, and remarked that during Cohen's retirement he would doubtless be able to amuse himself listening in to the dictators of the world: Hitler from Berlin, Mussolini from Rome, and Colonel Rey from Bechuanaland — dealing with his refractory Chiefs in the morning, and giving talks to Tiny Tots in the afternoon!
    This was a lovely dig at my autocratic government.

Friday 15 January
Three damn fool dispatches from Home raising fresh difficulties about my water, road, and wireless services. They are a lot of cursed idiots. They all pay lip service to the desirability of all my development work, and then do their best to stop it. But they won't succeed.
    All reports received so far regarding Foot and Mouth are satisfactory. If they continue so, it would appear to be a purely local outbreak, which we shall stamp out fairly easily and rapidly.

Saturday 16 & Sunday 17 January
A perfectly charming letter from Lord Clarendon. Clarendon is terribly upset at Duncan's appointment. He says: 'I am grievously disappointed that by consenting to an extended term of office, the old practice of selecting the Governor-General from Overseas has not been preserved. Departing from this precedent and appointing a politician is to my mind a grave error, and is moreover fraught with dangers politically as well as socially'.
    It is indeed a tragedy — part and parcel of the policy of disruption, scuttle, funk, and muddle which is increasingly pursued by Whitehall.
    The poor old British Empire, built up in spite of the British Government, is now being destroyed by the British Government.

Wednesday 20 January
A very hectic day. Lawrenson from Mochudi with his Chief, Mmusi, Arrowsmith from Gaberones and Mackenzie from Kanye, with their respective Chiefs, Seboko and Bathoen. Also the mining people (African-German Investment Company) who want to mine in the Bamalete and Bangwaketse Reserves.

Mmusi — whom we have put in place of Molefi — wanted to 'pay his respects', so no real difficulties occurred. He is doing fairly well. The ex-Chief is being a damn nuisance, going round and blackmailing traders into giving him £5 each under threat of boycotting their stores if they don't pay up.

The mining negotiations went very well with the others, especially Bathoen. Seboko was a bit nervous because he had already given an option on his mining rights to the British South Africa Company for £50 a year. However, I undertook to get him out of it, so he went away happy. The mining people, Hopkins and Roberts, were very pleased too.

I had a talk with Bathoen about the Proclamations, and I don't think we shall have any further serious difficulty with him about them now. He is worried about his crops, as there has been no rain there for six weeks — after good early rains.

Mmusi expressed the same fear, and asked me to come up and bring rain! He said that each time I had been up there it had rained afterwards — a wonderful reputation.

Thursday 21 January
Another interview with Sternau, the German Jew we are employing at the Lobatsi Fur Works. He is a very able, rather nice youngster. Had to leave Germany, because being a Jew he can't work as a master furrier, which he is, but only as an apprentice. It's a damn shame.

Friday 22 January
Tshekedi, who was married a year ago, has just declared in Kgotla that his recently born son is not his! (i.e. that he is not the father). He is divorcing his wife, and trying also to get her prosecuted for attempting to poison his mother![2] These enlightened Christians fill me with joy. All brought up and educated by the L.M.S. (London Missionary Society) — all earnest Christians.

Saturday 23 January
Hotting up again. Plague broken out in Northern Rhodesia. And as natives come from there thro' B.P. in large quantities to go to the mines, we are up against another danger — and have got to take elaborate precautions.

Sunday 24 January
The Union Government policy regarding natives and their treatment of them is amazing, and there is little doubt but that there will be big trouble one day — tho' it will take some years to blow up.

This proposed Mixed Marriages Bill is another indication of their attitude on the subject. Tho' the Bill itself, which prohibits marriages between whites and Asiatics or natives (but curiously enough not between whites and coloured), does not inflict any particular hardship on them, the speeches made shew the frame of mind — complete segregation, political and social.

Hofmeyer's[3] speech against the Bill was admirably reasoned: Grobler's in favour of it was puerile.

The Magistrates too give amazing sentences — two years hard labour to a native for stealing a goat, three years to another for stealing some mealies.[4] A white man has been charged here with stealing a pig. It will be interesting to see what sentence he gets. He has been let out on £50 bail.[5]

1937

Tuesday 26 January
All reports re Foot and Mouth disease are so far satisfactory: all being negative. And the disease is dying out within the cordon at Palapye.

Tshekedi brought the future Chief of the Bamangwato, his nephew Seretse, to see me this morning. The lad has improved a good bit, and seems pleasant enough and well grown. He is sixteen, so Tshekedi has only two more years to go, and then there will be trouble when Seretse succeeds.[6] Thank goodness I shan't be here.

Wednesday 27 January
What a country for disease! Locusts in the Union; Foot and Mouth and East Coast Fever in Southern Rhodesia; Rinderpest in Tanganyika; and Foot and Mouth here. And all the papers exaggerate and lie, and make things worse, and cause a lot of unnecessary trouble and suffering, to increase their beastly circulation.

Thursday 28 January
We have hundreds of reports from all over South Africa saying that our wireless station is out and away the best, and that the only other one that is any good is Berlin. It is such a pity that Daventry (B.B.C.) is so bad — bad reception and rotten programmes. It does us no good, but rather the reverse, and no one listens in. What is the good of an Empire broadcasting station when the stuff they put over is inaudible generally, and when heard is futile.

Friday 29 January
A long article in the *Star* today on my retirement. Quite inaccurate in most respects and generally futile. They say I am going at the end of this month!

Saturday 30 & Sunday 31 January
A long talk with old Chase, who wants to buy the Fur Factory at Lobatsi! He would make a wonderfully good thing of it, and is indeed the only man who could. He knows the country and the people, and all about skins, and is dead straight.

Wednesday 3 February
Our garden party — the last function we shall give here I hope — was a great success, thanks to Ninon's organising powers. We had a hectic morning getting everything straight — arranging the games in the garden, hiding the treasures; having the refreshment tables fixed; moving out the piano for the band. And my special job mixing three huge cans of Moselle wine cup.

Thursday 4 February
A very hectic day indeed at the Office. A long discussion all the afternoon with Gelman of the Federated Meat Industries re slaughtering and exporting from Lobatsi. The fact is that cattle prices have risen so much throughout South Africa, and the Union and the Southern Rhodesia Governments give such enormous bounties on meat export, amounting to as much as £5 to £7 per beast! — that it doesn't pay these people to slaughter at Lobatsi. Prices of B.P. cattle have risen from £2 to £5 per head, which makes all the difference, especially as we cannot afford to give a bounty of much more than ten shillings per head. It's all very difficult, but I think I can see a way out.

If we have 1,400,000 head of cattle, our exportable surplus should be five per cent — i.e. 70,000 head a year. If we can get the Union Government to give us

20,000 into Jo'burg, and 25,000 on the hoof into the Western Transvaal, we could levy ten shillings a head on them — which would give us over £20,000 a year to use as a bounty on the export of meat from Lobatsi. Say 20,000 head at £1 a head, and a total export of 65,000 head — that would be good enough. But all that means a lot of negotiation, and I don't suppose I shall have time to do that before I go.

Friday 5 February
European Advisory Council meeting all the morning — quite satisfactory. Then Ninon and I lunched with them at Dixon's Hotel. They gave us an excellent meal, and made themselves very pleasant.

After lunch we resumed the meeting, and each member made a speech about our going — quite affecting indeed. One member, poor old Glover, was so moved by his own eloquence that he burst into tears and had to stop! Very embarrassing.

Monday 8 to Thursday 11 February
The new hospital was opened at Maun in Ngamiland, and the new Chief of the Batawana 'Moremi' was installed at Maun. I sent wireless messages from our station on both occasions. Of course I ought to have been there, but it was quite impossible in view of the amount of work here.

It was rather a triumph getting my District Administration reorganisation scheme through at last, and all officers are very pleased. I have had very nice letters from them.

Friday 12 February
A wonderful rainfall at Palapye — ten inches in the last week, a record I should think. The aerodrome is a bog and Hobday, who has gone up there by plane, can't get back as his plane can't take off! The Lotsani River there which as a rule is as dry as a bone — a real South African 'sand river' — is running four feet deep. Cars are held up everywhere. It's simply splendid getting all this rain for the grazing and the crops. Our new dam at Mogobane, which holds up three hundred and fifty million gallons, ought to be a wonderful sight.

The new locust poison is a huge success, and it really looks as if we shall be able to cope with this curse in future. But I was surprised to learn from Arden-Clarke that they have used something of the sort in Nigeria for years. It is extraordinary that it should not have been known here. It just shows how much my Interstate Bureau for gathering and circulation information about animal disease and pests is needed.

Of course those blasted fools at the High Commission Office have mucked the arrangement I made with the Union Government people about cooperation with them in a Game Reserve in the South West corner of the Protectorate, bordering on the Union's Game Reserve for gemsbok. It is heartbreaking that fools should be allowed to interfere in matters they don't understand. And to cap it all, the press have got hold of the wrong end of the story. They have published a statement saying I have promised to give away a piece of Protectorate land! Life is really very trying.

Thursday 18 February
Saw Murray, our latest recruit. He is to run our Karakul sheep scheme at Ghanzi. He seems a very solid fellow, and is of course an expert at the job. We are starting with a pure-bred stud of eighteen rams and twelve ewes — costing about £20 each.

Two demonstration flocks — one consisting of about two hundred grade ewes, the other of about a hundred 'blink-eye' (native) sheep — so as to shew the farmers how to breed up. Our initial outlay will be about £200. But it ought to be a very good thing.

Friday 19 February
Got a telegram today to say that Molefi, the Bakgatla Chief I kicked out of Mochudi last year, has been arrested in the Union by the Police there for 'extortion'. He has been going round the traders on the Union side of the Bakgatla border, telling them that if they didn't give him £5 each he would prevent his Tribe trading with them. He is in gaol at Rustenburg, so I expect that is the end of him.

Also a telegram from Home agreeing to my proposal to slaughter all the infected Foot and Mouth cattle at Palapye, turn them into meat, and export the meat — after paying compensation. It's simply splendid, and now we'll be all clear in a month.

Tuesday 23 February
At last. Whitehall has agreed to my proposals for dealing with Molefi — indefinite suspension, but if he behaves properly we may review the decision after two years.

Monday 1 to Wednesday 3 March
Hectic days of discussion with our D.C.s. We were about twenty of us at the meeting, and covered a wide range of subjects — very interesting and useful. Russell England was present at one, and of course had a row with Nettelton.

Thursday 4 March
Opening of the Native Advisory Council in great style. Guard of Honour looking very smart. I let off an oration, and various Chiefs and others replied — all of them making very cordial and sympathetic references to Ninon. She certainly has made her mark on them. I left them the afternoon to yap amongst themselves, whilst I went on with the D.C.s. At 5, I had a very difficult and tricky meeting with Gelman the Managing Director of the Imperial Cold Storage Company, to arrange for the re-opening of the Lobatsi Meat Works, the slaughter of the fourteen hundred head of cattle from Palapye, and further purchase and slaughter of other cattle in the Protectorate. I was dog-tired at the end of it.

Friday 12 to Sunday 14 March (to Mahalapye)
Ninon and I off to lay the foundation stone of the Lawrence Hands Memorial Hall at Mahalapye. I had a row on the train with the new Customs officer who had the damn cheek to ask me where I was going — in my own Territory! I left a note at Lobatsi for Cuzen to telephone to Mafeking to report him. He will get hell when I get back next week.

A sleep after lunch, and then at 3.30 Ninon laid the stone. She did it magnificently and 'spoke her words' in a voice that was heard everywhere and with immense dignity. They presented her with a silver trowel — and everyone was full of praise for her. All the arrangements went off very well. Tshekedi was there looking rather sick and sorry: he had given the land for the Hall.

After changing from my top hat and tail coat, we got off at 5.

Thursday 18 to Saturday 20 March (back at Mafeking)
Tshekedi has got his divorce. I'm so glad the L.M.S. are so upset about it. The poison case (his wife trying witchcraft poison on his mother) won't come off just yet.

1937

Judge Watermeyer heard the appeal about costs in the Tshekedi case at Bloemfontein this morning, and I got a wire to say judgement reserved. Blakeway and Kelly went over from here, and Buchanan and his junior had to come all the way from Cape Town. I hope they were jolly well inconvenienced.

Sunday 21 March
A jolly run into Jo'burg.

Wednesday 24 March (at Johannesburg)
Official opening of the Rand Easter Show. We had the usual preliminary 11 o'clock tea there to meet Pirow, who is performing the ceremony.
The opening ceremony went off quite well. Ninon and I were in the 'Royal Box' as usual — Smuts quite close. Pirow made a long and rotten speech, funny for a clever man as he is. He spent the first half of it talking about railway expansion, and the expenditure of six and a quarter millions on stations and lines on the Rand — and the second half on talking absolute nonsense about agriculture. 'Rationalising' farm production is pretty hopeless in any country, and rank lunacy out here, where the farmers are the world's worst.

Thursday 25 March
I told Pirow that I thought the 'rationalising' among farmers that he had suggested wouldn't work. He said he quite agreed! But that one had to do something for the farmers, and it was much cheaper to give them something to think about and discuss and argue over than to dish out financial help. Also it took their minds of other things! Slightly cynical, and typical of the political mind.

Good Friday 26 March (to Mafeking)
We got off at 10, and had an excellent run into Ventersdorp. After lunch there, I had trouble with the Dutch police about a wretched native, son of the Mafeking headman. I saw this poor devil standing in the garage, frightfully knocked about. I discovered that last night he had run into a cow when motoring back from Jo'burg, and had been set upon by four Europeans (Dutch) in another car — who, he said, had robbed him after knocking him down and kicking him. The owner of the cow wanted compensation; the garage people wouldn't let the car go before being paid for repairs (£3.10s); and the police wanted the driver and his license. So, after much argument, I convinced the police that they couldn't hold the man; and the owner of the cow would have to sue in the ordinary way. And I lent the poor devil £3 to pay for his repairs. He was terribly grateful, apparently, but I am not regarding my £3 as a gilt-edged investment!

Saturday 27 (Easter Sunday) & Monday 28 March
We have won the Rand Easter Show gold medal, and were only just beaten by two points for the Empire Challenge Cup by ISCOR — the Government Iron and Steel Works, who put up a £25,000 exhibit.
I have a telegram from London to say they have approved my application for £58,000 for road development — and they have also approved my extra £2,000 for the additional wireless stations at Lehututu, Ghanzi, and Tsabong. So now the whole Territory will be linked by air and land. It is indeed a triumph. And if only they will approve my £130,000 water scheme before June, I shall depart happily.

Tuesday 30 March to Sunday 4 April
I had a talk with Tshekedi on Tuesday. He is very pleased at having got his divorce case through, but is now wanting to proceed with the witchcraft business. He is alleging poisoning of his mother by his wife, and talks of women consulting witchdoctors without their husbands' knowledge, and getting filthy love-potions. Tshekedi is also alleging conspiracy against him by (Disang) Raditladi, and Raditladi's son, Leetile,[7] the co-respondent in the divorce case. It looks like a nasty time ahead, thank goodness we shan't here.

I had a talk with Sir Walter Johnson, the medical expert who has come out from Home to advise us about our V.D. Campaign and medical work generally.[8] He was Director of Medical Services in Nigeria, and had just retired — a very pleasant and able man. Sir Cecil and Lady Fforde left Cape Town for England on retirement in the *Dunvegan Castle* on Friday 2. They have appointed Millin, K.C., to act in his place. He is the husband of Sarah Gertrude Millin, who writes all that stuff which people talk so much about — including a rotten life of Rhodes and a not good effort at Smuts.[9]

Monday 12 April
Better today. Went to the Office this morning. Had interview with Jeffares,[10] the engineer who is going to supervise our Okavango water development, for which we have got another £8,000.

I have been having the devil of a row with the Dominions Office about my pension. I wrote and asked them how much it was, and the figure seemed to me to be less than I ought to have. So I wrote back and asked them how they calculated it. To which they replied that they had recalculated it and that it was £40 a year *more* than they had said! Of all the dirty tricks!

Tuesday 13 April
There are a lot of repercussions about the Tshekedi divorce case, as I had feared. He is going for the co-respondent's family, and stirring up all sorts of trouble about witchcraft, conspiracy, etc. Fraenkel, the lawyer,[11] came to see me this morning. He has been retained by Raditladi (the co-respondent's father) to defend him, and is off to Serowe this afternoon.

There is no peace in this place, and never will be as long as the people at Home are so pathetically weak and influenced by those damn holy-bolies and Exeter Hall sob-stuff merchants.

Wednesday 14 April
More trouble. Lawrenson, our D.C. at Mochudi, came down to see me with Molefi. The latter has been offered a job by the local representative of the Mines for recruiting natives in the Bakgatla and Bamangwato Reserves. Of course it would never do, and would lead to all sorts of trouble. But to refuse will also lead to trouble — but of another kind. Molefi has to answer in our Court for embezzling £100 of Tribal money, and he has been condemned in a Union Court to a fine of £40 or three months imprisonment for extortion. What a Chief! It is a good thing we kicked him out of the Chieftainship; we shall now have to kick him out of the Reserve.

Thursday 15 & Friday 16 April
I finished off my confidential annual reports on Chiefs for the Dominions Office[12] — and the reports make pretty reading! There is hardly one of them that is

fit to be a Chief at all, or even a headman. A disloyal, incompetent, dishonest and rotten crowd.

And these are the people thro' whom we are supposed to administer the people in this unhappy country.

Fraenkel came in on his return from Serowe. Apparently Tshekedi is illegally endeavouring to try the Raditladi people. I sent him a telegram to say that he couldn't do it, so there'll be more trouble there.

He is an impossible devil to deal with.

Saturday 17 April
Knobel came down from Molepolole about the trouble that is going on there, in connection with the removal of the people from the hill to the vicinity of the Chief's house and Kgotla. We have fined or sent to prison nearly a hundred people for refusing to move, and are issuing another two hundred summonses! But we can't go on like this. It will mean putting half the Tribe in prison.

Knobel considers that the Chief, Kgari Sechele, is quite wrong in this matter, and that he has got ninety per cent of the Tribe against him. Knobel thinks we ought to reconsider our policy — but that's very difficult.

Anyhow I've sent for all three District Commissioners concerned — Ellenberger, Arrowsmith and Germond — and we are going to have a conference next week to settle this thing finally. I am sick of the weakness and stupidity of Kgari the Chief.[13]

That little devil Molefi has caused more trouble at Mochudi. He had elected to start a new religion in opposition to the Dutch Reformed Church, and started off with a meeting under some trees. In the course of this he observed that it was a shame to have to meet out on the veld when there was a perfectly good church in the village. So he suggested they should go and kick the people out of the church. Fortunately he was dissuaded from this. But he sent up to the D.R.C. minister to ask for six bottles of communion wine, as they proposed to celebrate communion! A more blasphemous and gratuitously offensive thing I have not heard of. The wretched minister has gone down with a heart attack, and I'm not surprised.[14]

On Sunday 24 January I referred to the cases of some natives who had stolen some mealies and in another case a goat, and got respectively three years and two years hard labour; and mentioned the case of a white man who had stolen a pig and had been remanded. The case was adjourned until 22 February. The sentence was £5 or one month — the sentence suspended for three years. In other words he got off with nothing. Justice!

Thursday 22 April
Fresh trouble at Mochudi: Lawrenson is worried. Kelly came to see me and reported that he had to drop the case against Molefi for embezzling the £100 Tribal money, as there is some flaw in the appointment of the trustees. It's a damn nuisance. However Molefi was found guilty on the other case — pinching Kgari's car, smashing it up, and refusing to pay for it — and has to pay £70. He was fined £40 in the Union in the case for extortion the other day — so he'll need some money.

The witchcraft trial at Serowe is in full blast. There's any amount of publicity about it in the papers. It's an amazing thing that this sort of superstition holds such sway even today. Anyway it is causing a lot of trouble.[15]

Friday 23 April
The Honours List was sent to me confidentially today. They are giving Ninon the O.B.E. She is so furious and disgusted at my being left out that she is refusing it, and writing to say so. Mrs Harris[16] is getting the M.B.E., but she was so upset and distressed at my being left out that she melted into tears! I am bound to say it is a goddam shame to think that, after all I've done here, they perpetrate such an act of injustice and ingratitude — when the idlest, stupidest, and most incompetent swine, who achieve nothing, get all sorts of rewards. I expect that double-crossing swine Priestman has had something to do with it. The bitter envy and jealousy of the office boys at the High Commission Office — and the utter inability of the people at Home to appreciate what had been done and the difficulty of doing it — have apparently combined to put this snub on the Territory and the whole of the staff.

Saturday 24 April
A deputation from Molepolole to protest against the removal of the village from the hill to the central position near the Chief's quarters — on which I have been insisting for years.

I had grave doubts as to these people representing anything or anyone but themselves. So I refused to discuss the matter with them until Monday, when the Chief and the District Commissioners concerned will be here. I sent them back with a flea in their ear.

A telegram from Mochudi to say that Molefi has broken out again and burned down seven huts. So I've had to send up some Police. I do hope there's not going to be big trouble again just before I leave.

Monday 26 April
Those Molepolole people, who came on Saturday, appear to have been lying heavily. They were not sent by the Chief or the Tribe — but merely by their own section of the village.

Saturday 1 May
All the morning in the garden discussing with the new Government Secretary, Forsyth Thompson.[17] He has arrived from Uganda: seems a very nice fellow, and able.

Sunday 2 May
Colonel Godley and Miss Archer left by car for Jo'burg. He is leaving finally, having done a very fine piece of work in Police re-organisation during the two years he has been here. We have now a really efficient Police force, trained — mobile — more Europeans — a proper system of recruiting — and a fine type of youngster joining.

Monday 3 May
The Order of the Silver Lion — a handsome silver badge on a blue ribbon — which has been presented to me by the Pathfinders Headquarters Council for my services to the movement, arrived this morning. Preston is going to invest me with it on the King's Birthday at Gaberones.

But I am not really interested in it, because they have not given Ninon anything, and she has done vastly more for the Pathfinders and Wayfarers than I have.

1937

Tuesday 4 May
Sir William Clark is supporting my request to be allowed to retire on 23 September instead of 1 September. The extra three weeks makes a difference of nearly £30 a year in my pension. I can't think that London will raise any difficulty. But they are a dirty lot of filthy swine at the Dominions Office. They ignore all I have done for the B.P. Then they try to do me out of £40 a year in my pension, which they have now admitted because I raised hell about it. And now I have to fight for this other £30. That makes £70 a year in all that they would have cut off my pension if I hadn't fought for it. My God, how I love them.

Wednesday 5 to Sunday 9 May
Further trouble at Mochudi. That little devil Molefi is really past praying for. Having turned him out of the Chieftainship, I have now decided to turn him out of the Bakgatla Reserve. That means a dispatch Home of course. But still it must be done.

'Coronation Tour'

Wednesday 12 May (at Gaberones)
Arrayed in full war-paint, with all our Christmas tree decorations hung about us, we started off at 9.45.

For the first time all my District Commissioners and Heads of Department are in uniform. I have been fighting for three years to get those damn fools at Home to agree, and they have done so at last. It makes a great difference from the native point of view.

Our first meeting was at Gaberones Camp, where there was a religious service for all Europeans — official and non-official. Arrowsmith did the service very well and then I gave an address. Ninon said it was the best speech I have ever made. I had no notes and had prepared nothing. It was of course on the subject of the King's Coronation.

Then on we went to Ramoutsa, where first we had to meet the Indian delegation with a combined Patriotic, Coronation and Farewell Address. A very charming document — but accompanied by some truly awful Indian delicacies to eat, which we had to try to swallow. Mercifully they gave us some quite good tea to wash it down. Otherwise I think we should have been sick. Then more speeches.

Thursday 13 May
A somewhat less strenuous day. I inspected the new barracks, stables, and other buildings that I have put up at Gaberones. They are all very satisfactory, except the stables which are damnable. It is obvious that the designer knows nothing about horses. They are too low, badly ventilated, stalls too short, absurd fixed iron bars between the horses. I have ordered drastic changes.

Saturday 15 May
Off to Mochudi for the day, just Ninon and I in 'Topsy'. We had tea at the Residency, then to the Kgotla which was held on the special open space which had been prepared for the Coronation. It was a great show.

They gave us a wonderful lion dance. Two regiments met us about half a mile from the Kgotla, and gave us a great greeting, and then came on with us. After the speeches, two men in complete lion skins, heads and manes and all, were pursued and 'killed' by other dancers with axes and knob-kerries after quite a realistic 'hunt'. There were others dressed in weird masks and headdresses, who also gave quite amusing performances.

My friend 'Mussolini' and one of the Chief's brothers made good speeches, following Mmusi, the Acting Chief. Mmusi is doing fairly well since we put him in place of his brother Molefi, who of course was not there.

Monday 17 May
Off to Serowe in 'Topsy' at 9.15. After morning tea at the Residency, we went to the Kgotla, where both Ellenberger and Tshekedi made very nice speeches which I had to answer. Then I had a longish interview with Tshekedi in Ellenberger's office. After lunch there was a big tea and tennis party at the Residency.

Tuesday 18 May (at Francistown)
The Coronation celebrations, all over the Territory, have been extraordinarily good. They reflect great credit on all our officials, and on the European settlers and natives — all of whom have entered into the thing wholeheartedly. We have presented ten thousand Coronation mugs to school children and bronze Coronation medals to hundreds. We have organised games and sports, and held services and meetings everywhere.

Wednesday 19 May
I had a talk with Simon Ratshosa about returning to the Bamangwato Reserve. He is prohibited from going there since the big rọw, and wants the ban lifted.

Thursday 20 May (back to Mafeking)
The train arrived at Mafeking at 9.30 am — an hour and a half late. The end of the 'Coronation Tour' — the last tour we shall make. I'm thankful it's all over. It's been very tiring, and Ninon and I have both had enough.

At all events we've done our 'bit' up to the end — in spite of the utterly damnable way in which we've been treated by that blasted Dominions Office. But I'll get a bit back on them after September.

And now to pack and clear out — and forget.

Thursday 20 May
I went down to the Office in reply to an S.O.S. from Arden-Clarke. We've had an utterly idiotic telegram from the High Commission Office about the application of the Proclamations to the Bamangwato Reserve — damning the negotiations that Arden-Clarke did in Serowe; and generally betraying the wanderings of a disordered mind. So I drafted a stiffish dispatch in reply. Arden-Clarke is off by car this afternoon to Pretoria, taking my dispatch with him, to try to reason with the fools.

Friday 21 to Tuesday 25 May
I settled all the details of the High Commissioner and Lady Clark's visit on the 29 and 30 May — down to the smallest detail, including where the white line is to be whitewashed for the car to draw up in the Camp! The staff-work must be perfect.

1937

Monday 31 May (to Kanye)
We went off for our last drive in 'Topsy' at 10 am — to pay our farewell visit to the Potts and to Chief Bathoen and the Bangwaketse at Kanye. We stupidly took the direct road, as it's shorter (75 miles) and very pretty, but it had got into a shocking state and we were badly bumped about.

Tuesday 1 June
Bathoen had assembled a good Kgotla meeting and made a really fine farewell speech. It was the best speech I have ever heard a native make in the eight years we've been here. Pott's speech was of course excellent. I had to reply, and the Kgotla gave us a great reception and presented us with a fine kaross. Back to lunch — and then off to Mafeking. This time we went back via Lobatsi (85 miles): a much better road. The drive from Kanye to Lobatsi is very pretty.
   The last view of the Protectorate we shall have.

Wednesday 2 to Sunday 6 June (at Mafeking)
Clearing up, handing over, and packing up. It was bitterly cold Wednesday, Thursday and Friday — especially Friday night, and we had to have fires going everywhere. A bit warmer again on Saturday.
   We handed over 'Topsy' on Wednesday morning, and took the Buick out for a trial spin in the evening. She is a beauty, very powerful, large and comfortable, and I think we shall like her.
   I had a very interesting interview at the Office with an old villain called Nicodemus, the Chief of the wild Damaras, whom we had met when we were trekking along the Botletli river up north. He and two of his headmen had come all this way to say good-bye. Extraordinarily nice of them.
   We are getting any amount for most charming letters, telegrams, and other messages of farewell. It is really very touching to see how many people seem to have appreciated what we have tried to do for them. One does not of course realise it at the time. Indeed one does not think of it at all.

Monday 7 to Friday 11 June
More clearing up, packing, and farewells. The latter are getting rather nerve-wracking, especially as we are both getting more and more tired.

Sunday 13 June
I finished off my last report on work done during my stay here, and signed the covering dispatch. It is a powerful effort, immensely condensed into forty five pages. I could have written four hundred and fifty, and then not covered the ground!

Monday 14 June
The heavy luggage went off at 9.30 partly by goods train direct to Cape Town, but most of it into the Government Store here to wait until our later plans are decided.
   I finished off the Introduction to Schapera's Report on Native Law and Custom, which I had promised to write for him. It is a huge report which he has taken three years, at intervals, to compile. That was another of my ideas — one that was of course pooh-poohed at first. Now everyone thinks it is wonderful, and they will do so even more when it is all printed and published.[18]
   I also finished off my notes on the Tshekedi trial, for inclusion in the Annual Report of the B.P.

I went down to the Office, and went into every Department and shook hands finally with everyone. They all seemed very sorry; some quite affected. Guigley could hardly speak.

I signed my last despatches. Then Ninon fetched me in the car, and I took my last look at the old Camp — the place that I have turned into a garden from the wilderness it was, planting nearly two hundred trees and generally improving, rebuilding, extending, etc.

Tuesday 15 June
Greatly to our surprise and pleasure, Forsyth Thompson and his wife, and practically the whole of the Headquarters staff turned up at Protectorate Government House to give us a final send-off. It was exceedingly nice of Forsyth Thompson — especially — he is the new Government Secretary — and indeed of all of them.

The Buick was packed full. (She takes an immense amount of luggage: a large trunk, two suitcases and etceteras in the boot alone.) After a last round of handshaking, Ninon and I climbed in, and we rolled out of the gates for the last time, and took our final view of Mafeking.

And so FINIS to this chapter in our lives.

It's been a wonderful experience, a most interesting and fascinating piece of work. Tremendously strenuous, very hard and difficult at times, but never dull.

One has the satisfaction of knowing that a whole country and its people have been put on the map in eight years — dragged from inertia and sloth to energy and progress, developed, made richer and more prosperous; its staff given better financial and living conditions and higher status; and the whole administration put on a higher plane which can now compare favourably with any in Africa.

It has been done, not with the help — but in spite of — the obstruction of the High Commission Office, who were bitterly jealous; and in spite of the similar tactics of the Dominions Office, whose attitude is well reflected in the fact that they have not even so much as sent me a letter of thanks or farewell.

But all the people of the Territory, white and black, official and unofficial — and all those outside who have been brought into contact with our work — they all know and appreciate, and have written me some wonderful letters. I would like to quote lines from Amery's letter — he was Secretary of State for the Colonies and Dominions (1926–1929):

> You have done a very fine piece of work, under very adverse conditions, which should have a permanent effect not only on the Bechuanas but also on the general problem of native policy in South Africa. I only hope that you yourself and Mrs Rey have not regretted your years of uphill endeavour with slender resources.[19]

A letter like that, from a man like that, is good enough. Added to the scores of others, and above all to one's own consciousness of results achieved and efforts made, it makes it possible to regard with a detached contempt the pettiness and small mindedness of those who — having failed to achieve results themselves, or to support the efforts of others — resent the attainment of a success which it was their duty to try for, and their obligation to recognize.

Editorial Notes

Notes for 1929

1. The Imperial Secretary was the head of administration for the British High Commissioner in South Africa, who at this time also held the office of Governor-General of the Union of South Africa. The High Commissioner had responsibility for the three High Commission Territories — the Bechuanaland Protectorate, Basutoland and Swaziland. These three territories were destined to be incorporated into the Union of South Africa under the terms of article 150 of the South Africa Act of 1909, provided that the Union Government satisfied certain conditions regarding its treatment of 'native' peoples within its borders. The British Government also made a promise that it would not hand over the High Commission Territories without consulting their inhabitants. The offices of Governor-General and High Commissioner were separated in 1931 when different individuals were appointed as Governor-General (the Earl of Clarendon) and High Commissioner (Sir Herbert Stanley).
2. Shirley Eales had served in the South African War of 1899-1902. He became Assistant Imperial Secretary in the High Commissioner's office in South Africa in 1923. In 1931 he succeeded Captain Clifford (see note 4 below) as Imperial Secretary. After the separation of the offices of Governor-General and High Commissioner his title was changed to Administrative Secretary, which post he held until 1934. He then became Member and Deputy Chairman of the Rhodesia Railways Commission until 1949. He died at Bulawayo in 1963.
3. The Earl of Athlone (Alexander Augustus Frederick William Alfred George Cambridge, 1874-1957), formerly Prince Alexander of Teck, was married to Princess Alice, grand-daughter of Queen Victoria, and was the youngest brother of Queen Mary. He was appointed Governor-General and High Commissioner of South Africa in 1923 — a post which involved an annual migration between Pretoria and Cape Town to open the Parliament of South Africa. He left in 1930 and was the last to hold the two positions simultaneously.
4. Captain the Hon. (later Sir) Bede Edmund Hugh Clifford was Imperial Secretary from 1924 to 1931. He was also the official representative of the British Government to the Union Government. When the post of British High Commissioner was separated from that of Governor-General this function was taken over by the High Commissioner. He left South Africa to take up a series of Governorships: Bahamas 1932-7; Mauritius 1937-42; Trinidad and Tobago 1942-6. He died in 1969, after publishing an autobiography entitled *Proconsul* in 1964.
5. Lt-Colonel Jules Ellenberger, born 1871, was Resident Commissioner of the Bechuanaland Protectorate from 1924 to 1927 and as such was directly responsible to the High Commissioner for its administration. He was literally born in a cave in Lesotho (Basutoland) in 1871, but it was the well equipped house of his famous French Protestant missionary family. He began his service in the Bechuanaland Protectorate in 1897 as Magistrate's Clerk at Gaberones, and died in Salisbury (Harare) in 1973 at the age of 102.
6. Vivien F. Ellenberger was the son of Jules, and served in the Bechuanaland Protectorate Administration as an administrative officer. He entered the service of the Bechuanaland Protectorate administration in 1915 as Clerk to the Resident Commissioner. In 1920 he became a Sub-Inspector in the B.P. Police and in 1934 a Resident Magistrate. He ended his career as First Assistant Secretary and Establishment Officer, retiring in 1951.
7. Lt-Colonel Rowland Mortimer Daniel succeeded Jules Ellenberger as Resident Commissioner in 1926 and was Rey's immediate predecessor — first as Acting Resident Commissioner from 1926 until January 1928, when he was made substantive Resident Commissioner. He joined the British

Editorial Notes for pages 2 to 7

South African Police in 1898 and transferred to administration as Assistant Resident Magistrate at Serowe in 1904. He then became Assistant (Resident) Commissioner for the Northern Protectorate based at Francistown in 1908. He retired to Bulawayo in 1930 and died there in 1957 — 'He served in the siege of Mafeking' — *Rhodesia Herald* (Salisbury), 16 December 1957.

8. Sir Henry Birchenough Bt. was born in 1863 and became Chairman of the Rhodesia and Mashonaland Railway Companies in 1925. He was also President of the British South African Company.

9. The Government Secretary was C.L. O'Brien ('Clob') Dutton. His position was as head of the Resident Commissioner's administration for the Bechuanaland Protectorate.

10. Khama III was the ruler of the Bangwato (usually called the Bamangwato by the colonial administration) who reigned from 1875 to 1923, with a brief previous year on the throne in 1872–3. He presided over the transition from independence to dependence of his kingdom after 1885, when the British declared their Protectorate over what is today Botswana. He was a devout Christian who enjoyed an international reputation as an example of successful missionary endeavour in Africa. In 1895 he travelled to London together with the rulers of the Bakwena and Bangwaketse to preempt Cecil Rhodes's attempts to take over the Bechuanaland Protectorate. He and his fellow monarchs met with success and ensured the continued identity of the Bechuanaland Protectorate under British rule. See Q.N. Parsons, 'Khama III, the Bamangwato and the British, 1895–1923' (University of Edinburgh: Ph.D. thesis, 1973).

11. Tshekedi was Khama III's second son. He became Regent of the Bangwato on the death of his elder half-brother, Sekgoma II, whose heir, Seretse, was a minor aged four. Tshekedi ruled as Regent until 1950 when, after having opposed his nephew's marriage to an English woman, he was rejected by the Bangwato who believed he was trying to deprive Seretse of his birthright. (Though he effectively ceased to be Regent in the eyes of the people when he went into voluntary exile in 1949, the British only withdrew recognition from him in early 1950). He died in 1959, having effected a full reconciliation with his nephew three years earlier. (See biography of Tshekedi Khama by Michael Crowder, in preparation.)

12. Seretse Khama, son of Sekgoma II and grandson of Khama III, was recognised as the Chief of the Bangwato by his people on his father's death in 1925 — by virtue of his being his only son in a monarchy where succession was by male primogeniture. His marriage to an English woman in 1948, before he returned from his studies in England to take over control of Gamangwato from Tshekedi, was opposed by the British — who feared the reaction of the South African government which would not tolerate a racially mixed marriage by a Chief in a territory it hoped to incorporate. Seretse was sent into exile in 1950, but was allowed to return in 1956 on condition that he renounced all claims of Chieftaincy of the Bangwato. In 1962 he became the first leader of the Botswana Democratic Party, Prime Minister of Bechuanaland in 1965, and President of the Republic of Botswana in 1966. Under his leadership the Republic experienced remarkable economic growth and political stability. He died in 1980.

13. The Resident Commissioner of the Bechuanaland Protectorate was ex-officio Officer Commanding the Bechuanaland Protectorate Police and as such enjoyed the title of Lieutenant-Colonel.

14. The field administrative officials who resided in the capitals of the major chiefs of the Bechuanaland Protectorate were known by the title Resident Magistrate up until 1936, when the title was changed to District Commissioner. Their primary function was administrative, but they had judicial powers to conform with their magisterial title.

15. The Kalahari (Kgalagadi in Setswana) is essentially a thirstland which supports a thin cover of vegetation as well as wild animals. Recent archaeology shows that parts of it had been used for cattle-keeping as well as for hunting and gathering for much of the past two thousand years. But over the last century, its people have been reduced by drought and trade to a life of exclusive hunting or to the position of servants of cattle-owners.

16. 'Ole Bill' is a reference to the famous First World War character portrayed by Captain Bruce Bairnsfather in *Old Bill* and *The Better 'Ole*.

17. The hut-tax which was introduced by the British administration in 1899 was the main source of revenue for the Bechuanaland Protectorate. It was imposed as a poll-tax on all adult males over the age of 18 on an individual basis, with a surcharge for an extra wife rather than as elsewhere on the number of 'huts'. It was collected by the Chiefs through the traditional *mephato* or age-regiments, of which all adult males were members. The Chiefs paid the bulk of the tax collected to the colonial administration, but retained a small portion for their own administration.

18. Daniel interviewed Tshekedi in connection with the issue of mining, with particular reference to Athlone's view that Tshekedi was disregarding his advice. Daniel then reported that Tshekedi was 'most careful not to do anything for which he will not be able to account in a satisfactory manner when the time comes to relinquish his regency' (Botswana National Archives File S46/18, 'Chief

Editorial Notes for pages 7 to 12

Tshekedi: Attitude towards Administration': Daniel to Imperial Secretary, 7 December 1929).

19. Kgaleman Tumedisho Motsete was born in Serowe in 1899 and educated at Tiger Kloof, where he gained his Junior Teacher's Certificate in 1918. He then went on to London University where he took Bachelor's degrees in Art, Theology and Music. He had been on good terms with Tshekedi, but they soon fell out as a result of Motsete's criticisms of what he considered Tshekedi's high-handed ways and autocratic administration. He founded the Tati Training Institution in 1931, and after some years in South, East and West Africa became first President of the Botswana People's Party in 1961. He died in the early 1970s.

20. Captain Gerald Enright Nettelton was born in Basutoland and joined the Bechuanaland Protectorate administration in 1914 after serving in the Native Affairs Department of the Union Government in Roodepoort. His first post was as a clerk in the Resident Commissioner's office. In 1917 he was appointed a Sub-Inspector in the B.P. Police. In 1924 he became a Resident Magistrate and was on a number of occasions Resident Magistrate in Serowe where his sister Madge was married to the trader Page Wood. Another, Bimbi, was married to Vivien Ellenberger. He himself married Helen Minchin, daughter of Spenser Minchin the Mafeking lawyer. Nettelton became Acting Resident Commissioner from July 1946 to January 1947 when he became substantive Government Secretary, a post he held until his death in 1950. Anthony Sillery, who became Resident Commissioner in 1947, wrote of him that he was 'cautious . . . cynical . . . mildly malicious . . . immensely knowledgeable about the Protectorate'.

21. Lobatsi (spelt Lobatse today) was a small railway town near the South African border in the extreme south-east of the Protectorate. It never, in fact, became the capital of the Protectorate which continued to be situated at Mafeking within the borders of South Africa. Apart from the expense of establishing a new capital town, there were fears that South Africa which expected eventually to incorporate the Protectorate would object to such a move. The Special Court of the Protectorate did however sit at Lobatse, which became the seat of the High Court in the 1950s.

22. W.J. (Jack) Chase, son of the Chief Veterinary Officer, W.H. Chase, was a Dairy Officer who on retirement in the 1950s founded the Chase-Me-Inn at Mahalapye where he died in 1985.

23. P.G.C. Adams was an influential white settler member of the European Advisory Council of the Bechuanaland Protectorate.

24. Hamilton William Dyke (1881-1961), born in Basutoland and educated in Scotland, graduating with a Glasgow doctorate in medicine and joining the Basutoland administration in 1913. After service in Palestine (1927-28) he became Principal Medical Officer of the B.P. 1929-35. He returned to Basutoland, where he retired in 1952.

25. The Colonial Development Act of 1929 was not as altruistic as its title suggests. Its main aim was to invest in the colonies in such a way that unemployment in Britain would be relieved. All orders for material and machinery connected with development projects financed under the Act had to be placed with British firms. Rey was to be assiduous in tapping the Colonial Development Fund established by this act. By 1937, when he left the Protectorate, the B.P. had received some £70,000 — compared with the £250,000 received by Nigeria with a population nearly a hundred times bigger.

Notes for 1930

1. Rey often confuses his employer in his Diaries. He was in fact employed by the Dominions Office, which was established in July 1925. The office of Dominions Secretary was held simultaneously with that of Colonial Secretary by L.S. Amery (1925-29), who offered Rey his appointment as Resident Commissioner of the Bechuanaland Protectorate. Amery's successor as Colonial Secretary, Lord Passfield (1929-34), also held the post of Dominions Secretary concurrently until J.H. Thomas took over the Dominions Office in 1930. This, together with the facts that the Dominions Office was housed in the Colonial Office building and the two shared staff under the rank of Assistant Under-Secretary and used the same library and typing service, may have been the source of Rey's confusion.

2. The Colonial Development Advisory Committee was established under the Colonial Development Act of 1929 to advise on applications for finance from the Colonial Development Fund.

3. Sir Drummond Chaplin was a Director of the British South Africa Company. He had been a Member of the Union House of Assembly 1910-14 before becoming the Administrator of Southern Rhodesia, which post he held until the territory became self-governing in 1923. He was also Administrator of Northern Rhodesia 1921-23. He died in 1933.

4. The Chartered Company refers to Cecil Rhodes's British South Africa Company and alludes to the

Editorial Notes for pages 12 to 14

Royal Charter granted by Queen Victoria in 1889.
5. The Royal Navy maintained a base at Simonstown near Cape Town.
6. The European Advisory Council was set up in 1921 to discuss matters affecting the European settlers of the Bechuanaland Protectorate. Members were elected to represent settler farmers as well as traders in the Reserves.
7. The Native Advisory Council was formed in 1920, with two representatives from each of the eight Tswana states that made up the Protectorate — though the Bangwato did not formally take up membership until 1939. Its role was purely advisory. In 1940 it changed its name to the African Advisory Council. Like its European counterpart it was presided over by the Resident Commissioner.
8. Simon Ratshosa was a grandson of Khama III, his father having married Khama's eldest daughter Bessie. He himself married Oratile, the daughter of Sekgoma II. With his brothers, Johnnie and Obeditse, he was a major power in the Bangwato state, both during the last years of Khama's rule and during Sekgoma's brief reign. During that time he and his brothers tried to exclude royal rivals from any position of influence, in particular the important Mphoeng and Raditladi families. But on the death of Sekgoma in 1925, Phethu Mphoeng managed to gain the sympathy of the young Regent Tshekedi, and ousted the Ratshosa family from power. Incensed by their elimination from power, the Ratshosas refused to attend a Kgotla meeting to which Tshekedi had summoned them. When they were forcibly brought before him, Tshekedi sentenced them to a thrashing. Simon and Obeditse escaped, got their guns and tried to assassinate Tshekedi. They were jailed for attempted murder, their property was destroyed by regiments led by Phethu, and when they finished their jail sentence they were sent into exile by the British along with Johnnie and Simon's wife, Oratile. Simon, however, proved resourceful and took up a skilful journalistic pen against Tshekedi, with accounts of his alleged autocratic behaviour and of the mistreatment of the Basarwa by the Bangwato, suggesting that they were little better than slaves. He proved a thorn in the side of Tshekedi until his death, still in exile, in 1939.
9. The attempted assassination took place on 5th April 1926. Tshekedi was slightly wounded on his left side above the hip, not in the arm as Rey asserts.
10. Isang was the Regent of the Bakgatla from 1920 to 1929 for his nephew Molefi. Like Tshekedi, Isang was a well educated man with strong ideas of local development. But he quarrelled bitterly with Molefi and was drawn towards collaboration with the South African Native Affairs Department. He died in 1941.
11. This is a reference to Molefi, *kgosi* of the Bakgatla from 1929 to 1936 when he was suspended by the British for his generally wild and eccentric behaviour. His younger brother, Mmusi, then acted for him. Molefi returned to rule in 1945 and died in 1958. He was the son of Linchwe's eldest son who had died before he could succeed his elderly father. By the rule of male primogeniture Molefi, a minor, was the rightful successor. Isang, as next in line, therefore acted as his regent.
12. This refers to Albert Jennings and Douglas Buchanan, who helped Tshekedi in his struggle to prevent the implementation of the British South Africa Company's 1893 mining concession in Bangwato territory. Jennings was current chairman of the South Africa District Committee of the London Missionary Society, which included the Bechuanaland Protectorate. He was a close friend and unswerving supporter of Tshekedi, who in turn continued to allow the LMS a monopoly of missionary activity in his territory. Buchanan, Cape Town lawyer, who came from an old LMS family, was an influential supporter of its activities. He became Tshekedi's personal lawyer in 1929, and also acted for the Bangwato Tribe. He was Tshekedi's closest European friend and confidant until his death in 1954. He was engaged in writing a biography of Tshekedi before he died. It formed the basis of Mary Benson's *Tshekedi Khama*, published by Faber and Faber in 1960.
13. Of course Rey means the Dominions Office. See Note 1 above.
14. Rey refers here to the border-gate between the Lobatsi Block (white farms) and the Bangwaketse Reserve, demarcated by a farm fence and a gate on the road to limit the movement of cattle between the two.
15. Allan Leckie Cuzen was Resident Magistrate and later District Commissioner at Kanye. He had served in the 1899–1902 South African War and then from 1902–1906 in the Cape Police. In 1906 he joined the Bechuanaland Protectorate Police, and in 1914 joined the administration as a 2nd Clerk to the Assistant Commissioner, Northern District. He was promoted to the position of Resident Magistrate in 1921.
16. Rev R. Haydon Lewis was the resident missionary of the London Missionary Society in Serowe from 1913 to 1929. He it was who first suggested to Tshekedi that he seek legal advice over the British South Africa Company's mining concession. The Administration were furious with him over this and tried to put pressure on the LMS to have him transferred from Serowe, which in any case the LMS were already planning. Lewis had been withdrawn, not 'kicked out', from

Editorial Notes for pages 15 to 20

Molepolole in 1913 to go to Serowe. He had fallen foul of Bakwena marital politics at Molepolole and not of the Administration. The missionary who was removed from Serowe by the LMS at the behest of the Administration 'for unknown reasons' was Albert Jennings, whom Lewis replaced and who had been there since 1902. The reasons for his removal are thought to be that he was indulging in trade. (See Parsons, 'Khama III, the Bamangwato and the British', *op. cit.*, p. 286).

17. Bathoen II was the young Chief of the Bangwaketse who was distantly related to Tshekedi. They had been at Lovedale School in South Africa together, and became lifelong friends. Bathoen frequently sought Tshekedi's advice on relations with the colonial administration. He took up the Chieftaincy in 1928, from his aunt, Ntebogang, who had acted as regent for him while he was at school. He reigned until 1969, when he abdicated in favour of his son so that he could fight for a seat in Parliament. He was duly elected and became Vice President of the leading opposition party, the Botswana National Front. He retired from politics in 1986 to become President of the Customary Court of Appeals.

18. A.G. Stigand, as Resident Magistrate, Ngamiland (1911-14), was the centre of a storm over revelations by the Aborigines Protection Society, which accused him of keeping concubines (notably two Herero women, Gaarebone and Pauline) and favouring their relatives. They accused him of violent behaviour towards the ruling Batawana minority, whose Chief, Mathiba, later ordered Stigand to pay maintenance for his children. Tshekedi Khama was to make much of this and other cases of 'miscegenation' by colonial officials in 1933 in his defence of his actions in the McIntosh affair. (See 1933 note 18 ff.) Stigand's brother. Chauncery Hugh Stigand (1877-1919), was the author of numerous books on the Sudan, Abyssinia and Kenya — including studies of wildlife and of the Kiswahili and Nuer languages. His memoirs of 1913 carried an introduction by Theodore Roosevelt (*Hunting the Elephant in Africa, and other recollections of thirteen years wandering*, New York: Macmillan).

19. Sebele II was the Chief of the Bakwena, and was considered very troublesome by the colonial administration, in particular by Rey who later had him deposed. Sebele's deposition was justified on the ground that the people wanted it. In fact, as the official records show, the mass of Bakwena still continued to support him and those hostile to him were a small group of royal relatives. He had come to the throne in 1917, but was never officially confirmed in his post by the British. He died in exile in Ghanzi in 1939.

20. For a detailed discussion of Tshekedi's dispute over the well see Michael Crowder, 'Tshekedi Khama and opposition to the British administration of the Bechuanaland Protectorate, 1926-1936', *Journal of African History*, 26 (1985) pp. 200-1.

21. This scientific expedition across Bechuanaland was led by Vernay and Laing on behalf of the Transvaal Museum at Pretoria, and resulted in numerous monographs including a classic work on prehistory and archaeology by C. Van Riet Louw.

22. Tshekedi had sailed to England in March 1930 to see the Secretary of State for the Dominions, Lord Passfield, to enlist his help in preventing the British South Africa Company taking up their mining concession in his territory. He also sought to obtain assurance from Passfield that the Bechuanaland Protectorate would not be incorporated into South Africa.

23. Edirilwe Seretse was Tshekedi's cousin, and acted for him as Chief in his absence in England.

24. The Bakalaka — Bakalanga as they call themselves — were a large subject group incorporated into the Ngwato state. John Mswazi, headman of one of the Kalanga sub-groups, had refused to contribute to the fund established to cover Tshekedi's expenses in travelling to England to see the Secretary of State. His conflict with Tshekedi was to be revived in the 1940s, in particular over levies for the construction of Bamangwato National College.

25. Makobamotse Regiment was a *mophato* (age-regiment) of Bangwato men, formed at an adolescent initiation school (*bogwera*) of 1894 and led by Kaelo.

26. Rey was correct in referring to the 'Church of Scotland' in that the United Free Church of Scotland had resumed sitting in the Assembly of the Church of Scotland in 1929, after 86 years of schism. But the UFCS had been running the great missionary institution of Lovedale, near Alice in the Cape, founded in 1841 — which Tshekedi Khama had attended from 1916 to 1920. It was also the UFCS which had signed a concordat with the London Missionary Society in 1930 to found a hospital and take over the LMS mission church at Molepolole.

27. This refers to Livingstone's naïve belief in the virtues of white colonisation around Lake Nyasa (Malawi) after the failure of previous missionary ventures. Rey's reference to cannibalism, derived from popular European literature on Africa, was reciprocated in many parts of Africa by popular belief that Europeans were cannibals.

28. Rey is referring here to the series of strikes that led to shootings by police and violence between white and black crowds during 1928-30. See E. Roux, *Time Longer Than Rope: A History of the Black Man's Struggle for Freedom in South Africa* (Madison: University of Wisconsin Press, 1966

Editorial Notes for pages 20 to 30

edn.), pp. 175–243, and J. Simons and R. Simons *Class and Colour in South Africa 1850–1950* (London: International Defence and Aid Fund, 1983 reprint), pp. 386–437.

29. Rev Alexander Sandilands, later chaplain to Bechuanaland forces in the Second World War, and author of *Introduction to Tswana* (Tiger Kloof, Cape: LMS, 1953). Retired to Canada.
30. Sir James Comyn Macgregor was Resident Commissioner of the Bechuanaland Protectorate from 1917 to 1923. He was married to Jules Ellenberger's sister, and had a long administrative career in Basutoland before becoming Government Secretary of the Bechuanaland Protectorate in 1912. He is best remembered as a translator into English (from French) of D.F. Ellenberger's *History of the Basuto* (Volume 1: London, 1912). He died in 1935.
31. The Basarwa, referred to in colonial times as Masarwa or Bushmen, were the predominantly hunting and gathering inhabitants of the Kalahari before the intrusion of the Bangwato and other Tswana peoples into the eastern Kalahari. To begin with the two peoples lived in a symbiotic relationship with the Basarwa producing hunting products for the Bangwato to sell to the Cape traders, and the Bangwato supplying them with imported goods, milk and meat in exchange. But the Bangwato soon extended their domination over the Basarwa, turning them into virtual serfs as herders of their cattle.
32. The majority of people around Kachikau (Kachekabwe) were Basubiya (Bekuhane, as they call themselves) subject to Chika Leshwane (Leshwane III). There was also a small village of Batawana under the widow of Sekgoma Letsholathebe, who had been deposed in Ngamiland in 1906 and had moved to Kavimba near Kachikau in 1912, dying in 1914.
33. Lord Passfield, the Dominions Secretary, was better known as Sidney Webb, the Fabian Socialist, husband of Beatrice. See 1930 note 1 above.
34. The 'Hottentots' referred to were livestock-herding immigrants, speaking Dutch, under the leadership of Simon Kooper (see 1931 note 7). The Bakgalagadi were herding people distributed over most of Botswana, and speaking a language closely related to Setswana and Sesotho. Bakgalagadi means people of the Kgalagadi or Kgalagari (Kalahari), i.e. 'dried up' country.
35. The two principal issues at stake were those of mining and the treatment of the Basarwa by the Bangwato. See 1930 notes 63 and 65 below.
36. General Hertzog, Prime Minister of the Union of South Africa, was a former Boer General who broke with the South Africa Party of Botha and Smuts in 1913 to form the National Party. His pact with the Labour Party in the 1925 election enabled him to defeat Smuts and brought him to power for the next fourteen years. He was the chief architect of Segregation and part of his design involved incorporating the High Commission Territories — especially the Bechuanaland Protectorate as *lebensraum* for South African blacks and Swaziland as more land for the whites.
37. Rey was exaggerating his position. The Resident Commissioner, like his Resident Magistrates, had judicial powers, but was in no way equivalent to a Chief Justice. Major cases that needed real legal expertise went before the Special Court of the Protectorate which was presided over by a Judge (or lawyer) from South Africa. The final court of appeal was the Judicial Committee of the Privy Council.
38. The Bangwato *mephato* or regiments had adopted a variety of regimental uniforms from the British military wardrobe, including the kilt, around 1913. The Chief of the Bangwato often dressed in the uniform of a lieutenant-colonel of the Royal Horse Guards. Such a uniform was given to Khama III in 1889, but appears to have been worn by Khama only in 1889 and subsequently by his son Sekgoma II — who was seen wearing it during the South African War and after his reconciliation with his father in 1916 during the First World War. Tshekedi ordered a replacement uniform for himself, a smaller man than Sekgoma. Both uniforms are now in the Khama III Memorial Museum, Serowe.
39. The Kgotla was the forum where justice was dispensed, administrative decisions were made, and public meetings were held. It was presided over by the Chief or, at the level of the ward or village, by the headman. Until the 1950s it was restricted in attendance to adult males, except where an adult woman was a litigant or a witness to a case.
40. Semane was a young commoner teacher who became the fourth wife of Khama in 1900. Khama had divorced his third wife, and his first two wives had died. Semane bore her husband five children — a daughter Bonyerile Victoria in 1901, Tshekedi in 1905, another son Ewetse in 1909 (who soon died) and twin daughters in 1913 who also soon died. Semane herself died in 1937.
41. It is not clear to whom Rey refers here. Tshekedi had a full sister Bonyerile, and one half-sister, Oratile, the wife of Simon, from whom he was bitterly estranged and who was at this time engaged in suing him in court over her father's estate.
42. Seretse's mother was Tebogo Kebailele, the third but only legitimate wife of Sekgoma II in the eyes of his father.
43. Rey characteristically exaggerated the complexity of his task in the Serowe *Kgotla* since only one

Editorial Notes for pages 30 to 40

language was used — Setswana — with occasional interpreting into English for non-Setswana-speaking officials like himself.

44. George Haskins and his two sons, Jimmy and Billy, of the local firm J.G. Haskins & Sons (founded 1897). James Haskins Jr was to become a leading politician in the 1960s and Speaker of the National Assembly in the 1980s. H.T. Gordon was Manager of the Tati Company.
45. Tati Concession Mining and Exploration Company in 1888 acquired a series of concessions in the Tati goldfields area which had been granted by Lobengula of the Ndebele to various companies and traders. It managed to remain independent of Rhodes' British South Africa Company, and its territory became part of the Bechuanaland Protectorate where it exercised some of the attributes of a Chartered Company.
46. i.e. the Rand Easter Show.
47. See note 32 above.
48. Mophane (mopani) a common tree in north-eastern and north-western Botswana, which often grows to the exclusion of other vegetation. It is deciduous and provides browsing for animals, particularly in times of drought.
49. In 1904 the Herero rose against German rule in South West Africa. The Germans ordered their extermination and indeed nearly accounted for three quarters of the Herero nation in their savage represssion of the revolt. Some 2000 Herero escaped to the Bechuanaland Protectorate, some settling in the Tawana state, others led by their ruler, Samuel Maherero, in the Ngwato state near Mahalapye.
50. Chief Mathiba of the Tawana (ruled 1906–1933) having succeeded to the throne on the deposition of Sekgoma Letsholathebe as Chief by the Resident Commissioner, Ralph Williams, in 1906. Among other achievements, he once banned the use of motor transport in his district, prompting the British satirical magazine *Punch* to publish the following ditty: 'When buses roll along the Strand/With people bound for Samarkand/ I'll book to Bechuanaland/Mathiba I will visit;/And all my heavy trunks shall go/From point to point by buffalo/In Bechuanaland the slow:/And by the way, where is it?*' To which the Editor added a footnote: '* To avoid correspondence I have found out.' (Source: Rey Autobiography, chapter xvii, p. 254 — Botswana Society, Rey Papers).
51. The Ratshosa brothers took a civil action against Tshekedi for compensation for the burning of their houses and the destruction of their property. The sum they claimed was substantial since their houses were in the European style and they were lavishly furnished and equipped. The Resident Magistrate dismissed their claim, but the Special Court of the Protectorate upheld it. Against the advice of the High Commissioner, the Earl of Athlone, Tshekedi appealed against the judgement of the Special Court to the Judicial Committee of the Privy Council. There he won, since the law lords regretfully agreed that under native law and custom he had been within his rights to have the Ratshosas' property destroyed for what had been a treasonable act.
52. Dr Alexander Logie Du Toit, South African-born (1878), qualified as a mining engineer and lectured in geology at Glasgow University in Scotland before returning home in 1903. He became geologist to the S.A. Irrigation Department and then to De Beers Consolidated Mines. He also expounded in scientific publications on the theory of Continental Drift. He died in 1948.
53. The Walvis Bay Railway scheme was pressed as Southern Rhodesia's own access to a West Coast port independent of Cape Town and Lobito in Angola (via the Northern Rhodesia Copperbelt). In the original manuscript Rey began by using the English spelling 'Walfish' but later reverted to the Afrikaans spelling 'Walvis'. (See 1931 note 39).
54. Sir Cecil Hunter Rodwell (1874–1953) joined Milner's 'kindergarten' in 1901 and was Imperial Secretary in South Africa from 1903 until 1918. Thereafter he was appointed to a series of governorships — Fiji (1918–24), Guiana (1925–28), and finally Southern Rhodesia (1928–34) — retiring to become a director of mining companies in South Africa.
55. General J.J. Kemp was a Boer General who distinguished himself in the South African war of 1899–1902. In 1915 he was sentenced to seven years in prison for his part in the pro-German rebellion of Boers who could not reconcile themselves to supporting their former enemy, Britain, against the Germans who had given them so much support during their war with the British. On his release he joined the National Party of Hertzog in 1920 and was elected to the House of Assembly. From 1924–34 he was Hertzog's Minister of Agriculture. He held various ministerial posts thereafter until Smuts ousted Hertzog as Prime Minister in 1939 over the issue of giving support to Britain in the coming European War.
56. Howard Unwin Moffat (1869–1951), Premier of Southern Rhodesia from 1927 to 1933, was son of John Smith Moffat and a scion of the famous missionary family. He had been manager of the Bushman Mine (copper) in the Bechuanaland Protectorate, and became Minister of Mines in Southern Rhodesia on self-government in 1923.
57. Sir Charles Patrick John Coghlan (1863–1927) was first Premier and Minister of Native Affairs of

Editorial Notes for pages 40 to 47

Southern Rhodesia from 1923 to 1927. Born in Cape Colony, he had proceeded to Bulawayo in 1900 to practise law and entered politics in 1908.

58. Oswald Pirow was South African Minister of Defence and Railways and was notorious for his ruthless repression of the Durban riots by black Africans in 1929 soon after his appointment as Minister of Justice and Police. He was pro-Nazi and in 1938 flew to Germany to discuss his plan for Africa south of the Equator to become a South African zone independent of British, Portuguese and Belgian control. He proposed that Germany should take back its former colony of Kamerun enlarged by neighbouring British, French and Belgian territory. When South Africa joined the British against the Germans, Pirow formed the New Order Group of the Reunited National Party which had open sympathy with National Socialism. He was Prosecutor for the South African Government in the Treason Trial of 1956-61.

59. William Ballinger was a Scottish trade unionist who had come out to South Africa in 1928 to help advise the black trade union movement (the Industrial and Commercial Workers Union) on its financial affairs. He and his future wife, Margaret Hodgson, a Lecturer in History at the University of the Witwatersrand, toured the Bechuanaland Protectorate in 1931 and wrote about it for various newspapers. At first Rey was very suspicious of Ballinger but warmed to him later, when Ballinger wrote articles critical of Tshekedi and his 'autocratic' behaviour. Rey even proposed Ballinger's name for membership of a Commission of Enquiry on the status of the Basarwa in the Bamangwato Reserve in 1931. Leonard Barnes was a freelance journalist, who had resigned from previous service in the Colonial Office because of his qualms about imperialism — as expressed in his *Caliban in Africa: an Impression of Colour Madness* (London: Gollancz, 1930). He subsequently published *The New Boer War* (London: Hogarth Press, 1932), which carried his impressions of Bechuanaland, Basutoland and Swaziland in relation to South Africa. In 1936 he became a Lecturer at Liverpool University, and transferred to Oxford University in 1947. After retirement in 1962 he began to travel in Africa again, and published books increasingly disillusioned with African independence.

60. Rey was historically incorrect. The Mmanaana group of Bakgatla had left the Transvaal because of Boer oppression in 1852, to live first among the Bakwena and then in relative independence by tribute to the neighbouring Bangwaketse. The 'Matebele' (Ndebele) of Mzilikazi (c.1790–1868) had left the Transvaal area in 1837–38. For Gobuamang, see note 77 below.

61. John Wallace Downie (1876–1940), Scottish railwayman who emigrated to Cape Colony in 1897 and Southern Rhodesia in 1902. Chairman of Coghlan's Rhodesian Party 1923-25, he sat in parliament holding different Ministries until 1930 — when he became Southern Rhodesia's High Commissioner in London (1930-34).

62. Piet Gert Wessels Grobler (1873–1942) had been a member of the Rustenberg Commando in the South African War and like Kemp had joined the pro-German rebellion during the First World War. He was sentenced to two years in prison for his part in it. He was elected to parliament in 1924 and became Minister of Lands under Hertzog. In the Fusion Government formed by Smuts and Hertzog in 1933, he held the critical portfolio of Native Affairs at the time Hertzog's segregationist policies were being consolidated by the Natives Representation Act of 1936, which removed black voters from the common roll in the Cape Province and thus ended all hopes of representation of blacks in Parliament on the same basis as whites.

63. This refers to the letter Tshekedi sent to the Resident Magistrate at Serowe on 30 August 1930 for onward transmission to the High Commissioner (BNA S 96/8 Tshekedi to Resident Magistrate Serowe, 30 August 1930). In it he criticised the High Commissioner, Lord Athlone, and questioned his authority in connection with the declaration he had made in October 1926 with regard to the status of the Basarwa. This stated that any Basarwa 'who wish to leave their masters and live independently of them should understand that they are at liberty to do so and that if the Mangwato attempt to retain them against their will, the Government will not allow it. It is the duty of the Chiefs and Headmen to help these people to stand on their own feet'. (BNA 43/7, High Commissioner to Secretary of State for Dominions, 13 August 1926). Rey was furious about the letter and insisted that Tshekedi withdraw it on the grounds that it would be 'obviously impossible to discuss matters on a friendly basis' until it were either modified or withdrawn. (BNA S 169/5. Note of Interview with Tshekedi, 2 October 1930). Eventually Tshekedi was persuaded to withdraw the letter.

64. This is now the Phutadikobo Museum. Oral tradition records that Mrs Rey was carried up the hill on a brass bedstead. (Personal communication from Sandy Grant).

65. Tshekedi met with Rey on 27 and 28 October 1930 to try and compose their differences. He was attended by six supporters. Apart from their disagreement over the status and treatment of the Basarwa, they discussed the matter of Quarantine Regulations, the BSA Co Mining Concession, financing of water suppliers in Serowe, and Oratile's case against Tshekedi. The transcript of their

Editorial Notes for pages 47 to 51

interview covers 50 pages. (BNA Bamangwato Tribal Administration C/3/627 — R-R 41, Minutes of meeting of 27 and 28 October 1930 at Mafeking).

66. Solomon Tshekisho Plaatje (1875-1932) was one of the most distinguished South Africans of his day: journalist, novelist, translator and linguist, he was an important figure in early Black nationalist politics in South Africa. He was founding Secretary of what eventually became the African National Congress and led opposition to the segregationist Natives Land Act of Smuts and Botha passed in 1913. See the biography by Brian Willan, *Sol Plaatje: South African Nationalist 1876-1932* (London: Heinemann, 1984).

67. Rey refers here to Dr Sebophiwa Molema, who graduated from Edinburgh University as a physician, and was brother of the more famous Dr Silas Modiri Molema, who graduated as a physician from Glasgow University. Dr Silas Molema became active in South African black politics, and was a historian of his people, publishing *Bantu Past and Present* in 1922. He died in 1965, while Sebophiwa was still living near Lobatse in 1986.

68. Henry James Edward Dumbrell (born 1885) was educated at St John's, Leatherhead in England, and after teaching in Huddersfield went out to South Africa to teach in Natal. There he eventually became Inspector of Schools in 1920. He then transferred to Swaziland, where he was appointed Inspector of Education for both Swaziland and the Bechuanaland Protectorate in 1928, but soon chose to live in and devote himself exclusively to the B.P. In 1935 he became the first Director of Education of the Bechuanaland Protectorate. He retired in 1945, having been awarded the O.B.E., and died at Pietermaritzburg in the 1970s.

69. Alfred John Haile, the son of a missionary in Madagascar born in 1888, was Principal of the (Arthington) Native Institution at Tiger Kloof in South Africa. His sister was a nurse at Serowe from the 1930s to the 1950s. Rey and other officials of the British Administration characteristically regarded the LMS missionaries with some disdain as non-conformists of lower middle class or even working class origin come to make good in the Colonies.

70. On 19 October 1930 eight Bangwato sent a petition to the Resident Commissioner complaining against what they alleged was oppressive rule by Tshekedi. The Resident Magistrate, Serowe, conducted an enquiry into the whole affair. He judged that the signatories were 'all people who can be classed as agitators' and that their petition originated from resentment at being called upon to undertake regimental labour on the new dam at Serowe. On the other hand he considered Tshekedi showed himself 'in his worst form in the course of this Enquiry. He has shewn all his bad features which is a pity because the Petitioners were able to score heavily'. Nevertheless he did not consider that the evidence presented by them warranted replacing Tshekedi as Chief. (BNA S 173/2-11, 'Tshekedi, Chief: Petition against: by certain members of the Bamangwato Tribe'.)

71. Rey was convinced that Tshekedi had been browbeating the Bangwato into opposition to mining in their Reserve. So he went personally to Serowe to tell them about the advantages mining would bring them and the consequences of embarking on legal proceedings against the BSA Co. Only three young men, however, spoke in favour of mining. Tshekedi ended the proceedings according to Rey not only attacking mining but all forms of European penetration. (*Correspondence relating to the Territories administered by the High Commissioner for South Africa* 20285/2, Rey to Athlone, 24 November 1930).

72. Finally the issue was resolved by the Company giving up rights in these lands in return for the Government's agreement to give some Crown Lands to the Bangwato in the North in compensation for the land in the Bamangwato reserve that the Company would be using for mining. Thus the Batlokwa were secured on their homeland.

73. Unfortunately we have been unable to track down data on the life of Wolfe (or Wolff) Davis.

74. Tshekedi's own view of the conditions in which miners worked was very different from that of Rey. As he told Lord Passfield in his interview with him: 'when I visted the Johannesburg mines, I felt more afraid than ever of having mines in my own country'. He also told him the miners' wages were inadequate. 'The money they earn at the mines they spend in food'. (BNA S63/9, 'Transcripts of Tshekedi Khama's interviews with Lord Passfield: Interview of 27th March 1930').

75. The Chiefs concerned were Seboko of the Bamalete, Bathoen of the Bangwaketse, Molefi of the Bakgatla. Nettelton, the Resident Magistrate, believed their objective was to draft a petition to call for the removal of Rey. Sebele of the Bakwena was also expected but it is not clear whether he did or did not participate. It seems that Rey was right and that Nettelton was over-reacting. (BNA S 173/2 Nettelton to Government Secretary and to Rey, 29 October 1930.)

76. There is no known record of Isang in this position. But Isang frequently impressed his ability on a new official at first meeting, subsequently losing the advantage as the official began to see him in more jaundiced light.

77. Gobuamang (1845-1940) became Regent of the Mmanaana-Bakgatla in 1889-1910 and then Kgosi

Editorial Notes for pages 51 to 56

in 1916. From the beginning he was antagonistic to Kanye to whom he and his people were administratively subordinate. This came to a climax in the 1930s because of Bathoen II's levy on the Mmanaana-Bakgatla for the Seventh Day Adventist Medical Mission. Guobamang on behalf of his people refused to pay the levy. Rey himself refused to allow the levy, but Cuzen his Resident Magistrate at Kanye allowed Bathoen II to go ahead with it. Hence the dispute. Rey himself did not realise that Cuzen had in fact allowed the levy. Cuzen supposed Guobamang's grandson, Philemon Dikgang Kabosetso Mosielele (still alive, 1986), to be a Communist because he had been to Adams College in Natal, coming back with a Junior Certificate. This Cuzen confused with going to Cape Town and becoming a Communist. He subsequently became a loyal colonial clerk. (We are grateful to Jeff Ramsay for the information on which this note is based.)

78. Orthography was always a contentious issue as far as African languages were concerned, not least Setswana, because it involved standardising the form of the language on the basis of a particular dialect and in relation to a common orthography with other Bantu languages. The competing 'standard' dialects were Setlhaping backed by the LMS, Serolong backed by the Wesleyans, and Sehurutshe backed by the Lutherans. There were the further complications of Setswana's close relationship with Sesotho, which was backed by the French Protestants, and the influence of the South African Native Affairs Department under whose jurisdiction the bulk of the Setswana-speaking peoples lived. In the eventual imposition of the 1937 orthography they were the dominant influences anxious to adopt a uniform orthography for the Sotho-Pedi-Tswana language group. The 1937 orthography was an unsatisfactory compromise which has only been slightly modified since, and has resulted in official Setswana usage in Botswana insufficiently reflecting the language as spoken within its frontiers.
79. 'Fat Albert' was the nickname originally given to a Hollywood star of the silent screen and was subsequently taken by various figures in the entertainment world.
80. For a full discussion of the dispute between Rey and the British administration on the one hand and Tshekedi and the Bangwato on the other over the issue of mining see Michael Crowder, 'Resistance and accommodation to the penetration of the capitalist economy in Southern Africa: Tshekedi Khama and mining in Botswana, 1929-1959', paper presented to the Botswana Society, Gaborone, 1984.

Notes for 1931

1. Evelyn Baring (1903-73) was destined to become British High Commissioner in South Africa from 1944 to 1951 and presided over the affairs of the Bechuanaland Protectorate at the most troubled period of its history: the crisis over the marriage of Seretse Khama to an English woman, Ruth Williams. He, more than any one else in the British administration, was responsible for the exile of Seretse in the face of South African pressure to prevent the installation of a chief married to a white woman in a neighbouring territory, which one day they hoped to take over. After leaving South Africa, Baring became Governor of Kenya. He had previously been Governor of Southern Rhodesia (1942-1944). He retired in 1959. He was knighted in 1942 and raised to the peerage in 1960 as Baron Howick of Glendale.
2. This refers to a case in which some Bangwato seized three Basarwa from a cattle post outside the Bamangwato Reserve and beat them so severely that one died. Rey and Tshekedi had a long-running dispute over the position of the Basarwa. Rey considered that they were little better than slaves of wealthy cattle owners who used them as herders without pay. See Suzanne Miers and Michael Crowder, 'The Politics of Slavery in Bechuanaland: Power Struggles and the Plight of the Basarwa in the Bamangwato Reserve, 1926-1940' in Suzanne Miers and Richard Roberts eds. *The End of Slavery in Africa* (Madison: University of Wisconsin Press, 1987).
3. The enquiry was conducted by Edward Samuel Bourn Tagart (1877-1956), former Secretary for Native Affairs in Northern Rhodesia, and published as *Report on the Conditions existing among the Masarwa in the Bamangwato Reserve of the Bechuanaland Protectorate and Certain Matters pertaining to the Natives living therein*. (Pretoria: Government Printer, 1933). Tagart was son-in-law of Sir Herbert Sloley, of the Basutoland Administration, who had conducted previous judicial enquiries in Bechuanaland.
4. The despatch in question is to be found in BNA S204/4, Rey to High Commissioner, 3rd February, 1931.
5. Even at this late date, after the position of Secretary of State for the Dominions was taken over by J.H. Thomas from Lord Passfield, who had held it jointly with his other office of Secretary of State for the Colonies, Rey still seems to have been confused as to who his ultimate master was.

Editorial Notes for pages 56 to 74

6. Headmen were drawn from the local community, and so were often not from the ruling clan of a Tswana state — the Bangwaketse in this case. However by 1948 Kokong had a Mongwaketse headman named Radikoro Moletshane.
7. Simon Kooper's Nama (probably called Khara-gei-khoin) crossed from German South West Africa during 1905 for refuge after the German-Nama War or Witbooi rebellion of 1904-5, and scattered as far as Lokgwabe near Lehututu and Tshane.
8. The Bechuanaland Protectorate Police are said to have acquired their camels from German South West Africa. There is also a tradition that the Cape Police acquired the first camels from a circus at Cape Town before 1900. Four-wheel drive vehicles finally replaced camels in the 1960s-70s, and today camels roam and breed semi-wild around Tshabong.
9. This is one of Rey's stock stories, told on his retirement in *The Star* (Johannesburg) and *Cape Argus* (Cape Town) of 23 September 1937, and in his Autobiography (chapters in Botswana Society, Rey Papers).
10. Tshekedi wrote to the Resident Commissioner as a result of this meeting: 'I have recently heard rumours and continue to hear rumours much to my surprise that during the recent joint visit of all the Protectorate Chiefs to Mafeking I behaved badly towards the Resident Commissioner . . . If these rumours have in fact got any foundation, why has your servant not been notified'. To this Rey replied: ' . . . I feel bound to say since you ask me that your demeanour, in the presence of the other Chiefs, at the meeting of the 2nd March in my opinion and in that of my officers who were with me left much to be desired, in particular, the fact that you went out of the room at the close of the meeting without any sign of respect.'
11. See Leroy Vail, 'The making of an imperial slum: Nyasaland and its railways, 1895-1935', *Journal of African History*, Vol. 16, 1976. pp. 89-112.
12. Dr Eric Arthur Nobbs. Born St Petersburg, Russia, in 1877. Educated in Germany and Scotland. Emigrated to South Africa 1900; Director of Agriculture in Southern Rhodesia 1908-1925. Thereafter consultant on animal husbandry in Africa. Died 1956.
13. Sir Herbert Stanley (1872-1955) was Resident Commissioner for Northern and Southern Rhodesia (1915-1918), Imperial Secretary in South Africa (1918-24), Governor of Northern Rhodesia (1924-27) and Governor of Ceylon (1927-31) before becoming British High Commissioner in South Africa. In 1935 he left South Africa to take up office as Governor of Southern Rhodesia. He retired in 1942.
14. The 'man' in question was E.S.B. Tagart. See note 3 above.
15. Tshekedi eventually agreed to mining operations in his Reserve in exchange for Crown Lands which would compensate him for any land alienated within his reserve as a result. For full details of Tshekedi's initial opposition to mining in this reserve see Michael Crowder, 'Tshekedi Khama and mining in Botswana, 1929-1959' in Alan Mabin ed. 'Organisation and Economic Change', *Southern African Studies*, vol. 5 (Johannesburg: Ravan Press, forthcoming).
16. *Bogwera* was the traditional Setswana initiation school for male adolescents, lasting a few months, at which initiates learnt the arts and secrets of adulthood — and were circumcised as the mark of their initiation. Each school then formed a *mophato* or age-regiment for life.
17. *Bojale* was the female adolescent school equivalent to *bogwera*. However there was no equivalent to male circumcision, except possibly a brand mark on the inside of the thigh.
18. These were eventually issued as Proclamations nos 74 and 75 of 1934 in January 1935.
19. Rey is referring to Ramsay MacDonald's second Labour Government. Stanley Baldwin was then leader of the Conservative Opposition. The Government was to collapse in August 1931, giving way to a Coalition or 'National Government'.
20. Rey really did write 'cucumbers' for 'concubines'.
21. Lotlamoreng (Letlamoreng), Chief of the Barolong at Mafeking (Mafikeng), came to the throne in 1919 and reigned until his death in 1954. The Barolong were divided between a Reserve in the Union of South Africa and the so-called Barolong Farms in the Bechuanaland Protectorate, but remained under a single Chief until after Botswana's independence.
22. The Scout Movement was racially segregated at this time between Scouts and Guides for whites, and Pathfinders and Wayfarers for blacks. Pathfinders and Wayfarers had been founded in the Northern Transvaal in 1922, and spread to 'native' areas such as Bechuanaland.

    The Life Brigade — under missionary rather than official patronage — was an alternative youth movement, founded as the Boys Brigade by William Alexander Smith in Scotland in 1883 for 'the advancement of Christ's Kingdom among Boys'.
23. The town of Molepolole had been founded on a hill, above the cave of Lepolole, in 1864. In 1900 the town was moved to a new site called Borakalalo, on the plain to the north of the hill. However, after his accession in 1911, Chief Kealeboga (Sechele II) moved back to the hill site known as

Editorial Notes for pages 74 to 78

Ntsweng, to separate himself from the political faction grouped around the London Missionary Society at Borakalalo. Most Bakwena followed him, and his son Sebele II (ruled 1918-31) stayed on there despite frequent attempts by the B.P. administration to get him and the people to move back to the plain. The stay on the hill became a matter of honour and of resistance to colonial dictation, as well as reflecting continuing factionalism among the Bakwena with so many royal uncles based at Borakalalo while the commoners stayed at Ntsweng. (See chapter by Jefferson Ramsay in forthcoming work, provisionally entitled *Birth of a Nation: the Making of Botswana*, edited by Ramsay and Fred Morton, to be published by Longman Botswana).

24. Kgari Sechele was a younger brother of Sebele II, chosen over an elder brother by the British to be Chief in place of Sebele II. Though he was to reign for three decades, Kgari Sechele lacked legitimacy in the eyes of his people, and there was no solution to the chronic factionalism of Bakwena politics.

25. Formal voting in Kgotla by raising of hands has been, and still is, rare. The consensus politics of the Batswana are traditionally based on the summing up of debate in Kgotla by the Kgosi (King or Chief) as president of the assembly.

26. Martinus Seboni (c.1900-63), well-educated son of a Headman at Molepolole, acted as Sebele II's secretary 1918-23, and then as a senior tax collector from 1926 to the 1940s — also sitting on the Native Advisory Council. Father of Professor Michael O. Martinus Seboni of Fort Hare University, and of Well-beloved ('Welly') Seboni, a populist politician and prominent businessman after independence.

27. The 'national office' was the only building that was not razed to the ground at Ntsweng (Molepolole Hill), because Phetego the mother of Sebele II and Kgari Sechele remained in it and refused to move.

28. When the British South Africa Company began to sell off farms to white settlers in the Gaberones Block in 1905, it was agreed not to disturb the Batlokwa from their land around Moshaweng (i.e. Tlokweng) until their obviously ancient Chief Gaborone (born c.1820) died. But when he eventually died in 1932 the Batlokwa had established effective occupation, and their land was then recognised as a native Reserve in 1933.

29. Rey is referring here to William Ballinger and Margaret Hodgson who wrote a series of eight very critical articles on the Bechuanaland Protectorate as a result of their visit which were published in the Johannesburg *Star* between 21 August and 3 September 1931, as from a 'Special Correspondent'. (See note 59 for 1930).

30. The Tuli Block is named after Fort Tuli at its northern end — the only part of Southern Rhodesia (Zimbabwe) south of the Shashe River, enclosed by a half circle of ten-mile radius and demarcated in 1899. The Tuli Block, up to twelve miles wide, ran along the western bank of the Limpopo for almost 350 miles. It had been ceded by Khama III of the Bangwato in 1895 to the British Crown, which then donated it to the British South Africa Company. It was sold off for white farms after 1905. Palla Ranch is named after Palla Camp, where German hunters shot *phala* (impala) in the last century.

31. Archibald John Morton Stuart was the second son of the 17th Earl of Moray (created 1561). After retiring from the Royal Navy he took up farming in the Tuli Block, returning to England in 1943 when he succeeded as 19th Earl of Moray. He died in 1974.

32. Benjamin 'Matebele' Wilson (1861-1959). Born in Cumberland, England, he emigrated to Kimberley in South Africa, and joined the Warren Expedition into Bechuanaland 1884-1885. He adventured as far as the Makgadikgadi salt pans and Bulawayo by 1888, and became an early Rhodesian settler, but eventually retired to Cape Town.

33. Jousse had succeeded in getting the Government to close down Khama's trading venture, which had threatened the commercial interests of the British South Africa Company group — for whose Limpopo Ranching Company Jousse continued to work. See Q.N. Parsons, 'Khama & Co. and the Jousse trouble, 1910-1916', *Journal of African History*, 1975, pp. 383-408.

34. Russell England was, despite his name, said to be of Polish origin. He was Chief Agricultural Officer of the Bechuanaland Protectorate. On retirement he established his own ranch and became Bechuanaland's 'Roy Welensky' or white settler leader — Chairman of both the European Advisory Council and the Joint Advisory Council. He was knighted in 1965, and was murdered in 1970.

35. Presumably Rey is referring to Headman Gaofetoge Mathiba of Magodu Kgotla, the former Chief Hut Tax Collector who was a member of the Bangwato royal family.

36. See note 15 above. Tshekedi was assiduous in inspecting the land that the Administration proposed to give the Bangwato in return for their agreeing to mining being undertaken in their territory.

37. Madge Page-Wood, sister of Gerald Nettelton, was married to 'Kissie' Page-Wood, a Serowe trader. A formidable woman, she supplied the South African press with news about the Bangwato

from the 1930s to the 1950s, and ran a boarding house for visiting whites.
38. Far from being Rey's idea, the dam was built at Tshekedi's insistence with the money Rey had originally wanted to use for a borehole. See Michael Crowder, 'Tshekedi Khama and opposition to the British administration of the Bechuanaland Protectorate, 1926–1936' *Journal of African History*, vol. 26 (1985) pp. 200–1.
39. See J.L.S. Jeffares, *Report on Rhodesia-Walvis Bay (Railway) Reconnaissance Survey* (Salisbury, Southern Rhodesia: Government Printer, Presented to Legislative Assembly, 1932). 65 pp + numerous plates and maps.
40. The Barolong of Samuel Moroka left their Barolong-baga-Seleka relatives at Thaba Nchu in the Orange Free State in 1884, being banished to Basutoland and then trekking to Tati District in Bechuanaland in 1898. The Tati Concessions Ltd. looked to the Barolong at Matsiloje (Madzilobge) to provide farm labour for white settler farms. More Barolong from Thaba Nchu, forced out by the Natives Land Act of 1913 in South Africa, joined Samuel Moroka in 1915–18.
41. See I. Schapera, 'The Native Land Problem in the Tati District', *Botswana Notes and Records*, Vol. 3 (1971), pp. 219–68.
42. John David Rheinallt Jones was born in Wales in 1884 and settled in Cape Town in 1905. In 1910 he married Edith Barton, and together they moved to Johannesburg in 1918. There he became Secretary of the Witwatersrand Council of Education and played a major part in the founding of the University of Witwatersrand, of which he became successively Assistant Registrar and Lecturer. He was also instrumental in the development of the Joint Councils of Europeans and Africans in Johannesburg and their spread to other parts of South Africa. In 1929 he was appointed Adviser on Race Relations to the newly formed South African Institute of Race Relations, while his wife became organiser of the women's section. He subsequently became Director of the Institute, a post he held until 1950, when he became its President. When they met Rey, he was Chairman of the Council of the Pathfinder Scouts, while his wife headed the Wayfarer Guides. Edith Rheinallt Jones died in 1934. J.D. Rheinallt Jones sat in the South African Parliament as Senator representing the Africans of the Transvaal and Orange Free State from 1937 to 1942. He founded and edited the scholarly journal at first known as *Bantu Studies* and later as *African Studies*. But he was never technically a Professor as Rey described him. He died in 1953, leaving his papers to the University of the Witwatersrand.
43. Moanaphuti Segolodi was an early supporter of Tshekedi but became disaffected over the question of tribal labour as a result of being flogged in 1930 for failure to fulfil his own regimental obligations. Thereafter he became an ardent opponent of Tshekedi, supplying the Ballingers with all the 'dirt' he could on Tshekedi's administration. See BNA S, 128/4 and S, 165/10.
44. Admiral Hugh Tweedie was Vice Admiral and Commander-in-Chief of the South African station from 1931 to 1933. He was promoted Admiral in 1935 and knighted. He retired the following year. One daughter, Mona, married Professor W.M. Macmillan. See note 54.
45. Sir Charles George 'Bongola' Smith (1858–1941). Born in London and sent to Natal as a child. He founded his own firm of sugar and cattle agents in 1888, extending into meat cold storage after 1902. He also developed interests in coal and gold mining, and in shipping, extending all over Southern Africa. See Michael Hubbard, 'Desperate games: Bongola Smith, the Imperial Cold Storage Company and Bechuanaland's Beef, 1931', *Botswana Notes and Records*, vol. 13 (1981), pp. 19–24.
46. Patrick Duncan (1870–1943), a barrister and Advocate of the Supreme Court of South Africa, was sometime President of the Special Court of the Bechuanaland Protectorate — and no friend of Tshekedi's, since he allowed the Ratshosas' claim for damage for having their houses burnt down following their attempt to assassinate Tshekedi in April 1926. While the Resident Magistrate's Court had held that Tshekedi had had the right to punish the Ratshosas for what amounted to treason in this way, Duncan awarded them damages. Tshekedi subsequently had Duncan's verdict overturned by the Judicial Committee of the Privy Council in 1930. Duncan went on to become the first native-born Governor-General of South Africa in 1937, which post he held until his death. He had previously served as a Minister under Smuts in 1921–24, and under Hertzog in his Fusion Government in 1933–36.
47. The South Africa Party (SAP) was the governing party of the Union of South Africa in 1910–24, at first under Louis Botha and then under Jan Smuts after 1919. It absorbed the predominantly 'English' Unionist Party in 1920, and returned to power in 1934 by uniting with the National Party in the United Party in the so-called Fusion Government — with Hertzog as prime minister and Smuts as his deputy. This resulted in Afrikaner nationalists and 'English' imperialists breaking away to form the new (Purified) National Party and the Dominion Party. (Cf. note 17 for 1936).
48. The Witwatersrand Chamber of Mines had two recruiting bureaux for African labour — the N.R.C. (Native Recruiting Corporation, for the Union, Basutoland and Swaziland, and Southern

Editorial Notes for pages 85 to 93

Bechuanaland) and 'Wenela' (Witwatersrand Native Labour Association). Between 1913 and 1923 'Wenela' recruiting stations were restricted to southern Mozambique. But much Witwatersrand mine labour came indirectly from further north, particularly from Nyasaland, and 'Wenela' looked forward to direct recruiting in the 'tropics'. This became imperative in the gold boom after 1932-33, when Witwatersrand gold mining could be indefinitely expanded with a guaranteed world gold price. But this expansion was blocked by the protectionism of Southern and Northern Rhodesian mines over the 'tropical' labour pool. Hence Northern Bechuanaland was seen as the key to unlocking Witwatersrand labour supplies to the north. By establishing recruiting stations at Francistown (main depot), Kasane, and Shakawe in Northern Bechuanaland, 'Wenela' could draw Southern Rhodesian, Northern Rhodesian and Angolan labour across borders, and thereby establish a strong bargaining counter for the negotiation with Southern Rhodesia and for access to Nyasaland and Tanganyika labour. Hence, even in 1931, Bill Gemmil of 'Wenela' had good reason to cultivate Rey's friendship, and his plans bore fruit in 1936 when his Bechuanaland stations opened and he moved his headquarters to Salisbury. (We are grateful to Alan Jeeves for making this clear at the African Studies Association, New Orleans, November 1985).

49. Samuel Weil (1862-1944), London-born Mafeking trader with many Bechuanaland and Southern Rhodesian trading interests, made his name and fortune during the famous siege of 1899-1900. He also developed interests in Southern Rhodesian mining and South African cold storage.

50. The old gallows were in the open at Hangman's Rock outside the Gaberones Goal. The new gallows were erected near the old fort (now next to water-tower and clinic).

51. Sir James Crawford Maxwell (1869-1932) graduated from Edinburgh University, and became a District Medical Officer in 1897 and then a District Commissioner in 1900 in Sierra Leone. He rose through the colonial administrations of Nigeria, Sierra Leone and the Gold Coast, until appointed Governor of Northern Rhodesia in 1927-32. Regarded as a follower of Lord Lugard, he tried to introduce to Southern Africa the West Coast colonial principles of Indirect Rule.

52. Tshekedi did not in fact sign the final agreement until March 22nd 1932. Rey's so-called victory was a somewhat Pyrrhic one since two years later the British South Africa Company abandoned the concession without having even located any mineral deposits they considered worthy of exploitation. See Crowder 'Tshekedi Khama and Mining'.

53. Tshekedi had followed Khama III and Sekgoma II in refusing previously to attend the Native Advisory Council. Khama III had refused to have anything to do with the Council from the time of its formation in 1919 as he saw the Council as incompatible with Ngwato custom since their representatives on the Council could make no decisions without first referring them back to the Kgotla. Tshekedi agreed to participate as an observer in 1931, presumably because the matter of the Native Proclamations was so crucial and he saw this as a forum in which he could rally his fellow Chiefs in opposition against them. See BNA S420/12 and Crowder, 'Tshekedi Khama's Opposition', p. 201.

54. Professor W.M. Macmillan was born in Aberdeen in 1874, but was brought up in South Africa where he became Professor of History at the University of Witwatersrand in 1917. His writings on the history, politics, social structure and economics of South Africa are still influential today. In 1934 he returned to Britain and eventually became Director of Colonial Studies at St Andrews University. He was a powerful advocate of colonial reform and his *Warning from the West Indies* published in 1936 was instrumental in the decision to give aid to the colonies in the form of the Colonial Development and Welfare Act of 1940. Macmillan returned to the Bechuanaland Protectorate in 1951 in the wake of the crisis over Seretse Khama's marriage to Ruth Williams. He went as a member of the ill-starred team of three observers sent out by the British Government to find out whether the Bangwato would agree to Tshekedi returning from exile to their Reserve as a private citizen. See Michael Crowder, 'Professor Macmillan goes on safari: the British government observer team and the crisis over the Seretse Khama marriage, 1951', in Hugh Macmillan with Shula Marks, eds. *Africa and Empire: W.M. Macmillan, historian and social critic* (Institute of Commonwealth Studies, London, in press).

55. The Reys were in the habit of visiting the Gubbins farm at Ottoshoop near Mafeking (see entries for 21 April and 13 to 19 October 1930). John Gaspard Gubbins (1877-1935) was an Englishman who had become a lawyer and then a farmer in the Transvaal, settling on the road between Zeerust and Mafeking. His interest in local history was sparked by his discovery near his farm of the grave of the first white woman to have died in the Transvaal (Mrs Jane Wilson, a Congregational missionary wife). His library became the basis of the Africana collection of the University of Witwatersrand, and he also founded the Africana Museum at Johannesburg. Among other things, the Christmas 1931 library fire at 'Wits' destroyed the papers of Dr John Philip (1775-1951) upon which Professor W.M. Macmillan had been working.

Editorial Notes for pages 94 to 103

Notes for 1932

1. For Kasane medicinal hot-spring see Botswana National Archives, File S.257/6. Schemes to erect a spa hotel, by Lonrho and others, did not materialise in 1945-47. The hot-springs lie between the Chobe River and the Kasane-Kazungula road, near the Chobe Brigades Centre.
2. The interview took place on 28 January and among the matters discussed by Tshekedi and Rey were land, problems relating to his half-sister, Baboni, and the case of Headman John Mswazi and his people who had rejected Tshekedi's authority. In a despatch on the interview to the High Commissioner Rey 'dwelt on the attitude of the Chief and the difficulties experienced in dealing with him'. (BNA S263/3, Rey to High Commissioner, 15 February 1932 referring to his despatch of 2 February).
3. Rey's confused geography of the Okavango area can be seen from any map.
4. Queen Mary had the reputation of being notoriously acquisitive, expecting to be given anything she admired, even when being entertained in a private house. It is said that hostesses hid objects that were likely to be admired by her.
5. Leopold Stennet Amery (1873-1955) was born in India, the son of a British forester. After a brief stint as a Member of Parliament, he joined the staff of *The Times* of London in 1899-1909, being seconded to South Africa in 1899-1900 where he came under the influence of Lord Milner — and subsequently compiled the seven volume *Times History of the South African War*. From 1911 to 1945 he represented various Birmingham constituencies as a Conservative Member of Parliament, becoming Assistant Secretary and then Secretary of State for the Colonies (1919-21 and 1924-29), adding the Dominions as a separate portfolio in 1925-29.
6. Sydney Charles, Earl Buxton (1853-1934) joined the London School Board after graduating from Cambridge University, in 1876. He then sat as a Liberal Member of Parliament from 1882 until 1914, rising through Assistant Secretary for the Colonies to President of the Board of Trade. He then became the British High Commissioner in South Africa 1914-20.
7. Sir Ernest Oppenheimer was born in Friedberg, Germany, in 1880. In 1896 he went to London to work for a diamond firm, and was sent to South Africa in 1902 as its representative. By 1917 he had established his own company, the Anglo-American Corporation, which in 1919 took over control of the diamond fields of South West Africa. In 1926 he joined the board of De Beers and in 1929 became its Chairman. Thereafter he played an important role in combating the depression in the diamond industry and in 1934 formed the Diamond Producer's Association and the Diamond Trading Company which effectively constituted a monopoly. He also played a major role in the South African gold industry and undertook major exploration and opening up of gold fields in the Orange Free State which reaped great reward when South Africa came off the gold standard in 1932. He was a close friend of Smuts, and represented Kimberley in the South African House of Assembly from 1924 to 1928. He died in 1945.
8. Sir George Albu was born in Berlin in 1857 and went out to South Africa in 1876 where he eventually became Chairman and Managing Director of the General Mining and Finance Corporation of Johannesburg. He was created a baronet in 1912 and died in 1935.
9. Colonel Sir William Dalrymple was born in 1864 and arrived in Johannesburg in 1888. He became Director of a number of mining companies, and was elected Vice-President of the Chamber of Mines on a number of occasions from 1899 to 1932. He was knighted in 1920 and became Chairman of Council of the University of the Witwatersrand.
10. John Martin was born in Scotland in 1884 and went out to South Africa in his mid-twenties to manage the *Bloemfontein Post*. By 1922 he had become Chairman and managing director of the Argus Printing and Publishing Company. Thereafter his interests switched to mining and despite his lack of experience he was very successful in the industry becoming on several occasions President of the Transvaal Chamber of Mines. He was a close friend of Smuts and during the Second World War was seen as a Cabinet Minister in all but name. He died in 1949.
11. Rey is referring to the 13th Session of the Native Advisory Council, which met at Mafeking on 31 March. No doubt its brevity was in part due to the absence of Tshekedi Khama.
12. The relationship between the Mmanaana and Kgafela branches of the Bakgatla is in fact rather remote and unclear: the split dates back two or three centuries.
13. Sir Philip Cunliffe-Lister, later Earl of Swinton, was Secretary of State for the Colonies 1931-35, and later went to West Africa as a resident Cabinet Minister (1942-44). Swinton later became Secretary of State for Commonwealth Relations (1952-55) and resigned as a Conservative Minister over the Suez Crisis in 1956.
14. Sir Alan Pim started his career as a British Indian civil servant in 1895. After retiring in 1930 he was

Editorial Notes for pages 103 to 111

asked to head Commissions of Inquiry into the finances of Swaziland and Zanzibar, and then into the Bechuanaland Protectorate (1932–33), Basutoland and British Honduras. In 1936 he headed a Commission of Inquiry into the Finances of Kenya, and in 1937 was appointed Financial and Economic Commissioner for Northern Rohdesia. The report he produced on the Bechuanaland Protectorate supported Rey's contention that the powers of the Chiefs needed defining. He published a number of books on Africa's economic problems. He died in 1958.

15. Stanley Langton, son of the Clerk to the Court of the Assistant Commissioner at Francistown. He burnt down the Resident Magistrate's Office at Kanye in order to destroy evidence of his embezzling of funds. His other 'beastly' crime was pornography. He habitually took photographs of naked women with the so-called Hottentot Apron (*labia minora* distended in childhood play). Langton continued to be a thorn in Rey's side in prison, complaining to the Dominions Office about poor diet, etc. (We are grateful to Professor Schapera for this information. Also see Sander L. Gilman, 'Black bodies, white bodies: towards an iconography of female sexuality in late nineteenth century art, medicine and literature', *Critical Inquiry* (Chicago), vol. 12, no. 1. 1985, pp. 204–242); Isaac Schapera, *The Khoisan Peoples of South Africa* (London, 1930) p. 55.

16. The Ottawa Conference of 1932 was held at the suggestion of the Prime Minister of Canada and brought together all countries of the Commonwealth. It met in the context of the world depression in trade and sought to increase trade among the countries of the Commonwealth as well as the British Colonies, which were represented by the British Government at the Conference. The Conference led to a series of agreements — eleven in all — one of which concerned South Africa on the one hand and the United Kingdom and the Colonies on the other. The United Kingdom and Colonies would give preference to some South African products, mainly agricultural, while South Africa would give preference to a large variety of manufactured products, an arrangement that benefitted industrial Britain though it had few advantages for the colonies.

17. Alfred (Lord) Milner, born in Bonn in 1852, became a journalist after education in Germany and England. He entered British government service in Egypt and made his mark as a brilliant administrator, moving to South Africa as Governor of Cape Colony and High Commissioner in 1897. Having provoked the Boer republics into war, he became Governor of the Transvaal and Orange River Colonies after their defeat and presided over the 'reconstruction' of South Africa until 1905 — assisted by the young administrators known to history as Milner's Kindergarten. After service in the War Cabinet during the First World War, and a brief stint as Colonial Secretary, he died in 1925.

18. The Gasetshware conspiracy was an attempt by a faction of the Bangwato to place Gasetshware as Kgosi in place of Seretse during the Regency of Tshekedi. Gasetshware was an older half-brother of Seretse, born to the sister of Sekgoma II's second wife. The conspirators, led by relatives of Khama III's first wife and of Khama's brother Kgamane, failed to place the Pretender on the Throne — and he was imprisoned for sedition and then exiled to Molepolole.

19. Frank G. Lee (born 1903) was a Secretary to the Commission on the Financial and Economic Position of the Bechuanaland Protectorate headed by Sir Alan Pim. He was a career Colonial Office civil servant who also served in the Dominions Office.

20. Samuel Milligan (1874–1954) was a British Indian Civil Servant who became Director of Agriculture for Bengal and in 1920 Agricultural Adviser to the Government of India. He retired in 1926 and became representative in South Africa of the Empire Cotton Growing Association. His role on the Pim Commission was as an agricultural and economic adviser. He also accompanied Pim on his Commissions in Swaziland, Kenya and Northern Rhodesia.

21. The Proclamations sought to limit and regulate both the administrative and judicial powers of the Chiefs. They were much resented by Tshekedi and the other Chiefs not only because they limited their powers but because they conflicted with traditional law and custom in particular with regard to the judicial reforms proposed by Rey. Here Tribunals were to replace the Kgotla, in which every adult male had the right to participate, as the means of dispensing justice. (See Crowder, 'Tshekedi Khama's Opposition').

22. Fourteenth Session of the Native Advisory Council, Mafeking 18 November 1932. Tshekedi's so-called rambling speech was in fact designed to delay discussion and therefore eventual implementation of the Proclamations. Members of the Council had just been presented with the reactions of the various Tribes to the draft Proclamations and Tshekedi argued that they had not had sufficient time to study them. (See Crowder, *ibid*. pp. 206–7).

23. Dingaan's Day (December 16) commemorated the defeat of a Zulu army by a Boer army in 1838 — Dingane having been the Zulu King, who did not take part in the battle. The day became a holy day, called the Day of the Covenant, among Afrikaner nationalists — and is now marked as a day of mourning among African nationalists.

24. Sir Basil Blackett (1882–1935) was a senior civil servant in the British Treasury who was Controller

252

Editorial Notes for pages 111 to 123

of Finance in 1919-22. Thereafter he spent six years in India as Finance Member of the Governor-General's Executive Council. On his return to England he became a director of the Bank of England and several companies including De Beers. He was Chairman of the Colonial Development Advisory Committee established in the wake of the Colonial Development Act of 1929.

25. James Henry Thomas (1874-1949) was an active and originally popular trade unionist who was elected Labour MP for Derby in 1910. He served briefly as Colonial Secretary in 1924 under Ramsay MacDonald. He lost support within the Trade Union movement when he opposed the General Strike of 1926. In 1929 he became Lord Privy Seal and Minister of Employment in Ramsay MacDonald's second Labour government, and in 1930 Dominions Secretary. In 1931 he joined the National Government. As a result he was repudiated by the Derby Labour Party but stood successfully as an Independent in his constituency. In 1935 he became Colonial Secretary. In 1936 he had to resign because of leaking budget secrets to friends who profited from the information, though he personally made no gain. In 1937 he published his autobiography, *My Life*.

26. *Letsholo* is a traditional large gathering of all male age-regiments (*mepatho*) held in the veld (open countryside), prior to communal hunting or war, or for discussion of great events requiring mass mobilization.

27. Thielman Johannes de Villiers Roos (1879-1935) was an early supporter of Hertzog and a founder member of his National Party. In 1915 he entered parliament and was the main architect of the National Party's electoral successes in 1924 and 1929. In 1924 Hertzog made him his Deputy Prime Minister and Minister of Justice. His relations with Hertzog became increasingly strained, however, and in 1929 he retired from active politics on the grounds of ill-health. In 1931 when the United Kingdom left the gold standard, Hertzog decided not to follow, creating financial and economic difficulties. Smuts, in opposition, called for the abandonment of the gold standard, but Hertzog obdurately stuck to it. In December 1932, Roos, recently returned to politics, campaigned for a national coalition to deal with the crisis. When it seemed likely that Smuts would join such a coalition with Roos and those who supported his approach, Hertzog agreed to abandon the gold standard and formed a coalition with Smuts in order to preempt Roos. Roos was not given a seat in the 'Fusion' cabinet and in pique formed a new party which failed to establish itself.

28. The opposition South African Party (under Smuts) had surprisingly beaten the Pact (National and Labour) government's candidates in Germiston and Roodepoort by-elections on the Witwatersrand. The SAP victory had prompted Thielman Roos to enter the political fray in December 1932 (see note above). On 28 December, the Pact government announced that South Africa had abandoned the gold standard for its currency. Ironically, this led to a boom in gold production for South Africa — now that the gold price was guaranteed in American dollars without the liability of a fixed gold standard for South African currency.

Notes for 1933

1. This refers to the coalition between Hertzog's National Party and Smuts' South African Party that was eventually formed after the General Election of 1934 with Hertzog as Prime Minister of what came to be known as the Fusion Government, and Smuts as his Deputy. It lasted until 1939 when Hertzog was overthrown by Smuts over the question of South Africa's participation in the coming war against Germany. The main significance of the coalition is that it enabled Hertzog to obtain the necessary two-thirds majority required to abolish the Cape Native Franchise in 1936.

2. The first airfields in Bechuanaland were in fact cleared in 1919. Palapye Road airfield was laid out as a staging post, with fuel dump, between Bulawayo and Pretoria on the Cape-to-Cairo civilian air route. Another airfield was cleared at nearby Serowe, the Bangwato capital, and the first planes from South Africa began to land at both airfields in 1920.

3. Sergeant Ndandala was a Muslim, said to be of Swahili origin, who had joined the King's African Rifles in Nyasaland — fighting against the Ashanti on the Gold Coast (Ghana), in British Somaliland, and in German East Africa. He won the Military Medal in 1916 for saving his wounded colonel, while — despite his own wounds — fighting off the enemy with a Lewis gun. After the First World War he enlisted in the Bechuanaland Protectorate Police and rose to the rank of sergeant. In 1934, aged about sixty, he visited Johannesburg and was interviewed by *The Star* newspaper. 'When are you going to retire?', he was asked. Standing 'straight as a pikestaff' and six feet tall, with rows of ribbons and medals on his chest, he replied: 'When I die.' ('Swahili warrior in town. Served king for 42 years. Not impressed by Johannesburg', *The Star*, 14 April 1934).

4. Tradition records that the 'weapons' were large wooden knitting needles — spears having long disappeared from use in the previous century. (We are grateful to Jeff Ramsay for this detail).

Editorial Notes for pages 123 to 135

5. The colonial military belief in aircraft having a salutary 'moral' effect on African 'natives' was first demonstrated in the Royal Air Force bombing of the Sayyid Muhammad ('Mad Mullah') resistance in Somaliland in 1919-20, followed by bombing of Bondelswart Nama dog-tax resisters in South West Africa in 1922. As recently as 1966, on Botswana's Independence Day, Harvard training aircraft of the South African Air Force crossed the border to 'buzz' the centre of Mochudi — a traditional town then considered the main centre of South African refugees.
6. Colonel Naus was a Belgian who claimed rank and military experience that raised scepticism among officials other than Rey. His method of damming the Okavango to increase the north-south flow of water was abandoned as futile by the Colonial Development Fund scheme of swamp clearance, under Brind and Drotsky, in the later 1930s and 1940s. (See Forsyth-Thompson to Rey, 5 August 1961 — in RHL Mss Brit Emp s384-5/2).
7. Potts, who succeeded Nettelton as Resident Magistrate at Serowe in 1931, found Tshekedi extremely difficult to deal with. In a special report of 1932 he wrote of Tshekedi: 'After twelve months official association with him, I can only say that he is an extreme Mongwato Nationalist, a past master in the art of obstruction when it suits him' (BNA S 262/3). For his part, Tshekedi complained that Potts and other officials encouraged the Bangwato to contact them directly without reference to their Chief (Tshekedi to High Commissioner, 26 July 1933 — BNA S 343/12).
8. William Seals-Wood (1880–1933), Chairman of Lever Brothers in South Africa and President of the South African Federated Chamber of Industries.
9. Rasebolai Kgamane was Tshekedi's first cousin, and son of the one-eyed Gorewang Kgamane who had acted as Regent during the illness of Sekgoma II in 1925. Gorewang was next in line to the Chieftainship after Tshekedi, and Rasebolai succeeded to that position after his father's death. Hence when both Seretse and Tshekedi became discredited in British eyes in the Chieftainship Crisis of the early 1950s, the Conservative Government tried to get Rasebolai elected as Kgosi. This failed, and Rasebolai became 'African Authority' (later 'Tribal Authority') during the interregnum.
10. Rey later refused to compensate Rasebolai — see BNA S 323/6. (We are grateful to Joslin Landell-Mills for this point).
11. Oribi and tsessebe are both species of antelope. Their names are derived from Khoi (*ourebi*?) and Setswana (*tshesebe*) languages respectively.
12. Dom-nut (*Hyphaene crinita*) is otherwise known as 'vegetable ivory'. Mukwa (*Pterocarpus angolensis*) is a fine dark red wood suitable for furniture.
13. Bees (*Trigona* sp.), rather than flies. (Again we are grateful to Joslin Landell-Mills for this point).
14. Sir Ronald Storrs (1881–1955) was a well-known British Arabic scholar and diplomat, also amateur archaeologist, who had been Military Governor of Jerusalem and Governor of Cyprus (and thus appears in accounts of 'Lawrence of Arabia'). He hated 'exile' in Northern Rhodesia. Lady Gore-Brown referred to him as a 'swollen potato' (Robert I. Rotberg, *Black Heart: Gore-Brown and the Politics of Multi-racial Zambia*, Berkeley and Los Angeles: University of California Press, 1977, pp. 149-50). He managed to be invalided out of the service after only two years as Governor of Northern Rhodesia (1932–34), but lived on to a ripe old age in England.
15. Rey was responsible for producing the Bechuanaland Protectorate's first definitive series of its own postage stamps, rather than an overprinting of Cape Colony or South African stamps.
16. Simvula and Chika were rival chiefs of the Basubiya on the Bechuanaland side of the Chobe River, after the death of Leshwane II in 1927. Simvula's village was Munga, and Chika's village was Sehongwane. The British recognised Chika as Leshwane III, and Simvula then crossed the river into the Caprivi Strip.
17. Makuba (Bakuba) — calling themselves Bayei — were indigenous people of the Linyanti (Middle Chobe) and northern Okavango swamps, whose language was related to the Hampukushu and other upper Zambezian peoples. David Livingstone called them Africa's Quakers because of their peaceful acceptance of Basubiya and Batawana bondage. Bayei constituted the great majority of the Batawana state in Ngamiland, whose capital from 1915 was at Maun.
18. See 1931 note 43 above.
19. A wild exaggeration, rendered as twenty years on page 44 and as fifteen years in Rey's *Report on Progress and Development in the Bechuanaland Protectorate 1929 to 1937*, p. 2, and in his draft Autobiography (Botswana Society, Rey Papers & RHL, Mss Brit Emp s384-5/3.) Makalamabedi lay athwart the main road from Serowe to Maun. Rey's immediate predecessor R.M. Daniel and J. Ellenberger were anyway familiar with Ngamiland *before* they became Resident Commissioners.
20. Makala Kopo, a Mokwena, Headman of Marapane Kgotla. Rakops (properly Rra-Kopo's) was named after his father or grandfather.
21. The Damara at Rakops (or Mopipi) under Nicodemus were refugees from the German-Herero War of 1904–05 in South West Africa, accepted into the Bangwato state. Herero royals and aristocrats

Editorial Notes for pages 135 to 138

lived in exile among the Bangwato at Mahalapye. For Nicodemus and Rey, see also page 235.
22. Rethatoleng Kelesemetswe, a Mokhurutshe, Headman of Kgonwe Kgotla.
23. See 1931 note 38.
24. Tshekedi followed his father in enforcing religious and political unity under an LMS State Church. The Bakhurutshe of Tonota had immigrated into Gamangwato from the Tati Company territory. Khama had made it a condition of their settlement in his territory that the Anglican Bakhurutshe should not openly practise their faith while under this jurisdiction. Soon after Tshekedi became Regent, some Bakhurutshe were reported to be openly practising their rite in Tonota. Tshekedi ordered them to leave their lands and settle in Serowe where he could keep watch on them. Thereafter there ensued a long battle between Tshekedi on the one hand and the British Administration and the Anglican Church on the other over the question of religious freedom. Rey was technically incorrect in referring to the 'Church of England' — that title was legally appropriated by the breakaway Anglicans of Bishop Colenso in South Africa.
25. Admiral Edward Evans, later Lord Mountevans, also 'Evans of the *Broke*'. Began his naval career on Scott's Antarctic expedition. Gained fame by a buccaneering action in 1917, when he rammed his frigate the *Broke* onto a German vessel in the Straits of Dover. Rose to Admiral and Commander-in-Chief of the Africa Station of the Royal Navy at Simonstown, near Cape Town. Also acted as High Commissioner August-December 1933 during Stanley's overseas leave. Tshekedi Khama considered suing him over his autobiography *Adventurous Life* (London: Hutchinson, 1946). Cf. Reginald Pound, *Evans of the Broke: a Biography* (London: Oxford University Press, 1963), pp. 221-228; and forthcoming biography of Tshekedi Khama by Michael Crowder.
26. Tshekedi irritated Rey and other British officials by his frequent failure to follow the correct administrative procedure with regard to correspondence. Formally every letter to the Resident Commissioner had to be passed through the Resident Magistrate and any letter to the High Commissioner through both these officials. Tshekedi frequently wrote direct to the Resident Commissioner and the High Commissioner. This he did, not through ignorance of the correct procedures, but it would seem as a deliberate act of provocation. If this was so, he certainly succeeded because Rey, and to a lesser extent Potts, became infuriated whenever he ignored procedures and the Administration kept files specifically devoted to Tshekedi's habit of writing to the High Commissioner direct. When it suited him, Tshekedi could be just as much a stickler for following correct procedures, especially where it concerned his own subjects approaching the Administration direct.
27. The European in question was a young blacksmith called Phineas McIntosh who together with his friend Henry McNamee had created general mayhem in Serowe, particularly by their amatory attentions to young Bangwato women. This shocked the puritan Tshekedi as much as it did members of the white community of Serowe. Tshekedi on several occasions asked the Resident Magistrate to take action on the matter, since he was well aware that he had no jurisdiction over the whites in his territory. Successive Resident Magistrates failed to deal effectively with the young men, and after McIntosh and a young Mongwato man fought over a girlfriend, Tshekedi decided to take the law into his own hands and had him brought before his Kgotla.
28. Rey adds, 'And it will become history.' See also his 'Notes on the Serowe Incident' on pp. 264-8.
29. Sir Percivale Liesching (born 1895), scion of a South African medical family, was educated at Oxford University and served in East Africa during the First World War, proceeding to work in the Colonial Office in 1920 and the Dominions Office from 1925. In 1928 he joined the High Commissioner's Office in Canada, and between 1933 and 1935 was Political Under-Secretary to the High Commissioner in South Africa. He subsequently rose to the rank of Permanent Under-Secretary at the Commonwealth Relations Office (1945-50) and High Commissioner in South Africa (1955-58).
30. The impetuous decision for the Navy to invade the Kalahari is sometimes attributed to Evans having been dining with members of the South African Cabinet when he first received the news of the flogging of Phineas McIntosh — source: Miss Irene Fletcher, London Missionary Society c.1968.
31. Leslie Blackwell was born in Sydney, Australia, in 1955. His family went to South Africa when he was ten. He served in the British army during the South African War of 1899-1902, and entered the Union Parliament in 1915 — holding his seat there until 1943. He fought in the German East African campaign and was awarded the Military Cross. Blackwell acted as part-time Legal Adviser to the High Commissioner, and as President of the Special Court of the three High Commission Territories, until he was succeeded in 1934 by a full-time appointee, Sir Arthur Fforde (see note 20 for 1934). Blackwell was appointed to the Bench of the Transvaal Supreme Court in 1943, and on his retirement in 1953 became for two years Professor of Law at Fort Hare University College.

Editorial Notes for pages 140 to 153

32. For the background to the Enquiry and details of the Enquiry itself see the Botswana National Archives S 349 and 350 series.
33. In fact the subsequent enquiry undertaken by Mr Percivale Liesching, of the High Commissioner's Office and the Resident Commissioner, while exonerating Resident Magistrates for failing to deal with specific complaints against McIntosh and McNamee brought by Tshekedi, concluded in the words of Liesching that there was substance in the complaints lodged by the Acting Chief on the general ground that the conditions from which these specific incidents arose were a matter in which responsibility for initiating remedial action rested with the Administration, irrespective of particular complaints by the Acting Chief, and that it appears that such remedial action of the fundamental character required was not in fact taken by the Administration'. (BNA S 349/12, High Commissioner to Secretary of State, Telegram 106 of 20 September 1933).
34. Despite the rivalries within the royal family, no-one would come forward to take Tshekedi's place as Acting Chief. (BNA DCS 19/4: 'Election of Ag. Chief of the Bamangwato'. Notes taken of a meeting at the Resident Magistrate's Office, 15 September 1933).
35. Rey had in fact hoped that the flogging incident would lead to the permanent exclusion of Tshekedi from the Chieftaincy. But apart from skilfully drumming up support in Britain from press, parliament and public opinion, Tshekedi ensured his reinstatement by formally acknowledging that he had no right to try whites in his Kgotla.
36. Tshekedi actually wanted to go to Britain to take up his case with the Secretary of State, as he had earlier done in 1930 when he was trying to prevent mining operations beginning in his territory.
37. Thomas Ellis (Lord) Robins (1884-1962) was born in the U.S.A. and became the first Rhodes Scholar from Connecticut to Oxford University. He became a British subject in 1912, and subsequently rose to be President of the British South Africa Company after a military career in Rhodesia.
38. Much as Rey admired Evans, in fact the latter's precipitate action in dealing with Tshekedi was to bring widespread criticism in Britain and especially in Parliament. As a result it was also to subject the Bechuanaland Protectorate administration to unwelcome scrutiny in the British and South African press, an outcome that Tshekedi had long been hoping for.

Notes for 1934

1. The *Watussi* was eventually scuttled by its captain off Cape Point at the beginning of the Second World War, defiantly raising the Swastika flag against South African Air Force bombers.
2. Rey's geography was very confused. Andara was on the Okavango River in the Caprivi Strip (marked as Lisho's on map).
3. In the interview held by the Secretary of State for the Dominions on 16 January 1934 with a delegation from the Anti-Slavery and Aborigines Protection Society on behalf of Tshekedi, Rev Albert Jennings falsely accused the B.P. Administration of failing to circulate the draft Proclamations in Setswana. He had to apologise formally to the Secretary of State and thereby to the High Commissioner and Rey for this 'lie'. (Rev A.E. Jennings to Mr J.H. Thomas, Secretary of State for the Dominions, 18 April 1934. Copies of his letter of apology were sent to the High Commissioner and to Rey. BNA, S 358/13).
4. See BNA DCS 16/19 'Interview between High Commissioner, Tshekedi Khama, Bathoen etc. Cape Town, 22-24 February, 1934'. Most of the talking was done by Tshekedi. (See Crowder, 'Tshekedi Khama and opposition', pp. 209-10).
5. L.S. ('Lou') Glover had been an officer in the Bechuanaland battalion of the South African Native Labour Contingent in France during the First World War. He was a prominent white settler representative in the B.P. until the 1950s, as chairman of the European Advisory Council and member of the Joint Advisory Council — sporting a large hearing-aid. His farm, Broadhurst, is now the northern suburb of the city of Gaborone, the site of the farm house being marked by a stand of exotic trees on the east side of Tsholofelo Community Centre.
6. For accounts of the visit of Prince George (Duke of Kent) see F. Leslie Burch, *With Prince George through South Africa* (London: Methuen, 1934) and A.A. Frew, *Prince George's African Tour* (London: Blackie and Son, 1934).
7. Presumably the Morula trees now just north of the Debswana skyscraper, in fact a few hundred yards from the railway station.
8. Du Plessis is presumably Senator J.A. Du Plessis, former Member of Transvaal Provincial Council representing Rustenburg.
9. Rey issued his own statement, carried by *The Star* (Johannesburg), 30 April 1934 — 'Interview

with Colonel Rey. What Bechuanaland is doing. Union statements denied.'
10. The only one of Rey's bright boys to distinguish himself was Arrowsmith who after serving in the Bechuanaland Protectorate from 1932 to 1938 headed the administration of a number of smaller British colonial territories. In 1952 he became Resident Commissioner of Basutoland and in 1957 became Governor of the Falkland Islands which from 1962 to 1964 he held jointly with the post of High Commissioner of the British Antarctic Territory. He was knighted and retired to become Chairman of the Royal Commonwealth Society for the Blind for fifteen years until 1986. (Interview with Sir Edwin Arrowsmith, Gaborone, 3 April 1987).
11. Batho was a white South African, with a Cornish name that was the exact replica of the Setswana word for 'the people'. He gained notoriety in June 1952 as the District Commissioner whose 'harsh impetuous' actions led to a riot at Serowe in which three policemen were killed — the only such incident in Botswana's history.
12. Sydney Vernon Lawrenson was also a white South African, born in 1907, who joined the B.P. Police in 1933 and rose steadily through the administration to the rank of Deputy Resident Commissioner and Government Secretary in the early 1960s. Described as 'sweet and paternal' by Mary Benson (1961).
13. See G.L. Steer, *Judgement on German Africa* (London: Hodder & Stoughton, May 1939), foldout maps of airline routes in Africa.
14. The Church Railway Mission was an Anglican mission, based on Bulawayo, which served whites on the railway line in Bechuanaland. Rev. Hands is commemorated by the Lawrence Hands Memorial Hall at Mahalapye. See page 228.
15. Sir Hubert Winthrop Young (born 1885) was Governor of Nyasaland between 1932 and 1934 before becoming Governor of Northern Rhodesia until 1938. His stay in Northern Rhodesia included a famous incident when his wife, a qualified pilot, was lost in her plane and was eventually found in remote countryside. Young moved on to become Governor of Trinidad and Tobago, and died in 1950.
16. Sir William Henry Clark, born in 1876, served in India on the Viceroy's Council (1910-16), in the Board of Trade as Comptroller-General of the Department of Overseas Trade (1916-1928), and as British High Commissioner in Canada from 1928 to 1934 before taking up his appointment in South Africa. He served as High Commissioner there until 1939 when he retired. He died in 1952.
17. Sir Dougal Orme Malcolm (1877-1955). Scottish-born, English-educated, he entered the Colonial Office in 1900 and became Private Secretary to Lord Selborne as High Commissioner in South Africa (1905-10). Elected to the Board of the British South Africa Company in 1913, he subsequently became its President.
18. Professor Isaac Schapera was Professor of Anthropology at the University of Cape Town, and conducted a large number of field research trips to the Bechuanaland Protectorate. He was therefore the obvious choice to undertake a study of Tswana Law and Custom which Rey saw as necessary to the implementation of his judicial reforms. The resulting research was published in his *Handbook of Tswana Law and Custom* in 1938. Schapera went on to a Professorship of Anthropology at the University of London based at the London School of Economics. His work on the peoples of Botswana was honoured in 1985 by the University of Botswana when it awarded him an honorary doctorate.
19. Professor A. Victor Murray lectured on education at Selly Oak Colleges in Birmingham, England. He was the author of *The School in the Bush: a Critical Study of the Theory and Practice of Native Education in Africa* (London, 1929), a classic work which criticised the romanticism of current ideas of 'industrial education'.
20. Sir Cecil Fforde was until his death in 1954 Judge President of the Special Courts of the Bechuanaland Protectorate and Swaziland, and Judicial Commissioner of Basutoland. He was in addition Legal Adviser to the High Commissioner. Before coming to South Africa in 1931 he had been Judge of the High Court of Punjab. He acted as High Commissioner in December 1935 and from May to October, 1936.
21. Presumably Dr S.M. Molema — see 1930 note 67.
22. Since renamed Voortrekkerhoogte.
23. Alfred Martin Duggan-Cronin (1874-1954). An Irish-born compound manager for the De Beers diamond mines at Kimberley, he became interested in capturing the vanishing traditional life of migrant labourers at home. To this end he toured South Africa compiling a massive collection of invaluable (albeit posed) ethnographic photographs, now housed in its own museum at Kimberley and partially published in a series of volumes.
24. See Paul Shaw, 'The desiccation of Lake Ngami: an historical perspective'. *Geographical Journal* (London), vol. 151, no. 3, Nov. 1985, pp. 318-26.
25. See entry for 11 September 1934.

Editorial Notes for pages 168 to 184

26. Dibolayang (ruled 1934–36) came from the powerful royal house of the Regents Meno and Dithapo Meno (ruled 1875–76 & 1891). He replaced Monna-a-Maburu (ruled 1932–34), the last surviving son of the great nineteenth century king, Letsholathebe.
27. Domboshawa was an 'industrial' and agricultural school, near Salisbury, founded by the Southern Rhodesian government in 1920 — followed by its equivalent at Tjolotjo near Bulawayo in 1921. The schools were controlled by the Native Affairs Department of Southern Rhodesia.
28. Possibly Victoria de Bunsen (née Buxton), mother of Sir Bernard de Bunsen the educationalist who made his mark in East African university development after the Second World War.
29. Jean Daniel Arnauld Germond, born 1904, came from the same Basutoland French Protestant missionary network as the Ellenbergers, Macgregor, Nettelton, Dutton, etc. He joined the B.P. administration at the age of 21 in 1925, and transferred to the British army from 1941 to 1946 as a major in charge of Bechuanaland troops in the Middle East, North Africa, and Italy. After a spell in Solomon Islands administration, he returned to the B.P. in 1950, and rose to Senior District Commissioner — retiring in the early 1960s. Decribed as a clever and convivial Frenchman by A.M. Tsoebebe (1986) and as a 'fascinator' by Mary Benson (1961), he was nevertheless convinced that he knew the best interests of Africans better than Africans themselves — and he frequently clashed with Tshekedi Khama.
30. Hyde Villiers, 6th Earl of Clarendon (1877–1955), had been Parliamentary Under-Secretary for the Dominions between 1925 and 1927 and Chairman of the BBC between 1927 and 1930, before becoming Governor-General and Commander in Chief of South Africa in 1931. When he retired in 1937 it was as the last British as distinct from South African-born representative of the Crown in the Union of South Africa. (See 1931 note 46). He subsequently became Lord Chamberlain, the censor of British theatre and a senior member of the British royal household.
31. Harold Eddey Priestman (1888–1956). Educated in Ireland, he joined the Ministry of Labour in London in 1919 after war service in France and India. He then joined the Colonial Office, working up from district administration in Nigeria back to an office job in London. After a short stint in The Gambia he became Administrative Secretary to the High Commissioner in South Africa 1935–49, and then retired.

Notes for 1935

1. Colonel Deneys Reitz was the son of the Chief Justice and later president of the Orange Free State. At the age of 17 he joined the Boer forces on the outbreak of the South African War of 1899–1902. He accompanied General Smuts on his famous raid into Cape Colony. At the end of the war he refused to take the oath of allegiance to the British Crown and spent three years abroad returning in 1905. He served on Smuts' staff in the German South West and East Africa campaigns in the First World War. He entered Parliament in 1920 as a supporter of Smuts. In 1923 he was appointed Minister of Lands. In the Fusion Government of Hertzog and Smuts he became Minister of Lands once again (1933). In 1935 he was appointed Minister of Agriculture and Forests and in 1938 Minister of Mines. He backed Smuts over the issue of joining Britain in the war against Germany and became Deputy Prime Minister to Smuts and Minister of Native Affairs from 1939–43. In 1943 he was appointed High Commissioner for the Union in London and held this post until his death in 1944.
2. The (Conservative & Unionist) British government of 1895–1905 was overthrown by a general election, in which the importation of Chinese semi-slave labour to the Witwatersrand mines was a major campaign issue of the victorious Liberal Party.
3. Rey always saw Bathoen as Tshekedi's 'running dog', following him without question. This was a grossly unfair assessment of Bathoen who, though he was clearly influenced by Tshekedi, his relative and 'senior' in terms of the time he had been a ruler, clearly had a mind of his own. Tshekedi for his part sought out Bathoen's advice and they held frequent meetings to discuss common action in relation to the administration. Interview with Bathoen Gaesetsiwe M.P. (former Bathoen II) conducted by Michael Crowder, 19 April 1985.
4. Lawrenson, the R.M. at Mochudi, noted a very healthy improvement in hut-tax revenue. Only a chance question to the Chief revealed its source. 'I asked Molefi where Mussolini (Kgari Pilane) was, and was told that Kgari Pilane was very busy 'making lots of wings for cattle' — i.e. smuggling cattle across the South African border. (Extract from letter enclosed in Botswana Society Rey Diaries, vol. ix, p. 63).
5. See also 'Lost mine of gold', referring to an area north of Ghanzi, in *Sunday Times* (Johannesburg), 24 February 1935.

Editorial Notes for pages 186 to 193

6. Harding, Batterbee and Whiskard were all senior Dominions Office officials, each reaching the rank of Assistant Under-Secretary of State — Harding 1925-30, Whiskard 1930-35, and Batterbee 1930-38. Sir Edward Harding briefly became High Commissioner in South Africa from 1940 to 1941, when he retired.
7. Margery Perham, later Fellow of Nuffield College and Reader in Colonial Administration at the University of Oxford, was the leading expert on colonial administration in Britain of her day. She was a personal friend and later biographer of Lord Lugard as well as of Sir Donald Cameron. She had great influence in the Colonial Office as well as the Dominions Office. Despite her close links with the colonial establishment she was a 'liberal' in her views on colonial reform and was always ready to write to *The Times* about what she saw as instances of colonial injustice. She opposed the incorporation of the three High Commission Territories into the Union of South Africa because of its 'native policy' and stated this opposition in print in her famous debate with Lionel Curtis in *The Protectorates of South Africa. The Question of their Transfer to the Union.* (Oxford: O.U.P., 1935).
8. Lionel Curtis served on Lord Milner's staff in South Africa and became Town Clerk of Johannesburg and held other positions in the Transvaal. On returning to Britain he became an important publicist for the Commonwealth and for South Africa. He was the author of a number of books including *With Milner in South Africa*. He was editor of *The Round Table*, the influential journal devoted to the British Commonwealth and Empire. He died in 1954.
9. Lord Hailey had almost as great an influence on British colonial Africa as Margery Perham and was Director of the African Research Survey that produced the 1938 *African Survey*. He came to this post in 1935 from India where he had been Governor of the United Provinces. In 1936 he was elevated to the peerage as Baron Hailey of Shaipur. He wrote widely on Native Administration in Africa and published a major survey of it in 1951 with a separate volume on *Native Administration in the High Commission Territories in South Africa* in 1953. He published a completely new edition of his *African Survey* in 1956. He died in 1969.
10. Major Sir Ralph Furse was Director of Recruitment for the Colonial Service from 1931 to 1948, and thereafter became adviser to the Secretary of State on Training Courses for the Colonial Service. He retired in 1950 and in 1962 he published *Aucuparius: Recollections of a Recruiting Officer*. Prior to his appointment as Director of Recruitment he had been Private Secretary to both Amery and Passfield at the Colonial Office. In effect he was instrumental in selecting every colonial officer between 1931 and 1948.
11. Allan Graham Marwick had served in the Natal Civil Service before joining the British forces in the South African War of 1899-1902. After the war he joined the British Administration in Swaziland, becoming Assistant Commissioner in 1907. In 1933 he became Deputy Resident Commissioner and in 1935 Resident Commissioner, a post he held for two years before retiring in Swaziland where he become a confidant and adviser of King Sobhuza II. He died in 1966. His nephew, Sir Brian Marwick, also became Resident Commissioner of Swaziland, and was author of *The Swazi* (Cambridge: Cambridge University Press, 1940).
12. In his autobiography, *Aucuparius* (pp. 245 and 249-51), Furse describes how — against the wishes of the High Commissioner — he hitched a lift in a trader's lorry from Palapye to Maun via Rakops, in order to get a taste of the 'real' Bechuanaland. He then discovered in the Okavango swamps 'above all other places I have seen, the world as God made it'.
13. Colonel R.S. Godley published his autobiography, *Khaki and Blue*, 1935, while his brother Sir A.J. Godley published an autobiography in 1939 under the title *Life of an Irish Soldier*. Both had played prominent parts in the 1899-1900 siege of Mafeking.
14. This refers to the offer by the Government of the Union of South Africa of a grant of £35,000 to the Bechuanaland Protectorate for development purposes. It was meant to be a sweetener that would persuade the Batswana that it was in their interests to accept incorporation into the Union. Rey correctly saw that it would merely alarm them. See BNA S 457/2, 'Cooperation of the BP with the Union'. Rey was also well aware that this offer was being made at the same time as Hertzog was pushing through his Bill to remove African voters from the common roll in the Cape (see note 17) which could only make the Batswana more apprehensive of a future under South Africa. He advocated that any decision on accepting the Union offer of financial assistance be deferred until the fate of Hertzog's Native Bills was known. '. . . So far as the B.P. is concerned,' he wrote to Sir Arthur Fforde, 'I am convinced that a hostile reception awaits the proposed line of action if launched now . . .' (Rey to Fforde, 25 December 1935).
15. Rey is alluding to Tshekedi Khama's process served in the High Commissioner, Sir William Clark, aimed at preventing him from implementing the Proclamations.
16. For a detailed discussion of Tshekedi's opposition to the Proclamations see Crowder, 'Tshekedi's opposition', pp. 206-12.

Editorial Notes for pages 193 to 205

17. Five hundred delegates to the All-African Conventon, chaired by A.B. Xuma, met at Bloemfontein in 1935 to protest against the Hertzog Bills — which enforced the colour bar in industrial employment and other forms of racial segregation, in order to deprive Africans of their South African citizenship and other human rights.

Notes for 1936

1. *Lebone* (i.e.*Lobone*) was a quarterly periodical in English and Setswana, which was started by the Department of Education of the Bechuanaland Protectorate with the first issue appearing in January 1936. According to the *Annual Report* for the Bechuanaland Protectorate for 1936: 'Matters of outstanding interest are published in the journal, and Natives are encouraged to contribute letters and articles to it in their own language. Some excellent articles by Europeans and Natives have already appeared.' (p. 52).
2. Edirilwe Seretse had sent in a letter of complaint against Tshekedi in July 1935. Rey agreed to see him, even though Nettelton, the Resident Magistrate at Serowe, warned that 'Edirilwe is a disgruntled and disloyal man so it is wise to accept his statement with reserve'. (BNA S 266/7: Nettelton to Assistant Resident Commissioner, Mafeking, 9 July 1935). Edirilwe's main point was that the Bangwato really wanted the Proclamations to which Tshekedi was objecting. He cited the opposition of the Raditladi family to Tshekedi. But he also accused Tshekedi of trying to keep the young Seretse away from his royal relatives, and of objecting to the High Commissioner's statement at Serowe 'when he told the Tribe that Seretse was their Chief and that Tshekedi had got to take care of things for him and was holding the place for him'. Edirilwe urged Rey to go to Serowe to emphasise that Tshekedi should not 'spoil things' for Seretse (typed memorandum 25 February 1936, in Botswana Society Rey Diaries, vol. xi, p. 12).
3. Hugh Ashton, author of *The Basuto* (London: Oxford University Press for International African Institute, 1952), moved on from Bechuanaland to Southern Rhodesia to direct the social welfare department of the city of Bulawayo — where he eventually retired.
4. Sir John Harris was Secretary of the Anti-Slavery and Aborigines Protection Society and a staunch supporter of Tshekedi. He had earlier been a missionary and traveller in Africa and on his return to Britain he entered politics standing for a number of different constituencies. He was elected as a Member of Parliament only once, in 1923 for North Hackney, and lost his seat the following year. This was however enough to give him the entry to the corridors of Westminster he needed as a lobbyist for humanitarian causes. He was also a prolific publicist and wrote a number of books including *Dawn in Darkest Africa*, and *Portuguese Slavery, Britain's Dilemma*. He died in 1940.
5. See 1934 note 18.
6. See BNA S 485/1 'Report of the Informal Committee of the Dominions Office on Future Policy with regard to the High Commission Territories, February 1936' and S 458/2 for Rey's reactions to the report.
7. As an inducement to the inhabitants of the Bechuanaland Protectorate to look more sympathetically on the idea of incorporation into South Africa, the Union Government offered a grant of £35,000 for its development. This was accepted by the British Government, but when it was announced in the various Tribal *dikgotla* it was received with general suspicion as a Greek gift. Indeed such was the outcry, which to be fair to Rey he foresaw as likely, that the British Government had to leave the Union offer in abeyance. Much as the Chiefs were aware of the need for funds for development during the lean years of the Great Depression, they would not accept them if, as they feared, the real price of acceptance would be incorporation into the Union.
8. *The Star* (Johannesburg), 24 April 1936.
9. Sir Lionel Phillips (1955–1936), Witwatersrand mining magnate, who had first come to Kimberley from England in 1875. Closely associated with Cecil Rhodes' partner Alfred Beit. He became a leading political agitator at Johannesburg against Boer rule, and was sentenced to death (commuted to a large fine) for treason in 1896. He retired to his estate at Vergelen outside Cape Town after the First World War.
10. Ernest Fredrick Waterymeyer (1880–1958) came from an old established Cape Colony legal family. Appointed to the Cape Bench in 1922, he became Judge of Appeal in 1937 and Chief Justice of the Union of South Africa in 1943.
11. The title of Resident Magistrate was changing to District Commissioner in 1936, thus bringing it into line with colonial practice elsewhere in British-ruled Africa. It further served to distinguish the Bechuanaland Protectorate administration from that of the neighbouring Union of South Africa where local administrative officials were still called Magistrates and Native Commissioners.

Editorial Notes for pages 206 to 217

12. K.T. Motsete (see 1929 note 19 above) founded the Tati Training Institution in 1931, near Tsessebe in the Tati Native Reserve. Dependent on Carnegie Corporation and Phelps-Stokes funds, the school faltered after Rey left as Government interfered and declined to back renewal of American aid. The school moved to Francistown in 1939 and closed in 1941–42. See Q.N. Parsons 'Education and development in pre-colonial and colonial Botswana to 1965', pp. 21–45 in M. Crowder, ed., *Education for Development in Botswana* (Gaborone: Macmillan for Botswana Society, 1984).
13. As there was no full-time position for an Attorney-General on the establishment of the Bechuanaland Protectorate administrative staff, a Johannesburg Advocate such as Blakeway was retained to act in this capacity when the need arose.
14. As late as 1984 Mr (now Justice) Isaacs was acting as a Justice of the High Court of Botswana. In an interview with him conducted by the editors at Lobatse on 3 April 1984 he recalled graphically his experiences as Junior Counsel to Blakeway in this case.
15. The 'loathsome crime' was bestiality with a goat, but the man has not been identified. (Interview with Sir Edwin Arrowsmith, Gaborone, 3 April 1987).
16. Charles Noble Arden-Clarke had been an administrative officer in Nigeria since 1920 before coming to the Bechuanaland Protectorate as Assistant Resident Commissioner in 1936. He was promoted Resident Commissioner in succession to Rey in June 1937, and during his five years' tenure steered through a new set of Native Administration Proclamations much closer to the Nigerian model than Rey's set which Tshekedi, in particular, felt were uncomfortably close in character to those of the Union of South Africa. Arden-Clarke, who was knighted in 1940 after only three years as Resident Commissioner — Rey had to wait until after he had retired — left for Basutoland in 1942 where he was Resident Commissioner until 1946. He was appointed Governor of Sarawak in 1947. In 1949 he became Governor of the Gold Coast and in close cooperation with Kwame Nkrumah oversaw its transition from British colony to independent state with the new name of Ghana. He became briefly its first Governor-General. He died in 1962.
17. Colonel Charles Frampton Stallard (1871–1971). An Oxford-educated barrister in the Transvaal, who fought bravely in the South African and First World Wars. He was elected to the South African Parliament in 1929, but resigned from Smuts' party to form his own Dominion Party in 1934. Regarded as a super-British imperialist (or 'Jingo'), he became Smuts' Minister of Mines in the Second World War. A 'confirmed bachelor', he died at the age of one hundred.
18. 'Little Englander' was the Germanic term of abuse applied to British anti-imperialists, contrasted unfavourably with those who wanted a 'Greater Britain'.
19. A customs agreement between the Bechuanaland Protectorate and Southern Rhodesia was necessitated by the withdrawal of Southern Rhodesia in 1935 from the South African Customs Union — of which the B.P. remained a member — in protest against the discriminatory measures such as the cattle embargo which the High Commission Territories suffered in silence.
20. Dr Hans Merensky (1870–1952), geologist and mining capitalist from Transvaal German missionary stock. He made his fortune from discovery of diamond fields at the mouth of the Orange River, the rights to which he sold to De Beers for more than a million pounds.
21. Dr Hans Pirow (1892–1945), brother of Oswald Pirow (see note 58 for 1930), was educated in Germany and England as a mining engineer. He became Government Mining Engineer in 1926.
22. Pirow's generous offer of South African Airways flights through the B.P. to South West Africa was part of an ambitious plan for SAA to dominate continental air traffic as far north as Angola and Kenya — leaving (British) Imperial Airways with the flying boat route along the East Coast. Pirow was a pro-Nazi and fitted in with German plans — see 1930 note 58, and 1934 note 13 above.
23. The so-called Philander Bastards held proudly to that name, as the descendants of the Orlam-Afrikaners of mixed African, Asian and European ancestry. Dirk Philander had defeated the leader of the Orlam-Afrikaners and proclaimed himself 'Captain of the Emigrant Bastards', settling in the 1860s around the Nossop-Molopo confluence area which was to be divided between German South West Africa and Bechuanaland Protectorate in 1885 (with the Protectorate ceding its portion in 1891 to British Bechuanaland, which subsequently became part of Cape Colony in 1895 and of the Union of South Africa in 1910). The Philanders were consequently attacked by Germans and Boers, and scattered between Rehoboth in South West Africa, white farms in Cape Province around Rietfontein, and independent hunters along the Nossop (Nossob) River. It was the Nossop hunters who were expelled from the Gemsbok National Park by the Union government finally in 1938.
24. Rey's Bechuanaland Protectorate radio (Station ZNB; 50.84 metres; 200 watts; daily 9–10 am, Sundays 9 am–1 pm and 3–5 pm) was short-lived. It was closed down almost immediately Rey left, though it was to be revived during the Second World War to carry news of Bechuanaland troops

overseas. See *Rand Daily Mail* (Johannesburg), 28 November 1936, & 'Stoep Talk' in *The Star* (Johannesburg), 8 and 9 November 1937.
25. But the Proclamations did indeed prove unworkable, and were revised in 1943. As Harold Robertson has put it, Tshekedi and Bathoen may have lost the battle but they won the war. (Harold H. Robertson, 'From Protectorate to Republic: a Political History of Botswana' Dalhousie University: PhD thesis, 1976, p. 166).
26. Indirect Rule was of course the model of colonial administration developed by Lord Lugard in Nigeria, and modified by Sir Donald Cameron in Tanganyika and Sir James Maxwell in Northern Rhodesia (see note 51 for 1931). Tshekedi and Bathoen argued that the real problem with Rey's Proclamations was that they did not conform to the principles of Indirect Rule elsewhere in British Africa. Tshekedi argued that Rey's Proclamations instead followed the principles of the 1927 Native Administration Act in the Union of South Africa, and made his point by a comparative survey of the laws. (Interview with Mr Bathoen Gaseitsiwe, former Chief Bathoen II, with Michael Crowder, 19 April 1985; see also Tshekedi to High Commissioner, 13 January 1934 in BNA S358/6).
27. The African national anthem was *Nkosi sikelel'i-Afrika* ('Lord bless Africa'), composed by Enoch Sontonga in 1892. But it was probably here sung in one of the Setswana translations rather than in its original Xhosa version.
28. Rey wrote to Arden-Clarke on 26 December 1936: 'I confess I can't quite understand the [agreement with Tshekedi]. It would appear that the arrangement confirms by law the Chief and Headmen as absolute and sole autocrats for the administration of justice by making them the whole tribunal and therefore excluding anyone else. I cannot see how this could possibly be regarded as coming within the letter of the law — it is very definitely against the whole spirit of it' (BNA S 422/7/1).
29. This passage was scratched from the carbon copy of the Botswana Society Rey Diaries in modern ballpoint pen, by a hand other than Rey's. Such atheism was certainly publicly inadmissable for a top colonial official, required to participate conspicuously in ritual ceremonies of the state religion.

Notes for 1937

1. Three months after Rey left the Protectorate in June 1937 the Administration was still trying to get Tshekedi to establish Tribunals. Rey's successor, Charles Arden-Clarke, came to the conclusion that Rey's Proclamations needed revision in consultation with the Chiefs, and in 1943 a new set, strongly influenced by Tshekedi's ideas, were introduced. The Tribunals were replaced by the *kgotla*, which the 1934 Proclamations had sought to abolish as a judicial institution.
2. Rey is referring here to the case brought by Tshekedi against his first wife, Bagakgametse, who was his first cousin, for adultery. When she became pregnant he insisted he was not the father and accused another cousin, Leetile Raditladi (see note 7 below) of committing adultery with his wife. He also accused his wife of using witchcraft to poison his mother who did in fact die shortly afterwards. Bagakgametse was divorced by Tshekedi. She was convicted of witchcraft, condemned along with Leetile for adultery, and the two were sent into exile by the British administration.
3. Jan Hendrik Hofmeyer, born Cape Town 1894, educated locally and as a Rhodes Scholar at the University of Oxford. First Principal of the University of Witwatersrand in Johannesburg. Entered politics and rose to Deputy Prime Minister under Jan Smuts. Widely regarded as the leading native-born white intellectual in South Africa. Died in 1948 and thus never succeeded Smuts as leader of the United Party.
4. Clippings from *Cape Times*, 22 January 1937, & *Mafeking Mail*, 23 January 1937, enclosed in Botswana Society, Rey Diaries, vol. xiv, p. 49.
5. See entry for Saturday 17 April 1937 below.
6. For the trouble that came when Seretse Khama was prevented from succeeding see W. Henderson, N. Parsons & T. Tlou, *Seretse Khama of Botswana, 1921-80* (Cambridge: Cambridge University Press, in preparation).
7. Leetile Disang Raditladi (1910-71), grandson of the Raditladi who had seceded from Khama in 1895, was born at Serowe. Educated at Tiger Kloof, Lovedale and Fort Hare, he came to prominence in 1937 when cited as co-respondent in Tshekedi's divorce case. He was banished from the Bangwato Reserve, working first as a clerk at Francistown and then as Secretary to the Queen Regent of the Batawana at Maun. During this time he wrote a number of historical plays, poems, love stories and a (now lost) biography of Khama III, which are recognised today as important Setswana literature — but often contained veiled critiques of Tshekedi's rule. Pioneer Francistown

trade unionist and founder of the Bamangwato National Congress in the early 1950s, he founded the Bechuanaland Protectorate Federal Party in 1958 but played no effective part in nationalist politics of the 1960s. His life awaits a biographer.

8. For details of the 'Venereal Diseases Campaign' see BNA S 403/6/1 'Venereal Disease and Measures for the Eradication of', in particular Rey's 'Note on the Deputation to the Secretary of State, 16 June 1936, for the Parliamentary Committee of the British Social Hygiene Council'. The seriousness of the situation is brought out by the fact that in 1935 there were 6,817 cases of syphilis reported, and the proportion of syphilitics to hospital out-patients was 25 per cent. Two years earlier it had been as high as 40 per cent. Compare this with British Army figures of 37 per cent of all soldiers suffering from venereal diseases in 1860, being reduced to 4 per cent by the 1920s — see Ronald Hyam, 'Empire and sexual opportunity'. *Journal of Imperial and Commonwealth History* (London), vol xiv, Jan. 1986, p. 47.

9. Sarah Gertrude Millin (1889–1968), Lithuanian-born South African popular novelist and biographer of the 1920s–40s. A particular obsession in her prolific novels was debilitation through racial miscegenation. She was married to Philip Millin (1888–1952) later Judge of the Supreme Court of the Union of South Africa.

10. For J.L.S. Jeffares see 1931 note 39.

11. Fraenkel ran the alternative law firm in Mafeking to Minchin & Kelly who usually represented Government. Fraenkel therefore took many cases against Government, including the representation of Seretse Khama in the later 1940s and early 1950s.

12. Rey's valedictory for Tshekedi read: 'Tshekedi's activities and mentality have been so much before the Government and are sufficiently well known that it would appear unnecessary to dilate on them in any great detail. Indeed to do so adequately would necessitate an extremely lengthy disquisition, but briefly it may be said that he is a man of exceptional intelligence, of good education but of a deeply suspicious turn of mind, definitely antagonistic towards the Government and to Europeans generally, quarrelsome and vindictive by nature, very industrious and hard-working; in other words a character of great possibilities spoilt by a strongly marked mental kink which makes it extremely difficult to work with him.' (Report dated 17 April 1937, BNA S433/10.)

13. For the problems resulting from Kgari Sechele's decision to move the site of his capital, see Titus Mnyamana-ja-Mbuya 'Legitimacy and succession in Tswana States: the case of the Bakwena, 1930–1963' (University of Botswana, B.A. History dissertation, May 1984).

14. Molefi's 'new religion' called Ipelegeng (meaning self-help), has been described as originating as 'a sort of Jacobite society designed to support the Chief financially and to secure his return to the Chiefship' — Anthony Sillery, *The Bechuanaland Protectorate* (Cape Town: Oxford University Press, 1952), p. 158. Ipelegeng became affiliated with and part of the Zion Christian Church (Z.C.C.), based in the Northern Transvaal, which was to become the largest Christian denomination in South Africa. Molefi offended the Dutch Reformed Church missionary and the British authorities by other rowdy behaviour too — by inviting a Johannesburg township jazz band to play at Mochudi, and by holding a lantern slide show of semi-naked bathing beauties projected on the church hall wall. (We are grateful to Fred Morton for this information). However, after a stint as a Regimental Sergeant-Major (like Kgari Sechele and Rasebolai Kgamane) in the Second World War, Molefi was again recognised as Chief of the British in 1945. He was killed in a car crash in 1958.

15. This refers to the witchcraft trial of Bagakgametse and her 'accomplices', much reported in the South African press of the time. (see also BNA S 345/8 & DCS 27/8 for the Enquiry, including statements by Tshekedi Khama in Kgotla on 10 May 1937).

16. Mrs Evelyn Harris was a formidable woman who headed the (white) Lady Clerks of the Mafeking Registry of the Bechuanaland Protectorate Administration.

17. Aubrey Denzil Forsyth-Thompson, born 1897, joined the Administrative Service of Uganda in 1921. On his transfer to the Bechuanaland Protectorate he became Government Secretary and when Arden-Clarke became Resident Commissioner he took over as his Assistant Resident Commissioner. He was made Resident Commissioner in 1942 on Arden-Clarke's transfer to Basutoland, and followed in his footsteps in 1947 when he was likewise named Resident Commissioner of that territory. He retired in 1951 and settled in Swaziland.

18. I. Schapera. *A Handbook of Tswana Law and Custom. Compiled by the Bechuanaland Protectorate Administration. With an Introduction by Lt-Col C.F. Rey CMG* (London: O.U.P., 1938). The Introduction is dated 14 June 1937.

19. L.S. Amery to C.F. Rey, 10 April 1937 (RHL Mss Brit Emp s384-1/1). Amery added: 'I wonder what you will be doing next.'

Appendix
NOTES ON THE SEROWE INCIDENT 1933

by C.F. Rey

There are a few points which it is essential to understand and to bear in mind if the full implications of the recent happenings at Serowe are to be appreciated.

The incident has been made to appear as the case of a harrassed native Chief punishing a scoundrelly European, because the Government could not, or would not, deal with him; and of over drastic action by the Government, as though this case of trouble with the Chief were an isolated instance.

A more grotesque distortion of the facts could hardly be imagined.

So far from the incident standing alone, or even of it being the real cause of the trouble, it was the culminating point of eight years' trouble with a swollen-headed youth whose openly expressed desire and ambition has been to be the ruler of an independent sovereign nation.

Trouble with this youth Tshekedi had started long before I became Resident Commissioner, and had been allowed to grow unchecked. For the last three years I have been negotiating two new Native Administration Proclamations which are designed to define, limit and regularise the position of the Chiefs; to establish proper native Councils and Courts; and to ensure proper administration of justice to the natives of the Territory. I may say that the administration of so-called justice in the Native Courts, especially at Serowe, has been an absolute scandal.

These proposals of mine which have been widely circulated to the natives and discussed by them, are designed for the benefit of the 200,000 people of the Territory, and as such, were naturally bitterly resisted by Tshekedi who was out for one thing — and one thing only — to maintain his present rights and privileges.

As I always have been, and still am, of the opinion that our duty is to safeguard the interests of the 200,000 natives — rather than to preserve the personal privileges of half a dozen autocratic, half-educated, and, to some extent, thoroughly rotten young Chiefs — I have pressed these proposals continuously and steadily and they are now within an ace of becoming law.

Realising this, Tshekedi determined to try at the eleventh hour to sidetrack the

Appendix

enactment of the new laws by raising a constitutional issue. He did this by the flogging of McIntosh.

It was a deliberate challenge to the Administration. He knew perfectly well that even under the existing law no white man, with or without his own consent, could be judged, on any excuse whatsoever, in any Native Court.

Nevertheless, Tshekedi dragged McIntosh before the Native Court, not — be it observed — on any immorality charge, but on a charge of common assault, namely striking a native. Tshekedi was not carried away by passion, nor did he do anything in the heat of the moment. He waited a whole month after the case had been before the Native Court, and then in cold blood, at the end of a month, without reporting the matter to, or notifying in any way any officer of the Administration, he ordered the man flogged.

Coming as this did on top of many years of opposition to the Administration and countless difficulties for which he had been rebuked on more than one occasion, it is perfectly obvious that this was, as I have said above, a deliberate challenge to the Administration.

Directly the news had been telegraphed to me I realised the position. There was no doubt about the facts. They were quite simple: the man had been sentenced to be flogged in a Native Court; and he had been flogged. Tshekedi had admitted that he had ordered him to be flogged; and he had even sent a Circular round to the European residents of Serowe saying he had done so.

That McIntosh was an undesirable person was equally admitted. There was no doubt about it at all. Two wrongs, however, do not cancel each other.

Each has to be dealt with on its own merits. Anyhow McIntosh was a side issue.

We had had trouble in another Reserve a little time ago where we had to remove a Headman (Gobuamang). He had only about a thousand men, but nevertheless the ten police whom I sent to do the work were roughly handled. The Headman was rescued from them, and had the Police not kept their heads I do not think that any of them would have escaped alive. We accordingly obtained the authority of the Dominions Office to borrow an armed force from Rhodesia to deal with this gentleman. But fortunately I was able to obtain the surrender of the whole Tribe before the Force was mobilised, so it was not necessary to bring them in.

Now, if it were necessary to do this for a minor Headman with only a thousand men, how much more necessary was a display of force in the case of the most powerful Chief in the Territory — the inhabitants of whose principal village, Serowe, numbered 20,000? To have gone up there either by myself, or with Admiral Evans alone, would have been to expose ourselves to what happened in the other case cited — which would have been an unthinkable and deplorable thing for the prestige of the Government.

It must be remembered that practically the whole of our Police Force is engaged on the seven-hundred-mile Cordon for controlling Foot & Mouth Disease. In any event, we have less than three hundred men to run a Territory larger than France; and of those men not more than forty are white, the rest being natives.

Consequently I recommended that a small force should be brought from the Fleet. As the High Commissioner was also the Admiral of the Fleet it would be a purely British force. It would afford a safeguard against any possible disturbance, and would produce a most valuable effect on all the Chiefs of the Territory — as showing the very definite interest which the Imperial Government took in the Territory, and the rapidity with which a force could be thrown into it if necessary.

Admiral Evans agreed to my proposals and about 165 men were sent up

Appendix

forthwith — hardly an excessive force to deal with the position.

The proceedings at Palapye Road have been grossly distorted. There was no question of a trial; no charge was made; neither the Crown Prosecutor of the Protectorate nor any other official legal representative was present. The facts were perfectly clear and were admitted by all concerned. It was merely an Administrative Enquiry in order that those facts could be properly recorded. The Acting Chief could add anything to them which he wanted to add; and the High Commissioner should be in a position with knowledge of all the facts to direct whatever Administrative action he thought fit should be taken.

In point of fact there was not really any necessity for an Enquiry at all, but I considered it better that there should be one.

Moreover, the Chief was allowed to have a Barrister from Cape Town and an Attorney from Mafeking to advise him. We made all the arrangements to get them up in time. They sat next to him at the Enquiry and they put into his mouth all the questions which he wished to ask, and the statements which he wished to make.

Tshekedi did not deny the facts, but he endeavoured to justify his attitude by claiming that he was exempt from the Territory's laws — an obviously and utterly impossible position. He stressed the undesirable character of McIntosh. We accepted that unreservedly, and it was consequently obviously unnecessary to hear unlimited evidence on that point — ample was given.

After the main Enquiry I personally, assisted by the Acting High Commissioner for the United Kingdom, who was an outside and unprejudiced person, held a second Enquiry into the alleged failure of the Administration to act. This Enquiry, plus a number of relevant documents, conclusively proved that there was no ground whatsoever for any such allegations. *Wherever these people, McIntosh and McNamee, had broken the law they had been brought before the Magistrate and punished.*

It must be remembered that the immorality side of their conduct was, unfortunately, not against the Law as the law stood, but the Magistrate had them up before him and censured them for their conduct. Our only possible action, as the law stood, was to turn them out of one district into another. (They were both born in the Territory and consequently we could not turn them out of the Protectorate.) This is a very important point to remember, because turning them out of one District into another is a rather futile measure which merely involves transferring the trouble from one place to another. It does not end the trouble.

On the other occasions when the Chief had complained he had been asked to produce evidence to enable the Magistrate to act, and by his own (the Chief's) admission had failed to do so.

Yet a further point to remember is that the general position, arising out of the sort of immorality practised by these men, had been dealt with by me over a year ago. We have a number of undesirable 'Europeans' here, and I have in fact turned out several. I had realised the evil, and the inability of the law as it stood to deal with it sufficiently drastically. I had accordingly issued a Circular to my Magistrates calling attention to this and asking them to consult with Doctors, Police Officers and Missionaries in the Territory with a view to suggesting a remedy. Amongst others, Tshekedi had been consulted and had replied that *he could suggest nothing*. This is another very important point.

Nevertheless, I drafted a law a year ago which provided for imprisonment for offences of this nature, which is under consideration. But, in view of that, we here could hardly be accused of not being alive to the trouble and trying to remedy it.

Appendix

As a result of the Enquiry, where — as I have said above — Tshekedi maintained an unrepentant attitude — he was temporarily suspended pending a decision as to further action. McIntosh and McNamee were turned out of the Native Reserve and sent to a place called Lobatsi, from which we have already received a bitter protest against having sent them there.

A few days afterwards Tshekedi sent a telegram, in which he abandoned his claim to try Europeans, undertook not to attempt any such course again, abandoned his claim to immunity from Protectorate Laws, promised to obey such laws — either existing or which may be passed in the future — and undertook to work loyally with the Administration.

We had thus gained our point. The drastic action taken in suspending Tshekedi has demonstrated to all the Chiefs of the Protectorate that any such pretensions as those advanced by Tshekedi would not be tolerated. His complete abandonment of them enabled me to recommend forthwith that the suspension should be brought to an end, which I did immediately. We have thus established a position which would never have been realised unless the drastic steps, which were taken, had been taken. The Secretary of State has refused to allow Tshekedi to proceed to England, and I think that we may now say that so far as this end is concerned we have cleared up the position.

Difficulties have been aggravated by the action of the London Missionary Society. I am prepared to believe that this Society has done good work elsewhere, but so far as this Territory is concerned they have done nothing but harm. They have endeavoured to establish a religious monopoly here and to keep out all other Missions; and so far as the Bamangwato country (the biggest Native Reserve in the Territory) is concerned, they have succeeded. But having kept out all other Missions from there, they have achieved nothing else. They have not a single Medical Mission or Medical Officer in the whole Territory, whereas the Dutch Reformed Church, the Seventh Day Adventists, the Roman Catholics and the Scotch Continuing Church have all got, or are getting, either Hospitals or trained medical people.

All these other Missions work loyally with the Government and are a great help to me. The London Missionary Society has consistently endeavoured to interfere in political and administrative matters, and has achieved nothing else. They are represented in the Protectorate by a poor type of individual, and at least two of these Missionaries have had to be turned out by the Government or at the request of the Government because of the trouble they were creating.

The man Jennings, who is now going to England to try and raise trouble, is the most troublesome specimen of them all. The Advocate, Buchanan, whose name has appeared in connection with this matter, is an amiable negrophilist who is doubtless merely doing the job he is paid for.

He and Jennings have, however, consistently fed the Press here with a series of misleading and even lying statements representing the facts in a totally untrue light; and of course, owing to my position, I have been unable to answer them.

The position may accordingly be summarised as follows:

1 The flogging of McIntosh by itself was really almost a side issue.
2 Tshekedi had been giving trouble to the Administration for years.
3 In order to force the issue he deliberately broke the law by flogging a European and raised a serious constitutional issue by claiming immunity from Protectorate laws, i.e. independence.

Appendix

4 The Administration took up his challenge and promptly suspended him.
5 He expressed regret, withdrew his claims, promised to obey present and future laws, and undertook to work loyally with the Administration.
6 As a result he was equally promptly reinstated.
7 The Administration were absolved from all charges of laxity in dealing with the matter.
8 The offending Europeans were expelled from the District.

EPILOGUE

by Neil Parsons

Bechuanaland was never the same again after Rey. Though the Protectorate was to regain some of its characteristic torpor, it was now blessed with the basic structure and personnel of a modern administrative state. Indeed, before Rey came it is possible to argue whether the Bechuanaland Protectorate constituted a state at all. It was little more than an imperial envelope around a cluster of 'native' states. Yet Rey's achievement was to create a core for the new state, rather than to bring the peripheral states into line. It was left to his more patient and personable successor, Charles Arden-Clarke (Resident Commissioner, 1937–42), to begin successfully the process of incorporating the peripheral states into the colonial state — enticing their traditional rulers by treating them as educated modern men, rather than bludgeoning them as archaic relics like Rey.

The peripheral 'tribal' states could not be really incorporated, nor could national development plans take off, until the 'tribes' (i.e. the populations of each old state or Reserve) came to identify with a sense of nationality synonymous with the borders of the colonial state. That long and gradual process, accelerated by the Second World War and reaction against South African government interference after the War, was eventually to bear fruit in the 1960s when Bechuanaland became the Republic of Botswana.

Rey after Bechuanaland
Though Charles and Ninon Rey left Mafeking in June 1937, he actually retired from the High Commission Territories service, after final leave taken in England, in September 1937. As readers of the diaries will have seen, Rey was determined to get his own back after retirement on 'that blasted' Dominions Office for 'the utterly damnable way in which we've been treated.'[1] He received few crumbs of comfort in London — only a semi-official letter from the Dominions Office thanking him for his work as Resident Commissioner.[2]

Rey's particular hurt was over not being knighted for his services, particularly because all but three of his predecessors as Resident Commissioner had been. The problem was not wholly solved in the New Year Honours of 1938 when King George made Rey a Knight Bachelor. This was the 'least prestigious' knighthood that could be awarded. The usual colonial honour was a knighthood within the Order of St Michael and St George (K.C.M.G. rising to G.C.M.G.), an Order in which Rey was already a Companion (C.M.G.).[3] But if he thought that the 'office

Epilogue

boys' of the Dominions Office had won their final insult, Rey was obliged to bear the slight in silence. Sir Charles and Lady Rey demonstrated their contempt for the 'imperial factor' by whiling out the rest of their days in colonial South Africa.

As an apparently embittered right-wing authoritarian, with experience and understanding of modern social engineering, Charles Rey might be said to have fallen among the 'marginal fascists' — who, as the historian Barry Kosmin has suggested, left Britain relatively free of fascism in the 1930s by playing out their frustrations in the Southern and East African colonies.[4] Rey was a racial paternalist, sometimes anti-semitic and increasingly anti-socialist, disparaging of liberalism and of humanitarian religion, with flashes of sympathy for Mussolini and even for Hitler. On his retirement, in a long newspaper interview, he openly praised the Italian invasion of Abyssinia as the harbinger of 'civilisation and development'. In March 1939 he contributed five articles to a Johannesburg newspaper on the Spanish Civil War, praising Franco as a 'really remarkable character' who had put down the 'Red Menace'.[5]

However, such 'marginal fascism' was consistent with the attitudes of much of the ruling class in Britain, and certainly with those of English-speaking whites in South Africa. Rey's 'marginal fascism' was a social attribute, rather than a pathological personality defect. As an obituary of Rey in the *Cape Times* was to point out: 'Although never one to suffer fools gladly, he always revealed — under seemingly strong opinions on a variety of subjects, spoken or written — a kind and understanding regard for human nature.'[6] Whatever Rey's initial sympathies with fascist authoritarianism, libertarian beliefs bubbled out when faced by a patriotic war. In 1937 Rey was beginning to believe that the Germans 'all seem to have gone mad' under Hitler's leadership. By November 1939 Rey was saying: 'The whole issue of this war is totalitarianism against democracy.'[7]

The Reys spent the first two or three years of their retirement touring the world and residing in the city of Johannesburg on the Witwatersrand — basking in the glow of publicity and approval of the local establishment. Rey became the editor of a Johannesburg magazine called *Africa Revealed by Word and Picture*.[8] He also made a living by contributing feature articles to newspapers. In February 1938 Rey contributed a very detailed six part article on the Bechuanaland Protectorate to the Johannesburg *Star* afternoon newspaper. The article called for an overhaul of Dominion Office control, and for the removal of white farm blocks to neighbouring colonies — the Tati Block to Southern Rhodesia, and the Tuli Block to the Union of South Africa. (This, presumably, was Rey's revenge on the Dominions Office, a month after his devalued knighthood.)[9] Thereafter, Rey was a frequent contributor to *The Star*, until early 1940, on a miscellany of international topics from the Suez Canal to the New York World's Fair of 1939.

Sir Charles and Ninon spent six months of 1938 touring in Europe and North America — where he was 'enormously impressed by the organisation and efficiency in New York.'[10] On their return to Johannesburg they became active members of Jan Smuts's wing of the United Party, the governing party of South Africa, within which Smuts overthrew Hertzog as Prime Minister — in order to get South Africa to support Britain in the war against Germany — by an internal coup in September 1939. Rey did not find it difficult now to champion white settler interests in Southern Africa, as is illustrated by the rather strange logic of his address to a women's branch of the United Party at Benoni, on the Witwatersrand, in February 1939:

Epilogue

We in South Africa are the only white sovereign state [in Africa]. In Africa there are some 145,000,000 people, 3,000,000 of whom are white. Two million of these whites are here; therefore we can regard ourselves as the potential leaders of Africa.[11]

Two months later, addressing another women's branch of the U.P. in nearby Boksburg, Rey played on mounting war fever by rehearsing the argument — against Hertzog's appeasement of Hitler — that the Witwatersrand could be bombed by German aircraft if South Africa succeeded in persuading Britain to hand Tanganyika back to Germany. 'The frontier of South Africa', said Rey echoing Smuts, 'is not on the Limpopo or the Zambesi, but on the Mediterranean.'[12]

The Reys maintained a life of travel and entertainment that must have strained their resources. In March 1939 they hosted an extravagant social evening at the largest hotel in Johannesburg. In July 1939, 'rubicund and monocled', Sir Charles was in London telling the press 'amusing stories of his journeys'. By August he was back in Johannesburg addressing a Rotary Club on labour problems, while Ninon opened a U.P. garden fete. Rey was a speaker much in demand at lunch clubs, and even addressed the Natal University College graduation of 1939. He also sat on the selection board of a flying club, interviewing trainee pilots. But he hankered after more substantial prospects, and stood for selection as U.P. parliamentary candidate for the Orange Grove constituency in Johannesburg. However, he failed to gain nomination within the party.[13] Ninon appears to have had more political success in heading a women's branch of the U.P., but the strain proved too great. She turned down the presidency of the Transvaal (white) Girl Guides, and began to discontinue public service. She took to the relaxation of painting of flowers in oils.[14]

At some time, probably in the early months of 1940, Sir Charles and Lady Rey opted to discontinue their careers in the industrial wilds of Johannesburg for the altogether more peaceful and picturesque Cape of Good Hope. They retired to Arthur's Seat Hotel, overlooking the sea at Cape Town, and lived a relaxed life. While Ninon painted and exhibited or sold her paintings for charity, Charles wrote newspaper articles less frenetically and became a well known voice on wartime South African radio — always ready with an opinion. At different junctures over the next three decades he was also reported to be working on nis memoirs.

In late 1946 and early 1947 Sir Charles Rey achieved some notability as an expert witness in the celebrated case of David Kgobe, alias W.J. Barker, alias Jousof Prince of Ethiopia. The Prince, arraigned on a charge of fiscal fraud, was shown to be an imposter by Rey, who thrilled the court with 'a series of word pictures rich and colourful with Amharic terms and idioms'. (Rather more serious was the 'African Legion' led by Kgobe alias Barker, which expected to share power in South Africa after the collapse of white rule 'in 20 or 30 years time'.)[15] Also in 1946, Rey received news of belated recognition for his work on Portuguese history in Abyssinia. He had been elected a Member of the Portuguese Academy of History in October 1945 upon the recommendation of a year earlier.[16]

In 1947 Rey's propagandistic talents were recruited by the South African Department of External Affairs to counter the new and unexpected overseas criticism of South Africa's 'native policy'. The world was beginning to tumble to the fact that Smuts' racist practices did not match up to the grand principles he had penned as the draughtsman of the Preamble to the United Nations Charter. Rey

Epilogue

wrote an extended justification of South African 'native policy' under Smuts, for publication in the United States. This was judged unsuitable for placing in the *New York Times*, and was instead published as a booklet by the South African Information Office in New York. Five thousand copies of the sixty page *Union of South Africa and Some of Its Problems* were printed, at the cost of almost fifty cents a copy, for distribution free in New York, Washington, and London.[17]

By the time the booklet appeared, in December 1947, it reported Rey as living in Southern Rhodesia. However the seventy year old Rey had not emigrated, but had merely rented a house in Salisbury, the capital of Southern Rhodesia, for a few months.[18] By January 1948 he was again writing from Arthur's Seat Hotel in Cape Town. Significantly, he does not appear to have been tempted to return north after the unexpected electoral victory in South Africa of the National Party under Prime Minister Malan during June 1948. It was that victory that boosted plans for a so-called Central African federation, based on Southern Rhodesia, as a British counterbalance to Afrikanerised South Africa — the very vision that had enthused Rey fifteen years earlier. Any qualms that Rey might have had about the Afrikaner nationalist government in South Africa seem to have been put at rest by 1950. In February of that year Sir Charles Rey, as President of the South African Association of Arts, a position that he had accepted in support of his wife's painting, was photographed laughing with the Prime Minister — while Minister of Justice ('Cat-o'-nine-tails') Swart glowered nearby.[19]

Rey returned to print on Bechuanaland in 1950, because of the interest aroused in South Africa by the marriage of Chief Seretse Khama to an English woman and their subsequent enforced exile overseas. Other commentators had seen this British colonial intervention, quite correctly, as appeasement of the South African and Southern Rhodesian governments.[20] In an article for the *Cape Argus*, reprinted in the *Bulawayo Chronicle* and then in an ultra-right Afrikaans journal dedicated to the new philosophy of *apartheid*, Rey preferred to diagnose the heart of the issue as the dangers of racial miscegenation, unchecked by incompetent forms of Bangwato and British colonial government.[21]

In April 1951 Rey ventured articles on the 'Future of the Protectorates' for the *Cape Times*. He had by now come full circle on the issue of incorporation into the Union. The incorporation of Basutoland, Swaziland, and the whole of Bechuanaland, was not only inevitable but desirable within two or three years. How otherwise could three territories that were 'geographically' part of the Union be British-administered without inevitable and undersirable conflict between Britain and South Africa? The articles were then reprinted by South Africa House, the Union's High Commission (embassy) in London, as a pamphlet for distribution within Britain.[22]

Sir Charles Rey, who after all was a cosmopolitan with fluency in at least two European languages, came to terms with Afrikanerdom to a degree then unusual among white English-speaking South Africans. As correspondence between them in 1949 shows, he and Amery had parted company over the issue of Afrikaner power. Amery saw Afrikanerdom as heading towards the reduction of South Africa to 'a small brown smear on a black continent'. He hankered instead for the experiment of 'the new greater Rhodesia'.[23] Rey on the other hand shows his colours in remarks scribbled on his copy of the South African *Hansard*, recording a parliamentary debate on Bechuanaland in 1954. 'Good' is scratched against the speeches of National Party leaders; 'Tripe' against the speech of the United Party leader Strauss. Rey also apparently approved of the *apartheid* blueprint for

Epilogue

territorial segregation, the Tomlinson Report of 1955, and disparaged people such as Father Huddleston who dared oppose *apartheid*. Rey was anxious that *Die Burger*, the Afrikaans newspaper that was the 'mass ventilator of apartheid theory', should be published in a weekly English language digest so that English-speakers could appreciate the niceties of Afrikaner politics.[24]

Rey was never unwilling to reminisce about his Bechuanaland days, even to the extent of being considered a bore on the subject. But his surviving papers indicate scant interest in current Bechuanaland affairs, except where they touched a chord of memory or material interests. In 1957 eighty year old Rey and others conducted a successful campaign to increase the pensions of High Commission Territories service officers, for which he received thanks from the even more ancient Jules Ellenberger who lived in retirement in Salisbury.[25] In 1961 Rey reacted to a *Cape Argus* report on a plan to pump water from the Okavango swamps to Serowe in eastern Bechuanaland, by writing a letter in praise of the eccentric Belgian water engineer, Charles Naus, whom Rey had left experimenting with weirs in the swamps. In response, Rey received a letter from Forsyth Thompson, Resident Commissioner of 1942–46 now also retired at Cape Town, who gently deflated Rey's opinion of Naus whom Thompson considered to have been a plausible fraud.[26] The sole references in Rey's papers to Bechuanaland's advance towards independence are on the building of Gaborone — the new capital, at last removed from Mafeking to a place inside the territory's borders. He told a newspaper columnist why he had never been back to Bechuanaland since 1937. 'Not a good thing, you know, to go back to the place. When you have been running a show, you never like to see it being done any differently.' However, he might be tempted to take a look at the new capital.[27] (He never did take a look.)

Ninon died on October 29th, 1958. Charles Rey was heartbroken and talked of suicide. But he was persuaded to take a new outlook on life by a friend and fellow artist of Ninon's, Mrs Fay Longhurst Murphy, herself a widow. She encouraged him to organise a memorial exhibition of Ninon's paintings, and to become involved in the St John's Ambulance Brigade — a voluntary organisation with uniforms and ceremonials that must have taken Rey back to his Bechuanaland days.[28] 'Colonel Rey' lived once again as patron of ceremonial details such as the trooping of new colours.

Mrs Murphy also encouraged Rey to turn his attention once more to his memoirs. He had a copy of his Bechuanaland Diaries to hand, and other papers on his career, though other diaries appear to have been destroyed by a fire in the London furniture depository where the Reys had left many of their belongings in the late 1930s. So Sir Charles Rey wrote an autobiography, in longhand, which he read out to Mrs. Murphy as he progressed. She advised drastic cuts in the more candid outbursts, after which the chapters went to be typed.[29]

During 1959 Rey nursed his grief but had not wholly lost his high spirits. When asked to send a message to the fiftieth anniversary celebrations of labour exchanges in Britain, his contribution was characteristically snappy:

> At 82, I still propel my automobile over the veld with some velocity, and am rarely caught by the police.
>
> . . . I am in the throes of giving birth to a book of libellous reminiscences spread over some 20 countries and 60 years. If completed, however, and a publisher of sufficient moral courage found to produce it, it is at least doubtful whether the Censor will be broadminded enough to pass it.[30]

Epilogue

The autobiography was completed by June 1961. The typewritten chapters now in the possession of the Botswana Society are disappointingly bland and contain sometimes misleading tales, re-told from but wanting the spice of the Bechuanaland Diaries. (The original handwritten rough draft of the autobiography was retained by Mrs Murphy as Rey's executrix.) But there is no doubt that the autobiography served Mrs Murphy's original purpose as a therapy of self expression for Rey to regain his grasp on life.

In 1963 Rey returned to the fray against a British High Commissioner in Pretoria, Sir Hugh Stephenson, the last holder of that position before it was abolished to make way for the independence of Botswana (Bechuanaland), Lesotho (Basutoland), and Swaziland. Rey put to Stephenson the case of pre-1947 High Commission Territories pensioners for improved pensions. Stephenson's reply was, as Rey noted, 'exactly what an official letter should be, i.e. polite, non-informative, non-commital, and non-human . . . and is so framed as to stymie our further action by attempting to lead us to believe that everything that could be done has been done, or is being done, or will be done, so rendering further action superfluous.' As a matter of tactics, Rey thought it best to lie low for a while, and then 'as soon as a reasonable interval has elapsed, return to the charge with vigour and a great sense of grievance.'[31]

During 1964 Rey was reported to be 'as brisk and bustling' as in the 1940s, though since encumbered by a hearing-aid. 'Blasted nuisance,' he complained: 'Doesn't work too well in a crowd. And I want to be able to hear if anyone calls me a damn fool!'[32]

Mrs Murphy remembers a man who was lively in wit and in physical vigour to the end. A man whose humour and basic compassion were appreciated by the African waiters who served them in Cape Town hotels, with whom he bantered and blustered. The Rey table always got the promptest and most friendly service.

The end came on March 30th, 1968. The ninety year old Sir Charles had been driven across the Cape Peninsula by Fay Murphy, for a picnic. When they returned home to Rey's residential suite that afternoon, Sir Charles was in expansive mood and went to get a bottle of champagne from the refrigerator. As he bent down to pick up the bottle, he felt pains in his chest. He yelped, and Fay came running. Telling her it had been nothing, he tried to open the bottle, spilling champagne on himself. He repaired to the bathroom to wipe off the spill. As he leant over the wash-basin he was sent reeling backwards by massive pains in the chest, and fell to the floor. Blood was pumping from a severed artery into the chest cavity.

Sir Charles Rey died a few hours later, in great agony, continually crying to doctor and nurse and Fay that he had no wish to die.

***

Sir Charles Rey was a minor character in the origins of the British welfare state, and a marginal figure in the history of Ethiopian modernisation; and he was arguably sent on a false trail to Bechuanaland. No doubt he would wish to be remembered as the 'live wire' — a man of decision and action. Ironically, he may now be remembered better as a man of observation and reflection. Those Sunday afternoons spent writing his diaries in the veld, with Ninon, 'Topsy' and Pongo, may after all have been more ultimately productive than all the energies spent on trying to make a reality of the fantasy of being 'Monarch of All I Survey'.

Epilogue

Notes

1. See p. 234 above.
2. F.J. Harding to Rey, 14 August 1937 (Rhodes House Library, Oxford: Mss Brit Emp s1384-1/1).
3. A.H.M. Kirk-Greene, 'On governorship and governors in British Africa', pp. 209-264 in L.H. Gann and P. Duignan (eds.) *African Proconsuls: European Governors in Africa* (New York: Free Press, London: Collier-Macmillan, and Stanford, California: Hoover Institution, 1977). The three Resident Commissioners referred to were F.W. Panzera (1906-16), J. Ellenberger (1923-28), and R.M. Daniel (1928-30).
4. Barry Kosmin, 'Colonial careers for marginal fascists — a portrait of Hamilton Beamish', *The Wiener Library Bulletin* (London), vol. XXVIII, nos. 30-31 (1973-74), pp. 16-23. See also Lewis Hastings, *Dragons are Extra* (Harmondsworth, Middlesex: Penguin Books, 1947); Raphael Samuel, 'The middle class between the wars', *New Socialist* (London), no. 9 (Jan-Feb. 1983), pp. 30-36; no. 10 (March-April 1983), pp. 28-32; no. 11 (May-June 1983), pp. 28-30.
5. *The Star* (Johannesburg), 3, 4, 6, 7 and 8 March 1939.
6. J.G. Herring-Cooper, 'Sir Charles Rey — a tribute', *Cape Times* (Cape Town), 5 April 1968.
7. See Botswana Society, Rey Diaries (Mss), entry for 17 April 1937; 'Sir Charles Rey on international affairs', *Rand Daily Mail* (Johannesburg), 13 November 1939.
8. *Africa Revealed by Word and Picture* (Johannesburg), vols. 1-6, 1935-39. Rey contributed features as well as editing the whole journal — cf. C.F. Rey, 'Matters of interest and personal recollection of some parts of Africa', *Africa* (Johannesburg), Dec. 1937, in the first issue edited by Rey.
9. 'Bechuanaland. A half century of neglect', *The Star*, 1 February 1938(I), 2 February (II), 3 February (III), 4 February (IV), 5 or 7 February (V), 7 or 8 February (VI).
10. 'Sir Charles Rey's tour', *Cape Times* (Cape Town), 31 October 1938.
11. 'Union's chance to guide Africa'. *The Star*, 17 February 1939; *Rand Daily Mail* (Johannesburg), 17 February 1939.
12. *The Star*, 22 April 1939, cf. G.L. Steer, *Judgement on German Africa* (London: Hodder & Stoughton, 1939).
13. 'An explorer returns', *Evening Standard* (London), 17 July 1939; *Rand Daily Mail*, 16 August 1939; 'Friend of the Negus wants to be an M.P.', *Sunday Express* (Johannesburg), 19 November 1939 — RHL Mss Brit Emp s1384-6/2.
14. 'Sir Charles Rey's reception at the Carlton', *The Star*, 31 March 1939; 'The daily social scene: Lady Rey in Durban', *Natal Mercury* (Durban), 18 May 1939 — Botswana Society Rey Papers.
15. *Cape Times*, 30 September and 10 October 1946, and 27 March 1947; *Cape Argus* (Cape Town), 10 & 11 October. 1946.
16. Certificate in Botswana Society Rey Papers.
17. RHL Mss Brit Emp s1384-6/4.
18. Interview with Mrs Fay Longhurst Murphy, Cape Town, 27 June 1979.
19. *Cape Argus*, 27 February 1950, p. 1 — RHL Mss Brit Emp s1384-6/2. Rey as Life President of the South African Society of Arts was disparaging of modern painting. He was identified with the South African settler painter Tretchikoff, whose naturalistic portraits often in lurid colours were sold in chain stores, and the landscape artist Sydney Carter. See *Sydney Carter*, (Johannesburg: Swan Press, 1948), and Botswana Society Papers and Photographs. See also note 32 below.
20. cf. W. Henderson, N. Parsons, and T. Tlou, *Seretse Khama, 1921-1980: a Biography* (Cambridge: Cambridge University Press, forthcoming).
21. *Bulawayo Chronicle* (Bulawayo), 22 and 23 March 1950; Charles Rey, 'Background of the Bamangwato', *Journal of Racial Affairs* (Stellenbosch), vol. 1, no. 3 (April 1950), pp. 6-11.
22. *Cape Times*, 16 and 17 April 1951; C.F. Rey, *The Future of the British High Commission Territories in South Africa* (London: South Africa House, 1951) 8 pp.
23. L.S. Amery to Rey, 29 August 1949 and 27 April 1953 — RHL Mss Brit Emp s1384-1/1.
24. Union of South Africa, *House of Assembly Debates (Hansard)*, 12-14 April 1954, cols. 3769-3783, 3784-3804 and 3804-3823 (RHL Mss Brit Emp s1384-5/5); Rey to A.L. Geyers, n.d. (ibid 6/1). For *Die Burger* see T.R.H. Davenport, *South Africa, a Modern History* (London: Macmillan, 1977), p. 253.
25. Botswana Society Rey Papers; J. Ellenberger to Rey, 1 October 1957 — RHL Mss Brit Emp s1384-6/1.
26. Forsyth Thompson to Rey, 3 July 1961 — RHL, Mss Brit Emp s1384-5/2.
27. *Cape Times*, 17 September 1964 re new capital at Gaborone (ibid 5/5), Botswana Society Rey Papers. For an author so prolific on Abyssinia, Rey was remarkably reticent in publishing on Bechuanaland. His only major article was 'Ngamiland and the Kalahari', *Geographical Journal* (London: Royal Geographical Society), vol. 80 (1932), pp. 281-308. He never wrote the book he

promised on retirement (cf. *The Star*, 23 September 1937, p. 20), though his six-part article in *The Star* in February 1938 (see note 12 above) may have summarised the substance of the planned book.
28. Botswana Society Rey Papers and Photographs; interview with Mrs Fay Longhurst Murphy, Cape Town, 27 June 1979.
29. Interview with Mrs Fay Longhurst Murphy, June 1979. Only the Bechuanaland chapters of the typed autobiography (chaps. XVI–XIX, pp. 237–319) are in the possession of the Botswana Society. The rest were auctioned off by Rey's executrix through Sotheby's in London.
30. Copies in Botswana Society Rey Papers and RHL Mss Brit Emp s1384–1/6.
31. Botswana Society Rey Papers.
32. 'Talk at the Tavern of the Seas' (column) *Cape Argus*, 6 April 1964. The interview was on the occasion of Rey opening an exhibition of water colours by Mrs Fay Longhurst Murphy. 'Mrs Murphy is a good painter', said Rey: 'I can't stand these modern daubers.' After criticising British press coverage of South African events ('What a lot of rot . . . Trying to solve our problems and they don't know the first things about us.'), he ordered the *Argus* to use a photograph of Mrs Murphy and not of himself on the column.

INDEX

Abel-Smith, Captain, 12
Abyssinia, viii, xiv, xv–xvi, 199, 204, 270
Abyssinian Corporation, viii, xiii, xiv–xv
Adams, P.G.C., 8, 239n.23
Aerial survey, 155
African Flying Service, 155
African-German Investment Company, 216, 224
African Legion, 271
Afrikanerdom, viii, xvii, 272
Agricultural, experimental work, 200, 203; Demonstrator, 62
Aircraft Operating Company, 100, 153
Air services, 156, 157, 161–2, 182, 182–3, 216, 253n.2
Albu, Sir George, 100, 251n.8
Alice, Princess, 2, 12, 52, 237n.3
'All Red Route Committee', xii
Amery, Leopold, viii, xvi, xvii, xix, xxi, 99, 236, 239n.1, 251n.5, 272
Angola, 36, 49, 145, 146, 158
Anti-Slavery Society, 200
Apartheid, 272, 273
Arden-Clarke, C.N., 210, 213, 214, 216, 221, 223, 234, 261n.16, 269
Arrowsmith, Edwin, 153, 154, 176, 184, 185, 213, 257n.10
Ashton, Hugh, 199, 200, 210, 260n.3
Athlone, Earl of, 2, 4, 11, 12, 24, 38, 39, 51, 52, 237n.3

Baden-Powell, Lady, 201
Baden-Powell, Lord, 154–5, 201–2
Bakalaka tribe, 18, 32, 241n.21
Bakgalagadi tribe, 24, 58, 73, 176, 242n.34
Bakgatla, Reserve, xx, 44; tribe, 13, 41–2, 44, 70, 74, 84, 110, 121, 173, 174–5, 212, 244n.60
Bakwena, Reserve, xx, 173; tribe, 66, 69, 83, 84, 187, 232
Ballinger, William, 41, 76, 244n.59, 248n.29

Bamalete Reserve, 218
Bamangwato (Bangwato), Reserve, xx, xxi, 37, 80, 234; tribe, 4, 6, 16, 18, 29, 48, 54, 55, 66, 69, 81, 100, 106, 117, 141, 242n.31, 242n.38
Bangwaketse, Reserve, xx; tribe, 41, 81, 101, 121, 125, 173
Barclay's Bank, South Africa, 12
Baring, Evelyn, 54, 246n.1
Barnes, Leonard, xvii–xviii, 77, 244n.59
Barolong, district, 120; tribe, 72, 80, 249n.40
Basarwa see Marsarwa
Basubia tribe, 33, 34, 132, 242n.32
Basutoland(Lesotho), xvii, xviii, xx, 49, 84, 177, 189, 204
Batawana, Reserve, xx; tribe, 35, 102, 132, 133, 167, 195
Batho, Mr, 153–4, 257n.11
Bathoen I, xi
Bathoen II, xx, 15, 41, 44, 57, 70, 74, 85, 96, 101, 105, 106, 120, 125, 173–4, 212, 235, 241n.17; opposition to Proclamations, 183, 188, 195, 203; trial, 208–9, 218, 219–20
Batlokwa tribe, 49, 70, 88
Batterbee, Sir Henry, 186
Bayei see Makuba
Bechuanaland, After Rey, 269: Before Rey, xvii–xx; Rey's appointment, xx–xxii
Bechuanaland Protectorate Police, 2, 11, 14
Bechuanaland Protectorate Relief of Distress Fund, 127–8
The Bechuanaland Torch, 197
Bekuhane see Basubia Tribe
Beveridge, Sir W., vii, xii
Bezeidenhout, Colonel, 184
Birchenough, Sir Henry, 2, 238n.8
Bisley, 27
Blackett, Sir Basil, 111, 252n.24
Blackwell, Leslie, 138, 144,
160, 255n.31
Blakeway, Mr, 195, 196, 207, 208, 209
Bloemfontein, 193, 229
Board of Advice on Native Education, 48, 88, 164–5
Board of Trade, xii, xiv
Botletli River, 136
Botswana, Republic of, 269, 274
Botswana Society, viii, ix
Boy Scouts, 196, 216
Brind, Mr, 7, 8, 9, 42, 181, 207, 211
Brinton, Major, 184, 185
British Foreign Legion, 31
British Industries Fair, 98–9
British Navy, 138, 139, 140, 265
British South Africa Company see Chartered Company
British South Africa Police, xviii, 40
Broadcasting stations, 217, 218, 226, 229
Buchanan, Douglas, 53, 139, 192, 208, 209, 219, 240n.12, 267
Buckingham Palace, 102
Bulawayo, 38, 39, 81, 85, 88–9, 89–90
Bulawayo Chronicle, 128, 272
Bull Camps, 181, 186, 201, 220
Die Burger, 273
Bushmen, 24, 168
Buxton, Lord, xx, 99, 251n.6

Cambridge, Lady May, 52
Campbell, Alec, ix
Cape Argus, xx, 272, 273
Cape Colony (Province), 4, 62, 98, 197
Cape Mounted Rifles, 31
Cape Times, 223, 270, 272
Cape Town, 1, 11–12, 24, 52–3, 65, 68, 90–1, 93–5, 143–5, 146–7, 148, 178–81, 185, 187, 193–4, 204, 221–4, 271
Caprivi Strip, 33, 101, 145, 146, 200
Cattle, exporting, 92, 92–3, 95, 97, 98, 99, 144, 172, 190, 196, 220; running, 13, 20,

277

Index

118, 199, 203; smuggling, 189, 190, 203, 206
Chamberlain, Joseph, xvi, xix
Chaplin, Sir Drummond, 12, 49, 239n.3
Chartered Company, 12, 22, 30, 37, 40, 49, 53, 67, 76, 88, 90, 142, 161, 239n.4
Chase, W. H., xx, 8, 9, 19, 27, 28, 33, 36, 37, 56, 57, 60, 64, 68, 69, 78, 80, 92, 98, 104, 115, 116, 118–9, 142, 145, 146, 147, 151, 154, 156, 158, 167, 186, 239n.22
Chief's Island, 166
Chief's powers, 13, 69, 94, 107–8, 126
China Tariff Commission, xii
Chobe River, 33, 95
Church of England, 39, 75, 88, 136
Church of Scotland mission, 19, 147, 267
Church Railway mission, 155, 257n.14
Circumcision (Bogwera), 67, 69–70, 247n.16
Clarendon, Lord, 176, 217, 224, 258n.30
Clarendon, Lady, 176, 181
Clark, Mrs, 180, 184
Clark, Sir William, 159–60, 180, 181, 184, 185, 187, 189, 192, 194, 209, 214, 215, 218, 220, 223, 224, 233, 257n.16
Clifford, Captain the Hon. B.E.H., xxi, 2, 11, 81, 82, 87, 95, 237n.4
Coghlan, Sir Charles, 38, 40, 243n.57
Colonial Development Act, xx, 9, 239n.25
Colonial Development Advisory Committee, 12, 39, 47, 98, 178, 239n.2
Colonial Development Fund, 97, 109, 143, 181
Colonial Office, xvii, xix, xx, 12, 14, 24, 30, 66, 68, 70, 84, 85, 86, 87, 91–2, 93, 96, 116, 124, 144
Commonwealth Relations Office see Dominions Office
Communism, 26, 51, 146
Compatriots Club, 99
The Congo, 82, 85, 88, 89, 93
Copper, 89
Cowper, William, xxii
Crocodile River, 100
Cromer, Lady, 54
Croneen, Captain, 125, 139, 148, 213
Crown Lands, 9, 49, 80, 133
Cunliffe-Lister, Sir Philip, 102, 103, 251n.13
Currency question, 111, 114, 115; Gold Standard, 111, 113

Curtis, Lionel, 187, 259n.8
Customs Conference, 182
Cuzen, Allan Leckie, 14, 15, 19, 41, 42, 43, 44, 45, 57, 176, 208, 240n.15
Cuzen, Mrs, 41, 57

Dairy Control Board, 84
Dalrymple, Sir William, 100
Damara tribe, 35, 69, 135, 235, 254n.21
Daniel, Mrs, 2, 3, 13, 19
Daniel, Lt.-Col. R.M., 2, 3, 4, 7, 9, 11, 12, 13, 14, 16, 19, 22, 31, 237n.7
Davis, Wolfe, 49–50, 142, 172
De Beers Company, 161, 209
de Bunsen, Victoria, 174, 258n.28
De Havilland Aircraft Company, 118, 155
Desert Patrol, 6
Diamonds, 161, 184, 209
Dibolayang, Chief, 168, 169–70, 195, 258n.26
Dingaan's Day, 111, 252n.23
Disraeli, xi
Dombashawa, 170, 258n.27
Dominions Office, vii, xvii, xxi, 12, 14, 24, 30, 91–2, 103, 106, 107, 117–18, 119, 148, 150, 152, 171, 174, 178, 186, 198, 201, 231, 232, 239n.1, 269
Douglas, Captain, 100, 118, 155
Douthirt, Mrs, 56, 57, 62
Downie, J.W., 43, 103, 244n.61
Drew, Dr, 31, 79
Drew, Mrs, 79
Drought, 129, 130, 134, 135, 191
Drury, Merrivale, 7, 8, 13, 41, 52, 55
Drury, Mrs, 41, 52, 55
Drydale, Major, 145
The Dual Mandate, xxi
Duggan-Cronin, A.M., 166, 257n.23
Duke, Dr, 51
Dumbrell, H.J., 48, 73, 106, 161, 164, 204, 245n.68
Duncan, Patrick, 84, 85, 94, 106, 112, 119, 217, 218, 249n.46
Duncan, Mrs, 106, 181, 217–8
Du Plessis, J.A., 153, 256n.8
The Dutch, 4, 5, 18, 41, 127
Dutch Reformed Church, 39, 45, 116, 136, 267; missionaries, 76, 213
Du Toit, Dr, 37, 38, 42, 47, 51, 161, 186, 209, 243n.52
Du Toit, Mrs, 47
Dutton, C.L. O'Brien, xx, 3, 8–9, 19, 38, 62, 80, 91, 96, 238n.9

Dyke, H.W., xx, 9, 33, 36, 43, 56, 57, 58, 60, 69, 78, 147, 156, 168, 239n.24

Eales, Shirley, xx, 1, 11, 84, 95, 98, 106, 123, 138, 140, 178, 180, 237n.2
Economic Commission, 106–7
Edirilwe, Seretse, 18, 19, 22, 23, 78, 197, 241n.23, 260n.2
Education, 48, 88, 104–5, 106, 164, 164–5, 170
Edward VIII, 195, 219, 220, 221, 222
Ellenberger, Lt.-Col. Jules, xvii, xix, 2, 12, 22, 36, 37, 116, 237n.5, 273
Ellenberger, Vivien F., 2, 28, 92, 105, 164, 165, 171, 186, 195, 208, 212, 213, 237n.6
Encyclopaedia Britannica, xvi
England, Mrs, 70
England, Russell, 64, 67, 70, 78, 81, 84, 163, 196, 203, 209, 221, 248n.34
European Advisory Council, 13, 17, 39, 41, 52, 64, 83, 87, 97, 176, 176–7, 184, 195, 227, 240n.6; incorporation into the Union, 184, 185; cattle export, 196
European poll-tax, 96
Evans, Admiral Edward, 137–8, 140, 141, 142, 143, 179, 180, 255n.25, 265
Evans, Mrs, 137–8
Expedition, river Gambia, xi
Experimental Grass Cultivation Station, 50
Export trade, 142, 144, 145, 154, 172

Fascism, 270
Federated Meat Industries, 173, 198, 226
Fforde, Lady, 165, 230
Fforde, Sir Cecil, 165, 177, 178, 180, 189, 190, 192, 195, 198, 209, 223, 230, 257n.20
Flying postal service, 155, 157
Foot and Mouth disease, 64–5, 66, 68, 70, 80, 81, 83, 84, 86, 97, 115–17, 154, 157, 158, 160, 161, 169, 223–4, 226, 228, 265; cordon, 118, 119, 120, 122, 126, 142, 154, 155, 200; inoculation against, 116–7, 120, 123, 127, 137
Foreign Jurisdiction Act, 209
Forsyth-Thompson, A.D., 232, 236, 263n.17, 273
Fraenkel, Mr., 230, 231, 263n.11
Francistown, 22, 31–2, 54–5, 79, 85, 86, 87, 88, 89, 97, 110, 151, 162–3, 205, 234; Creamery, 90, 98, 110

278

Index

Franco, General, 270
Furse, Major Sir R., 189, 190, 259n.10

Gaberones (Gaberone), xviii, 16–18, 20, 35, 44, 45, 46, 70, 76, 83, 86, 149, 150, 174, 206, 233, 273
Gaberones, Chief, 88, 206
Gambia, River expedition, xi
Game, 132–3, 184; Reserves, 227; Kruger Park, 138; Nossop River, 217
Garraway, Sir Edward, xx
Gash, Captain, 23, 24, 62, 70–1, 74, 174
Gelman, Mr, 198, 226
Gemmil, Bill, 85, 100, 119
George, H.R.H. Prince, 148, 150, 151
George V, 194–5
Germans, 155, 179
Germany, xii, 146, 270
Germond, J.D.A., 174, 258n.29
Ghanzi, 67, 71, 168–9
Girl Guides, 150, 181, 196
Glassman, Mr, 151
Glover, L.S., 150, 184, 190, 227, 256n.5
Gobbleman see Gobuamang
Gobuamang, Chief, 41–2, 44, 45, 51, 74, 101, 105, 120, 121, 173, 245n.77, 264; attempted arrest of, 122–3; surrender, 124–6
Godley, Colonel R.S., 190, 232, 259n.14
Gold Producers Committee, 49
Gomo, 135
Gomoti River, 166
Gordon, H.T., 31, 79, 110
Great Makarikari Salt Lake, 129–30
Grobler, P.G.W., 43, 187, 190, 192, 216–7, 225, 224n.62
Gubbins, J.G., 47, 48, 93, 250n.55
Gungwe Reserve, 205, 206
Gunther, John, 222

Haile, Rev. Alfred John, 48, 98, 152, 190, 245n.69
Hailey, Sir Malcolm, 188, 259n.9
Hale-Carpenter, Dr, 47
Hands, Rev., 155, 164
Harding, Sir Edward, 186, 259n.6
Harris, Mrs Evelyn, 232, 263n.16
Harris, Sir John, 200, 260n.4
Harrison, Sir James, 65
Haskins, Billy and Jimmy, 31, 88, 243n.44
Haskins, George, 31, 154, 243n.44

Hay, Mr, 18, 172, 173
Henderson, Dr, 105, 124, 135, 164
Herero rebellion, 35, 243n.49
Hertzog, General, xix, 26, 108, 109, 152, 185, 242n.36, 270
Hex River Mountain Pass, 11
High Commission Office, 234, 236
High Commission Territories, xvii, xviii, 196, 214, 237n.1, 274
Hitler, Adolf, 128, 146, 270
Hodgson, Margaret, 77, 244n.59, 248n.29
Hofmeyer, J.H., 216, 217, 225, 262n.3
Holbeck, Captain, 81, 82, 100, 106, 162, 163
Holland, xiii, xiv
Hope, Lt., 29, 33, 66, 82, 85, 119, 121, 153
Hopkins, Captain, 89
'Horn of Africa', xiv
Hottentots, 24, 58, 59, 242n.34
Huddleston, Father, 273
Huggins, Dr, 157, 182
Hukuntsi, 59
Hurndall, Mr, 92
Hut-tax, xix–xx, 6, 24, 58, 69, 79, 97, 105, 134, 238n.17

Immigration Proclamation, 87
Imperial Airways, 155
Imperial Cold Storage Company, 50, 68, 85, 87, 90, 94, 117, 142, 144, 146, 172
Imperial Institute, xii, xiv
Imperial Reserve, 3, 17, 91, 101
Indian Civil Service, 54
Indian Mutiny, 31
Indirect Rule, 218, 262n.26
Inside Europe, 222
Inter-Allied Commission, xiii, xiv
In the Country of the Blue Nile, xvi
Irrigation, 98, 133
Isaacs, Mr, 207, 261n.14
Isang, ex-Chief, 13, 46, 51, 70, 74, 86, 110, 111, 112, 113, 149, 152, 165, 171, 174, 178, 197, 240n.10

Japan, 152, 198
Jeffares, J.L.S., 231
Jennings, Albert, 25, 51, 53, 55, 67, 153, 240n.12, 267
Jews, 43, 128, 146, 147, 158
Johannesburg, 43, 49–50, 85–6, 118, 142, 155; Empire Exhibition, 211, 212; Easter Show, 32, 39, 64, 99–100, 229; University, 47

Kabosetse, Headman, 74, 121, 122, 123, 126
Kachikau, 33, 131, 132
Kalahari, xx, xxi, 6, 9, 15, 19, 56–62, 92, 184, 238n.15
Kanye, 14–15, 41, 44, 73, 81, 104, 121–2, 163, 235
Karakul sheep industry, 169, 190, 227–8
Kasane, 20, 23, 33, 36, 88, 131; Hot water springs, 95, 131, 251n.1
Kazuma, 130
Kazungula, 33
Kelly, Mr, 195, 196, 207, 221
Kemp, General, 40, 70, 81, 109, 118, 142, 145, 147, 151, 176, 181, 243n.55
Keppel, Major, 119
Kgampu, 41
Kgari Pilane, 175, 248n.24
Kgari Sechele, 74, 75, 83, 231, 248n.24
Kgobe, David, 271
Khakea, 57
Khale, 172
Khama III, xi, xvii, xix, 4, 77, 238n.10, 241n.40
King Solomon's Mines, 34
King Williams Town, 74
Knollys, Lord, 12
Kokong, 58
Kooper, Simon, 59, 247n.7
Kosmin, Barry, 270
Kruger Game Reserve, 138

Labia, Count, 179, 183, 186, 187, 194
Labour Corps (France), 76
Labour exchanges (Germany), xii
The Lady, or the Leopard, xvi
Laing, Dr, 18, 34
Langton, Stanley, 104, 112, 113, 252n.15
Lawrence Hands Memorial Hall, 228
Lawrenson, Sydney Vernon, 48, 125, 154, 212, 213, 230, 257n.12
League of Nations, 108, 196
Lebone loa Betsoano, 197, 260.1
Ledeboer, Mr, 20, 46–7, 105, 107, 173, 199
Lee, Frank, G., 106, 252n.19
Leeson, Mr, 42, 47
Leetile Disang Raditladi, 230, 262n.7
Lehututu, 55, 56, 59, 184
Leshwane III, 33–4, 254n.16
Lesotho, 274
Letsholo, 112, 253n.26
Lever Brothers, 127, 128
Lewis, Rev. Haydon, xvii, xx, 14, 73, 240n.16
Liesching, Sir Percivale, 138, 139, 140, 141, 147, 178, 225n.29

279

Index

Linchwe, Chief, 113, 177
Livingstone, 88, 89, 131
Livingstone, David, 20, 33
Lloyd George, David, vii, xii, xiii
Lobatsi, xviii, 7-8, 13-14, 22, 26, 27, 37, 41, 46, 66, 72-3, 81, 82, 105, 111-12, 120, 163-4, 172, 202, 239n.21; Cold Storage Works, 41, 72, 82; Creamery, 117; Hospital, 41, 111; Meat Works, 198, 202, 228; Tshekedi's 'case', 207-9
Locust, campaign, 54, 147; conference, 160; plagues, 67-8, 90, 176; poison, 227
London, 85, 102-3, 186-7
London Missionary Society (LMS), 14, 16, 19, 20-1, 23, 24, 26, 30, 39, 48, 51, 53, 55, 56, 62, 67, 73, 75, 98, 132, 152, 170, 174, 190, 267
Lotlhamoreng, Chief, 72, 185, 247n.21
Lotsani River, 79, 227
Lovedale, 19
Lucan, Dr, 133
Lugard, Lord, xxi, 88
Lusaka, 89
Lutherans, 88

Mabuasehube pan, 61
MacDonald, Dr, 86
MacFarlane, Mr, 70, 83, 84, 87, 150, 184, 196
Macgregor, Sir James, 12, 22, 181, 242n.30
Machaneng, 205, 206
Macmillan, Prof. W.M., 91, 250n.54
Mafeking, xviii, 2-7, 8-10, 11, 13, 14, 16, 19, 24, 35, 43, 47, 48, 51, 54, 62, 65-8, 69-71, 80, 81, 86, 87-8, 90, 91-3, 95-8, 101, 103-5, 106-8, 109, 110-11, 113-17, 118-21, 124, 126-8, 137-8, 141, 142, 147-8, 149, 150, 152-5, 155-61, 172-5, 176-8, 181-5, 187-92, 195-202, 203-4, 204-5, 207, 216, 217, 224-8, 228-9, 229-33, 234, 235, 273
Mahalapye, 27, 28, 163, 203, 228
Maitengwe River, 130
Makalaka tribe, 22
Makala Kopo, 135, 254n.20
Makalamabedi, 134
Makobamatse Regiment, 19, 241n.25
Makuba tribe, 35, 133, 254n.17
Malaria, 156
Malcolm, Donald, 188
Malcolm, Sir D.O., 161, 257n.17
Manchester Guardian, 212

Mangan, Mr, 19, 20, 121, 122, 125
Mangwato tribe, 23
Martin, Alistair, 222
Martin, Captain and Mrs, 176
Martin, John, 100, 251n.10
Martinus Seboni, 75, 248n.26
Marwick A.G., 189, 192, 259n.11
Mary, Queen, 99, 251n.4
Masarwa tribe, 23, 54, 55, 66, 67, 69, 80, 129, 242n.31
Masterman, Captain, 153, 184
Masunga, Chief, 32
Mathiba, Chief, 35, 243n.50
Matopos, 38
Maun, 19, 34, 35, 133, 166-8, 170-71
Maxwell, Sir J.C., 88, 89, 250n.51
McIntosh, Phinehas, 255n.27, 265, 266, 267
McNamee, Henry, 255n.27, 266, 267
Meat Board Conference, 220
Meat Control Bill, 118
Meat export, 106, 109, 142, 151, 172, 173, 183, 186, 188, 197, 226-7
Meat Quota Board, 186
Merensky, Dr Hans, 216, 261n.20
Metsemotlhaba River, 78, 112, 174, 175, 206
Meysing, Bishop, 76, 128, 147, 197
Midgeley, Mr, 36, 198-9
Milligan, Samuel, 106, 116, 181, 186, 252n.20
Millin, Philip, 230
Millin, Sarah Gertrude, 230, 263n.9
Milner, Alfred, xix, 106, 252n.17
Mining, concessions, 53, 67, 91, 100, 161, 218, 224, 225; Law, 89, 91; Monarch mine, 151; Proclamation, 87; recruitment of labour, 85; Tati gold mines, 162-3; treatment of Africans, 50-1
Ministry of Labour, xii, xv, xvi
Ministry of Munitions, xiii
Ministry of National Service, xiii, xiv
Missionaries, 19-20, 38, 45, 51, 63, 132, 141, 147, 152, 174, 205
Mitchell, Philip, xx, 81
Mmanaana *see* Bakgatla
Mmusi, Chief, 165, 216, 225, 234
Moanaphuti Segolodi, 81, 86, 133, 249n.43
Mobile dispensaries, 199, 219
Mochaba River, 132
Mochudi, 45-6, 76, 86, 109-10, 112-13, 136, 165-6, 171, 174-5, 205, 206, 212-13, 215-16, 233
Moffat, Howard Unwin, 40, 103, 243n.56
Mogobane dam, 227
Molefi, Chief, 46, 76, 86, 101, 163, 171, 175, 178, 183, 187-8, 197, 205, 206, 208, 212, 213, 217, 225, 232, 233, 240n.11; arrest for extortion, 228, 231; conflict with Isang, 70, 86, 109-10, 111-12, 149, 152-3, 174; new religion; 231, 263n.14; suspension, 214, 215-16, 228
Molema, Dr Sebophiwa, 48, 165, 188, 245n.67
Molema, Dr Silas, 245n.67
Molepolole, 15, 19, 72, 73, 74, 83, 88, 188, 205, 247n.23
Monna-a-Mabura, Chief, 168
Mopipi, 135-6
Moremi, Chief, 45, 147, 195, 218, 221
Morning Post, xvi
Moroka, Samuel, 80
Moseley, Lt., 24, 58, 59, 60, 111, 112
Moshupa, 44, 74, 122, 123, 124-6
Motsete, Kgaleman T., xxi, 7, 23, 206, 239n.19, 261n.1
Mswazi, John, 18, 19, 22, 32, 241n.24
Murphy, Fay Longhurst, 273, 274
Murray, Prof. A.V., 165, 257n.19
Mussolini, Benito, 187, 202, 270
'My Book on Bechuanaland Protectorate', xvii

Nata River, 130
Natal Mercury, 223
National Council of Women, 219
National Insurance Act (1911), xii
National Party (S.A.), 272
Nationalists (S.A.), 90, 117
Native Administration Proclamations, 126, 137, 148, 178, 183, 188, 192-3, 218, 219-20, 221-2, 234, 252n.21, 264
Native Advisory Council, 13, 17, 20, 21, 69, 87, 91, 101, 107-8, 137, 183, 205, 228, 240n.7
Native Affairs Conference, 84
Native Agricultural Show, 67, 81
Native Courts of Justice, 69, 94, 107, 108, 126, 264
Native Labour Recruiting Association, 85
Naus, Charles, 124, 152, 166, 167, 190, 254n.6, 273

Index

Ndandala, Sgt., 122, 123, 125, 160, 253n.3
Neale, Captain, 20, 38, 39, 66, 71, 73, 74, 76, 83, 84, 85, 123, 125, 132, 139, 140, 145
Nettelton, Captain G.E., 7, 20, 23-4, 29, 30, 47, 48, 79, 139, 140, 195, 208, 239n.20
Newton, Sir Francis, xx
New York Times, 272
Ngami, Luke, 167
Ngamiland, 35, 69, 85, 92, 170; Game Reserve, 88
Nobbs Dr E.A., 63, 64, 247n.12
Northern Rhodesia, xxi, 33, 44, 85, 88; Government, 101; Legislative Council, 89, 92, 93
Notwani River, 172
Nyasaland, 40

Okavango River, 35, 133, 178; swamps, 166
Oppenheimer, Sir Ernest, 100, 209, 251n.7
Orange Free State, 80
Orthography Conference, 51
Ottawa Conference, 106, 109, 252n.16
Ottoshoop, 22, 47, 99

Page-Wood, Madge, 78, 248n.37
Palapye Road, 48, 78, 79, 139-41, 171, 205, 206, 266
Passfield, Lord (Sydney Webb), 24, 30, 239n.1
Pathfinders and Wayfarers movements, 80, 101-2, 106, 137, 151, 173, 196, 206, 216, 220, 221, 232, 247n.22
Perham, Marjorie, 187, 259n.7
Philander Bastards, 217, 261n.23
Phillips, Sir Lionel, 204, 260n.9
Pim, Sir Alan, 103, 106, 114, 115, 116, 117, 149, 178, 251n.14
Pirow, Oswald, 40, 41, 216, 229, 244n.58
Pirow, Dr Hans, 216, 261n.21
Plaatje, Sol, 48, 245n.66
Portuguese South West Africa *see* Angola
Potts, Captain, 81, 96, 106, 126, 135, 139, 140, 167, 221, 234, 254n.7
Pretoria, 1-2, 43, 44, 50, 81, 84-5, 87, 105-6, 108, 118, 123, 138, 139, 142, 175-6, 187, 189, 192-3; University, 47, 50
Priestman, H.E., 178, 191, 192, 193, 207, 223, 232, 258n.31
Privy Council, 37, 196, 198, 212

Railway Company, 27, 53, 55, 207
Railway Mission, 163
Rakops, 134-5
Ramaquabane, 32, 79, 83
Ramatlabama, 18, 119, 200
The Rand, 50
Rand Club, 100, 216
Rand Daily Mail, 100, 118, 159, 233
Rasebolai Kgamane, 129, 254n.9
Ras Tafari Makonnen (Haile Selassie), xiv, xv, xvi
Ratshosa, Oratile, 37, 243n.51
Ratshosa, Simon, xvii, xx-xxi, 13, 37, 234, 240n.8, 243n.51
The Real Abyssinia, xvi
Reilly, Captain, 21, 73, 82, 95, 106, 114, 122, 123, 125, 126, 174, 175, 178, 180, 210, 213, 214
Reilly, Mrs, 73, 82, 173
Reitz, Colonel Deneys, 158, 186, 190, 191, 258n.1
Report on Native Law and Custom, 199, 200, 235
Resident Commissioners Conference, 188-9, 214
Rethatoleng Kelesemetswe, 136, 255n.22
Rey (née Graham), Adina Elidia, xi
Rey, Arthur Anthony, xiv, xv
Rey, Edmond Fernand, xi
Rey (née Webster), Nina (Ninon), xiii-xiv, xv, xvi; First Lady, 197; death, 273; O.B.E. 232; involvement with Pathfinders and Wayfarers, 80, 106, 173, 220, 221
Rey, Roderick, xiv, xv
Reynick, Mr, 45, 46, 76, 84, 86, 111, 112, 121, 124, 174, 175
Rey's Mounted Murderers (R.M.M.), 24
Rheinallt Jones, Mrs, 80, 101, 102, 106, 151, 216, 249n.42
Rheinallt Jones, Prof. J.D., 80, 249n.42
Rhodes, Cecil, xvii, 11, 168; house (Groote Schuur), 223; grave, 40
Rhodesia, 23, 41, 43, 55, 66, 80, 272
Rhodesia and Nyasaland Airways (RANA), 182
Rhodesian Cooperative Creameries, 88-9, 90, 97, 98, 99
Richards, Mr, 189, 204
Robins, Thomas Ellis, 37, 142, 256n.37
Rodwell, Sir Cecil Hunter, 39, 40, 159, 243n.54
Roman Catholic Church, viii, 25, 26, 39, 76, 128, 267

The Romance of the Portuguese in Abyssinia, xvi
Romyn, Dr, 80, 81
Rondebosch, 65
Roos, Thielman Johannes de Villiers, 71, 113, 114, 253n.27
Royal Aeronautical Club, xiv
Royal African Society, xvi, 99, 102
Royal Empire Society, 99
Royal Geographical Society, xvi, 99, 102
Royal Military Academy, xi
Royal School of Mines, xi
Rutherford, Mr, 111, 112, 113, 171

Salaman, Peggy, 125
Sandilands, Rev. Alexander, 242n.29
Santandibe River, 166
Satsarogo Pan, 34
Save the Children Fund, 174
Schapera, Prof. Isaac, 183, 199, 200, 235, 257n.18
Schools, 72-3, 75, 135, 164, 170, 206
Seals-Wood, William, 127, 254n.8
Sebele I, xi
Sebele II, 15, 38, 39, 66, 68, 69, 70, 71-2, 74-5, 76, 83, 169, 241n.19
Seboko, Chief, 218
Sekgoma Letsholathebe, xxi
Sekunawe River, 79
Selika, 28
Seretse Khama, xxi, 29, 226, 238n.12, 272
Serowe, 14, 19, 20, 28-31, 37, 48-9, 78, 81, 82, 117, 129, 136, 138-41, 142, 205, 206, 234; aerodrome, 166; dam, 88, 129
Seventh Day Adventists, 88, 147, 168, 170, 171, 267
Sillery, Anthony, xviii
Simonin, Dr, 179
Simonstown, 12, 179
Sinvala Konguena, Chief, 34
Skin and fur factories, 190, 197, 207, 209
Smith, Sir C.G. 'Bongola', 82, 85, 87, 89, 90, 249n.45
Smuts, General, 84, 177, 204, 212, 223, 270
Socialists, Socialism, xxi, 42, 59
South Africa, vii, xvii, xviii, xix, xx, 26, 33, 36, 63, 91, 97-8, 108, 160, 184, 186, 270, 272; colour-bar, 196; coalition government, 117, 118, 119; customs agreement with B.P., 220; Government, 47, 68, 100-1, 109, 114, 117, 118, 127, 128, 172, 199, 202; Mixed

281

Index

Marriage Bill, 225; Native Bill/Policy, 193, 197, 198, 271; inclusion of Protectorate, 153, 155–6, 157, 191, 204, 272; treatment of natives, 225
South Africa Party (SAP), 84, 117, 249n.47
South African Police, 21, 107, 199, 203, 220
Southern Cross, 6
Southern Kalahari, xxii, 24, 45
Southern Rhodesia, xx, 33, 38, 39, 40, 85, 92, 108, 116, 272; customs agreement with S.A., 182; Government, 97, 98; Railway Company, 119
South West Africa, xx, 39, 43, 59, 145–6, 156
Stallard, Colonel C.F., 211, 261n.17
Stanley, Lady, 65, 81, 82, 83, 100, 105, 148, 150, 180, 212
Stanley, Sir Herbert, 65, 68, 81, 82, 84, 90, 94, 98, 100, 106, 107, 108, 143, 144, 150, 154, 155, 159, 162–4, 175, 178, 180, 247n.13
Star, 159, 212, 226, 270
Stephenson, Sir Hugh, 274
Stigand, Captain, A.G., 15, 19, 21, 66, 73, 80, 241n.18
Stigand, C.H., 241n.18
Store, Gordon, 125, 145
Storrs, Sir Ronald, 131, 254n.14
Stuart, Hon. A.J.M., 77, 118, 157, 248n.31
Stud farms, 181, 186
Sturrock, R.C., 84, 108, 177
Sun and Agricultural Life, 85
Swakopmund, 145
Swaziland, xvii, xviii, xx, 49, 84, 189, 204, 274

Table Mountain, 1
Tagart, E.S.B., 80, 84, 246n.3
Tanganyika, xxi
Taoge River, 167
Tati, 83, 115, 120
Tati Concessions Company, 31, 32, 79, 80, 90, 103, 110, 151, 243n.45
Tati Goldmines, 156
Tati River, 79
Taxation of Africans, xix–xx, see Hut-tax
Tebogo Kebailele, 29, 242n.41
Thamalakane River, 133, 166
Thomas, James Henry, 111, 153, 174, 186, 239n.1, 252n.25
Thornton, Mr, 181, 182, 189
Tiger Kloof, 48, 98, 110
The Times, 187
Tlapen, 18
Tomlinson Report (1955), 273

Toteng, 167
Townsend, Deaconess, 205
Transport Conference, 211, 212
The Transvaal Chamber of Mines, 49
The Transvaal, colour-bar, 196; government, 65
Tsabong, 60, 61, 92
Tsane, 58, 59
Tsessebe, 32, 83, 205, 206
Tsetse fly, 34, 39, 54
Tshekedi Khama, vii, viii, xix, xx, xxi, 4–5, 6–7, 13, 14, 16, 18, 23, 24, 25, 28, 29, 30, 37, 45, 47, 48, 49, 55, 56, 62, 67, 69, 78, 82, 83, 84, 90, 91, 96, 100, 108, 117, 130, 136, 153, 166, 171, 184, 185, 188, 210, 234, 238n.11; address to H.R.H. Prince George, 147–8; divorce, 225, 228, 231; locust campaign, 147; Mining concessions, 161, 162; opposition to Proclamations, 126, 137, 138, 148, 183, 189, 190, 196–7, 203, 219–20, 223; report to Dominions Office, 230; suspension/flogging of Europeans, 138–41, 264; trial, 207–9, 218
Tswana, xvii, xviii, xix
Tuli Block, 77, 78, 79, 86, 118, 205, 248n.30
Tuli Block Farmers Association, 27
Tweedie, Admiral H., 81, 249n.44

Unconquered Abyssinia, As It Is Today, xvi
Unemployment: A Problem of Industry, xii
Unemployment Grants Committee, xv
Unemployment Insurance (1912), xii
Union of South Africa see South Africa
Union of South Africa and Some of Its Problems, 272
United Free Church of Scotland, 241n.26
United Nations Charter, 271
United Party (S.A.), 270, 271
United States of America, xiv, 270

Van Rensburg, Mr, 137, 184
Venereal Disease Campaign, 230, 263n.8
Venning, Colonel, 94–5
Vernay, Mr, 18, 102
Vernay-Laing expendition, 18, 34, 241n.21

Veterinary conference, 158, 159
Victōria, Queen, xi
Victoria Falls, 33, 36, 88, 131
Viljoen, Mr, 216, 217
Vukwe, 83

Wallace, Edgar, xxii
Walvis Bay, xx, xxi, 145, 146
Walvis Bay conference, 43
Walvis Bay Harbour Board, 94–5
Walvis Bay Railway, 39, 40, 42, 80, 81, 94, 103
Walvis Bay stock route, 109, 111, 144, 145, 146, 182
Warren, Sir Charles, 208
Water schemes, 37, 38, 41, 42, 61, 189, 206, 210, 228, 230, 273; conference, 47; dams, 167
Watermeyer, E.F., 204, 209, 229, 260n.10
Watermeyer, Mrs, 209
Watussi (German boat), 145, 256n.1
Wayfarers see Pathfinders
Webb, Sydney, see Lord Passfield
Webber, Major, 140
Weil, Samuel, 85, 250n.49
'Wesleyanys', 88
Whalehan, Colonel, 176
Whiskard, Sir Geoffrey, 186
White Dominions, xvi, xvii, xxi
White Train, 51
Wilkins, Colonel, 184
Williams, Colonel, 90, 106
Williams, Ralph, xviii–xix, xxi
Wilson, Benjamin 'Motebele', 77, 248n.32
Wilson, Woodrow, 196
Wireless/telephone communication, 155, 218, 226, 229
Witchcraft, 60, 225, 228, 230, 231
Witch-doctors, 60, 121, 135, 149, 160, 230
Witwatersrand mining companies, viii
Witwatersrand Native Recruiting Corporation Compound, 49
Witwatersrand University, 51, 77, 93,
Wood, Major, 155

XL Bazaar, 86

Young, Sir H.W., 157, 257n.15

Zambesi Bridge, 63
Zambesi River, 33, 95, 98
Zauditu, Empress, xiv

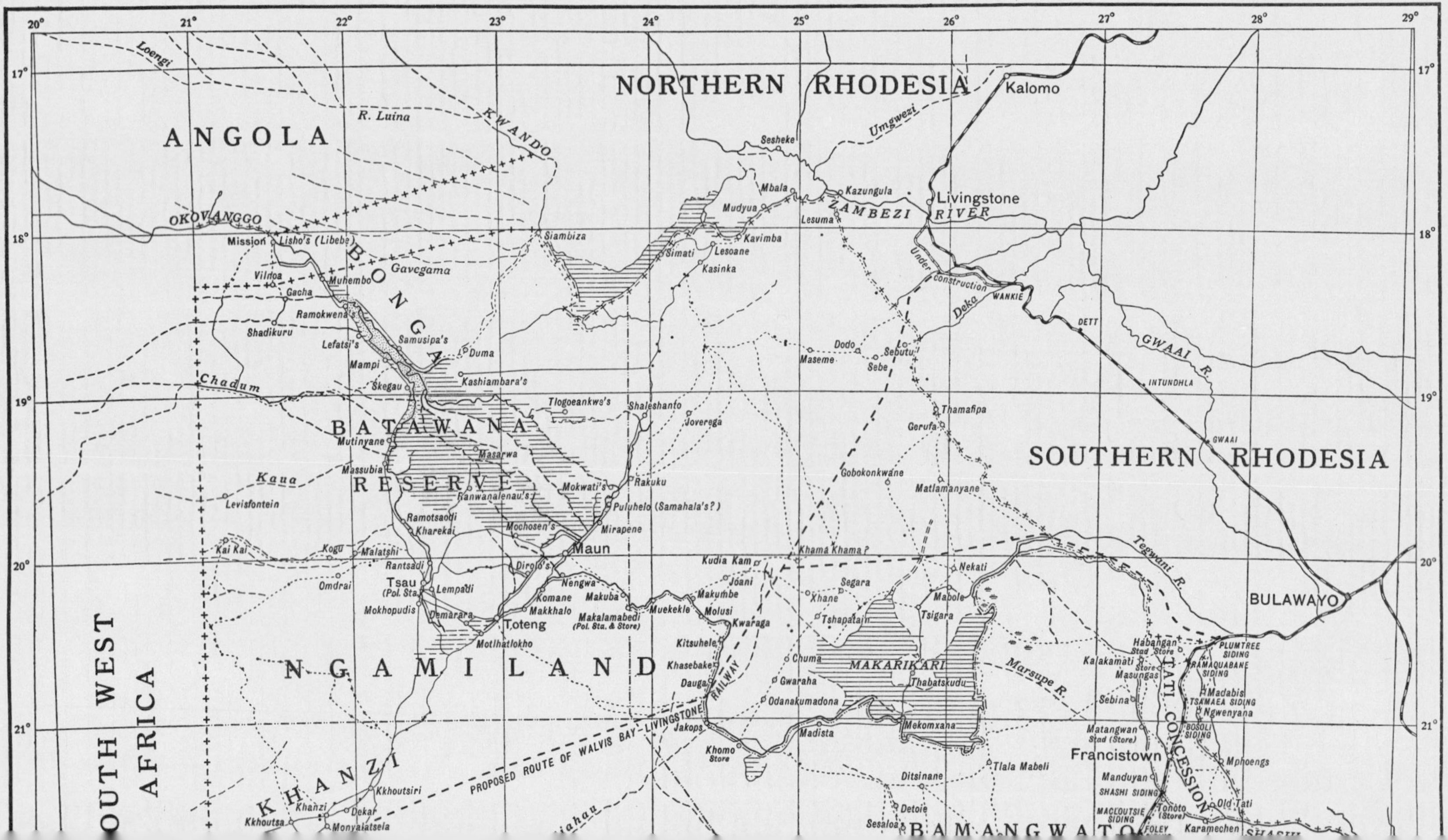

NORTHERN RHODESIA
SOUTHERN RHODESIA
ANGOLA
SOUTH WEST AFRICA
NGAMILAND
BATAWANA RESERVE
BONGA
KHANZI
BAMANGWATO
TATI CONCESSION
MAKARIKARI
Kalomo
Livingstone
ZAMBEZI RIVER
Kazungula
Sesheke
Mbala
Mudyua
Lesuma
Kavimba
Lesoane
Simati
Kasinka
Siambiza
KWANDO
R. Luina
Loengi
Umgwezi
OKOVANGGO
Mission
Lisho's (Libebe)
Gavegama
Villoa
Muhembo
Gacha
Ramokwena's
Shadikuru
Lefatsi's
Samusipa's
Duma
Mampi
Kashiambara's
Skegau
Chadum
Tlogoeankwe's
Shaleshanto
Joverega
Mutinyane
Masarwa
Massubia
Kaua
Levisfontein
Ranwanalenau's
Mokwati's
Rakuku
Puluhelo (Samahala's?)
Ramotsaodi
Kharekai
Mochosen's
Mirapene
Maun
Kai Kai
Kogu
Malatshi
Rantsadi
Dirolo's
Omdrai
Tsau (Pol. Sta.)
Lempadi
Nengwa
Komane
Makuba
Makkhalo
Mokhopudis
Demarara
Toteng
Makalamabedi (Pol. Sta. & Store)
Muekekle
Motlhatlokho
Makumbe
Molusi
Kwaraga
Kudia Kam
Joani
Khama Khama?
Kitsuhele
Khasebake
Dauga
RAILWAY
LIVINGSTONE
PROPOSED ROUTE OF WALVIS BAY
Jakops
Khomo Store
Kkhoutsiri
Khanzi
Dekar
Kkhoutsa
Monyalatsela
Under construction
WANKIE
Deka
DETT
GWAAI R.
INTUNDHLA
GWAAI
Dodo
Maseme
Sebutu
Sebe
Thamafipa
Gerufa
Gobokonkwane
Matlamanyane
Segara
Xhane
Tshapatain
Nekati
Mabole
Tsigara
Chuma
Gwaraha
Odanakumadona
Thabatskudu
Madista
Mekomxana
Tlala Mabeli
Ditsinane
Detoie
Sesaloa
Tegwani R.
Marsupe R.
BULAWAYO
Habangan Stad Store
Kalakamati Store
Masungas
Sebina
Matangwan Stad (Store)
Francistown
Manduyan
SHASHI SIDING
MACLOUTSIE SIDING
FOLEY
Tonoto (Store)
Karamechen
Old Tati
Mphoengs
PLUMTREE SIDING
RAMAQUABANE SIDING
Madabis
TSAMAEA SIDING
Ngwenyana
BOSOLI SIDING
SHASHI
17°
18°
19°
20°
21°
22°
23°
24°
25°
26°
27°
28°
29°